SENEGAL: ESSAYS IN STATECRAFT

edited by
Momar Coumba Diop

Senegal: Essays in Statecraft

First published in 1993 by CODESRIA

Copyright © CODESRIA

CODESRIA is the Council for the Development of Social Science Research in Africa head-quartered in Senegal. It is an independent organization whose principal objectives are facilitating research, promoting research-based publishing and creating multiple fora geared towards the exchange of views and information among African scholars. Its correspondence address is: B.P. 3304, Dakar, Senegal.

ISBN   2-86978-032-x (Soft back)
        2-86978-033-8 (Hard back)

Cover designed by Ousmane Ndiaye Dago
Typeset by Hadijatou Sy, CODESRIA
Printed by Antony Rowe Ltd.
Distributors: ABC, 27 Park End Street, Oxford OX1, IHU
Copyediting: Foster and Philips
Translation: Ayi Kwei Armah

CODESRIA would like to express its gratitude to the Swedish Agency for Research Cooperation (SAREC), the International Development Research Centre (IDRC), the Ford Foundation, the Norwegian Ministry of Foreign Affairs and the Danish Agency for International Development (DANIDA) for support of its research and publication activities.

Senegal: Essays in Statecraft

Contents

Acknowledgements ii
Notes on contributors iii
Acronyms v

1. Introduction: From 'Socialism' to 'Liberalism':
   The Many Phases of State Legitimacy 1
   Momar Coumba Diop
2. Economic Mechanisms in Historical Perspective 28
   François Boye
3. The State of the Groundnut Economy:
   A 30 year Crisis 85
   Mohamed Mbodj
4. Environmental Policy: A Management Critique 130
   Paul Ndiaye
5. Population and 'Development': The Search for
   Policy Options 167
   Mohamed Mbodj, Babacar Mané, Waly Badiane
6. Urban policies: Management and Development 195
   Lat Soucabé Mbow
7. Beyond Patronage and 'Technocracy'? 221
   Mamadou Diouf
8. The Future of Tradition 269
   Souleymane Bachir Diagne
9. The Democracy of the Literati 291
   Aminata Diaw
10. The Regime and the Press 324
    Moussa Paye
11. Reform Options for the Educational System 370
    Abdou Sylla
12. Student Unionism: Pluralism and Pressure Politics 420
    Momar Coumba Diop
13. Trade Unions, Political Parties and the State 470
    Babacar Diop Buuba

Acknowledgements

We would like to express our appreciation for the material support provided by CODESRIA, without which the production of this work would have been an impossible assignment. There were no strings attached: we had complete freedom to define our objectives and approach. We thank the CODESRIA management, and hope they will continue the positive if difficult effort to prove that African intellectuals can nurture indigenous institutions capable of expanding their inventory of analytical tools and concepts.

Our work benefited significantly from criticisms and suggestions advanced by an assessment committee comprising Boubacar Barry, Abdoulaye Bathily, Francine Kane and Charles Becker. In addition, we received analytical comments on some of the articles in this volume from the following scholars: Djibril Samb, Penda Mbow, Edouard Dim, Kader Boye, Amadou Ly, Mamoussé Diagne, Fatou Sow, André Lericollais, Ibrahima Thioub, Ousseynou Faye, René Collignon and Babacar Fall Baker. René Collignon, a seasoned publisher with an eye for the well turned phrase, offered valuable comments.

To all colleagues who thus helped in the production of this work, we here express our profound gratitude. Needless to say, beyond that the responsibility for the content of this volume is entirely ours.

Notes on Contributors

Momar Coumba Diop: Lecturer and Research Fellow, Cheikh Anta Diop University, Dakar. Recent publications include *Le Sénégal sous Abdou Diouf: Etat et Société* (with Mamadou Diouf), Karthala, Paris, 1990; 'Les successions légales: les mécanismes de transfert du pouvoir en Afrique' (with Mamadou Diouf), Working Document 1/1990, CODESRIA, Dakar. Currently engaged in research on relationships between central government authorities and local communities.

François Boye: Lecturer; Director, School of Economics and Management, University of Saint-Louis; Member, Macro-Economic Research Network, World Institute for Development Economics Research, Helsinki.

Mohamed Mbodj: Lecturer. Head, Department of History, Faculty of Humanities, Cheikh Anta Diop University, Dakar; Director, Laboratory of Historical Demography. Author of numerous publications on the history of the groundnut economy. Member, Editorial Board, *Journal of African History*. Assistant Editor of the journal *Sociétés-Espaces-Temps*.

Paul Ndiaye: Lecturer, Department of Geography, Faculty of Humanities, Cheikh Anta Diop University, Dakar; Director of the Bio-geographic Laboratory. Editor of the newsletter *Notes de Biographie*. Member of the production team for the *Etude Prospective Sénégal 2015*, Ministry of Planning and Cooperation, 1989. Consultant to the Senegalese Government.

Babacar Mané and Waly Badiane: Population experts and statisticians, Ministry of Economics, Finance and Planning.

Lat Soucabé Mbow: Lecturer, Department of Geography, Faculty of Humanities, Cheikh Anta Diop University, Dakar. Author of numerous articles on urban geography. Inspector-General in the Ministry of National Education since 1983. Member of the production team responsible for the document *Etude prospective Sénégal 2015*, Ministry of Planning and Cooperation, 1989.

Mamadou Diouf: Lecturer, Department of History, Faculty of Humanities, Cheikh Anta Diop University. Publications include *Le Kajoor au XIXème*

siècle: Pouvoir ceddo et Conquête coloniale, Karthala, Paris, 1990; *Le Sénégal sous Abdou Diouf: Etat et Société*, (with Momar Coumba Diop) Karthala, Paris, 1990. Editor of the journal *Sociétés-Espace-Temps*.

Souleymane Bachir Diagne: Lecturer, Department of Philosophy, Faculty of Humanities, Cheikh Anta Diop University, Dakar. Publications include *Boole, l'oiseau de nuit en plein jour*, Belin, Paris, 1989.

Aminata Diaw: Lecturer, Department of Philosophy, Faculty of Humanities, Cheikh Anta Diop University, Dakar; Member, CODESRIA Research Network on Ethnic Conflicts in Africa.

Moussa Paye: Journalist, Ministry of Communication. Contributor to numerous journals and author of several articles on trade union activities. Founding member, Information and Communication Professionals' Union, Senegal, as well as of the Sud Com Group, publishers of the magazines *Sud Hebdo* and *Sud Magazine*.

Abdou Sylla: Research Fellow, IFAN-Cheikh Anta Diop University, Dakar; specialist in African aesthetics and education. Publications include *Création et Imitation dans l'Art africain traditionnel*, Initiations et Etudes Africaines, No.34, IFAN, Dakar, 1988; and *L'Ecole future pour qui?*, Etudes et Recherches No. 108, ENDA, Dakar, 1987.

Babacar Diop, Buuba: Lecturer, Department of Ancient Civilizations, Faculty of Humanities, Cheikh Anta Diop University, Dakar. Author of numerous articles on ancient African history. Secretary-General, Independent University Staff Union from 1985 to 1990. Member, Executive Committee, African Literacy and Adult Education Association.

Acronyms

ANJS	National Association of Senegalese Journalists
ASACE	Senegalese Insurance Agency for Foreign Trade
BCEOM	Central Office for Overseas Studies
BDS	Senegalese Democratic Bloc
BHS	Senegalese Housing Bank
BM	World Bank
BNDS	National Development Bank of Senegal
BOM	Organization and Methods Bureau
BSD	Senegalese Development Bank
CCCE	Central Fund for Economic Cooperation - France
CED	Coordination of Dakar University Students
CES	Coordination of Secondary School Pupils
CESTI	Centre for Information Science and Technique
CFPS	Special Centre for Pedagogical Training
CGTDS	Senegalese General Confederation of Workers
CGTS	General Confederation of Democratic Senegalese Workers
CNREF	National Commission for Educational and Training Reform
CNTS	Senegal National Confederation of Workers
CPSP	Price Compensation and Stabilization Fund
CRAD	Rural Development Assistance Centres
CSS	Senegalese Sugar Company
EBAD	School of Librarians, Archivists and Documentalists
EISMV	Inter-State School of Veterinary Science and Medicine
ENCRB	Bambey National School of Rural Cadres
ENEA	National School of Applied Economy
ENEP	National School for Pre-School Education
ENS	National Training College
ENSUT	University College of Technology
EPT	Thiès Polytechnic
FCFA	African Financial Community francs
FIDES	Investment, Funds for Economic and Social Development
ICS	Senegalese Chemical Industries
INDR	National Institute for Rural Development
IST	Institute of Earth Science
JORS	Official Gazette of the Republic of Senegal
OCA	Agricultural Marketing Board
OHLM	Council House Board
ONCAD	National Agricultural Produce Marketing Board
PENG	Price of Groundnut Fertilizer (francs per kg.)
PDES	Economic and Social Development Plan
SAR	African Refining Company
SATEC	Technical and Co-operative Assistance Company

SEIB	Industrial Electric Company of Baol
SENELEC	National Corporation for Electric Power Distribution
SICAP	Cap-Vert Building Society
SIES	Senegalese Fertilizer Corporation
SISCOMA	Senegalese Industrial Company for Mechanical Engineering and agricultural Equipment
SNTI	National Industrial Tomato Corporation
SODAGRI	Agricultural and Industrial Development Corporation
SODEVA	Agricultural Extension and Development Corporation
SONACOS	Senegalese National Oilseed Marketing Corporation
SONAR	National Rural Supplies Corporation
SONEES	National Water Corporation
SOSAP	Senegalese Fisting Company
SOTRAC	Cap-Vert Transport Corporation
STN	New Lands Corporation
SUDES	Democratic Teachers Union of Senegal (see also UDEN)
UDEN	Democratic Teachers Union of Senegal
UMOA	West African Monetary Union
UNCA	Senegalese National Union of Agricultural Co-operatives
UNDES	National Democratic Union of Senegalese Students
UPS	Senegalse Progressive Union
PS	Socialist Party

1. Introduction - From 'Socialism' to 'Liberalism': The Phases of State Legitimacy

Momar Coumba Diop

The idea for the research presented here dates back to 1988. At that time, while finishing a different book (Diop and Diouf, 1990a), we became convinced that a number of points called for further study to shed more light on the critical situation in Senegal. Such an undertaking required more energy than we had at the time, in addition to inputs of expertise beyond our own. We contacted a number of colleagues, requesting their participation in a dynamic interactive process designed to yield responses to questions raised by the sub-region's crisis.

This book fits in with a range of recent analytical works on Senegal. In 1988, under the aegis of Djibo Kâ, the Ministry of Planning and Cooperation launched a prospective study entitled Senegal 2015.

The study, conducted partly by lecturers and researchers from Cheikh Anta Diop University in Dakar was guided by short range utilitarian concerns, in so far as it was intended as a preparatory step in the elaboration of policy guidelines for the Eighth Development Plan (1989-95). The working group came up with perceptive ideas on change in Senegalese society. But the way in which their insights were selected, then incorporated into the Plan document, robbed them of any coherence, blunted their analytical thrust, and weakened their instructive impact.

In this way, the historical background study centred on an analysis of six main topics and was used for drafting a 'Scenario of Trends and Strategic Options for Medium Term Orientation Plans'. In the process, aspects of the study considered irrelevant to the planners' concerns were edited out. To obviate the loss of substantial quantities of data generated in that exercise by national specialists, we asked members of the Senegal 2015 group to make a fresh presentation of their historical analyses of Senegalese society in this volume. In the resulting text, we have taken care to incorporate their various contributions within a framework designed to highlight their principal insights.

On a different plane, this book complements our work *Sénégal sous Abdou Diouf* (Diop and Diouf, 1990a). In that book we had challenged selected publications on political and legal sociology. We thought, in effect, that in order to understand the socio-economic and political issues at stake, it was important to take stock of the accelerated pace of events since Abdou Diouf took over the presidency of Senegal from Senghor in the late 1970s. The new approach required that we steer clear of the principal emphases of the existing literature, which tended to accent relationships between the State, organizations revolving around religious elites and the groundnut economy, or the ability of the ruling class to construct an integrated State. In analyzing relationships between State and society, we offer this contribution to the debate on the role and status of the State in the development process - a debate made more sharply relevant by economic crisis and the implementation of structural adjustment programmes.

At independence, the State was seen as an efficient machine primed to stimulate economic growth. Today, judging by the tone of ruling class organs as well as publications issued by funding agencies, the State looks rather like a parasitic monster. Accused of poorly public resources and wasting investment opportunities, it has taken a great deal of bashing from the media. By examining evolving relations between State and society, our study sheds clearer light on economic stagnation, withdrawal and resistance within civil society.

The chapters from our individual contributors cover precise sectorial fields, but the general coherence of the work is enhanced by a common approach that uses the crisis of State power as a reflective prism. The chapters lay bare the complex skein of relationships binding the State to the economic and social order, examine the kinetic interplay of conflict and collaboration between different claimants to legitimacy, and identify and describe transformations affecting the structure of power in Senegal, and the individuals which manage it. In our analysis of the crisis of the State, we have accented internal political and economic dynamics along with the roles of indigenous actors. In so doing we have adopted an approach based on insightful remarks by Terray (1987), who argues that while the influence of external causes should not be denied, imperialism is not the sole actor on the African political stage. The resulting framework is calculated to enhance our understanding of the role and status of social actors, the structures they have designed for themselves, and the difficulties posed for the ruling class by the crisis of the state.

A clear analysis of basic premises guiding the rhetoric of the central power structure, coupled with an assessment of its effectiveness, facilitates an understanding of the scope and meaning of social behaviour that tends to upset the system-maintenance strategies of the ruling class and its allies. In this connection, questions have arisen about the viability of the Wolof model that has so far provided the basic paradigm for the construction of the

Senegalese State. Confronted now with challenges from the urban, regional and ethnic 'peripheries', that model might be in danger of falling apart. The political class in its entirety now faces a hurdle. It has to come up with new strategies of political mobilization in a situation where ordinary people, angered by the absence of forward-looking social programmes, might very well drift into acts of uncontrollable violence.

In our study of the State, we have stuck to precise disciplinary guidelines, focusing only on factors relevant to our analytical framework, and working only on topics for which specialists were available. The period selected for study stretches mainly from independence to the present. There are two contributions, however, in which the authors extend their focus into the past, to facilitate an in-depth examination of the course run by the post-colonial State. In chapter 7, this provides a historical background for most of the studies in this volume, in sufficient depth to facilitate a reconstruction of production conditions over a given territory, as well as of methods used to control its inhabitants.

Each contributing author, drawing on hard data, presents an assessment of State behaviour patterns, together with explanations of the current crisis mechanisms. It would have been possible, for example, to conduct a study of the agricultural crisis by emphasizing food crop farming, or by shifting the focus from the groundnut basin onto other regions. Other foci could have provided suitable bases for research: technical changes in the agricultural sector since 1960; land management; dynamics and constraints in the agricultural sector. But bearing in mind material constraints affecting the production of such a collective work, Mohamed Mbodj decided to exclusively focus on the crisis of the groundnut economy. His contribution is complemented by explanatory information offered in Chapter 2 on the government's agricultural policy, chapter 7 on the rural political system, and chapter 4 on the environment.

A deliberate effort was made to ensure that wherever possible, contributions from different authors would dovetail into each other. It was not our aim, however, to produce an encyclopaedic tome. Our objective was to break intellectual ground for subsequent work of a more detailed, more comprehensive nature, on a topic whose complexity we understand all too well. In our desire to breathe new life into research on the history and current condition of the State, we have paid the closest possible attention to the social, economic and political constraints that have marked its development, the better to identify and describe the ups and downs of the formative process. Our resulting assessment gives us a means to assess cyclical patterns in the growth of the State. Concurrently, it enables us to show in what ways the crisis, once it broke into public view in the late 1970s, tended to weaken the support system on which the legitimacy of the ruling elites reposed. To do this, we have had to identify social forces confronting each other in their drive to shape the country's political and economic options.

This work proffers no panacea for ailments revealed by ongoing political, social and economic changes in Senegal. The team of scholars here includes no secular missionaries[1]. The aspiration informing it is the desire to facilitate better comprehension of present realities. The analyses emphasize the wide range of issues raised by ongoing changes in Senegalese society. A number of contributions also probe the likely consequences of these changes in the short-term. On the whole, even though the authors leaned over backwards in the interests of objectivity, the tenor of these articles is a pervasive feeling of pessimism about 'the Senegalese condition' that is hard to gloss over.

Our analyses shed light on two processes. The first is the attempt of the ruling class that acceded to power in 1960 to create a basis for its hegemony. The second is the parallel set of crises related to upheavals in the process of political integration and to the depressed economy. In practice, the hegemonic dream of the ruling class meant merely the adoption of neo-patrimonial guidelines. Such an approach was not guaranteed to create an integral State. However, the ruling class did succeed in co-opting selected members of the opposition who challenged its legitimacy. The increasing marginalization of the State can be dubbed 'the revenge of African societies.' It is the same process Mbembe (1988:23) sees as indicating a 'pagan revenge' on formal norms of State life established since independence. While we would not go as far as Mbembe, we recognize that numerous forces have risen to block State expansion.

The first such force is the peasantry. Senegalese peasants have deployed strategies of resistance which, while evading direct confrontation with the State, enable them increasingly to 'escape' (Fatton 1988:256) into a no-man's land beyond the reach of official economic norms (Senegal/CES 1976). The fact that such 'escape' strategies are possible at all means that there are areas of economic and political life open to ordinary people, which the State has a hard time asserting its control.

Sandbrook (1987:19) asks how unintegrated peasant societies might be studied and comprehended in situations where there is absolutely no legitimate authority. The answer to that question is clear enough: the network of Muslim marabouts keeps the peasantry under effective lock and key. Now Sandbrook supposes the marabouts could flatly reject the role of social activists and monitors, and turn instead to challenging the legitimacy of the State. But rural networks affiliated to the ruling class have blocked the creation of peasant communities likely to challenge or compete directly with the State. In the urban areas, political and social life is segmented into ineffectiveness, while continuous attempts are made to silt up channels of self-expression that might prove useful to protest movements.

As a result of these tactics, groups challenging the legitimacy of the ruling class have developed a 'riot culture'. Rural networks operated by the Muslim marabout clergy ensure that forces hostile to the ruling class cannot penetrate into rural society to change established political game rules. In times of economic hardship, however, systems based on such support are difficult to manage. In an attempt to cope with their dwindling purchasing power, peasants withdraw into political and economic sanctuaries not yet corralled by the State. The nature of relations between the ruling class and the opposition shows that the ruling class has failed to assert lasting moral and intellectual leadership over the society. It has been unable to ensure obedience from intellectuals without the use of force.

In the early 1960s, the ruling class pushed for considerable expansion of the economic base of the State. From 1960 to 1963, recalcitrant opposition parties and internal power struggles within the ruling class sorely tested the coherence of official institutions. In subsequent years the State began to restructure these institutions to better contain the continuous infighting between sections of the elite which had led the country to independence. Through a complex system of co-optation, mergers and banning orders, the ruling class created a situation in which, by 1966, all opposition to the government was defined as criminal (Hesseling 1985: 257).

During this period, an authoritarian regime nurtured State institutions while actively suppressing the potential development of any autonomous source of power. In the first decade after independence, one institution - the army - played a vital role in the self-perpetuation of the ruling class. It did this by pushing normal military defence duties onto the back burner and concentrating on the business of political pacification. This is one reason why in time the army grew into an organization for brokering domestic power relationships.

Because it is continuously engaged in duties related to the maintenance of order, and because it has become the umpire in conflicts within the ruling class, the army is an important player on the national political scene. In strengthening mechanisms of obedience and discipline, and in umpiring civil conflicts, it has taken care to safeguard military values and to protect the privileges of the officer class. The ruling class, for its part, has offered these privileges with a view to winning the allegiance of the military leadership, so that they can help put down those social forces challenging its writ. However, faced with insurrectionary situations, the army has had to come up with innovative solutions, whose outcomes are uncertain (Touré 1989).

For though the army has acted when called upon, it has balked at direct involvement within the framework of the political system.

By keeping aloof from politics, the army has been better able to handle internal tensions provoked by such factors as ethnic conflicts and clashes between line and staff officers. It has also avoided trends towards disintegration and disturbances in its hierarchy that would definitely have surfaced if it had taken direct political control. The army has continually taken on social pacification assignments on behalf of the ruling class because the police force has not proven itself either large enough for such duties or capable of effectively dominating insurrections.

Such steady reliance on military support (Lo 1986, 1987) could lead the military into the conviction that it is indispensable to the regime. From that attitude it is only a short step to the temptation of a coup d'état. To obviate this possibility, the ruling class has boosted the army's professional status. The top officer classes work in a system of power sharing between branches of the armed forces. The top brass have outstandingly cushy salaries, emoluments and perks. Beyond that there is French control over the military establishment. All these factors have helped to maintain military loyalty. Furthermore, State oversight of the officer class is ensured through the creation of an extravagantly equipped proto-militia known as an operational field force unit (Légion de Gendarmerie d'Intervention). Lastly, the esprit de corps of the officer class is deliberately diluted by incessant reshuffles in the command hierarchy.

Army officers are part and parcel of the ruling class. As such, they also harbour personal aspirations to power and wealth. These aspirations are met through the steady improvement of the army's professional status, the appointment of army officers to selected civil service positions, and the naming of retired generals to diplomatic posts. The army has thus remained the armed fist of the ruling class, helping to maintain the kind of situation described by Obasanjo:

> *From the moment of their accession to power, some of our nationalist parties began to take themselves for something they had never in fact been, that is to say, authentic and unique embodiments of our countries' objective social will. In time power became concentrated not in the hands of a party but in those of an individual supported by an army of informers. In traditional African society, opposing viewpoints had always had an honoured place, but now dissent came to be viewed with a misguided hostility that made it practically synonymous with treason. This political intransigence caused the sources of our people's creativity to dry up* (quoted by Anyang' Nyong'O 1989:14).

Despite the authoritarian climate, the activities of underground political groups did not come to a complete halt. Among clandestine groups there were student and teachers' unions. However, through a combination of harsh repression and the co-optation of selected opposition leaders, the ruling class succeeded in consolidating its power base. In the first decade of independence, which was also the decade of the providential State, there were several showdowns between rival segments of the Westernized political elite. The end of that decade also signalled the closing of a cycle characterized by a marked degree of continuity with the colonial system: the economy was dominated by foreign companies dating back to the colonial days; the educational system was ill-suited to national needs; the agricultural system was notoriously inefficient; and the political system was based on the purchase of allegiances. Such was the profile of the governmental model under Senghor.

The ruling party, a single party in all but name, stifled the free expression of divergent points of view. As Moussa Paye demonstrates in his analysis, under these conditions the existence of a free press was unthinkable. The State was self-appointed judge and umpire. Throughout the period, State control over the media was rarely relaxed. At the end of the first decade of independence, the State was reorganized. But in the 1970s, there continued to be confrontations with militant student and teachers' unions. In response the government banned all hostile political organizations. The only remaining avenue for such opposition groups was underground work. This was a time of structural economic problems marked chiefly by a steep drop in agricultural production a factor of intense concern for government and the oil factories (Senegal/CES 1976:44-48).

To defuse the situation, the Government decided on a political amnesty in 1974. Thereafter, President Senghor authorized the creation of the Parti Démocratique Sénégalais (PDS). In the newly liberalized political climate, the press became a closed field for unequal political combats. Despite the vitality of the Journalists' Union and the so-called independent press, the Government maintained its stranglehold on the media. It also refused to lift its monopoly on television and radio broadcasts in the national interest[2].

The economic and social crisis of the late 1970s resulted in a major personnel overhaul within the power structure, along with an ideological restructuring that pushed Senghor's philosophy of Negritude into the background, yielding centre stage to a hazy doctrine of *'sursaut national'*.

In 1981, when Abdou Diouf came to power, his team managed to short-circuit a number of claims staked by the urban petty bourgeoisie. This was a result of the advent of unfettered multi-party politics. By encouraging a proliferation of political platforms, the new order weakened the impact of political and intellectual discourse. Meanwhile, the system could do nothing to halt the downward economic slide; youth were abandoned to despair; low income earners were pushed deeper into poverty. All these signs underlined the weakness of the ruling power bloc, a feature of which was an increasing urge to coopt intellectual power. It was a tactic calculated to hijack the moral authority of the intellectual establishment by yoking it to political power. This is the process highlighted in chapter 9 by Aminata Diaw in her analysis of 'the democracy of the literate elite'.

The political reforms instituted after 1974 did not threaten the regime because the people, especially the rural population, were in the main uninvolved in party political activities. The ruling class showed appreciable skill in manoeuvring[3], between the Senegalese people on the one hand and the foreign funding agencies on the other, to ensure its own survival. On this last point, Berg (1990) pulls no punches:

The Senegalese authorities are in the habit of solving problems of scarce resource allocation more by relying on money from the funding agencies than by making hard choices involving sacrifices. This is understandable enough. Which government would not do the same if it could? Suppose a Minister has a project requiring funding. Suppose also, that in the normal process of public budgetary allocations, his project is axed. His solution is to turn to a foreign sponsor. Under normal circumstances the search is not unduly difficult. If budgetary credits are insufficient to cover recurrent expenditure, it is generally possible to get some funding agency to finance part of local expenditure... The outcome is an Alice-in-Wonderland situation in which normal management rules need never be observed (Berg 1990:43-44).

The 'irregularities' revealed in the operations of the National Recovery Corporation, set up in the wake of a restructuring of the banking system, after only one year of activity, perfectly illustrate this point.

Meanwhile, the ruling class is confronted by structural problems amplified by a policy of political pacification underlying its economic initiatives since independence. It is a remarkable fact that neither foreign donors nor the local population give the economic record of the ruling class a passing grade. Intellectual backing for its economic programmes has been lukewarm (Berg 1990:42). In the opinion of intellectuals within the power bloc, these economic policies are at loggerheads with established financial circuits set up to pump money into the 'bread and butter economy'. The implementation of formulae suggested by the funding agencies leads to a shrinkage of the political and social base of this strategic socio-professional group which grew up in the shadow of the State, causing the public sector to swell considerably in the process.

The democratization of the country's political life stimulated the rise of a variegated press. One salient feature at the time was the emergence of a professional union of communications staff. A second was the emergence of a generation of better trained journalists much more determined than their predecessors to live up to the image of serious professionals. The ruling regime reacted in a rather surly fashion. The Government passed a controversial press law, and the State has maintained its monopoly over audio-visual media. These are symptoms of a determination to keep control. On this issue the record provides no indication that the regime has ever changed its attitude.

Those groups responsible for intellectual production and the creation of a relatively autonomous culture have not escaped the impact of political and economic change. Their muted claims are often totally smothered under the load of daily material and financial survival problems. To make matters worse, the ideological models they formerly advocated have been discredited. As for institutions responsible for intellectual production and reproduction, they too, shattered by the general crisis, have slumped into near ruin. In the process, they have become theatres of major political confrontations. Throughout the period of State construction, wave after wave of radical student protest has presented itself as the advocate of intellectual interests and a defender of democratic rights in society at large.

In the 1960s, in response to nationalist pressures of the independence era, the activities of this movement were identified as part of the struggle against 'Imperialism and its African puppets'. The fathers of independence were trying to establish and consolidate a political order. The younger generations were shaking the foundations of that order. The regime adopted stringent measures designed to derail the political plans of its younger opponents, but the latter survived in spite of official repression. The problem, however, was that the student leadership, coming from the opposition parties, got embroiled in various conflicts between Marxist groups competing for a following among the urban petty bourgeoisie. In spite of these contradictions, opposition groups were able to mount a series of major confrontations with the State in the period under study.

Another objective of the militant student and teachers' trade union movements was to demand a high-quality educational system. As Chapter 2 shows, the history of the Senegalese educational system is that of an administration improvising policies on the fly. There has been a discernible rise in school attendance, but enrolment is still less than 50% of the school-age population. Classrooms are overcrowded. Failure rates are high. At every level in all cycles, dropout rates are spectacular. An educational reform project has been in the offing ever since the nation-wide Congress of Educational and Training Staff (1981), the sessions of the National Commission on the Reform of Educational and Training Institutions (1981-84), and a series of educational innovations adopted along the same lines, especially by Iba Der Thiam, Minister of National Education from 1983 to 1988. But, in the mean-time there are chronic shortages of personnel, material resources and money, while the population grows apace. As a result, educational standards have fallen, and pupils and students, teachers and parents have all slumped into despair. The education of the country's elites is now threatened by a pervasive lowering of standards.

Our findings indicate that an increased dependence on intervention by international institutions has become a fact of life in Senegal. This has chipped away at State power, influence and legitimacy. The regime habitually claims a democratic record, but now that opposition parties are demanding access to the media and reforms in the Electoral Code, these official claims sound rather hollow. In some neglected outlying regions, segments of the population have clashed with the State over issues which are hard to characterise[4].

It was probably in a bid to block such developments that large scale political moves similar to those that followed Senghor's resignation (Diop and Diouf 1990a) were made beginning in March 1991. They followed clashes in the wake of which leaders of the PDS and other parties were either imprisoned or violently assaulted and humiliated by the police (*Sud Hebdo*, 131, 15 November 1990) as happened during the march organized by the National Conference of Heads of Opposition Parties to demand access to State media[5]. This was the sequel to the failure of various attempts made as from 1988 to foil assaults mounted by opposition leaders on the government (Diop and Diouf 1990b), at a time when State authority had been eroded by a proliferation of protest movements. In the new phase, efforts were made to co-opt opposition leaders into the State structure, and to defuse conflicts with so-called separatist groups in the Casamance (*Le Témoin*, 36, 2 April 1991; *Le Soleil*, 10 April 1991).

By encouraging alliances between a number of nominally autonomous trade unions and the National Workers' Confederation of Senegal (CNTS), Senegal's leaders tried to create divisions on the labour front, thus accentuating the political atomization indispensable for the implementation of the structural adjustment programme. A constitutional reform revived the post of prime minister, abolished in 1984, extended the term of office of the parliamentary speaker from one to five years, reintroduced censure motions, and gave the President of the Republic the power to dissolve the National Assembly (*Le Soleil*, 22 March 1991). In addition, the government established a post of ombudsman in Act Number 91-14 dated 11 February, took opposition demands into consideration in reforming the Electoral Code, (*Le Soleil*, 21-22 September 1991), and appointed five opposition leaders, including the PDS leader Abdoulaye Wade, to ministerial posts.

These moves, designed to lower the political temperature, came at a time when the government's economic policies had obviously failed. For that reason, it is possible to interpret them, following Fatton (1987), as a new manifestation of Senegal's 'passive revolution'. In Fatton's view, the political reforms of the Senghor years, officially described as a 'democratic opening', were intended to alleviate the crisis of the State in the 1970s. Partial under Senghor, the opening became complete with Abdou Diouf's accession to power. Diouf accomplished a 'passive revolution' by strengthening the bases of liberal democracy.

There was a special aspect to the 1991 reforms: they happened at a time when the ruling establishment ideas of technocratic nationalism and liberalization were facing mounting difficulties. It is too early to make a definite assessment of the new configuration. For one thing, the new game rules are somewhat opaque, and their impact on the tenor of Senegalese political life is correspondingly hard to evaluate. It is already clear, however, that they in no way change the basic structural features of the economy.

Mamadou Diouf, beginning with the colonial heritage, describes the numerous metamorphoses of the Senegalese State in its relations with society. In the process, he shows how, by being drawn into the adjustment programme, the State has been penetrated by groups promoting an ideology based on technocratic illusions. In the context of the restructuring of the national economy, the function of these groups seems to be the management of dependency. Backed up by the President's Office which, under Jean Collin (1981-90) became the effective political and administrative policy-making centre of the State of Senegal, members of these groups were used as a resource pool to blunt the effectiveness of the political system built up by Senghor and his collaborators.

The implementation of structural adjustment programmes resulted in a reshaping of relationships between the State and certain social protagonists such as the country's 'business community', which claimed the status of a 'national bourgeoisie'[6]. These were people who had amassed fortunes thanks to the connivance of a friendly State. They constituted a 'national bourgeoisie' which had so far failed to take control of any key sector of the national economy. Understandably, they felt increasingly threatened by the steady abolition of protectionist government measures.

Two considerations may be highlighted as far as political developments are concerned. First, within the ruling Socialist Party, attempts were made to decompress structures, mainly through the overhaul of political office holders. Party leaders sharpened competition for positions without fixing or clarifying ground rules. At the same time they were able, until April 1991, to paralyze every attempt to co-opt opposition leaders into the decision-making structures of the State. They did this by exploiting Jean Collin's manoeuvering skills and contacts to the hilt. Collin regularly snuffed out any source of power likely to disturb his game rules, entirely geared to the watchful maintenance of the neo-patrimonial establishment.

In its efforts to fragment the opposition, the ruling group was consistently faithful to its own traditions. Moreover, it got considerable help from the structural shortcomings of the opposition groups themselves. For example, the latter remained broken up into ill-coordinated sectarian grouplets, and the level of their theoretical insights into the State and social stratification was low. Ever since independence, numerous attempts had been made to unify the opposition. But they had invariably foundered against ideological incompatibilities and ill-concealed personal rivalries. So the opposition had been unable to find a unified approach to the construction and inspiration of a well-structured social movement with deep roots among the ordinary people. It therefore remained exclusively tied to the urban intelligentsia.

That urban intelligentsia provided a shaky base at best. In its behaviour and performance, it slavishly followed ideologies and thought patterns produced by cultural bureaucracies and political establishments abroad. This made it essentially a comprador bourgeoisie. And that made the design of applicable strategies and tactics of struggle intended to shatter the dominant local regime dauntingly complicated.

Since the late 1960s, a series of reform programmes had been tried, with attempts to rationalize the regime and give it a technocratic orientation. But the Senegalese State, addicted to a style of patron-client relationships, could not change its spots. Neither could it drop its old habit of seeing politics solely in terms of social pacification. The State therefore, had no power to halt its own drift into crisis. Economic reforms were attempted. In social terms they exacted a high toll; yet their material yield was disappointingly low. The ruling policy was heavily geared to addressing external imbalances. Operative sectors open to the State were shrinking. This led to intense competition between aspirants for a dwindling number of opportunities for pillage and embezzlement, while those already in such positions fought tooth and nail to keep rivals out. As a result, insecurity became the order of the day, with incumbents in elite sectors finding it increasingly difficult to stabilize their power bases. Structural adjustment policies worsened political imbalances at a time when the leadership was increasingly debilitated by factional infighting. In a word, the existing model of accumulation, whose main achievement was to plunge the country into economic paralysis, was on its last legs.

Today there are numerous symptoms of this social impasse. People have no expectations whatsoever that their living conditions will improve. The youth are chronically frustrated (*Le Soleil*, 19 March 1922:7-9). Urban youth from the proletarian strata, struggling to survive under unprecedented conditions of poverty, their misery made more bitter by the showy lifestyles of privileged groups, erupted in the period from 1988 to 1990. Their riots were uncontrolled, because they operated outside the framework of established political parties. Their violence was the outcome of ruptures in the social fabric. Taking advantage of the commotion, people long confined to the shadowy fringes of society emerged to loot goods they could not afford, or simply to smash property beyond their dreams. Apart from brief spells of activity during election campaigns, the level of youth involvement in the programmes of opposition political parties is low. This is a result of the inability of these parties to come up with strategies and programmes other than unrealistic futuristic rhetoric meant for the consumption of an 'educated' minority.

Chapter 2 makes it plain that from a macro-economic point of view, the country has no self-sustaining growth mechanisms. In 1960 the ruling class did a great deal in an effort to consolidate the country's economic bases. The result of its endeavours was an expansion in the scope of State intervention. This voluntarist policy faced a series of stiff challenges, including the 1962 coup d'état, the abolition of French price guarantees for oil seeds in 1967, the disturbances of 1968, the cycle of droughts that began in the 1968-69 farm season, and the first petrol crisis. But it was not until the second petrol crisis hit that it ended in failure, so that by the eve of the third decade of independence the country was obliged to swallow the pill of structural adjustment policies.

Broadly speaking, towards the late 1970s, the economy began to face increasingly severe problems. Despite a series of vigorous reforms, the low rate of growth in the rural sector has been a constant feature in the recent history of the country. During the 1980s, industrial production also declined markedly. Given its unusually high input costs and the overvalued monetary unit, the CFA franc, Senegalese industry has not been competitive on the international market. The interventionist State has therefore seen its freedom of manoeuvre steadily reduced by skyrocketing recurrent expenditure the economy has been too weak to fund.

The country's water resources have deteriorated badly, and the downslide has been accelerated by climatic hazards. The combination of these natural calamities with human behaviour patterns has led to the kind of serious environmental changes described by Paul Ndiaye. Often, human consumer needs go far beyond levels conducive to environmental regeneration. For that reason, nature-based production systems have registered substantial drops in productivity. However dynamic other sectors may have been, the series of droughts devastated them all, and none have been able to alleviate the impact.

The overvaluation of the CFA franc in relation to currencies outside the franc zone has blocked the growth of an export sector competitive enough to power the national economy into the international market and to make up for fluctuations in export volumes and prices for groundnut products. Membership of the franc zone makes it possible for Senegal to bring in imports without having to pay up outstanding current account deficits. This has made domestic consumption independent of domestic production. Concurrently, it has made domestic savings inadequate to finance investment necessary for sustained growth.

Investments in the agricultural sector have been colossal, but yields have been too chancy to help modernize the country's agricultural system. Numerous reports have laid bare the causes of the crisis in the groundnut production system (Parti Socialiste 1988; France/MRE 1985; Kane 1986). In the absence of any economic process capable of replacing the deteriorating groundnut sector as the dynamo of the Senegalese economy, the crisis has been deepening steadily, and rural incomes have fallen just as constantly (France/MRE 1985).

Groundnuts have played a key role in local socio-economic development since the mid-nineteenth century (Mbodj 1978). From 1967, Senegal stood at the end of the period referred to by Mamoudou Touré as the 'phase of relative quiet (Touré 1985:9). The immediate manifestation of this situation was an atmosphere of 'peasant malcontent'. In their analysis of this phenomenon, government experts sometimes blamed official economic policy guidelines:

Senegal, geared as it is to groundnut export production in the form of seed or oil, has overlooked the rational, systematic organization of a diversified economy that might have helped meet the nutritional needs of its citizens and facilitated the emergence of new economic sectors, an industrial sector in particular. The country was caught in a specialized role within a colonial economy dominated by France. Within a colonial context the arrangement had its rationale. However, it is simplistic to argue that since as a colony Senegal drew certain "advantages" from that system, it was reasonable for an independent Senegal to continue within that specialized role. What the present situation proves is quite the opposite: that Senegal still has a colonial economy, and that the country would be well served by a radical change in its economic orientation. Such a change would require structural adaptations (Club Nation et Développement 1970:8).

State interventionist policies have had a marked impact on the peasant environment, especially in the area of groundnut production. State interventionism dates back to colonial times, but was intensified from 1970, with a proliferation of public and parastatal organizations running up higher and higher deficits. There is little doubt the State wanted to control groundnut production upstream and downstream because the crop was so pivotal in the economy. But the main criticism of the official approach, as it emerges from official documents, repeatedly indicates that State management practices were negligent, that guidelines were confused (Kane 1986:21), and that a number of other factors that had led to the inefficient running of public enterprises applied in this sector also.

State intervention was compromised by rampant corruption, with officials embezzling funds and misusing State property in neo-patrimonial style. An outstanding example of the resulting waste was the National Development Aid and Cooperation Board (ONCAD), as Chapter 3 makes crystal clear. The government's poor economic performance was also due to its habit of subordinating objectives detailed in its development plans to political contingencies of the kind explained in this volume. On this issue, Jean Collin had this much to say in 1966:

All too often, directors of public enterprises have avoided taking imperative measures because they are too weak to stand up to their staff. Sometimes they are afraid to offend their clients, and I use that word clients advisedly. Sometimes they fail because of simple carelessness, because of a feeling that once they present the State with a fait accompli, it will inevitably bail them out without any punishment. Even in extreme cases where they face the prospect of sanctions, they can still hope for a transfer that is in some cases as good as a promotion (Dakar Matin 26 April 1966).

The deterioration of groundnut farming in the subsistence sector is a remarkable feature of the peasant situation, characterized by pauperization, low levels of productivity and mechanization, shoddily organized transportation and distribution systems, etc.

The causes of the crisis that has wiped out the Senegalese agricultural system are multiple. Seasons of successive drought have upset agrarian ecosystems. The rural exodus has resulted in some loss of available labour power. Unfavourable changes in the structural relationship between input prices and agricultural producer prices have left peasants with insufficient incomes (Kane 1986:72).

In the 1970s these problems worsened, leading to lower export yields and earnings. The policy of agricultural diversification, backed by the establishment of regional development corporations with poorly coordinated functions (BIT/PECTA 1980) ran into structural management problems. Reforms undertaken in the early 1980s led to the abolition of ONCAD and the institution of a New Agricultural Policy (Senegal/MDR 1984).

The State eased certain of its responsibilities onto the shoulders of the peasantry. Groundnut farmers retaliated in various ways. Some cut back on fertilizer use, making soil regeneration harder (Parti Socialiste 1988: 28). On this issue, government experts have noted, correctly, that:

> *serious problems remain as far as fertilizer use is concerned. They will have to be solved before intensive farming methods can be applied. One aspect requires State involvement. It is the supply of fertilizer designed to help regenerate soils. The other aspect, the use of fertilizer to intensify crop yields, depends on agricultural producers* (PS 1988).

With the winding up of the agricultural programme, available equipment was inadequate for intensive farming. Findings from various sources indicate that structural adjustment measures penalize peasants producing groundnuts:

> *The main impact of price adjustment measures on cereal and groundnut production has been to siphon off producer earnings. Urban incomes have been relatively less affected, since the price of the national staple, broken rice, has remained stable. Agricultural incomes, on the other hand, have decreased very substantially on account of drops in the selling price of cereals and groundnuts in particular* (France/MRE 1985:66).

The shortfall in cereal production is a structural fact of economic life in Senegal. It has forced the authorities to import supplementary cereal stocks amounting to about 400,000 tonnes, and to rely on international food aid. Prevailing consumer patterns have turned rice imports into a dictatorial imperative the government is powerless to cope with. In the estimation of the Economic and Social Council, cereal harvest volumes averaged 660,000 tonnes from 1972-73 to 1978-79. This met about 60% of the country's needs (Senegal, CES 1985:63). More strikingly, the Economic Council points out that production levels in the agricultural sector have risen a mere 1.3% since 1960. If, as the authorities claim, local production is to meet 80% of domestic consumption by the year 2000 (Parti Socialiste 1988: 18), then productivity in the cereal farming sector will have to be boosted to 4% (Senegal, CES 1985:63).

The policy aimed at getting the population to eat local cereals in place of imported rice is hampered by low yields and the deterioration of farm soils.

Furthermore, if the cost of rice were raised in accordance with suggestions from donor agencies, already hard pressed populations might respond in politically damaging ways. The authorities have tried to encourage the consumption of local cereals by raising prices paid to producers of local cereals as well as prices charged consumers of imported rice. But results have been unsatisfactory.

The development of hydro-agricultural systems in the Senegal River valley could alleviate the country's dependence on food aid. That would presuppose lower costs for the production of local rice, the marshalling of resources so far unavailable from national savings, and the settling of conflicts with neighbouring Mauritania. Quite apart from problems related to the prohibitive cost of development projects, to the tendency to relegate livestock herders to the fringes of society, and to the frequency of land tenure disputes worsened by claims to social legitimacy based on archaic power structures, the situation remains fraught with considerable ambiguity. The overriding concern behind State intervention in this region is the repayment of debts contracted to pay for development projects, and the need to meet such strategic imperatives as nutritional self-sufficiency. Neither concern is necessarily compatible with the need to guarantee adequate and stable peasant incomes.

The agricultural sector and the rural areas have been put through a decade of structural changes and reforms. But end results have been poor. François Boye offers a clear explanation for the failure:

The rhetoric of the NPA says the agency exists to promote agricultural production. In practice it discourages production. SONACOS, for instance, could close down its oil production factories, import refined oil and make handsome profits from domestic sales. The NPA also encourages dependence on foreign food supplies. Why bother to finance increases in cereal production when large profits can be realized on rice imports on a pro rata basis? In addition, the NPA puts the groundnut sector deeper into the red. For how can balance sheets in that sector become positive again when foreign markets do not support producer prices, and on the domestic scene peasant producers, taking their cue from the high selling price of groundnut oil, grind up their own nuts? For all these reasons, instead of helping to wipe out State losses in the agricultural sector, the NPA actually increases the deficit. In the process, while making State disengagement a matter of urgency, it also makes it harder to achieve. After all, it would be unthinkable simply to let the agricultural sector slide unchecked into bankruptcy (Boye 1988:9).

In the present situation, peasant incomes are inadequate for meeting vital needs. This has aggravated the crisis in Wolof society. Paternal authority, according to A B Diop (1985), is under increasing attack, divorce rates are on the rise, young people migrate more frequently now without parental permission, and communal farms are being turned into individually owned plots. Peasants throughout the country face subsistence problems, and Wolof peasants are the hardest hit. The government has intensified its intervention, but that has not stopped the obvious stagnation of the peasant economy.

This dynamic is among the reasons for intensified social stratification in the rural areas, especially in the groundnut basin, where a majority of peasants earn incomes way below subsistence levels. In sharp contrast to this group, there is another, emergent group comprising beneficiaries of the groundnut programme, mostly marabouts and large-scale producers. Disparities have been worsened both by State arbitration in the groundnut sector and by the imperatives of political life (Caswell 1984). These weaknesses in the groundnut sector are to a large extent the causes of migratory movements in the rural areas. Some of these movements have become a regular part of the subsistence lifestyle of rural populations (Roch 1975).

The State has tried to ease population pressure in the Groundnut Basin. It has also attempted to channel migratory movements towards the New Lands in eastern Senegal, in particular through the establishment of the Société des Terres Neuves (STN). There are many reasons for the peasant exodus into the urban areas, but in certain regions the main cause is the crisis in the groundnut production system. Migrants include women as well as men. Various authors have noted movements of job-seeking young women and girls into the urban areas (Guigou and Lericollais 1988).

In Chapter 6 on urban administration and management, Lat Soucab Mbow shows clearly that urbanization has not been brought under control. The process involves the interplay of economic, political, social and cultural factors all subject to varying degrees of inertia. The problem is that the planning tools used here are either inadequate for dealing with imbalances in the urban structure, or made obsolete by an extremely fluid and dynamic reality. Official programmes take too long to design, while there is a notorious lack of co-ordination between institutional protagonists in charge of complementary programmes. Urban facilities and organizations are in a crisis of operational incapacity. In their day-to-day existence the urban populations have ample proof of the impasse, caused by an economic environment in which the operational capabilities of the public authorities have been whittled down.

In an attempt to solve problems thrown up by rapid urban growth, the State took control of large sectors in the first two decades after independence. Laws and by-laws were issued in floods, and public funds were liberally allocated. Yet the operational crisis in the urban areas remained intractable, and imbalances in the urban infrastructural network became even more pronounced. These problems are rooted in general conditions governing the development of Senegal's domestic resources. One result of the present crisis is a shift in relations between the State and the urban communities, with the latter shouldering an increasingly heavier burden through the process of decentralization.

Given the combined impact of poor management and accelerated population growth, urban environments have deteriorated to the point of crisis, especially in Dakar. The improvement and use of limited zones with well-defined potential have raised identical problems concerning ecological balances. The examples mentioned by Paul Ndiaye underline the role of mining operations and dams, which on the local scene create conditions similar to those observed throughout the country, but at higher levels of intensity.

An analysis of policies applied reveals a number of trends that tend to frustrate the implementation of measures designed to check various forms of environmental degradation. Paul Ndiaye shows that Senegalese officialdom has gotten into the habit of drafting impressively large volumes of legislation, but that implementational mechanisms are notoriously lax. Little by little, public attitudes have been changing, with citizens increasingly willing to get involved in environmental protection activities, whether these are initiated by the authorities or not.

Urban populations intent on meeting basic needs have had to cope with real impoverishment. Certain public services continue to be available, but under increasingly difficult conditions. The health system is a case in point. Government experts, noting this, observed at the time the Vth Plan was being drafted: 'The development of health services has not kept pace with population growth.' (Senegal/MPC 1977:123). The contribution from Mbodj, Mané and Badiane shows that the situation tends to get worse because of the growth rate (3%) of a population that is remarkably young, and whose geographical distribution is especially lopsided.

As in many countries, the health system emphasizes therapy to the detriment of prevention. It has to make do with insufficient equipment poorly distributed over the national territory. For instance, from 1960 to 1988 the number of hospitals rose from 7 to 18. Official statistics for the same period indicate that the population per hospital bed rose from 1,294 to 2,109. Health centres rose in number from 34 in 1960 to 47 in 1988, with the population-per-bed index rising from 4,064 to 8,695. Medical personnel, insufficient to begin with, are concentrated in the urban areas. For each 100,000 inhabitants there are 6.6 doctors, 2.9 pharmacists and 0.8 dentists.

In the period from 1966 to 1976, health expenditure was less than 10% of the national budget. From 8.4% in 1965-66, the percentage fell to 6.6% in 1975-76, to 5.5% in 1983-84, and to 5% in 1987-88. These data are corroborated by Gérard Chambas (1991), who underscores the fact that allocations for health are a low priority item in the recurrent budget of the State. Chambas observes that health allocations dropped steeply in the 1970s, levelling off at approximately 5% in the structural adjustment period.

The proportion of budget expenditure allocated for personnel emoluments is high. From 55% in 1965-66, it rose to 66% in 1976-77, and to 68.7% in 1986-87. It has therefore been impossible to increase expenditure for equipment and medical supplies. An analysis of expenditure patterns for the health system based on official sources[7] indicates that 86% of budgetary allocations for medicines in the Ministry of Health goes to hospitals. Expenditure for purchases of equipment has remained low, at 14% for the period from 1966-67 to 1975-76, and 15% in 1986-87. On this issue the Economic Council, examining the draft fifth Plan during an ordinary session held on 14 April 1977, had this to say: 'In health matters Senegal seems to have fallen two Plan periods behind. The time has come for the country to catch up. Otherwise sooner or later, there will be a price to pay' (Senegal/CES 1977:49).

The country's sanitary facilities are dilapidated. Official statistics give a false impression of this reality. It has become quite routine, for instance, to get substandard service at the country's hospitals from poorly trained staff, while the sick and dying tend to get increasingly unequal treatment depending on their social status. Such unequal treatment has been harshly reinforced by the outbreak of such illnesses as AIDS in this time of economic depression.

Socio-economic differentiations revealed by the foregoing analysis are modulated, however, by systems of solidarity generating substantial cash flows. The catch is that while these systems of solidarity do compensate for social disparities, they also destroy the capacity to build up household savings. Given the linkages between the crisis and cultural changes, the authorities have put forward a number of political solutions. In the past, Leopold Sédar Senghor and his collaborators advocated an ideology called Negritude which offered a two-track domestic cultural agenda based on the concepts of enracinement (local roots) on the one hand, and ouverture (receptivity to foreign influence) on the other. Since Senghor, his heirs have attempted to create a surrogate ideology called the sursaut national (national pride). This also is a two-track concept. Its promoters fabricated an official set of values intended to encourage the country's youth to internalize certain cultural and socio-political values. The rationale for this move was as follows:

> The most serious threat to the future of the Senegalese school system, and therefore to the future prospects of Senegalese society as a whole, is the absence of moral training and public spirit among our youth. The country's youth are capable of demonstrating positive determination in numerous fields of activity. But they have inherited ambivalent cultural attitudes; they are subject to the penchant for ideological confusion inevitable in all periods of crisis; they are tempted to imitate foreign lifestyles and mindsets. They are habitually under-supervised, and sometimes simply abandoned to their own devices. Psychologically, all this makes them extremely vulnerable. (Sénégal d'Aujourd'hui, 34, September 1985:4-11).

Strenuous efforts have been made to shore up the cultural foundations of Senegalese society through a campaign against 'cultural alienation' the centrepiece of which is a draft Cultural Charter 6:

> The important role played by culture in the lives of human individuals and societies; the cultural identity crisis threatening the Senegalese nation as it emerges from colonialism, a key alienating factor; the rise of a world history dominated by great powers imposing their cultural models; the economic problems confronting this country - all this necessitates the drafting of a Charter designed to define a policy of hard-headed options, generous in its principles and guidelines but realistic and cognizant of our still-developing country's limited resources, capable of working out practical solutions to real problems without betraying or abandoning cultural principles or priorities (Senegal/MC: n.d.).

The purpose of the two operations described above was to control the impact of the current crisis on the bases and distribution channels of the existing power structure, and to contain the erosion of the political regime's bases of legitimacy. This, at any rate, is among the objectives identified by Diouf et.al:

> The crisis in the value system (the values in question being those of our ancestors, needless to say) is at bottom nothing other than the clash between an open system and a closed one... Confronted with the increasingly powerful gravitational pull of foreign values, the traditionalist rhetoric that comes stuffed with old proverbs and extolls ancestral values to the skies might be no more meaningful than priestly incantations.

In this connection, Pathé Diagne is quite right when he wonders:

> What remains of the feeling of honour when battalions of immigrants from the Sahel are left to wallow in ignorance and criminality, often ready to

try every possible hustle in the struggle to survive? What is left of respect for elders or of kinship bonds when differences in living standards are so spectacularly great'? (Diagne 1985:22).

Hence the question posed by Diouf et al.:

> Does the dominant model followed by the ruling class in fact express the cultural values advocated in such official rhetoric? Is it sensible to pick out so-called positive ancestral values and restore them without first reinstating the very ancestral socio-political system which gave them their underlying coherence, and which was definitely set against equality? (Diouf et al.:82-83).

In this volume, the problems confronting the two operations mentioned above are analyzed by Souleymane Bachir Diagne. Taking off from a study of official cultural rhetoric, he lays bare the holes in statements based on an assumed dichotomy between traditional and foreign values. His contribution provides proof that:

> the incantatory aspect of the remembrance of traditional values with which official speeches are so liberally seasoned is an indication of the fact that those values are under assault. Indeed, the speeches advocating those old values often bear the ineffectual stamp of simple moral preachments (Diouf et al.:83).

With these observations behind us, we thought it high time to turn to considerations outside the State. After all, 'to understand the State we need standpoints outside the State' (Dandurand 1983:10). One investigative route leading out of the State was the analysis of social movements: 'that have risen to bang against the bulwarks of the State apparatus, undermining them, eroding their bases and probably getting shattered in the process' (Dandurand 1983:10).

The social movements at the core of our study are basically student and teachers' unions. The struggles of teaching staff in the 1970s, addressing all problems facing the Senegalese educational system, were sometimes led by veterans of the May 1968 days. The context of these struggles was the sociological remix of teachers' unions. The outcome was the convocation of a General Congress of Educational and Training Staff (EGEP) and the challenging of the educational system established since independence.

Radical though the teachers' trade union movement was, it was a poor camouflage for ideological differences splitting various factions of the left. Babacar Diop shows that the trade union movement was an extremely active component of the independence struggles. But from 1960, linkages between trade unions and political bodies became problematic. The chronic swing from structural unity to schism characteristic of trade unions and political organizations once more became the dominant pattern, as indicated by the history of the UNTS.

Then came the vogue for 'responsible trade union participation'. That, however, did not signal an end to conflicts in the workplace or at union headquarters. Later, when so-called autonomous trade unions made their appearance, plans to form a central trade union body independent of the official CNTS went into operation. Because of internal conflicts within the opposition, however, the baby steps of the new organization were difficult. From 1981, political reforms gave trade union pluralism a more solid base. Structural adjustment policies provoked trade union upheavals and struggles, with the CNTS now taking an active part. Various political parties tried before, during and after the February 1988 elections to take advantage of this situation. Today the so-called autonomous trade union movement is split in two. All signs point to an imminent realignment of trade unions.

This book is an attempt to trace the slow transition from a voluntarist development policy to economic regression. Basic changes outlined indicate how liberalism came to be the explicit official doctrine of the State. Under the aegis of the new ideological options, the public sector is accorded lower priority.

The liberalization programme has taken the form of punitive privatization exercises, sometimes aimed at the transfer of "dud" enterprises from the public to the private sector. On balance, the privatization programme has been a financial failure. Following the restructuring of the banking sector, there has been a tendency to give less and less attention to vital national interests. The implication is that certain categories of economic operators will be denied bank credits. Meanwhile, the reforms in question have not halted the economic downslide. Neither have they reduced social disparities. Political safety valve operations conducted since 1960, including constitutional reforms and games of political musical chairs, have facilitated short term political balancing acts but left social claims unsatisfied. The temporary balancing acts are shaky in any case, given the parlous state of the economy and the power plays pitting political office-holders against each other. It is a situation that has driven the government into increasing dependence on foreign aid as a crisis-management expedient.

The dominant school of thought now among donor agencies, argues that aid given to Senegal in the 1980s was used to frustrate the adjustment measures the government ought to have been implementing. What then is to be done to stop the trend? In the opinion of François Boye in (Chapter 2), it will be necessary :

to let the coalition of interest groups that has held together the State since independence fall apart. The financial cost of an expanded clientele is prohibitive.

Still, questions remain. Does the country, here and now, possess any social and political forces capable of spearheading such structural change? And, outside the framework of structural adjustment policies, is there an economic programme coherent enough to organize and manage such change? These remain open questions.

Notes

1. The phrase is borrowed from Mamdani (1990), who used it during his confrontation with certain participants at the Carter Center Seminar held at Emory University from 17-19 February, 1989. See *CODESRIA Bulletin*, 2, 1990. pp. 7-12.
2. French capital, which henceforth controlled the most business-like printing operation in Senegal, the Nouvelles Imprimeries du Sénégal, tried to launch a daily evening paper after the launch of a cable television channel. An FM radio channel was allocated to Radio France International, 'the world radio station', which through its sensational and unbalanced coverage of the Senegalo-Mauritanian crisis certainly exacerbated tensions between the two countries. These changes in the local media scene threatened not only the official press but also the fledgling "independent" private press. (*Sud Hebdo*, 161, 13 June 1991:4-5; also *Le Témoin*, 44, 28 May 1991:4; also see feature articles published in the local press on manipulative and stonewalling tactics used to stall implementation of the structural adjustment programme. Cf. *Wal Fadjri*, 258, 19 April 1991:4-5; and 259, 26 April 1991:4-5.
3. In its coverage of relationships between the government and the funding agencies, the local press expresses contradictory demands. Sometimes it castigates the government for imposing draconian hardships under pressure from international financial institutions. At other times, using supposedly confidential documents leaked from the funding agencies, it highlights government resistance to the wholehearted implementation of adjustment prescriptions. Such leaks are particularly frequent in cases where the funding agencies are shown pressuring the government. Recent analyses of the government's economic policies (Berg 1990:42-43) indicate that in power relations between the government and funding agencies, the ruling class has a certain degree of elbow room. That is why, in our opinion, interpretations of the power equation based on the assumption of straightforward impositions by the funding agencies are unwarranted simplifications of the real situation.
4. Since 1990, there has been a series of particularly bloody clashes between the army and groups described as 'separatists' in the Casamance region. These clashes have taken place in a situation of worsening relations between Senegal and its neighbours. There have been armed clashes with Guinea-Bissau, a conflict with Mauritania, and the collapse of the Senegambian Confederation. Considerable military resources have been deployed in the attempt to crush the so-called separatist movement. Yet frequent attacks on government representatives and symbols of 'Northern imperialism' have continued. As part of a general effort to settle conflicts between segments of the

Westernized urban petty bourgeoisie and to end conflicts between Senegal and its neighbours, negotiations were conducted between so-called separatists groups and the government. They resulted in an agreement on the liberation of 355 persons (*Le Soleil*, 30 May 1991), coupled with the signature of an agreement with Bissau (*Le Témoin*, 45, 4 June 1991:4-5; and *Wal Fadjri*, 264, 31 May 1991:4-4). These agreements indicated a change, with the government apparently ready to refrain from the use of military and police violence in the handling of the 'Casamance crisis'. Certain factions calling themselves the Movement of Democratic Forces of the Casamance responded by escalating their demands. The emergence of large segments of the leadership of this politico-military organization from underground, and their semi-official recognition by the central authorities, strengthened the legitimacy of their claims to independence. For that reason, even while avenues to a compromise were being explored, the issues at stake in the conflict over the status of the Casamance remained unresolved. Witness the new turn of events from December 1991. That month, after distributing a communique accusing the authorities of 'duplicity', groups claiming to be affiliated to the MFDC assassinated the Member of Parliament Mamadou Cissé. Little by little, the region was once more taken over by insecurity, despite the mediation of a Peace Commission created at the Bissau Conference. Once again, demands posing a more radical challenge to central government authority were presented: an end to political meetings; the abolition of rural taxation in the area; and restrictions on government troop movements. The government was obliged once more to negotiate another agreement with the MFDC at Cacheu in Guinea-Bissau, in April 1992. It is too early yet to assess the impact of these decisions on the region's stability.

5. This was the Conférence nationale des Chefs des Partis de l'Opposition, (CONACPO), created in February 1990 (*Sopi* 163, 21 November 1990). A year later, however, CONACPO was plunged into a crisis by the decision of its main component, the PDS, to withdraw (*Sopi* 176, 29 March 1991). For a detailed discussion of problems encountered by the opposition in its attempts to transcend its fragmentary tendencies, a basic structural characteristic, see Diop and Diouf (1990a).

6. For a profile of this bourgeoisie, see El Malki's description of the distinguishing traits of Third World bourgeoisies (El Malki 1989:199-213).

7. Information contained in the ensuing section comes from the following sources: Senegal/MPC (1977 and 1989); Senegal/MSP (1989).

Bibliography

Anyang' Nyong'o, Peter, 1989, 'Démocratie et instabilité politique: réponse aux observations de Thandika Mkandawire', *CODESRIA Bulletin*, 1, pp.13-15.

Bayart, Jean François, 1983, 'La revanche des sociétés africaines', *Politique Africaine*, 1, pp.95-128.

Berg, Elliot, 1990, 'Ajustement ajourné: réforme de la politique économique du Sénégal dans les années 80', (Mimeographed summary in French prepared for USAID).

BIT/PECTA, 1980, Mission interdisciplinaire sur l'emploi, Avant projet de rapport, Dakar, 15 février, multigr.

Boye, François, 1988, 'Le modèle de la Banque Mondiale au crible de l'expérience sénégalaise', Paper delivered at the Colloquium on the Agricultural Crisis in Senegal, Dakar, 19-23 December.

Caswell, Nim, 1984, 'Autopsie de l'ONCAD: la politique arachidière au Sénégal', *Politique Africaine*, 14, pp.39-73.

Chambas, Gérard, 1991, 'Politique d'éducation et de santé face à l'ajustement: le cas du Sénégal', Paper delivered at the Colloquium on the State and Society in Senegal: Social Crises and Dynamics, Bordeaux, 22-24 October.

Club Nation et Développement, 1970, 'Contribution à la solution du malaise paysan et une nouvelle approche du développement au Sénégal', Dakar, May.

Dandurand, Pierre *et al.*, 1983 ,'L'Etat et la société', *Sociologie et Sociétés*, XV, I, pp.3-12.

Diagne, Pathé, 1985, 'Des systèmes sahéliens de valeurs', miméo, Dakar.

Diop, Abdoulaye Bara, 1985, *La famille wolof: tradition et changement*, Karthala, Paris.

Diop, Momar Coumba and Mamadou Diouf, 1990a, *Le Sénégal sous Abdou Diouf: Etat et Société*, Paris, Karthala.

Diop, Momar Coumba and Mamadou Diouf, 1990b, 'Léopold Sédar Senghor, Abdou Diouf, et après?', *L'année Africaine*, 1989, pp.189-215.

Diouf, Mamadou *et al.*, 'Etude prospective de la société sénégalaise en l'an 2015. Synthèse de l'analyse rétrospective', mimeo Dakar.

El Malki, Habib, 1989, *Trente ans d'économie marocaine 1960-1990*, Paris, CNRS.

Fatton, Robert, 1987, *The Making of a Liberal Democracy: Senegal's Passive Revolution: 1975-1985*, Lynne Rienner, Boulder.

Fatton, Robert, 1988, 'Bringing the Ruling Class Back: Class, State and Hegemony in Africa', *Comparative Politics*, April.

France, (Republic of), Ministry of External Relations, Cooperation and Development, 1985, 'Déséquilibres structurels et programmes d'ajustement au Sénégal', 3 volumes, mimeo, March.

Guigou, Brigitte and André Lericollais, 1988 , 'Crise de l'agriculture et marginalisation économique des femmes en pays sereer siin (Sénégal)', Paper delivered at the Colloquium on the Agricultural Crisis in Africa, Dakar, 19-23 December.

Hesseling, Gerti, 1985, *Histoire politique du Sénégal*, Paris, Karthala.

Kane, Cheikh Hamidou, 1986, 'La nouvelle planification du développement économique et social', Paper delivered before the National Council of the Socialist Party, Dakar, 26 April.

Lo, Magatte, 1986, *L'heure du choix*, Paris, L'Harmattan.

Lo, Magatte, 1987, *Syndicalisme et participation responsable*, Paris, L'Harmattan.

Lo, Magatte, 1991, *Le temps du souvenir*, Paris, L'Harmattan.

Mamdani, M. 1990 'Coup d'oeil sur les études africaines à l'Américaine', *CODESRIA Bulletin*, 2, pp. 7-12.

Martin, Michel, 1973, 'Un aspect de l'insertion des militaires dans le processus de développement national en Afrique: étude de quelques contradictions', *Revue Canadienne des Etudes Africaines*, VII, 2, pp.267-285.

Mbembe, Achille, 1988, *Afriques indociles: Christianisme, pouvoir et Etat en société postcoloniale*, Paris, Karthala.

Mbodj, Mohamed, 1978 'Un exemple d'économie coloniale: le Sine Saloum (Sénégal et l'arachide, 1887-1940. Culture arachidière et mutations sociales', Doctoral dissertation, Paris VII.

Parti Socialiste, 1988, 'Réflexions sur les conséquences sociales du Programme d'ajustement structurel à moyen et long termes', Dakar, 30 May.

Roch, Jean, 1975 'Les migrations économiques de saison sèche en bassin arachidier', Humanities Series, *Cahiers de l'ORSTOM*, 1, pp.55-80.

Sandbrook, Richard, 1987, 'Personnalisation du pouvoir et stagnation capitaliste: l'Etat africain en crise', *Politique Africaine* 26, pp.15-37.

Senegal, (Republic of), Economic and Social Council, 1976, 'Etude sur les mécanismes de réajustement des prix et des salaires: périodicité et niveau des réajustments', Dakar.

Senegal, (Republic of), Economic and Social Council, 1985, 'Le Sénégal face aux problèmes démographiques'.

Senegal, (Republic of), Ministry of Planning and Cooperation, 1977, 'Draft Vth Four-Year Economic and Social Development Plan, 1977-1981', Volume III, June.

Senegal, (Republic of), Ministry of Culture, undated, 'Charte culturelle: document d'orientation'.

Senegal, (Republic of), Ministry of Rural Development, 1984, 'La nouvelle politique agricole', Dakar.

Senegal, (Republic of), Ministry of Planning and Cooperation, 1987, 'Deuxième réunion du groupe consultatif. Paris, le 31 mars et 1er avril 1987. Le programme d'ajustement économique et financier à moyen et long termes (PAML) 1985-1992', Volume 1 and Volume 2.

Senegal, (Republic of), Ministry of Planning and Cooperation, 'Etude prospective Sénégal 2015', Dakar, July.

Senegal, (Republic of), 1989, 'Projet de Plan d'orientation pour le développement économique et social 1989-1995 (VIIIth Plan)', Dakar, October.

Senegal, (Republic of), Ministry of Public Health, 1989, 'Déclaration de la politique nationale de santé', Dakar.

Terray, Emmanuel, 1987, 'Introduction', in Emmanuel Terray, (ed.) *L'Etat contemporain en Afrique*, Paris, L'Harmattan.

Touré, Babacar, 1989, 'Histoire vraie d'un faux complot', *Sud Hebdo*, 49, 20 April and 50, 27 April.

Touré, Mamoudou, 1985, 'Politique d'ajustement économique et financier', Paper presented before the National Council of the Socialist Party, Dakar, 11 May.

2. Economic Mechanisms in Historical Perspective

François Boye

Introduction

National economies are complex realities, and cannot be fully understood through a single analytical or heuristic approach. This chapter lays no claim to methodological exhaustiveness. Neither does it proffer a comprehensive study of the Senegalese economy. Its purpose is precise and limited: to situate the Senegalese economy within the dynamic background of its historical development. Given the current reality of structural adjustment in the country, our approach draws heavily on macroeconomic data, analyses and statistics, for four reasons:

- First, current economic policies are targeted at specific imbalances. These imbalances are normally expressed as statistical indices. The examination of such indices is therefore a pre-requisite to any clarification of economic realities.
- Second, data generated by the National Statistics Board constitutes an invaluable source of information. So far there has been a tendency to overlook them, the excuse being that they are approximations, not dead accurate figures.
- Third, there is no way to explain the country's recurrent deficits, especially in its balance of payments and public finances, unless we first take the trouble to understand underlying macroeconomic mechanisms.
- Fourth, all economic policies draw their relevance from a given macro-economic context.

Our argument, designed to clarify ongoing trends and to suggest the contours of coming changes, is structured in three sections. The first section presents an analytical overview focused on an examination of balances in the following sectors: employment and resources; the balance of payments; public finances; and financial flows and volumes. The second section treats the foregoing analytical overview in greater detail by looking at specific economic sectors and assessing their macroeconomic impact. The third section focuses on economic policies pursued since independence, evaluating their suitability and gauging their efficiency.

An Analytical Overview

The Balance of Employment and Resources

Judging by calculations based on constant prices (see Table 1, Appendix), tabulated within the framework of the readjusted Sixth Plan and updated in DPC reports on the country's economic prospects, Senegal has never registered high economic growth rates. Its annual growth rate has averaged 2.71%, but there have been large fluctuations in specific years. Overall, by its twenty-seventh year of independence, the country's gross domestic product had scarcely doubled.

During the first decade of independence in the 1960s, when annual growth rates of 5% were commonplace on the international scene, Senegal sauntered along at an average annual growth rate of only 3%. In the 1970s, rocked by a series of external shocks including the abrogation of the gold standard in foreign exchange transactions and the establishment of floating exchange rates in 1973, the first and second petrol crunches of 1973 and 1979, the dizzying fall in raw material prices after 1975, and severe droughts in 1971, 1973, 1977, 1978 and 1980, the growth rate dipped under 2%, falling as low as 1.45%. Tentative data for the 1980s suggests the beginnings of an upswing. For the period between 1981 and 1987, the average annual rate of growth was 3.92%. Assuming that rate holds, the 1980s should turn out to have been more productive than the preceding couple of decades.

Wild swings in growth rates for specific years have not been a feature simply restricted to a particular decade in Senegal's economic history. Indeed, ever since independence, annual growth rates have been widely variable in every decade, with differences as high as ten percentage points separating the lowest and highest annual rates registered.

The drought affecting the country since the late 1960s has been one of the reasons for fluctuations in the annual growth rate. The gross domestic product has fallen every time a drought has eroded production levels in the agricultural sector, with a consequent slump in the primary sector as a whole. The years 1971, 1973, 1977, 1978, 1980, 1981 and 1984 were cases in point. There is obviously a correlation between value added in the agricultural sector and that in the overall production system. However, the correlation in no way indicates a preponderance, in macroeconomic terms, of the primary sector. Neither does it prove that the secondary and tertiary sectors have no dynamism of their own. To begin with, in real terms value added in the primary sector has never been more than 50% of GDP. In fact, the tertiary sector has registered consistently higher value added. Furthermore, in times of depression, negative growth rates in the primary sector have always been lower than GDP rates. Lastly, in the crisis years of 1971, 1977, 1978 and 1981, real growth rates in the secondary and tertiary sectors were actually positive.

There is a popular misconception to the effect that the two components of the production picture, viz.: domestic production and foreign imports, grew in inverse proportion, with the foreign component displacing domestic production in importance and *vice versa*, during or after the cycle of natural disasters that marked the 1970s. Certainly, in 1967, 1977, 1981 and 1984, import volumes increased while GDP fell. It is also true that import levels have tended to be elastic as compared to GDP (m). But seen from a long-term perspective, this has never resulted in the substitution of foreign for national production.

From 1960 to 1970, the average annual economic GDP growth rate of 3.08% was compatible with practically steady levels of imports (-0.27%). From 1971 to 1980 the average rate (m) was 1.48 (2.15%: 1.45%). From 1981 to 1987 it dropped almost one percentage point without changing the complementary pattern of domestic production and foreign importation maintained from 1960 to 1987 (on the average, m = 1.32%: 2.71% = 0.48).

The close long-term correlation between agricultural value added, economic GDP and imports evaluated at constant prices indicates a degree of independence between permanent balance of payments deficits (with the national current account in the red and net external assets at negative levels) and the national demand for foreign goods and services. During the 1970s, imports did not decrease to compensate for the cumulative shortfall in Senegal's foreign exchange balances, as we shall see below. Stabilization programmes established in the following decade admittedly slowed down the quickening pace of importations. In 1982, for instance, in economic GDP growth rate of 17.2% coincided with an 0.8% drop in the rate of importation. But these developments did not turn the demand for foreign commodities into a manipulable variable that could be used to redress the country's external account balances. In other words, never has feedback from the impact of balance of payments on the overall economy changed import patterns in a way to slow down growth rates in Senegal.

The various aspects of changing overall demand have not kept pace with each other as much as the corresponding aspects of overall supply have. Average foreign demand, after increasing in volume in the 1960s on account of the preponderance of groundnut product exports (over 50% of total exports) and the gradual replacement of unshelled groundnut exports with exports of crude or refined groundnut oil, began to fluctuate along with GDP levels as from 1971. This happened in spite of the emergence or reinforcement of non-agricultural exports such as fishery products, phosphates, fertilizer and petroleum products, and despite the volume of international commerce, which grew at average rates of 7.7% and 3.5% in the periods from 1967-1977 and from 1977-1986 respectively (*World Economic Outlook* 1985: 63).

Exports did little to alleviate the impact of the economic depression during the years of drought. Private consumption at constant prices, however, dipped steeply (1969, 1972, 1973, 1980) over the 1960-87 period. It had a less mercurial growth rate than any other item in the overall demand picture between 1960 and 1987. Furthermore, on the average it was higher than all growth rates registered in the national accounts except for public consumption. For that reason it was able to maintain the domestic market, keeping it from shrinking under the impact of foreign shocks or climatic hazards. In other words, private consumption remained dynamic, but at a price. It dried up household savings, so that gross domestic savings were negative overall. It also pushed the public sector into heavy debt whenever the State attempted, in the 1970s, to revitalize the national economy by launching ambitious projects such as the Senegalese Sugar Complex, Dakar Marine and the Industrial Free Zone. On the other hand it had a positive impact in that without it, the real growth rate of economic GDP, low enough since 1970, would doubtless have fallen lower still.

While Senegalese households boosted domestic demand, creating conditions for overall negative[1] savings, the volume of public consumption was unable to play a compensatory role, even after the establishment of stabilization programmes. Quite the contrary: it did not cease growing as from 1972, when it decreased slightly. In subsequent years it continued eating into public savings, swelling the financial needs of the civil service (see below), and putting pressure on the country's foreign accounts by driving it to borrow from foreign lenders and to import commodities.

In terms of volume, the contribution of gross fixed capital to the expansion of overall demand over the long term has always been negligible. In the first decade after independence, the loss of the West African market and the dwindling of French administrative agencies in Senegal reduced a substantial portion of industrial production capacity installed after the end of World War II to non-viability. That is why in real terms, FBCF levels in 1970 were lower than in 1960. Furthermore, over the 1960s, average annual investment growth rates amounted to zero.

Beginning in 1974, the State and the public sector went on a spending spree, buying up investment goods. The binge was encouraged by soaring export incomes (1974, 1975, 1976), by low interest rates on international money markets between the two petrol crunches, and by structural adjustment programmes after 1979. Nevertheless, the bottom line was not a steady rise in investment volumes. The reason was that prices of investment goods, most of which Senegal habitually imports, increased at much higher rates on account of exceptional inflation rates in the OECD countries from 1974 to 1981, while exchange rates often fluctuated after 1971. In 1979, FBCF calculated in constant prices came back to 1975 levels after having decreased continuously in the intervening years. From 1980 the trend turned upwards, but the annual increase was negligible because the drop in public investments during the crisis in public finances in 1981 and 1984 prevented average annual growth rates from going over 2% between 1981 and 1987.

The Balance of Payments

Two sets of statistical data - the first from official reports covering the 1968-88 period and published by the IMF, the second from unofficial evaluations published by the DPC, tell the same story: The accounts of the State of Senegal have always been in the red, except for the year 1972. Prior to 1980, the chronic deficit in the country's current account was caused mainly by shortfalls in its trade balance, always extremely high when compared to net positive unilateral transfers, something Senegal has always enjoyed. In the 1980s, debt service payments began to deepen Senegal's balance of payments deficit on a regular basis, pushing the nation into an increasingly uncomfortable posture on the international money market.

The Trade Balance

The relationship between variations in economic GDP volumes and those in the trade balance calculated in constant prices has in general tended to be inverse. The level of the country's invariably negative commodity trade balance has always decreased whenever overall activity contracted, except in 1976. In all recovery years (1972, 1974, 1979, 1982) it has risen. The pattern being so regular, it is unreasonable to hold the international situation responsible for Senegal's external position. The fact is that no matter what changes take place on the international economic scene, Senegal's trade balance remains negative. This was true before 1973, when inflation rates in the OECD countries were low. It was true when, after 1974, inflation rates hit double digits in those same countries. It was true during the international trade boom before 1976, as well as in the slump following the first half of the 1970s decade. It was true when dollar exchange rates rose in 1973, 1980 and in the first half of the 1980s decade, and when primary material prices rose between 1973 and 1980. And it was true when, after 1980, primary material prices fell. All this indicates that the real causes of Senegal's chronic trade deficit are to be found within the national economy.

Never have Senegal's export earnings fully paid for the country's imports. The reason is that Senegal's non-agricultural exports (fishery products, phosphates and petroleum products) differ from manufactured products. Outlets for the latter in the northern countries (the European Economic Community, the USA, Canada) have registered high growth rates. Second, increases in the agricultural export trade have never been sufficient to absorb the impact of macroeconomic changes and climatic hazards ravaging the production and export of groundnut products. Third, volumes and/or prices of products imported into Senegal have tended to stay above a given floor[2].

One explanation could be that as far as the international economy is concerned, the products Senegal has to offer are only of marginal value. A second is that the country's export industries outside the agricultural sector have proved incapable of turning into growth poles. One telling point is that since 1977, production indices in the extractive and chemical industries have been trending downwards. There is a third explanation, related partly to the fact that Senegal operates as a price-taker on the international market, and partly to the fact that instead of concentrating on intermediate goods, whose prices tend to be relatively elastic, depending on levels of activity, the country's import structure emphasizes consumer commodities and petroleum products, because of the jump in petrol prices since the 1970s. Prices in both of the latter categories are rigid.

The Balance of Services

Before 1979, Senegal's balance of services followed a rational pattern independent of changes in economic GDP volume levels or the trade balance. It registered a positive balance whenever net foreign exchange income from the tourist industry, the airport and seaport services and disbursements by foreign administrative agencies installed in Senegal sufficed to pay for all demands for foreign services. That was the case in 1970, 1971, 1972, 1973, 1974 and 1978. In the opposite case, when demand for foreign exchange related to freight services, commodity insurance, the use of foreign transportation services and transfers of profit abroad exceeded foreign exchange earnings from Senegal's own services to foreign buyers, the balance became negative.

It was the need to borrow from foreign sources to finance the chronic deficit in the country's current account that in the end brought the service balance also into line with the overall economy's tendency to stagnate. In 1980, interest payments began to exceed FCFA 10 billion (African Financial Community Francs). The upward spiral has been phenomenal since then. In 1985, for instance, interest payments amounted to FCFA 55 billion. For that reason, the balance of services has shifted definitively into the red, and the downward trend is set to worsen.

Unilateral Transfers

Unilateral transfers, such as gifts, grants and remittances etc., are the sole item in the current accounts picture (out of three) which are always contributed positively to the country's foreign exchange resource base, even in times of economic crisis. But gifts, grants and remittances are symptoms of increasing numbers of Senegalese migrants working abroad, as well as of a dependence on foreign aid. These are not indices of economic progress. In macroeconomic terms, unilateral transfers have not helped the country to balance its current accounts. Neither have they enabled the country to postpone national debt rescheduling to some never-never date. So far, all they have achieved is to make up for net outflows due to transfers of profits and interest payments, which take up an increasing proportion of Senegal's economic GDP value. Were it not for the generosity of allies, the solidarity of migrants with their kin back home, the high inflation rate which has kept GDP value (in current prices) rising despite ups and downs in overall production volume, and the lackadaisical attitude of the Senegalese civil service, which has never cut back on aggregate personnel emoluments, the national income[3] would have shrunk dangerously as from 1979 (see Appendix, Table 6).

Financing the Current Account Deficit

In the past quarter century, net direct foreign investment has not kept pace with Senegal's balance of payments financing needs. In the first place, while the deficit has been getting steadily larger, investment has been erratic in a completely insensitive way. Worse still, foreign investment has occasioned the repatriation of profits at higher levels each succeeding year, e.g.: FCFA 3.4 billion as against FCFA 6.5 billion in 1977; 5.5 billion as against 6.2 billion in 1978; 2.1 billion as against 7.3 billion in 1979; 1.6 billion as against 5.4 billion in 1980; 2.3 billion as against 7.8 billion in 1981; 3.8 billion as against 8.0 billion in 1982.

Foreign exchange reserves could do little to cushion the country during the first half of the 1970s when climatic hazards and international economic shocks threatened the national economy. In 1962 Senegal's foreign exchange reserves had stood at $78.1 million. From then until 1969 they decreased steadily until they amounted to no more than $6.2 million. From the second decade of independence, foreign borrowing became the only way to finance the current account. 1979, besides yearly borrowings have taken the principal form of long term public capital loans. Prior to 1981, the process had caused no explosive interaction involving debt service payments, the current account and the economy's need for foreign exchange financing. This was because its pattern of evolution up to that point was rather haphazard, following no specific trend. In the 1980s, however, the country reached a juncture where it had to fall back on debt rescheduling[4] to avoid being placed on foreign exchange rations or getting sucked into a vicious cycle of increasing new debts to pay old and ever-rising debt service charges. To say that Senegal's current account deficit has always been financed is merely to utter an accounting truism. Coupled with a top-down view of the balance of payments, in which the top of the chart determines what appears at the bottom, such a statement is also tantamount to an observation that no imbalance in the balance of payments has ever produced a backlash on the real sector in such a way as to cause subsequent corrective action. Senegal, in plain words, has never had to tighten its belt, in the sense that it has never had to cut down on imports of goods and services. By the same token, it has never had to reduce its economic GDP in volume terms, with a view to squeezing out foreign exchange surpluses adequate for paying off debt service charges.

Cash Flow Volumes and Counterpart Entries

According to international monetary statistics published by the IMF, changing cash flow volumes (M2) in Senegal (see Appendix, Tables 1 and 3) have gone through three phases. From 1960 to 1969, when the country's foreign assets showed a positive net balance, the characteristic trend was for cash flow volumes to go downwards. It was not until 1971, for instance, that M2 rose above 1961 levels. There are two explanations for this: public sector credits were stagnant, and the Public Treasury maintained a status of creditor with regard to the banking system. During the 1970s, neither the tailspin that brought Senegal's net foreign exchange assets down from a positive balance of F CFA 4.4 billion in 1971 to a deficit of F CFA 87.1 billion in 1980 as a result of the recurrent deficit in the balance of payments, nor the repeated slumps in business as a whole, brought down the volume of cash in circulation in the country. As a matter of fact there was a literal explosion in the volume of cash in circulation, which registered an annual rate of increase of 17%. This bore no relation whatsoever to inflation or to the volume of economic GDP.

One reason for this independent behaviour of credit with regard to the economy is that the Senegalese Public Treasury shifted from its old position of creditor *vis-à-vis* the monetary system to a new position of borrower. To this day that shift has been steadily accentuated. Second, the State pursued a voluntarist policy aimed at integrating local business people into various key sectors of the national economy. But in the 1980s, when structural adjustment programmes went into operation, the trend was broken off. There were years in which the volume of cash in circulation grew at double-digit rates. In 1981 and 1982, for instance, the rates were 21% and 22% respectively. Nevertheless, from 1983 to 1987, the annual rate of increase was divided by an average factor of five each year[5].

This reduction in cash volume throughout the economy is not so much the result of a deliberate policy of monetary austerity as a consequence of the sterile effect of stiffening deflationary pressures exerted on M2 by the deterioration of Senegal's foreign exchange position. In 1985, for instance, Senegal's net foreign liabilities amounted to 258 billion F CFA, three times the 1981 level. It would have been impractical to fix a ceiling on internal credit from the outside. In the first place, the public finances were in such a state of imbalance that it was impossible to ration advances requested from the Public Treasury (see below). Moreover, the increasingly debt-ridden position of Senegal on the international scene would have meant that the volume of cash in circulation would have had to continue indefinitely shrinking.

In any consideration of the various component aspects that go to make up the volume of cash in circulation, the salient fact after a little over a quarter century of independence is, oddly enough, the hefty size of fixed term deposits. It is often said that in Senegal, savings are an unknown phenomenon. People who mouth this platitude sometimes know no better. At other times, they base their conclusions exclusively on readings of economic accounts that indeed registered negative savings rates between 1980 and 1981. But that is only part of the story. Accounts of second-level banking institutions show that business people in Senegal do have certain financial capacities. Prior to 1973, these savings were far below 10% of cash in circulation, but from 1974 to 1984, the relative proportion rose above 15%, and in 1984 the figure was actually double that percentage, i.e.: 30%. Since 1983, fixed term deposits have consistently exceeded fiduciary issues and maintained levels approximating those of current account deposits. In 1985, fixed term deposits made up 10% of GDP value.

Prices

Senegal has never been subject to the type of inflationary mechanisms (see Appendix, Table 4) that paralyzed most underdeveloped countries in the second half of the 1970s. Even when, as in 1973, 1977, 1978, 1980 and 1981, economic recession resulted in lower export levels, Senegal did not suffer from inflationary shocks provoked by the rationing of scarce imported goods and services necessitated by dwindling foreign exchange resources. The reason is that exchange resources are managed within a community structure, the franc zone. This has helped Senegal to keep up its import capacities even though its net external balance has been negative since 1973. Senegal's national reserves have shrunk, but this has not led to successive devaluations of the CFA franc induced by speculation and tending to perpetuate inflation. The reason is that the CFA franc is not a national currency. It therefore does not reflect specific features of any particular national situation.

Whenever an external shock has been provoked by increases in raw material prices and/or the dollar exchange rate, the national economy has been shaken by double-digit inflation[6]. That is what happened in 1974-75, 1982, 1984-85. The fact that the result was not a permanent inflationary spiral is further proof of the absence of inflation-multiplier mechanisms in Senegal.

Neither has inflation been a drawback on the export market. Senegal's two leading export outlets are France and the Ivory Coast. In both markets real exchange rates have not tended to increase, since over a 27-year period, Senegalese prices have not shifted significantly from local price levels. Needless to say, real interest rates paid out to holders of savings accounts have been negative. That fact, however, has not dampened enthusiasm for fixed term deposits. Quite the opposite: there has been a spectacular upward surge in fixed deposits in the banking system since 1980 (see above).

Lastly, over a long period inflation has not worsened terms of trade between the primary and secondary sectors in any systematic way. In the 27-year period from 1960 to 1987, the rate of growth of the deflationary factor of value added in the primary sector has been equal, on the average, to that of value added in the secondary sector. In plain terms, it would be wrong to blame the low growth rate of the national economy on any supposed inflationary crisis.

Public Finances

Because the public finances in Senegal are currently in a state of crisis, there is a popular supposition that patterns of public finance have changed remarkably since independence. That view is erroneous. As Table 8 in the Appendix shows, civil service accounts and public finance parameters have changed little.

a) Taxes and duties have always been the mainstay of the country's public finances. This remained true even after the expansion of the public sector after 1968 and increased State participation in the private sector after the first petrol crunch.

b) Income taxes have never superseded customs duties and sales taxes, etc. as the most productive tax base.

c) Households have consistently paid higher taxes than enterprises, even though gross operating revenue from the three sectors have at all times amounted at least to double the total of salaries, wages and social expenditure.

d) The bulk of government revenue has invariably gone to pay salaries and wages plus social expenditures.

e) Gross government savings have never been adequate for funding planned investments. As a result, the country has always needed to rely on foreign funding.

f) Senegal started life as an under-taxed nation. It has never changed that status. One index of this reality is that tax revenue is still lower than 25% of GDP[7]. A second is that income taxes have rarely amounted to 5% of GDP.

g) Import duties continue to provide relatively little revenue, because only in exceptional years has the State been able to collect more than a quarter of amounts really due.

h) Salaries, wages and social expenditure have consistently taken up approximately half of tax revenue.

Given the above observations, one might wonder why the crisis of the country's public finances only began recently, that is to say, at the end of the 1970s, instead of coinciding with the first days of the Republic. On the basis of the principal trends enumerated above, we are in a position to advance a categorical answer: the State of Senegal did not plunge into a financial crisis because of any injudicious changes in its normal methods of financial accounting and book-keeping. It is a series of foreign shocks which have driven the State into shrinking its operational scope since 1980. As early as the 1960s, foreign indebtedness was among the principal means whereby Senegal financed its capital goods budget. At that time, however, debt service charges were lower than 5% of tax income, and the State was actually a creditor as far as the banking system was concerned.

How, it might be asked, was such a miracle possible? There were two reasons. First, this was the first development decade, when financial arrangements available to the Third World tended to be more like outright aid packages than impositions of world market conditions. International financial markets then were small, and the USA discouraged the expansion of the Eurodollar market (cf. the Interest Equalization Tax). The financial market was also somewhat hermetic, since deregulation and the free flow of capital had not yet come into fashion. Exchange rates and currencies tended to be stable, and despite the inflationary slippages provoked by the Vietnam War, double-digit inflation was regarded as an academic hypothesis. To all intents, exchange rates were fixed, and wild fluctuations in interest rates belonged in the realm of science fiction scenarios.

In the 1970s the State of Senegal was hit by a series of changes following fast after each other. Budgetary expenditure for personnel doubled between 1973 and 1978, after wage levels were raised following the first petrol crunch. The public service swelled. Equipment expenditure trebled between 1970 and 1978 as a result of numerous investments in that period (in terms of current prices, public and private investments rose from F CFA 30 billion to F CFA 100 billion between 1970 and 1980). Debt service charges on loans taken to fund the investment boom increased fourfold. Transfers and subsidies paid out to companies also quadrupled.

These were major changes, certainly. But they were not necessarily time bombs. It would have been possible to keep up the pace if the 1974-75 context that made such changes possible in the first place had lasted. That would have meant rising terms of trade, low real interest rates on the world market, the maintenance of excellent credit ratings, the earning of exceptional income from the sale of oleaginous crops, and the reaping of superb profits from the CSPT. Unfortunately, rainfall levels were lower than normal in 1977, 1978 and 1980. Second, from 1976 the international climate changed steadily until the trends that had started with the first petrol crunch ultimately became crushing.

Under such circumstances, the crisis of the public financial system since 1979 turns the spotlight on the ways in which successive governments have tried to adjust to new contours on the international scene.

- The moment fluctuating dollar exchange rates and interest rates create an external upward trend in debt service charges, the low variability of the ratio of personnel emoluments to tax income begins to appear like a factor of budgetary imbalance.

- Given the inelastic floor of personnel emoluments and the constant increase in the weight of debt service charges, capital expenditure and transfers have to be reduced to prevent an explosive spiral caused by government funding needs, foreign loans and debt service charges.

- When primary material export prices stay depressed over long periods, the State, gaining less and less profit from the phosphate industry while paying the deficit run up by the groundnut industry, is forced not only to halt its subsidies to peasants and make them pay going market prices, but also to cease subsidizing unprofitable public enterprises by liquidating them.

In the 1980s, various stabilization programmes incorporated these economic policy guidelines into their overall implementational approach. So far, however, they have not reshaped Senegal's public finances:

- Recurrent expenditure still eats up the bulk of State tax income.

- Public savings are still a pittance compared to the cost of necessary investment.
- The State of Senegal is bound to remain dependent over the long term on donor agencies to meet its funding needs. In other words, foreign lenders have to agree to reschedule debt payments and to continue to finance the State budget.
- Debt service charges keep growing, eating constantly into public savings.

In sum, Senegal is still caught right where it was in 1979. The country is confronted with the same conundrum: in an international environment that has turned more hostile, what are the appropriate budgetary policies that would help the nation adjust to the changed situation?

Sectorial Analysis

The Primary Sector: Contribution to Growth

Turning points in primary sector business activity have tended to coincide with turning points in the economy as a whole since 1967 (see above). That does not mean that the primary sector has played a preponderant role in the overall economy since 1960.[8] Only in the unstable, depressed decade of the 1970s did changes in value added in the primary sector (see Appendix, Table 5) determine the rate of growth of economic GDP (rp = 133% on the average). By contrast, in the 1960s as well as after 1980, the increase in average economic GDP volume growth rates (see above) reflected a substantial fall in the contribution from the primary sector (rp = 11% on the average between 1960 and 1970; average rp = 57% between 1981 and 1987).

The inverse relationship between the growth rate of economic GDP and the parameter rp is also corroborated when the period from 1960 to 1987 is split into two, facilitating the comparison of years of high growth with years of low growth or recession. The primary sector makes a 37% contribution on the average to overall growth for the range of years when the variable TXGDPE is at least equal to 4%. For the range of years when the variable TXGDPE is lower than 4%, the contribution is 95% on the average.

What the share of the primary sector reflects above all is the development of the agricultural sub-sector. Over the entire period from 1978 to 1987, the impact of this sub-sector on the annual growth rate of the VAP variable was over 60%. (For other periods there are no available statistics on levels of intersectorial value added). Only in 1987 did the situation change: in that year, for the first time, volume levels of value added in the agricultural sub-sector (-1.3%) and in the primary sector (2.8%) developed along inverse lines. On the whole, the preponderance of the agricultural sub-sector is more a consequence of its great relative weight and the range of its fluctuations than of efficient performance. For even though in the 1978-1987 period the agricultural sub-sector received three quarters of investment funds allocated to the primary sector (Senegal/MDR 1982: 27), it registered levels of value added constantly below those for the animal husbandry and forestry sub-sectors, while its average growth rate (2.72%) was lower than that of the animal husbandry sub-sector (3.1%).

Detailed studies of the agricultural production system (cf. Appendix, Table 9) show that over the 1960-1987 period, productivity in the sub-sector was also low:

a) Millet yields were exceptionally high for two consecutive harvests in 1973-74 and 1984-85. Even so, the peak yield of 753 kg per hectare attained in 1978 was only 46% higher than the 1960 yield.

b) In 26% of all cases, (1962, 1965, 1977, 1980) the expansion of acreage planted with millet coincided with actual drops in yield levels.

c) Since 1980, millet production levels have attained at least double the 1960 level in only one year, 1986.

d) Annual rice production levels over the second half of the 1980s only matched 1969 levels, i.e., about 140,000 tons.

e) Average groundnut yields per hectare during the 1960s (865 kg) were higher than those for the ten planting seasons (767 kg) following 1976.

f) In 27% of all cases (1963, 1968, 1970 and 1980), even though the total area planted with groundnuts expanded, yields dropped.

g) Average annual groundnut production levels in the 1960s (920,000 tons) was far higher than in the decade after 1976 (792,000 tons).

For the stagnation in the agricultural sub-sector indicated by these figures, there are two underlying explanations. First, is ecological factors. From the end of the 1960s, desertification and overpopulation in the Groundnut Basin combined to reduce fallow land, destroy soils and aggravate deforestation. Yields for the period, reflecting lower and lower levels of fertilizer and other farm inputs, tended to fluctuate unpredictably, like rainfall.

The second explanation is organizational factors. Prior to 1980, the rural world functioned under a bureaucratic administrative system. Red tape often delayed deliveries of adequate quantities of good quality seed and fertilizer to peasants. Even after government intervention in the sector was reduced in 1981, these input levels remained low. The new game rules required seed and fertilizer costs to be deducted from prices paid to groundnut producers. Wishing to cut their losses, peasants sought to escape from official marketing channels by selling on the parallel market (80% in 1984) and reducing their demand for groundnut seed and fertilizer. Since 1981, fertilizer consumption has gone down.

What this means is that the preponderant contribution of the agricultural sub-sector to growth in the primary sector (and thus to overall economic growth) does not signify that it operates as a growth pole, i.e., as a sub-sector whose technical and economic efficiency are high enough to catalyze growth in the rest of the economy.

Contribution to the Balance of Payments

The primary sector impacts on the country's balance of payments along four channels. Exports of raw or semi-processed materials are the first. Even though exports of groundnut products, fresh fish and canned fish have consistently brought in less than 50% of export value since 1980, they have always earned more than any other Senegalese export. Despite fluctuations in raw material prices and other changes on the international market since 1971, ups and downs in the value of these exports have by and large tended to reflect changes in the national production system.

Second are cereal imports. The gap between the national demand for cereals (rice and wheat) and national production levels has led to an increasing reliance on foreign production. Thus, rice imports increased three-fold from 109,000 tons in 1960 to 336,000 tons in 1985. Nevertheless, Senegal's dependence on foreign food supplies has not become so serious as to lead to balance of payments problems. For one thing, the fact that foreign exchange is not rationed means that the country has never had to choose between food imports and imports of capital goods. Besides, even if cereal imports had been abolished from the onset of the structural adjustment programme, the current account deficit would have been cut by less than 40%.

Third are foreign loans for investment financing in the primary sector. Because 75% of investment in the country's development plans is financed through foreign resources (Lemoine 1982), the primary sector accounted for at least 20% of Senegal's long-term indebtedness between 1976 and 1981.

Fourth, are induced effects in other sectors caused by primary sector activity. The primary sector induces a range of activity in the secondary (canneries, oil factories) and tertiary sectors (trade and transport). Through these channels, primary sector activity affects all imports of goods and services. It is easy enough to understand how Senegal's balance of payments posture is affected by the relationship of these activities to the primary sector. However, the precise manner in which the canneries, the oil manufacturing industries and the trading sector have impacted on that posture has been far from straightforward.

Export volumes of groundnut products have always been insulated from changes in prices of oleaginous products on the international market. The country's oil manufacturers (before 1976) and SONACOS (after 1976) have invariably exported the equivalent in oil and oil cake of all oil seed delivered to them for processing. The reason is that whenever there was a difference between prices paid to national producers and international market prices for oleaginous products, the CPSP (before 1986) or the Groundnut Guarantee Fund (since 1986) subsidized groundnut inputs. The point is that if SONACOS had been forced to operate on the basis of real market prices as from 1981, it would have had to ration the amount of oil seed processed and sold, handling only those quantities guaranteed to maximize the profitable operation of its plants as determined by their productivity and relative market costs. Had that happened, Senegalese peasants would have been brought into line with well-defined but variable demand levels of oil seed required by the factories. The State finances would have improved, since compensatory subsidies would no longer have to be paid to groundnut producers. Also, in order to boost production and profits, the oil factories would have had to make steady cuts in costs[9] (Senegal/MDR 1988).

Rice imports have trebled in 25 years because government intervention in the rural sector has never enabled the country's peasants to produce enough surplus millet or rice to meet the urban demand for cereal. One underlying reason for this failure is that Senegal's agricultural policy has been geared to a constant: the maintenance of groundnuts as the most profitable cash crop. The gap in producer prices for groundnuts and millet rose from FCFA 5 in 1960 to FCFA 20 in 1987 in favour of groundnuts[10]. Furthermore, the millet market is felt to be small, while public support for rice farming is considered prohibitively expensive. Rice grown on irrigated perimeters in the Senegal River valley has always had to be subsidized by the Compensation Fund. In any case, peasants in Senegal have long thought of cereals as something to be cultivated mainly to meet subsistence needs, and only secondarily for sale. In addition, rising demand for rice in the urban areas has been encouraged by price differentials between imported rice and locally produced millet flour. In practice, the policy has been to keep urban purchasing power relatively high. One way this has always been done is through the maintenance of minimal prices for broken rice (the staple, known as SIAM), and the privatization of subsidies. Millet not sent to the flour mills attracts no subsidies. As a result, it is unlikely that the price of millet flour will ever drop lower than that of imported rice.

Foreign loans used to finance primary sector investments have risen steadily. This is because during the 1970s, when the Compensation Fund balance for groundnut sales was firmly in the black, CPSP resources were partly used to keep urban purchasing power high through consumer commodity subsidies, as well as to fund costly bureaucratic structures and agro-industrial projects like the Senegalese Sugar Complex. Had surpluses extracted from the primary sector been ploughed back exclusively into that sector, the dependence on foreign loans would not have become such a knee-jerk reaction.

Contribution to the Public Finances

Because the primary sector is connected to every other sector in the national economy, it has had a permanent impact on every item of public expenditure. It is possible, however, to get a more specific understanding of its contribution to the financial posture of the State through an examination of operational agencies created by the State since 1960 within the framework of public intervention in the rural areas.

In the wake of independence the State set up numerous public agencies in quick succession as replacements for the firms that had dominated the colonial trading economy. The new agencies included the Senegalese Development Bank (BSD), Agricultural Marketing Board (OCA), Rural Development Assistance Centres (CRAD), and the National Agricultural Produce Marketing Board (ONCAD). At the time, these corporations could be supported comfortably enough from national resources. The fledgling Republic had healthy balances in its Treasury, and the PNG was a lender, not a borrower. The country had substantial foreign exchange reserves, amounting to $78 million in 1962. France was buying groundnut seed at prices above world market levels, so that fat profits from sales were still possible. Broken rice (SIAM) was cheap, enabling the Treasury to rake in a profit from the Compensation Fund. But in 1968 France pulled the plug by stopping subsidies for Senegalese oil seed. From then on the country was hit by a series of shocks and financial vicissitudes, and the economy has been reeling since.

- The fall in the export price of groundnut seed was passed on to the national producer. To add insult to injury, rainfall totals were low in 1968. The result was a 25% drop in the quantity of groundnuts offered for sale to ONCAD, the State purchasing board, in 1969.
- Reduced cash income in the rural economy as from 1969 worsened peasant poverty, pushing many into bad debts. This endangered the financial stability of ONCAD and the BNDS.
- Worsening peasant insolvency meant lower demand for fertilizer and agricultural inputs. The result was less business for regular suppliers of ONCAD such as SISCOMA and SIES.
- The shrinkage in rural cash transactions and the low level of production inputs made farmers turn to planting millet as a replacement for groundnuts.

When the EEC provided funds for cushioning the country against shocks caused by its exposure to world market prices for oleaginous products, it seemed as if the impact of successive waves of bad economic news could at last be softened. But in 1971 and again in 1973 the drought struck, converting the recession into a long-term depression. The State has since then been involved in crisis-management, trying to hold back the threat of chaos.

In 1973, for instance, public funds had to be marshalled to underwrite a rescue plan (Senghor, 1974) including price rises for farm producers, a 4-franc bonus for groundnut farmers, the payment of bad debts owed by insolvent peasants to ONCAD (F CFA 3.5 billion), the distribution of F CFA 410 million worth of foodstuffs to tide consumers over until the next harvest, the provision of free animal feed (F CFA 250 million), the expenditure of F CFA 686 million for boreholes and maintenance work on wells, and the freezing of prices of essential commodities. When the world economy was rocked by upheavals in the second half of 1973, the impact of these crisis arrangements was intensified. For despite the high cost of subsidies the State imposed on the Price Compersation and Stabilization Ford (CPSP), the new financial agency created in 1974 to guarantee price freezes, the upward surge of raw material prices after the Yom Kippur War, together with the effect of three bumper harvests between 1974 and 1976, boosted the State's financial capacities tremendously.

The result, for the primary sector in particular and the economy in general, was a series of expansionist decisions. For instance:

a) Prices paid to producers increased at rates above 25% in 1975 (from F CFA 29 to F CFA 41.5 in the case of groundnuts).

b) Subsidies paid out to the Rural Development Mutual Fund, intended to support the agricultural programme, increased fourfold between 1973 and 1976.

c) Sugar from the CSS, approved under the Industrial Code since 1970, was not competitive on the world market. However, it was agreed that the CPSP should subsidize it.

d) New rural development agencies (SNTI, STN, SODAGRI) were created.

e) The State bought up oil factories dating back to colonial times and set up its own facility for marketing oleaginous products, the SONACOS, in 1975.

f) The public sector became overcrowded.

This expansionist trend was compromised by two successive years of drought, 1977 and 1978. Furthermore, as from 1976, world market prices for oleaginous products and phosphates both went into a tailspin. The State was therefore forced to bring domestic prices for food commodities into line with world market prices for rice and oil. That took some of the heat off the CPSP. But, owing to its strained financial situation, the State was still unable to stop the recurrence of cycles of economic depression, even though its past policies were designed precisely to do that. It could therefore not avoid the downward slide into the agricultural and financial crisis that ended in the abolition of ONCAD in 1980.

From 1981, the State began steadily cutting back on its commitments in the public sector. But as far as the public finances were concerned, State disengagement has so far proved no less costly than State intervention. The liquidation of ONCAD left the State holding the bag for accumulated liabilities, some F CFA 67 billion in 1980. Poor rains that year caused a 26% drop in groundnut production (488,000 tonnes), making it necessary for the CCCE to lend the "National Rural Supplies Corporation" (SONAR) funds for rebuilding seed stocks (120,000 tonnes). To cover heavy expenditure for the transport and distribution of seeds, SONAR was given a subsidy from the CPSP. The same CPSP had to compensate the Senegalese National Oilseed Marketing Corporation (SONACOS) for its part in marketing groundnuts. In 1986, the State had to raise producer prices for groundnuts by 28.5% (from F CFA 70 to 90) in an attempt to limit the expansion of the parallel market[11]. The government had to subsidize groundnut prices as from 1986, and the production of sugar and irrigated rice also had to be subsidized.

Contribution to Cash in Circulation

Despite its substantial macroeconomic influence, over the years the primary sector seems to have lost a great deal of its former impact on changing levels of cash in circulation (see Appendix, Table 7):

- Farm season credits had in the past imparted a cyclical rhythm to volumes of cash in circulation. This was because during the first quarter of the year liquidity levels were pumped high. They were just as regularly lowered in the rainy season. Subsequently, however, the agricultural credits that had nurtured these cycles lost their overwhelming importance due to economic stress. In the first place, their average share of total credit fell below 25% from 1975 to 1987. As a result, off-season credits grew at an average rate higher than the overall growth rate for all credits. Second, the steady increase of medium and long term credits (which made up over 35% of total credits after 1985) with little or no connection to the primary sector, reduced fluctuations in economic credit levels. That gave the volume of cash in circulation a more even rhythm. This was in marked contrast to the pattern of short term credits and fiduciary issues of currency, still strongly influenced by the rhythms of the yearly agricultural cycle.

Neither the rapid increase in injudicious loans following the disastrous farming seasons of the 1970s nor the heavy liabilities left by the wound-up ONCAD had any significant effect on the normal routines of the monetary system. Interest rates on debts and credits were not suddenly boosted to exorbitant levels to attract savings or to maintain bank profits in the teeth of dwindling financial capacities. Discount rates were not raised unduly to punish inefficiently run banks. The share of the Central Bank in refinancing operations involving credits allocated to second-echelon banks did not decrease sharply. So banks short of cash were not forced to attract available savings or to increase in-house capital.

- Net foreign assets have decreased steadily since 1973 quite independently of business slowdowns in the primary sector. This has been true even though: a) value added in the primary sector has consistently varied in accordance with the volume of economic GDP; b) Economic GDP volumes and the trade balance have maintained a consistent inverse relationship; c) the trade balance and the current account balance varied inversely only in exceptional years (1975, 1979, 1983); and d) the current account deficit was financed not through deductions from foreign exchange reserves but from loans.

- Only the Government's net deficit with the monetary system, worsening steadily since 1973, may be imputed to the influence of the primary sector. That is because the deficit, at least in part, is symptomatic of huge shortfalls the public finances have had to absorb on account of climatic hazards and the impositions of the world market, filtered through ONCAD, the CPSP, SONAR or SONACOS (see above).

Development and Impact of Primary Sector Prices

It is a widely held supposition among development economists that over the long haul, primary sector prices (DVAP) have not lagged behind general price levels (DPIBE or the deflationary factor in the value of economic GDP). The opposite is in fact the case. In the period from 1961 to 1987, the average growth rate of the variable DVAP has been higher than that of the variable DPIBE (6.95% as against 6.37%). This has been the observable result in every decade of the post-colonial era, the exception being the period from 1981 to 1987.

As compared to the African consumer price index (PCM), prices in the primary sector (see Appendix, Table 4) do not support the hypothesis according to which in developing countries, market costs dependent on prices paid to rural producers have been decreasing with time. The difference between average growth rates of PCM variables and the DVAP over the period 1967 to 1986 (9.23% minus 9.20%) has been infinitesimal.

The picture that emerges from a study of available sectorial data for the period 1978-87 is that prices in the agricultural sub-sector have registered the highest average growth rate (14.6%). Other sub-sectors follow in descending order: animal husbandry (8.49%); fisheries (8%); forestry (4.51%).

Price increases in the primary sector do not seem to have had a major impact on the rate of inflation (the rate of growth of the variable DPIBE) since 1960. In years when the variable DVAP grew at a rate of 10% or higher (1961, 1966, 1968, 1973, 1975, 1982, 1986), it was rare for the rate of inflation in that year or the next to reach double digits. Now the function of the CPSP and its forerunner organizations was precisely to prevent the passing on of sudden producer price hikes down to consumers of primary products. Might these patterns indicate a high rate of success in fulfilling that function?

Lastly, a detailed examination of agricultural production (Appendix, Table 9) does not support the conclusion that price fixing plays a decisive role in farmers' decision to produce one crop other than the other.

- In 50% of all cases (1967, 1974, 1980, 1982, 1986), net producer prices for groundnuts varied in inverse proportion to total hectarage planted with that crop;
- In 44% of all cases (1971, 1975, 1982, 1986), as producer prices for millet rose, the area under cultivation shrank, or vice versa;
- In 54% of all cases (1961, 1963, 1965, 1967, 1971, 1980), peasants reacted to every change in the price differential between groundnuts and millet by increasing the area planted with both millet and groundnuts.

The Secondary Sector

Contribution to Growth

The volume of economic GDP did not double in the 27 years from 1960 to 1987. By contrast, the volume of value added in the secondary sector, increasing at an average annual growth rate of 4.15% over the same period, doubled as early as the mid-1970s[12]. No doubt about it: this achievement indicates that the secondary sector operates with a certain dynamism of its own. In the first place, despite the gravitational pull of the primary sector and its multi-faceted impact on the food industries, primary and secondary sector growth patterns have not really been dependent on each other. For instance, the average growth rate in the primary sector from 1960 to 1987 was 2.57%. Second, in 1967, 1969, 1971, 1977 and 1981, the volume of value added in the secondary sector grew at a rate of at least 2%, at the same time as the volume of overall economic GDP was shrinking. Meanwhile the following sub-sectors maintained industrial growth even during some periods of general recession: a) the energy sub-sector: expansion here continued steadily; b) phosphates: the sub-sector grew steadily until 1974, after which date it entered a cyclical pattern of boom and bust; c) the chemical industries: their growth in the 1960s and 1970s was followed by decline in the 1980s; and d) the textile industries: experienced steady growth, albeit at low rates.

Its independent dynamism notwithstanding, the secondary sector remained marginal as far as its average contribution to overall growth was concerned. In the 1960s the average rate was 19.11%; in the 1970s it was 5.84%; from 1981 to 1987 it was 11.9%. The explanation is that the secondary sector has relatively little weight, accounting for less than 33% of the overall economy in terms of the volume of value added. It is this lack of weight that has neutralized the impact of the sector's growth rate, whose dynamism is inversely proportional[13] to that of the economy as a whole.

From 1978 onwards, the oil factories contributed no more than 10% on the average to the volume of value added in the secondary sector. But even though their relative weight in the sector decreased, they maintained a preponderant influence on sectorial growth rates. On the surface this was a paradox. But from 1978 to 1987 it could be explained by the amazingly wide range of volume growth rates registered by the oil manufacturing enterprises. Between the lowest and highest rates registered, the difference was a staggering 346 points. No other industrial sub-sector had such wild variations between its peaks and troughs. Ultimately, the reason for this anomaly was the highly unsteady rainfall.

That said, it must be admitted that Senegal's oil factories are far from being paragons of efficiency. In the 1978-86 period, they registered value added figures consistently below 25%, a threshold just as regularly exceeded by such other sub-sectors as the Public Works Department, the energy industry, the chemical industries, textile factories and the mining industries. From 1978 to 1982, average productivity in the oil factories, calculated in constant prices, was lower than that in the extractive industries (2.96 million as against 3.65 million). What this means is that in the secondary sector just as much as in the primary sector, the sub-sector making the highest contribution to growth in the past has no outstanding capacity for efficient performance to contribute to the overall economy.

Contribution to the Public Finances

The secondary sector, as we have just observed, has demonstrated its capacity to grow at higher rates than the economy as a whole. But that does not mean it has made major contributions to the public coffers.

During the 1960s, indirect taxes and duties paid by the secondary sector never reached 15% of all indirect tax monies paid in to the State budget. In the 1970s, the substantial increase in the share of indirect taxes contributed by the secondary sector (30% in 1979) was offset by the need for the State to pump increasing subsidies into industries hard hit by price changes brought on by the two petrol crunches.

From 1980 to 1986, net indirect taxation after deduction of operational subsidies dropped from F CFA 48.97 billion (11 times their 1970 level) to 2.76 billion, after thrice dipping below zero (1982, 1984 and 1985).

With the exception of 1974, 1976 and 1977, taxes on BIC paid by industrial establishments, calculated as a percentage of total direct taxation, never rose above 25%. Substantial dividends paid out to the State in the 1970s, especially in 1974 and 1975, proved to be a flash in the pan when phosphate prices plummeted as from 1976.

Because the State was committed to the maintenance of the public industrial sector, as well as to its expansion after the first petrol crunch, it was obliged to go into direct borrowing, to guarantee loans and to write off international loans that it had to pay back when the financial crisis of 1978-82 pushed the entire public sector into bankruptcy. Soaring prices for imported intermediate goods and high energy costs in Senegal forced the State to subsidize exports in the fisheries, phosphates, textile and footwear industries as from 1981.

The low level of net contributions from the industrial sector to the public finances indicates the failure of Senegal's industrial policy as defined in six investment codes[14]. The official idea was that the establishment of new industrial units would be governed by fiscal and other concessions including preferential tariffs. But capitalist investors have not responded to such State inducements by honouring the rule of reciprocal advantages. The State may have absorbed the loss of initial tax income as a means of helping most of the enterprises in question to run profitably (for example, in the 1970s). But in return, it has gained no additional tax revenue from new industrial business or inter-industrial spin-off. The result has been the opposite. For apart from the period 1972-77, tax exemptions have kept direct tax revenue accruing to the State from gross business earnings in the secondary sector below 10% since independence.

Preferential treatment given certain lines of business under the investment code has forced the State to subsidize other industrial sub-sectors victimized by external losses (such as exorbitant costs charged by monopolies), tottering under the impact of international competition, and/or struggling to cope with inflationary spirals caused by external factors such as the two petrol crunches. In according special recognition and juridical status to such enterprises as the CSS, the BUD and Dakar-Marine, the State has pushed the public sector into absorbing losses in such public sector enterprises as SENELEC and the National Water Works Corporation (SONEES). Sometimes the State has compensated by offering subsidies; at other times the expedient has been to tap foreign loans guaranteed by the State.

All in all, the State has been unduly generous in its eagerness to guarantee loans as a means of encouraging industrial investment. The policy has saddled it with colossal losses from white-elephant enterprises that strutted a grandiose while before collapsing into bankruptcy. Names like SOSAP, BUD and SEIB come to mind. Against such a background, it becomes understandable that the New Industrial Policy was launched in the teeth of the crisis in Senegal's public finances. The step was, needless to say, in part a response to the need to create a healthier climate for enterprises geared to the international market, which offers vaster opportunities than the local market. But beyond that the principal impetus came from the desire of the State to serve notice to capitalist investors that henceforth it was no longer going to baby non-competitive enterprises, and that it had decided to make normal rates of taxation the standard towards which all investors benefiting from initial concessions would inexorably shift, because all starting advantages would automatically decrease to zero in a fixed schedule of years (see Act 87-25).

Contribution to the Balance of Payments

The contributions of the primary and secondary sectors to the country's exports are inseparable. The processing of primary materials for the export trade has in no way changed the pattern of the dominance of groundnuts and fishery products in the export picture. This continued dominance cannot be attributed to either the primary or the secondary sector alone. Since 1960, no specific secondary sector export has proved to be in competition with primary sector exports. In 1974, phosphates brought in F CFA 25 billion worth of earnings. This reflected a 400% growth rate following the first petrol crunch. In the 13 years following that, the figure was exceeded only twice (28.7 billion in 1984; 27.3 billion in 1985). Petroleum products have not undergone notable changes in quantity since 1973. However, their value has swollen or dwindled in tune with price levels fixed by OPEC. Production of phosphoric acid at the Senegalese Chemical Industries complex (ICS) is too recent a development to have generated useable growth statistics. It seems clear, nevertheless, that prospects there are none too radiant. At the moment, the world fertilizer market is in a glut, and the ICS has been facing problems as a consequence. There is also a world-wide surplus in cereal production.

The secondary sector consumes such imported inputs as wheat, petroleum, powdered milk, spun yarn, liquid sulphur, ammonia, potassium, chemical colouring, lubricants, vinyl and metal products. It specializes mainly in the processing of light industrial goods (capital goods are imported). It therefore has a measurable impact on the country's import picture. It must be remembered that 50% of all imported capital goods comprises equipment earmarked for the industrial sector. So in terms of value, imports connected to the secondary sector[15] have always been preponderant. Since 1970 they have accounted for over 50% of Senegal's demand for foreign goods and services.

The industrial sub-sector has made appreciable contributions to Senegal's trade balance. Its exports (groundnut products, fishery products, phosphates, petroleum products and fertilizer) have consistently been higher than its imports, except in those years when groundnut production took a drastic fall (1973, 1978, 1980, 1981). On the other hand, the sub-sector is partly controlled by foreign capital and upper management staff. This causes permanent inroads on the country's current account balance.

As indicated above, foreign investments in Senegal have yielded repatriated profits far in excess of the sums originally invested. Because of outstandingly hefty salaries and transfers paid out to upper-level expatriate executives, Senegal has either registered negative net unilateral private transfer balances (according to IMF statistics, such was the case from 1979 to 1983), or a negligible positive balance in the public sector (from 1984 to the present). If we add the fact that increased debt service charges in the late 1970s indicate that the country's major industrial investments (the CSS, Dakar-Marine, the Industrial Free Zone, and the purchase of the former West African Water and Electricity Corporation) yielded little profit in comparison with total interest payments occasioned by their dependence on foreign financing, we might justifiably conclude that it is the industrial sector that pushed the national economy under foreign control for a whole decade.

Contribution to Cash in Circulation

The impact of the secondary sector on the volume of cash in circulation has never been different from that of the economy as a whole. The effect of the secondary sector was indistinguishable from that of the primary sector during the years of the agricultural boom. In 1967, 1969, 1971 and 1981, when the secondary sector stood out like a booming island in a sea of recession, the increase in the volume of cash in circulation did not reflect the fact that as far as the allocation of short term credits was concerned, the industrial sector had superseded the trading sector, and that in the allocation of medium and long term credits it had also superseded the construction sector (public works, real estate and private housing).

The Banking System

Contribution to Growth

The banking system has supported growth in two ways. First, it has financed the agricultural programme, in the sense that it has provided funds to facilitate the production and marketing of agricultural produce. This is a line of business left over from the colonial era. Despite its seasonal and sectorial nature, it does make a contribution to growth. One index is the fact that years of accelerated growth in Senegal have invariably been those times when major corporate capital has underwritten a production and marketing boom in the agricultural sector. Such an outcome has been possible because the country's monetary policy has never straitjacketed the domestic agricultural programme under foreign norms likely to limit opportunities of major corporate refinancing, or to make such capital more expensive.

Such preferential treatment has brought the banks some prosperity. It has been observed, for instance, that whenever business in the agricultural sector is particularly slow, value added in the banking sector shrinks accordingly. Still, the preferential policy has brought its share of major risks. Since the 1970s, the Senegalese banking system has piled up an impressive backlog of bad debts and litigious loan cases. The bankruptcy of ONCAD only made matters worse. That debacle, as a matter of fact, could have brought the entire monetary system in the country to a halt had the Central Bank not agreed to avoid penalizing second-level banks by making access to refinancing facilities prohibitively expensive for them.

Public rumour would have it that interest rates on loans are high in Senegal. This is quite false. Compared to interest rates on loans abroad (especially in France), and considering the country's chronic deficit in financing capacities, Senegalese interest rates have stayed consistently low. But what, in practical terms, does such an assertion mean? For one thing, that the Central Bank, right from its establishment, has never fixed bank rates according to contemporary international monetary standards. Second, that second-level banks, acting under local banking regulations, have charged interest on loans at rates lower than might have been possible in the light of international economic practice and imbalances between their assets and liabilities.

These low local interest rates have insulated the national economy from the international money market, which even after 1979, the year Paul Volker took office at the Fonds Européen de Développement (FED), remained mercurial. That protection has prevented Senegal from sliding into a monetarily induced recession of the type experienced in the United States in 1982. The down side is that the maintenance of such low interest rates over such a long period has cost the banking system a great deal. First, it has led to missed opportunity costs. Second, it has limited the system's capacity to offer positive interest rates on credits with a view to attracting savings placed abroad or in the informal sector. Third, it has discouraged foreign borrowing to finance national economic development. Fourth, it has made the system permanently dependent on the Central Bank. Finally, the result has been a monetary policy doomed to take lax attitudes unless it is prepared to stall the entire banking system.

Contribution to Public Finances

The bank has regularly made a contribution equivalent to 20% of tax income for the previous budgetary period. In practice, this has not been tantamount to a refusal on the part of the banking system to finance the expansion in State activities since independence. Through its support for the agricultural programme (understood in the sense described above), and through its constant financial underpinning of the impressive public sector, the banking system has regularly supported the State budget by underwriting the public finances. As matter of fact, had it not been for all kinds of bank loans extended to the public sector, the State would have been obliged to pay out more subsidies and to borrow more heavily in order to keep alive its various tentacles in all sectors of the economy. That would have worsened the budget deficit.

The banks have been experiencing a crisis since 1978. That crisis provides precise proof that the '20% rule' is limited in its application. In fact the rule applies only to funding for the Public Treasury. It would never have been invoked if credit allocations to public sector enterprises had not become so huge, comparatively speaking, that the non-repayment in full of credits advanced to the State threatened to plunge the banking sector into a liquidity crisis. In other words, had management practices in the public sector been stricter, the State would have been in a position to get the banking system to finance its expanded schedule of activities indefinitely. The current dependence of the Senegalese State on foreign donor agencies is an aberration from the normal rules of the franc zone.

Contribution to the Balance of Payments

The banking system has played a significant role in the continued deterioration of Senegal's net foreign assets on account of its operational rules. The fact that capital may freely be transferred within the franc zone has enabled second-echelon banks to operate on a permanent external deficit. Since 1976, this deficit has increased steadily despite parallel increases in credits financed by the Central Bank and the low percentage (less than 20%) of bank liabilities occasioned by foreign commitments. Because the 20% rule is automatic[16], and refinancing arrangements for the agricultural programme equally non-negotiable, it has been impossible, in statutory terms, to implement any monetary policy likely to shrink domestic demand severely enough to make imports of goods and services compatible with any targeted level of the current account balance and net foreign assets. This is the reason why stabilization programmes, even though they went into operation in 1980, have done nothing whatsoever to increase net foreign assets or to improve the current account balance (see below).

Contribution to Cash in Circulation
Within the operational framework of the banking system, the volume of cash in circulation (M2) is a resultant of interactions between the Central Bank and second-echelon banks (the monetary base), as impacted upon by the behaviour of factors external to the financial system (e.g., the demand for fiduciary currency) as well as by institutional constraints (such as the reserve coefficient). In Senegal, the monetary base has always been made up mainly (i.e., to the tune of 75% at least) of fiduciary currency. This is because there is no legal reserve coefficient obliging the country's banks to keep a high percentage of their deposits 'frozen' at the Central Bank. In practice, the proportion thus held is less than 10%. As for the currency multiplier index which mainly reflects variations in treasury constraints imposed on banks by their customers (deposit-based fiduciary issues), it rose steadily until 1977 (from 1.83 in 1962 to 2.93 in 1977). From that date it has been chronically unpredictable: (2.84 in 1978, 3.14 in 1984 and 1985, 2.50 in 1987).

Since 1960, counterpart entries for the monetary base have changed so as to factor in all fluctuations in counterpart entries for the volume of cash in circulation. Up until 1974, Senegal's net assets abroad were in the black but dwindling. From 1976 they declined steadily, slipping deeper and deeper into the red. Government accounts retained a low net credit balance until 1975. In 1976 they slumped past zero point. Since then they have grown increasingly negative, the deficit growing by a multiple of 38 from 1976 to 1983. Until 1972, bank claims had been equivalent to a percentage of the monetary base, usually around 90%. Nowadays they are more than half as much again. In other words, as from 1976 Central Bank accounts reveal that attempts were made to adjust monetary aggregates to a deteriorating balance of payments and a worsening situation in the nation's public finances. Monetary policy, in other words, was accommodating.

Policy Analysis

Within the framework of the IMF and World Bank paradigm (Khan, 1987) designed to monitor stabilization programmes submitted to these financial institutions for approval, economic policy comprises the following elements:

a) A demand policy intended to reduce discrepancies between overall demand and production capacity;

b) A structural policy designed to expand production capacity;

c) An exchange rate policy intended to boost export production;

d) An external borrowing policy designed to ensure the continuous funding of the national economy by foreign capital.

Because these four economic policy objectives are interdependent, they also have to be basically compatible with each other. For it is easier to control overall demand if production capacity is expanding. The nation's international credit rating improves as excess demand for goods and services falls, and *vice versa*. The production of exportable goods contributes directly and indirectly to the expansion of national production capacity. And because the production of exportable goods has a positive impact on the balance of payments, it provides a continued incentive for foreign investors to pump capital into the national economy. Implementational means used to achieve these policy goals, however, diverge.

Monetary and budgetary policies are instruments of demand policy. Monetary policy is tantamount to a control mechanism used by the Central Bank to try and influence credit demand through the manipulation of interest rates. When domestic demand has a tendency to grow independently of domestic production, monetary policy has to be austere. It should, in other words, leverage interest rates upwards. Its efficiency depends first on capital movements which can neutralize its effects with greater or lesser speed; secondly on the flexibility of price and income structures, which can make any shrinkage in overall demand more or less temporary; and thirdly on the elasticity of investment as related to interest rates. In the absence of such elasticity, monetary policy is deprived of a major transmission belt.

Budgetary policy affects domestic demand directly through its impact on public demand for goods and services, and indirectly through the inhibiting effect of taxation on individual purchasing power. It is all the more effective when it does not produce a backlash in the form of variations in interest rates that tend to cancel out its initial impact on overall demand.

Price policy is the instrument of structural policy. It involves the suppression of all distortions tending to work against the economy's growth potential by discouraging producers and owners of production factors. In practical terms, it should make it possible for market mechanisms to replace institutional and legislative mechanisms that protect the domestic market in a way that inhibits export growth. It should prevent agricultural resource allocations that are counterproductive within the framework of the international price structure. And it should abolish negative real interest rates incompatible with the buildup of domestic financial capabilities. That these prescriptions are effective is proved by the outstanding success of the Newly Industrialized Countries, which structured their economies in line with world market realities.

The axiom is obvious to the point of tautology: the instrument of exchange rate policy is the exchange rate itself. Exchange rates should vary in such a way as to keep the national economy competitive. This means that the nation's producers should be able to market their produce on the world market at prices identical to their competitors'. This requirement in turn means that exchange rates have to be fixed at realistic targets capable, within limits, of making up for the differential between inflation levels on the national and international markets. This is a tricky feat since domestic inflation has to factor in a degree of imported inflation.

The instrument of an external borrowing policy is the foreign loan. Foreign loans should be used to finance capital accumulation on condition that the export sector can generate the foreign exchange resources needed to repay them. Unless this condition is met, foreign loans are likely to turn into an obstacle to growth as heavy debt service payments drag national income inexorably downwards.

Economic policy packages are made up of specific combinations of these instruments. Typically, macro-economic adjustment packages include a restrictive monetary policy, an austere budgetary policy, partial or total liberalization of economic sectors, the devaluation of national currency, and a damper on external borrowing. The question before us is this: prior to IMF and World Bank intervention in Senegal in 1979, were the economic policies in force more different from the adjustment package model than those in subsequent years? That is the key question we shall be addressing below, in our evaluation of macroeconomic management since independence.

Monetary Policy

The monetary policy followed by Senegal during the 1960s, if available statistics are anything to go by, can in no way be described as expansionist.

Prior to 1973, credits paid in to the Treasury were subject to a 240-day stipulation. Before its abolition in the 1973 Reform, this clause acted as a disincentive minimizing government loans from the banking system, which never exceeded a peak of F CFA 3.5 billion. The clause kept non-governmental loans below zero.

Individualized rediscount ceilings were imposed on financial and non-financial agents. This effectively blocked the tendency of credits to the economy to offset the decrease in net positive assets that followed the withdrawal of numerous French administrative agencies from Senegalese territory and the establishment of a network of Senegalese diplomatic missions throughout the world (resulting in lower levels of official unilateral transfers)[17]. This tight check on monetary demand was abolished in the 1975 Reform.

Checks on monetary demand maintained M2 below its 1962 level until 1970. There was no inflation due to monetary causes. Between 1962 and 1967 prices (the deflationary factor for the value of economic GDP) rose steadily, but the volume of cash in circulation (M2) remained tight. Real additional receipts decreased. Prices (the deflationary factor for the value of economic GDP) increased twice as much on the average as the volume of cash in circulation (1.81% as against 0.91%). From 1960 to 1970, internal demand increased steadily in volume terms, the only exception being 1969. The macroeconomic consequences followed a similar upward curve. Given the above picture, it is clear that these growth patterns were not caused by decisions taken by the monetary authorities. In the 1970s, on the other hand, observers of the Senegalese economy generally agree that monetary policy began to show all the imbalances typical of the economy as a whole.

The arguments put forward have served as a basis for stabilization policies implemented since the start of the current decade. The fact that after 1971 rediscount rates were not in line with international money market rates encouraged capital transfers abroad, worsening the depletion of Senegal's foreign assets. Ballooning PNG as from 1976 was not offset by a brake on credits to the private sector. There was therefore an expansion in domestic demand at a time when successive years of drought had led to a decrease in the supply of goods and services.

The cumulative loss of net external assets after 1972 did not stimulate the adoption of a counter-cyclic management strategy designed to deal with overall demand and based on the reduction of credits to the economy intended to improve both the current account balance and the net value of the country's foreign assets.

Between 1971 and 1980 the supply of money in terms of real value grew at exceptionally[18] high average rates (10%). This happened under circumstances of imbalance that led to the introduction in the 1970s of an economic and financial recovery programme. Still, it does not follow that there was a causal relationship between these developments. Neither does it follow that the causative move was the decision of the monetary authorities to stimulate overall demand despite the decline in productive activity. True, there was a situation of excess liquidity in the 1970s, but that did not modify the trend of domestic demand in volume by an iota. It grew at the same average rate (3.08%) in the first two decades of the post-colonial era. As a result, the trebling of the deficit in the trade balance between 1975 and 1978 (from F CFA 26.8 billion to F CFA 76.8 billion) and the downward slide into a negative savings posture in 1980 should be imputed to the drop in economic GDP and overall GDP caused by successive years of drought between 1970 and 1980.

It was not monetary policy that caused the imbalances of the previous decade. Because it did not become contra-cyclic, monetary policy did not become geared to those imbalances. Now this statement would in itself provide a further basis for criticism if the monetary authorities exercised direct or indirect control over all counterpart entries making up the volume of cash in circulation. But the fact is that the statutory regulations of the West African Monetary Union (UMOA) have always denied them this power. Within the UMOA framework there is only one rediscount rate. Therefore Senegal does not have the authority, through its National Credit Committee, to take unilateral action to stop the deterioration of its net external assets by bringing market rates within the domestic economy into line with French money market rates. Incidentally, from 1970 to 1980, Togo, Benin and Niger were not in this situation. As for the Ivory Coast, it came under this regime only in 1978. Automatic refinancing of credits in the agricultural programme meant that in years of good rain, monetary policy could not set a desired target for external assets if credits for the agricultural programme and their macro-economic fallout worked against a shrinkage of overall demand. The 20% rule had the effect of an *a priori* imposition of a floor for monetary issues no matter what the size of *ex ante* macroeconomic imbalances at times when the PNG mainly reflected[19] the level of loans extended to the government by the monetary system.

This chain of reasoning makes it clear that monetary policy in the 1970s was geared to internal realities. It also makes it plain that the monetary authorities were not guilty of mismanagement. In my opinion it indicates, in addition, the reasons why the various stabilization programmes tried out since 1980 have failed to reverse the trends followed by the PNG and the country's net external assets. The point is that there will be no long-term decrease in the PNG as long as the State Treasury is empty, and as long as the 20% rule pegs government loans to a variable that keeps rising because it incorporates a built-in inflationary factor: tax income. There will be no tendency towards a balance in the country's net external assets as long as such a balancing act would necessitate reductions in credits to the economy incompatible with both the 20% rule and the automatic refinancing of credits allocated to the agricultural programme.

By positing these conditions we do not mean to overlook the increase in net external assets registered in 1986. Nor do we intend to dismiss the decrease in the PNG in 1987[20]. But we maintain that these were one-off events, not trends. As such, they signalled an unequivocal decision by the monetary authorities to break with past habits. They therefore serve all the more strongly to remind us that an exogenous monetary policy is a prerequisite to the success of any adjustment policy.

The reform of monetary policy instruments (BCEAO, 1990) that began in September 1989 and remained in force until September 1991 was informed by the same concern. The regular practice of fixing bank rates higher than international money market rates was intended to direct banks with net deficit accounts towards the money market and to discourage the BCEAO from refinancing second-echelon banks. The fact that possession of time deposits on the money market was made a condition for access to Central Bank credits meant that portfolio management standards were more stringent. This made it impossible for excessively high money supply levels to push the banking system into underwriting cumulative imbalances. Under the new schedule, bank rates were no longer used to direct efficient money management but to penalize mismanagement. Banks could determine their own interest rates, provided they did not overstep the 16% ceiling, considered the acceptable boundary. Instead, the new rates penalized banks with a shortage of available resources unable to meet their financial needs on the money market. In the process, they would stimulate competition between banks, reduce the demand for BCEAO credits, and impose more rigorously dissuasive conditions for the allocation of economic credits.

For some time it had not proved feasible to reconcile the refinancing of agricultural credits and the balance of payments recovery policy (see above). But the incorporation of agricultural credits into the overall contribution from the Central Bank to the economy was to end the impasse.

In sum, it was almost an entire decade after the country officially embarked on an adjustment programme that the BCEAO acquired the instruments for the implementation of an adjustment policy. Only time will tell whether it will use that instrument to spark expansionist or deflationary developments.

Meanwhile, one can only view with alarm the new banking context in which all monetary policies will have to operate. Throughout the UMOA zone, banks based on African capital are moribund or definitely dead. The vacuum left has been filled mainly by subsidiaries of French financial institutions.

In Senegal, this circumstance has created a surplus on a money market fed by solvent and profitable financial intermediaries since the banking sector was restructured. That is the up side. The down side is that the country's strategic interests are increasingly ignored by the banking sector. The way things are moving, it seems more likely that the new instruments of monetary policy will work to deny Senegalese business persons access to credit, instead of stimulating the recovery of the national economy.

For it was quite impossible, once the Central Bank had taken a hands-off attitude to the management of second-echelon banks, that the resulting rise in the cost of credit would ever be compensated by additional subsidies from the Treasury. After all, the Treasury itself was having to make do with rationed funds. So the allocation of credits to the economy was likely to turn into an unsolved problem hampering the advancement of private initiative and support for new supply policies (NPA, NPI), if the totality of funds available for refinancing had to go into helping out the impecunious Treasury as well as underwriting credits to the locomotive sector, agriculture.

The new policy pegs the availability of farm credits to projected levels of export income. Furthermore, a protocol dated 29 December 1989 places SONACOS under an obligation to pay back farm credits for each previous year. This opens up a harrowing possibility: a drop in the price of oil seed could lead to SONACOS purchasing less than the volume of groundnuts produced by farmers, either because of financial problems linked with the necessity of reimbursing agricultural credits, or because farm credits were inadequate. (NB: producer prices are not pegged to international prices for oil seed).

Exchange Rate Policy

A casual observer might suppose that Senegal has never had an exchange rate policy. After all, the exchange rate for the CFA franc has always remained fixed. If, however, we take the exchange rate to be the price differential between national and foreign products, it becomes clear that Senegal has always had an exchange rate policy. It takes the form of interventionist approaches to domestic price levels as well as import and export prices.

Before 1980, there was no policy whatsoever regarding export prices, except that until 1967, France paid preferential prices for oil seed from Senegal. The overriding aim of the State was to modify consumer prices of imported commodities as a way of providing relief for urban consumers (of rice,) and peasants (fertilizer, at any rate before the establishment of SIES). A parallel aim was to induce foreign capitalists to invest in Senegal, through exemptions from customs duties and protective provisions in the investment code. There was also the concern to balance the public finances, expressed in such measures as the revision of subsidized prices.

The results of this interventionist policy have been disappointing, to say the least. Because of its numerous and miscellaneous objectives, the price modification policy involving imported and national products was incoherent. For one thing, it tended to devalue the CFA franc in real terms, since protectionist prices for investment products approved on the investment code raised prices. At the same time, it had an aspect of revaluation, because imported food was subsidized through the stabilization scheme. The various investment codes discouraged the production of export commodities other than raw materials. They did this by facilitating domestic marketing, at a profit, of products unlikely to make it on the international market. Additionally, it imposed surplus charges on potential exporters that tended to make their products even less competitive on the international market. Lastly, the absence of an interventionist export price policy actually disturbed groundnut exports. For the need to fix producer prices for groundnuts below an international price level that was already low enough (except for the boom times of 1974-1978) meant that most of the time the purchasing power of peasants was getting whittled down^{21}, leading to the replacement of groundnuts with millet on the farms, or the emergence of parallel markets for groundnut sales (see Sectorial Analysis Section).

As from 1980, Senegal's exchange rate policy underwent two innovative changes. The first was an interventionist approach to export prices. The second was a decision to let market forces determine price levels. The first innovation was tantamount to a devaluation of the CFA franc. It started with subsidies for selected exports including fish, fertilizer, textiles and footwear. The subsidies were later extended to all exports, in a bid to make them more competitive.

The second innovation produced an effect similar to an upward valuation of the 'national' currency. It was part of an all-out reform process complete with a new customs schedule, a new investment code, the NPI and the NPA. Its aim was to bring consumer prices of imported commodities into line with import prices, and ultimately to integrate the domestic market fully into the world economy.

Most probably, it is yet too soon to draw up even a preliminary balance sheet. Provisional indications, however, suggest neither a strengthening of subsidized exports nor the emergence of new export commodities capable of holding their own on the world market. What, it might be asked, are the reasons for the failure of subsidized exports to take off?

First, supplies have fallen off. The fish population in Senegal's territorial waters has been thinning out steadily. Second, the international economic climate is unfavourable. The fertilizer market, for one, is in a state of glut. Third, there is the basic consideration that most local industries are quite unequipped to cope with international competition, even if the NPI is bent on plunging them into it. That is the case, for instance, in the textile and shoe industries.

No new industries have emerged because there has been no comprehensive restructuring of the national economy to bring it into line with the opening onto the world market. The reason is that supplies of local goods and services (cement, sugar, energy, etc.) are still subject to excessive overheads. As far as imports are concerned, the exchange rate policy based on the new supply policy package has also been disappointing. It has not facilitated the rise of a productive sector capable of replacing imports with more new local products. The explanation is clear: right from the start, Senegalese producers were not dynamic, innovative producers hampered by the disincentive of price differentials. What they really constituted was a group of handicapped manufacturers hobbling along on the crutch of an interventionist State (see below). Moreover, the policy did not end the overvaluation of the CFA franc. As a result, manufactured goods imported from South-East Asia, Spain, Italy and the United States are relatively cheap. This makes the trading sector at the moment more dynamic and important than the uncompetitive industrial sector. Meanwhile, the balance of payments is unfavourable, net external liabilities exceed assets, and the public finances are in the red because rampant smuggling and under-invoicing starve them of funds.

Structural Policy

The Agricultural Sector

In theory, the New Agricultural Policy is supposed to follow anti-interventionist principles. Yet agricultural development has always been designed and run as a process dependent on State intervention. Prior to the onset of adjustment programmes, State intervention was total. The State fixed prices to be paid to agricultural producers; it provided organizational staff to work in cooperatives, operational companies, the CPSP, BNDS, SONACOS, etc; it provided the organizational framework for the production and marketing of agricultural produce; it provided extension services to peasants, and controlled the provision of inputs and production factors in the rural areas, etc.

It was the successive years of drought plus the attendant economic crisis which revealed the counter-productive character of total State control of agriculture in Senegal. The evidence came in the following forms:

a) The deduction of substantial sums from groundnut sales to finance the work of ONCAD and the BNDS pushed peasants into selling their harvests on parallel markets in Senegal or abroad, mainly in Gambia.

b) Under the old system of joint co-operative responsibility, better organized peasants who paid their debts promptly were penalized by regulations that made it impossible for them to take out individual loans. Demand for inputs and production factors, dependent on credit, which in turn was limited by the peasants' collective ability to repay past debts, was accordingly low.

c) Every time the groundnut yield fell, the rebuilding of seed stocks was jeopardized.

d) With prices paid to producers pegged neither to input costs nor to the consumer price index, the peasants' purchasing power was weak. This hampered the spread of modern planting techniques.

e) When faced with urgent financial need, peasants were in the habit of selling their agricultural equipment.

f) Falling farm incomes led peasants to shift from groundnut production to millet planting.

g) Peasants could not initiate activity in the agricultural sector; only the State could, no matter how unbalanced the public finances might be from the word go.

For all these reasons, there was no way the Senegalese State could avoid making changes in its agricultural policy. In the late 1970s it adopted a new set of options for its overwhelming financial needs. After the abolition of ONCAD, policy and practice in the agricultural sector were reformed in accordance with three main guidelines: the reduction of State involvement; liberalization; and the adoption of market prices as the decisive yardstick.

Now we come to a question no assessment of adjustment policies can dodge: have the new policy options put an end to the old production disincentives? Judging by the experience of the past eight years, the answer is no. The reasons are as follows:

a) Since 1981, peasant earnings have been subject to deductions for fertilizer purchases. This has reduced the use of fertilizer even further.

b) Deductions for fertilizer and seed stocks brought down net prices paid to groundnut producers from 1983 to 1985.

c) In 1986, the net producer price for groundnuts was increased from F CFA 70 to F CFA 90. But the move coincided with a shrinkage in total hectarage planted with groundnuts.

d) Average groundnut production from 1981 onwards (767,000 tons) was lower than the average in the final six years of the 1980s (883,000 tons).

e) Because prices paid to peasant producers were not pegged to a general cost of living index, peasant purchasing power fell. This led to a reduction in the percentage of the groundnut crop sold on the official market (41% in 1984, 19.4% in 1985) between 1983 and 1985.

f) Increased financial payments occasioned by deficits run up by SONAR, SONACOS and the Groundnut Stabilization Fund (see Sectorial Analysis) forced the State to disregard the guideline requiring adherence to real market prices by maximizing its profits from imported rice and locally produced and consumed groundnut oil.

g) The surcharge on imported rice did nothing to help local cereal production. Quite the opposite: in the first place it served as an incentive for increased rice importation, with the result that rice imports since 1981 have exceeded the annual average for any period since independence. Second, the increase in average levels of millet production (up from 566,000 tons between 1975 and 1980 to 620,000 tons between 1981 and 1986) was inadequate to provide a saleable surplus commensurate with the urban demand for rice.

h) The exorbitant cost of locally consumed oil increased opportunities for profit on the parallel market. Moonlighting local oil manufacturers seized them.

The Industrial Sector

Prior to the launching of the New Industrial Policy, industrial policy in Senegal was geared to two objectives. The first was to attract foreign investment. The second was to bring strategic sectors of the economy under State control. The first objective was the fundamental result of Senegal's weak financial capabilities, coupled with the shortage of skilled industrial personnel. The second objective, given an increasingly sharper profile from the 1970s on, was a requirement of the socialist ideology of the ruling party.

It is perfectly true that the resulting industrial policy gave rise to a large number of industrial units. Just as undeniably, it created lots of jobs (see the section on employment in the public industrial sector)[22]. But the same policy has also imposed on the overall economy an accumulated series of costs that have ended up jeopardizing its survival. The costs involved are as follows:

a) The State has suffered substantial losses in fiscal revenue, making it incapable of generating enough funds of its own to finance public sector investment (see Sectorial Analysis).

b) The State has gone deeply into debt on the external money market to finance investment, as well as guaranteeing public and private sector loans under the investment code (see Sectorial Analysis).

c) The public enterprises involved are chronically mismanaged. It is their lifelong vocation to live on State subsidies.

d) Goods and services on the domestic market coddled with protective tariffs and buffeted by a series of droughts are exorbitantly priced.

e) Price structures in the industrial sector encourage import substitution but make Senegalese products uncompetitive on the world market.

f) As from the 1980s the industrial sector became incapable of providing work for all skilled personnel. It was therefore necessary to redefine industrial policy. In February 1986, an inter-ministerial council session focused on the industrial sector came up with a set of policy options popularized under the name of the New Industrial Policy. Was that the appropriate response?

The numerous factory closures since 1986, all pushing the economy deeper into depression, indicate that the policy is a failure. On the other hand, we do not have a regular series of annual statistics to support the argument that 1986 was a turning point. So we have decided, in the ensuing part of our discussion, to suspend judgment on that issue. Instead, we shall assess the capacity of the New Industrial Policy to reshape the mechanisms of the national economy.

The opening up of the country's frontiers (meaning the lowering of customs tariffs and the abolition of quotas) is a positive step. But it cannot help to make the industrial sector productive and competitive unless domestic costs are brought into line with foreign costs. The trouble is that as matters stand now, some of the mechanisms of the present economic policy frustrate the achievement of this goal.

First, given the fixed exchange rate of the CFA franc and the normally low inflation rates in the South-East Asian countries, labour costs in Senegal will invariably remain high as compared with labour costs in the free zones of Hong Kong, the Philippines, Malaysia and Thailand.

Second, as long as Senegal continues to support public sector enterprises (SONEES, SENELEC), along with protected banks as well as mixed corporations like the SAR, the country will always have to face surcharges detrimental to an adjusted schedule of production costs.

Third, in order to lower costs through heightened productivity, massive investments are needed to modernize the country's industrial units, dating essentially from the colonial days. But at the moment, the domestic market and the size of projected profits are too puny to justify such investments.

As the labour market becomes more 'flexible' with the abolition of the public Employment Agency and the prospect of indefinite renewals of short-term labour contracts within a climate of increasing joblessness, the total wage package is bound to shrink. That will mean a further narrowing of outlet opportunities available to competitive enterprises serving the domestic market. State withdrawal, involving the abolition of State-supported enterprises, the systematic scaling down of tax breaks offered in the investment code, and the sale of selected public enterprises, cannot generate gross positive savings and a renewed capacity to finance investment from national funds, unless losses of tax revenue caused by the winding up of uncompetitive enterprises can be made good through all sorts of private investment attracted by the provisions of the New Industrial Policy. That consummation is far from certain.

For one thing, recessionary pressures set in motion by the current wave of corporate closures could snowball if public demand continues to be too feeble to spark an expansion. Second, the new schedule of scaled-down tax breaks is likely to turn off potential import-substitution industries unless other compensatory advantages can be found for them. Lastly, new export-oriented industries are unlikely to be enchanted with the prospect of having to put up with the surcharges imposed on the economy to this day by the former State-supported enterprises (SAR, SOCOCIM, CSS, etc.).

Export promotion (involving export subsidies and the creation of the ASACE) cannot provide a basis for export-led growth unless monopoly rights granted to public sector and State-supported enterprises are abolished. Otherwise exports would have to be permanently subsidized to compensate the export sector for the loss of opportunity costs occasioned by the implicit protection of the import-substitution sector in its inter-industrial relationship with the export sector. The dilemma is that on the one hand, the State has no desire to go all out in the liberalization of the national economy. On the other hand, it does not have the financial resources to continue eternally subsidizing all the country's export enterprises, present and future.

Whichever way we look at it, then, the New Industrial Policy seems quite incapable of initiating a process of structural change in the Senegalese industrial sector thorough enough to provide a new and viable growth model. No doubt, actual developments in the years ahead will be more complex than the macro-economic projections presented above. But given the state of the economy in Senegal today, these projections are likely to prove, broadly speaking, correct.

Budgetary Policy

Like monetary policy, budgetary policy has had to adjust to the various macro-economic imbalances that hit the Senegalese economy in the 1970s. The growth rate of public demand (consumption and investment) in volume terms rose by nearly two points during the second decade of the post-colonial era (3.31% to 5.18%). It thus contributed to inflated domestic demand at a time when overall supply was low, and it would have been more judicious to scale demand downwards accordingly. Instead of containing the expansion of income distributed within a general context of shrinking supplies, public service salaries taken as a proportion of GDP remained constant (12.5%) in the 1960s and 1970s.

The pressure of taxation grew by an annual average of 1.4 points between 1971 and 1980. But it was still insufficient to curtail the volume of private consumption. Monetary policy at least had certain institutional checks. The policy of support for overall demand after 1970, however, had no such institutional constraints whatsoever. It was a reflection of the State's expansionist policy after the first petrol crunch (see Sectorial Analysis). There was no let-up in its financing even though the public finances deteriorated sharply as from 1976. Three facts attest to this state of affairs.

First, there was no deduction from domestic financial capacities to match the expansion in government financial requirements. Indeed, it was in the 1970s that the grand upswing in indebtedness began. What the government did was to borrow massively from foreign sources from 1973 to 1980, mainly to finance increased public spending.

Second, even though the PNG ballooned continuously as from 1976, the normal discount rate increased only once[23], after the first petrol crunch (in 1975). This made the cost of loans quite independent of the explosive imbalance in the public services.

Third, on account of the 20% rule which insulates advances to the Treasury from the impact of total government deficits, monetary policy (by which we mean the determination of contributions in general) has not made it possible to treat the refinancing of economic credits and government financial needs as interchangeable realities.

Ever since the onset of adjustment programmes, budgetary management has become markedly more austere. Because of the boom in foreign debt service charges (from F CFA 11.7 billion in 1981 to F CFA 40 billion in 1986), and also because of its commitments to the IMF, the State was forced to freeze practically all its expenditure for equipment and transfers between 1982 and 1985. It was also obliged to modify concessionary prices for products on the stabilization schedule (for example, the series of sudden price increases decided upon in August 1983) in an attempt to reduce the CPSP deficit; to liquidate the SONAR in a bid to stop it from further draining the public finances; to reduce payment arrears as from 1982, and to increase indirect taxation (for example, the rise in TVA in 1981) as a means of increasing stalled tax revenues. In 1986 the current operations deficit was reversed - a feat highlighted in DPC reports.

It would be premature, however, to take this for proof of real macro-economic adjustment. In the first place, public demand in volume terms has consistently pushed up the level of general demand, except in the years from 1981 to 1984. The average increase in the growth rate of demand over the 1981-87 period was 2.6%.

Second, since 1980, budgetary policy has not driven down the disposable income of private individuals. The proportion of government wages and salaries in the GDP pie increased by 1.5 points on the average (12.28% between 1971 and 1980, 13.88% between 1981 and 1988). Furthermore, the percentage of tax revenues fell back to 1960 levels, 1.3 percentage points lower than the 1970s level (18.12% as compared to 19.52%). Third, the volume of the trade deficit after 1980 was higher on the average (F CFA 52.15 billion) than it was in the years from 1970 to 1980 (F CFA 41.3 billion).

The best indication that any improvement in the public finances as from 1986 was negligible is the fact that since 1988 the Public Treasury has been bedeviled by an acute cash flow logjam. It is true, of course, that numerous formidable external causes have worsened the crisis: the socio-political disturbances that followed the February elections; the locust infestations that ravaged the countryside; and the low world prices for oil seed as compared to producer prices for groundnuts in Senegal. But there were internal causes as well. The national wage package was in no way trimmed to reflect the need to honour the State's foreign commitments. Neither was it modified to take into account the changes in the tax collection schedule over the 1980s. The policy of liberalization drove down the revenue from customs duties. As for the privatization of public enterprises, it was a financial fiasco.

So far, the government has balked at radical measures designed to contain the causes of financial imbalance. Instead of taking a bold decision simply to dismiss as many civil servants as required to meet public debt servicing requirements and reduce the financial needs of the public sector, it opted for a programme of voluntary retirement (January 1990) funded by the World Bank within the structural adjustment programme framework. This compromise approach was aimed at reducing civil service employees by a total of 4,800 employees by June 1992. Instead of straightforwardly liquidating all public enterprises dragging the public finances into the red, the government chose to persist in its privatization programme. Lastly, the increased tax schedule of 1989, even though it occasioned some public protest, was not designed to reinstate the old protectionist system (the minimum rate for customs duties rose from 10% to 15%); its real aim was to broaden the tax base.

When all is said and done, the current status of the public finances and the economy as a whole is one of worsening stagnation. Why? One reason is that economic policy decisions have been characterized by a lack of courage. Given the objective obstacles to their effective application, there is no way they can succeed. Take the programme of voluntary retirements for instance. For obvious political reasons, its execution has been spread out over time. Thus diluted, it cannot possibly be of any use to a Treasury faced with urgent short-term problems. Even in the medium term, it cannot produce the expected improvement in the State's budgetary operations unless it can be guaranteed that the savings it is supposed to generate from personnel emoluments will not be eaten up by extra interest payments necessitated by the World Bank loan that made the programme possible in the first place.

The privatization programme, no matter what its implementational modalities, cannot possibly provide the State with sufficient resources to release it from the stranglehold of financial dependence, thus leading to a recovery in its budgetary policies. To begin with, the public enterprises up for sale offer little that could attract potential investors because with one or two exceptions they all operate chronically at a loss. Second, the current value of these enterprises must be heavily discounted by Senegal's macroeconomic prospects, which are unequivocally deflationary. Under such circumstances it would be a foolhardy foreign investor indeed who would rush in where the entrepreneurial State now fears to tread. Finally, the national banks which could have supported a stronger commitment on the part of private Senegalese investors have disappeared from the economic scene.

Even the increased tax schedule is of extremely limited effectiveness. Already, it has come up against the problem of a shrinking tax base, with both income and business transactions feeling the impact of the current depression as enterprises close, wage earners are laid off, and public spending on capital goods gets cut. The medium and long-term adjustment programme (or the New Industrial Policy), proscribes support in the forms of increasingly higher customs tariffs until 1992. Last but not least, it labours under an iron necessity to sustain domestic demand, because it is the rise and fall of that demand that determines the hopes and fears of private investors capable of making the liberalization policy really work.

All these mechanisms are clear as daylight. But because the fiscal measures adopted in 1990 (the individual income tax surcharge and the generalized VAT) refused to take them seriously that they ended up looking like assaults on the economy.

Conclusion

This chapter has not revealed the existence of any economic mechanism capable of energizing the Senegalese economy over the long-term. The agricultural system is not sufficiently productive to facilitate a long-term growth strategy based on the substitution of local cereals for imported rice and the greater integration of peasants into the modern urban sector. Exports are so inelastic as compared to international economic growth that they cannot guarantee the continuous growth of the national economy. The industrial sector is so uncompetitive that the hope of steadily increasing Senegal's world market shares is just a nice pipe dream. In comparative terms, inputs here are so expensive as to make any growth strategy presupposing the attraction of direct foreign investments a non-starter.

The fact is that over the past 30 years, changes in the Senegalese economy have not followed a pattern of growth recognizable by an school of economic thought since the industrial revolution. Every passing year, admittedly, there has been a gross accumulation of fixed capital. Considering, however, the probability that this capital gets obsolete at an exponential rate, there has been no accumulation of capital in any sector that has continuously increased productivity, cut production costs, improved the competitive value of national products and, as a result, boosted domestic income. The reality has instead been one of a series of booms and busts. It may be pointed out that the root cause of this cyclical pattern is the unpredictable pattern of rain and drought. That merely underscores the fact that the Senegalese economy, taken as a system, lacks an internal engine. It depends entirely on external haulage for its starts and stops. Hence the perdurance of all styles of deficits over such long stretches of time.

From 1960 to 1988 the outside world paid off the country's deficits. That made it possible for domestic income to grow independently of the slow-growing economy. Now the World Bank and the International Monetary Fund have moved in. It looks as if aeons have passed since either organization issued flattering report cards on the Senegalese economy. Now they are busy burning into the national consciousness the reality that it is time to come back down to earth. Through their various programmes, especially the Shadow Programme that started in March 1990, they are making it clear that if Senegalese incomes are low, one reason is that the productive capacity of the economy is weak.

Common sense would indicate that all this is merely normal. The catch is that once we have gotten used to a roller-coaster of cumulative imbalances over an entire decade, it seems downright dangerous to come down to level-headed common sense. There will, for instance, be the cold turkey necessity of getting by without the injections of foreign resources needed to keep up our living standards. Meanwhile, it will be necessary to reorder our economic policy priorities. It will be necessary to face up to the fact that our cherished national sovereignty is nothing grander than a certificate of impotence at a time when the international economy is getting restructured, where blocs are forming around America, Japan and Europe, where free trade is in practice stalled, and where the Eastern European countries have emerged on the international scene. It will be necessary to face the anger of urban populations for whom it is no longer possible to guarantee jobs, purchasing power or public services. It will be necessary to leave peasants, whose agricultural inputs such as seed and fertilizer can no longer be subsidized, to fend for their poverty-stricken selves. It will be necessary to stop promoting the interests of local business persons, because in any case no one here has more than token control over public markets and contracts and the banking system. It will be necessary to let the coalition of interest groups which has held the State together since independence fall to pieces. Because the extended support base of clients on which it rides has become financially prohibitive to maintain. In sum, the Senegalese nation has hit hard times.

Notes

1. This is the conclusion indicated by official national accounts published from 1959 to 1981.
2. Since 1970, total annual import value has decreased in only two years: 1978 and 1980.
3. National income = Economic GDP + civil service emoluments + net unilateral transfers - net transfers abroad of income factors.

4. F CFA 14.7 billion A in 1981; 25.5 billion in 1982; 28.6 billion in 1983; 36.1 billion in 1984; 35 billion in 1985.
5. 4.2% in 1983; 5.1% in 1984; 4% in 1985; 11.2% in 1986; -0.5% in 1987.
6. Inflation = Growth rate of the value of the deflationary economic GDP factor. According to the World.
7. Bank report on World Development in 1988, taxation in the industrialized countries today amounts to 30% of economic GDP.
8. Given that Economic GDP = VAP+VAS+VAT
   with VAP = Value added in the primary sector
   VAS = Value added in the secondary sector
   VAT = Value added in the tertiary sector

$$TXPIBE_t = \left[\frac{VAP}{PIBE}\right]_{t-1} \times TXVAP_t + \left[\frac{VAS}{PIBE}\right]_{t-1} \times TXVAS_t + \left[\frac{VAT}{PIBE}\right]_{t-1} \times TXVAT_t$$

where TX = growth rate.

The contribution of a given sector J to growth in a given year t is known as the ratio

$$r_{jt} = \left[\frac{VAJ}{PIBE}\right]_{t-1} \times \left[\frac{TXVAJ}{TXPIBE}\right]_t \quad \text{where } j = P,S,T$$

9. The cost of groundnut seed processing at SONACOS is twice as much as the cost in European factories.
10. The gap between producer prices for groundnuts and millet widened from 5 to 20 Francs between 1960 and 1987.
11. In 1984, 60% of the groundnut crop was sold outside the official marketing channels. In 1985 the figure was 80%.
12. The precise year was 1976, when the level reached 107.6 billion, i.e., 2.04 times the 1960 level.
13. Unlike the primary sector, the secondary sector makes a bigger contribution to the overall growth of the economy the stronger that economy is. In those years when the overall economic growth rate was at least 4%, the secondary sector contributed averaged 24%. For other years the rate was negative on the average.
14. JORS: Acts 62-33; 72-43; 77-91; 81-50; and 87-25.
15. Wheat + petrol + intermediate goods + 1/2 capital goods.
16. The Central Bank has no right to turn down Treasury requests for advances in keeping with the 20% rule.
17. In the absence of balance of payments statistics figures for the years between 1960 and 1967, this is my explanation for the drop in foreign assets.
18. M2 grew by an average of 17.6%, while the deflationary factor of economic GDP grew in value terms by 7.7% on the average.
19. Government deposits do not fluctuate much.
20. Previous increases in net external assets and decreases in the PNG both dated back to 1975.

21. This was because of independent variations in their tax liabilities (fertilizer) and/or the price of food commodities, or because of their excessive indebtedness.
22. From a demographic viewpoint, Senegal's industrial landscape in 1986 was far different from what it had been in 1960.
23. This reflects the fact that thew rate, being fixed within the framework of the West African Monetary Unit (UMOA), does not mirror the circumstantial peculiarities of any particular country.

Bibliography

BCEAO, 1990, 'La politique et le dispositif des taux d'intérêt dans l'UMOA', *Notes d'Informations et Statistiques,* June.

Khan S Moshin, 1987, 'Macroeconomic Adjustment in Developing Countries: A Policy Perspective', *The World Bank Researcher Observer.* 1 January.

Lemoine, Guy, 1982, 'Note sur les investissements du plan'. Mimeo, Dakar.

Senegal, Republic of, Ministry of Rural Development, 1982, 'Bilan global des réalisations du Gouvernement en faveur du monde rural depuis l'Indépendence'. Mimeo, Dakar.

Senegal, Republic of, Ministry of Rural Development, 1988, 'Etude sur la filière arachide au Sénégal', Mimeo, Dakar.

Senghor, L Sédar, 1974, 'Discours d'ouverture de la première session du Conseil Economique et Social', Mimeo, Dakar.

World Economic Outlook, 1985.

Table 1: Employment and Major Resources
(in Million Francs CFA 1977)

	PIBE	IM	CVMN	CVADM	FBCF	EX
1960	263	173.3	211.9	54.1	57	158.4
1961	278.8	161.3	228.0	54.1	50.7	150.0
1962	288.3	180.4	248.0	60.6	51.8	145.0
1963	300.9	179.3	271.7	61.9	46.2	133.3
1964	306.1	174.3	272.7	65.0	49.8	131.8
1965	320.5	169.1	281.9	65.8	47.1	132.0
1966	330.3	179.1	291.1	69.0	38.6	141.0
1967	323.7	187.5	293.5	69.8	41.6	140.1
1968	354.2	176.4	306.2	62.1	43.4	147.6
1969	335.5	160.2	274.1	53.9	44.3	145.4
1970	358.1	178.5	293.5	59.4	54.8	158.6
1971	355.3	172.9	295.6	62.1	56.5	140.6
1972	380.6	172.7	293.4	61.3	64.3	160.2
1973	357.1	171.5	291.6	61.1	62.8	140.2
1974	376.4	174.8	300.5	65.8	68.1	149.8
1975	406.2	195.3	328.0	66.9	70.5	168.5
1976	437.5	217.8	361.1	75.8	67.0	196.9
1977	422.6	251.7	363.6	77.9	62.2	209.2
1978	389.4	216.9	365.0	84.8	62.5	140.1
1979	430.3	255.1	388.4	90.9	68.8	182.0
1980	404.9	206.6	376.5	94.7	78.3	133.1
1981	399.3	228.1	397.2	92.9	65.7	141.9
1982	468.1	226.4	413.7	97.1	70.5	189.4
1983	476.3	224.6	413.6	101.1	75.6	191.9
1985	465.1	228.3	442.2	106.8	72.6	166.3
1986	502.2	242.8	433.4	113.5	87.4	191.4
1987	522.7	245.4	445	118.6	92.5	194.2

Source: DPC

Table 2: Structure of the Money Stock (in billion francs CFA)

	M2	QM	DCT	CUR
1962	36,50	1,23	14,23	18,59
1963	31,92	1,04	13,06	15,01
1964	30,95	0,87	11,80	15,75
1965	30,00	1,04	11,99	14,72
1966	2,81	0,70	12,76	12,56
1967	26,05	0,74	13,04	0,21
1968	29,64	1,28	14,48	11,92
1969	29,73	1,76	14,66	11,58
1970	37,27	2,77	17,26	15,24
1971	38,05	2,84	17,35	15,94
1972	42,83	3,72	20,99	16,49
1973	52,37	8,17	23,02	19,45
1974	77,26	9,49	36,89	28,96
1975	86,10	10,92	42,85	29,46
1976	113,60	18,76	58,63	33,74
1977	130,97	21,85	66,70	39,47
1978	158,83	32,31	76,54	46,23
1979	161,12	39,91	74,28	42,94
1980	177,69	39,75	81,97	51,36
1981	216,92	53,69	85,12	73,61
1982	262,34	73,34	98,73	84,49
1983	273,00	83,85	106,06	78,28
1984	287,12	95,47	109,58	77,32
1985	300,11	106,62	103,44	86,22
1986	333,50	106,68	117,15	104,30
1987	332,80	118,41	109,67	100,70

Source: IMF, International Financial Statistics

Table 3: Counterparts to the Money Stock (in billion francs CFA)

	NAVEXT	CRECO	NCRGO	CRPRIV	RFN
1962	15,35	23,54	-10,76	34,30	7,87
1963	11,40	23,60	-10,67	34,27	11,36
1964	9,08	26,25	- 8,92	35,17	13,33
1965	7,09	27,89	- 6,65	34,54	14,02
1966	9,51	22,05	- 8,76	30,81	11,79
1967	7,95	22,56	- 4,52	27,08	8,39
1968	2,93	30,24	- 2,39	32,63	12,89
1969	- 0,23	34,91	0,17	34,73	13,01
1970	5,21	37,52	- 0,03	37,56	13,50
1971	4,40	39,87	0,05	39,82	13,50
1972	5,83	47,22	- 0,04	47,26	12,94
1973	- 3,39	65,68	2,19	63,49	25,20
1974	- 5,91	90,69	1,04	89,65	38,50
1975	-10,31	108,81	1,87	106,94	39,40
1976	-10,69	136,99	14,02	121,92	42,80
1977	-12,93	162,73	16,66	144,62	44,30
1978	-35,83	213,35	16,0	196,14	71,10
1979	-63,30	250,59	18,76	223,92	78,10
1980	-87,17	293,57	28,67	261,52	107,60
1981	-133,21	368,88	51,64	313,46	146,80
1982	-172,84	441,01	98,26	338,96	169,60
1983	-198,76	477,10	116,31	356,12	175,30
1984	-225,30	489,89	131,13	353,61	156,00
1985	-258,87	530,83	150,70	373,43	182,00
1986	-208,25	535,67	153,5	374,34	167,40
1987	-206,56	538,88	146,02	385,02	158,90

Source: IMF, International Financial Statistics

Table 4: Prices

	TDPIBE	TDPIBE^F	TIC	TDPIBE^{CI}
1960	-0.44	3.6	-	-
1961	4.88	3.4	-	-
1962	1.71	4.7	-	-
1963	-0.24	6.4	-	-
1964	3.79	4.1	-	-
1965	0.47	2.2	-	-
1966	0.32	2.9	-	-
1967	1.60	3.2	-	-
1968	-2.03	4.3	-	-
1969	4.86	6.5	-	-
1970	4.65	5.6	-	-
1971	3.05	5.8	-	-
1972	4.26	6.2	3.00	-
1973	7.17	7.8	5.75	-
1974	17.75	11.1	5.75	-
1975	10.00	13.4	6.00	-
1976	4.40	9.9	6.00	19.2
1977	8.60	9.0	6.00	32.0
1978	8.50	9.5	6.00	4.7
1979	7.60	10.4	6.0	6.9
1980	5.90	12.2	6.25	9.4
1981	8.70	6.25	6.25	1.5
1982	12.28	12.62	8.25	4.2
1983	9.9	9.5	7.25	15.4
1984	12.10	7.2	7.25	-
1985	11.70	5.8	7.25	-
1986	8.80	5.1	6.08	-
1987	1.80	2.8	5.25	-

Note: All the figures are percentages except for the CPI which are indices.

Table 4: (continued) Prices

	TDVAS	TDVAP	CPI
1960	0.95	-0.20	-
1961	4.13	2.60	-
1962	0.30	5.40	-
1963	-0.45	29.50	-
1964	2.7	6.50	-
1965	1.26	4.30	-
1966	2.09	6.30	-
1967	2.0	2.50	100
1968	-3.06	2.70	101
1969	8.21	-0.10	103
1970	0.55	49.00	107
1971	2.80	5.30	111
1972	4.42	9.20	117
1973	2.48	6.20	131
1974	33.18	6.10	153
1975	12.0	8.22	201
1976	-0.06	-11.80	207
1977	6.01	14.10	228
1978	15.50	-17.70	235
1979	6.1	16.9	257
1980	14.4	-0.06	279
1981	4.2	5.49	296
1982	4.5	-3.31	347
1983	12.6	-18.5	388
1984	20.8	24.6	427
1985	15.6	-3.8	490
1986	5.3	21.4	-
1987	0.5	0.3	-

Source: DPC

Table 5: Contributions from the Primary (CTRA) and Secondary (CTRI) Sectors to Economic Growth

	CTRA	CTRA
1960	1,347823	0,391304
1961	-0,826088	0,239131
1962	2,010526	0,326316
1963	0,158730	0,150794
1964	0,057693	0,807690
1965	0,743055	0,152778
1966	-1,142858	0,142858
1967	-1,287884	-0,46969
1968	0,016393	-0,08852
1969	-0,106952	-0,09090
1970	0,269911	0,287611
1971	6,571388	-0,78570
1972	0,877470	0,067193
1973	0,791489	0,072340
1974	1,160622	0,502591
1975	0,167785	0,080537
1976	0,578275	0,335463
1977	0,657719	-0,36912
1978	0,942771	0,278729
1979	0,672372	0,278729
1980	0,925197	0,712599
1981	1,053569	-3,74999
1982	0,357538	0,254360

Source: Calculated from DPC.

Table 6: Breakdown of National Income (in billion francs CFA)

	VPIBE	SADM	UT	DTTE	RN
1971	2.161.000	.109.999	1.339.767	1.106.001	2.594.927
1972	2.407.000	3.290.001	1.626.550	1.861.998	2.880.035
1973	2.431.000	3.510.001	1.269.242	2.494.000	2.883.964
1974	2.994.000	3.939.999	1.527.134	3.008.001	3.510.633
1975	3.592.000	4.719.998	1.795.518	4.440.002	4.199.152
1976	4.028.000	5.650.000	2.549.409	3.903.000	4.808.911
1977	4.226.000	6.100.000	2.638.836	4.960.003	5.050.284
1978	4.250.000	6.970.001	2.723.300	6.899.998	5.150.330
1979	4.982.000	8.370.001	2.135.507	1.290.000	5.903.551
1980	5.066.000	1.064.000	2.546.407	1.170.000	6.267.641
1981	5.473.000	1.225.000	4.643.414	1.830.001	6.969.341
1982	7.075.000	1.366.000	5.840.758	2.670.001	8.758.076
1983	7.984.000	1.501.000	5.955.603	3.690.000	9.621.560
1984	8.506.000	1.649.000	6.046.380	4.440.001	1.031.564

Table 7: Evolution of Credits

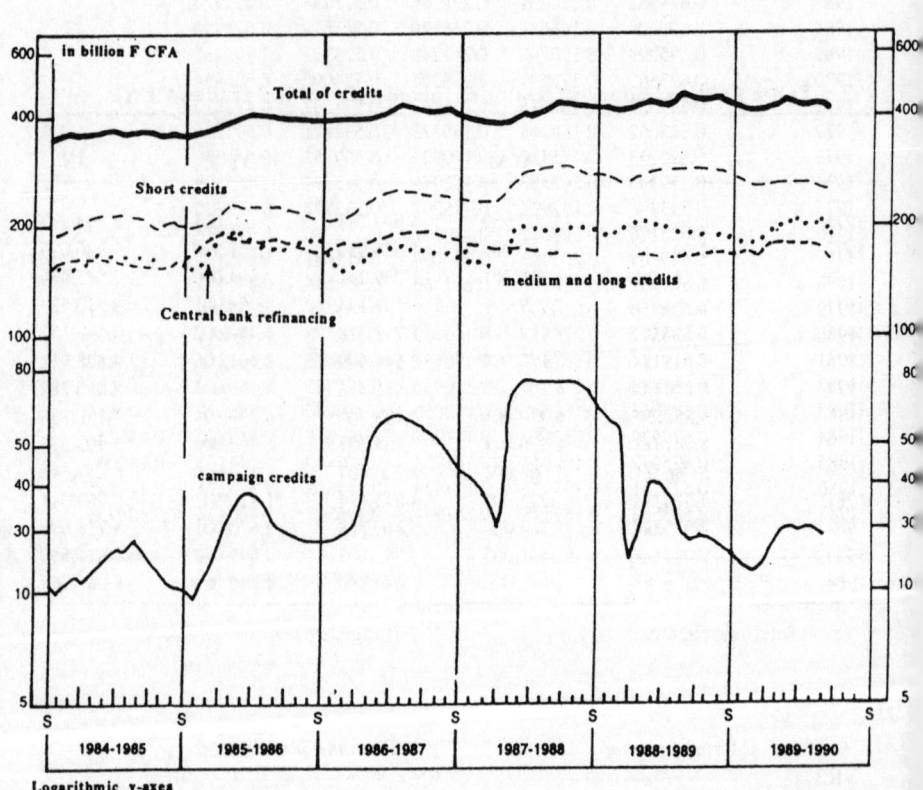

Source: BCEAO *Statistiques économiques et monétaires* No. 397, Octobre 1990.

Table 8: The Ratios of Public Finance

Year	R1	R2	R3	R4	R5	R6
1962	0.647331	0.201799	0.101845	0.420181	0.406304	-
1963	0.653100	0.190269	0.089546	0.460500	0.416386	-
1964	0.604628	0.193852	0.268937	0.472341	0.418157	-
1965	0.584089	0.180206	0.252791	0.486478	0.445890	-
1966	0.617457	0.171993	0.267500	0.507461	0.484440	-
1967	0.624582	0.174404	0.298754	0.517234	0.493220	-
1968	0.606609	0.166634	0.236320	0.523629	0.521979	-
1969	0.595099	0.179746	0.217248	0.523392	0.498831	-
1970	0.623560	0.172499	0.218294	0.534090	0.502354	-
1971	0.649027	0.182548	0.236842	0.535232	0.478372	-
1972	0.622062	0.168746	0.190873	0.537871	0.503736	-
1973	0.592153	0.185514	0.170929	0.569353	0.535530	-
1974	0.559306	0.202857	0.152976	0.545194	0.465138	-
1975	0.553998	0.197997	0.175597	0.532192	0.459908	-
1976	0.626166	0.187272	0.180747	0.512786	0.473946	-
1977	0.643704	0.203935	0.164068	0.511689	0.445190	-
1978	0.699761	0.217123	0.217762	0.504546	0.470157	-
1979	0.630750	0.210689	0.174658	0.463106	0.537520	0.658823
1980	0.538572	0.225612	0.169319	0.562173	0.526371	0.635803
1981	0.619124	0.187369	0.153763	0.502726	0.661355	0.425837
1982	0.661883	0.179955	0.150932	0.496785	0.610270	0.406639
1983	0.678063	0.186801	0.152850	0.489040	0.572080	0.409266
1984	0.670539	0.186509	0.151267	0.491018	0.562830	0.496241
1985	0.625972	0.189844	0.145924	0.507490	0.511203	0.440000
1986	0.523111	0.193927	0.174429	0.514826	0.477291	0.444445
1987	0.533562	0.189698	0.187094	0.496347	0.466438	0.408955

$$R1 = \frac{\text{Transaction taxes}}{\text{Internal revenue}} \qquad R4 = \frac{\text{Personnel expenditure}}{\text{Budgetary operating costs}}$$

$$R2 = \frac{\text{Internal revenue}}{\text{Gross domestic Product}} \qquad R5 = \frac{\text{Personnel expenditure}}{\text{Internal revenue}}$$

$$R3 = \frac{\text{Import tax}}{\text{Import value}} \qquad R6 = \frac{\text{Taxes on profits(BIC + BNC)}}{\text{Taxes paid by households(ITS + IGR)}}$$

Source: Ministry of Economy and Finance

Appendix 9: Agricol Sector

	DVAP	DVAS	CPI	DVAP/DVAS	DVAP/CPI	PQARch	CGRND	PQRZ	CRZTH	FMDR	TDPIBE	TDPIBEf	TDPIBEd
1960	42.80	52.90		0.80		22.00	48.00	18.00	30.00		-00.44	03.60	
1961	55.00	55.00		1.00		22.00	47.00	18.00	33.00		04.28	03.40	
1962	46.90	55.10		0.85		22.00	41.00	18.00	37.00	580.9	01.71	04.70	
1963	45.40	54.90		0.82		21.50	42.00	18.00	35.00	537.4	-00.24	06.40	
1964	47.80	56.20		0.85		21.50	45.00	21.00	33.00	438.6	03.79	04.10	
1965	47.80	56.90		0.84		21.50	50.00	21.00	33.00	516.8	00.47	02.20	
1966	56.90	58.10		0.97		21.50	45.00	21.00	40.00	803.0	00.32	02.90	
1967	47.60	59.20	100.00	0.80	0.47	21.50	44.00	21.00	54.00	400.0	01.60	03.20	
1968	54.4	57.50	101.00	0.94	0.53	18.00	40.00	21.00	50.00	356.2	-01.85	04.30	
1969	48.0	62.10	103.00	0.77	0.46	18.00	53.00	21.00	47.00	139.2	06.02	06.50	
1970	51.7	62.40	107.00	0.82	0.48	18.50	63.00	21.00	39.00	545.7	04.35	05.60	
1971	55.4	64.10	111.10	0.86	0.49	19.50	69.00	21.00	36.00	880.3	03.05	05.80	
1972	58.4	66.90	117.50	0.87	0.49	23.00	63.00	21.00	37.00	717.1	03.97	06.20	
1973	64.8	68.50	131.30	0.94	0.49	23.00	86.00	21.00	65.00	851.7	07.64	07.80	
1974	67.5	89.00	153.10	0.75	0.44	29.00	177.00	21.00	129.00	1192.1	16.84	11.10	
1975	98.9	100.30	201.50	0.98	0.49	41.50	92.00	21.00	77.00	5080.1	11.17	13.40	
1976	97.5	94.30	207.20	1.03	0.47	41.50	100.00	41.00	60.00	3525.8	04.11	09.90	19.20
1977	100.0	100.00	228.30	1.00	0.43	41.50	133.00	41.50	66.00	1968.1	08.60	09.00	32.00
1978	103.3	117.00	235.00	0.88	0.43	41.50	141.00	41.50	82.00	2786.5	09.14	09.50	04.70
1979	108.4	123.40	257.30	0.87	0.42	41.50	119.00	41.50	70.00		06.08	10.40	06.90
1980	114.1	141.50	279.80	0.80	0.40	45.50	102.00	41.50	91.00		08.06	12.20	09.40
1981	121.9	146.40	296.30	0.83	0.41	50.00	168.00	41.50	130.00		09.54	11.80	01.50
1982	149.8	152.10	347.60	0.98	0.43	70.00	125.00	41.50	96.00		10.27	12.60	04.20
1983	157.5	170.00	388.20	0.92	0.40	70.00	132.00	51.50	105.00		09.65	09.50	15.40
1984	162.5	207.10	427.00	0.78	0.38	70.00	152.00	51.50	109.00		14.10	07.20	
1985	189.2	239.20	490.50	0.79	0.38	70.00	156.00	60.00	97.00		11.70	05.80	
						90.00							

3. The State of the Groundnut Economy: A 30-Year Crisis

Mohamed Mbodj

The word crisis has become standard in the vocabulary in African affairs.[1] Before it became a descriptive master-key for every sector, however, it had long been particularly applicable to the agricultural sector. To this day agriculture occupies centre stage in the general crisis of African economies and societies. The shift from complacent to generally critical analyses of performance in the agricultural sector occurred in the wake of the catastrophic droughts which began the 1970s.

Before then, the literature on African agriculture had favoured dithyrambic strains. Socialist advocates waxed eloquent about the qualities of the continent's 'peasant societies'. The argument was that they bore the seeds of a socialist or communist future. Not to be outdone, capitalist commentators for their part dreamed of 'green revolutions', harbingers of an equally radiant free market future. Left and right, both visions looked forward to a development process primed by the agricultural system.

Later in the 1970s euphoria gave way to more realistic views. At times the analyses became frankly gloomy. Their main weakness, prior to the early 1980s,[2] was that they were seldom comprehensive. Furthermore, their premises invariably conditioned their conclusions. They therefore remained, for the most part, trapped within their own ideological trammels. Lastly, they often skipped over the 1960s decade, frustrating an accurate understanding of the depth and features of the crisis.[3]

Senegal, a Sahelian country, has an overwhelmingly rural economy dependent for success or failure on a number of climatic, structural and circumstantial factors. Over all these factors the country has infinitesimal control.

To begin with, agriculture in this country is rain-fed. It is therefore highly dependent on climatic conditions. Chief among these are the abundance or dearth of rain, and the evenness or unevenness of its distribution over time and space. The soil is in many places sandy and light. Dry winds blowing in from the Sahara desert pose a constant threat, and droughts are commonplace. To these natural constraints must be added the weight of human pressures. Farmland tends to be parcelled out into tiny, overworked family units. The climatic imbalance, in sum, is worsened by the fragile ecology of a degraded environment.

Working together, these factors often create a condition of immanent crisis distinctive enough to give Senegal a peculiarly high profile in the new 'crisis literature'. The gist of that brand of literature is an overwhelmingly negative assessment of the dominance of the national economy by the speculative groundnut farming system. One main development that helped to highlight the crisis was the cycle of increasingly frequent years of drought that began in 1971. A second was the premature implementation, in 1984, of a New Agricultural Policy under the aegis of the World Bank and the International Monetary Fund.

Warnings about the danger of the groundnut hegemony had been sounded as far back as 1960 (Gaye, 1960:239). Since then, a number of different policies, designed (at any rate in theory) to remedy this state of affairs, have been tried. Yet the sector continues to provide direct employment for over a million persons, takes up more than 40% of cultivated land, and has consistently dictated the general tenor of economic life in Senegal (*The Economist*, December 1989:13-21).

Over the entire stretch of the country's independent existence, there have been three main agricultural policy packages or simulacra thereof. Within each package there have been considerable differential changes. Between the starting date (1960) and the present, our periodization is organized around two pivotal dates. The first marks the beginning of what is commonly known as the cycle of drought, in 1971. The second marks the installation of a structural adjustment policy, around the time when the National Agricultural Produce Marketing Board (ONCAD) was abolished, that is to say, in late 1979.

- The period from 1960 to 1971 was the high tide of 'nationalization' in the agricultural sector. Overall policy then was framed within a framework of socialistic planning. The system's sole operational mode was the establishment of various institutional mechanisms designed to cement the domination of the power elite comprising the State and the Muslim religious leadership, the marabouts. As early as 1967, 'peasant disturbances' had shaken up the system, indicating that all was not well. It took the devastating drought that began in 1971 to lay bare the full extent of its shortcomings.
- The period from 1971 to 1979 was a time of trials. It started with an avalanche of climatic disasters that revealed the shakiness of the system, exposed the inadequacy of the State's coping capacity, and showed how skilfully the marabouts could use the crisis to boost their influence. From the early 1980s, with help from the World Bank and the IMF, the State acknowledged the seriousness and scope of the

crisis. There was a change of regime, which prepared the ground for painful policy changes.
- The main development of the period from 1979 to 1990 was the design of a structural adjustment policy, implying a re-examination of sectorial policies and the implementation of ensuing modifications. In this process the high point was the design of a New Agricultural Policy between 1982 and 1984. The new policy differed from its predecessors in one central sense. Hitherto, the State had been unchallenged master in policy matters. Now the game plan called for it to withdraw from the playing field, leaving market forces free to call the shots.

Our approach calls for a description of each succeeding phase followed by an analysis that emphasizes the absence of any medium and long-term policy. In plain words, agricultural policy in Senegal has had more to do with knee-jerk reactions to changing circumstances and the claims of political and social structures than with any clear-eyed attempt to achieve real control over the sector. It is not our intention, within the limits of this chapter, to offer an exhaustive analysis of the entire Senegalese agricultural system since 1960. Our aim is to focus mainly on policy in the groundnut sector. One reason is the sector's overwhelming economic and political importance. A second is that agricultural policy, generally been designed along sectorial lines, has usually presented an incoherent image. A third reason is that such an approach is both handy and feasible.[4] The ensuing remarks, then, apply essentially to the Groundnut Basin.

The Period of the Peasant State: 1960-71

The contours of the Senegalese economy were established by colonialism. A brief historical background is therefore a useful way to understand the adoption of groundnut cultivation in Senegal, before we move to the contemporary period. For in the latter period, the original option is by no means challenged. Instead, attempts have been made to implement various structural reforms. So far, unfavourable rainfall and circumstantial conditions have deeply compromised the results.

Origins

Broadly speaking, the colonial period in Senegal lasted from 1887 to 1960.[5] That was the period when France brought together within a territorial unit named Senegal a core of natural regions and traditional political environments which shared a number of similar features and which, more significantly, had in earlier times carried on more or less sustained economic relationships with each other.[6] The groundnut crop was the kingpin of the economic system established by French colonialism. Groundnuts, a typical cash crop introduced into the Senegambian area in the sixteeth century, were to become the key to the area's economic dependence in the twentieth century.

Senegal began its serious involvement with groundnuts in the 1840s. At that time it was a lucrative item of trade, especially since the abolition of the slave trade had mired the trans-Atlantic trade circuit in depression. Gum arabic and rubber were given a try, but they failed to create a buoyant economy. The region was prey to constant political instability, and gum and rubber, dependent on the gathering process, were extremely vulnerable to the vicissitudes of time and place. Groundnut cultivation offered this difference: it was subject to no existing social code. Peasants were therefore free to invest their labour in it. Until that point, cotton had been one of the few agricultural products sold on the market. The groundnut crop now replaced it.

The advent of groundnut farming meant a real advancement in the status of the peasantry. Individual peasants now moved into roles that used to be reserved for the aristocracy at the time of the slave trade: they could now be producers, sellers and buyers. These had already begun in the second half of the nineteenth century. The colonial regime accelerated them. There was the new pressure of taxation. There was administrative control. Above all, there was a new lifestyle that gave high prestige to factory-made cotton textiles and rice as major consumer items that could be bought with groundnut earnings. In the late nineteenth century, French currency replaced barter in the area's markets, installing a potent cash nexus for the new trade. More generally, cash had a considerable impact on social relationships. The normal rites of passage punctuating all the population's lives - marriage baptism and assorted ceremonies - now required cash for purchasing cloth, imported cola, etc.

With money making ever-widening inroads, ambitious individuals competing for social prestige, and social networks getting wider, every social event required more and more cash. All this pushed peasants into increasing dependence on loans from traders. In the 1910s, Native Insurance Companies (SIP) began to play an active part as providers of credit to peasants. Interest rates ranged from 30% to 300%. To pay them, peasants had to pledge their future crops to traders when emergencies struck, which was often. After the 1905 famine, it became normal for peasants to live permanently in hock. Three decades later, that is to say, in 1933, the SIP actually gained total control over all groundnut seed in the country.

From that point on, peasants were caught up in the cogs of an increasingly relentless machine that deprived them of any control over their economic options. In the interests of increased yields, an agronomic plantation and a research station were set up in Bambey in the early 1920s. Research done there focused on plant varieties and mechanization. In spite of the establishment of these 'modernization' structures, however, there were no significant changes in the production system before the 1960s.

Up until 1945, the colonial system had invested little in Senegalese agriculture. But when the Overseas Territories Investment, Economic and Social Development Fund (FIDES) was set up within the framework of France's first Plan, the stage was set for locking the country deeper into dependency. At that time, France drafted a comprehensive Plan costing a total of FCFA 134 billion for its West African colonies, with Senegal as centrepiece. There was an attempt to mechanize groundnut farming in the central and southern regions (Eastern Saloum and Middle Casamance), along with rice farming in the Lower Senegal River basin.

In the upshot all these sectorial programmes failed. Nevertheless, they did reinforce the French economic presence, aggravating the corollary extroversion of the Senegalese economy and its dependence on the groundnut crop. The most visible index was the steady development of groundnut exports in the colonial period. The only exceptions came during the two world wars and the great depression of 1929 (see annexe 1).

Rural Socialism: 1960-1966

The impact of the colonial heritage was enormous. It was France, after all, which programmed the country to specialize in an outward-oriented agricultural economy highly vulnerable to world prices for agricultural produce and energy. Senegal's farmers concentrated on export production while the country was forced to import rice, which became an essential commodity in the Senegalese diet. This was in accordance with a tacit division of labour during the colonial era. At independence the new State did not condemn the system. It busied itself mainly with agriculture and the marketing of agricultural produce, content to leave the industrial sector mainly under foreign control. Furthermore, Senegal's new government authorities acquiesced in the nineteenth-century colonial idea according to which the country's sandy soil was really unsuitable for any crops other than the God-sent groundnut (JORS, 1965:227).

Bureaucratic and extension structures set up to organize the groundnut economy were top-heavy. This was to prove an enormous handicap when the time came for Senegal to adapt its economic policies to changing conditions on the world market. It seems that at the time of independence, the country's leaders had no accurate idea of the size of this handicap. Thus, without waiting for definitive findings from an exhaustive study of the economic situation (it ultimately filled 15 volumes[7]), the government passed a law dated 13 January 1960, establishing two major levers of the fledgling State. One was the Agricultural Marketing Board (OCA). The other was the

Senegalese Development Bank (BSD). At one stroke, then, Senegal nationalized the entire groundnut trade, ending a system that had lasted over a century.

Apart from offering the national community substantial pickings from the system, the government wanted to mark in symbolic terms a radical break with the colonial past. To this end, the OCA was empowered to meet three objectives. First, it was to exercise sole control over agricultural trade and groundnut exports. Second, it was to take sole charge of the country's cereal imports. Third, it was to promote rural development through co-operative associations.

The Act of 20 May 1960[8] established new-style co-operatives. Their function was to collect farm produce for delivery to the OCA, which in turn was expected to supply them with foodstuffs, seed, equipment and other necessities of rural society. The system was financed by the BSD, a State bank.[9] The stated ambition inspiring the system was 'to shift from the old trading economy to a modern, rationally planned economy inspired by socialist ideals and operating on cooperative principles' (Péhaut 1984:407).

Nevertheless, private buyers supplying the OCA, known as stock agencies (OS) remained active until 1967. In the meantime, membership of the new co-operative associations was theoretically optional. The hope was that rebates offered to members by the co-operatives, representing the difference between wholesale and retail prices, would make them more attractive than the usual trading circuits. These policy instruments having been established, the next step was to endow them with functional guidelines and objectives.

Among the principal operational guidelines was the need to solve the problem of the dominance of the groundnut sector.[10] The Minister of Development and Planning, Karim Gaye, drawing the major conclusions indicated by a study by CINAM-CERESA (1963), summed up the matter in laconic fashion on the eve of the definition of the First Plan: 'This economy, dominated as it was by the groundnut crop, was profoundly unbalanced' (Gaye 1960:239). The newly defined agricultural policy tried to meet this key challenge head on.

The first measures intended to solve the problem were incorporated in the First Four-Year Plan (1961-65), unveiled before the National Assembly on 4 April 1961 by the President of the Executive Council, Mamadou Dia (1961:207-215). Mamadou Dia presented the package as part of 'the revolution' inspired by 'African socialism', a first stage in 'the expected evolution of our economy over the next quarter century'. The agricultural sector, allocated 13.4% of total planned investment, was assigned the following major objectives, in order of priority: to provide extension and supervisory services for the rural areas; to treble the amount of food crop production offered for sale, to develop water supply services in the rural areas, and to extend zones of intensive cultivation so as to boost agricultural development.

The leading objective, then, was the provision of extension and supervisory services in the rural areas. The objective was informed by what Mamadou Dia (1961: 212) referred to as 'the African socialist ethic'. The principal ambition at that time was to mobilize the people for the construction of a socialist, humanist nation. The rural extension service was supposed to spark 'a revolutionary process within the country that would establish an African socialist system conceived by our people, established by our people, and working for the benefit of our people' (Cissé, 1963:124). The primary aim was to create an atmosphere of trust between the peasantry and the government, largely lacking in the past on account of the high-handed habits of the colonial administration. To begin with, chieftaincies would be abolished. Meanwhile, 'civil servants and others manning the technical infrastructure would have to put themselves at the service of the cooperative movement, ready to hand over progressively to that movement as soon as it acquired sufficient dynamism and technical know-how to take full charge of its responsibilities'. (Dia, 1962). The basic unit in this structural system was to be the village. Operating as a central productive unit using collectively-owned equipment, it would be guided by a team of all-round extension officers and endowed with a marketing co-operative handling groundnuts. Together these agencies would take charge of local development programmes. Step by step, all responsibility was to devolve directly onto the peasants themselves. According to the rhetoric of the policy-makers, the peasantry was to become the instrument of its own liberation.

Beneath the high-flying rhetoric of participatory and outright democratic dreams lay the grit of reality: the struggle for political and social control over the rural areas. The Director of Rural Organization minced no words about that aim. His mission, he said, was principally political. It would be necessary to fight against the trading system, against debt traps and usurious interest charges set up by traders, and against the traditional privileges enjoyed by the rural nobility. Furthermore, it would be necessary to restrict customary chiefs to their administrative functions, and to shift villages beyond their old, narrow-visioned role as organizations based on family kinship solidarity, exclusively devoted to mere subsistence (Cissé, 1963:115-121).

The system called for the organization and supervision of rural society mainly by rural extension teams working with producer co-operatives. In this way it was planned to kill two birds, one socio-political, the other economic, with one policy stone. Co-operatives were expected to supply all peasant families with a basic minimum of equipment. All would be entitled to it, and it would enable them to work without having to leave their home territories. Agricultural machinery had already been introduced in the colonial era. Now its use expanded greatly, thanks to a policy of equipment credit that opened up prospects of higher harvests and larger farm units. For example, in the short period from 1957 to 1963, the number of farms using draught animals rose from 200 to 5960. Farms using light machines increased from 0 to 4,782, and the number of ploughs rose from 1,111 to 5,170. Now peasants took out more loans for equipment purchases than for off-season subsistence (Ecrement, 1965:61, 134).

The National Domains Act of 17 June 1964 underlined this voluntarist, communal vision. In the first place, it transferred land tenure control in the rural areas to the community, while individual rights to land were vested in persons directly working it. By the mid-1960s, this embryonic agricultural policy had begun to bear apparently satisfactory fruit. Peasants gave top priority to groundnut production. Development programmes helped out. Above all, there was a sustained effort to modernize farming practices and equipment. For these reasons, production in 1965 reached a record high: 1 million tonnes. Average production figures from 1960 to 1971 were 937,000 tons. Average yield per hectare was 879 kilos.[11] Never since have those figures been bettered.

Before 1960, co-operatives had collected only 15% of the total produce. By the mid-1960s their share had risen to 70%. In their rise they had reduced the private trading circuits to relative insignificance. France continued to pay preferential prices far above world market prices for Senegalese nuts. In 1966, the groundnut sector accounted for 80% of the country's exports. Productivity in the oil-manufacturing sector was at its peak. In sum, everything seemed to be going according to the best-laid plans of the State, and in accordance with the findings of the CINAM-CERESA research team. Under the sheen of success in this period however, the cracks of crisis had begun to appear, though some did not develop into full blown fissures until the ensuing period.

Problem number one was that more than ever before, the country's economic structure had become dependent on the groundnut crop. As early as 1965 the Economic and Social Council had expressed some anxiety on this head (JORS, 1965:226), arguing that the low level of foodstuff production was particularly dangerous. An initial, independent scientific assessment supported this conclusion, pointing out that 'the overriding preoccupation of the Senegalese cooperative movement is the groundnut trade. That situation is likely to prevail for a long time to come' (Ecrement, 1965:132).

Problem number two: abundant rains had helped achieve the flattering results of the early 1960s. They had thus worked to cover up a number of problems that would surface later. From 1960 to 1968, rainfall was normal. Its distribution was relatively even (see Chapter 4 in this volume). Indeed, rainfall totals for the period were actually 15% to 25% higher in the northern regions as compared to average figures from 1931-1960 (Ndiaye, 1988).

Problem number three: in addition to the above technical and physical problems, socio-political problems arose to influence agricultural policy. In the absence of detailed information on the operations of co-operatives before 1962, the comparison is bound to be relatively unreliable. But all indices point to a real success story. In 1961 there were 638 co-operatives; by 1966 the number had reached 1,467, and in 1971 it rose to 2,378. Of the total, 1800 or almost 80% were devoted exclusively to groundnut farming (Frélastre 1982:58). In the same period, the market share of the co-operatives rose from 20% of the groundnut crop to 75%. In the fallout, the number of stock agencies dropped from 3,000 to 510.

One intriguing landmark in this successful advance was Circular Number 32 of 21 May 1962, issued by the Council Chairman, M Dia. His purpose was clear enough: to leave his brand unmistakably on an institution so pivotal in rural life that it could turn out to be decisively important in the ideological and political power struggle developing between him and Senghor.[12] The circular's main principles were as follows: as the co-operatives increasingly demonstrated their capacity for self-management, they would become progressively independent of State control and support. Groundnut co-operatives were to be transformed into multi-functional and multi-sectorial structures. Lastly, the co-operative movement was to be vertically integrated at local, regional and national levels (Dia, 1962; Gellar, 1987:125).

The conflict between Senghor and Dia reached its paroxysm in December 1962, After that, agricultural policy in Senegal underwent an adjustment. Indications are that prior to 1962, it was Dia who wielded the greatest influence in the shaping of agricultural policy. His ambition was to end the exploitation of peasants by the trading companies, the rural aristocracy and the religious leadership, thus enabling peasants to take direct control over their own lives. As an instrument, he aimed to use the apparatus of theUnion progressiste sénégalaise (UPS), a *de facto* single party with a strong tradition of rural mobilization.[13] He could also count on the Rural Extension Service.

Senghor's vision was less populist, more technocratic. It was that vision that was to get developed after December 1962, after Dia's expulsion from power (Gellar, 1987).

The Technocratic Temptation: 1966-70

Once Dia was out of the way, Senghor was free to drift unchecked along a top-down technocratic course. The orientation was clear enough at the start, but it was only in the late 1960s that it was fully defined.[14] In the initial stages, he curtailed the operational reach of cooperatives by abolishing their responsibilities in the consumer area and ending their attempts at integrated development as early as 1963. State oversight was reinforced through the auditing of co-operative accounts. Local structures were also empowered to fix priorities in local development activities. In July 1964, Rural Development Assistance Centres (CRAD) were put in charge of the inspection of rural co-operatives (Péhaut, 1984:409). That same year, the technocratic drift negotiated another meander when a foreign technical operations company, the Technical and Co-operative Assistance Company (SATEC) was called in. Its terms of reference were to take charge of expanded agricultural activity in the Groundnut Basin. The move marked the return to public development agencies. Gellar (1987:130-131) calls it the beginning of the long-term triumph of the 'productivist' or technocratic approach. Now the co-operatives were to all intents pushed back to the status they had endured under colonial rule, when they were known as the SIP. In that capacity they served as nothing more than produce collection depots and obedient tools for the transmission of the State's economic policy directives.

The new approach found support in the findings of a study commissioned by the Economic and Social Council on the economic situation in Senegal as of 1965. The study pointed out that the rate of agricultural growth, barely matching that of the population, was low. To break through that low ceiling, there would have to be a 'technological revolution. Indeed, that revolution was considered inevitable (JORS, 1965:226). In earlier years the Muslim marabouts, large-scale producers who had felt threatened by the rise of populist co-operative structures, breathed easier. They could now continue their old game of domination over the co-operative movement, either by setting up their own co-operatives or by taking control of local co-operatives established by their followers.[15] As a matter of fact, the rural aristocracy used co-operatives to build up or strengthen their political, economic and social bases as well as to boost their personal prestige and authority.

When Senghor assigned a set of more technical objectives to be followed by the Rural Extension Service, marabouts understood clearly that the new policy offered them certain advantages. To begin with, it would enable them to infiltrate an apparatus that could potentially be used to challenge traditional authority. Beyond that, it put them ahead of the queue of potential beneficiaries from the spread of new agricultural techniques. State officials, too, were generally pleased with these developments. After all, now they knew they were finally dealing with people with a stake in the status quo. Besides, they could count on the support of powerful men, and their own social prestige could only improve as a result (Coulon, 1981:230).

As long as there was no threat to the revenues of the UPS party-state under Senghor, and as long as the system ensured the continued loyalty of the population, the major plantation-owning marabouts were given free rein (Copans, 1980). Government agencies gave them preferential treatment. For instance, they could draw on juicy lines of credit at the Banque nationale de développement du Sénégal (BNDS); they were paid excellent wholesale prices for their groundnuts, and some, like Cheikh Mbacké, were allowed direct access to the world market. They were awarded quotas for seed and agricultural equipment. They were the first to profit from technical innovations. They received direct subsidies from the Price Stabilization Fund, an organization founded in 1966 and given autonomous status in 1973 under a new name: the Price Compensation and Stabilization Fund (CPSP). All this was done in the name of the development of production and the stimulation of innovation.

From 1966 to 1973, the Fund distributed F CFA 3,017 million in subsidies. Of this total F CFA 1,040 million, that is to say, 34.5%, went to major plantation-owning marabouts between 1970 and 1973. For that period they represented 43.6% of total disbursements, at a time of particular hardship (Jammeh, 1987:237). That was a typical instance of the formidable confluence of interests between the government and the marabouts in the rural areas. And the venue for this confluence was the co-operative movement.

There was one catch. The arrangement worked only as long as peasants continued to trust the co-operative association as a viable economic partner. Above all, it worked only so long as the stratum of leaders and dignitaries continued to benefit from artificially inflated prices, subsidies, over-generous bank loans and free support from the rural extension services under their control. What changed this entire grab bag was the economic swing that brought Senegalese groundnut prices into line with world market prices. Up until the mid-1960s, Senegalese groundnuts had enjoyed a double price bonus on the French market. First, these prices were in CFA francs, pegged to the French franc at a 50-1 rate that had remained unchanged since the 1940s, even though the French franc had been devalued by 37% since 1955 (Péhaut, 1984:412). The result was that Senegalese produce was considerably over-valued in relation to world prices for tropical oil seed priced in pounds sterling. Moreover, in line with the workings of the French colonial system since 1933, produce from competitor countries was subject to a surtax on entering France.[16]

In the mid-1960s, the bubble burst. Advances in the world food industry in the area of cooking oils and oil cake used as animal feed had shifted preferences increasingly away from groundnuts. And as from 1 January 1968, the implementation of a common agricultural policy within the European Economic Community, coupled with the Yaoundé Convention, ended the implicit subsidy. The government had known since 1963 that these changes were coming, but it did practically nothing to cushion the blow. It began reacting only in 1965, and even then the measures it took were lily-livered. It urged producers to boost production as a way of maintaining income in the teeth of falling prices. Such was the assignment conferred on the SATEC: to raise groundnut production by 25% from 1965 to 1969, mainly by juggling such technical factors as mechanization, planting techniques, selected seeds and fertilizer (Waterbury, 1987:193-199).[17] The government also made producers pay the cost of marketing arrangements, especially transport. The oil factories and the OCA no longer wanted to bear these costs since they compromised their competitiveness and aggravated their cash flow problems. For the first time since independence, the camouflaged drop in groundnut prices impinged directly on peasant incomes. From that point on, that became the rule.

In 1971, a Permanent Committee on Major Agricultural Products was set up, but the move did not change the situation one whit. In August 1971, Senegal decided to process its entire groundnut crop locally. To do this it bought up most of the country's oil factories. Indeed, with the groundnut harvest dwindling steadily, there was no other option if the struggling national industries were to be guaranteed a minimum operational base. The move had little effect on the international market. Senegalese oil remained under strong pressure from international competitors. As for Senegalese oil cake, the campaign against aflatoxine gave it a bad press. The bottom line was that the total farm season income package dropped from FCFA 22 billion in 1965 to a mere FCFA 10 billion in 1970. Péhaut characterizes the crisis as follows:

> *between 1960 and 1968, Senegal shifted from a system of groundnut produce marketing that was liberal on the domestic market but protected on the international market, to the opposite: State marketing arrangements ended downstream in a competitive market where coping was hard!* *(Péhaut, 1984:414).*

Meanwhile, by 1966 the Senegalese State had become sufficiently aware of the long-term risks entailed by the new situation of vulnerable groundnut prices. It therefore decided to make some economies of scale. Specifically, it began to reduce operating costs of various governmental structures throughout the land by merging them into a single monster, ONCAD on 30 June

1966.[18] ONCAD absorbed the CRAD, the co-operative service, and the OCA. The old stock agencies were finally abolished, so that the State monopoly had total control over groundnut marketing. In subsequent years its terms of reference were constantly expanded in the name of the same principle on which it had been founded: improved efficiency. Everyone was too busy to notice that the new monopoly had ballooned beyond its critical mass.

ONCAD had now taken over the supervision of the entire groundnut economy. What this meant in practice was simply that it bought the crop from producers and resold it to local or foreign oil factories. It then deducted trading costs and its own operating expenses, turning the balance over to the CPSP. If the balance was negative, the CPSP made good the loss. In this way the State moved from a situation in which its role was to stabilize world market prices for groundnuts, to one in which its objective was to maintain a relationship between foreign agricultural prices and domestic consumer price levels (for sugar, rice, tomato paste, oil and wheat flour). At the hub of the system, ONCAD ended up importing and distributing rice as a sub-contractor for the CPSP, because it had both international marketing facilities and a wide domestic network.

The suitability of all these reforms was doubtful in any case. What was worse, their timing was particularly bad. For beginning in 1966, the region entered a cycle of major droughts that kept worsening into the 1980s. From 1968-69 to 1970-71, production fell steadily. In 1971-72 it picked up momentarily, only to fall again, and so forth. In short, the rainfall regime became so staggered that it no longer made any sense to forecast annual production levels. The one thing everyone could be sure of was that the trend was downwards. For instance, the average yield level from 1960 to 1973 was 832 kg/ha. From 1960 to 1966 it was 939 kg/ha, but from 1966 to 1973 the figure was only 740 kg/ha (Frélastre, 1982:52). The figures give a good indication of declining production after 1966. Meanwhile, the general fall in world market prices for agricultural raw materials only aggravated the situation.

Because the government had great faith in the efficiency of technocratic structures, ONCAD grew so important that after 1967 the State delegated the responsibility of managing the country's entire agricultural system to it. The board's annual programme statement and annual business reports were tacitly considered a sufficient control panel for the whole agricultural economy. On the ground, ONCAD had enormous power, and its officials exercised it with gargantuan zest. The board supervised co-operatives, implemented the agricultural programme, managed the supply of such agricultural inputs as seeds, pesticides, fertilizer and machinery, organized produce freight, supplied rice, and ran practically all rural services. It co-ordinated the work of huge specialized regional services known as Regional Development Agencies (ARD): SODEVA, which managed groundnuts in the Groundnut Basin; SAED, in charge of rice planting in the Senegal River valley; SODESP, in charge of animal husbandry in the Ferlo area; SOMIVAC, responsible for rice production in the Lower Casamance; and SODEFITEX, the cotton agency operating in Eastern Senegal, Eastern Saloum and Upper Casamance.[19]

Pretty soon ONCAD grew into a monster incapable of controlling its own expansion, unable to manage its own affairs, and submerged by all the problems of rural society, especially in the Groundnut Basin. So serious were its problems that in 1969 the State called in an Italian company, ITALCONSULT, to conduct a financial and organizational audit. After two years of toil the mountain gave birth to a mouse: extension services for peasants were reorganized, management procedures were amended, and computers were introduced to run the business side. The board itself was not directly shaken. It was not even challenged (Péhaut, 1984:410; ITALCONSULT, 1970).

In the period from 1966 to 1970 a number of serious trends began to surface. Eventually they combined with the impact of the devastating droughts of the 1970s to cause a major crisis that carried over from the late 1970s into the early 1980s.

The ONCAD Hegemony: 1971-79

The main feature of the crisis of the 1970s was that there was, strictly speaking, no policy. Nowhere were objectives identified or resources located for their achievement. Nor were there any ideological guidelines designed to ensure their coordination within a coherent dynamic. In place of all this there was ONCAD. And its impact was so decisive that it became the main cause and venue of the agricultural crisis in Senegal during the 1970s. ONCAD also provided the most visible symbol of the failure of agricultural policy in Senegal.

The ONCAD System

A good way to approach an analysis of the failure of ONCAD is to look at selected essential parameters such as its size, its management style and its relations with the political authorities, the marabouts and the co-operatives.[20] ONCAD was grossly over-sized because it was expected to do too many things at once: groundnut marketing, the management of seed stocks and other inputs, supervision of some 1,800 co-operatives, and the import and distribution of rice. The personnel roster was accordingly overcrowded. There were 4,500 employees in all, 1,799 of them permanent, 2,153 temporary, and 535 expatriate or other technical assistance staff. The organization also had enormous quantities of underused equipment, including 639 storage depots and, in 1980, over 1,000 motor vehicles, poorly maintained for the most part (Péhaut, 1984:421).

ONCAD's overheads were therefore huge. ITALCONSULT, for instance, estimated that a staff totalling just 1,609 persons could have done the job (Caswell, 1984:65). There is no telling how much ONCAD cost in all, but between 1973 and 1976 alone, its operating costs amounted to 87.2% of its business turnover, and in 1980 to 30% of earnings from groundnut sales (Frélastre, 1982:63). All this merely confirms the wry Senegalese perception that like many other public sector enterprises, ONCAD really had just one main purpose: to look after itself, its employees and their bosses.

ONCAD's gargantuan size made management unavoidably problematic. The computerization of its business brought no improvement. Management was so badly organized that serious supervision was out of the question. There were too many internal decision-making centres. Management practices were decentralized and riven with procrastination. This created juicy opportunities for numerous intermediaries, weaving in and out of labyrinths of red tape. The corporation drifted along in a permanent haze. In 1975-76, ONCAD's expenses topped the recurrent budget of the State of Senegal. Worse still, none of this expenditure took into account the country's real resources. In fact, ONCAD splurged with no awareness whatsoever that the nation in general was in dire economic straits. By the time it was wound up, ONCAD had thus piled up an official deficit of F CFA 72 billion. With interest rates added, the total exceeded F CFA 90 billion. More than a few observers concluded that a large portion of the deficit was embezzled.

The point was well taken. Rural extension organizations had a long and varied record of embezzlement. Under ONCAD, however, such cases were more frequent, the amounts involved larger. Co-operative units became notorious for tales of phantom loads and tampering with scales. Groundnuts were mixed with chaff, payments were made to nonexistent transporters and co-operatives[21], different grades of seed stocks (ordinary grade refinery groundnuts, top quality table nuts and selected seed)[22] were manipulated, agricultural equipment, seedlings and rice were sold on the parallel market at home and abroad[23], etc. Once headquarters accounts were computerized, large-scale instances of embezzlement began to surface as from 1971[24]. And that was by no means the end.

The most popular embezzling techniques included fake invoices of all types, absurd purchase orders, the temporary placement of large corporate funds in private bank accounts where they drew interest for the beneficiary before being forwarded, cash vouchers that became untraceable at accounting time, in-house sales of equipment at huge discounts, the issue of fake transport permits and licences, the allocation of unearned travel allowances and other bonuses, the payment of salaries and wages to ghost employees, etc. Needless to say, politicians, civil servants and religious leaders all participated in the grab fest, either personally or on behalf of their hangers-on. ONCAD was a good place to find jobs for relatives, friends and dependents. Contracts with ONCAD gave many enterprises, big and small, their livelihood. The board distributed rice quotas, provided equipment, housing, vehicles and fuel for political and civil service big shots on the go. In some cases the perks were permanent giveaways[25].

In the 1970s, ONCAD took a number of important strategic decisions that were to affect the rural situation long afterwards. The problem was that the ONCAD system, internally rotten as it was, could not possibly take reasonable long-term decisions. One example was the agricultural equipment distribution system. From the mid-1970s it had become clear that the equipment already distributed was adequate, yet ONCAD continued supplying equipment at the initial rate. The mismanagement was most durably harmful in the area of transport facilities and processing machinery. Transport arrangements had become more complicated because the cooperatives served as trading posts. In the late 1950s there had been only 300 such collection and distribution points, but now there were 1800. Trucks had knocked out or pushed aside every other kind of transportation, including barges, pack animals and railroad traffic, even though trucking costs sometimes made the shift senseless[26].

As far as the industrial structure was concerned, ONCAD financed a programme that doubled the processing capacity of Senegal's oil factories between 1964 and 1971. But this feat was accomplished at one of the worst possible junctures. Groundnut production was falling; foreign markets were shutting their doors; less fancy oils were becoming a fashionable staple; and the exchange rate of the franc had risen. Groundnut shelling capacity was boosted according to the same absurd logic, and with similarly catastrophic results: the Senegalese industry boosted its capacity beyond the ability of producers to supply it, and beyond the absorptive capacity of its market outlets.

The most disastrous misstep, however, was that ONCAD pushed the co-operative movement into a dead-end situation. The country's peasants had been led to expect good times ahead in the 1960s. What they got instead was a slump, and it created a particularly strong climate of depression in the countryside. Admittedly, economic conditions had worsened for the entire country as from the mid-1970s. It was also true that neither the government nor ONCAD had the power to root out the main causes of the general crisis. Terms of trade for all raw materials save petroleum had fallen. Droughts had become a chronic feature of Senegalese life. But potent as these two causes were, they did not exonerate the State or its principal instrument from 1966 to 1980, ONCAD.

All things considered, it is hard to lay the blame on any particular agricultural policy. In all seriousness, there was no such thing. ONCAD spent little time trying to develop a coherent policy and an efficient implementational style. What it did was to take off busily in every possible direction. Policy, intelligently understood, is the establishment of a clear order of programmed priorities, followed by the disciplined accomplishment of the tasks thus ordered, resulting in the transformation of the natural environment and the human situation. In that precise sense, there was no agricultural policy in Senegal during the heyday of the giant organization, ONCAD.

The Absence of a Genuine Agricultural Policy

In the 1960s, with encouragement from the State, Senegal's peasants got together to form co-operatives. At the time their overriding aim was to get the best possible price for their crops, in an attempt to break through a vicious cycle of indebtedness that was making them lose control over their lives. The co-operative movement then offered them guaranteed prices, rebates at the end of the farm season, subsistence loans to tide them over off-season lean times, seed and fertilizer at low interest rates, hire-purchase terms for otherwise unaffordable machinery, and the solution of transport problems through the creation of numerous new collection and supply posts. The hope was that as they got more familiar with the organizational side of co-operative affairs, they themselves would eventually take over (Cissé, 1963; Ecrement, 1965).

That heart-warming dream vanished in short order after Dia's fall from power. From then on extension service officials, politicians and marabouts all took advantage of a situation created by direct State control. Conflicts of interest, corruption, embezzlement and influence-peddling became the rule[27]. A number of deontological guidelines had been set out in Circular Number 32, but now they were simply shoved aside (Gellar, 1987:130).

Up until 1966, good harvests had camouflaged the rot. But in the 1966-67 farm season, the drought began. The world market price for groundnuts also dropped. Most peasants were therefore in no position to repay their debts. Increasing numbers actually gave up trying, and from 1970 to 1980, the country-wide debt repayment rate fell to an average of 60% (Tuck, 1987:163). The situation got so bad that peasants who managed to repay their individual debts suffered because the principle of co-operative liability imposed two penalties on them. First they paid their own debts. Then they suffered because their colleagues could not pay theirs[28]. In addition, the makeshift agricultural policy[29], such as it was, was poorly understood. Increasing numbers of officials were getting exposed as incompetent; equipment and inputs were getting issued late; corruption was common; debt collectors used violent methods; off-season subsistence credits were cut; marketing operations were subject to longer and longer delays. The peasants, understandably, slid into a condition that came to be known as the rural malaise.

From 1971 to 1980, as years of drought followed each other, that condition worsened. Some of the consequences, according to Gellar, were declining orders for inputs and equipment; failure or refusal to repay debts; disappointment with price levels, ONCAD and the co-operative movement; the withdrawal of peasants from co-operative and Rural Development Agency activities; and lastly the dynamic growth of a parallel market (Gellar, 1987:132). We might add the following trends to the list: a tendency to depend on periodic handouts of imported food; the resale of equipment and sales vouchers; and rising apathy among the majority of competent, formerly hard-working officials (Caswell, 1984:56-57). One accurate pointer was the default rate in the repayment of loans taken by members of cooperatives. In the 1970s, peasants tended to pay roughly in accordance with the abundance or meagerness of their harvests. But there was a definite long-term tendency to let arrears grow, and the rate of repayment kept falling. From 1970 to 1980[30], accumulated debts increased at an average annual rate of 10.7%.

The government tried strong-arm tactics, but the combined impact of intercession by marabouts and the introduction of multi-party politics brought such attempts to a quick end. In many zones, marabouts made themselves advocates of the people against particular impositions. In general, they also reinforced their hold on rural society and confirmed their status as special spokespersons in dealings with the State (Coulon, 1981:283-87). All this while they remained the main beneficiaries of shifts in income and production capacity on the local and external scenes.

The State lurched along with no new agricultural policy, in fact with no agricultural policy of any kind. It seemed resigned to the buffetings of climatic hazards and the world market. Unable to stop these disasters from hitting the peasantry, it decided at least to soften their impact. The main cushioning method turned out to be the writing off of debts. In four farming seasons (1970-71, 1972-73, 1979-80 and 1980-81), peasant debts were entirely written off. In the 1977-78 season, they were partially written off. In five out of eleven[31] seasons, then, debts were written off. Out of some F CFA 23,719 billion loaned out from 1970 to 1980, only 46.5% ever were paid back (Tuck, 1987:160-187).

The write-offs, however, did not mean a genuine transfer of resources to rural producers. For quite often, peasants used loans as a means of supplementing their ever-dwindling incomes. They would borrow from the co-operatives more seed, equipment etc. than they needed, with the hope of flogging the surplus, no matter how cheaply, to make ends meet when the going got tough. It might be said, in other words, that peasants used co-operative loans as a surrogate for what they really needed: a system of wage guarantees in the teeth of climatic and economic uncertainty. By getting into the habit of wholesale write-offs, the State was promoting an ultimately perverse cycle of inflationary speculation based on the fact that loans taken out in boom times would be written off when the bust came. A side effect of the process was to make any effort to improve farm productivity look rather silly.

It seems clear enough that the writing off of all peasant debts would be counterproductive to any well-thought-out agricultural policy. It was more of a political expedient than an economic measure. The reasoning behind it was in any case suicidal. It deprived the State of the only normal means of coercion available to it. Moreover, it turned circumstantial crises into a structural imbalance. The habit underlined the need for a real agricultural policy. After all, it was hard to imagine such aberrations continuing if the country's agricultural system was really to develop.

For a long time, reforms indispensable to agricultural recovery had been postponed. In time they became urgent. The need became all the more desperate because the State, already on its knees, was almost too broke to continue honouring its financial obligations. Groundnut production levels had fallen. The entrepreneurial State was bankrupt. It therefore had little leverage in negotiations with international capital. By the same token, it could hardly envisage far-reaching reforms at home (Mbodj, 1991:121-22).

Reforms Under the Adjustment Programme

As the decade of the 1980s began, Senegal was in dire straits. Officially, the culprits were the drought and deteriorating international trade terms. These factors were presented as monolithic, gigantic and permanent facts of life. Little was said about the responsibility of a bureaucracy which had embezzled or wasted a substantial portion of public assets[32]. Perfunctory diagnoses of this sort became standard incantatory fare at various congresses and National Council sessions of the ruling party, the UPS, from the mid-1970s. Since the country's leaders had no rainmaking skills, and since they had no leverage over world market prices for raw materials, it was the kind of argument that had nowhere to go. Pretty soon it became untenable, especially when accompanied by higher taxes[33] on urban incomes.

At the end of the 1970s the tone of official rhetoric changed. The primary impetus for the shift came from a young 'technocrat', Abdou Diouf, who had been appointed Prime Minister. Diouf's main goal was to return the financial management of the country to orthodox norms. He wanted first of all to get the major macroeconomic balances on course. Only after that did he envisage recovery and growth[34]. Given that perspective, the main thrust of a three-phase reform package was to cut deficits, to reform structures, and then to boost production. We can now turn to an examination of these three phases, represented by the abolition of ONCAD (1978-80), the reform of extension structures (1980-85), and the final phase: the installation of a New Agricultural Policy (as from 1984).

The Abolition of ONCAD

There were two direct ways to cut deficits. One was to plug money drains. The other was to bring in fresh capital. The first required the abolition of budget-guzzling organizations, a category including most public and parastatal enterprises, along with cutbacks in the total national wage package and social welfare expenditure. The second meant the attraction of aid funds, mainly from the World Bank and the International Monetary Fund. The lead-up to the first was a wide-ranging debate on the cutting of the huge deficit in the public sector. Two factors provided opportunities for the proceedings. The first was an internal political debate that started in 1974 and grew sharper during the 1978 general elections. It was given plenty of fuel by accounting and auditing missions conducted by the Organization and Methods Bureau (BOM). The second factor was the fact that Senegal's traditional suppliers of financial aid, namely France, the EEC, the oil-rich Arab countries of the Gulf, and especially the International Monetary Fund and the World Bank, believers in orthodox liberal capitalism themselves, were not too keen to continue pouring money into structures whose operational methods often ran counter to the principles they held dear.

The internal debate ran from 1979 to 1980. It took little time for it to zoom in on ONCAD[35]. This was understandable. After all, the agricultural sector was an economic heavyweight, employing 70% of the Senegalese population. Taxation had risen sharply, the official explanation being that it was necessary to lighten the burden on the rural population. Lastly, the huge deficit run up by ONCAD was particularly glaring in view of its corpulent presence in all aspects of national life. One particularly prestigious forum for the debate was the *Club Nation et Développement*, a think tank that brought together the bulk of the country's intellectuals who either belonged to the ruling party (now called the Socialist Party), intended to join it, or were closely affiliated to it. This is probably an appropriate place to point out that the very idea of such a think tank was a major innovation initiated by the government itself. It marked more than a mere change in style. It meant that the government now sought to base its legitimacy on its technical competence. Significantly, it was getting frustrated in that quest by fossilized and overly personalized structures set up by the Socialist Party[36].

The debate did not make giant waves among the public. One possible reason was that there were few people ready to argue on behalf of ONCAD. Neither its basic principles nor its operational methods were defensible. It was therefore rapidly outflanked. Four main points emerged from the debate:

- The cooperative movement was a fiasco;
- ONCAD was in dire need of reform;
- The Rural Development Agencies (RDAs) would have to become efficient and responsive to rural needs;
- The rural population should assume greater managerial responsibility over their own affairs.

As far as the diagnosis went, there was general agreement on these four points. When it came to prescriptions, however, the consensus broke apart. Three schools of thought advocated different solutions each based on a different diagnostic point. One group was for making ONCAD reform the key issue, cutting State intervention to the bone, and rationalizing the groundnut production and marketing circuit. Members of this group were mainly technocrats from the Central Government and the BOM in the President's Office. Their principal worry was to honour neo-classical economic principles.

With equal determination, a second group emphasized the RDAs, placing their bets on decentralization. To this school belonged the SODEVA officials along with the majority of local and international development agencies. The third group was rather close to the second. Its goal was to revitalize cooperative activity within a broad programme giving greater responsibilities to the rural population. Adherents of this school were mainly old timers dreaming of a return to the heady socialistic agricultural policies of the early 1960s. To some of the most active, the famous Circular Number 32[37] was still a sort of manifesto.

In an effort to resolve these differences, a National Commission was appointed in February 1979 to trace out an acceptable path[38]. Its recommendation was a package deal: co-operatives were to be promoted under the aegis of an autonomous national department. Rural Development Agencies were to be retooled as service and training agencies working with co-operatives. ONCAD was to continue functioning as a funding and implementational agency for the national agricultural programme. Lastly, selected cooperatives were to be allowed to market their produce without the ONCAD imprimatur.

In May 1980 the National Council of the Socialist Party adopted these proposals, stressing the need to involve the rural population in the impending reforms, and to give them greater responsibilities. The gestation period had been long. It had spawned a great variety[39] of studies and ideas. Now, it seemed, the government was ready to come out with a policy for reforming ONCAD.

Suddenly, however, the National Assembly, meeting in an extraordinary session, voted to abolish ONCAD. Before the national debate could amble to a logical conclusion, the country's obligations towards the World Bank/International Monetary Bank duo had preempted the issue. As early as the last years of the 1960s decade, it had been common knowledge that Senegal was in serious economic difficulties. The only new development in 1978-79 was the revelation of the size of the country's debt. In 1972, debt service charges had taken up only 4% of export earnings. By 1978 the percentage had risen above 15%. Foreign exchange reserves were vanishing, and the balance of payments was negative[40]. Senegal was thus short of cash on both the domestic and international fronts. In September 1978 it approached the World Bank. That institution had just put together a mechanism for handling structural adjustment loans. It was happy to have Senegal offer itself as a guinea pig. The IMF agreed to participate. In December 1979 an agreement was signed with the World Bank. In August 1980 another was signed with the IMF. The upshot of the two accords was an Economic and Financial Recovery Programme for 1980-85, coupled with an Economic Policy Declaration focused on taxation, currency, price levels, parastatal organizations and agricultural policy[41].

These developments sounded the death knell for ONCAD. As far as the funding agencies were concerned, the Marketing Board had become a symbol of the worst possible aspects of mismanagement under the former socialistic economic policy[42]. Taking advantage of the wave of revulsion created by new revelations of embezzlement in August 1980, the government rammed through a motion dissolving the board. At one stroke it thus wiped out one of the sources of imbalance in the public finances, broke up one of the major obstacles in the way of a liberal economic policy, and cut a lot of fat off the bloated public wage package.

ONCAD, then, looked like the first victim of the new adjustment policy. As we have seen, it was a most convenient victim. It would have been hard, in any case, for Abdou Diouf, the prospective President, to simply take over ONCAD. It had become an enormous torpedo at the service of Senghor's power system, working for a party which was yet very far from accepting the younger Diouf as its boss. It would have been dangerous for him to let a debate that had shaken the party at every level continue. It would have been equally hazardous had he waited until his first year in office to dissolve the organization. After all, he needed to have that first year go down as a time of smooth consensus.

It seems clear that Abdou Diouf fought tooth and nail to get the measure approved. After the dust had settled, explaining his move in 1981, he said that ONCAD

had lost the capacity to fulfill its terms of reference. Moreover, it had become impossible for the cooperatives to continue coexisting with such a top-heavy and ubiquitous organization. The Board tended to reduce them to simple groundnut collection depots, which they were in fact about to become. We remain committed to the objective of liberating rural society from the bureaucratic red tape and excessive official interference hampering its development[43].

The breakneck speed[44] of ONCAD's abolition gave rise to three explanatory hypotheses. The first was that the struggle for Senghor's succession was already on. The second was that even at that time there was deep distrust between the party apparatus and its future leader. The third was that the downfall of ONCAD was among the first of Abdou Diouf's major political victories. Meanwhile, a number of smaller organizations were set up in place of ONCAD.

New Structures: The SONACOS/SONAR Tandem

ONCAD had bitten the dust, but that did not mean the State was determined to follow a different policy. The State's main preoccupation was to achieve better results without investing such a lot of money. The search, in other words, was more for efficiency than for a radically different agricultural policy. The two main agricultural policy instruments in the post-ONCAD period were SONACOS (the Senegalese National Oilseed Marketing Corporation) and SONAR (the National Rural Supplies Corporation). The latter in particular came to be perceived as the successor to ONCAD. It also gave the impression of following the defunct board's policies.

SONAR was born during the same session that voted the dissolution of ONCAD. Its task was to supply the rural areas with agricultural inputs and equipment. SODEVA continued to function as its specialized agency in the Groundnut Basin, while other regional corporations played similar roles in their respective areas. The SAED, for instance, covered the Senegal River valley, SOMIVAC covered the Casamance, etc. But in time SONAR moved beyond the simple mandate of production development to get involved in a whole range of rural welfare activities.

SONACOS was established on 1 October 1975. At its inception its responsibility was to sell groundnuts to the oil factories and to look after the public interest in that sector. But gradually it took over monopoly control of the oil market (June 1978), and then of the entire oil industry after the State bought the oil factories on 1 January 1980. From 1980, SONACOS took charge of the processing and marketing of the entire groundnut crop. The SEIB, operating with 51% public capital, was given similar responsibilities in Diourbel region and the district of Linguère.

SONACOS did all the work formerly handled by ONCAD, except that freighting of the groundnuts to collection points was left in the hands of the cooperatives, while the rice trade was handed back to the Compensation Fund. SONACOS and SONAR were clearly an improvement over ONCAD. More lightly structured, they were more efficient and less expensive to run. SONACOS and SEIB together had a marketing staff of just 500 as compared to over 2,000 for ONCAD. Their activities were also more streamlined. Many collection points were abolished. Seed stocks were managed by the cooperatives, but individual producers' contributions and accounts were tracked. Loans for machinery were held in abeyance for five years. All purchases were now cash down. The only input now subsidized was fertilizer.

These changes were positive. Nevertheless, the international climate remained harsh; the fallout from the recent past remained damaging; and the peasantry remained discontented. The combined effect of these factors was that in the mid-1980s, agricultural yields and production were less than brilliant. To begin with, the reform programme seemed to have got off on the wrong foot, because it was started smack in the middle of the farming season. The groundnut harvest in 1980-81 was the worst registered by Senegal since the 1950s. Marketing figures were even more disappointing. Oil factories worked at less than 30% of capacity. SONACOS and SEIB had a combined total processing capacity of 900,000 tons, but in 1980-81 they received only 260,000 tons (29%). SONACOS had earned the State substantial profits up until 1979. But it carried the simultaneous burden of having to deal with ONCAD's backlog of liabilities. It therefore slumped into the red (Péhaut, 1984:430). The situation got so tight that Senegal actually had to import foreign oil to meet its foreign commitments.

Trying to cope with this catastrophe, the government quashed producers' debts in April 1981 and raised producer prices in the middle of the farming season. These incentives came too late to help ordinary producers, and only the large scale plantation-owning marabouts and certain traders were able to benefit from them. Most peasants, driven to despair, preferred the safer route to the parallel market[45].

The government was much affected by the disaffection among peasants. Its economic consequences were disastrous, but what upset government officials even more was the lack of confidence it revealed. Some actually thought of it as ingratitude. Transport arrangements were stymied, since transport owners either could not or would not invest in vehicles. They were waiting to see how the new system would perform. It was also plain that the co-operatives were failing in their major role as managers of groundnut collection depots.

In the wave of reforms from 1978 to 1980, the government had hoped to cut down the number of individual co-operatives by getting as many as possible to merge[46]. Peasants, especially those in the Mouride areas, hated the idea. From 1981 the Co-operation Service began to put its finger accurately on the four main reasons for their resistance[47]. Some villages were going to have to pay transport costs for the first time; others would see their transport costs go up. The marketing process involved a lot of wasted time because so many people had to be concentrated at one particular sales point. Villages that had formerly had their own cooperative agencies were unhappy at losing prestige along with some benefits. Lastly, the added distance away from home gave ordinary peasants little control over cooperative activities. Even more bitter resistance came from rural dignitaries and Socialist Party officials. On paper, the reforms said village units would enjoy financial autonomy. In practice, this meant problems regarding control over cooperative resources[48].

In spite of all these problems, the reform programme got into gear in September 1983, with the issue of financial autonomy shelved. In place of 1,887 co-operatives, there were now 314 so-called 'development co-operatives'. Each rural community had at least one. The 314 headed a total of 4,200 village units. There was a special effort to involve other agricultural sectors and cash crops (cotton, market gardening, animal husbandry and fisheries) that had formerly been ignored in cooperative activities. Co-operatives in these other sectors were generally more efficient, better managed and more popular because they included young people and women. As a counterweight to administrative structures, the State sponsored the Senegalese National Union of Agricultural Co-operatives (UNCA) in May 1978. This umbrella body was expected eventually to take over the management of the entire cooperative system, by-pass such intermediaries as SONAR, and organize welfare activities at the grass roots level.

The reforms were long postponed on account of the 1983 elections. By the time they finally got into operation, they had entirely lost the impact the old faithfuls of Circular No. 32 had hoped they would have. For one thing, control over the co-operative movement as a whole remained in the hands of large plantation-owning marabouts and Socialist Party big shots. The reform process did not jeopardize their interests. Besides, people continued to view the reforms as a top-down mechanism imposed by the State. The perception was that the State was keen to shift its responsibilities (read problems) onto peasant shoulders, but had no intention of shifting economic decision-making power (read potential benefits) in the same direction. Lastly, the co-operative movement was the ground-level economic lever in the countryside, and the sharp political struggle for control over rural society necessarily affected it[49].

The mid-1980s, then, saw no breakthrough. The continuing impasse was proof that the hasty reforms, contemptuously dismissed as 'petty reforms' by the opposition, were silly. Above all it indicated a continuing, urgent need for a well-defined and serious agricultural policy addressing all sectors of activity in the rural environment within a coherent framework conceived in the national interest. In 1981, the Senegalese government called in one of the fiercest critics of its agricultural policy over the previous 20 years, René Dumont.

The renowned agronomist presented his proposals as simply his personal 'opinions, not advice'. His published report nevertheless reached beyond the usual condemnation of the urban bias of the country's economic stance to propose a list of measures to be taken if the rural situation were to be salvaged. Peasants, he suggested, should be freed from the oppressive hierarchy of co-operative chairmen, weighing clerks, transport owners and traders battening on State and party. Soils in the Groundnut Basin should be revitalized. Peasants should then be organized into credit unions. A three-tiered programme should be established to oversee rain-fed agriculture in the south, small-scale water works projects, and the use of draught animals to work small perimeters in the Senegal River valley (Dumont and Mottin, 1982).

Indications are that not much positive attention was paid to Dumont's 'opinions'. In the preface to his report, the Minister of Rural Development merely observed that it 'deserved a constructive response'. There is an intriguingly symptomatic footnote to this episode. For in the end it was left to foreign pressure to initiate the New Agricultural Policy (NPA). That policy subsumed a number of Dumont's opinions.

The New Agricultural Policy

Almost everywhere in Africa, the food crisis of the 1970s yielded place to an agricultural crisis. The general head-scratching that ensued culminated in the Berg Report, published in 1981. The World Bank/IMF duo adopted its findings as their operational policy basis for the design of economic policy packages for countries requesting their guidance. It should be clear enough why the two institutions imposed measures aimed at reversing prevailing trends in the country's economic affairs when Senegal appealed to them in October 1979. In a pretty standard approach to relations between the State and the economy, Berg locates the roots of agricultural crisis in a number of policies pursued by African governments. He puts a special emphasis on a tendency to butter up the urban strata with artificially low (subsidized) prices for foodstuffs, generous resource allocations to import substitution industries and wage-earning workers, and a generally overvalued currency.

In the October 1980 Economic and Financial Recovery Plan, Senegal announced a set of fiscal, monetary and financial reforms, a priority investment schedule, the break-up of parastatal organizations, a new price policy and a list of incentive measures[50]. During this first phase, the overriding aim was to re-establish a balance in the public finances. Results ranged from lukewarm to downright disappointing. Berg (1990:XV) actually described what happened in the 1980-84 period as a 'false start'. It was therefore necessary to draft a second Medium and Long-Term Economic and Financial Adjustment Programme for the period from 1985 to 1992. Over the medium term the programme stayed on course as far as control over inflation, budget totals and the balance of payments deficit were concerned. Long term additions included economic restructuring, the improvement of productivity and the recovery of production.

In the primary sector, this meant the implementation of a New Agricultural Policy (NPA)[51]. As Abdou Diouf himself admits in his preface to the final document[52], it seems that foreign pressure played a decisive part in the decision. In presenting the New Agricultural Policy to Senegalese public opinion, the government argued that it was justified because progress in the agricultural sector since independence had been so mediocre. The causes indexed were mainly political and economic. Climatic conditions had been hazardous; circumstances had generally been unfavourable for groundnut production, but a main compounding factor had been the lack of a water resource development policy. Extension organizations in the rural areas had been inefficient. Production incentives had been weak. Farmers had little capacity for self-financing, and last of all, the State had been overburdened with heavy costs.

This was the first time an analysis of the causes of the country's agricultural woes had removed climate from its usual honoured place as the mother of all problems. The government now linked the sector's poor performance with problems besetting the agro-industrial sector, the balance of trade deficit, the fall in rural living standards, and the heavy debt owed by both the State and the peasantry to the national and international banking systems.

The proposed solution was to create conditions for the recovery of production within a framework of increased participation and responsibility for the rural population in which the State would only serve as a catalytic agent (Senegal/MDR 1984).

The New Agricultural Policy was based on the idea that henceforth the agricultural sector should generally operate according to market norms, with peasants tuned in to the profit motive[53]. In practice, this meant that the rural areas had to be reorganized, with the State playing a reduced role. For example, it would no longer supply fertilizer or subsidize machinery purchases. It would have a significant role only in two areas. The first would be the promotion of local cereal production and marketing so as to help make up the country's food deficit and reduce the high import bill for rice and wheat. The main mechanism for this policy would be price controls. The second would be to spearhead a soil regeneration campaign[54].

In all practical terms, then, the State adopted a hands-off policy. It no longer supplied seed, agricultural equipment, fertilizer or any type of input whatsoever. All it did was to arrange to have inputs available for producers able to pay cash. SONAR was therefore wound up in 1985, and SODEVA sacked 75% of its staff. The State, however, has continued to guarantee an official price for groundnuts. In addition, it supervises groundnut processing factories, working through SONACOS. It is up to private entrepreneurs to organize the collection and transport of the groundnut crop, along with the entire trade in foodstuffs.

As far as the State is concerned, the category of 'private entrepreneurs' includes a vast array of operators of all stripes, from ordinary middlemen through traders and large plantation-owning marabouts to the former cooperatives now modified into Economic Interest Groups (GIE). A rural bank known as the National Agricultural Credit Fund of Senegal (CNCAS), run jointly by the State and the co-operative associations, is supposed to provide the necessary financial support for the system.

The real purpose of the New Agricultural Policy is to establish a new division of labour between the State, the population and private participants. The State will deal solely with organization and co-ordination. Peasants will be responsible for development activities, and private entrepreneurs will ensure linkages between State and peasantry. The three main policy foci of the new system are taken care of by three priority sub-programmes. The first is the re-establishment of financial balance. The second is the maintenance of cash crop production levels through price incentives, but without subsidies. The third is the long-term food self-sufficiency sub-programme.

The New Agricultural Policy has multiple implications. Here we shall focus on its political and socio-economic aspects. The Senegalese government plans to use prices as incentives. What it forgets is that price fixing is a thoroughly political activity. For the decision to raise prices of imported cereals while freezing the purchasing price of groundnuts in order to encourage local cereal production is a political option (Jammeh, 1987:223-224). Like all political choices, it presents advantages and disadvantages. In other words, the issue is to determine who will gain from the new rice structures. The matter can be put more crudely: on whose side is the State going to be? If we consider the Senegalese territory as a marketplace for commodities and capital, the point is to determine from which group capital and commodity resources are to be shifted, and to which other group these resources are to be delivered.

Once all subsidies for fertilizer and seed stocks are withdrawn, there is little doubt that it is the large-scale producers who stand to benefit[55]. In fact, these characters are actually in a position to replace the State by tightening their old control over rural credit[56]. The storage of groundnut seed poses particular problems to peasant producers. Very few have the means to stock adequate quantities of seed without risking deterioration in quality. Risks associated with makeshift storage are high[57].

As far as fertilizer use was concerned, the alternative to commercial purchase was not the use of home-made fertilizer but the use of no fertilizer at all. Formerly, peasants had benefited from a rebate that ranged between 50% and 80% of the market price (Gaye, 1988:6; Berg, 1990:83). When that rebate (in fact a subsidy) was abolished, the real price peasants had to pay for fertilizer rose 400% between 1982-83 and 1984-85 (Gaye, 1988:6). Little wonder, then, that peasants simply gave up fertilizer use. From 1984-85, they used less than 30% of the quantities they had formerly used, even though those quantities had been far lower than the minimum recommended by the agricultural services (Commander et al., 1989:163).

To deal with the situation, funding agencies were obliged to agree to a 50% subsidy that was to be phased out between 1985 and 1990 (Berg, 1990:84). Meanwhile, the aim of improved productivity remained a pipe dream. It was always possible for peasants to exploit family ties or patronage to make up scarce seed stocks. Fertilizer stocks, however, could not be hustled up so easily. The expedient went counter to the objective of giving ordinary peasants greater responsibilities within the cooperative framework. The inherent risks of rain-fed agriculture could only be borne by large-scale producers, whose interests did not always override those of the small peasant.

The socio-economic implications of the New Agricultural Policy were linked to the political aspect. It was hoped, for instance, that a new alliance between small peasants and large-scale producers would take the place of the old one between urban wage-earners and large-scale cash crop planters[58]. The substitution of a new 'rural priority' for the old urban bias would entail a long-term loss of influence for urban groups. If it went far enough, it would cause the loss of some part of the existing industrial base[59]. That in turn would mean a slow but sure process that would bring the organizational mouthpieces of the urban wage-earners - trade unions and orthodox political parties - to heel.

The catch is that in Senegal, there is no guarantee that such a scenario would pan out. For the regime has nothing to offer urban groups in return for their acceptance of the new deal: no job security, no distribution of dividends. The best it can do is to proffer symbolic recognition to the so-called informal sector as an 'honourable' part of the national economy and society. In any case it is doubtful if anyone can build a coherent sense of national solidarity while laying the burden on social strata whose purchasing power has been shrinking ever faster since the 1970s, and whose members have no direct or indirect responsibility for the management of the situation. There is no question of continued belt-tightening unless the payoff is going to be an improvement in the living conditions of the poorest peasants. And that is far from likely.

It is, needless to stress, too early yet for an accurate evaluation of the performance of the New Agricultural Policy. But the Senegalese Government is decidedly up-beat about it. There are indications that their high spirits are partly justified. Groundnut production, for instance, after dropping from 682,000 tons in 1984-85 to 587,000 tons in 1985-86, rose to 841,000 tons in 1986-87, 963,000 tons in 1987-88, and 723,000 tons in 1988-89 (Berg 1990:106). In 1984-85, the oil factories had operated at a mere 20% of capacity; but in 1987-88 they climbed back up to over 60% of capacity (*The Economist*, 1990:13-43). Most significant of all, local cereal production has been making substantial advances since 1984-85 (CILSS, 1990:5). All these advances have been made while producers have been getting better prices. Add to that the prospect of 240,000 hectares of irrigated land coming into production soon around the dam scheme in the Senegal River valley, and it becomes easy to understand the euphoria of some Senegalese officials in mid-1988. The media made much of their optimism.

A more detailed examination of these figures leads to the conclusion expressed by Berg, namely: that the key explanation is that since 1985, climatic conditions have generally been good (1990:105). World market prices for oil seeds have continued to go down. Groundnut oil prices, for instance, swung from US$1,016 per ton in 1983-84 to $500 in 1986-87 and then to $750 in 1988-89. All this while the State continued paying steady prices to producers, at the rate of FCFA 50 per kilo in 1983-84 and 1985-86;

F CFA 90 per kilo from 1985 to 1988. This translated into a stabilization subsidy of F CFA 30 billion for oil in 1987-88. The State was bleeding money. In 1988-89 the producer price was lowered to F CFA 70 per kilo to stop the haemorrhage.

The CNCAS played no part in the advances registered. In all, it delivered seed to a grand total of just 599 peasants. Local pundits argue that the reasons for its failure include its exorbitant interest rates (15%), and the stipulation that borrowers pay an initial deposit of 20% (Sarr, 1990:6). For our part, we remain unconvinced that the rural bank could lower these rates and still stay in business.

The reasons are many. The State wants to cut out all subsidies. The local market faces a severe cash flow crisis. The only collateral ordinary peasants offer is their next harvest. Besides, they find the bank sites and operating methods inconvenient. The State, for its part, has based its projections on the assumption that producers would make decisions solely on the basis of 'economic rationality'. It is an unjustifiable assumption that ignores a well-known reality: the emergence of entrepreneurial producers is a long-range process. It presupposes a basic minimum of economic and sociological conditions. In Senegal at the moment, it is rather difficult to tell if these preconditions are really in place.

The same degree of caution would be advisable in any assessment of the more technical matter of inputs. The fertilizer supply crisis continues. Since fertilizer prices are sky-high and credit availability abysmally low (Gaye, 1988), peasants use fertilizer as if it were some precious metal. The wish to see private entrepreneurs move into the fertilizer trade remains a cynic's prayer. On paper the profit margins offered look exciting. But traders know conditions on the ground would make payments impossible to collect. To make business possible, there would have to be effective demand in the form of cash. So far all that exists is human need far removed from effective purchasing power. In such a situation angels would fear to trade.

In the handling of seed stocks, peasant producers performed well. They were able to lay by reserve stocks after good harvests. SONACOS had in turn planned to sell 100,000 tons of selected (meaning expensive) seed in 1989-90. In the event it sold no more than 12,000 tons (Sarr, 1990:6). Other problems have remained unsolved. One is the preservation of seed quality. This requires good protective arrangements for genetic stocks, plus periodic renewals of plant inventory. In the period after 1960, one clear success achieved by the Senegalese government was the mechanization of groundnut production on individual farm units. But today that achievement is threatened by the NPA policy of cash sales. To start with, the rural areas do not have the cash flow necessary for such investment and re-investment.

Moreover, very often, the trade in agricultural machinery is based on inter-village credit arrangements. In the long run such arrangements work to the benefit of lending parties, and in the rural areas these are the big plantation-owning marabouts.

It is a major concern of the New Agricultural Policy to motivate producers, especially cereal producers. That, incidentally was the putative purpose of the Cereal Plan, a forerunner of the new policy established in 1986. It was expected to take charge of the cereal sector as well as to arouse interest in local cereal production. To make the idea work, the government took an opposite tack to the former policy option requiring the avoidance at all costs of higher food prices (Bates, 1981). Technically speaking, this was feasible, for agricultural prices were fixed by a select cabinet committee in which the Finance Minister normally had a preponderant vote. That vote could be overridden by a decision of the President, and in the 1980s the President began to use that prerogative with increasing frequency (Jammeh 1987).

The new prices were all the more attractive because the price of the main imported foodstuff, rice, remained fixed considerably above the cost price on the world market[60]. It was hoped that the new price structure would provide sufficient incentives for rural traders to invest in the system. The State therefore thought it had set up conditions for a viable rural market in foodstuffs on which the urban areas could depend. What it forgot was the axiom that no market can function without credit, and the rule of thumb that credit for rain-fed agriculture is inherently high-risk. To compound the anomaly, where rural credit did exist, it was to be tied to the groundnut crop, which carried a guaranteed price, instead of being linked to cereals.

There was a further problem. Growers need special storage facilities to stock large quantities of cereal. For the time being, such facilities are a monopoly of parastatal institutions. In any case, prospective rural capitalists can hardly afford them. Hovering above all these problems is a major question mark: how long will the old price-fixing system survive now that the State has decided on the eventual deregulation of the rural commodity[61] market? Lastly, how far could the government possibly afford to go, in political and social terms, in letting prices of imported rice and wheat rise? Those two items, after all, have been pinpointed by the World Bank and the IMF as the main obstacle to the development and consumption of local cereals.

Conclusion

On paper, Senegal was proclaimed independent in 1960. In reality, the country has lived under the same system, more or less, from 1890 to the present. Throughout that period, the trading sector, private as well as public, has consistently siphoned off most of the potential profit from groundnut production. Under the circumstances, the State has been content to improvise policy from moment to moment. Most of the time that policy did not go beyond the agricultural programme.

Admittedly, at the start of the period under study (1960-62) and at its end (1985-90), there were well defined policies that gave the multiple activities of the State a coherent framework. But all such policies had a fatal flaw: they were directly influenced by considerations that had nothing to do with rural society. In the earlier period, a voluntarist ideology inspired attitudes and structures ill suited and ultimately hostile to rural interests and official objectives. In the 1980s, the situation imposed reforms designed within the framework of national financial recovery. The new reforms, however, suffered from the same old voluntarist ideological bias. They therefore put the country's peasants through an unduly stressful cold-turkey process of withdrawal. The harsh 'weaning' traumatized them.

Now the advocates of these same 'adjustments' argue that even if there has not been sufficient time for an in-depth discussion of NPA results, it is clear enough that in the final analysis, Senegalese agriculture has not undergone much of an 'adjustment' (Berg, 1990:107). Achievements have been assessed as worse than disappointing. Funding agencies, which from 1980 to 1987 put up a brave show of unanimity, have lately degenerated into squabbles, with which officials and the local press are only too glad to regale public opinion. Does that mean, then, that nothing has changed?[62]

There are those who think the root of the entire problem lies in the option in favour of a cash crop such as groundnuts. Dumont, and many leftist commentators, argue that a substitute must be found for that crop. Some advocate abandoning it altogether. Such views find occasional echoes in the media, especially when the crisis grows particularly acute.

They are, however, utterly unrealistic. Besides, they reveal a lack of familiarity with realities of life in Senegal that may be due to ideological blinkers. Of the total population 61% live in the rural areas. More than half are in the Groundnut Basin[63]. This population is made up of followers of the great marabouts, who figure among the most solid pillars of the ruling regime. These marabouts and most dignitaries of the ruling party owe their economic power and social prestige to the groundnut economy. Why on earth should the ruling regime choose to commit *hara-kiri*, destroying the peasants and their leaders into the bargain, simply in order to drop groundnuts and embrace some other crop that would probably demand as much if not more labour, be as vulnerable to climatic inclemencies, and get just as mercilessly kicked around on the world market?[64]

Increased cultivation of local cereals, especially millet, could of course help ease the situation, especially by cutting heavy food import bills. But these crops complement groundnuts; they do not require their abandonment. Meanwhile, post-production infrastructural support and the regular fixing of guaranteed prices continue to encourage groundnut production. There is also the fact that the stabilization fund for rice imports provides the State with an appreciable source of liquidity. For a cash-thirsty State that is a huge plus, and it is the surest argument against the State adopting any pricing policies or privatization measures that would dry up the source. For all these reasons, the powers that be will continue depending on the groundnut economy, and commentators will have to face the fact of its continued importance.

So the imbalance that emerged in the 1960s continue^{65}. In fact it has grown worse. Furthermore, productivity has stalled, and the groundnut sector has settled in the red. To cap it all, nothing points to imminent change, nor even to relief in the medium term (Bonnefond and Couty, 1988:319-340).

The State is still the main protagonist in the rural areas. Its activity shapes life at every level^{66}. Senegal continues to import agricultural foodstuffs. Rice and wheat flour remain the leading staples. Local cereal production and marketing are still largely inadequate and of secondary importance in every respect. Whether production rises or falls depends mainly on the weather. Yields remain unpredictable, fertilizer use is inadequate, mechanization is regressing, and all indices show that productivity has stagnated, perhaps even declined.

In absolute terms, rural incomes have declined (Bonnefond and Couty, 1988:333), though it may be a matter of some small consolation that urban incomes dropped much more sharply (Bonnefond and Couty, 1988:333; Berg, 1990:75). On the whole, the situation might actually be said to have deteriorated. After all, all other sectors of the country's economy have been hit by the crisis. It was unlikely that agriculture could prove the exception. Development through agriculture, such as advocated by international organizations led by the World Bank and the International Monetary Fund, remains, for Senegal, an objective. The question is whether the country can attain it.

Notes

1. Jonathan Barker, in the introduction to his work (1984:11-31), distinguishes between various features of this type of crisis literature. Depending on the weighting of different parameters, the emphasis is usually on dependence (local versus external factors), structural imbalances (production or exchange systems), or the relationship between the State and relevant economic forces. Our approach here is essentially history-based. Designed to take comprehensive stock of the entire situation, it tries to factor in all relevant data with no preconceived bias. For while we recognize the role played by ideological stances in the drafting and implementation of political

decisions, we are much more impressed by the fact that quite often, as we shall see, realities on the ground make a mockery of theoretical presuppositions.
2. A good example of the new approach was the Eliott Berg Report (1981), though there were antecedents, all from the World Bank (1974).
3. Michael Loftchie's article (1985:160-187) offers an excellent introduction to the component thematic foci of the literature in question, in addition to a fine overview thereof.
4. As a rule, government agricultural policy in Senegal has been made up of a series of sectorial policies called 'Plans'. These Plans take into account one or two types of produce organized into 'Branches'. There is thus a Cereal Plan and a Seed Plan, along with a Cotton Branch, a Rice Branch, etc. On the other hand, there is no coherent government policy labelled known as a 'Groundnut Policy'. The reality is a matter of trial and error. The 'New Agricultural Policy' is the first attempt at a comprehensive organization of agricultural policy with clearly defined objectives, resources and implementational modalities.
5. On the history of the groundnut economy in Senegal, see Samir Amin (1971), Founou Tchuigoua (1981), Mbodj (1978).
6. Curtin (1975) provides a good introduction to the area's economic history before the colonial era.
7. This key study has remained in mimeograph form. It deserves to be properly published, if not in its entirety, then at least in summary form. It is popularly known as the Lebret Report, after the Dominican priest who acted as Coordinating Editor for it. An alternative name is the CINAM-CERESA Report, after the official designation of the multidisciplinary team that produced it. Drafted by a team of economists and researchers from other disciplines working on detailed field studies, it was begun in October 1958 and finished in July 1960. Its findings were strongly influenced by the contemporary school of thought led by François Perroux at the Institute for the Study of Economic and Social Development (IEDES). Among its main ideas was the advocacy of a 'humanist' socialism, or socialism 'with a human face'. The enterprise seems to have been unique in Africa at the time. It is still an unequalled achievement in Senegal today.
8. In fact the new co-operatives had antecedents dating back a long time into the colonial period. Specifically, they were successors to the Native Insurance Company (SIP), the Rural Mutual Assurance Company (SMPR), the Rural Mutual Development Company (SMDR) etc. For further details see Camboulives (1967); Mbodj (1978).
9. By virtue of a legislative act passed on 26 May 1964, the BSD became the National Development Bank of Senegal (BNDS), with identical terms of reference.
10. It became the fashion among officials to talk of a 'groundnut monoculture'. This, of course, was a disingenuous use of language, but at least it showed the extent of official uneasiness (or guilt?) regarding the crop that had come to symbolize all the disadvantages of colonial rule. As a matter of fact the same uneasy feelings informed by the same negative perceptions are discernible among Senegalese officials to this day.
11. By way of comparison, average annual production figures in the 1950s were just 699,000 tons. There was, in effect, an increase of 34%. Averages for earlier periods were of course lower. The difference is even greater if the period is restricted to the very first years after independence. From 1960 to 1966, average annual production was 982,000 tons.
12. Scholars have paid scant attention to the immediate circumstances motivating this circular (Gellar, 1987:123-159). It is noteworthy that on 12 November 1962, at the height of the crisis between Dia and Senghor, a difficult ministerial reshuffle enabled

Dia to appoint one of his closest collaborators, Ibrahima Sarr, as Minister of Development in place of Karim Gaye, a Senghor supporter. Just after the fall of Dia, Gaye was again appointed Minister of the Rural Economy. All this seems to indicate that the rural sector was a key prize in the conflict between the two leaders.
13. It was Mamadou Dia who drafted the two basic documents of the modern cooperative movement in Senegal (Dia, 1952 and 1962).
14. According to Mark Gersowitz and John Waterbury (1987:8), President Senghor, addressing a UPS congress session, said the principal roadblock in the way of Senegal's economic development was the absence of trained technicians, managers and administrators.
15. Historically, the first co-operatives directly established by Senegalese citizens with no interference from the authorities were created in 1947 by certain marabouts who were major producers: Cheikh Mbacké founded and directed a co-operative in Mbacké; Bassirou Mbacké directed one in Diourbel, Ibrahima Niasse ran one called the Senegalese Mutual Agricultural Cooperative (COMAS) in Kaolack; and Fodé Diouf organized one at Kahone. The first three were top-ranking marabouts. The last was a district chief, a direct descendant of the old Saloum kings.
16. The system was established following the notorious 'Groundnut Battle' in the French Parliament. For details see Mersadier (1966:826-77) and Marseille (1984:285-99).
17. This is an appropriate point for a brief aside on basic technological changes introduced first by SATEC then by SODEVA in the second half of the 1960s. Their main thrust was the increase of yields through improved farming techniques, the use of selected seeds, the use of fertilizer, and the popularization of the use of draught animals. The experiment was a definite success. But given the enormity of the ravages caused by drought in the 1970s and 1980s, it turned out to be just a drop in the bucket.
18. The article by Caswell (1984) provides a trenchant analysis of ONCAD.
19. These Regional Development Agencies operated as fiefdoms independent of each other. They tended to guard their autonomy jealously, arguing that ecological peculiarities in their operational zones made this necessary. In the late 1970s I was personally able to observe the extent to which the SODEFITEX and SODEVA, both operating in the Thyssé-Kayemor area in Eastern Saloum, remained aloof from each other's business. This was an indication of the low-level of co-ordination, or even a total absence thereof, in the conduct of agricultural policy. The agencies in question had a pronounced technical bias, and their key staff tended to be expatriates, so they could hardly communicate productively with the majority of peasants. One telling pointer was that most Rural Development Agencies targeted an elite of model peasants or pilot groups for their programmes.
20. Caswell's article (1984) offers a painstaking analysis of the ONCAD experience, with an emphasis on the political aspect. I have drawn heavily on it here.
21. By 1965, 2,481 permits for the groundnut transport business had been issued, even though there were only 915 trucks. In other words, there was a highly profitable parallel market in ONCAD freight contracts. The public got to know of these dealings as a result of lawsuits involving insurance companies when accidents occurred, or when drivers were accused of theft (see Péhaut, 1984:426).
22. Such shenanigans had a catastrophic impact on agricultural policy. The supply of adequate quantities of selected seeds has always been a key objective in all policies aimed at improved yields and higher production levels. In 1971, ONCAD, with help from the EEC, started a seed supply service. By 1976 the entire system had broken down. In 1980, more aid was needed from France to get the scheme going again.

23. According to an article in the 27 August 1980 issue of the daily newspaper *Le Soleil*, during the 1970-80 farm season, 5,000 items of minor equipment disappeared in the region of Diourbel alone.
24. Ironically, a few years later the Division of Computer Services was itself rocked by a similar scandal.
25. Caswell (1984:66-69) gives a good description of such deals, with an emphasis on the role of marabouts. She asserts that ONCAD was definitely a key centre for 'clan politics', a pivotal component of the State-as-private-property that has been such a dominant feature of life in independent Senegal and Africa as a whole.
26. ONCAD used to advance loans to so-called transporters to buy trucks. The latter then turned round and signed contracts allowing ONCAD to hire these trucks. The ruse enabled them to acquire brand new vehicles without having to pay a single CFA franc. The 'transporters' involved were mostly politicians, marabouts or their cronies. This was one of the causes of the deep distrust between the State and those genuine professional transport operators who got marginalized as a result of such deals. They were often obliged to become sub-contractors or to buy up vehicles that had already made a profit for their original owners, and were in any case dilapidated.
27. Copans (1980:195) cites the case of a marabout who was also chairman of a co-operative. In 1966 he was sacked for embezzlement. But that did not stop him from getting reelected in 1967.
28. No such problem troubled the peace of marabouts. They had always assumed that their loans were favours rendered by a grateful State. Incidentally, the CPSP used to pay large subsidies to selected marabouts, the sole purpose being to help them pay off their loans.
29. From 1964 there were frequent reforms, and many new structures were created. Peasants at the receiving end took all the busy shuffling to mean that the State was hesitant and confused, that it hardly knew what it wanted to do. This view is related to the conclusion that from 1966 to 1984 the State had no agricultural policy to speak of.
30. Tuck (1987:160-87) presents a good analysis of the phenomenon.
31. The 1977-78 farm season was the first time the government attempted to establish an accounting system in which write-offs would be based on real production shortfalls calculated on a region-to-region basis. But general elections were imminent, and the regime feared it might be accused of favouritism. It therefore reverted to the practice of across-the-board write-offs.
32. This was particularly true of the rhetoric favoured by Senghor and his followers. It was based, very selectively, on the work of economic dependency theorists such as Samir Amin, the leading exponent on the local scene. One reason for this preference was the government's inability to take determined action to deal with targeted causes of the crisis. Accusations directed against external forces diverted attention from internal responsibility. Official rhetoric therefore made use of 'dependency theory' while skipping over aspects of it critical of local performance, such as the observation that foreign exploitation was possible only because there were local stooges to ensure its continuation.
33. This was the time of such compulsory taxes and deductions as the 'Drought Tax' and the 'Emoluments Tax'. While ordinary people were thus being urged to tighten their belts, the high-flying lifestyles of State officials and the corrupt practices of State and parastatal officials continued unchecked. In organizations like ONCAD, they got worse.

34. It is generally estimated that from 1960 to 1979, GDP only increased at an average annual rate of 2.5%, lower than the population growth rate of 2.7%. Even the 2.7% figure for the average growth rate, in our opinion, is a gross under-estimate (Lewis 1987:293).
35. It was the new Finance Minister, Ousmane Seck who brought the debate into the public sphere with early talk of a 'Recovery Plan' and arrangements to get ONCAD to repay sums owed the State, during a National Council session on 19 September 1978 (Zuccarelli, 1988:150).
36. Considering a hypothesis put forward in the debate, the change killed two birds with one stone. ONCAD had become, according to reports, so powerful that it was uncontrolable. Starting out as an instrument of power, it had become a source of political power facilitating the creation of a support base independent of government influence (Caswell, 1984:71-72). This was of course unacceptable within the competitive framework of the new politics of the 'democratic opening'. It was also unconscionable against the background of sacrifices imposed by the structural adjustment programme.
37. Gellar (1987:133-36) offers an excellent report on this debate.
38. Its initial terms of reference required it to study practical modalities for the implementation of structural changes in the co-operative movement in the regions of Thies and Diourbel. These were problematic regions because marabouts were powerful there, groundnut farming was a long-established practice there, ecological conditions were particularly delicate, and excess population pressure had led to over-exploitation of the land.
39. These hesitations were probably related to the unwillingness of President Senghor to confront what had been a key aspect of his policies for 15 years. It is only correct to add that all manner of people who knew the abolition of ONCAD would hurt their interests, especially rural politicians and dignitaries, certain administrators in the groundnut-farming areas, assorted so-called businessmen, and most employees of the Board, did their best to keep the talk flowing, the better to avoid too quick a surgical strike, to gain time to wangle new arrangements that could prove as cushy as the old (assuming the reform was like so many others that had gone before). Some of them also hoped the public would grow tired of the debate, and let the creamy status quo continue.
40. On these financial developments and the background to Senegal's relations with the World Bank/IMF duo, (Lewis, 1987:283-325). Lewis pinpoints Abdou Diouf as the key architect of the accords. This helps clarify a detail: that the initiative really came from the Senegalese government.
41. The description by Durufflé, 1987 of the process leading to the adoption of structural adjustment policies focuses on Senegal.
42. Lewis (1987:305) says the World Bank, the International Monetary Fund and the International Development Agency all regarded ONCAD as a 'black sheep'. It must have looked all the 'blacker' for wearing the pinkish camouflage of the socialism they so hated.
43. The quotation is from an address to the Economic and Social Council cited by Diop and Diouf (1990:66).
44. It was accomplished in August, right in the middle of the farm season. Producers were thus given no chance to mount a reaction.
45. The peasants were suspicious of the new system initiated so late in the farming season. Furthermore, the new President's hard-nosed talk had alerted peasants to the fact that the government was broke. They hardly expected to get another debt write-off, and

were afraid the supposed write-offs would in fact be deducted from their prospective earnings. They therefore preferred to sell their crop at a discount but for cash behind the back of the State. The buyers were large-scale producers and middlemen who sometimes did not hesitate to resell the crop in neighbouring countries. The principal destination was Gambia, where sellers could obtain slightly higher prices, in cash.

46. The average amount of groundnuts marketed by individual cooperatives was 350 tons. But estimates showed that to cover marketing costs, the minimum quantity would have to rise to 1,500 tons. (Gellar, 1987:137).
47. An appreciable amount of the data used in this analysis of cooperative reforms comes from Gellar (1987:137-57).
48. This was one of the very few facets of the reform that ordinary peasants found to their liking. Funding agencies gave it their wholehearted backing. They figured it was an indispensable step towards giving producers greater responsibilities and narrowing down opportunities for corruption. The old-style cooperatives had no incomes at all. By contrast, the reformed cooperatives kept F CFA 1 for every kilo sold.
49. Diop and Diouf (1980) describe Senegalese political life as a 'single-party culture'. The advent of multi-party politics did nothing to change that reality. Furthermore, with the dwindling potential of the State, the value of structures and positions still capable of bringing in hidden incomes, helping in the establishment of new support bases, or facilitating the maintenance of existing loyalties, went up (see also Magassouba, (1984:230-231).
50. This chapter is not focused on recovery policies or adjustment programmes in general. François Boye's contribution in this volume deals with the issue of major macroeconomic balances. We shall therefore limit ourselves, in this chapter, to assessing their direct impact on sectorial implications of the New Agricultural Policy as from 1985. We intend to pay particular attention to the groundnut sector. Incidentally, in 1986 the NPA was supplemented by a Cereal Plan which stated, for the first time ever, that henceforth the Number One priority would be shifted to cereals.
51. Discussions on a New Agricultural Policy had begun during an Interministerial Council session in May 1983. A first policy draft was presented to Senegal's foreign partners in October. The programme was adopted by the Interministerial Council of 28 March 1984.
52. The type of Recovery and Adjustment Plan that is now common throughout Africa got off to an early start in Senegal. This circumstance has given rise to documentary material too abundant for exhaustive listing. A representative sample includes Durufflé (1985), Gersowitz and Waterbury (1987), Bonnefond and Couty (1988), Commander, Ndoye and Ouedraogo (1989) and Delgado and Jammeh (1991).
53. Symbolic of the necessary shift to capitalism was the profile of the new Minister of Rural Development, Amadou Bator Diop. Trained as an agricultural engineer, he had also worked as an entrepreneur. The change was particularly striking because the man he replaced had been a plodding researcher. The new minister's cabinet colleagues, generally more 'political' than this technocrat, found themselves having to explain at length, and with some difficulty, that the Socialist Party had not really abandoned its socialist orientation.
54. The policy of soil regeneration is a key to the survival of Senegalese agriculture, but I shall not be discussing that topic here (see the chapter by P Ndiaye in this volume). One things is quite clear. Individual peasants do not possess there sources needed for the success of this policy. Neither do peasant associations on their own. The failure of this aspect is symbolized by the fact that in regions where the degradation of soil quality is an urgent threat, deforestation continues. For example, 40,000 hectares of

woodland in the Khelkom area were recently removed from the list of classified forest reserves and given to a plantation-owning marabout who would no doubt parcel some of the land out among his followers.
55. The provision of fertilizer is linked to the issue of soil regeneration in areas degraded because of being cultivated for too long a time by too large a population. The aim is to improve yields and the problem is particularly acute in the old groundnut basin of Sine, Baol and Cayor. Official rhetoric may assume there is a division of labour, but in reality all initiatives are left to the peasants. That means they also have to bear the attendant costs.
56. During our tour of the zone between Louga and Touba in October 1985, we were particularly struck by the prevalence of this phenomenon.
57. On the average, each groundnut seed can be expected to produce a ten-fold yield. In their calculations for the 1985-86 farm season, Commander *et al* (1989:162) estimated that peasants would have had to save 38% of their harvests if they were to cope with the various climatic hazards, population growth and the need to maintain income levels. But during the same period (from 1984-85 to 1985-86) the purchasing price of groundnut seed sold on the market rose 50% (Gaye, 1988:4).
58. This is further proof that the generality of African farmers, faced with a predatory State and exploitative plantation owners, do not really have the will to withdraw from cash crop production. In my opinion, what such peasants actually do is to maneuver and to jockey for position, with the aim of negotiating a better cut. They do not really envisage withdrawal, much less a total break.
59. The analytical stance favoured by this school reminds one of René Dumont's well-known positions. It is thoroughly anti-urban in its bias, its rhetoric emphasizing the imagery of cities as bloodsucking leeches, urban dwellers as exploitative parasites, the cities as pillagers of the countryside, etc. And it loves to hate Africa's elites. Beyond that, the solutions advanced tend to be rather vague, or stuck in the rut of 1960s politics. It is therefore unable to give due attention to problems in all their complexity. One stream within this school, however, has come up with more modulated analysis (Hyden, 1985:188-217).
60. Since 1971, the differential has averaged more than 50%. The resulting surplus has gone to fund CPSP business, including the activities of the groundnut sector. In effect, old trends were reversed, with the urban areas now subsidizing the rural.
61. Assuming, for instance, that the agricultural market was totally liberalized, what leverage could the State then use to consolidate its plan for self-sufficiency in food by the year 2000?
62. There have, of course, been changes. One principal change has been a matter of approach. In the 1960s, vast multidisciplinary studies were conducted as a prelude to the formulation of policies. The New Agricultural Policy covers a great deal more ground than the policies of those earlier years, but it was preceded by only a very general set of agro-economic studies.
63. Office of the President (1989:4).
64. Incidentally, according to *Cyclope* (Chalmin, 1991:165), a publication specializing in market forecasts, 1990 and 1991 were supposed to be good years for the groundnut crop.
65. The problem goes farther back, if we examine the historical background to groundnut production. For instance, the first agricultural crisis caused by this imbalance dates back to 1904-1905. It was indeed that crisis that led to the creation of the SIPs, prototypes of rural cooperatives, in the Sine-Saloum region in 1907 (Mbodj, 1978).

66. When the State began withdrawing from the rural areas, many observers hoped fondly that non-governmental organizations would help prepare peasants to look after their own interests. In the event, most of these organizations have proved unimaginative, addicted to easy success, and dependent on handouts from European and American charities, etc. They have therefore succumbed to the same temptations as the State in the 1960s and 1970s. For example, they have distributed inputs free of charge, doled out camouflaged subsidies, and stifled peasant initiatives with their ubiquitous staff playing the role of arrogant 'donors'. Through simple conformity, certain organizations have played favourites with traditional leaders of local communities, etc. Additionally, their approaches tend to be myopic, with a proliferation of identical projects that end up wasting financial resources.

Bibliography

Amin, Samir, 1971, *L'Afrique de l'Ouest bloquée: l'économie politique de la colonisation, 1880-1970*, Paris, Editions de Minuit.

Barker, Jonathan, 1984, *The Politics of Agriculture in Tropical Africa*, Beverly Hills-London, SAGE.

Bates, Robert H, 1981, *Markets and States in Tropical Africa: The Political Basis of Agricultural Policies*, Berkeley-Los Angeles, University of California Press.

Berg, Elliot, 1981, *Accelerated Development in Sub-Saharan Africa: An Agenda for Action*, World Bank-IBRD, Washington D.C.

Berg, Elliot, 1990, *Adjustment Postponed: Economic Policy Reform in Senegal in the 1980s, Dakar*, USAID.

Bonnefond, Philippe and Philippe Couty, 1988, 'Sénégal: passé et avenir d'une crise agricole', *Tiers-Monde*, N°.114, April-June, pp. 319-340.

Camboulives, Marguerite, 1967, *L'organisation coopérative au Sénégal*,Paris, Pédone.

Caswell, Nim, 1984, 'Autopsie de l'ONCAD: la politique arachidière au Sénégal 1966-1980', *Politique Africaine*, 14pp. 39-73.

Chalmin, Philippe, (dir.), 1991, *Cyclope (Rapport sur les cycles et les orientations des produits et des échanges): les marchés mondiaux*, Economica.

CILSS, 1977, *Marketing, Price Policy and Storage of Food Grains in the Sahel*, 1, CRED/USAID.

CILLS 1990, *Problématique des politiques rizicoles en pays sahélien*, Vol. 3, *Le Sénégal*.

CINAM-CERESA/ Ministry of Rural Development, 1963, 'Rapport général sur les perspectives de développement du Sénégal', Dakar.

Cissé, Ben Madi, 1963, 'L'Animation rurale base essentielle de tout développement', *Afrique-Documents*, pp. 68-69.

Colvin, Lucy, G (ed.), 1981 *The Uprooted of the Western Sahel*, New York, Praeger.

Commander Simon et.al., 1989, *Structural Adjustment and Agriculture. Theory and Practice in Africa and Latin America*, Overseas Development Institute, London, Porsmouth, J Currey, Heineman.

Copans, Jean, 1980, *Les marabouts de l'arachide: la confrérie mouride et les paysans du Sénégal*, Paris, Le Sycomore.

Coulon, Christian, 1981, *Le marabout et le Prince*, Paris, Pédone.

Cruise O'Brien, Donal, 1984, 'Des bienfaits de l'inégalité - L'at et l'économie rurale au Sénégal', *Politique Africaine*, 14:34-8.

Curtin, P D, 1975, *Economic Change in Precolonial Africa. Senegambia in the Era of the Slave Trade*, Wisconsin University Press, Madison.

Delgado, Christopher and Sidi Jammeh (eds.), 1991, *The Political Economy of Senegal Under Structural Adjustment*. Praeger, New York.

Dia, Mamadou, 1961, 'Discours devant l'Assemblée Nationale, le 4 Avril 1961', in *Afrique-Documents*, 59, September-October: pp.207-215.

Dia, Mamadou, 1962, 'Circulaire N°32 du 21 Mai 1962', Office of the Council President, Senegal, *JORS* 2 June 1962: pp.952-955.

Dia, Mamadou, 1952, *Contribution à l'étude du mouvement coopératif en Afrique noire*, Présence Africaine, Paris.

Diop, Momar Coumba and Mamadou Diouf, 1990, *Le Sénégal sous Abdou Diouf. Etat et Société*, Karthala, Paris.

Dumont, René and Marie-France Mottin, 1982, *Le Défi sénégalais: reconstruire les terroirs, libérer les paysans* Etudes et Recherches séries, pp.74-82. ENDA, Dakar. (Preface by Djibril Sène, Minister of Rural Development).

Durufflé Gilles, 1987, L'ajustement structurel en Afrique (Sénégal, Côte d'Ivoire, Madagascar, Karthala, Paris.

Ecrement, Marc, 1965, 'Mouvement coopératif et développement rural dans la République du Sénégal', EPHSS Thesis (VIth Section), Paris.

Founou-Tchuigoua, Bernard, 1981, *Fondements de l'économie de traite au Sénégal*, Paris, Silex.

Frélastre, Georges, 1982, 'Evolution de la politique agricole du Sénégal', *Le Mois en Afrique*, January-February.

Gaye, Karim 1960, 'Le Sénégal dans la voie du développement économique', *Afrique-Documents*, 54, November-December, p.239.

Gaye, Mactar, 1988, 'Le désengagement de l'Etat et la problématique des intrants agricoles au Sénégal', Paper delivered at the International Colloquium on the Crisis in African Agriculture, University of Dakar, 19-23 December.

Gellar, Sheldon, 1987, 'Circulaire 32 Revisited', in Gersowitz, Mark and John Waterbury (eds.), *The Political Economy of Risk and Choice in Senegal*, London, Frank Cass, pp.123-159.

Gellar, Sheldon, 1982, *Senegal: An African Nation Between Islam and the West*. Boulder, Westview Press.

Gersowitz, Mark and John Waterbury (eds.), 1987, *The Political Economy of Risk and Choice in Senegal*. London, Frank Cass.

Hyden Goran, 1985, 'Urban Growth and Rural Development' in Carter G M and O'Meira P eds., *African Independence, the First Twenty Five Years*, Indiana University Press - Hutchinson, Bloomington-London.

Italconsult-Ministry of Rural Development, 1970, 'Rapport général sur la coopération'. Dakar.

Jammeh, Sidi, 1987, 'Politics of Agricultural Price Decision-making in Senegal', in Gersowitz, Mark and John Waterbury (eds.) pp.223-44.

Journal Officiel de la République du Sénégal (JORS), 1965.

Lewis, John, 1987, 'Aid, Structural Adjustment and Senegalese Agriculture', in Gersowitz, Mark and John Waterbury (eds.) pp 283-325.

Loftchie, Michael, 1985, 'Africa's Agrarian Malaise', in Carter, Gwendolyn M. and Patrick O'Meara (eds.). *African Independence, The First Twenty Years*, Bloomington, London, Indiana University Press, Hutchinson.

Loftchie, Michael, (ed.) 1986, *Africa's Agrarian Crisis: The Roots of Famine*, Boulder, L Rienner.

Magassouba, Moriba, 1984, 'La participation en milieu rural dans un pays en voie de développement: les communautés rurales au Sénégal', in *Annuaire du Tiers-Monde*, VIII, (1982-1983), Paris, Nathan, pp.225-234.

Marseilles, Jacques, 1984, *Empire colonial et capitalisme français. Histoire d'un divorce*, Paris, Albin Michel.

Mbodj, Mohamed, 1978, 'Un exemple d'économie coloniale: le Sine-Saloum et l'arachide, 1887-1940', Doctoral thesis, University of Paris VII.

Mbodj, Mohamed, 1991. 'Politics of Independence in Senegal, 1960-86', in Delgado, Christopher and Sidi Jammeh (eds.) pp. 119-26.

Mersadier, Yves, 1966, 'La crise de l'arachide sénégalaise au début des années trente', *Bulletin de l'IFAN*, B, XXVII, 3-4 pp. 826-77.

Ndiaye, Paul, 1988, 'Rétrospective de l'environnement et de l'équilibre écologique du Sénégal, Rapport sectoriel pour l'Etude prospective de la société sénégalaise en l'an 2015', July.

Péhaut, Yves, 1984, 'De l'OCA à la SONACOS', *L'Année africaine*.

Sarr, Yoro, 1990, 'La Nouvelle Politique Agricole, Cinq ans après', *La Tribune de l'Economie Africaine*, 1, February.

Schumacher, E J, 1975, *Politics, Bureaucracy and Rural Development in Senegal*, Berkeley, University of California Press.

Senegal, Republic of. Ministry of Rural Development, 1982, *Bilan global des réalisations du Gouvernement en faveur du monde rural depuis l'Indépendance*, Dakar.

Senegal, Republic of. Ministry of Rural Development, 1984, 'Conseil Interministériel sur la Nouvelle Politique Agricole: Rapport de Présentation', Dakar, March.

Senegal, Republic of. Ministry of Rural Development, 1984, *Document de présentation de la Nouvelle Politique Agricole*, March-April.

Senegal, Republic of. Ministry of Rural Development, Office of the President, 1989 Committee on Economic Policy and Planning, Statistics and Projections Unit 1989, 'Les Principaux résultats provisoires du Recensement de la Population et de l'Habitat du Sénégal de 1988', Dakar, December.

Senegal, Republic of. Ministry of Rural Development, Statistics Board, 1984, *Situation Economique du Sénégal*, Dakar.

The Economist, 1989, 'Country Profile 1989-1990: Annual Survey of Political and Economic Background (Senegal, The Gambia, Guinea-Bissau, Cape Verde)', London, December.

The Economist, 1990, 'Country Report N°4: Senegal, The Gambia, Guinea-Bissau, Cape Verde, 1989-90', London.

Touré, A, 1982, 'Bilan céréalier dans le Bassin Arachidier depuis 1960 et Perspectives des années 1980', Dakar, SODEVA.

Tuck, Laura, 1987, 'Financial Markets in Rural Senegal', in Gersowitz, Mark and John Waterbury (eds.) pp.160-187.

Waterbury, John, 1987, 'Dimensions of State Intervention in the Groundnut Basin', in Gersowitz, Mark and John Waterbury (eds.), pp.193-199.

World Bank-IBRD, 1974, *Senegal: Tradition, Diversification and Economic Development*, Washington D.C.

Zuccarelli, François, 1988, *La vie politique sénégalaise (1940-1988)*, Paris, CHEAM.

Annexes

Table 1: Groundnuts Marketed from 1887 to 1959 - Five-Year (Averages in Tons)

1887	025 000
1890-94	045 000
1895-99	069 000
1900-04	123 000
1905-09	169 000
1910-14	235 000
1915-19	192 000
1920-24	318 000
1925-29	439 000
1930-34	404 000
1935-39	538 000
1940-44	263 000
1945-49	407 000
1950-54	435 000
1955-59	691 000

Source: Periodic Reports of the Colonial Administration, ARS 2 G.

Table 2: Five-Year Average Groundnut Production Figures, 1960-1989

Five-Year Period	Production (Tons)	Yield/ha (kilos)
1960-1965	942 180	914
1965-1970	918 450	828
1970-1975	761 237	723
1975-1980	962 187	785
1980-1985	746 820	737
1985-1989	778 425	985

Source: Berg (1990: 62).

Table 3: Groundnut Producer Prices*, 1968-1989

Period	Net Producer Price
1968-69	16.5
1969-70	16.5
1970-71	17.6
1971-72	22
1972-73	25
1973-74	25
1974-75	40
1975-76	40
1976-77	40
1977-78	40
1978-79	40
1979-80	43
1980-81	46
1981-82	60
1982-83	60
1983-84	50
1984-85	60
1985-86	90
1986-87	90
1987-88	90
1988-89	70

* The producer price is what peasants actually get paid at the weighing-in counter per kilo of groundnuts after all deductions have been made, and before any potential rebates. Figures are in current Francs CFA.

Sources: Ministry of Rural Economics; *The Economist* (1990); *La Tribune de l'Economie Africaine* (1, 1990); Jammeh (1987); Bonnefond & Couty (1988).

4. Environmental Policy: A Management Critique

Paul Ndiaye[*]

Environmental issues have a low priority in the political decision-making processes of African States. There is no organized body of opinion sensitive to environmental concerns. The only exceptions are pockets of the urban population, often closely linked with concerned non-governmental organizations (NGOs). The ecological debate, now drawing in influential groups as well as increasing numbers of individuals in the developed countries, attracts little attention on the African political and social scene. It might seem surprising, then, in a book on the role of the African State in economic and social development, to devote a chapter to the environment.

It seems that many officials and ordinary citizens do not perceive the environment as part of a commonwealth, a resource of quantifiable value. Such a mind-set obviously gives those intent on arguing that the environment deserves protection and rehabilitation a hard row to hoe. For conservation programmes require funding. Given the long list of more urgent social and economic needs competing for scarce finances, such funding is unlikely to materialize. So the public, obsessed with daily survival hustles, pushes the environment to the fringes of its consciousness. The State, hard pressed to raise implementational funds for its economic programme, in turn neglects the environment.

Still, the environment is not a neutral medium. It cannot be pushed completely out of mind. Consciously or not, State officials constantly refer back to it to explain their economic failures, or to justify new policy directives, depending on the prospects of acceptance or rejection. In sum, the environment serves as an excuse for failure to tackle real problems.

The purpose of this chapter is to present a historical analysis, covering the past 30 years, of the environmental situation in Senegal. The topic covers an enormous range, and the existing documentation is copious. We have therefore focused our study on the four main aspects of production systems; the urban environment; the behaviour of the population; and the attitude of the public authorities.

The chapter is based on data from a bibliographical base comprising 75 titles. We have drawn liberally on personal experience and observation in

---

[*] Oumar Wane, Abdourahmane Samoura, Ibrahima Sow, Thiécouta Ngom and Aminata Diaw provided invaluable help in the processing of data used in this chapter.

the description of trends, as well as in the identification of indices of imminent change significant enough to be seen as relevant to the future development of the system.

The Deterioration of the Natural Environment

Rainfall

Senegal's development over the past three decades has been characterized by the decisive impact of fluid and erratic climatic factors that have affected the functioning of all terrestrial and aquatic ecosystems. From 1960 to 1968, rainfall totals were more or less normal. Seasonal distribution patterns were also, broadly speaking, normal. Indeed, in the northern regions of the country, average rainfall in the Sahelian areas for the 1960s was 15% to 25% higher than the average for the three previous decades, 1931 to 1960.

In the period from 1968, the trend reversed with a chronic drop in rain. The fear was that this was the start of a desertification process. In years like 1972-73, 1983-84, conditions were particularly harsh. Rainfall totals were 40% to 60% lower than usual in the northern regions, and 30% to 35% lower in the south. Yearly fluctuations in that period were wider than normal. New minima were registered that went far below record minima for the previous half century. Rainfall statistics for the 1971-80 decade show how widespread the process was: throughout the northern third of the country, the drop in rainfall precipitation was nearly 60%. This was one aspect of a general deterioration in regional conditions, and it resulted in a southward extension of the Sahelian zone. The general historical pattern becomes clear from a study of statistics from three Senegalese meteorological stations, one in the extreme north (Podor), one in the extreme south (Ziguinchor) and the third in between (Bambey).

Table 1: Rainfall Statistics from Three Stations

Station	Period	Annual Rainfall (mm)	Variation (%)
Podor	(1)	333.5	-
	(2)	215.0	36
	(3)	279.5	16
Bambey	(1)	680.1	-
	(2)	508.1	25
	(3)	599.0	12
Ziguinchor	(1)	1547.0	-
	(2)	1276.8	17
	(3)	1424.0	08

Source: Leborgne 1988.
Period (1) = 1931-1960;   Period (2) = 1961- 985;   Period (3) = 1931-1985.

Rainfall statistics taken over the long term (at least 25 years) indicate a significant decrease in both the 1931-60 and 1961-85 periods, with the shortfall widening steadily from south to north. The average decrease suffered by Ziguinchor in the south, for instance, was -17%. For Podor in the north, the figure was -36%. In some years the situation was markedly more disastrous. In 1983, for example, rainfall totals over practically the entire country were more than 30% lower than average. Table 2 for the particularly dry years of 1972 and 1983 shows the geographical spread of zones experiencing decreases in rain precipitation.

Table 2: Extension of the Drought Over the National Territory

Decreasing Rainfall Totals (%)	70%	50%	30%
		Zone Decrease	
1972	Dagana-Lac de Guiers Cape Verde Peninsula	North of the Foundiougne-Diourbel-Bakel axis	North of the Kolda Tamba-Kidira axis
1983	North of the Mbour-Thiès-Saldé axis	North of the Bignona Matam axis	North of the Salemata-Kédougou-Saraya axis

Source: Goudiaby 1984.

An examination of certain key isohyets makes it easier to understand fluctuations in precipitation in Senegal over the past 20 years. In 1968, the 1,000 mm isohyet was situated along the northern frontier of the Gambia. In subsequent years it moved southwards, ending up along the Bignona-Sédhiou-Kédougou axis in 1984. There was a similar shift in the position of the 600 mm isohyet, which marks the boundary of the Sahelian climatic zone. That isohyet shifted more than 100km southwards in roughly three decades. In the 1941-50 decade it used to lie in the same latitude as Tivaouane; by 1971-80 it had shifted to the latitude of Fatick.

Needless to say, this change reconfigured the national landscape. In the past, the area to the north of the 600 mm isohyet, i.e., the Sahelian climatic zone, covered some 77,000km^2, equivalent to 40% of the national territory. The recent shortfall in rain precipitation has extended that total area by 45,000 km^2. So now the percentage of national territory in the Sahelian zone has risen to 60%. The area in the Sudanese and Sudano-Guinean climatic zone has shrunk accordingly.

The drought, then, became a permanent reality in Senegal. A number of attendant atmospheric factors worsened its impact: sandstorms and dry mists became more intense, while the frequency of humid mists and fog dropped sharply. Concurrently, there was also a steep rise in aerosol use. The result was a series of blockages in the evolution of the natural environment with the ensuing problems of less water available from rain precipitation; number of days of useful rainfall, often by as much as a third; frequent anomalies that punctuated what was left of the rainy season. The season might start too early, or come late. Rains sometimes stopped in mid-season for variable lengths of time. Sometimes they fell in unusually concentrated and violent bursts, etc.

Hydrological and Hydro-geological Factors

It goes without saying that the new situation produced enormous modifications in the country's agricultural and agro-pastoral sectors. The changes were also ecological, involving the entire hydrological system, for the decrease in rain affected the supply of surface water as well as underground resources. River flood tides were relatively low and short-lived. Water tables close to the surface rose only briefly, and seasonal marshes dried up too fast. The deteriorating rainfall, in other words, had a direct impact on surface water resources. Average annual rainfall over the national territory from 1968 to 1981 was 552 mm, a figure 33% below normal. The total volume of rain precipitation yielding that average was 108.6 billion m^3, distributed as follows:

- Direct evaporation: 75.4% = 81.5 billion m^3
- Runoff water: 24.0% = 26.4 billion m^3
- Underground seepage: 00.6% = 00.7 billion m^3

It should be noted that low rainfall results in comparatively higher rates of evaporation as compared to runoff and seepage. Average flow volume in the Senegal River has dropped steadily since 1968. In 1984 it was down to just 72% of the modular average for the period from 1903 to 1978. Indeed, it was 37% lower than the figure for 1971, the last year in which hydrological statistics for the Senegal River's flow volume were higher than the modular average. Other permanent rivers in the region, such as the Gambia and the Casamance, which, together with the Senegal River, account for the outflow of one-quarter of total rainfall volume in the country, have undergone similar changes.

To begin with a recapitulation of the conditions for the resupply of some underground water-bearing strata. First, the resupply of strata close to the surface depends on the seepage of a tiny percentage of total rainfall. An examination of the comparative table of available underground water resources and amounts actually used shows that whether rainfall totals for a particular year are low or high, renewable water resources are more than enough to meet Senegal's underground water requirements.

Table 3: Comparative Table of Underground Water Availability and Use Levels

	Annual Volume (million m^3)	%/volume used	Daily Volume (m^3/day)
Minimum	500		1,357,000
Max. Renewable Resources	700		1,900,000
Senegal	153	31 min.	420,000
Senegal (including Dakar)	61	12 max.	166,000

Source: Sénégal/MPN/MPC 1985

When we consider the specific case of Dakar, however, the situation looks quite different. By the end of the 1970s, all available resource bases in the area around Dakar had been brought on tap. At times the resources were exploited beyond the natural rate of renewal. For example, underground water-bearing strata lying within a 60km radius of Dakar have been tapped to the point of over-exploitation.

Table 4: Underground Water Resource Out-take Levels in the Dakar Area in Normal Years

	Renewable resources (m3/day)	Out-take levels (m^3/day)
Infra-basaltic stratum	18,000	21,000
Peninsula sand stratum	47,000	00,000
Sebikotane Paleocene stratum	20,000	31,000
Pout Paleocene stratum	35,000	35,000
Resource potential	120,000	127,000

Source: Senegal MPN/MPC 1985.

The disturbing aspect of this exploitation of shallow water-bearing strata beyond their natural capacity for self-replenishment is that it aggravates other consequences of the decrease in rainfall. For one thing, lower rains mean that water-bearing strata near the surface do not get fully replenished. This leads to a rapid drop in the water table, making moisture inaccessible to the roots of most perennials. The ecological fallout from this situation can be seen in two areas. First, natural vegetation cover has been disappearing much faster than before. A telling illustration is the disappearance of palm groves in the Niayes region. Second, following the drop in the water table, sea water has been making inroads into the shallower water-bearing strata as over use exhausts their natural water content.

Over the past couple of decades, strikingly unpredictable climatic changes have aggravated the deterioration of the natural environment. However, it is the combination of their effects with those of a number of human activities that has led to large-scale transformations in the overall environment. The principal consequence of these changes has been the steady lowering of the country's life-support potential.

Dwindling Biological Potential

The climatic change that occurred in the early 1970s was one of the causes of the lowering of the region's biological potential. That diminution provoked a number of catastrophic conditions often described as consequences of desertification. Under the combined impact of harsh climatic conditions and the over-exploitation of the region's ecosystems, the environment as a whole was degraded. The degradation took the form of the heavy depletion or outright destruction of plant and animal life. At the same time, the rapidly increasing human population needed more products derived from both plant and animal resources to meet their needs. The human factors most frequently involved are overgrazing, excessive exploitation of woodlands adjoining the urban areas, the extension of farmland into ecologically fragile zones, and the frequency of bush fires.

Generally speaking, in the period from 1971 to 1982, the total land area under cultivation increased from 11% to 12% of the national territory. The increase occurred at the expense of non-agricultural land. In effect, it was the result of attempts to make up for poor yields in years of low rainfall. However, the increase in the area under cultivation did not result in increased production, since the average annual yield for major crops fell from 0.69 tons to 0.64 tons per hectare.

As for vegetation cover along the usual livestock grazing ranges, especially in the Ferlo area, observations conducted from the start of the drought indicate a general downward trend in productivity, with occasional upswings during exceptionally rainy years. Furthermore, the digging of increasing numbers of deep boreholes has led to more intense consumption of the meagre vegetation cover in the area with the greatest concentration of such watering points.

Senegal's livestock resources developed along different lines from 1971 to 1984, depending on species. There was an 18% drop in total head of cattle, but the number of sheep and goats rose by a modest 5%. This new situation was parallelled by spectacular changes in the spatial organization of the predominantly Sahelian northern regions (Saint-Louis, Louga, Diourbel), and the predominantly Sudano-Guinean regions (Kaolack, Fatick, Tambacounda, Ziguinchor and Kolda). In 15 years, the latter regions became the dominant livestock areas, superseding the traditional pastoral regions. The trend is especially clear-cut as far as cattle herding goes. It is the result of a fall-back strategy necessitated by unfavourable climatic conditions in the northern parts of the country, which decimated livestock herds.

Wildlife, for its part, suffered directly from successive years of drought. Animal habitats were destroyed, watering points and foraging grounds became scarce. Among indirect effects, there was the expansion of farmland, intensified poaching, etc. Throughout the entire northern half of the country, large animals survive only in tiny pockets. Wildfowl have grown fewer following the early drying-up of watering points and hydro-agricultural ponds along the Senegal River. As for reptiles and aquatic mammals, they have vanished from the area. Only small wildlife are present in normal numbers, but even they have to cope with the competitive thrust of expanding farmland.

Table 5: Livestock Numbers in the Northern and Central Regions as Percentages of the National Total

Year	Northern Regions	Central and Southern Regions	Livestock
1971	53%	42%	CATTLE
1983	39%	55%	
1971	61%	29%	SHEEP / GOATS
1983	46%	42%	

Source: Senegal MPN/MPC 1985.

The impact of the drought on inland fishing has been severe. In part, the drought caused a fall in the volume of water in such bodies as the Senegal River and the Lac de Guiers. But in other areas the effect was indirect, as in the case of rising salt levels in some rivers and streams in the Casamance and Saloum regions. In 1960, the Senegal River provided about 17% of the protein intake of the riparian population; but from 1972 the proportion decreased to an insignificant figure. Quantities of fish caught decreased steadily from 1967 to 1977. By the end of the period, production had dropped by 80%. Part of the reason was the generally low flow volume. But fishing equipment had also been modernized, and conservation rules were widely disregarded.

On the whole, then, the trend has been one of dwindling resources caused by a harsh physical environment and the pressure of consumption requirements often exceeding sustainable rates of resource use, jeopardizing the natural capacity of the environment to replenish itself. The trend has shattered the region's ecological balance, with devastating consequences for the environment as a whole.

The Performance of Natural Production Systems

Climatic conditions over the past three decades have had a marked tendency to push the production and reproduction capacities of plant and animal resources downwards. Senegal's woodland vegetation, broadly speaking, continues to show the effect of the pressure it has been under. That pressure is an outcome of the environmental context coupled with patterns of resource use which determine the self-replenishing capacity of the country's woodlands.

The General Breakdown of Ecological Balances

Senegal's woodland reserve cover has spread rapidly in recent decades. In 1976, there were 192 reserves covering a total area of 3,940,000 ha. By 1988 the total had risen to 199 reserves covering 5,948,000 ha or 31% of the national territory. An additional area of 1,126,000 ha makes up six national parks. Classified as reserves or not, the country's woodlands have been hard hit by exceptionally harsh climatic conditions. The result has been a decrease in vegetation cover.

Woodlands along river valleys (gonake groves), dependent on river flows for water, have been damaged by low flow levels since 1968. All have registered high mortality rates ranging from 25% to 40%. In some particularly ravaged areas as much as 80% of vegetation cover has been lost. Rehabilitation efforts have made slow progress. Large patches of mangrove vegetation along the Casamance River estuary, in the Saloum area and along the coast south of Dakar have been disappearing. Plant mortality rates in these areas have risen to between 30% and 35% due to changes in salinity levels.

Vegetation cover in unsubmerged areas has also suffered substantial losses. Gum groves in the north have lost between 25% to 75% of their population in places. In the Niayes area, palm stands are threatened with extinction, and even in the Casamance they are under threat. Some economically less significant crops have also been ravaged. There are places where dried-out trees stand as if in some huge tree cemetery, with people raiding them for wood before bush fires consume them. At the moment there is widespread thinning of the country's vegetation cover. Woody trees have come up underdeveloped. In the northern regions, grass cover has become disturbingly sparse due to the combination of climatic inclemencies and human depredations.

The evidence suggests that in the 1980s, there was an inverse relationship between the substantial expansion of the total area classified as reserves, and therefore protected areas in principle, and the actual extent of vegetation cover, which decreased. Apparently there was a desire to attenuate the effects of the new situation through stronger conservation measures. On the other hand, classification as a reserve does not guarantee that vegetation cover will be spared the impact of uncontrollable depredations. The most serious threat comes from over-exploitation. Furthermore, industrial or mining complexes, roads and other infrastructural facilities are sometimes constructed on such reserves, with damaging consequences.

The Consumer Impact on Fragile Environments

A study of Senegal's forestry potential conducted in 1980 indicated that the country's woodland reserves covered 11 million ha, over which the total volume of live timber was 80 million m^3. Out of this resource base, the annual consumption of timber and wood is 3.6 million m^3. Since, under the best conditions, the average productivity of the country's natural woodland base is no more than 600,000 m^3 per year, the conclusion is clear: Senegal consumes more timber and wood than its woodlands can produce. Every year, 4.5% of the existing resource base is used to meet timber and firewood needs. In addition, some 60,000 ha of woodland are brought under cultivation each year. These figures indicate the scope of the human consumer impact on the woodland base, already diminished by climatic inclemencies.

Generally speaking, population growth has pushed up consumption levels for the entire range of woodland products normally used for household needs (cooking, pharmacology, carpentry, etc.). Rising consumer demand has in turn caused rapid decreases in resources. Furthermore, the unfavourable climatic situation has affected vegetation such as acacia plants (the source of gum arabic) in the north of the country. High extinction rates caused a 90% drop in gum production, from 3,170 tons in 1971 to 693 tons in 1982. The trend was aggravated by uncontrolled tapping, haphazard pruning and frequent bush fires.

With increasing demand from the urban areas for firewood and charcoal, the out-take from woodland resources has risen accordingly. Worse still, urban dwellers prefer charcoal. Since it takes 100 kg of wood to produce less than 20 kg of charcoal, the impact of urban consumers on woodland resources is three times heavier than that of rural households depending solely on firewood. Let us look at the example of Dakar. There are times when the total quantity of charcoal officially registered nation-wide is smaller than the quantity monitored at entry points into the city of Dakar, or the quantity actually consumed in the city. This was the case in 1972. This raises doubts about the accuracy of officially registered production figures. Incidentally, the quantity of charcoal consumed in Dakar increased from 1972 to 1987, while firewood consumption decreased considerably.

A further factor in the consumer impact on the fragile environment is the prevalence of bush fires. These aggravate the ravages of human exploitation and climatic hazards.

Table 6: Wood-Based Fuel Consumption in Dakar (in tons)

		1961	1972	1984
Nation-wide product.:				
	Charcoal	30 700	69 661	107 300
	Wood	47 840	80 169	54 288
Quantities Entering Dakar:				
	Charcoal	-	74 017	98 213
	Wood	-	78 190	25 064
Estimated Real Consumption: Dakar				
	Charcoal	-	96 222	127 676

Source: DEFC/DCSR 1987.

Table 7: Patterns of Bush Fire Occurrence in Recent Years

Period	Number of Bush Fires	Area Burned (Ha)
1975 - 1976	276	3 100 000
1981 - 1982	205	402 037
1986 - 1987	444	128 702

Source: DEFC/DCSR 1987.

The steady increase in the urban demand for wood fuel and other woodland products has taken a heavy toll of the woodland resource base. Every year, 200,000 ha are affected in one way or another. Wood cutting and the clearing of woodland for new farms both worsen imbalances in the regional distribution of woodland resources, with only three regions (Ziguinchor, Kolda and Tambacounda) capable of covering all their fuel needs. As far as national firewood requirements are concerned, the master plan for forestry development projects a 9% increase in the 1985-95 period. National consumption, on the other hand, is expected to increase by 42%. This indicates that pressure on the nation's woodland resource base will become increasingly intense. The latter projection needs to be modified, however, because part of rural consumption is regularly met from wood gathered on cultivated and fallow land, sources unaccounted for in official statistics.

It is interesting that charcoal prices rise less often than those of other fuels. Each rise is also smaller. From 1962 to 1987, for instance, charcoal prices rose only five times (over 25 years). By contrast, petrol prices rose 14 times in 10 years. Butane gas prices rose six times in six years, though admittedly they also fell once. The main point is that forestry is a highly important sector from the social and economic points of view. But the figures also indicate that the use of forest and woodland resources is dangerously intensive.

Over the past 15 years, the incidence of bush fires has been steadily reduced. In the early 1970s, the total area burned annually exceeded 6,000,000 hectares. Since 1978, the combination of hard work and low rainfall has lowered the figure. In 1980 it was down to 200,000 ha; by 1987 it had decreased further to 130,000 ha. This achievement is the result of public information campaigns, improved equipment for the forestry service, and the creation of village-level bush fire brigades.

Declining Productivity and the Rehabilitation of the Environment

The combined effect of the pressures described above has been a serious deterioration of the nation's vegetation cover. There is a real threat of long-term destruction. It is necessary, therefore, to protect and rehabilitate plant cover by various means, including the establishment of reserved zones, the promotion of rational resource use, etc. Another approach emphasizes reforestation programmes and public information campaigns. It was in line with that approach that an intensive reforestation policy based on voluntary participation and geared to boosting the productivity of natural production systems was initiated in 1968.

The first reforestation campaign in Senegal was organized in 1936. At that time teak and gmélina trees were planted in the Casamance. The next campaign started with the planting of trees intended to stabilize sand dunes along Dakar's north coast in 1947. From 1960, several mass campaigns were organized. They included a National Tree-Planting Week, the distribution of saplings to urban and rural groups, the planting of trees along major road arteries, etc. In the late 1960s, worsening climatic conditions led to the implementation of a first series of forestry development projects which factored in the changed ecological circumstances and fixed a comprehensive set of objectives designed to cope with the problem. In 1981, Senegal came up with a plan for the sector. It took the form of a master plan for forestry development in which long-term policy guidelines were spelled out. The implementational strategy was organized around the improvement of natural groves, an indispensable aspect of rational resource management; the proliferation of national reforestation sites working to strengthen the country's woodland base in order both to protect the environment and to raise productivity; and large scale tree planting by communities and individuals in the rural areas, urban outskirts and urban areas.

A lot of water has gone under the bridge since then, and the master plan is now somewhat dated in terms of its diagnosis and its planning options. It is time, therefore, to update the programme and breathe new life into the project schedule.

An ever-rising number of increasingly ambitious projects have been drawn up, with larger and larger numbers of the rural population participating in organized groups. In the beginning, achievements were modest in scale. From 1977, however, the implementational tempo picked up speed. From 1977 to 1981, for instance, the area reforested averaged 2,450 ha per year. The plan had projected a reforestation rate of 7,500 ha per year for the period. The implementation rate was therefore 33%. From 1981 to 1985, the target was 10,000 ha per year, and the area planted was 9,784 hectares per year. In 1986 and 1987, the areas planted exceeded plan targets set at 14,000 ha.

Results, in other words, have been positive. Nevertheless, it would be unrealistic to overlook one fact: reforestation cannot proceed fast enough to catch up with consumption needs, especially for wood fuel. Still, in the face of ever-rising national demand, intensified reforestation efforts are of course a good idea. The gradual increase in Senegal's vegetation cover is the result of public information campaigns. Thanks to such campaigns, private and community groves in the rural areas caught up with official plantations in 1981. Since then they have been much more numerous. Old trends have thus been reversed, partly because of the extremely high cost of regular public sector tree planting exercises.

The shift had repercussions on the Forestry Code. Published in 1965, the code is now being revised to incorporate new forestry development policy guidelines. The revisions include provisions guaranteeing private property in forestry resources, and making it possible to recoup the cost of forestry products in a way that reflects their economic value. The aim is to encourage people in general to play a more active role in agro-forestry activities.

This much is clear: in Senegal today, national policy on plant resource protection, reforestation and soil conservation is becoming clarified and acquiring organizational shape. In the worst-hit zones such as the Senegal River valley and delta, the woodland and pastoral zone and the endangered farmlands of the Groundnut Basin, there are plans to establish rational resource use patterns and improve the natural resource base along sound ecological principles.

With regard to soils, a decisive new factor has been introduced: there is currently a high level of involvement in the development of structures responsible for protecting and rehabilitating soils, with special attention to judicious water use in the dry regions. Attention is also being paid to specific water resource problems such as saline and alkaline levels in areas set aside for intensive land use.

Poor Control of the Urban Environment

The urban population growth rate in Senegal has been extremely high and steady. The rise in the number of urban areas with over 5,000 inhabitants (the threshold defined by the Urban Code) is shown in Table 8.

Table 8: Number of Urban Areas and Rates of Urbanization

Year	No. of Urban Areas	% Total Population
1955	14	18.8
1964	22	26.6
1970	30	32.3
1973	31	35.0
1984	37	39.6

Sources: MUHE, 1982; MUH, 1986.

From 1960 to 1976, Senegal's urban population grew at an average annual rate of 5.1%, while the population as a whole grew at a rate of 3.2%. If current trends hold, by the year 2000 the urban population in Senegal will make up 48% of the total. About 40% of the urban total will be made up of migrants, the remainder from natural increase. Dakar and its suburbs will account for 56% of the urban total.

In the decade from 1965 to 1976, a number of towns grew spectacularly. A total of 14 towns doubled their populations; four towns tripled theirs, and one urban area saw its population rise four-fold. From 1955 to 1965, only six towns doubled their populations, and only two tripled theirs.

Such rapid growth has had and will continue to have far-reaching consequences on the urban environment, especially with regard to the adequacy of infrastructural facilities, planning and the maintenance of law and order.

An analysis of urban space occupation patterns shows that there is an administrative structure backed up by a formidable array of laws and regulations providing a framework for decision-making in the urban planning process. Numerous implementational trends surfaced in the 1960-90 period.

On the whole, urban planning in Senegal is half-baked and piecemeal. Its inadequacies are visible in the disorganized state of road traffic and various services in many neighbourhoods, especially those on the urban outskirts. This is all the more disturbing given the high level of demand for housing. The supply of new housing units in the urban areas is no longer enough to meet demand. The housing shortage in Dakar is particularly acute. A striking feature of the land and real estate situation is the absence of any central management. Moreover, unauthorized building and squatting often forces the hand of the urban planning system, seriously disturbing development plan schedules. Relocation operations, apart from being costly, also present thorny political and social problems.

In all urban areas (Saint-Louis, Thiès, Ziguinchor, Kaolack and Dakar) special no-construction zones have regularly been taken over for housing. Occasionally, the State itself takes the initiative. Most often, however, it is ordinary people, mainly new migrants and low-income families, who put up such housing. In Dakar there are numerous instances of vacant lots being officially allocated to builders. It is also common to find all sorts of unauthorized tradespersons, repairers, chop bar operators, hawkers, etc. occupying sidewalks. The disorganization stretches to the corralling of livestock in public places and the piling up of building gravel on sidewalks. All this leads to a general deterioration of sanitation and health standards. One clear reason for the fall in standards is that since 1960, the Sanitation Service has not been much in evidence, and where it has been present, its work has been inefficient. Other urban services are equally inefficient, as we shall discuss later.

Dakar deserves particular attention. For one thing, from 1960 to 1990, the city grew according to officially approved urban plans. Other urban areas did not have that advantage. This positive trend has continued, even though there have been inadequacies and failures in plan scheduling. Urban space use in the Dakar area has been regulated under three master plans. The plan adopted in 1961 was really a modification of the 1946 master plan defining urban zones. The 1967 master plan envisaged a projected population of about 1 300,000 by 1980. The 1980 master plan updated the 1967 plan to cope with a projected population of 2,800,000 by the year 2001. Preliminary studies were completed as early as 1982, but work on the master plan is yet unfinished. Most likely, developments on the ground will outstrip the plan even before it is officially unveiled.

The 1980 master plan focuses on the country's third municipality, Rufisque. That town still contains 84% of the land area available for urban development in the Dakar region. It seems clear enough that previous master plans did nothing to remedy initial imbalances. Nevertheless, it is possible to perceive intimations of impending change. In the Dakar region, for instance, the municipality recently set up a demolition brigade to combat squatting near public highways and open spaces.

There are signs of similar trends elsewhere. The new Urban Code now awaiting approval, for instance, contains a number of fundamentally innovative provisions more suited to Senegalese realities. That is a far cry from the old Urban Code, in force since 1966, based mainly on French urban planning regulations.

One common feature of Senegalese towns and cities is that they set aside very little space for parks and green belts. People in general are yet to understand the role of such spaces. Upkeep and maintenance costs for such parks are high, and municipalities have an increasingly hard time paying water bills entailed by such improvements. On top of that, livestock tend to wander over parks, destroying work done. Other aggravating factors are the lure of real estate speculation and the absence of effective regulations forcing developers to create and maintain green areas. Dakar offers a clear example of this downward trend. As existing green areas deteriorate, the municipal authorities patch them up. But in all the new housing estates developed over the past decade or so in the northern section of the peninsula, not a single new green belt was incorporated.

The innovations we see now, then, have to do with public information campaigns promoting the maintenance of existing green areas. Indeed, the new Urban Code now awaiting approval is expected to incorporate the issue of green areas.

Production and Processing Urban Waste

In Senegal, the city facing the most acute waste production and disposal problems is Dakar. It is a fast-growing city built on a tiny peninsula. Furthermore, most of the country's industrial infrastructure is crammed there, making Dakar a particularly congested area in comparison with other urban areas in the nation. Partly on account of these reasons, and also because the city has been more thoroughly studied than others here, we shall concentrate mainly on Dakar.

The Solid Waste Cycle

The main source of waste is household trash. Recent statistics indicate that the average city dweller in Dakar produces 0.5 kg of waste per day. In 1981, the city's waste output totalled 570,000 m^3. If we factor in the urban growth rate, we should get a figure of 1,000,000 m^3 for 1990. Table 9 of quantities of solid waste collected in Dakar shows that the quantities have risen quite steadily over the years.

Table 9: Quantities of Solid Waste Collected in Dakar

	1957	1971	1980	1985
Quantity/day (T)	173	325	620	850
Quant./day/inhabt./(kg)	0.67	0.48	0.52	0.55
% differential	4.00	6.00	2.00	7.50

Source: Wane 1981.

The reason for the steep increase in waste collected is not so much a large increase in actual quantities of waste output, as the introduction of a more efficient collection system with the hiring of a private garbage collection company, SOADIP, in 1971. It seems, furthermore, that variations in tonnage collected from different neighbourhoods depend to a large extent on the level of urbanization there. In 1985 a mixed company, the SIAS, took over from SOADIP. The new contractor's terms of reference were expanded to include industrial waste disposal, tree pruning and the cleaning of areas not covered by the former contract.

Waste Processing and Disposal

At the moment, collected waste is transported to the Mbeubeusse dump at the north-eastern tip of the peninsula. Dakar is in the peculiar position of having no genuine waste processing plant. From 1967 to 1970, there was an attempt to install a plant designed to turn urban waste into compost. In the end that effort was abandoned. The only remaining disposal system depends on the physical transport of waste to the Mbeubeusse dump, operated mainly by the SIAS, which accounts for about 83% of waste disposal in Dakar. One disturbing aspect of the process is that the Mbeubeusse dump is a disposal lot controlled by no one, open to everyone. It therefore raises serious problems of hygiene. Besides, it is quite likely to get saturated, yet so far no alternative site has been selected.

Apart from household waste, there are numerous waste products for which there is no regular collection routine. Such waste piles up on makeshift waste disposal sites on many vacant lots in the urban areas. Typical contents include wrecked vehicle chassis, industrial waste and such heavy household waste as tree branches.

For over two decades now, the main problem has been the elimination of rapidly increasing quantities of waste. Other towns besides Dakar are in a similar situation. Municipal authorities routinely dump urban trash in abandoned quarries, or simply stash it somewhere outside the town. In Thiès, for example, garbage is dumped within the city limits, at the western highway exit towards Dakar. From time to time the accumulated waste is burned at the dump site. In Kaolack, waste is haphazardly dumped in a belt of 'tannes' ringing the town. In Saint-Louis, waste is frequently dumped along the banks of the Senegal River. In Diourbel, waste is dumped in a nonchalant fashion, mostly near the southern and eastern entries. Such flimsy garbage disposal arrangements have given Senegalese towns a dirty reputation. There are many reasons for this state of affairs.

The country has, on paper, stringent laws regulating the dumping and disposal of household waste. But it seems the inhabitants routinely disregard the rules. Such behaviour has an impact on the condition of existing infrastructural facilities, as well as on the waste problem itself. Public arrangements for the collection of household waste in containers are unsatisfactory. There are too few containers. The distance between one container and the next is discouragingly long, and people improvise temporary dumps between containers rather than walking 50 to 500 metres to get to them. In Dakar, one regularly sees piles of refuse on the ground around practically empty containers. This makes refuse collection points zones of serious pollution. Those close to markets are especially hazardous.

In Thiès and similar towns, household refuse is collected in built-up areas twice a week at the most, because of a shortage of equipment. This encourages the piling up of rubbish in unauthorized locations in built-up areas as well as in squatter neighbourhoods normally inaccessible to collection trucks anyway. The municipal authorities would be well advised to consider an alternative solution: the use of horse-drawn tipcarts capable of reaching the least accessible neighbourhoods. Costs for such a system are yet to be calculated, but there is little doubt that its creation and maintenance would solve local health problems without straining the budgets of medium-sized towns.

Large quantities of solid waste are often dumped into open drains intended to evacuate rainwater. Sometimes the waste includes dead animals, making the drains particularly unhealthy in the dry season. There is a peculiarly unpleasant aspect: the systematic ransacking of private garbage pails, public containers and the Mbeubeusse dump by rag dealers who recycle everything that is not absolutely rotten, working under questionable conditions. Thanks to them, part of the city's garbage gets brought back almost to square one, and is recycled after cursory cleaning into the distribution circuit. It is not so much the fact of recycling itself that is disturbing; garbage is recycled under conditions that endanger public health. Currently, a number of specialized job hustles have developed around the recycling process near the Mbeubeusse dump. They supply an active trade circuit in the popular neighbourhoods of Dakar and certain inland towns. As long as there are no regular arrangements for waste processing, any idea of stopping such activities would seem to be wishful thinking. There is an urgent need to set up a waste treatment plant and to take active steps to prohibit access to dump sites. In Dakar, there seems to be a real determination to improve the situation. The necessary resources also seem to be available, or might soon be. Other urban areas are less lucky. All the municipal authorities there seem able to do is to burn their garbage from time to time when it piles up too high at dump sites.

Sewage and Water Drainage

Liquid waste disposal arrangements in urban areas include the collection, treatment and drainage of waste water along with rainwater. Typically, however, Senegalese towns have few private or public facilities for such treatment and drainage. Sometimes this lack of equipment creates serious environmental problems.

Collection and Drainage

According to the Sanitation Code, the collection and drainage of liquid waste is the responsibility of local communities. In practice, the Ministry in charge of Sanitation has delegated part of its responsibilities to the National Water Works Corporation (SONEES). SONEES already enjoys a monopoly over the production, piping and distribution of drinking water in the urban areas. To this, the responsibility for public sanitation operations was added in 1983.

It is SONEES, then, which is responsible for the purification and drainage of most liquid waste passing through the underground sewage system in municipal Dakar. The system includes 150 km of rainwater drains, 450 km of waste water drainage pipes and 25,000 lines feeding into the drainage pipe network. To help the corporation meet the cost of its sanitation assignments, it is empowered to put a surcharge on every cubic metre of water it sells.

Sanitation Systems
Here again Dakar is in a different situation from the other urban areas. Dakar has separate systems for the drainage of rainwater and waste water, even if many neighbourhoods remain unconnected to the systems. By contrast, municipal authorities in the inland towns, even if they are in places able to invest in rainwater drainage systems to prevent flooding in the poorer areas, still have only token waste water drainage systems. Rufisque, Thiès, Kaolack and Ziguinchor are all in this situation. Worse still, none of these towns has a waste water treatment plant. Their liquid waste is channelled into seepage areas, or in some cases drained directly into the ocean.

Rainwater drainage is a big headache now. Numerous unauthorized channels pour waste water into rainwater drainage channels. Another problem is that since Dakar has only a modest rainfall regime, drainage channels tend to get clogged up with sand, thus becoming useless in the rainy season. Furthermore, some low-lying areas that used to serve as sewage evacuation areas have now been built up. This sometimes leads to floods in such places as the dual carriageway, the junction near the Prestations Familiales building, and the Castors neighbourhood.

Dakar has two sewage treatment plants sited north of the city, a purification plant at Patte d'Oie and the other at Dagoudane Pikine. Each is supplied by a sewage network. There are plans to build a third purification center and sewage network complex to serve an adjacent zone. The Patte d'Oie Builders station, built in 1970, operates inefficiently because it is chronically overloaded. It used to supply a downstream irrigation network with treated water that market gardeners could tap. But for some time now the network has been blocked. In reaction, market gardeners have smashed the main pipe to get at untreated water and use it to irrigate their fields. The resulting public health and sanitation conditions are deplorable. It is possible that such conditions are responsible for the outbreak of local epidemics of such diseases as typhoid fever. In any case, over the past several years the incidence of such diseases in the Dakar area has been unusually high.

The second station under construction is intended to serve the newly built up area of Grand Yoff and a large part of Pikine. Waste water treated there would either be channelled into the sea near Cambérène or used for irrigation. Unfortunately, there is every reason to fear that this station will face the same management problems that have stymied work at the Patte d'Oie Builders station. Operations were scheduled to begin in 1987, but were delayed until recently.

The majority of the urban population makes do with more or less elaborate individual sanitation facilities in those places where waste water cannot be drained into public sewage networks. The level of sophistication of such facilities depends on the users' social status, the nature of surrounding soil, the urban zone in question, and the amount of space available. People in the poorer strata normally have no special facilities. Waste water from households is simply poured out on sidewalks or vacant lots, as in Fass and Colobane. With upward social mobility comes more sophisticated equipment with a less disagreeable impact on the surroundings. Waste water goes into containers periodically emptied into the public sewage system or in individual cesspools, sometimes right along the sidewalk. Faeces go into individual latrines without flushing arrangements. Alternatively, people use public toilets, often poorly maintained.

In households with more adequate sanitation facilities, all waste liquid is channelled into a septic tank with supplementary drainage into a soak-away cesspit. Septic tanks are often so small that they have to be emptied frequently.

Liquid Industrial Waste

Dakar is practically the only city that has to deal with the disposal of liquid waste from industrial sources. Industrial development in the Dakar area has produced increasing quantities of industrial waste of all kinds. Practically all of it gets dumped into the sea with no appropriate treatment. Liquid industrial waste, some of which is channelled into the sea at high temperatures, contains various mineral and organic substances, chemicals with toxic effects on marine flora and fauna, heavy metal like lead and mercury, etc.

Most industrial establishments channel their liquid waste into the urban rainwater and sewage networks. Network channels are regularly blocked by large solid matter. The Hann Bay area, where the biggest evacuation pipes from the adjacent industrial zone end, has been seriously polluted.

There are two clear trends in the evacuation of urban liquid waste. In places such as Saint-Louis, Kaolack and Ziguinchor, liquid waste is poured into rivers or the ocean. In the case of Dakar, the evacuation point is a ten-metre deep tank situated 300 metres offshore. Normally, there is no special treatment. In some areas such as Dakar's Soumbédioune Bay, this kind of arrangement has caused a disturbing increase in the germ count.

Liquid waste sucked out of private septic tanks is transported in tankers and emptied out in open spaces close to the collection points, with no regard whatsoever for environmental damage. It is hard to quantify the damage done by the evacuation of industrial waste into such outlet areas as Dakar's Hann Bay. What is clear is that existing legislation on pollution prevention and the handling of industrial waste is extremely lax. Furthermore, the enforcement style is laid back.

Still, behaviour patterns among the population have been changing perceptibly. People are increasingly willing to do their best to install improved private sanitation facilities in areas without public sanitation networks. The Grand Yoff neighbourhood provides an example of what a determined community can accomplish with help from the public services. From 1982 to 1986, people there agreed to pay one-third of construction costs for cesspits and disposal tanks for liquid household waste. The result was an improvement in basic health conditions.

Air and Noise Pollution

Atmospheric and noise pollution take various forms, almost entirely concentrated in the Dakar area. This is because Dakar is the site of considerable industrial activity. It also has the lion's share of the nation's motor traffic.

Industrial activity accounts for a large share of this kind of pollution. The most widespread atmospheric pollutants include waste sulphur derivatives from petrol, kerosine and other fossil fuels in industrial plants and households. Factories producing chemicals, cement and other building materials give off fine dust and different kinds of aerosol fumes. Admittedly, because of Dakar's peninsular location, winds blow most such atmospheric pollutants out to sea. But air pollution caused by various types of motor vehicles is a more serious matter. For one thing, the number of vehicles on the roads has risen at a steady rate of about 12%. In 1984 there were 120,000 vehicles. Exhaust gases contain nitrogen oxides, hydrocarbons and lead compounds. At times of peak traffic, emissions of such gases reach critical levels on the main roads converging on Sandaga market. The trend is worsening with the rapid conversion to diesel fuel of all types of vehicles, especially small cars.

The harm caused by noise pollution is real but difficult to identify. Noise pollution can come from a great number of sources. Sometimes the root cause is the non-observance of residential zoning regulations. At other times noise is caused by people using broken-down equipment. One clearly important factor is the tendency to keep using obsolete machinery without taking steps to reduce noise emission. In addition, the installation of workshops and factories in residential neighbourhoods means high decibel levels throughout the day. Officials in charge of enforcing existing legislation are generally indulgent towards culprits, and force of habit has ended up making an anomalous situation seem normal.

Large numbers of motor vehicles on the roads are virtual antiques. Roadworthiness tests are lackadaisical. The combined effect is to drive decibel levels way beyond average levels of tolerance. Some noise pollution comes from the social environment itself. Family ceremonies and religious celebrations often involve the use of loudspeakers; so do political meetings and the activities of permanent or temporary sports clubs and entertainment centres. For those living in the built-up areas growing up around Dakar airport, air traffic is a further source of sound pollution.

In Senegal, social attitudes to air and noise pollution are rather unusual. While social norms are quite stringent in other respects, air and noise pollution are not frowned upon. Indeed, some patterns of community behaviour indicate habitually high tolerance levels for such pollution. Only rarely do officials or communities attempt to stop it. There is no attempt to inform people about the physiological, psychic and general health risks related to air and noise pollution. Everyone, in effect, seems accustomed to a high-decibel, high-pollution lifestyle. It is intriguing, in this respect, that broadcast messages urging people to lower the volume of their radio sets at given times stopped after the 1960s. Their cessation clearly indicates that even if individuals still complain about noise, the society as a whole has given up trying to do anything about it. There are laws and regulations, but their effect is negligible. The reasons, most likely, are sociological.

In all coastal villages and towns along the Petite Côte, there are makeshift herring smoking hearths, the greatest concentration being in Mbour. The smoke they generate adds to air pollution. Each time the public authorities have attempted to relocate the hearths away from the urban areas, they have run into stiff resistance. This is a further indication that the population is used to this particular kind of pollution, closely linked to local occupations.

The Coastal Strip and the Inland Zones

Almost invariably, development decisions, whether they entail resource extraction or infrastructural construction, have a strong impact on the environment. That impact is particularity powerful when the projects in question involve industrial plants or major public engineering works. In Senegal, over the period 1960-90, the environment has been under particularly intense attack in specific geographical zones where the coastal strip has undergone urban development, where underground resources have been exploited, and where hydro-electric and other water resource facilities have been constructed.

In the coastal areas, the Senegalese coastline has almost never been known to remain stable for any long stretch of time. The normal situation features more or less rapid fluctuations. Often, the Senegalese coastline recedes after a period of active erosion. We should point out that there are some exceptions to this rule along the Senegalese coast. For instance, in areas such as the strip from Saint-Louis to Kayar and the southern Saloum coast, the shoreline has indeed advanced seaward. Other sections (from Kayar to Yoff, for instance) have stayed more or less stable. But between the Cape Verde peninsula and the promontory of Sangomar, the shoreline has been receding at an average speed between 1.2 and 1.5 metres per year. The highest recession rate has been observed in the town of Rufisque, where in the space of 47 years (from 1933-80) the sea advanced 122 metres inland.

Shoreline erosion is not seen as a decisive threat to the environment except in the urban areas, where it can cause spectacular and catastrophic damage. On occasion it has resulted in the destruction of housing units, forcing the public authorities to relocate the population, as happened in certain neighbourhoods in Rufisque, or more recently in Palmarin (1987). It would be possible, in technical terms, to limit shoreline erosion. But the engineering structures involved would entail substantial cash outlays. For that reason, only token implementational steps have been taken.

Exploitation of Surface and Underground Resources

From 1960 to 1980, Senegal had no mining laws apart from Decree Number 61-356 of 1961 which laid down stipulations governing quarry workings. The decree distinguished between two types of quarry. Permanent quarries were defined as those producing an output above 200 m^3. Quarries with an output lower than that figure were classified as temporary. In theory, both permanent and temporary quarries might be sited on private land or public land. In practice, temporary quarries were nearly always sited on public land.

Quarry Products

Quarrying is done by handicraft-type or semi-industrial enterprises. The materials quarried are such hard rocks as basalt (in the Dakar and Thiès regions), sandstone (Dakar, Thiès, Saint-Louis, Tambacounda), limestone (mainly in the Dakar region, at the SOCOCIM quarry in Bargny), and such friable materials as shells (Dakar, Thiès, Kaolack, Fatick), clay, laterite and especially marine, river or desert dune sand, available practically all over the country.

Incidentally, the need to preserve the environment led to the prohibition of basalt extraction in the Dakar area in 1972. As far as friable materials such as sand are concerned, in theory the regional mining and geological services are there to ensure their rational management and exploitation in conformity with norms of ecological balance. Since the 1960s, one notable feature of resource extraction patterns has been the steady level of high demand. The prime factor here is the development of the housing construction sector, the main consumer of these materials, along with the public works sector, particularly active in road construction.

Three enterprises in particular warrant particular attention:

- The Senegalese Phosphate Company of Taïba (CSPT) has been quarrying limestone phosphate deposits in Taiba since 1958. Since that date, 18 billion m^3 of raw mineral have been extracted, but that is only 20% of the total volume excavated. It should be pointed out, though, that quarrying operations at the Taïba site are automatically followed by land refills.

- The Senegalese Phosphate Corporation of Thiès (SSPT) quarries aluminium phosphate and limestone phosphate reserves as well as attapulgite at its various concessions in Tivaouane, Thiès, Sebikotane, Warrang and Mbodiène. As of 1986, over 6 million tons of phosphate and 500,000 tons of attapulgite had been extracted after the stripping away of non ore-bearing strata averaging 13 metres in thickness. These figures give an inkling of the extent of environmental depredation at the quarry sites.

- Since 1986, PROCHIMAT has extracted some 40,000 tons of attapulgite at Pout and Nianing. The company regularly fills in excavated surfaces after its quarrying operations.

These three enterprises are regulated under Decree N°. 61-367 of September 1961. The decree contains no specific stipulations requiring quarrying enterprises to take any measures to safeguard the environment. Neither does it require them to replant tree cover on their concessions.

In all these cases, one salient fact is the absence of any environmental conservation legislation. That has been the situation since independence. Mining and quarrying are growth industries in Senegal. Their effect on the environment is clearly deleterious. Oddly enough, the Mining and Geological Service cannot approve permits for the opening of quarries without favourable recommendations from such departments as the Lands Department, the Cadastral Survey Service, the Forestry Service, the Local Government administration, etc. Such recommendations and approvals are subject to the payment of rehabilitation and reforestation fees. Yet in those few places where quarry sites have been refilled after excavation, and where trees have been replanted, it was the enterprises themselves which took the initiative. That was the case at the SSPT quarry in Pout and at the CSPT quarry in Mboro. The PROCHIMAT quarry at Pout, according to the official fee schedule, was supposed to pay for reforestation at the site. But that work has never been done.

Another trend involves small-scale clandestine quarrying in recently urbanized zones or squatter areas. An example is the north shore of Dakar, where there have been numerous infractions of existing legislation, likely to expose inhabitants living closest to the shoreline to serious risk. Steps are now being taken to remedy the situation, through the passage of appropriate legislation in particular. For the need to draw up a mining code in line with new policy guidelines for the mining industry has become quite clear.

There were no specific stipulations in Decree No. 61-356 concerning environmental protection. The main issue addressed by that decree was the protection of quarrying and mining companies. The new Mining Code and the Decree designed to further its implementation both make small-scale and industrial mine and quarry operators responsible for environmental protection. The Code was scheduled to become operative in 1988. Its application would give the State greater control over its mineral resources. At the same time, it would bring mining regulations into line with changes in land and real estate legislation in Senegal.

Dams and Salt-water Barriers

The country's humid zones, rivermouths and river basins have been selected for the construction of hydro-agricultural infrastructures. The aim is to enhance water resource control as a means to agricultural recovery. The risk, however, is that completed or ongoing programmes might end up changing the natural environment in profound ways. Forested regions are likely to be transformed, arid and semi-arid zones will become irrigated perimeters, and vast quantities of water will get backed up behind dams. It is assumed that any development policy designed to minimize negative fallout will make environmental protection an integral part of all construction projects.

In the Senegalese countryside, dams fall within the category of imported technology. A number of ethnic groups, however, have developed farming techniques based on water management practices. One example is rice growing on saline soils in mangrove swamps among the Diola, proof of their capacity to solve environmental problems through the use of appropriate technologies. Still, the development of such farms does have a number of environmental side effects. The substitution of rice for mangrove stands destroys or transforms the natural vegetation. It also modifies soil make-up in significant ways. The trouble is that only the cultivated topsoil gets desalinated. Salt deposits remain deeper below the surface. This is dangerous for the rice fields, because salt might resurface in the dry season. The Diola response is to leach out the soil again in the very first weeks of the rainy season.

Toucouleur farmers construct ponds in flood basins. The work they do around these ponds depends on the use of a simple but appropriate technology, coupled with rational and coherent space utilization. One striking aspect of such space utilization is that several different occupational groups get to use the same sites cooperatively, without competition. This is a good instance of ecological management in action. Occupations in flood basins include fishing, agriculture, animal husbandry and forestry.

Diola and Toucouleur communities demonstrate an ability to adapt to natural conditions through control of water resources achieved without unnecessary inroads into natural ecosystems. These lifestyles depend for their balanced continuation on the permanent interaction of various factors: people, construction and management techniques, the healthy functioning of various parts of the ecosystem, including water, soil, flora and fauna. That balance was abruptly shaken after the drought of the 1970s. Infrastructural changes followed, culminating in the adoption and implementation of a policy on dam construction.

Two main areas were selected for the construction of reservoir dams. Construction work on the Anambé Dam in Casamance began in 1982. The dam was planned as a multi-phase project, the first phase being the construction of a swish dam and the improvement of a 1,000 ha hydro-agricultural perimeter capable of yielding a double harvest thanks to water from a 10 km long reservoir with a capacity of 50 million m^3. The area irrigated was expected eventually to cover 16,000 ha. The Diama Dam, situated on the lower Senegal River, was completed in 1986. Backing up water over an area of 23,500 ha with a storage capacity of 250 million m^3, the dam provides water for irrigating perimeters in the delta area. It also facilitates the steady resupply of the Lac du Guiers with water. These dams are expected to help meet two objectives: the first is to cut the country's cereal production deficit, mainly by reducing rice imports. The second is to enhance agricultural diversification.

It should be noted that the Diama Dam also functions as a salt-water barrier by keeping seawater from flowing up the lower Senegal River valley when river flow levels are low. It is the Casamance, however, where it has proved most urgent to construct dams and barriers to help rehabilitate about 50,000 ha of land rendered agriculturally unusable by the flow of salt water up the entire lower and middle river basin. To keep briny water from flowing up to selected sites, it has been found advisable to construct a series of linked dikes served by a drainage network. Alternatively, salt-water barriers, also reinforced with efficient drainage networks, have been constructed. To prevent the acid content of upstream soils from rising excessively during the dry season, sea water is let in to keep soils in the lower basin moist.

The salt water barrage, as currently designed, is not a long-range solution to the soil salinity problem. In a search for more permanent solutions, an experimental station was constructed for testing an implementational model for the development of saline soils in the Lower Casamance rivermouth area. The project, known as the Guidel Dam, was stared in 1962-63, but because of funding problems it was not completed until the early 1980s. Other projects are under construction at Bignona, Affiniam, Simbandi-Balante, Nyassia, Baïla, Kamobeul and Soungrougrou.

Dam construction is a recent development in Senegal. It is therefore too early yet to pinpoint trends. All we can state now is that the new dams have certainly demonstrated their potential for causing the kinds of major transformations they were planned to bring about. An additional consideration is the fact that dams constitute a response to other challenges posed by changing climatic conditions. It is the general crisis created by these changes, after all, that so seriously affected the supply of water and raised salinity levels in the rivermouth areas.

A noteworthy feature of salt-water barriers in the Casamance basin is that they do not include water-retention dams. This makes their efficient operation dependent on rainfall levels a serious drawback. For when rainfall is low, salt-water barriers do not have enough water to wash out and improve salinated soils. Hence our conclusion that a lot remains to be done before complete control of water resources for agriculture is achieved. Meanwhile, the existing infrastructure is effective, strictly speaking, only in stopping salt-water from flowing up the river basin during the planting season.

In any case, the construction of dams and barriers in the Senegal River basin and in the Anambé area will cause profound environmental changes. These dam-related changes happen mainly because when water backs up behind a retention dam, the result is an ecological system completely different from the original water resource environment. There are several hydrological aspects: land gets flooded over, the surface area under water grows larger, evaporation increases accordingly, there are changes in water quality and clarity, etc. Biological factors also change: fish species that formerly migrated upriver and seawards get eliminated, water takes longer to get reoxygenated, and water-borne diseases or illnesses related to the presence of water (cholera, typhoid, bilharzia, malaria, etc.) reappear.

Evaluations have been conducted of the environmental impact of dams in selected occupational sectors along the Senegal River. Once the flow of the river is regularized by dams up- and down-stream, nearly 9,000 ha of woodland will be lost outright. An additional 3,000 to 4,000 ha will be lost each year as hydro-agricultural development work advances. To alleviate the negative impact, the Senegal Valley Development Authority (OMVS) action programme recommends reforestation around dam sites, more stringent enforcement of laws protecting woodland and forestry resources, and the development of a mass forestry campaign. There will be a definitive drop in the volume of fish caught as a result of the impact on sea-fish and salt-water fish of modifications in salt content. The average annual loss is projected at 4,000 tons.

Irrigation is a novel farming technique in Senegal. As such it presents an ecological danger, the risk of making soils sterile. Rice planting practices on the more or less saline soils of the lower Senegal valley, which does not involve deep drainage, causes soil desalination through inputs of large quantities of good, fresh water. The desalination process affects only the surface layers of soil. It also raises the water table which often has a high salt content, and can therefore provoke dangerously high alkaline levels in the soil. Research studies indicate that to bring 250 000 hectares of saline land on the left bank of the Senegal River under cultivation following the retention of water behind the Diama Dam, 2.5 billion m^3 of fresh water will have to be supplied, while the total amount of water to be pumped out will be 600 million m^3. There will therefore have to be a skilfully designed network of deep drainage channels. In addition, soil conservation plans will require anti-alkalinization measures and the evacuation of drainage water below pumping stations.

Conservation and Rehabilitation Campaigns

There are numerous local and national programmes designed to alleviate environmental degradation caused by the current drought or by injudicious exploitation of natural resources. Some of these programmes are aimed at straightforward conservation. They follow more or less strict regulations. Others are intended to rehabilitate degraded areas. One constant feature in all instances is that the initiative invariably comes from the administrative authorities.

Conservation measures take many forms, including checks on development, the establishment of no-trespassing zones, and the classification of national domains.

The threat of environmental degradation has led to the adoption of numerous measures imposing restrictions on development since the early 1970s. In the forestry sector, for instance, the authorities have had to forbid firewood cutting in all the northern regions of the country where before, people were still allowed to go and strip off dead wood from stricken trees. Now the only regions where wood-cutting is openly permitted are the Casamance, Kaolack and Tambacounda. But even there the number of cutting licenses has been reduced. The restriction and prohibition of wood-cutting was accompanied by publicity urging people to use other fuels such as gas. Reinforcement was provided in the form of sales tax incentives. The result was a relative easing of consumer pressure on woodland areas, even if consumption rates remained high.

The establishment of no-trespassing areas was mainly tried on an experimental scale. The principal venue was the sylvo-pastoral zone, where a number of development projects incorporated the concept into their animal husbandry programmes. Vindou-Thiengoly, Labgar and Rao provide good examples of this approach. The no-trespassing zones in question have always been small in size. So far, therefore, findings from this type of experiment are of little relevance once we shift to the national scale. Furthermore, fences put up to create no-trespassing zones are prohibitively expensive. And then guards have to be posted to ensure compliance. All this makes it unlikely that this approach will be implemented on a wide scale.

In our discussion of natural production systems, we noted that the total land area classified as reserves increased greatly in the past 12 years. It was decided to classify increasingly large areas as the environment deteriorated. This has certainly been an area of spectacular progress in conservation, even if there have been instances of encroachment aggravated by the shrinkage in the resource base.

The invariable purpose behind rehabilitation measures has been to improve the productivity of ecosystems. The main aim of reforestation campaigns is to increase supplies of firewood or timber. Reforestation campaigns have been particularly intense in the central and southern regions. They have produced large, systematically ordered plantations of fast maturing species within forest reserve perimeters. On account of their prohibitive cost, the programmes were phased down in the early 1980s. Instead, the emphasis shifted to community-based reforestation campaigns producing village woodland lots. These campaigns have yielded some results, even though so far there is no reliable land tenure legislation that could provide greater incentives for individuals to plant more trees.

Attempts have been made to rehabilitate leached out soils in the Groundnut Basin through the plantation of Acacia albida (Kadd) trees. Alternatively, the same result has been sought by protecting the natural tree cover. The objective is to use the nitrogen-fixing capacities of the acacia species to enrich impoverished soils, especially in the regions of Louga, Thiès, Fatick and Diourbel.

As from 1973, a great deal of useful work was done in the replanting of gum-producing stands in the Ferlo zone. The idea was to give the gum arabic industry a new lease of life. A lot of effort also went into reforestation programmes on irrigated land in the Senegal valley designed to make the provision of tree cover an integral part of hydro-agricultural projects. But it was not until the period from 1980 to 1984 that reforestation projects really proliferated. The increase was particularly spectacular in the Saint-Louis region during the final phase of the Senegal River development project.

The coastal sand dune stabilization project and the protection of market gardening basins in the regions of Saint-Louis, Louga, Thiès and Dakar began in the colonial period. At that time most work was focused in the Malika area. Implementation got a major boost after 1975 when several projects undertook reforestation work on over 13,000 ha between Kayar and the Gandiolais zone.

A large number of projects were undertaken with the aim of safeguarding existing potential or rehabilitating degraded resources. The proliferation of such projects after 1970 was apparently the result as much of the extent of environmental degradation observed as of the determination of the public authorities to contain the threat. For that reason, all regions were involved, to one degree or another, in the adoption and implementation of campaign strategies. The positive change in official attitudes seems to be a long-range trend.

It should not be forgotten, nevertheless, that there are still numerous hitches. For example, there is a wide variety of conservation and rehabilitation efforts. However, the total area involved is very small when compared with the large tracts cleared for cultivation, and given the decreasing productivity of natural ecosystems. Also, companies in special zones set aside for mining and quarrying operations are charged fees supposed to be ploughed back into the rehabilitation of those zones. However, the money has so far never been used for the intended purpose. There is an obvious shortcoming here, due to the failure to check that companies fulfill their contractual obligations. Persons and groups given licenses to cut wood are never required to replant trees. In practice, no logical connection has been established between the right to cut wood and the responsibility of planting trees. The reason is that the State has become practically the only entity that initiates tree planting activities. Now new guidelines are emerging which make room for local community participation in reforestation operations. There is an urgent need, however, to define community privileges and decision-making prerogatives regarding the use of reforested areas.

The above trends are also affected by a number of embryonic changes, of which two deserve special attention. There was a change at the political level with the establishment in 1983 of a government ministry directly in charge of environmental protection. Significantly, the change enhanced the coordination of various programmes hitherto administered by different services. The result was a powerful boost in measures designed to combat environmental degradation. On a technical level, public information campaigns focused on the need to save energy have led to profound behavioural changes. One indication is the rapid spread of the use of improved stoves designed to alleviate consumer pressure on forest resources. Overall results, however, remain modest.

Conclusion

For a long time the public authorities maintained a rigid posture: they were bent on keeping a monopoly on responsibility for environmental matters. This was part of a more general mindset characteristic of the first years after independence. At that time, the State was the sole agency making and implementing decisions. In those early years, however, ecological balance and other environmental matters were not considered burning issues. In the 1970s the situation changed entirely.

In legislative and administrative matters the government plays a decisive role. For all environmental activities depend on the interpretation and implementation of regulations affecting various aspects of the environment. One striking feature here is the great diversity of laws and regulations governing some aspect or other of the environment. There is a Forestry Code, an Urban Planning Code, a Sanitation Code, a Health Code, a Mining Code, and so forth. All these codes reflect the practical responsibility assumed by the State for environmental affairs. They also indicate the importance accorded to the sector.

Since laws and regulations governing environmental resources are embodied in a variety of sectorial codes, official approaches to the environment tended to be piecemeal, not integrative. That situation began to change between 1983 and 1990, when a major Ministry took over responsibility for the sector. We may expect the various regulatory texts to get streamlined in coming years, even though in practice, a number of responsibilities attributed to the new Ministry were withdrawn in March 1990.

There is another characteristic of the government's regulatory texts. They are rather heavy on repression. Sanctions often outweigh incentives. The logical result is the adoption of militaristic procedures. Public health officials, forestry guards and keepers at the national parks are all drawn to the regimental style. Even Dakar has fallen in step, with the recent creation of its own environmental inspection brigade. The military style, though admittedly it signals an important change, is no guarantee of efficiency. The number of officials has risen, but that has in no way prevented continuing environmental degradation. In any case, human depredations are still widespread.

The speed of administrative action is also notoriously slow. This contrasts sharply with the fast-breaking pace of environmental developments in real life. For example, certain legal amendments designed to deal with processes that started years ago have only now been passed. Some are still pending. The Forestry Code and the Urban Planning Code provide good instances of this state of affairs. A time-honoured feature of administrative review procedures is their rigidity. A second is that they take forever. Furthermore, even those laws already in existence are very loosely and carelessly enforced. There is no other explanation for the filthy state of the environment, especially in the urban areas. As a matter of fact, little is ever said out loud about infringements.

These drawbacks have to do with long-standing habits. Real as they are, they should not blind us to the fact that public attitudes have changed a great deal. For one thing, local groups and communities are getting increasingly involved in decision-making processes affecting their lives directly. The government monopoly on decision-making is being gradually relaxed. This has given non-governmental organizations room to organize more programmes. What is more, in their public utterances, government officials now recognize the need for a comprehensive, integrated approach to the environment. In addition, there has been a quantum leap in official awareness of the fact that environmental problems transcend national boundaries. The main guideline in this respect is now the need to work together on a multinational basis.

As far as the people are concerned, for years on end the only way they participated in environmental protection programmes was to get mobilized to provide unpaid labour in 'self-help' campaigns. Participatory programmes of that kind were frequent in the rainy season. On the whole they ensured acceptable standards of cleanliness. But in the 1960s those public agencies responsible for organizing such programmes slackened in their work. Popular participation lapsed accordingly in those towns where clean-up programmes had in the past been organized by official agencies. In the end the activities were abandoned outright. Since then, however, deep changes in attitudes have taken place under the combined influence of educational programmes initiated by the State, upward social mobility among individuals, and public awareness of the fact that unfolding climatic changes might turn out to be permanent.

Care should be taken to approach environmental issues differently according to the milieu - rural or urban - involved. In the urban areas, the population tends increasingly to see the environment in terms of sanitation. People say they want to live healthy lives; but their behaviour patterns foul up the environment. Still, there is a marked tendency to clean up private homes and spaces. So far, there is no such desire to clean up public spaces. For now, the level of public discipline is too low to justify any expectation that this situation will improve. One only has to look at the foul state of almost all markets to be convinced of this. In general, individuals do their best to keep the interiors of their homes clean. Oddly enough, the moment they get out in public, they behave with the utmost abandon, scattering used packaging and wrappings, especially plastic bags, over sidewalks and in downtown commercial areas. People, in other words, behave as if the only environment they have to care about is the space under their direct individual responsibility. Clearly, a long and steady educational process will have to be conducted to change this attitude.

In the rural areas, the environment was perceived first of all in terms of the shattering impact of ecological changes on farm production systems. People were suddenly forced to change their attitudes. The main result was the very high level of sensitivity to various aspects of 'desertification' among the rural population. The environment is seen mainly in terms of the production of resources jeopardized by the malfunctioning of one or more ecological variables over which human beings have little control, even if they can temper some of their consequences.

The fact bears repeating: environmental attitudes among the population change in a series of gradual shifts. Most often, these shifts are caused by various constraints. In the Senegalese situation, there has been a real rise in consciousness concerning environmental issues. It has in fact led to instances of individuals getting involved in environmental protection activities without waiting for official initiatives. That is a noteworthy fact indicating that the seeds of change have been sown in this society.

In the urban areas the outstanding feature of environmental participation is that those involved, mainly young people, spontaneously get involved in projects. Sometimes they set up neighbourhood committees and local groups to remove cumbersome piles of garbage, clear the streets of sand, construct playgrounds, etc. Such activities occur most frequently in newly settled zones not yet served by the municipal authorities. There is another form of participatory involvement, in which youth organizations are mobilized to work on holiday work site projects. By definition, these are projects of limited scope. But they do symbolize the willingness of part of the youth to identify with certain common causes.

The increasing commitment of the rural population to activities aimed at solving environmental problems takes two main forms. First, there are rural women's organizations, which have showed great understanding of issues related to firewood and played a leading role in popularizing improved stoves and hearths. Their impact on the environment is indirect, but it is important to highlight its positive influence in helping to popularize the new type of stoves, made to use less firewood and charcoal.

Second, there are public information campaigns against bush fires, coupled with village reforestation projects, a high-priority component of the rural contribution to the recovery of a threatened ecological balance. Over the last few years, bush fire brigades have been formed in all regions. Their presence has brought about a remarkable decrease in the area affected by bush fires. Village reforestation projects have also provided additional financial earnings to rural populations in a matter of years. They have given an impetus to the national reforestation programme, as pointed out above.

An examination of popular attitudes and various forms of involvement in environmental protection programmes reveals several positive aspects. Most are embryonic indicators of future changes, and they date back to the last 15 years. It would be wrong, however, to gloss over one constant reality: so far, there is no national consensus fixing a series of common programmes, mobilizing the public at large, based on a collective approach determined by precise programmatic objectives. The national authorities have sometimes attempted to reach that goal by arousing patriotic feelings or using incentives such as food handouts. But they have never achieved lasting results. Furthermore, they have been unable to avert conflicts of interest, all the more acrimonious because reforestation and other environmental projects produce substantial economic and social benefits.

Environments are necessarily historical phenomena. It is necessary to begin by committing the population at large, the principal protagonists, to environmental activities throughout practically the entire extent of the environment. But in addition, it is equally necessary to find methods to change public attitudes in ways designed to ensure the sustained coherence of such programmes across time. The public authorities would be well advised to incorporate among their objectives just such a process of sustained, comprehensive environmental development.

Bibliography

Baldé, P, 1987, 'Problèmes de pollutions et nuisances dans la ville de Thiès'. Paper presented at the Regional Training Seminar on Ecological Approaches to Human Premises in Sub-Saharan Africa, BREDA, Dakar, 26 - 30 October.

Barral, H, et al. 1983, 'Systèmes de production d'élevage au Sénégal dans la région du Ferlo', Final Report on Findings from a Multidisciplinary Research Study, AC-CGRIZA(LAT) - Action de coopération concertée - Groupe de recherches interdisciplinaires en zones arides (Lutte contre l'aridité en milieu tropical).

BCEOM, 1978, 'Collecte et traitement des déchets solides dans la région du Cap-Vert et de six capitales régionales', A General Report, MTUPT, Dakar, July.

BCEOM, 1986, 'Etude des systèmes de gestion des déchets et de récupération des ressources dans la zone métropolitaine de Dakar', UNEP/FAC/World Bank, September.

Bonfils, M, 1987, *Halte à la désertification du Sahel*, Paris, Karthala.

Ciss, B, 1984, 'Les aspects fonciers de la construction. Problématique des réserves foncières', Seminar on Recovery in the Construction Industry, MUH, Saly, 6-7 January.

Cissokho, C A K, 1980, 'Communication sur la politique forestière du Sénégal Réalisations et perspectives', National Council of the Socialist Party, SEEF, Dakar.

Dabo, M, 1983, 'L'aménagement hydro-agricole du bassin de l'Anambé'. Paper presented at the Thiès Colloquium on Earth-filled Dams and Rural Development in Africa, Ecole polytechnique de Thiès (EPT).

Degeorges, A and I Samba, 1983, 'Planification des impacts d'aménagements hydrauliques pour le développement des zones rurales en Afrique', Paper presented at the Thiès Colloquium, EPT.

Dia, I, 1988, 'Sociologie et écologie dans la problématique des aménagements hydro-agricoles dans la moyenne vallée du Fleuve Sénégal (Rive gauche)', Doctoral Thesis, ISE, Dakar University.

Diallo, S, 1982, 'Evolution géomorphologique du littoral sur la Petite Côte à Rufisque', Master's Thesis, FLSH, Geography Department, Dakar University.

Dieng, O, 1983, 'La pêche au Lac de Guiers, in Le Lac de Guiers: Problématique d'environnement et de développement', Papers of the ISE Colloquium, Faculty of Science, Dakar University.

Diouf, P S and T Bousso, 1988, 'Fleuve Sénégal: environnement aquatique et pêche: Synthèse bibliographique', Scientific Papers No. 108, CRODT-ISRA, Saint-Louis.

Diouf, P S, T Bousso and A Fontana, 1988, 'Compte-rendu du Séminaire sur l'environnement aquatique et la pêche dans le delta et la vallée du fleuve Sénégal', MDR, CRODT-ISRA, 9-11 February, Saint-Louis.

DITT, 1983, 'Etude de valorisation des déchets ménagers et industriels de la ville de Dakar', Mission Report.

Doyen, A, 1983, 'Impacts sur l'écosystème forêt de petits barrages: le cas du bassin versant du marigot de Baïla (Basse Casamance)', Paper presented at the Thiès Colloquium.

Dumont, R, 1986, *Pour l'Afrique, j'accuse*, Paris, Plon.

Engelhard, P and T Ben Abdallah, 1986, *Enjeux de l'après-barrage, Vallée du Sénégal*, ENDA/ Ministry of Cooperation, Republic of France.

Environmental Development in Africa - Relais urbain participé (ENDA-RUP), 1986, *Normes et restructuration de l'habitat*, ENDA-RUP.GTZ, MUH.

Fonds des Nations-Unies pour l'alimentation et l'agriculture (FAO), 1984, *Politique de lutte contre la désertification et de protection de la nature dans un pays d'Afrique de l'Ouest, du Maghreb et du Soudan*, Summary Report, Dakar, 18-27 July.

France, (Republic of), 1983, *Développement urbain en Afrique noire, quel habitat promouvoir. Expériences et pratiques* No. 54. Ministry of Foreign Relations, Cooperation and Development, June.

Gaye, O and P P Vincke, 1983, 'Problèmes sanitaires et mise en valeur de la vallée de Guidel (Basse-Casamance), Sénégal', paper presented at the Thiès Colloquium.

GFCC and ORGATEC, undated, *Evaluation des effets sur l'environnement d'aménagements prévus dans le bassin du fleuve Sénégal*, final Summary Report by Gannet Felming Cordry and Carpenter (Harrisburg, Pennsylvania, USA) and ORGATEC, Dakar, USAID/OMVS, Dakar.

Goudiaby, A, 1984, 'L'évolution de la pluviométrie en Sénégambie de l'origine des stations à 1983', Faculty of Humanities, TER, Dakar.

Hervy, J P, 1983, 'Retentissements possibles, en Afrique, de la création de barrages sur différentes maladies à vecteurs ou à hôtes intermédiaires', Paper presented at the Thiès Colloquium.

Institut sénégalais de normalisation (ISN), 1987, *Rapport de synthèse de l'atelier de normalisation. Qualité-Batiment-Génie civil*, Inst. Sen. Norm./MPC Seminar, 26-29 October.

Kane, C H, 1984, 'Conseil interministériel sur les perspectives et stratégies de développement de l'après-barrage', Ministry of Planning and Cooperation, Dakar, November.

Konté, C A K, 1985, 'La gestion des déchets à Dakar-Sénégal. Contribution pour une politique de traitement des déchets ménagers par incinération avec récupération d'energie', Postgraduate diploma thesis, Ecole nationale des cadres ruraux (ENCR) - University of Paris XII, September.

Labonte, R, 1983, 'Problématique des aspects écologiques et des problèmes de l'eau', Paper presented at the Thiès Colloquium.

Langley, P, 1986 'Notion d'urbanisme, aspects analytiques', Ecole nationale d'économie appliquée (ENEA), Dakar.

Leborgne, J, 1988, 'Pluviométrie au Sénégal et en Gambie', Faculty of Humanities, Dakar, 95 pp.

Loyer, J Y, and J Y, Lebrusq, 1983, 'L'influence de l'intensification des cycles de riziculture sur la basse vallée du fleuve Sénégal', Paper presented at the Thiès Colloquium.

Madeley, J, 1983, 'Les projets de grands barrages: investissement rentable ou développement non viable?' *Mazingira* 7, No. 4, 28 pp.17 -23.

Mbengue, A, 1987, 'Aménagements hydro-agricoles et agro-industries dans la région du lac de Guiers; évolution depuis 1954 et impacts socio-économiques', Doctoral dissertation, ISE, Dakar.

Nejjar, A, 1983, 'Impacts des barrages sur l'environnement', Paper presented at the Thiès Colloquium.

Ngom, T, 1976, 'Les équipements urbains des capitales régionales du Sénégal'. Graduate thesis, Institute of Urban Planning and Land Development, Faculty of Applied Sciences, Free University, Brussels.

Organisation de la mise en valeur du fleuve sénégal (OMVS), 1983, 'Le programme de l'OMVS, son contenu et ses effets sur l'environnement dans le bassin du fleuve Sénégal'. Seminar on Environmental Management in the Senegal River Basin: Monitoring the Saint-Louis Area, 12-19 December.

Pélissier, P, 1966, *Les paysans du Sénégal. Les civilisations agraires du Cayor à la Casamance*, St. Yrieix, Fabrègue.

Reizer, C, 1983, 'La technique des petits barrages est-elle concevable en grande plaine d'inondation?', Paper presented at the Thiès Colloquium.

Reizer, C, 1986, 'Impact sur l'environnement des aménagements hydrauliques en Sahel fluvial. Faut-il construire des barrages sur le Sénégal?', Symposium on the Environmental Impact of Major Hydraulic Development Projects, Paris, UNESCO, 27-31 October.

Rural Equipment Service, Ministry of Water Works, 1983, 'Les barrages anti-sel au Sénégal', paper presented at the Thiès Colloquium, Direction de l'équipement rural (DER).

Sakho, F, 1986, 'Normes d'aménagement et de construction', Survey of Squatter Housing, Department of Urban Planning and Architecture, Gesselschaft für Technische Zusammenarbeit (GTZ), 34 pp.

Sakho, L A, 1986, 'La maitrise de l'eau dans la mise en valeur agricole du Sénégal à l'après-barrage', Seminar on the New Agricultural Policy, CREA, University of Dakar, 7-10 May.

Sall, M, 1982, 'Dynamique et morphogenèse actuelles au Sénégal occidental', Doctoral dissertation, Institute of Geography, Louis Pasteur Institute, Strasbourg.

Sène, E H, 1975, 'Reforestation du pays. Intérêt majeur à mettre en oeuvre', Paper presented at the Officers' Conference.

Sène, E H, et al., 1977, 'Rapport national du Sénégal - Conférence des Nations-Unies sur la désertification', Nairobi, Kenya, 29 August - 9 September.

Senegal, Republic of, 1961, *Décret No. 61-356/MTPHU-MI.G*, Decree dated 21 September, fixant le régime d'exploitation des carrières au Sénégal'.

Senegal, Republic of, 1961, *Décret No. 61-357/MTPHU,-MIG*, Decree dated 21 September, réglementant et codifiant le régime des substances minérales au Sénégal à l'exception des hydrocarbures ou gazeux', 28 p.

Senegal, Republic of, 1966, *Code de l'Urbanisme: partie réglementaire*, Decree No. 66-1076 of 31 December.

Senegal, Republic of, 1966, *Décret No. 66.586 du 12 juillet modifiant les limites d'exploitation des carrières*.

Senegal, Republic of, 1972, Décret No. 72.868 du 13 juillet modifiant le décret No. 61.356 du 21 septembre 1961 fixant le régime de l'exploitation des carrières au Sénégal et abrogeant certaines de ses dispositions.

Senegal, Republic of, 1972, Loi No. 72.27 du 19 avril relative au régime de l'exploitation des carrières.

Senegal, Republic of, 1976, Direction des eaux, forêts et chasse (DEFC), Situation forestière au Sénégal, Consultation CILSS-UNSO-FAO sur le rôle de la forêt dans un programme de réhabilitation du Sahel, DEFC, Dakar, March.

Senegal, Republic of, 1982 Ministère de l'urbanisme de l'habitat et de l'équipement (MUHE), Etude du plan-directeur d'urbanisme de Dakar, Livre blanc, SONED AFRIQUE/BCEOM/MUHE, October.

Senegal, Republic of, 1982, Rapport annuel 1981-1982, DEFC, Dakar.

Senegal, Republic of, 1984, Promotion de l'habitat social en milieu rural et semi-urbain, Projet SEN/82/005/CNUEH-PUD: le financement de l'habitat social en milieu rural et semi-urbain; Rapport intermediaire. URBAPLANAN, Lausanne, January.

Senegal, Republic of, 1984, Direction de l'environnement (DE), Comptes rendus de visites de contrôles d'établissements industriels, Technical Report No. 218, Environmental Board, Ministère de la protection de la nature (MPN).

Senegal, Republic of, 1984, Ministère de la protection de la nature (MPN), 'Face au désert, 1979 - 1984', Rétrospective des différentes campagnes de reboisement, Ministry for the Protection of Nature, Senegal.

Senegal, Republic of, 1985, Conseil National de l'Urbanisme et de l'Environnement consacré à l'Environnement, Environmental Board.

Senegal, Republic of, 1985, Protéger l'environnement pour un Sénégal encore plus beau, National Seminar on an Environmental Protection Policy Under the Joint Auspices of the Environmental Board and the Industrial Sector, Environmental Board, Ministry for the Protection of Nature, Dakar, 18-19 January.

Senegal, Republic of, 1985, 'Communication au séminaire national sur la désertification', Saint-Louis, MPN-MPC, 22-26 April.

Senegal, Republic of, 1985, MPN/MPC, 'Rapport introductif du ministère de l'Hydraulique', Séminaire national sur la désertification, Saint-Louis, 22-26 April.

Senegal, Republic of, 1985, 'Les ressources végétales et la lutte contre la désertification', paper presented at the National Seminar on Desertification, Saint-Louis, 22-26 April.

Senegal, Republic of, 1985, 'Rapport de la Direction de l'Elevage sur le cheptel sénégalais', paper presented at the National Seminar on Desertification, Saint-Louis, 22-26 April.

Senegal, Republic of, 1985, 'Sécheresse et pêche continentale', paper presented at the National Seminar on Desertification, Saint-Louis, 22-26 April.

Senegal, Republic of, 1986, Ministère de l'urbanisme et de l'habitat (MUH), 'Les équipements urbains à Dakar, croissance et gestion urbaines en Afrique', MUH/CRHUA, Draft.

Senegal, Republic of, 1986, Workshop Symposium on the Importance of Appropriate Technologies for Durable Economic Development, Environmental Board, MPN/Ministry of Environmental Affairs, France, Dakar, 12-15 January.

Senegal, Republic of, 1987, DEFC/DCSR, 1981-1987: Rapports introductifs de la conférence préparatoire des campagnes de reboisement.

Senegal, Republic of, 1987, Direction de la conservation du sol et du reboisement (DCSR), Communication sur la participation du P.S. à la campagne nationale de reboisement, Conseil national du Parti socialiste, 23 May.

Singleton, M, 1983, 'Présence et absence de barrages en Afrique', paper presented at the Thiès Colloquium.

Vu Van Thai, undated, Le développement en milieu soudano-sahélien: le cas du bassin du Fleuve Sénégal, *Formulation pour l'environnement*, IDEP/UNEP/SIDA, Dakar.

Wane, O, 1981, 'Contribution à l'étude de l'environnement au Sénégal', Matières résiduaires et disparités urbaines dans une ville africaine, Doctoral dissertation, Paris.

White, G, 1978, L'irrigation des terres arides dans les pays en développement et ses conséquences sur l'environnement, *Notes techniques du MAB, 8*, UNESCO.

5. Population and Development: The Search for Policy Options

Mohamed Mbodj, Babacar Mané, Waly Badiane

In the Third World as a whole, and in Africa in particular, crisis has dominated discussions of population issues since the early 1960s. In the 1980s, however, there was a significant shift. Before then, Africa's population had been seen simply as an element contributing to the slow rate of economic growth, indeed of the development process as a whole. Now, population was itself perceived as the cause (Jemai, 1987:1). The central factor was the high population growth rate. For some time there had been attempts to dissociate demographic analyses from the concept of a crisis but the shift meant, for the moment anyway, that these attempts had failed (Savané, 1988:9-10). Considering the vast scope of the problem, some analysts have gone so far as to see the population problem as a time bomb (MacNamara quoted by Savané, 1988:178). The paradox, in the face of such a serious issue, is that most African states waited 30 years before coming up with a clear and coherent population policy.

Available data indicates that, the salient feature in Senegal's demography was the quickening population growth rate. Of this reality the Senegalese government took only tentative stock. Measures taken in the 1960s, for example, were indirect, and were no more than variations on hoary public health and land development policies. Most lacked imagination. In the late 1970s, awareness of the seriousness of the problem began to rise. Even so, implementational responses remained stuck in the old inefficient rut. Then came a series of recommendations from various international platforms, coupled with the implementation of structural adjustment programmes. The cumulative impact speeded up the process. From the mid-1980s it began to bear fruit in the articulation of a population policy.

The Stakes Behind the Population Craze

Senegal has a high population growth. The population is also overwhelmingly young. The most urgent issue, however, is not a matter of size. It is in part the rate of increase, and in part the way the total population is distributed over the national territory.

Population Size and Growth Rate

Steady population growth has been a fact of life throughout the twentieth century. It was not until the 1960s, however, that the high growth rates typical of recent years began to attract attention. Two factors underlie current high levels of population growth. The first is the high and steady fertility rate. The second is the regular drop in mortality rates. In 1904, the population of Senegal totalled 1,130,000 (Senegal 1904). In 1960, according to the National Population Survey of 1960-61, it was three million. In 1976 it reached five million (Senegal, 1981b), and by 1988 it had climbed to 6.9 million (Senegal, 1988). Even adjusted to compensate for under-estimates of approximately 15% before the 1976 census (Becker and Mbodj, 1987:14), these figures indicate high growth trends. The average annual population growth rate has followed a steady upward curve, from 1.8% between 1904 and 1960 to 2.3% between 1960 and 1970, to 2.5% between 1970 and 1975, and to 2.7% between 1976 and 1988.

For the period from 1976 to 1988, the natural growth rate was estimated at nearly 3%, a figure indicating a doubling of the population every 25 years. Such a situation is clearly out of control. Estimates based on assumptions of constant fertility rates and steadily decreasing mortality rates give a projected growth rate in excess of 3% for the 1990s. Should they prove accurate, Senegal's population could total 11 million by the year 2001 (Bâ, 1985).

Judging by preliminary findings from the 1988 General Population and Housing Census, the Dakar region, with an average annual growth rate pushing 4%, has registered the highest population growth rate since 1976. Next comes Diourbel (3.2%), then Thiès (2.8%). Growth rates in all other regions fall below the national average. The high population growth rate in the Dakar region aggravates an already notable imbalance in the geographical distribution of the population. An analysis of specific categories reveals even higher growth rates. For example, the population of children under 15 years old has been increasing at an annual rate of 3.8%. The active population, for its part, grows at an annual rate of 3.6%, while the urban population growth rate is 3.8%. These differential rates have a direct effect on the make-up of the population.

Internal Composition of the Population

Senegal, a country with an extremely high fertility rate, has a population structure heavily dominated by the young. A break-down according to major age groups shows a large proportion below 20 years old. That proportion has increased steadily since 1960. In 1960, the under-20 proportion was 50%. In 1975 it stood at 53%, and by 1988 it had reached 58%. Census figures for 1988 show a gender differential within this age group, the male population being younger than the female. Specifically, 54% of the male population is under 20 years of age, as compared to 52.6% of the female population. Conversely, the adult percentage has been dropping steadily. In 1960 it was 44%, in 1976 it was down to 40%, and by 1988 it had decreased further to 37%. The proportion of the senior category, 60 years and above, has also dropped, from 6% in 1976 to 5% in 1988.

The youthfulness of the population has certain socio-economic implications discernible in the index of dependent children. This index, arrived at by taking the number of children under 15 years old as a percentage of the adult population aged from 15 to 59, now stands at 97%. The coefficient of economic dependency - the ratio of children under 15 years old plus seniors over 65 years old to the active population aged between 15 and 64 years - also highlights the large size of the dependent population. That figure stands at 104%. In 1976 the first index was 82%, the second 89%. It should also be noted that there are population growth differentials between administrative regions as well as between rural and urban zones.

Spatial Distribution

In 1988, average population density in Senegal was 35 inhabitants per square kilometre. That figure might lead one to suppose that this is a country with a sparse population spread out over a relatively small land area, 196,722 square km in all. But the index of population density has risen vertiginously this century. For in 1976, the figure was only 25 inhabitants per km^2, and back in 1904 it was just 5 inhabitants per km^2. These averages also conceal significant disparities in the changing situation.

At the beginning of the twenth century, the eastern region of Senegal was sparsely populated, and the Cape Verde peninsula was not heavily settled either. Thiès, the Senegal River Valley region, and Louga, were then the most densely populated areas, with 54% of the total population living there (Becker *et al.*, 1987:79). By independence, the pattern had changed entirely. The population was shifting southwards. The most densely populated regions were Sine-Saloum (22% of the total population), the Casamance (18%), and Thiès (14%). But the Cape Verde peninsula also had grown to 11%. The pattern remained unchanged up to the 1976 census. The outstanding development then was the growth of Cape Verde (18%), which by then had practically caught up with Sine-Saloum (20%). Other regions declined.

In 1988, the geographical distribution pattern of the population showed a pronounced imbalance between a densely populated west and a still sparsely populated eastern half. The western and central regions (Dakar, Thiès, Diourbel, Fatick and Kaolack) together contained two-thirds of the population. There were also vast differences in space occupation patterns among politico-administrative regions. The Cape Verde region, renamed Dakar after the territorial reform of 1984, moved into first place with slightly more than 22% of the population. The former Senegal River Valley region, renamed the Saint-Louis region, declined along with Louga, while population percentages in other regions remained stable. The problem is that in terms of space, Dakar region is the tiniest in the country, with a mere 0.28% of the country's total land area. At the other extreme, Tambacounda, geographically the largest with 30.3% of the national area, is the most sparsely populated, with six inhabitants per km^2.

Space occupation levels in Dakar region are therefore extremely high. The ratio rose from 1,711 inhabitants per km^2 in 1976 to 2,710 per km^2 in 1988. Next to Dakar in order of decreasing density come the regions of Thiès (102 inhabitants per km^2 in 1976, 144 in 1988) and Diourbel (97 inhabitants per km^2 in 1976, 142 in 1988). The regions of Kaolack, Ziguinchor and Fatick, registering between 51 and 60 inhabitants per km^2, are above the national average, while Saint-Louis, Louga and Kolda regions, registering between 15 and 29 inhabitants per km^2, have population densities lower than the national average.

One factor exaggerating the imbalance in the spatial distribution of the population is the accelerated pace of urbanization in recent times. In 1904 the urban population made up only 9% of the total population. In 1960 it made up just 22%, but by 1976 it had risen to 34%, and in 1988 it reached 39%. From 1976 to 1988, the urban population grew at an average annual rate of 3.8%. Regional patterns, however, indicate that the urban population growth rate was not highest in Dakar. In Ziguinchor and Thiès, annual growth rates exceeded 4%. Comparisons of municipal areas indicate that the fastest growing are Pikine and Mbour, with annual rates higher than 6%, while Fatick, Kolda and Ziguinchor average 4.5% annually. The comparable rate for the municipality of Dakar is only 2.8%. Growth rates in Matam and Podor are practically zero.

Key Factors in Population Dynamics

Demographic dynamics are complex phenomena basically dependent on the ratio between fertility and the birth rate, on the one hand, and mortality on the other. In Senegal, that ratio has been expanding steadily since independence.

Fertility

According to the 1988 (Senegal, 1989a), Senegal has a gross birth rate of 47 pour mille. According to the 1986 Population Health Survey (EDS), the average woman in Senegal ends up producing 6.6 children in a lifetime. These statistics make Senegal a country with a high fertility rate. There are four main significant factors accounting for this. First procreation begins early. People tend to get married relatively young, and women are likely to enter the procreation cycle almost as soon as they are physically ready. According to the 1978 Family Health Survey (ESF) and the 1986 Population Health Survey (EDS), the median age of Senegalese women entering marriage is between 15.6 and 16.6 years. The age at first birth is relatively low, averaging 18.3 years in 1978 and 19.7 years in 1986. A total of 35% of women have their first child before reaching the age of 18 (Senegal, 1988). Second, the likelihood of pregnancy is high. The focus on marriage is particularly intense, since wedlock is an essential aspect of social life in Senegal. In the 1986 survey, 76.2% of women between the ages of 15 and 49 years were married. After divorce or widowhood, second marriages are swift and frequent. The overwhelming majority of Senegalese women spend the fertile period of their lives as wives. In that situation they are constantly open to the possibility of pregnancy. Third, contraception is not widespread. According to the 1986 Population Health Survey, the percentage of women making regular use of modern contraceptive methods is still low, involving only 2.4% of married women. The percentage using the entire range of methods is 11.3%. Given such a situation, it is highly probable, especially among young mothers, that within five years of a first birth, a second will follow. In 1977, that was the situation of 77% of the women. Fourth, is fertility preferences. According to the 1986 survey, the average number of children women between the ages of 15 and 49 considered ideal was 6.8. Education was a factor here too. The ideal number of children for women who had never been to French-language schools was 7.4; among women with a primary school education the number fell to 5.6; women with a secondary education or higher wanted an average of 4.5 children.

However, a comparison of the number of offspring produced by women aged between 40-49 years (7.3), in 1978 with a current fertility statistic (the Overall Fertility Index) based on the 1986 Population Health Survey for the period 1983-86 (6.6) reveals a modest downward trend in fertility. Thus, from 1978 to 1986, the circumstantial index of fertility fell from 7.1 to 6.6 children per woman. Over the same period, overall fertility dropped by 9%. The decrease was traceable mainly to the younger generations, especially those under 30 years of age. The tendency of education to push fertility rates downwards was particularly clear. In 1986, the Overall Fertility Index was 5.9, while the average number of children produced by women between 40 and 49 years who had a secondary school education was 3.8. Urbanization was a further factor: urban women averaged 5.4 children as compared to 7.1 children for rural women.

Mortality

Though mortality rates have dropped since independence, they are still quite high among the population at large. The gross mortality rate dropped from 26.6 per mille in 1960 to 19.3 per mille in 1978, and to 17 pour mille in 1989 (Antoine et al., 1987:5; UNICEF, 1990:110). During this period, life expectancy figures, a better index of overall mortality, rose from 37 to 48 years (UNICEF, 1990:110). These statistics mean that Senegal is among the countries with the highest mortality rates. Comparable average life expectancy figures for various parts of the world are as follows: developed countries: 73; Latin America: 64; Asia: 54; Africa:50 (Vallin, 1986:48).

The figures given above are gross statistics and averages. As such, they conceal substantial variations from group to group. For instance, mortality rates are generally higher among men than among women, except for women of child-bearing age. More remarkably, mortality rates among children aged from 0 to 5 years are still extremely high. One child in five dies before the age of five (Senegal, 1986). Several socio-economic, cultural, sanitation and other factors account for this high rate of mortality. There are a number of variables, however, which impinge more directly on infant mortality rates. These include the age of the mother and the spacing of births. For example, children born to women at either end of their reproductive lives - start and finish - suffer higher mortality rates than children born in the middle period. Similarly, babies born less than two years after siblings are twice as likely to die within one year than those born at least four years later (EDS 1986).

The main causes of death and sickness among children 5 years old and younger are malaria (39%), diarrhoea (23.8%), respiratory ailments (23%), measles (10.9%), tetanus (5.4% and meningitis (3.5%) (Basse et al., 1990). The evidence suggests that malnutrition is a serious problem in the rural areas. It is undoubtedly a major cause of high infant mortality rates.

Much less is known about the main causes of mortality among adults. However, the following factors are prominent: cholera, tuberculosis, yellow fever and cancer. Complications related to pregnancy and childbirth also constitute a major factor. The impact on women is definite. Maternal mortality rates from 1980 to 1988 were evaluated at 6 per 1,000. That is high, especially when correlated with comparable rates in the developed countries, i.e., between 0.05 and 0.2 per mille (UNICEF, 1990:114-115). Meanwhile, a much more devastating outbreak of pandemic proportions, Aids, hovers just around the corner. At the moment, its incidence is still low. As of 1 September 1989, the officially declared rate of infection was three inhabitants per 100,000. But population patterns in this country, characterized by rapid rates of increase, high mobility and an urban explosion, could contribute to the rapid spread of the disease (Amat-Roze, 1989:344-347).

As was the case with life expectancy figures, national mortality statistics also conceal regional disparities. Rural mortality rates, for instance, are almost twice as high as urban mortality rates. Mortality rates among children five years old and younger average 135 per mille in the urban areas, as compared to 250 per mille in the rural areas (Senegal, 1986). Rural mortality rates are higher partly because health facilities are more numerous in the urban areas. Furthermore, urban income levels are higher. The urban population is therefore in a position to make more frequent use of health facilities and to pay closer attention to hygienic norms. That is probably why mortality rates among children and youths are lower in Dakar than elsewhere in the country. For Dakar contains a third of all hospitals in Senegal, and has one medical doctor per 7,855 inhabitants. The figure for the inland town of Louga, for instance, is one medical doctor per 162,000 inhabitants. Difficulties related to the drought and the agricultural off-season are also more acute in rural than in urban areas - a further cause of the difference between rural and urban mortality rates.

Migratory Patterns

One major obstacle hampering the conduct of studies on migration is the dearth of data. Information from the General Population and Housing Survey of 1988, for instance, is to this day not fully available. It is clear, even in the absence of all the data, that migratory movements, just as much as fertility and mortality patterns, play a decisive role in population dynamics. The impact of such movements on population levels and spatial distribution patterns varies from situation to situation.

The number of people involved in internal migratory shifts is enormous. According to the 1979-80 Migration and Labour Survey, in 1980 alone, 731,000 Senegalese, or 18% of the country's total population, moved from one region to another. This is a high index, and it has been typical since 1960.

Table 1: Numbers of Persons Involved in Internal Migratory Movements

Year	1960	1971	1976
Total	329,520	502,982	655,397
Percentage of total resident population	10	13	13

Sources: Senegal, 1960; Senegal, 1971; Senegal, 1981b.

An examination of the inter-regional migratory balance (the difference between numbers of outgoing and incoming migrants in various administrative regions) reveals a number of disparities (see Table 2). Up until 1976, the regions of Dakar, Sine Saloum and Tambacounda (from 1971) were the only regions with positive immigratory balances. Dakar was the region with the greatest drawing power, while Diourbel, Saint-Louis and Louga experienced the highest migratory outflows.

Table 2: Regional Migratory Balances, 1960-1976

Region	1960	1971	1976
Dakar	+ 112,340	+ 213,595	+ 262,320
Casamance, Kolda & Ziguinchor	9,940	24,164	37,323
Diourbel	90,540	96,932	42,185
Saint-Louis	46,040	82,537	83,495
Louga	-	-	- 80,932
Tambacounda	-06,960	+ 7,139	+ 3,289
Sine-Saloum (Fatick & Kaolack)	+ 77,500	+ 3,556	+ 1,513
Thiès	-36,360	- 20,637	- 23,187

Sources: National Population Survey (EDN), (Senegal, 1960) and (Senegal, 1971); (Senegal, 1981b).

Along with large-scale migratory movements, the tempo of urbanization has accelerated. The prime source of urban immigrants is the massive rural exodus provoked by the unbalanced distribution of socio-economic and cultural facilities in the urban and rural areas, to the detriment of the latter. In the hope of finding better living conditions in the urban areas, young people from the rural areas flee their home situation and flood into the towns. Dakar receives the largest inflow, especially in the municipalities of Dakar, Pikine, Guédiawaye and Rufisque, which now total more than one and a half million inhabitants (Senegal, 1989a). It is estimated that over 20,000 migrants move into the region in years of normal climatic conditions. In poor years the total might logically increase (Le Brun, 1973:7).

So far, available data on international migrations do not provide an adequate basis for a detailed study. The situation is further complicated by the fact that migrants often have a precarious legal status. Incoming migrants may therefore find it advisable to keep a low profile within the Senegalese population. Some do not bother to declare their destination. Enough is known, however, to enable us to assert that Senegal is a country where both incoming and outgoing migratory currents are strong. The 1976 census listed 118,782 foreigners, equivalent to 2.3% of the total population, as officially resident in Senegal. The 1988 General Population and Housing Census showed that their numbers had stagnated in absolute terms (122,340). In relative terms, however, the immigrant population had declined to just 1.8% of the total population. A major cause of the change was the series of recent political changes in the neighbouring countries of Guinea Bissau and Guinea Conakry. Moreover, many second-generation immigrants were integrated into the national population.

The exact number of Senegalese citizens abroad is unknown. For instance, only about 30,000 Senegalese migrants are registered at the Senegalese Consulate in Paris, and yet some estimates place the actual number of Senegalese migrants in France at 180,000 (Becker and Mbodj, 1987:11-12). The majority of Senegalese migrants are job-seekers. Their favourite destinations are France, the Ivory Coast, Gabon, Congo, Zaire, Zambia, Cameroon, Saudi Arabia and the United States.

Economic, Social and Ecological Effects

The combined effects of rapid population growth and massive urbanization feeding on the rural exodus are numerous. Population growth tends more or less to obscure changes in economic performance while invariably straining the economy. Total gross domestic product rose from F CFA406 billion in 1970 to 617 billion in 1989 (at constant prices). That meant an annual growth rate of 2.6%. Nevertheless, over the same period, per capita GDP slid downwards on account of population growth. The resulting negative growth rate was 0.5%. Final household consumption totals rose from F CFA 293.5 billion in 1970 to F CFA 453.5 billion in 1989, indicating an annual rate of increase of 2.7%. On the other hand, per capita consumption levels fell at an annual rate of 0.4%.

Given the country's high rates of population growth and urbanization, the shortage of job opportunities has led to unemployment and under-employment. According to estimates derived from the RAPID II model (Rapid Awareness of Population Impacts on Development), the official unemployment rate in Senegal rose from 15% in 1976 to 18% in 1986, and to 20% in 1988. Because the population is predominantly young, there has been a downward trend in the ratio of the active population to the total population. The percentage dropped from 44% in 1972 to 41% in 1986 (Senegal/MPC, 1989:10). By 1988 the drop had become even steeper: 34% (Senegal, 1989a:20). The negative trend illustrated by these figures gives a good indication of the deepening economic crisis that has lasted over the past 20 years.

The increase in the school-going population has overloaded educational facilities, dragging educational standards down (see the article by Sylla in this volume). Because of the rapid rate of increase of the school-age population, Senegal is still far behind in the achievement of national educational objectives. Gross school attendance rates at the elementary (55.2%), middle (19.9%) and secondary (8.2%) levels for the year 1988/89 still fell short of official targets. Girls still have lower school attendance rates, up from 40% in 1979 to 40.6% in 1988 (Sénégal/MPC 1989: 88). The gap is likely to continue over the long term. It might even widen, since average rates of increase for the in-school population, which rose from 6% between 1961 and 1978 to 6.7% between 1978 and 1985, fell back to a mere 3.9% between 1985 and 1988 (Sénégal/MPC 1989: 87).

Turning to health facilities, we find that the number of hospitals per 10,000 inhabitants fell from 9.7 in 1970 to 7.2 in 1988. Figures for the number of inhabitants per available hospital bed are even more instructive. In 1960 the ratio was 1 bed to 1,294 inhabitants; by 1988 it had dropped to 1 bed per 2,109 inhabitants (Senegal/MPC 1989: 85). The shortage of health facilities affects all social strata. For instance, even though Dakar region is often perceived as a well-off area, the ratio of available maternity hospital beds to women there, 1 to 300 in 1960; had dropped to 1 to 550 by 1982 (Diouf, 1989:55). The official programme promises health care for all Senegalese by the year 2000. The way matters stand now, the attainment of such an objective is unlikely.

Housing is a serious problem, most acute in Dakar region, where rapid population growth and the rural exodus have aggravated an already serious shortage. A great deal of effort has gone into attempts to solve the problem, but the supply still falls short of the ever-increasing demand. From 1960 to 1973, for instance, 15,000 new housing units were constructed. Compared to the demand, that was a drop in the ocean. From 1973 to 1980 there was a lull in construction pending the creation of the Housing Bank of Senegal (BHS). That turned a bad situation into a disaster. Construction picked up again in 1980, but business in the housing sector has yet to make up the accumulated shortfall (Sénégal/MPC 1989: 95-96). In particular, it is hard for planned housing programmes to keep up with exploding demand. At the same time, private individual construction often has a maverick character, the developers' overriding concern being to cram as many people into each building as possible. In their attempts to cope with tremendously high demand for hous:ng, certain big city neighbourhoods such as Dakar's Médina are increasingly taking on the look of slums (Tall-Thiam, 1989:43-51).

Rapid population growth has been aggravating the imbalance between population levels and available natural resources. The impact on the environment is the most visible aspect (see Ndiaye's chapter in this volume). For example, from 1973 to 1983, the total forested land area decreased by 6.4%. Charcoal and firewood consumption increased substantially, from 4.250.000 m^3 in 1976 to 6.760.000 m^3 in 1986 (Senegal, 1988b:9). It is in the countryside, however, that the most serious immediate impact was registered.

In the rural areas, population growth has pushed people into over-exploiting land, causing premature soil exhaustion. The drought has multiplied the effect, causing a reduction in the total cultivable area, and indeed of the land area actually cultivated. Thus, the total land area under cultivation rose from 2,021,000 hectares in 1960 to 2,265,000 in 1971, then to 2,411,000 in 1981; but it declined thereafter to 2,137,000 hectares in 1989 (Sénégal/MPC 1977: 90; Kelly and Delgado 1991: 101). The drop was particularly noticeable in the 1980s. The average cultivated land area decreased from 2,255,000 ha during the 1981-85 period to 2,137,000 ha during the 1986-89 period (Kelly and Delgado 1991:101). The situation could result in a shortage of cultivable land in the most populous western areas.

Food production has also gone down. Cereals suffered the steepest decline, due mainly to the population upswing. The per capita index of cultivable land has not kept pace with population growth. Between 1970 and 1982, the area of arable land per inhabitant dropped from 1 hectare to 0.86ha In the time between the First and Sixth Plans, the cultivated area per inhabitant dropped from 0.58ha to 0.35ha. Over the same period, the area planted with food crops per inhabitant decreased from 0.30ha to 0.19ha The even more significant ratio of the average land area actually cultivated by a single person dropped from 1.4ha in 1981 to 0.8ha in 1989 (Kelly and Delgado, 1991:112).

The combination of rapid population growth in the rural areas, people entering the work force early and quitting late in life, has intensified pressure on land resources. This is especially so since farming techniques have remained essentially unchanged. Thus, while the population increased by 71% from the First to the Sixth Plan period, cereal production increased only 28%. The result was a 26% drop in per capita cereal production, assuming we take the First Plan period (1960-64) as the base. If this situation does not change over the long term, as in all probability it will not, there will be no chance of achieving the national objective of self-sufficiency in food.

Population Policy: Ends and Means

In April 1988, the Government of Senegal adopted a Population Policy Declaration (DPP). The move indicated a growing awareness of the importance of population issues in the development process. It also marked a U-turn from the Senegalese position in 1974, when the country's delegate to the Bucharest Conference asserted that "Africa must opt for development today. The contraceptive pill can come tomorrow, if at all" (quoted in Vallin, 1989:113). The Senegalese itinerary was no different from that of other African countries (Savané, 1988:9-17). All Africa may have been shocked in 1965 when President Johnson declared that it was better to invest five dollars in population control programmes than a hundred dollars in economic development (Lieberson, 1986:102). But by 1987, 31 out of 49 African countries thought it was time to lower their population growth rates (Ekanem, 1988:8.3.18). Still, the Senegalese situation had certain specific features. It also changed at its own pace. The change in viewpoint resulted mainly from two major events. The first was the 1976 General Population Census. The second was even weightier: the debate that began in the early 1980s on the implementational impact of structural adjustment policies. In the transitional decade during which issues related to these key events were thrashed out, the seeds of change took root.

It is not really feasible in this chapter to conduct a detailed assessment of the government's population policy from 1960 to 1988. But it is possible to state the inescapable conclusion from such a detailed evaluation: government policy was piecemeal in conception, incoherent in execution. In the 1960s and 1970s, the dominant attitude was blithely optimistic. Faith in the power of human determination seemed boundless. Programmes were often begun without prior in-depth planning, and before adequate institutional structures had been established. The general run of activities included the drafting of territorial development and public health policies incorporating demographic data. The following programmes were established: a maternal and child care programme; a family health and population programme; a family welfare programme; and a series of population unit programmes.

Because serious questions arose concerning the efficiency of some of these programmes, legislative measures were tagged on. One such measure was the adoption of the Family Code in 1973. Another was the cancellation of the 1920 Act prohibiting contraceptive advertising, which had until then blocked the implementation of family planning programmes.

Since independence, then, the government had taken a series of measures falling, roughly speaking, within the framework of a tentative population policy. In the 1970s, however, there was a change in style. In the 1960s, the socialistic official rhetoric had repeatedly called for the mobilization of citizens. In the 1970s, the new buzz-word was management. In line with the new style, the population was now referred to as human resources. The government's technocratic approach spawned a variety of sectorial policies designed to address a multiplicity of problems arising from the day-to-day unfolding of the development process. We cannot cover all these sectorial policies here. What we can do is to highlight typical scenarios in the sectors of education, health and employment.

The educational process has been caught between the anvil of high population growth rates among the young and the hammer of dwindling financial resources. The bind has sometimes resulted in acute crises (see the chapter by Sylla in this volume). Different strategies emerged as suggestions for coping, beyond individual crises, with the situation in general. They included more rational use of teaching staff and educational infrastructure, cheaper but better adapted equipment, a lowering of dropout rates, and a search for more varied sources of financial support beyond the government budget, mainly through contributions from direct beneficiaries and greater support from non-governmental organizations. For example, the 1988 Human Resource Development Project (PDRH) included a vocational training and education component under which it was planned to recruit nearly 710 teachers and to build 320 elementary school classrooms on the average per year (for more information see *Le Soleil*, 24 September 1991).

The strategy for the middle and secondary school cycles was based on the rehabilitation of existing educational premises and the passage of legislation to ensure efficient management of the school population in order to achieve high educational standards (see Sylla in this volume). The general aim in higher education was to boost development dynamics. In addition, both the Women's Welfare component of Phase I of the PDRH programme and the Priority Action and Investment Programme on Population (PAIP-1) included substantial literacy campaigns targeted at specific groups within the context of Human Resource development.

In the field of health, priority guidelines focused on the campaign against maternal and infantile mortality. Thus, in keeping with the Alma Ata (USSR) Declaration of 1978, Senegal was committed to the implementation of a basic health care system emphasizing mainly health education, the promotion of good nutritional habits, mother and child care, and the implementation of a family planning programme as well as an extensive vaccination programme. In the same vein, and with a view to improving the country's health standards, Senegal undertook a series of reforms outlined in the 1989 Declaration of National Health Policy. The main points were the following: greater participation of the population, the private sector and non-governmental organizations; the rationalization of the production, purchase, distribution and use of medicines, greater decentralization; the boosting of the capacity of support structures at central and regional levels; improved management of human, material and financial resources, and the structural overhaul of the public health training system. Incidentally, the Human Resource Development Project includes a Health component which, when implemented, should help to achieve objectives set out in the DPP.

In the field of employment, the Senegalese Government, in concert with donor agencies (bilateral and multilateral aid agencies), established the following policy for the creation and support of enterprises:
a) The provision of credit for the creation and support of enterprises;
b) Training and productivity-boosting programmes for entrepreneurs; and

c) Training and technical aid programmes backed up with credit opportunities.

In practice, the entire range of policies ended up at best producing results just a shade more comprehensive than the old-style territorial development programmes. The big drawback of the approach was that it broke up inextricably interlinked problems into several units, frustrating their solution. No part of it was designed to take comprehensive charge of all population problems. Population was acknowledged as important, but it was treated as a simple datum, at best a variable among others. It was not until more than 20 years after independence, at a time when the country had reached a dead end on all fronts, that a serious approach taking all demographic issues into consideration was adopted.

An Integrated Approach to Population Issues: 1976-88

Data from the first census of 1976 provided an instructive turning point. The Director of the Statistics Board, the parent body of the National Census Bureau, was of the opinion that the new data invalidated initial estimates underlying the Fifth Plan, for the period 1977-81 (Thiongane 1987:17). For instance, those estimates had projected annual population growth rates of 2.2% to 2.5%. These were ridiculously low compared to the actual rates registered, ranging from 2.7% to 2.8%. The introduction to the Sixth Plan document therefore sounded the alarm, pointing out that population growth rates had been grossly under-estimated since 1960. The population problem, the document added, has now taken on a more urgent aspect (Senegal/MPC 1977:17). The government thus acknowledged two major points: first, there was a real population problem, and it was not a simple matter of territorial distribution or development. Second, the conundrum of population growth rate had to be solved.

The administrative style of that period habitually responded to all unforeseen problems by creating new, specialized structures and mandating them to come up with solutions. Naturally, then, in 1979, a National Population Commission was established, along with a Human Resources Board that later became a government department. These were significant steps forward. Unfortunately, they were not part of a coherent policy with clearly defined objectives. They were rather more like knee-jerk reactions to an emergency. It was not until the adoption of the Population Policy Declaration of April 1988 that a programme framework for population-related activities and measures was defined.

The government then deployed, for implementational purposes, an array of ideological, scientific and politico-economic instruments. These institutional facilities were an integral part of the context, helping to create and maintain it in an interactive process. They were set up at different times, but in the end they all worked together to create a determinant synergy in the late 1980s.

On the ideological level two major factors were worth highlighting. The first was the burning issue of women's rights, especially the right of women to control reproduction. The second was the opportunity provided by the Alma Ata Conference and its corollary, the policy of universal primary health care. To begin with, in the wake of International Women's Year and the Mexico Conference 1984, there was a very clear blending of a number of issues: women's health, women's right to control their bodies and reproductive capacities; contraception; and even birth control. The Alma Ata Conference of 1978 confirmed the trend. It had a tremendous impact on the Senegalese scene, resulting in the adoption of the priority objective of providing primary health care for all human beings on earth by the year 2000. Like other African governments, the Government of Senegal was committed to the objective. However, it understood easily enough that it would be hard to attain as long as the population doubled every quarter of a century. Since it could not realistically hope to generate the necessary resources, it was logical for the government to begin flirting with the idea of limiting population growth. That would mean finding ways to justify such a birth control policy and to create a national consensus around the issue. In effect, it would not be hard to mobilize the majority of the population around the idea of universal health care and women's rights. The innovation would be the additional linkage of population growth with environmental problems, a regular motif propagated by the World Watch Institute through its influential yearbook *The State of the World*.

Scientific and intellectual legitimation was provided by an increasingly copious stream of literature establishing a new field of study known as Population and Development (Gavreau et al., 1986:1-10; Gregory and Piché, 1986:11-46). In short order, the new tandem became the dominant focus of publications and research activities, with generous support from United Nations (UNFPA) and government agencies (USAID) as well as private foundations (mainly the Ford and Rockefeller Foundation). Private foundations are particularly active in the field. Quite often, their names encapsulate full-scale programmes: World Watch Institute, Zero Population Growth; Population Crisis Council, and so forth.

The political and intellectual culture thus established rides, consciously or not, on a neo-Malthusian approach. It has turned many African researchers, technicians and officials involved with population issues into transmission belts, mouthpieces and kept experimenters working for an intellectual culture sounding one exclusive note. Jemai (1987:18-22) provides an accurate description of this process typified by formulae that impose the solution in the statement of the problem. Some of the key concepts used are quite unscientific: overpopulation, explosion, challenge, natural law, brake, obstacle etc. They come with programmed responses: birth control, childbirth spacing, family planning, etc. As a finishing touch, impressive statistical paraphernalia are brought in. One result of this situation is that during the 1970s, the bulk of population research in Senegal focused on issues of fertility and migration. Other issues such as mortality and the family were pushed aside.

Political legitimation took longer to work out. Oddly enough, the circumstantial context and foreign intervention proved decisive factors. The United Nations played a leading role, setting up the United Nations Fund for Population Activities in 1973. The Fund's terms of reference covered population and family planning. It was particularly active in the organization of various World Population Conferences. The Bucharest Conference (1974) may have been considered a victory for supporters of high birth rates. But at the Mexico Conference (1984) the majority of Third World countries adopted population policies and action programmes. China and Algeria, formerly defiant champions of the opposition to negative linkages between population and development, executed an about-face symbolizing a new trend (Basse *et al.*, 1990: 5). From the 1980s on, then, many of the requisites of political legitimation were present. In 1982, Senegal agreed to trial runs for a model designed by the Futures Group. Its objectives were clearly outlined in its acronym, RAPID (Rapid Awareness of Population Impacts on Development). The project, put together by a University of Michigan team, was explicitly designed to persuade the government that it was necessary to adopt measures to curb high population growth (Ekanem, 1988:831-837).

That was just the beginning. It was only in the mid-1980s that a real consciousness of the need for a comprehensive policy emerged in response to demand from both the government and public opinion. There was a change, for instance, in structural adjustment programmes which had come into force in the 1980s: now they incorporated population issues. Within the framework of measures to deal with the social aspect of adjustment, Senegal and the World Bank/IMF tandem worked out an initial declaration stating an explicit population policy in 1988.

During the mid-1980s there was a debate about accusations that structural adjustment policies disregarded the interests of the disadvantaged majority, especially by cutting budgetary allocations for education and health. One defensive argument advanced by advocates of adjustment was that without adjustment, the situation would have been worse for all concerned. Given such a context, a population policy was considered just as crucial as economic reform (World Bank 1986). The UNFPA/ILO expert in charge of drafting a population policy in Mali admitted that it was a response to the social aspect of structural adjustment (*Pop Sahel*, 1990:32). From then on, it was clear that Structural Adjustment Programme 3, then being negotiated, was going to incorporate population issues. Such an outcome was all the more likely because in 1984, the Economic Commission for Africa, restating conclusions reached by the African Population Conference held in Arusha in January 1984, recommended that population be accorded central importance in development policy design (Sai, 1988:321-24). The Arusha Conference, incidentally, had acknowledged that at the present time, demographic problems are hampering the development of the African region (Basse *et al.*, 1990). The OAU went even farther, recommending the design and adoption of an appropriate population policy (Basse *et al.*, 1990:22).

By the late 1980s, then, all necessary elements for a break with past practices were in place. In April 1987, the Human Resources Board in the Ministry of Planning brought together a multidisciplinary group of academics, top civil servants and experts from various areas. Their assignment: to draft a series of sectorial studies on population covering data, situation and structure, fertility, mortality and the family. After a year of work in separate committees, a summary of all sectorial reports was examined by the National Population Commission. The document then went to the Inter-Ministerial Council of April 1988. That body adopted it, making it the Population Policy Declaration of 1988.

The Population Policy Declaration (DPP)

In a passage on typology, Savané (1988:153) presents three distinct types of population policy; policies designed to limit population growth; policies designed to encourage population growth; and policies emphasizing spatial distribution.

Savané places Senegal in the first category. The classification is justified, for the preamble to the Population Policy Declaration stresses the need for Senegal to solve its population problems which still constitute serious obstacles to its development (1988:2) by adopting a definite and determined policy. The DPP then shifts to a series of factual observations, ending with a statement of general policy guidelines for Senegal:

In both national and international circles, a full-scale debate is now going on about correlations between population growth and economic growth. All agree, however, that the population's living standards cannot be improved unless the economy generates additional resources at a rate faster than the rate of population growth.... In the Senegalese situation, population growth has wiped out economic achievements (Sénégal, 1986:5).

The Population Policy Declaration follows orthodox principles based on respect for individual rights and the preservation of the family. Its objectives fall into two categories. In general, they aim at improving living standards, reducing ill health, mortality and fertility rates along with growth rates, evening out regional imbalances of all types in order to halt the rural exodus, and lastly, improving the quality of scientific knowledge. In strictly demographic terms, what is involved is simply the advocacy of orientations derived from the RAPID studies, the reason being that in the absence of reliable scientific data, it would be premature to fix quantified demographic objectives (Sénégal, 1988b: 11).

The achievement of these aims depends on a strategy designed to meet a number of objectives including the following: improved health care for mothers and children, lower fertility, voluntary birth spacing, educational and information campaigns for women and especially for youth, preservation of the family, the slowdown and if possible the reversal of migratory movements, a more intensive territorial development policy, reduction of unemployment and under-employment, support for population studies and research, and lastly the formulation of appropriate legislative and statutory regulations. To implement this package, it was necessary to set up an institutional framework along with programme implementation mechanisms. Population policy was given an institutional framework in the form of a decision-making body, the Inter-Ministerial Council on Population; a consultative structure called the National Population Commission; plus a Technical Committee for Supervision and Assessment in charge of planning, coordination, supervision and evaluation. In addition, there were implementational structures, agencies detailed to conduct studies and research, and other support facilities.

The operational instrument for the implementation of population policy was the first Action and Priority Investment Programme for Population Issues (PAIP). This was a huge programme with a total budget of F CFA 19 billion. It comprised 17 components. External donors were to provide practically all necessary funding. Money, however, was not the biggest obstacle.

Implementational Problems Facing Population Policy

With the definition of a comprehensive forward policy, an important first step had been taken. But policy definition is one thing; implementation is quite another. Past analytical studies had often clarified solutions and strategies. Just as often, they had been inadequate in their practical approaches. For example, their understanding of the types of difficulties likely to be encountered, as well as of their intractability, was faulty. The trouble was due to a degree of confusion between explanatory and implementational approaches. The accent on programmatic action had, in particular, divorced population problems from their ecological, political and social contexts. This had resulted, in a sense, in a loss of historical perspective. There was also the problem of a technocratic bias. Jemai 1987:21 discusses it in terms of an inherently static approach... which transforms tools into concepts.

It was an approach that favoured one-sided viewpoints and gave overwhelming weight to external factors. One typical result was that throughout the preparatory work leading to the Population Policy Declaration, no expert or commission ever paid systematic attention to potential problems. These problems are of two basic types, and between them they create difficult interfaces that need to be highlighted. The first set of problems derives from socio-cultural constraints. The second set has to do with political and financial constraints.

Socio-Cultural Constraints

In the preliminary remarks, the Population Policy Declaration merely presents a perfunctory summary of socio-cultural factors. The issue, though, is not a simple matter of acknowledging the existence of this or that problem. The point is to go beyond simple observations, to grapple, in practical terms, with actual obstacles, and to overcome them. There is no room here for an exhaustive listing of the obstacles referred to. But we can indeed put a precise finger on the main constraints which, in our opinion, now weigh down heavily on Senegal's stated population policy, and will continue to do so for a long time yet.

Of these the first, possibly the most important, and probably the least likely to be completely overturned in the near future, is the perdurance of social attitudes generally favourable to high procreation rates. These attitudes are nurtured by Islam, Christianity and the traditional religions.

Islam is the declared religion of over 90% of the Senegalese population. Islam attracts a great deal of attention on account of its acceptance of polygamy. Beyond that, it also makes marriage a supremely desirable consummation. It condemns calculated approaches to population, preferring to exalt trust in the will of Allah, who supposedly fixes in advance the number of children allotted each couple (Bâ, 1989:60-61). Given such circumstances, procreation is substantially outside the control of individual believers.

There is a nuance, though. For Islam, unlike the Roman Catholic religion which has a Pope appointed to express the will of God, recognizes no central authority or spokesperson. Islam therefore exercises no pressure for or against population policy. It is this inertia which presents a danger. For it can be exploited by any religious leader or group wishing to take advantage of difficult circumstances or to promote various ambitions. And the active intervention of a secular state is a sure-fire way to provoke such a reaction in Senegal, a country divided between religious confraternities and rival groupings. Theologians at Al Azar University have issued a conciliatory *fatwa* on the issue, quoted by Senegal's Director of Human Resources, a woman:

> *For countries whose resources are incompatible with their population density and which are obliged to import most of their subsistence requirements, birth control is desirable, indeed required* (Sène, 1989:22).

But even that edict would not suffice to prevent problems over the issue. For the Senegalese strain of Islam is, on the whole, impervious to this kind of advocacy coming from foreign sources. The reason is that none of the really important religious structures transmit such news, the principal confraternities least of all.

A second constraint is the high level of illiteracy, most pronounced among women. It is generally acknowledged that women educated in the French-language school system get married later, are less likely to contract polygamous marriages, and use modern contraceptive methods a great deal more (Sarr, 1988:15). Uneducated women constitute the prime target of family planning programmes. The expectation is that uneducated women will compare their living standards with those of their educated sisters and draw the right conclusions. But that approach faces two drawbacks. First, educated women are urbanized, while the majority of Senegalese women live in the rural areas. Second, according to the General Census on Population and Housing, the school-going rate for girls between the ages of 7 and 12 is 36%, compared to 51% for boys. But the rate of absolute illiteracy among women over 15 years old is over 82% (Senegal, 1989a:17). In other words, the impact of women's education on population policy is likely to remain restricted to social strata which already accept planned parenthood.

There is a third and final constraint: the failure to take stock of the family unit as the group venue for decisions on reproduction. In the first place, the habitual emphasis on women's responsibilities could backfire if women's decisions are perceived as assaults on the family. For at the moment, the role of men within the family unit is often overlooked. This creates opportunities for a strategy based on distrust and confrontation, thus postponing the kind of consensus needed for the implementation of any population policy. The biggest thorn, however, is the ultimate population policy objective: significant reductions in family size. This runs counter to past, present and future realities at the centre of economic and social life in Senegal. Survival strategies are rooted in large families. The current economic crisis has reinforced that role. The point is that here the perception of the family simply as a reproductive unit is incomplete. It is also a productive unit, and the social protagonists involved still see that role as crucial (Gregory and Piché, 1986:27-38).

Clearly, these constraints are serious enough to compromise the officially stated policy. They might even frustrate it altogether. The most vulnerable aspect of the policy is the implementation of fertility-related measures, mainly within the framework of operational family planning programmes. The Population Policy Declaration, addressing the issue, argues the need for a campaign based on information, education and communication and geared to the socio-cultural context, with a view to overcoming these constraints. The point is well taken. A word of warning, though. It is perfectly reasonable to persuade people to change their behaviour patterns. But asking them to jettison their survival strategies is a much tougher proposition.

Politico-Financial Constraints

To cope with a series of situations we might define as financially and politically straitening, the Population Policy Declaration advocates various measures. One such situation is the current tax schedule, coupled with the social system, which encourages large families, implying attitudes favouring high birth rates. The system is biased in favour of wage earners with numerous offspring.... It is necessary to correct this attitude and to make provision, if need be, for disincentive measures (Senegal, 1988b:18).

The knot to be unravelled here is the conflict between social and fiscal legislation, on the one hand, and population policy objectives, on the other. Pure logic would dictate legislation to overturn the present system. But the country is in a situation of permanent crisis; the ruling party is allied to the largest trade union organization in the country, and lastly, the challenge to the entire system provoked by any such move would be tremendous. For all these reasons, such a logical approach is for now merely academic.

Already, the reception given to the New Agricultural Policy and the New Industrial Policy has been so unenthusiastic that it is difficult to envisage anything now beyond maintenance of the status quo. In a political context of democratic competition for power, any party that advocates logical reforms of this sort is certain to lose the support of an electorate determined to defend benefits deemed to have been acquired through fierce struggle against the colonial regime. As socialist regimes go, the Senegalese government might be rather watered-down, but even so, if it allowed itself to seem less interested in the welfare of the toiling masses, it would be signing its death warrant. Besides, it is only an assumption that there is a correlation between the tax schedule and family size. Neither in this country nor anywhere else has it been conclusively proved.

Needless to say, to implement population policies, a lot of funding has to be mobilized. The 1988 Population Policy Declaration gives no statistical data, but in the present context of latent economic crisis and strict controls on public spending, it is hard to imagine how Senegal can raise the resources needed for the achievement of its objectives. So external funding has to be the key.

The first PAIP called for some F CFA 19 billion. Practically the entire amount came from foreign partners. The same agencies financed the drafting of the Population Policy Declaration, along with various population surveys and studies. In effect, foreign donors have invariably wielded real influence. Sometimes their impact has been decisive. At times it has been indispensable. They allocate funds to such sectors as information/education/communication; maternal and infant health care; family planning; population dynamics, women's advancement; programmes for youth and emigrants; and support facilities for the co-ordination, monitoring and evaluation of population policy.

By contrast, there are so far no support arrangements for aspects focused specifically on employment, the environment, statutory regulations, etc., even though they are vitally important. All in all, it is possible that the lack of financial independence could compromise the Senegalese government's own desired population policy options. In the long-run, this type of financing results, under the best of circumstances, in lop-sided programmes. In the worst case they might lead to incoherent implementation. How rational is it, after all, to divorce sanitation from the environment, or to try and collect reliable statistical data without a continuous programme of activities designed to impact on various indices drawn from these data? Often, foreign funding installs a degree of dependence on foreign sources into the public consciousness. The national will abdicates, and in the end national interests are disregarded. Seen in the light of hostile reactions to structural adjustment policies imposed by the IMF and the World Bank, there is the danger of population policy coming to be seen as part and parcel of the adjustment package. And as everyone knows, adjustment has left a sour taste in the public mouth, to put it mildly.

Conclusion

Our analysis clarifies a number of principal foci around which population policy in Senegal has been organized since independence. In particular, the analysis of changing patterns from 1960 to the Population Policy Declaration of 1988 provides a basis for the identification of current policy.

Population policy developments in Senegal provide an almost perfect illustration of the process described by Cordell and Piché (1990:299-300). Initially, the argument was that small families would emerge and spread as a result of socio-economic development. In other words, economic and social structures would first have to be modernized; demographic attitudes would be modernized along with them, or follow suit. In this paradigm, sociology and economics were viewed as allies of demography. Such was the attitude in the 1960s and 1970s, and it was aptly illustrated by the speech of the Senegalese delegate to the 1974 Bucharest Conference, quoted above.

In subsequent years, faced with an upward surge in population growth, the analytical focus shifted to the type of values and attitudes to be promoted to instigate behavioural change. Cause and effect were thus reversed, and population policy became coterminous with family planning. In the Senegalese situation, the upshot was that population growth levelled off, then dropped. Management, education and communication have all become allies of demography. The new situation is exemplified by the jargon of the 1980s - human resource management - and the inclusion of the information-education-communication trio as a standard fixture in all projects. Senegal's Population Policy Declaration brings this country closer to the Indian model, with its emphasis on persuasion, than to the Chinese model, which is much more collectivist and coercive (Savané, 1988:155).

Like population policies adopted practically everywhere in Africa, Senegal's policy aims primarily at cutting the population growth rate. But the policy, like the vision which spawned it, is reductionist, in the sense that it isolates a small number of factors from a complex *Gestalt*. In this case the isolated factor is fertility. The intellectual stances resulting from such an approach sometimes border on cynicism. For instance, on examining the findings of Senegal's 1986 Population and Health Survey, we find that apart from the generalities contained in the introductory chapter, the five other chapters treat the following issues: Marriage and Pregnancy (II); Fertility (III); Contraception (IV); Fertility Preferences (V); and lastly Maternal and Infant Mortality and Health (VI). Admittedly, there are plans to publish other analyses, but the fact that this one was published first speaks volumes. In the first place, the title is disingenuous. It also demonstrates the perverse effects of a reductionist approach often promoted by funding agencies that care little for the national interest.

Analytical studies based on approaches of such dubious credibility skip over economic and social relations in which demographic behaviour patterns are rooted. By that stroke they occult the historical background of original realities behind current data. Thus, by linking underdevelopment with excessively high population growth rates, they put the blame on individuals who decide to have children, or simply let nature take its course. Cordell and Piché (1986:38) in fact describe this attitude, which supposes that survival tactics adopted by poor people and peasants are actually the cause of their condition, as cynical. People who reason that way forget that the human beings involved are social beings motivated, as such, by considerations far beyond their isolate selves. It is hard to see why individuals should begin conforming to individualistic norms when they live in a context where their survival still depends overwhelmingly on their families. It is the reductionist attitude that makes the government so eager to forget an essential aspect, an indispensable protagonist in any credible population policy in present-day Senegal: the family. For example, there is a sub-section of the population policy document entitled Preservation of the Family. But even though the issue is described as one of the main foci of the Population Policy Declaration, it rates a grand total of six lines, if that, in an early draft. That allowance gets whittled down to two lines in a later edition issued in January 1989 (Senegal, 1988b; Basse *et al.*, 1990).

Granted, the Population Policy Declaration acknowledges some of its shortcomings, but it does so from the perspective of design, not that of approach, the key issue here. The document recognizes that while considerable progress has been achieved in the study of fertility and the condition of the population, significant gaps remain as far as mortality and migratory movements are concerned. And yet the definition of a national population policy requires the simultaneous incorporation of data on birth rates, mortality rates and migrations in the definition of a national population policy (Senegal, 1988b:16).

Even with regard to the campaign against excessively high fertility rates, the policy acknowledges that a large part of work done on the national and regional levels to promote childbirth spacing is entirely out of the control of the State, although it needs data accumulated in the process of such work in order to play its proper role as catalyst and co-ordinator (Senegal, 1988b:17). The part played by non-governmental organizations in this situation is all too clear. There is no need to stress the potentially negative effects of an attitude likely, in the long-run, further to compromise the results expected from the population policy. The public authorities also bear part of the blame. For they have adopted an exclusively sectorial approach that often obscures the kind of interdependent relationships typical of all societies.

In the final analysis, there is a need to re-examine the description, explanation and interpretation of population problems in order to understand measures adopted by Senegal. Demographic behaviour patterns are simultaneously individual and familial responses to historical and circumstantial challenges. It is therefore imperative to situate demographic phenomena back in their historical context. We agree whole-heartedly with Cordell and Piché when they argue that in order to understand demographic change, we have to comprehend transformations in production structures.

On the whole, we also support the kind of programmatic activities they envisage. We find particularly cogent the argument that it is necessary to accept the concept of the reduction of inequalities in the effort to deal with fertility, in the same way as that concept is now accepted as an integral part of any effort to curb mortality (Cordell and Piché, 1990:304-306). The point is to improve the real conditions of human reproduction, meaning material living conditions. Every population policy ought therefore to incorporate significant socio-economic measures.

The practice of isolating fertility from other factors must, for that reason, stop. And migratory movements should once more be given central importance in policy design. By that we do not mean it will be sufficient merely to repeat the usual hand-wringing about the rural exodus and wanderlust. What we need to do is to design migration policies in terms of retention (Marcoux, 1988) instead of falling into the usual negative groove that explains migration in terms of repulsion and attraction. The main thing is to motivate people to stay in their home villages, not to stop them from leaving. A policy shift towards retention, however, is impossible unless it is understood that for most rural families, migration is a crucial survival strategy, indispensable for the satisfaction of consumption needs left unmet under local conditions.

Bibliography

Amat-Roze, J M, 1989, 'L'infection à VIH et le SIDA en Afrique noire: facteurs d'épidémisation et de régionalisation', *Les Cahiers d'Outre Mer*, No 168, Oct.-Dec.

Antoine P, H Bâ and F G Mbodj, 1987, 'La mortalité au Sénégal', Dakar, Preparatory Commission of the Inter-Ministerial Council on Population Policy. Mimeo, Nov.

Bâ, H, 1985, 'Projections démographiques à partir de l'ESF' in Y Charbit, L Guèye and S Ndiaye, (eds),'Nuptialité et fécondité au Sénégal,' *Travaux et Documents Séries*. N°112, Paris, INED, PUF.

Bâ, H 1989, 'Contraception et Planification familiale au Sénégal,' *Historiens et Géographes*, No. 4-5, pp.58-61.

Basse, M A, B Mané and L Savané, 1990, 'Les programmes et politiques de population,' Papers presented at the Evaluation Seminar on Documentary Educational Files on Population Education (Mimeographed), Saly, Population Studies and Training Group (GEEP), November.

Becker, C and M Mbodj, 1987, 'Histoire du peuplement et évolution démographique au Sénégal: 1904-1986.' Paper presented at the Colloquium on Source Documents on the Demographic History of Sahelian Countries (Mimeographed), Dakar, Sahel Institute, March.

Becker, C, M Diouf and M Mbodj, 1987, 'L'évolution démographique régionale du Sénégal et du Bassin Arachidier (Sine-Saloum) au vingtième siècle, 1904-1976,' in Cordell, D and

J Gregory (eds.), *African Population and Capitalism.* Boulder and London, Westview Press.

Cordell, D and V Piché, 1990, 'Grandeur et misère de l'analyse matérialiste en démographie: une application au domaine des politiques démographiques', *Révolution et Population - Chaire Quételet 1989.* Academia, Institute of Population Studies, Louvain-la-Neuve, Catholic University of Louvain, pp.295-310.

Diouf, P D, 1989, 'Santé familiale et croissance démographique au Sénégal,' *Historiens et Géographes,* No. 4-5, pp.52-57.

Ekanem, I I, 1988, 'African Population Policies: Formulation and Implementation in the 1970s and 1980s,' in *African Population Conference/Congrès africain de population.* Liege, UIESP, 8.3.1 - 8.3.19.

Gauvreau, D et al, 1986, 'Population et sous-développement: pour un renversement de tendances,' in Gauvreau D, J Gregory, M. Kempeneers and V Piché (eds.), *Démographie et Sous-Développement dans le Tiers-Monde.* Montreal, Centre for Developing Area Studies, McGill, pp.1-10.

Gregory, J and V Piché, 1986, 'Démographie, impérialisme et sous-développement: le cas africain,' in Gauvreau, D, J Gregory, M Kempeneers and V Piché (eds.), *Démographie et Sous-Développement dans le Tiers-Monde.* Montreal, Centre for Developing Area Studies, McGill, pp.11-46.

GEEP (Population Studies and training Group), 1990, 'Documents du séminaire, d'évaluation des Dossiers Pédagogiques, Documentaires sur l'Enseignement de la Population'. (Mimeographed), Saly, November.

Historiens et Géographes, 1989, Special issue: 'Population: compter avec l'école' No. 4-5, 2nd Semester.

Jemai, H, 1987, 'Pour une approche matérialiste des problèmes de population et de développement en Afrique,' in Jemai, H (ed.). *Population et développement en Afrique,* Dakar CODESRIA, pp.1-68.

Kelly, V and C L Delgado, 1991, 'Agricultural Performance Under Structural Adjustment,' in Delgado, C L and S Jammeh (eds.). *The Political Economy of Senegal Under Structural Adjustment.* New York, Praeger, pp.97-118.

Le Brun, O, 1973, 'Mécanismes de dissolution-conservation-développement de l'artisanat et problèmatique de l'éducation dans les zones urbaines d'Afrique', BREDA, February.

Lieberson, J, 1986, 'Sommes-nous trop nombreux sur cette planète.' *Jeune Afrique,* No. 1355-56, 24 and 31 December, pp.100-114.

Mané, B, 1986, 'Croissance démographique et problèmes alimentaires au Sénégal.' Final graduate paper in Population Studies, Yaoundé, IFORD.

Marcoux, R, 1988, 'Emigration rurale et capacité de rétention des populations: étude d'une centaine de villages dans la vallée du fleuve Sénégal.' Paper presented at the Conference of the Canadian African Studies Association, Kingston, May.

Mbodj, M, G Ciss and P Baldé, 1987, 'Etat et Structures de la population du Sénégal.' Mimeographed, Dakar, Preparatory Commission of the Inter-Ministerial Council on Population Policy, October, 25pp.

Mbodj, M and C Becker, 1989, 'A propos de l'histoire et des populations de l'Afrique Noire: propositions pour de nouvelles approches,' *Revue Canadienne des Etudes Africaines,* No. 23, 1, pp.40-53.

Metge, P, 1966, 'Le peuplement du Sénégal.' 2 volumes, mimeographed. Ministry of Planning, Development and Territorial Development.

Sai, F T, 1986, 'Population and Health: Africa's Most Basic Resource and Development Problem,' in Berg, R J and J Whitaker-Seymour (eds.), *Strategies for African Development.* pp.129-154.

Sai, F T, 1988, 'Key Issues and Problems in African Population Policy in the 1990s,' in *African Population Conference/Congrès africain de population*. Liège, UIESP.

Sarr, I, 1988, 'Etude de la situation démographique à partir de l'analyse des sources.' Mimeographed, Dakar, Preparatory Commission of the Inter-Ministerial Council on Population Policy, 25 pp.

Savané, L, 1988, *Populations - un point de vue africain.*, Anvers, EPO, 219 pp.

Sène, R, 1989, 'Il est nécessaire de maitriser la fécondité afin d'atteindre nos objectifs.' Interview, *Pop Sahe*, N°. 9, May, pp.20-23.

Senegal (Republic of) 'Recensement général de l'AOF', National Archives, 1904, 22 G 19.

Senegal (Republic of) 1960-61, Direction de la Statistique - Enquête Démographique Nationale (EDN).

Senegal (Republic of) 1965, Enquête Démographique Nationale (résultats) in L Verrières, thèse University Cheikh Anta Diop, faculté des sciences économiques.

Senegal (Republic of) 1977, Ministère du Plan et de la coopération, 'Projet de 5ème Plan quadriennal de développement économique et social 1977-81', Tome III, juin, p.245.

Senegal (Republic of) 1980, Statistics Board. 'Situation économique du Sénégal'.

Senegal (Republic of) 1981, 'Enquête sénégalaise sur la fécondité (ESF/1978): Rapport national d'analyse.' 2 volumes.

Senegal (Republic of) 1981, 'Recensement Général de la Population d'avril 1976 (RGP/1976) - Analyse des résultats nationaux', 101 pp.

Senegal (Republic of) 1988, *Enquête Démographique et de Santé au Sénégal - 1986*. Statistics Board and the Institute for Resource Development/Westinghouse. 174 pp.

Senegal (Republic of) 1988, 'Projet de Développement des Ressources Humaines.' Human Resources Division.

Senegal (Republic of) 1988, Ministry of Planning and Cooperation. 'Déclaration de la Politique de Population (DPP).' Human Resources Division. April, 21 pp.

Senegal (Republic of) 1989, 'Les principaux résultats provisoires du Recensement Général de la Population et de l'Habitat du Sénégal (RGPH/1978)', December, 21 pp.

Senegal (Republic of) 1989, 'Déclaration de la Politique Nationale de Santé.

Senegal (Republic of) 1989, 'Plan d'orientation pour le développement économique et social 1989-1995 (VIIIème Plan).', 261 pp.

Senegal (Republic of) 1990, 'Tableau de bord annuel de la situation sociale au Sénégal', Human Resources Division, 77 pp.

Senegal (Republic of) 1991, Planning Board, 'Synthèse de la situation démo-économique et sociale du Sénégal.' Human Resources Division, 155 pp.

Senegal (Republic of) 1991, 'Premier Programme d'Actions et d'Investissements Prioritaires en matière de population (PAIP)', Human Resources Division, February.

Tall-Thiam, K, 1989, 'Démographie et Urbanisation à Dakar: le processus de la 'taudisation' de la Médina Est.' *Historiens et Géographes*, No. 4-5, pp.43-51.

Thiongane, A, 1977, 'Un avenir incertain parce que les ressources se font rares.' Interview, *Pop Sahel*, No. 3. July, pp.16-17.

United Nations Children's Fund (UNICEF), 1990, *La situation des enfants dans le monde. 1991*, 128 pp.

United Nations Fund for Population Activities, 1990, *Relever le défi démographique*. Washington D.C., 52 pp.

Vallin, J, 1989, *La population mondiale*. Paris, La Découverte, 129 pp.

Verrière, L 1965, 'La population du Sénégal', Thesis presented at the Law Faculty, University of Dakar, 220 pp.

World Bank, 1986, *Rapport sur le Développement dans le monde*, Washington D.C.

World Bank, 1989, *L'Afrique subsaharienne: de la crise à une croissance durable - Etude de prospective à long terme*, Washington D.C.

Zachariah, K C and N K Nair, 1980, 'Sénégal: Structures des migrations internes et internationales au cours des dernières années', *World Bank Staff Working Paper* 415, Washington, 39 p.

6. Urban Policies: Management and Development

Lat Soucabé Mbow

By the time Senegal achieved independence, the urbanization process was already in full swing. Over 20% of the population lived in urban areas. Since then, urbanization has intensified. In the process, it has left its stamp on the organization of the national environment, just as it did in the colonial period:

- towns are concentrated in the western and central regions, and
- the pattern of their development is lop-sided, with by far the lion's share going to the capital in practically all respects.

The purpose of this chapter is to assess the efficacity of public sector intervention in coping with complex problems involved in the improvement of living conditions for urban dwellers, and in the provision of development and extension services for the rural areas from urban bases. An examination of work done during the past three decades reveals a radical transformation of relationships between the State and the urban areas following certain political and economic changes since 1981. Before then, the central government authorities had ruled unchallenged over the urban scene thanks to a stifling array of legislative provisions and the massive use of public capital in development programmes conceived and implemented by State agencies. Then, in reaction to a number of emergent challenges, the central authorities began to back-track. In their retreat they left room for local-level authorities and the population at large to assume part of the responsibility for urban management. The State was thus free to concentrate more effectively on its leadership, co-ordination and supervision functions.

Vicissitudes of Recent Urbanization

Under the combined impact of various factors, the country's population has been undergoing major shifts throughout the national territory since independence. The shifts mainly favoured the urban areas, which therefore grew rapidly in size. However, lacking resources needed to cope with such rapid growth, they ran into an urban crisis. That crisis has compromised the fulfilment of inhabitants' aspirations and dampened business in the modern economic sector.

Population Shifts Into Urban Areas

In 1961, the urban population in Senegal was 697, 058, equivalent to 22% of the national population, and was distributed among some ten urban areas. A decade and a half later, the urbanized percentage had reached 32%, while the number of urban areas rose to 22. By the time of the 1988 census, the urban percentage had climbed to 39%. For the 1961-88 period as a whole, the Senegalese population grew at an overall average rate of 3% per year. The urban population, however, grew at an annual rate of 5%.

The urban upsurge affected all the country's regions, but it was particularly intense in the western regions. Table 1 shows the changing rates of urbanization in various regions of Senegal over the past two decades.

Table 1: Regional Urbanization Rates in Senegal 1976-88 (%)

Region	1976	1988	Variation 1976-88
Cape-Verde	96	96.4	+0.4
Casamance	17	21.0	+4.0
Diourbel	26	38.0	+12
Fleuve	25	27.5	+2.6
Louga	08	10.8	+2.8
East. Senegal	8.9	13.8	+4.9
Sine Saloum	2.5	16.3	+3.8
Thiès	25	32.0	+7.0

Source: Compiled by author.

Dakar region (Cape-Verde), with its extremely high urbanization rate, is far ahead of the others, although now the ratio of rural to urban inhabitants there is becoming stable. In the hinterland, the majority of the population is still rural, but every succeeding census indicates an increasing shift towards the urban areas. Particularly strong growth in Diourbel was due to a tendency of the population at large to cluster around the most dynamic poles in the environment while able-bodied members continue their drift out of the region. Population increases registered by towns in the outlying regions were far from negligible: +4.9 points in Eastern Senegal; +4 in the Casamance; +2.5 in the Senegal River Valley (Fleuve). Unless steps are taken to reverse current trends, within a generation, over half the population of Senegal will be living in the urban areas. Furthermore, the lop-sided trend towards concentrated settlement in the western regions will continue[1].

The reversal of old population patterns has been so extensive because of the active role played by migratory movements as well as the internal dynamism of the urban population. There are as yet no reliable studies on the precise contribution of migrations to urban growth. The closest indices can be obtained by comparing individual birthplaces with current areas of residence. That index suggests that in 1976, the percentage of the population born in most of Senegal's urban centres was generally equal to that of the immigrant population. Extreme cases were Dakar, Kaffrine and Tambacounda, where the proportion originating from outside was markedly higher. Moreover, it was clear that outside the regional capitals where migrants came from far afield, smaller district towns got their incoming population from much closer by. As a rule, migrants there came from within the district or local administrative area[2].

The rural exodus remained the major source of urban immigration as ever-increasing numbers of people, fleeing the shock of the agricultural crisis, moved from the countryside. But the urban economy was also reeling from the impact of structural adjustment. It therefore offered only an increasingly diminishing number of opportunities. Obviously, were it not for the attenuating effects of business in the so-called informal sector, together with networks of family, ethnic and religious solidarity, social tensions resulting from high job demand and low supply opportunities would have been much sharper.

Data from the 1978 Family Health Survey (ESF) indicates that despite prevailing socio-economic constraints, fertility levels remain high in the urban areas. In fact, it turns out that fertility rates among urban women are higher than among rural women, except for those whose first marriages come relatively late in life[3]. No doubt, this seemingly paradoxical situation has to do with the effect of migratory movements, which bring young adults of both genders into the urban areas. Additional factors are the fact that sexually active persons have shifted away from traditional birth control methods without substituting modern techniques for them; and mother and child care facilities are more effective in the urban areas.

The last advantage applies to infantile mortality as well. In the urban areas, infant mortality rates are estimated at 130 per thousand; the national average is 156 per thousand, while the rural rate is 240 per thousand. The effect of these parameters on the make-up of the urban population is mainly visible in the size of the youth population, whose most urgent problems are related to training and employment.

At the bottom of the population structure we find those age categories making up the majority. According to the 1976 General Population Census, between 40% and 50% of the population in the major urban areas was made up entirely of people below 15 years of age. Young adults between the ages of 15 and 44 accounted for some 30% to 35%[4]. Because the economic crisis narrowed opportunities for self-fulfilment open to youth in this category, some were pushed to the fringes of society, where they are likely to find protest against the social status quo increasingly attractive.

Urban Structures

The evolving urban situation in Senegal may also be analyzed in terms of the distribution of the population among towns. In this respect, ever since World War II, there has been a widening imbalance between Dakar and the country's other urban bases. In 1961, 41.8% of Senegal's urban population lived in Dakar. By 1976, that percentage had risen to 49.9%. In the same period, the size gap between the country's largest and second largest urban areas widened. Specifically, at independence Dakar had a population five times that of Kaolack. By the time of the 1976 General Population Census, Thiès had superseded Kaolack in second place, but the population of Dakar had grown seven times greater than that of Thiès. The top-heavy pattern of urban development at the national level is repeated at the regional level, as Table 2 shows.

Table 2: Size Ratios Between Largest and Second-Largest Towns in Senegal's Hinterland Regions

Year	Casamance	Diourbel	Fleuve Senegal	East Senegal	Sine Saloum	Thiès	Louga
1961	5.5	3.9	8.1	3.5	9.7	4.3	4.6
1976	4.8	2.1	6.7	3.3	9.1	3.1	4.9
1988	5.6	2.0	3.9	3.7	8.9	2.3	5.3

Source: Compiled by author.

In comparison with the size differential between Senegal's leading urban areas, however, imbalances between top regional towns are tending to diminish. This is proof that the current surge in urban populations is part of a wider process embracing small and medium towns as well as certain particularly dynamic rural centres in the hinterland[5].

The rank-size distribution curve shows this trend towards denser concentrations along the middle and lower strata of the Senegalese urban network. The graph was extremely steep in 1961, because at that time there were almost no really significant towns of medium size below Dakar, with its population of 374,700 inhabitants. Only Thiès (69,560 inhabitants) and Kaolack (69,140) came within the category of towns with between 50,000 and 100,000 inhabitants. By 1976, three other towns (Saint-Louis, Ziguinchor and Diourbel) had joined the group. The number of towns with populations between 25,000 and 50,000 increased from two to five. One of the five was Touba, the religious centre, which underwent a spurt of phenomenal growth[6]. Other towns that in 1961 were only rural villages or little towns grew to join the category of towns with 10,000 to 25,000 inhabitants. There had been ten such towns in 1961; by 1976 there were 14. In the course of time, then, the graph of leading urban areas came to resemble a parabola, a sign of impending saturation at the level of missing linkages.

Constraints on Rapid Urbanization

In the Western world during the nineteenth century, it was the demand for labour from an emergent industrial system that provoked the rural exodus into the urban areas. The rural exodus in Senegal today follows a different pattern. It is a consequence of transformations within a country enduring numerous constraints imposed by a harsh environment: drought, population pressure, deteriorating trade terms, inflation, external debt. Given the limited resources of the State and local communities, and under prevailing conditions, it has proved impossible to make investments commensurate with the demand for jobs, housing and urban services. Over the past 20 years, while Senegal's population growth rate remained high and constant[7], the economic growth rate was low. Manufacturing industries were expected to boost economic capacity in the urban areas. But following the crisis in the agricultural sector, with which the industrial sub-sector is inextricably linked, and under the impact of foreign competition, industry stagnated. Investment in the sub-sector failed to generate large-scale employment, their capitalistic organization notwithstanding[8]. Many able-bodied persons found access to work only within the traditional economy.

Small towns with fewer than 50,000 inhabitants had the highest percentages of persons working in the primary sector[9]. That was perfectly predictable, since modern business had only a tentative presence in such towns. The only modern sector activities there were decentralized civil service departments responsible for administering the rural hinterland, plus a few handicraft shops and nondescript trading enterprises serving the local market. It was a narrow job market, insufficient to keep the rural labour force in place. As a rule, able-bodied persons migrated to larger urban areas.

The population tended to cluster most thickly in the leading urban areas because job opportunities there were much more regular. In addition to the same type of work available in the smaller towns, larger towns offered openings of a more substantial kind in such areas as large-scale industry and sophisticated trading. This type of activity requires the presence of a sizeable population, plus appropriate accommodation and other facilities. The main prerequisite is an urban infrastructural and equipment base good enough to facilitate communication links serving the most active poles of activity. There lies the great advantage of regional capitals and the national capital.

The so-called informal sector experienced a boom in the larger urban centres because low-income households there offered a potentially vast market. The sector is also particularly dynamic because its operational mechanisms are exceptionally flexible. As a matter of fact, a number of occupations in the informal urban economy are extensions of such traditional caste occupations as iron-smithing, wood-work and leather-craft. As such they do not require particularly advanced vocational training from rural migrants practising them. Orthodox economic analyses have long looked down upon these trades as parasites of the formal sector. But now these small urban occupations are getting rehabilitated. There are those who argue that in the present depressed state of the economy, it is the informal sector which is most likely to provide alternative avenues to the improvement of the urban job situation. Such advocates highlight two features of the sector: the low rate of investment it demands, and its greater capacity to create jobs[10].

Still, a substantial fraction of the active population in the urban areas remains jobless. In the regional capitals, 1976[11] figures for unemployed men of working age ranged from a quarter to a third of the active population. In the absence of greater job opportunities, which is to say, unless living standards are improved, Senegal's urban areas are likely for a long time to face operational and equipment problems. Such basic services as sanitation, water and street lighting have been kept up, more or less. But the maintenance of existing services is likely to raise such severe problems as to make any thought of renovation a pipe dream. The drinking water supply system is one of the very few public services where demand has not yet exceeded critical limits. There are problems in that service too, but they are mainly technical. They arise mostly because supply stations are too far from consumer outlets[12], or because parts of the water supply network are too old. The cost to municipal authorities of electricity and water grids has prevented them from improving their coverage, especially in the poorer neighbourhoods[13].

The housing problem appears to be the thorniest infrastructural constraint. One reason is the fast pace of population movements. A second is the severity of economic hardship, restricting sources of funding. Year in, year out, as young families are formed, they look for opportunities to escape from having to share accommodation with relatives. At the same time, immigrants flow into the urban areas. Those unable to build, buy or hire housing shack up with relatives, creating different degrees of overcrowding. Meanwhile, prospective home builders face enormous obstacles. There is, in theory, an official price schedule for real estate. But in practice, building plots tend to cost a lot. In situations where the government takes no steps to influence supply patterns by providing free plots, speculation in real estate booms. There is a lot of shady dealing. Squatter areas thus built up cause extremely complicated problems when attempts are made to bring them under legal urban planning norms. Furthermore, building material prices have risen steeply[14] in the past two decades. As a consequence, the pace of construction in the parastatal sector (SICAP and the OHLM) has fallen off considerably. At the end of the Third Economic and Social Development Plan Period (1973), housing units constructed totalled 15,000. From 1973 to 1981, however, the total dropped to 5,000.

Rising rents have reinforced a characteristic trend towards social segregation in planned housing projects. The Parcelles assainies experiment in Dakar and Thiès with World Bank support admittedly helped provide low-income housing. But it was restricted to those selected regions. It therefore could not help meet demand in all the country's urban areas.

Public housing underwent a resurgence from 1981, thanks to the overhaul of the funding system. The Senegalese Housing Bank (BHS) was established to provide a credit facility, creating opportunities in real estate development for larger numbers of private entrepreneurs. It also gave public housing agencies more favourable conditions for backing up the recovery of their construction programmes[15].

Given the complex nature of the problems outlined, which are incidentally only a sampling of constraints inherent in the urban process, it seems clear that Senegal is fairly overwhelmed by the development of its urban areas. Investments earmarked for solving the problem only serve to finance stopgap or rehabilitation measures. To make up accumulated deficits in various areas, the country needs hard-to-get resources.

Urbanization Under the State

The 1980s marked a turning point in Senegalese development. Following changes in the leadership of the State, economic and social reforms had a new lease on life[16]. The reforms resulted in the definition of a set of new policies such as a New Agricultural Policy, a New Industrial Policy, a New Educational Policy etc. In line with the new context, the national territorial and urban development policy led to an updated programme necessitated by the drafting of a new planning system designed to bring greater cohesion into long-term development activities[17]. The challenge, as far as territorial development was concerned, was to reverse trends inherited from the colonial past while promoting an urban system equipped to fulfil a double function: first as a support system for a balanced development process; and second as a living environment for the fulfilment of human aspirations.

To achieve these objectives, the State, whose approach was derived from socialist paradigms, arrogated to itself in the immediate post-independence period far-reaching prerogatives that left little room for private initiative in the creation and management of urban environments. On the social level, it has to be admitted that this policy had some patently positive results. The trouble was that its maintenance depended closely on the ability of public bodies to function as providers and allocators of resources. Now during the 1970s, the financial situation deteriorated, making an adjustment in the relationship between the State and the urban areas necessary.

State Control of Urban Management

The urban system Senegal inherited at independence was admittedly modest. Nevertheless, it was sufficient to attract sizeable migratory movements, chiefly from the rural areas. Aid programmes run by the former colonial power were designed more to stimulate production than to bankroll social amenities. For that reason, existing urban infrastructures did not offer satisfactory living conditions[18] for incoming migrants. Under these conditions, infrastructural facilities and equipment installed under the colonial regime began with time to fall apart under pressure from increasing demand. The degeneration of living conditions in the urban areas was most obvious in the housing sector, because there were practically no plans whatsoever setting out conditions governing future growth[19]. To make matters worse, allocation arrangements for residential purposes were notoriously slow. To circumvent them, home builders started maverick neighbourhoods without the most basic services. Dakar, with its many teeming shanty towns[20], exemplified this trend in spectacular fashion. The resulting poor housing conditions constituted a serious health hazard for inhabitants.

Construction work done by the SICAP housing corporation, created in 1952, was insufficient on its own to make up the housing shortage in the capital city, and utterly incapable of making a real dent in the housing shortage in other towns. Generally low living standards proved a handicap to private sector initiatives. In 1960, Senegal's 100,000 wage earners (out of a total population of 2,500,000 inhabitants) took home an average wage packet estimated at F CFA15,000 (Sidibé, 1961:33). It might have been possible for local communities to supplement government programmes. But the modest sums available to the municipal administrations were squandered in non-viable operations instead of being invested in investment of clear public benefit.

The authorities of the new nation, then, inherited a difficult situation. In addition, the urban network was unbalanced in many respects, a fact which contributed to the polarization of the national environment. In the unsettled period leading up to independence, the urban environment was profoundly marred by individual acts of vandalism. Only a force different from the population itself, in other words the public authority, was capable of restoring respect for rules safeguarding the common interest.

The commitment of the new authorities to the urban process took the form of the creation of a series of agencies mandated to alleviate the deterioration of structures built up under the colonial regime. They were also required to spell out guidelines for a new policy. As early as the transitional period of internal self-government, a Commission for Urban Development and Housing had been set up. From 1960 on, a ministry was formed to deal with the two sectors.

Legislation taken over from the French colonial period provided a basis for an urban policy. But while the metropolitan French approach to housing was a decentralized one, in Senegal decisions concerning guidelines for urban development[21] were the prerogative of the highest political bodies. To be specific, the Urban Development Code states that it is the President of the Republic who determines the basis of urban planning policy. He is assisted by the National Urban Planning Council, whose members include ministers and heads of major national departments serving the urban areas, as well as the government's Urban Planner or Architectural Adviser[22]. Regional Urban Planning Commissions were also consulted in an advisory capacity on issues related to regional development and connected with urban planning and housing.

The stated policy aim was to:

provide for the gradual and forward-looking development of urban areas within a general policy framework geared to economic development and social progress. (This policy) is intended, mainly through rational land use, to create for the population as a whole a living environment conducive to its harmonious physical, economic, cultural and social development[23].

The policy paid lip service to a comprehensive approach, but in fact it reduced the urban environment to the various city and town boundaries. From that point of view, all that was needed to promote the welfare of the population was to develop the area thus delimited. The question of urban extension services for adjacent hinterland areas was left in abeyance. Subsequently, this aspect of urban planning policy was taken up with the creation of the Department of Territorial Development (1967). The accompanying forward planning draft for the period up to the year 2000 emphasized the need to change conditions governing the polarization of the national environment. This was to be done through the upgrading of selected regional capitals into balance-inducing metropoles. The idea was to offset Dakar's predominant pull among the leading urban areas[24].

The key mechanism the public authorities depended on for the rational management of the urban environment was planning. The term was given multiple connotations. It meant investment programming within the PDES framework, in keeping with the government's State-oriented development perspectives. Simultaneously, it meant controlled land allocation. Spatial expansion within the municipalities, towns and other urban agglomerations was made conditional on the compulsory drafting of development plans including master plans, urban planning schemes and detailed drafts. Most often, these were designed at the central level.

Implementational work on these frameworks was not finished in due time because of shortages of funds. Quite frequently, urban planning documents designed to deal with some fast-breaking urban situation were rendered out of date by events happening just at the time of their final presentation.

As an antidote to the incompetence of elected municipal officials, and in an effort to place the modest resources of the municipalities at the service of their populations, the central government established new management structures for administrative supervision. Regional capitals were thus placed under a dispensational common law regime. The effect was to bring them under the strict supervision of the State as represented by the regional governor or the municipal administrator[25]. Furthermore, a municipal administrative Code was promulgated[26] in order to lay out guidelines for proper conduct in the use of local funds. It should be pointed out that these measures made it possible to clean up the municipalities. They had been paralyzed by the combination of poverty and excessive politicization. However, the impact of the measures was limited by two factors. The first was the lack of adequate funds. Even though allocations were transferred to the municipalities from the State budget, large debt backlogs impoverished the municipal treasuries.

The second drawback was the low level of popular involvement. Elected local officials had had their wings clipped. They therefore became unenthusiastic about mass mobilization campaigns.

Funding the Urban Sector

In the first two decades after independence the State was by far the biggest provider of funds to the urban sector. This was in keeping with the dominant role the State had arrogated to itself in the urban process. Its self-appointed function was to steer the process towards a retrieval of territorial equity while creating within the various urban environments an atmosphere conducive to the material and spiritual welfare of the population.

Public funding was not limited to budget allocations from State and municipal agencies. It also included investments by parastatal organizations engaged in the provision of infrastructural equipment throughout the national territory. Among public sector programmes, those initiated by the municipalities were relatively small in scale. They still are.

Until 1976, resources allocated for equipment within the national budget were distributed among various ministries working in the urban areas. From 1976, however, the allocation mechanism was streamlined with the establishment of a specific allocation for the development of urban planning and housing, the FAHU. An annual total between F CFA 1 and 2 billion, made up of deductions from wages and earnings of private companies together with part of the fiscal income from real estate transactions[27], was poured into the fund. Until the creation of the BHS, all this money was turned over to the OHLM and SICAP as subsidies. Part of it was used to finance the development of plots allocated by the public housing agencies. The rest was used to fund research and other work in urban planning conducted by the government. This subsidy to planned housing helped to reduce unit costs and bring housing within the economic reach of purchasers.

A correlation of the relative value of urban investments in the national economic budget and the rate of urbanization in Senegal shows a bias in favour of the urban sector. In the Fifth Economic and Social Development Plan period (1977-80), for instance, even though the urban population comprised only 30% of the national total[28], it absorbed 49.2% of invested funds. Population pressure, however, tended to bring down the level of per capita[29] investment. Expenditure patterns showed a regular bias in favour of services providing urban amenities and keeping up the urban traffic network (transport, water resources, sanitation and plot development, housing). Depending on circumstances, 20% to 25% of budget investments were allocated to resource supply networks (energy, telecommunications) or human resources (education, health, sports).

One point needs highlighting: dependence on foreign funding means that a great deal of uncertainty[30] surrounds the implementation of planned projects. In the first decade after independence[31], the investment capacity of the municipalities was practically zero. The reason was that their operational costs, including a heavy personnel emoluments package, ate up all their income. In subsequent years the situation improved because the State adopted a set of measures designed to make the municipalities refocus on their principal functions. The measures included the allocation of selected taxes (basic tax, patent and licensing fees)[32] to the municipal budget; and the allocation of support funding to finance municipal[33] equipment purchases.

These innovations notwithstanding, such investments very rarely amounted to more than 5% of budgetary disbursements. Their make-up reveals subtle variations in priorities adopted by the municipalities. In Dakar, almost all funds were invested in urban amenities, the transport network and utilities grids. In the regions, allocations were much more biased towards the primary sector, because of the rural character of the towns involved.

Numerous parastatal enterprises were active in the urban areas. In the 1960-70 decade, the best known were the housing agencies SICAP and the OHLM, along with the utility corporations: SENELEC, the National Water Works Corporation (SONEES), SOTRAC and the Posts and Telecommunications Agency. The only parastatal making a profit from its operations. None of them could have implemented their programmes without State loans and subsidies. Such a funding policy could only be sustained under conditions of steady economic growth, which would have facilitated the mobilization of cheap capital from the State, eked out with funds from the private banking sector. But from 1968, Senegal began to face a profound crisis brought on by a combination of many external factors: drought, deteriorating trade terms, inflation, etc. The crisis caused huge macro-economic imbalances and complicated Senegal's financial commitments abroad. Recovery measures were adopted as from 1979. Their consequences included cuts in public expenditure, which in turn meant decreasing subsidies for loss-making enterprises.

State Intervention in Urban Construction

A look at various ways in which the State intervened in the creation of the urban environment reveals a pattern of continuity between the post-World War II period and the immediate post-independence period. Experience had shown that two obstacles still had to be surmounted if urban development programmes were to be implemented. The first was the land tenure problem. The colonial regime[34] had encouraged private individuals and groups to acquire land. This had sparked speculation and hampered increased production and access to urban facilities. The second obstacle was the dysfunctional nature of the State's production system. The public accounting system had the speed of a snail. If operational structures created by the government were to work efficiently, they would have to be placed under autonomous management regimes free of red tape.

To generate financial resources indispensable for its territorial development programmes, the colonial State had set up in those areas where it did not have total control over land an extended regime comprising the public domain on the one hand and the private domain on the other. In point of law, the public domain comprised the following areas: the sea adjoining Senegalese territory[35]; navigable waterways together with their banks; land corridors on either side of communications infrastructures; military installations; museum collections, general merchandise and food markets. The State was empowered to cede portions of land in the public domain to public or private corporate bodies as well as to individuals[36].

The private domain included land acquired as a result of legal registration, deeds of purchase, exchange, pre-emptive purchase, confiscation, expropriation, donation or inheritance. Until 1964, registration requests were extremely common. But with the passage of legislation establishing the national domain, the number of such requests went down. On the other hand, cases of expropriation for purposes of public utility multiplied after 1945 as a result of the opening of numerous work sites in the urban areas for the construction of roads, sanitation networks, or housing[37]. Land in the private domain not transferred to the public services could be ceded to private individuals in the form of permits to live on or use the premises, or of concessions. They might also be leased or sold[38].

The primary targets of the National Domain Act were in the rural areas, where land tenure structures constituted obstacles to the implementation of development programmes designed after independence. In order to forestall any misunderstandings, however, Articles 4 and 5 stated that the Act applied equally to urban areas. The category of National Domain included land in both the urban and rural areas not classified as belonging to the public domain, not registered under any name, and title to which was not inscribed in the Mortgage Register.

In theory, once this law had been passed, all land formerly under customary jurisdiction ought to have come under State control, and the State would have been recognized as the sole administrator of such landed property. In practice, various individuals, invoking sometimes real, sometimes mythical prerogatives derived from tradition, have continued selling or otherwise disposing of land. The result of such illicit dealings has been a swell of disorderly squatting on urban space. To deal with it, public authorities have sometimes been compelled to bulldoze squatters off occupied land before reorganizing occupation patterns in line with regular urban planning norms.

Similar obstacles have blocked efforts to impose urban planning guidelines in the area of transfers of land tenure rights. There is an official price tariff. Indeed, it is periodically updated. It was designed to counter speculative price gouging, currently widespread in real estate deals. But the only practical use of the official price list is to provide a basis for calculating compensation in case of expropriation for public use, and to fix amounts payable to secure leases and occupation permits from the public authorities. In real estate transactions, trickery is the order of the day. That is because the rate of taxation on such deals is high[39]. There is legislation empowering the public authorities to pre-empt property sales, and it is intended to combat such shady dealing. But to exercise such rights, the authorities would have to come up with sufficient funds to accomplish the pre-emptive purchase of the property in question, within the stipulated time limit[40].

The capital city provides the best venue for measuring the impact of private land tenure regulations on the creation of the urban environment. Since the government started charging a real estate tax, land values have shot up, with prices mounting in step with the addition of amenities in new urban zones. Access to land in the urban areas has come to be determined by the capacity to pay costs. In other words, the urban environment is a theatre of social segregation. Commuting has intensified, complicating transport organization within urban areas.

In 1960, faced with a set of urgent operational and equipment problems in the urban areas, the State had no choice but to create implementational agencies independent of official red tape while still remaining under State control. In truth there was no innovation involved here. The colonial government had defined statutes for national corporations along with mixed economy corporations. SICAP, for instance, was thus created in 1952, and its objectives then were more ambitious: to improve urban and rural housing throughout Senegal.

In the second decade after independence, the operational structures of the State were reinforced. They were also extended to cover urban development domains other than building construction. When, in the 1970s, the petrol crunch sparked increases in value added as a result of widespread increases in the cost of production factors, the State responded by boosting its capital shares in corporations contracted to supply such services as water, electricity and telecommunications. The expansion of the parastatal sector did not stifle private initiative, however. Even where there were monopolies, as in Dakar's public transport system and the electricity supply system[41], private suppliers became active because the State sector was manifestly incapable of meeting total demand.

The public authorities led the way in encouraging the establishment of complementary sectors in the interstices between the public and private spheres working to create the urban environment. Thus, even though the State set up a number of housing agencies to implement its policies, it rejected every approach that would have resulted in an integrated public system incorporating the building construction phase within a public or parastatal corporation. Instead, keen to promote job creation and the development of small and medium size enterprises, the State opted for the method of public tenders and bids from competing individual enterprises. The policy has helped some Senegalese entrepreneurs to move closer to the big time.

Apart from the shortage of funds for their development programmes, the various institutional agencies have very often been unable to operate efficiently because of a lack of co-ordination. The only level at which their sectorial approaches were brought into a semblance of interconnection was that of the overall development plan. Worse still, under the old planning system the only real co-ordination involved was geared to the limited purpose of exploiting economies of scale at the project implementation phase. Otherwise, each institution followed its own priorities. On the ground, this scattershot approach sometimes left loose project ends hanging. For instance, housing projects were built with no commercial centres to serve them, no health facilities and no schools, because the municipality and the ministries involved were preoccupied with other concerns. In the urban areas of Senegal, such stories are still common today.

Urban planning policy in the 1960-70 period was least successful in its attempts to reshape urban infrastructures with a view to re-establishing a balance in the polarization of the national environment. It would be no exaggeration to say the status quo remained unchanged. As in the colonial past, when the bulk of the country's economic infrastructure was installed in the western regions, those regions remained ahead. Certain observers have tagged the zone productive Senegal. Dakar remains the national metropole, towering above all other major urban areas. Senegal's externally-oriented economy has continued operating to the capital city's advantage, reinforcing its productive capacities, job opportunities and incomes as it continues to serve as the country's gateway into the wider world.

It had been expected that selected regional capitals would grow to serve as poles of attraction counterbalancing the preponderant influence of Dakar, but, lacking adequate resources for that mission, they failed to accomplish it. Oddly enough, the fastest growth rates were chalked up by much smaller towns[42]. Unfortunately, there were not enough such dynamic little towns to create a dense network of intermediate towns bringing economic and social progress to the rural areas and thus keeping the population there from having to migrate.

Institutional measures taken in the attempt to decentralize production units clustered in the Dakar area had little impact[43]. The trouble was that production units relocated outside Dakar merely went to zones nearby: Thiès, Diourbel, Kaolack. Similarly, major tourist projects launched in the 1970s were mostly sited along the coast. On the whole, therefore, these developments reinforced disparities between the western regions and the rest of the country.

It would have been possible to decentralize modern economic activities by siting production units in the *unused-Senegalese* hinterland. But for that to happen, two conditions would have had to be met. The first would be to achieve control over the investment resources which with which to underwrite a determined development policy for the national environment. However, official ideology notwithstanding, the public authorities favoured free enterprise in sectors of economic activity outside agriculture. In the First Economic and Social Development Plan, this attitude was clearly spelled out:

In the industrial sector, the Plan looks forward to large scale participation from private capital. Nevertheless, the State does not plan to remain passive. It intends to play an energizing role by defining an industrial programme, by commissioning studies and research indispensable to the installation of new industries, and by acquiring shares whenever necessary[44].

Meanwhile, even in its newly assumed and limited role of facilitator, the State was slow to act in creating requisite conditions for the expansion of industrial infrastructure in the hinterland. Not until the establishment of the SONEPI did ancillary facilities needed for the establishment of small and medium enterprises begin to get installed in regional capitals[45].

The second condition was the creation in urban centres in the hinterland a socio-cultural environment that would provide an incentive for qualified personnel, often in short supply, to want to settle there. Such staff normally expect certain housing, entertainment and cultural standards to be met if they are to settle in areas far from the nerve centres of modern life[46].

The record of State intervention in the urban areas is a mixed one. Clearly, State investments helped improve living conditions for the population in many respects. Sanitation facilities were provided, potable water was connected, housing units got constructed, etc. Yet, considering the scale of chronic distortions in the urban tissue, and in the light of certain unhealthy aspects of life in the urban areas, one is tempted to say Senegal's urban planning policies have failed. We need, however, to see the urban crisis as an phenomenon affecting all countries forced to live under conditions of economic dependency. Foreign investors looking for labour in the peripheral regions focus on business likely to bring in high profits. They therefore cluster around economically viable environments offering the lowest production costs. To overcome the lethargy of territorial structures inherited from colonialism, Senegal has the following options: the first is to open itself up to foreign decision-making centres, while creating conditions for a more equitable development process favourable to the hinterland regions. The second option is to break entirely with past patterns and begin an inner-directed development process within a framework of West African integration. In the decades ahead, it is likely that urban planning and territorial development policies in Senegal will be determined by a combination of the two options.

Conclusion: A Forward-looking Programme

Against the background of the international economic crisis, a debate of great import for the future of Third World countries got under way in the 1980s. Its focus: the role of the State in the process of economic and social development.[47] It had wide reverberations in Senegal, especially because the democratization of public life created openings for the free expression of critical opinions on relationships between the State and the economy, polity and society.[48]

By the evidence of official rhetoric, the new development strategy gave the State a less overweening social and economic role than it played in the past. Henceforth, the State was expected to stimulate private operators, to act as umpire in disputes between them if need be, and to coax them into working in the public interest, all without cramping their creativity and their freedom of action. This was a radical departure, and it inevitably required the reorganization of projection mechanisms, implementational modalities and management strategies applied to urban and territorial development in general.

As far as projections were concerned, official bodies responsible for co-ordination and policy design in the public sector were allowed to continue in their functions. The innovation was in the greater accuracy with which they handled their projections, and the care they took to harmonize them with each other as well as with the nation's long-term strategic options. The State, in line with its policy of withdrawal, gave local communities and civil society greater opportunities to engage in the creation, use and maintenance of urban facilities.

Towards the Third Millennium: Development Scenarios for Senegal

In the final decade of the Second Millennium, Senegal broke away from past paradigms, thus beginning the reformation of its planning system. The key innovation introduced by the new approach was the drafting of forward-looking scenarios based on background studies covering 30 years of change, coupled with a structural analysis of the way the society works, culminating in a series of scenarios of possible developments in all aspects of national life over the coming generation. These prospective scenarios were designed to provide clear information to public officials involved in selecting strategic options for the attainment of future goals. They were also intended to help define supplementary programmes designed to achieve set goals[49].

If trends established over the past 30 years continue, it is highly probable that both the country's business activities and its population will get crammed into the most dynamic areas. In other words, the concentration of activity in Dakar region and areas close to the capital city will get accentuated.

And if the climate remains unpredictable, the long-term result is bound to be a deterioration of the natural resource base. That is likely to be aggravated by human pressure on environmental resources, leading to an ecological crunch. As in the past, lower rains would first mean a drying out of surface water and a drop in the water table. Vegetation cover, deprived of suitable nourishment, would become more vulnerable to the various forces preying on it. It would become more imperative to construct water resource development facilities in order to exploit underground water and improve management of waterway volumes. Such improvements might slow down the tendency of the natural production system to become less productive.

In this context, where harsh natural conditions would make life in the rural areas even more precarious, the likelihood is that the rural exodus would become the only survival strategy available to the active rural population. It would then be hardly surprising if, after a generation, over 60% of the Senegalese population came to be squeezed into Dakar and in the Groundnut Basin (the regions of Thiès, Diourbel, Fatick and Kaolack)[50], while over 50% of the remainder lived in urban areas, with differences in size between various centres getting larger.

As a matter of fact, if current economic and demographic trends continue, the level of urbanization in Senegal will reach 56.4% by the year 2006. In other words, 10,235,800 of the total population of 18,136,630 would reside in the urban areas. The effective boundary of the national metropole would cover Dakar, Thiès and even Mbour, with a population of 6,493,400 inhabitants, or 35.8% of the national total and 63.4% of the urban total. A long way behind Dakar, the remaining leading towns would include: two cities with more than 500,000 inhabitants each: Kaolack and the conurbation of Touba-Mbacké; three towns with populations over 300,000: Ziguinchor, Saint-Louis and Diourbel; and four towns with between 100,000 and 300,000 inhabitants: Tambacounda, Kolda, Louga and Tivaouane.

If economic activity in the nation is to be maintained at 1978 levels (48.5%), 156,000 new jobs will have to be created every year, 84,000 in the urban areas. But the recently completed Seventh Plan projected only 7,000 to 8,000 new jobs per year over the four-year period it covered. Under such conditions, the risk of worsening unemployment and heightened social tensions becomes all too clear. Social tensions are likely to be sharpened not only by fierce competition for jobs and incomes, but also by the failure of various public services to meet the population's needs. Economic losses caused by the breakdown of these services could in turn lead to dwindling investment in productive activities even if rising numbers of able-bodied unemployed persons bring down labour costs.

If that happened, it would take a long time to stop the vicious spiral. For with every withdrawal of capital investment not counterbalanced by relocation elsewhere on the national territory, the macro-economic consequence would be a decrease in national production, a worsening of the country's financial imbalance, and the probability of increasing foreign indebtedness. Overall, if current trends continue, all projected scenarios are likely to push Senegal into various dead ends. That is why it is imperative to find ways to steer clear of the abyss ahead.

A number of variables on which the Senegalese system depends for its dynamism (population, the rural exodus, economic extroversion) exert a powerful pull against change. For that reason, any strategy designed to find a solution to the problem posed by current trends is likely to take a long time yielding results. That is why the impending National Territorial Development Programme projects the break-down of policy for the balanced development of territorial structures into two phases. The first phase covers the period from 1989 to 2006. The aim during that phase would be to influence unfolding trends positively by making a series of adjustments in inherited patterns of territorial development geared to planned economic and social measures. The second phase would begin in the year 2006. That is when conditions for the balanced occupation of the national territory would converge.

The long-term expectation is that balanced settlement will be achieved by enabling those regions whose share of the population would decrease (assuming current trends continue) not merely to hold their own increasing population in future, but also to attract some of the extra population from the most densely populated regions. According to that scenario, nearly 1,400,000 persons who would otherwise have settled in Dakar, Thiès and Diourbel would be redistributed to Saint-Louis, Ziguinchor, Kolda, Kaolack, Fatick, Louga and Tambacounda[51].

In the same vein, urbanization rates would drop slightly, from a 2021 level of 56.4% under the first evaluation scenario to 50.4% in the phase of balanced development. To achieve that goal, the rural areas would be given greater resources to facilitate increased settlement there of the active population. Investments in modern sector activities would be relocated into secondary towns. This would slow down Dakar's growth by offering alternative destinations to opportunity-seeking migrants. Such a revival of smaller urban centres, linked with the fulfilment of increasingly important functions by urban centres of different calibres, would logically lead to the development of a more balanced pattern of urban growth more suited to the extension needs of the rural hinterland[52].

Breaking the Current Spiral

Investment policy produces different effects depending on priorities. In the decades ahead, economic and financial recovery measures taken by the public authorities should raise internal savings from their chronically low levels and boost investment. In the medium-term, resources mobilized for implementing development projects will be channelled into greater productivity, in line with major guidelines envisaged in the 1989-85 Plan. According to this scenario, it is possible that future Economic and Social Development Plan allocation patterns will follow the same lines as the four previous plans. This means that the secondary sector, among the main pillars of economic growth in the crisis period, will continue to account for a preponderant share of investment. Since small-scale enterprises will be accorded priority treatment in investment allocations, the job situation should improve. Small enterprises have the advantage of not requiring large capital inputs; they also create many jobs, and react more flexibly in crisis situations.

Whether the enterprises involved are small or large, however, capitalist investment invariably flows into areas where business can be conducted at the lowest cost. Unless this tendency is modified, more investment will be attracted to urban areas with major economic potential. Towns offering fewer opportunities for marginal investment costs would be disadvantaged. Regional imbalances would become aggravated. To stop this from happening, the State should intervene by promoting conditions conducive to the expansion of the national industrial infrastructure in the areas it intends to develop. The solution is applicable everywhere. It requires the development of accommodation facilities for decentralized enterprises, coupled with the provision of advantages designed to compensate them for losses of opportunity entailed by their relocation from major urban centres[53].

Meanwhile, the State and local communities should share in creating around such relocated enterprises an environment attractive enough for the permanent settlement of technicians and executives working there. During the installation of technical equipment for these enterprises, various housing, cultural and entertainment programmes should be organized in a bid to make daily life in the hinterland less frustrating. Successful industrial decentralization might stimulate significant synergies in other areas of economic activity, especially in the tertiary sector. The areas of Taïba-Mboro and Richard-Toll provide excellent examples of such development. Tertiary sector activities of one type can generate other types of activity in the same sector. For example, the creation of a university in Saint-Louis is bound to have a significant impact on local trade, transport and other services. The well-thought-out decongestion of selected extension services and decision-making functions bunched up in Dakar could produce similar effects without in any way diminishing the capital city's pre-eminent role.

But none of the initiatives outlined above can facilitate the creation of a balanced pattern of territorial occupation if the rural hinterland continues to be buffeted by economic crisis and climatic hazards. For in that case people will continue migrating to the cities. Migrations might even intensify. To guard against such a possibility, public authorities and private agencies will be working to generate supplementary incomes in the rural areas. It is quite possible to achieve this objective if the potential resources of the rural environment are optimally developed.

For example, irrigation-based water resource control will place agricultural production on a more reliable footing. In addition, it will help produce a wider variety of crops than possible with rain-fed farming. As dams on the Senegal, Casamance and Gambia Rivers come into operation, opportunities will improve for greater water resource use. That in turn should help intensify cereal and market gardening production. At the moment, the country is heavily dependent on foreign sources for these staples. However, State withdrawal from the primary sector might prove to be a handicap unless institutions called upon to step into the gap left by disappearing State agencies really fulfil their appointed role. In the past, the State's agricultural programme supplied farmers with production inputs. Now that the programme has been abolished, there is a need to create conditions facilitating access to credit. The trouble is that apart from land, there is little property in the rural areas that banks might want to accept as collateral. It would be a decisive improvement if land tenure rules in the rural areas were changed to make it possible for those actually farming land to own it. Such a transformation would help change mind sets and land use methods[54].

Together with these activities designed to help stabilize the rural population on its own home grounds, other, more specifically demographic measures are envisaged. Their aim would be to keep urban population growth down to levels compatible with the country's economic resources. Senegal has tried out monetary techniques as a means of limiting fertility in the long term, to little avail. It has therefore decided in favour of family planning. In this endeavour, special attention is devoted to the education of target groups and the expansion of services conducive to lower birth rates. With increasing school education, urbanization and awareness of medical and sanitation norms, attitudes of the younger generations towards marriage and procreation are likely to keep changing[55]. The most optimistic projections envisage a 50% reduction of the fertility index by the year 2016[56].

As far as urban development is concerned, it is probable that part of the public savings generated from the economic and financial recovery programme will be invested in the urban areas for the general purpose of maintaining and expanding the national infrastructural base. Municipalities should get more active in fund allocation thanks to improved revenue from local duties and taxes, together with the imminent provision of community credit. Repayment charges on loans will doubtless have an impact on conditions of access to public services. Instead of their being provided free of charge, such services could carry a charge sufficient to cover costs. That would be an efficient way to guarantee high-quality public services.

As the State withdraws and various development agents assume greater responsibilities, urban management will increasingly become structured along two levels. At the lower level, local neighbourhoods will be given greater responsibilities for such routine general-purpose duties as public stand-pipe management and the cleaning and beautification of public parks and squares. Higher-level urban management will require a comprehensive vision and matching operational resources that only the State and municipal authorities can afford.

The foregoing analysis shows that far from being neutral environments, urban areas grow in line with processes of political, economic and social organization impinging on the development of territorial resources. Their rapid growth these past decades reflects the fact that the modern sector economy has been more dynamic than the rural economy. The persistence of imbalances in the urban network indicates that this dynamism has favoured certain urban areas more than others.

Public intervention has been ineffective in its attempts to promote balanced urban development. This was because the degree of control over unfolding circumstances was variable. In particular, the fact that the State arrogated such a gargantuan role to itself in the development process led to a dispersal of its resources. An additional factor was the nation's dependence on foreign funding for investment.

All projections indicate that in the imminent future, urban areas will dominate the Senegalese landscape. We have identified the stakes involved in such a transformation, and outlined solutions to problems arising. To flesh out these proposals, what remains is to redefine roles in accordance with the capacities and abilities of all agents involved in the development or use of Senegal's urbanized environments and the national territory surrounding them.

Notes

1. According to demographic projections from the Ministry of Territorial Development, if current trends continue, by the year 2021 the rate of urbanization in Senegal will have reached 56%. The regions with the highest percentages will be Dakar (97%), Ziguinchor (79%) and Diourbel (60%). All three are in the west.
2. We can give two examples here; a: In 1976, Zinguinchor's 69,649 inhabitants included 51% born outside, while the 2,482 inhabitants of Oussouye included 41.5%; b: The 88,665 inhabitants of Saint-Louis included 31.2%; Podor's 6,760 inhabitants included 29.5% born outside.
3. Data generated by the 1978 Family Health Survey suggests that only the category of rural women over 25 years old register higher fertility rates.

4. In 1976, percentages of persons under 15 years of age inhabiting the regional capitals were as follows: Dakar: 44.9%; Ziguinchor: 45.2%; Diourbel: 43.4%; Saint-Louis: 53%; Kaolack: 44%; Thiès: 47.2%; Louga: 47.3%.
5. From a total of eight urban areas in 1961, Senegal's urban structure grew to 22 towns in 1976. Of the 22 grew from rural or semi-urban nuclei (totalling between 1,000 and 10,000 inhabitants).
6. Touba, the centre of the Mouride religious confraternity, had a population of 2,666 inhabitants in 1961. By 1976 it had grown to 29,734. Preliminary data from the 1988 General Population Census indicates the town numbers over 100,000 now.
7. In the period from 1977 to 1983, Senegal's GDP rose at an annual rate of 1.6% in constant terms, while the population growth rate was 3%.
8. During the Fifth Plan period, it took a total investment of F CFA27 million on average to create a single job. The average for major enterprises was F CFA55 million.
9. In 1976, the percentage was as high as 31.7% in Kaffrine (11,430 inhabitants), 15.8% in Kaolack (104,154 inhabitants), and 3.7% in Dakar (813,317 inhabitants).
10. According to Ministry of Planning and Cooperation data on the Fifth Plan period, it took from F CFA 27 to 55 million to create a single job in the industrial sector; the investment required for one job in the handicraft sector was F CFA5 million.
11. In Dakar and Kaolack, for instance, the percentage of active unemployed males was 27%; it was 28% in Louga and Fatick, 32% in Thiès, 34% in Ziguinchor, and 36% in Saint-Louis.
12. To meet the water supply needs of the capital, whose processing plants cannot meet current needs, a 270-kilometre pipe was laid to bring in water from the Lac de Guiers in the Senegal River valley.
13. Of municipal bills 94% are made up of public water fountain supply costs. The municipal authorities have now fallen behind in such payments.
14. Given a base index of 100 for the year 1972, the construction cost index had risen to 331.6 by 1981, according to Ministry of Equipment data.
15. BHS operations facilitated the construction of 5,542 housing units and the development of 1,847 plots from 1981 to 1987.
16. Deteriorating public finances in the 1970s pressured the government into adopting a short term stabilization plan (1979-81).
17. Opportunities for the updated programme came in the form of the 'Senegal 2015 Prospective Study' and preparatory work for the National Territorial Development Programme (Territorial Development Plan).
18. It was the first 'Fonds d'investissement pour le développement économique et social' (FIDES) (1948-53) that emphasized funding for housing construction. Subsequent plans shifted the accent to economic development, especially in the rural areas.
19. Only a few urban centres had urban planning programmes prior to 1960: Dakar, Saint-Louis and Rufisque. Whatever planning took place in other towns was the work of enlightened administrators.
20. In 1963, out of Dakar's total population estimated at 415,000 inhabitants, 78,000 were slum dwellers, and a further 63,000 lived in unhealthy neighbourhoods.
21. Article 1, Title 1 of Decree Number 66-1076 dated 31-12-1966 on the Urban Code (Section on Regulations).
22. Prior to the installation of the National Urban Planning Council in 1964, urban planning and housing issues of major national concern were handled by the Inter-Ministerial Council under the chairmanship of the President of the Republic.
23. Article 1, Act No. 66-49 of 27 May 1966, abrogating and superseding the Urban Planning Code (JORS, 25-6-1966. p.705).

24. There were to be five such balance-inducing metropolitan areas: Kaolack, Ziguinchor, Saint-Louis, Tambacounda and another town to be defined later. These metropoles would be decision-making and planning centres endowed with infrastructures adequate for those functions.
25. The special statute removing regional capitals from the regime of full scale communal departments came into force in Dakar in 1964, in Saint-Louis in 1965, in Thiès 1966, and in Diourbel, Tambacounda and Ziguinchor in 1970.
26. The Municipal Administrative Code was adopted on 30 June 1966. It has undergone several amendments since then.
27. This fiscal income was made up of 2% deductions from public and private sector wages and salaries, the same percentage of the total wage packet paid by private sector employers, plus a 1% value added tax in the real estate sector.
28. MPC-CEGIR, 1986, 'L'intervention allocative publique dans le secteur urbain sénégalais et sa gestion, analyse et rétrospective'.
29. In the Fifth Plan period, per capita investment stood at F CFA 22,539 in current values and F CFA 18,672 in constant values. During the Sixth Plan period, these amounts fell to 19,269 and F CFA 10,121 respectively.
30. During the Fifth, Sixth and Seventh Plan periods, the national State budget has depended on foreign sources for between 60% and 70% of its funding.
31. For example, in the financial years 1963-64 and 1964-65, respective investment percentages were as follows: Kaolack: 2% and 3%; Ziguinchor: 4% and 0%; Saint-Louis: 0.09%; Tambacounda: 1% and 12%; Diourbel: 1% and 1.19%; Dakar: 5.6% and 1.05%.
32. This tax reform came into force on 1 January 1977.
33. This fund, totalling F CFA 4 billion in 1977-78, was financed through a 1% surtax on BIC totals.
34. The basic relevant text was the Land Tenure Decree of 1906, amended in 1932. It established title deed registration and made registers accessible to both French citizens and the indigenous population.
35. The coastal domain consists of a strip of land about 100 metres wide as measured from the farthest reaches of the sea at high tide. In proto-colonial legislation, its equivalent was the zone of 50 surveyor's steps.
36. Under an Act passed on 2 July 1976, such transfers entitle beneficiaries to do construction or road works, carry on mining or quarrying enterprises, or to conduct diverse economic and social activities on the land acquired.
37. Reasons for which the Expropriation Act might be invoked are spelled out in Article 2 of Act No. 76-67 of 2 July 1976.
38. Persons to whom land in the public domaine is ceded have to pay an annual fee.
39. Taxation on real estate transfers goes as high as 20% of declared value.
40. Article 22 of the State Domains Code stipulates: 'Within three months from the registration of the deed or declaration, the State may exercise pre-emptive rights to the purchase of premises and real estate rights put up for sale'.
41. A number of private enterprises such as the SEIB of Diourbel, the SEIC of Ziguinchor (before they were nationalized) and the Senegalese Sugar Company at Richard Toll have been selling electricity to the SENELEC network.
42. In the period from 1961 to 1976, only two towns, Touba and Richard Toll, registered growth rates higher than 10% per year.
43. The main one was Decree No, 78-036 of 16 January 1976 on location permits. It was intended to help control the installation of projects throughout the national territory.
44. First Four-Year Economic and Social Development Plan (1960-63).

45. With help from foreign funding agencies, SONEPI, established in 1969, set up industrial zones in most regional capitals designed to attract industrial and handicraft enterprises.
46. For instance, the Senegalese Sugar Company, one of the country's largest enterprises, was obliged to build for its executives a housing estate with a wide range of modem amenities.
47. See *Tiers-Monde*, XXIV, 93, January-March, 1983.
48. In 1974, Senegal reverted to pluralist democracy. Initially the experiment was limited, but eventually it opened up to multi-party politics. Thanks to the new climate of opinion, it became possible for opposition voices of liberal and even Marxist persuasion to subject the activities of the government and the Party-State to regular analytical criticism.
49. The prospective study, conducted from February 1988 to July 1989, comprised: a background study of Senegalese society and its natural environment which facilitated the identification of changing trends and the seeds of change; a structural analysis clearing the way to the prioritized classification of variables determining the functioning of the Senegalese socio-economic system; and a prospective study presenting possible scenarios for various components of the system over the long term.
50. According to the final draft of the National Territorial Development Programme, if rates of population growth registered over recent decades continue, by the year 2021 the population is likely to be concentrated in the following proportions: Dakar: 30.9% as compared to 21% in 1988; Dakar and Thiès: 45% as compared to 35.4% in 1988; Dakar, Thiès, Diourbel, Fatick and Kaolack: 69.2% as compared to 63.4% in 1988 With the exception of Tambacounda, the percentage of the national population in the other regions would be likely to decrease from 1988 levels.
51. If current trends continue, regions outside the Dakar metropole are set to lose population. But if these trends are halted either through determined programmes or by natural developments in the regions of Dakar, Thiès and Diourbel coupled with economic decentralization, 1 378 300 persons could be redeployed to the outlying regions.
52. The final draft of the National Territorial development Programme proposes an urban network including the following components: a national metropolitan complex (Dakar, Pikine, Rufisque, Thiès), excellently equipped and therefore acting as a pole of attraction for the entire country; 4 national centres of balance (Kaolack, Saint-Louis, Tambacounda, Ziguinchor); 10 regional centres of balance (Richard Toll-Dagana, Matam, Bakel, Kédougou, Kolda, Louga, Diourbel, Touba-Mbacké, Fatick, Mbour); plus 50 local development poles.
53. However, not all enterprises in Dakar have the same potential for decentralization.
54. The law on the National Domain referred to here vests eminent domain in land unregistered by 1964 in the nation, with the State exercising management rights thereto.
55. The overall fertility index dropped from 7.2 children in 1978 to 6.6 in 1988. Between the two dates, the average age at which Senegalese women began their reproductive lives increased from 18.3 to 19.7 years.
56. Fertility index projections for the year 2016 range from a high of 4.5 children per woman to a low of 3.5.

Bibliography

Senegal (Republic of),Territorial Development Board, 1989,'Esquisse finalisée du Plan d'aménagement du territoire', Dakar.

Senegal (Republic of), Ministry of Planning and Cooperation, 1989, 'Etude prospective: Sénégal 2015', Dakar, 150 pp.

Sidibé, Yoro, 1961, 'L'urbanisme et l'habitat au Sénégal', *Africa* 13-14.

Tiers-Monde, 1983, 'Le rôle de l'Etat dans le Tiers-Monde', N°. XXIV, 93.

United Nations Development Programme, 1987, 'Définition d'une politique urbaine; mission d'analyse stratégique', Dakar.

USAID, 1984, 'Evaluation du développement urbain au Sénégal'. Dakar, 101p.

7. Beyond Patronage and 'Technocracy'?

Mamadou Diouf

The drive towards democracy is a central issue in African political debates today, along with its corollary and practical expressions, multi-party politics, freedom of association and freedom of speech. For two decades at least, the ethos of the single party provided the basic rationale for the construction of nation-states determined above all, if only in the words of their advocates, to achieve the messianic goals of national unity, economic development and social justice. Even the most liberalized regimes were not free from the devastating impact of this ideological current. As the continent slid into economic crisis and consequent structural adjustment programmes, and ideological pressures mounted in favour of respect for human rights; as political conditions were attached to economic salvage measures; and as the populace showed its disaffection by evading taxes and customs duties, shirking civic duties or playing the political game with studied duplicity; and as violence and insurrection became commonplace especially in the urban centres, it became clear that African societies were seeking to break out of the old round of single-party politics.

This is, in a sense, a case of the nationalist chickens coming home to roost, after the shift from the protest phase (1945-60) to the implementational phase of the post-colonial period. Right now, it is still hard to determine how deep the cracks that have knocked into the official structures and institutions responsible for co-ordinating and regimenting post-colonial society (trade unions, the media, etc) by the repeated onslaughts and demands of 'civil society' really go. That difficulty remains, even though, given its 'protean nature' (Mbembe, 1990:1), civil society tended to find its fullest self-expression outside the arena of central political power (Amin, 1988)[1].

Single-party government was, according to Mbembe (1990:1), a 'nightmare that practically all African countries south of the Sahara had to endure'. Senegal was among the first to explore a way out of that nightmare. The process of awakening was gradual and controlled. It began in 1974 with a multi-party system restricted to three, then to four parties. In 1981, the political arena was opened up completely to all currents. The resulting system was an incomplete democracy if ever there was one. It was run by a new elite of 'technocrats' who rudely upset the old post-colonial social compromise in the attempt to establish their own political and economic supremacy, but were incapable of controlling and channelling the forces unleashed by the constraints of economic crisis and the catastrophic social fallout from structural adjustment programmes. For a decade now the technocratic elite has tried to manage the new crisis situation. In that exercise the institutionalization of multi-party politics was expected to serve as a key instrument. However, various parts of the society seem to have turned their backs on that instrument, preferring the imperatives and the rhetoric of ethnic homelands. Their disaffection has fissured the unitary ethos, threatening the territorial integrity of the nation-state.

That unitary ethos had informed the incumbent rulers' approach. But now it is inadequate to rein in pluralistic social groups bent on autonomy and democracy. At the very least they intend to gain greater freedom and scope at the expense of a State bedeviled by economic problems of alimentary survival (Bayart, 1988) and tethered by the ropes and stays of multilateral financial organizations (Dieng, 1990).

The purpose of this chapter is to examine the three decades of change following independence. Our analysis will begin with the pre-colonial and colonial legacy, then move into an assessment of changing interrelationships between State and society in post-colonial Senegal. We shall also assess the rhetorical arsenals they have deployed in their attempts to create and legitimize their bases, as well as to confront and proscribe each other through social agents operating in environments circumscribed by plural, countervailing legitimacies.

Here I find myself in agreement with Foucault (1989) who, in response to the question: 'Of what does the art of government consist?' defines two objectives of governmental power: control over a given territory, and over the population occupying it. His approach, within the Senegalese situation, is pregnant with insight, because of its implied opposition to what we shall characterize as the ethos and rhetoric of homelands, the structural basis of Senegal's largest communities. According to Mbembe:

the post-colonial compromise involved a specific identity associated with a given historical trajectory, that of societies just then emerging from the colonial experience (Mbembe, 1988).

We might therefore trace the history of such a society, in this specific case the history of Senegal, by using a set of clearly defined questions as a probe.

The questions raised in this chapter focus on an examination of relations between the State and specific social agents, with attention to the range of factors influencing. Our inquiry aims to identify the interplay of various social actors occupying a given environment, that of Senegal.

The post-colonial State assumed a messianic mission. For that reason, the pioneering generation of nationalists defined their role as educational. Their self-assigned task was to impose the truths they believed in on the consciences and in particular on the imaginations of those they ruled. That approach led to the characteristic presentational style of post-colonial government: the ruling regime assumed itself to be coterminous with all society. It was the only agency qualified to interpret reality, to organize the endowment of events and phenomena with meaning, and to map the contours of the grand highway to economic development and social justice.

We shall need, obviously, to identify ways in which power-wielding coalitions were formed. By the same token, we shall have to assess the impact such coalitions, with their integrative, all-encompassing visions based on State power, had upon society. That society itself, let us stress, habitually expressed itself in ambiguous ways, and acted in unfocused ways along divergent paths covering an enormous gamut from resistance to escapism, from commitment to withdrawal and the reproduction of authoritarian mind-sets. (Mbembe, 1988; Bayart, 1985, 1988). It might be usefully observed, in effect, that there is a measure of common ground between rulers and subjects. That shared ground includes the acceptance of common reference points, and participation in dramatically choreographed shows of power involving well-rehearsed production techniques, all calculated to guarantee order and inculcate obedience. Sometimes, inevitably, the common ceremony of power also degenerates into disorder and 'rowdiness'[2].

To test these probes in the specific context of Senegal, it will be necessary to follow a precise investigative approach that examines in an orderly sequence the antecedents of the post-colonial State, the establishment of a system of political patronage, the rise of the 'technocratic' elite with the imposition of structural adjustment on Senegal, and finally the first stirrings of an embryonic civil society, seen through instances of resistance and protest against the established order from selected social categories, almost exclusively urban (students, schoolchildren, civil servants, young lawyers, teachers and journalists). These groups share a single common reference point: democracy.

Our approach should facilitate the examination of complex, unstable relationships between State and society. It should also enable us to explore answers to crucial questions: Which agents are responsible for the reproduction of various parts of Senegalese society at the present time: the State, selected social classes, political parties, trade unions, youth movements, religious brotherhoods, etc? What is their informing ethos? To what degree are political institutionalization and popular participation effective? How do all these factors interact? How are the symbolic and rhetorical arsenals of various homeland claimants deployed within the post-colonial dream of the integral State, the territorial environment and the Nation under construction,[3] in the daily confrontation with the *master fictions*[4] of State power?

The Creation of a Colonial Environment

The colonial system was structurally based on a long history interacting with a set of social and political practices deeply etched into the collective memory of the population. Senegal is a product of colonial drives that took the form of political conquest and the pursuit of economic interests. Colonial patterns are still discernible in the behaviour patterns of the post-colonial State. The colony of Senegal comprised a collection of villages, districts, areas, mixed and full-fledged municipalities, and assorted hamlets all brought together in economically related regions. Directly or indirectly, these communities were shaped and designed to fit in with the objectives of the colonial system: the mobilization and efficient management of the indigenous labour force, at low cost, to meet metropolitan requirements for raw materials.

The colonial environment was standardized and unified through the fusion of environments and communities which in pre-colonial times had been separate, discrete. In time its organization was systematized, before its regime ended after World War II. Colonialism shook up the internal dynamics of Senegalese societies, sometimes shattering them. But despite the official claim of a 'civilizing mission'[5], the colonial system was unable to wipe out all traces of their specific roots in the environment. These roots differed in depth and tenacity from group to social group, in accordance with varying degrees of integration into the colonial economy, and the extent of indigenization. The colonial dynamic did not simply fail to eradicate pre-colonial social and political formations and attitudes. Even in its attempts to bring them to heel, the colonial administration adjusted to them in the interests of efficiency. The subjugated societies, for their part, invented various adaptive, underhand stratagems to help them sidestep the full impact of the colonial system without undue strain. It was this nexus of interactions that produced indigenous colonial society.

The historical reconstruction that took place then resulted, first of all, in the diversion of interdependent social networks and economic spheres from old centres to new ones growing up along the Atlantic coastline. Initially these were the trading factories of the slaving era. Later they became the urban centres of the colonial system, with their down-town business areas and ancillary native quarters. Over the long haul, the evidence indicates that various homelands caught up in the new system cooperated or clashed, all within a heterogeneous territory, Senegambia. In that area, even though the communities had separate origins, they shared a number of economic, ecological, ideological and political linkages. The stage-by-stage transformation of the territory that became Senegal affected the various historical phases of the area's political system. The transformation also determined the behaviour of protagonists under varying situations through a variety of interactive processes. At each point in the process the pattern of change helped to define a focus of identity around which processes and modalities for the invention and redeployment of numerous historically dated power plays and codes revolved. Those codes still operate to this day. We shall attempt to describe and analyze this accumulated succession of ideational systems produced by the ruling class in its effort to structure the operational environment of the ruled. And the purpose of our analysis will be to shed light on the creation of the post-colonial Senegalese State.

Pre-colonial Antecedents

Initially, the pre-colonial Senegambian environment was an open space into which flowed successive migratory waves, leading to combinations of population groups along with various social, cultural, political and economic structures. On the basic strata thus formed, the imperial constructs of the western Sudan had a more or less pronounced impact, from the creation of the Ghana empire to the emergence of the Wolof empire of the Jolof. The successive political systems in this region from the eleventh to the thirteenth century did not cover the entire Senegambian area. Often, they did not go beyond the political integration of subject populations. The proximity of trans-Saharan trade routes stimulated the emergence of State structures in the ethnic homelands of northern and central Senegambia. In the outlying zones, however, homeland systems unburdened with the need to ensure security, and not needing to extract taxes from commercial routes and networks, facilitated the maintenance of more loosely organized power systems. The differentiating influence of the great empires, coupled with Islam, the ideological accompaniment of trans-Saharan trade, had a profound impact on the two types of communities present in pre-colonial Senegambia: one hierarchical[6], the other described as egalitarian[7].

It was during this period that a dissociation occurred between the territorial system and the homelands comprising village communities, marking out different areas of legitimacy, with more or less pluralistic systems operating with varying degrees of autonomy depending on their geographical closeness to the seat of territorial power. Integration then was exclusively political. The State was defined solely to mean the Sovereign, his allies and clients. The main attributes of these individuals and groups close to the centre of State power were a propensity to self-enrichment, the use of violence and coercion, the deployment of symbols, a particular code of honour, and diverse ostentatious trappings. The history of the State, in its primordial determination to control all sources of accumulation (roads, commercial networks and mineral wealth), was marked by the systematic subordination of local power through violence or co-optation, along with the weakening of centres of countervailing power. In reaction, local village communities concentrated solely on the maintenance of their autonomy and leadership.

The dynamic tension between the territorial imperative of centralization and the centrifugal search for autonomy in the homelands led to punitive, predatory wars mounted by the ruling aristocracies, countered by resistance campaigns waged by peasant communities. This tension was also the source of segmentary approaches on the part of both rulers and ruled, in their search for economic wealth, social prestige and political power. The resulting process of constant social fragmentation was a perfect framework for patron-client networks. The system was motivated more by considerations of political integration and the control of subordinates than by economic profit. For the aristocracy, living as it did by warfare, the control of trading circuits and the ownership of mineral wealth, was often able to avoid undue exploitation of productive forces[8] under its domain. The patron-client culture thus established was so effective in practical terms that even those Muslim communities that developed under the influence of the trans-Saharan trade were integrated into the framework defined by relationships of solidarity and/or resistance in the territory.

In time, however, the direction of major trade got reversed as the Atlantic trade was established. The change had a tremendous impact on the reorganization of the environment as well as on the reshaping of social groups and economic priorities. As the Atlantic trade gradually superseded trans-Saharan trade, and as it focused increasingly on a single commodity, slaves, it reorganized the Senegambian environment. From the sixteenth century onwards, the new trading system placed greater emphasis on routes penetrating inland along the Senegal and Gambia Rivers. At the same time it established trading posts all along the Atlantic shoreline. In so doing, it diverted trade from its former foci, condemned the old trans-Saharan trading centres to decline, and afforded the formerly insignificant sea-board provinces an opportunity to achieve their independence. An economy of violence spread throughout the area, and autocratic styles of royal rule became the order of the day as rulers tried to tame rival power structures and to control local centres of authority. Royal administrative systems organized local village communities under tight reins. These communities in turn reshaped themselves around the administrative systems that developed. Community leaders either lost their clout or were integrated into patron-client networks. The tendency of local leadership to become fragmented or co-opted gave the State and the various patron-client networks scope to develop and expand. Meanwhile, the struggle for the control of the Atlantic trade accentuated violence and fragmentation within the ruling class. At the same time it encouraged patron-client strategies, to the detriment of institutional approaches. The resulting political fission has been aptly detailed by Barry (1988)[9].

States in the region became highly militarized during the period of the trans-Atlantic trade. The military focus had a political corollary, coercive centralization, that drew Islam into a warlike, militant phase at the expense of discredited traditional religions. Islam redefined and re-created the community as a horizontally integrated social unit cutting across ethnic boundaries in the confrontation with the old kingdoms. The ongoing economy of violence in these old kingdoms was exacerbated by the economic depression that followed the abolition of the Atlantic slave trade and the rough transition of the Atlantic trading system from illegal to legal commercial norms. This was also a time when the search for protection led to expanded patron-client networks as threatened individuals sought patronage. From now on the road to power lay through the capacity to attract a large following and to deploy violence for defensive purposes (protection) as well as for offensive ends, principally to facilitate access to resources.

Environments constructed by such means were chronically unstable. The resulting State systems were fragile, and turnover rates in the ruling class were high. The political topography was constantly shifting, along with social systems, especially at the time of the abolition of the slave trade. The prevalence of elite power struggles, meanwhile, weakened the hold of old hegemonic codes. Centres of power and conditions governing the exercise thereof grew fluid and changeable, weakening communal habits of obedience and shrinking the range of domination. All these factors, at the moment of conquest, defined the limits of State power.

That is why, in those regions previously endowed with State structures, colonial conquest, beneath its military aspect, involved considerable co-optation of segments of the ruling elite. In the egalitarian communities, however, resistance to colonial integration was tougher and longer-lasting.

The Construction of an Indigenous Society

The colonial State planned its integration of Senegalese societies in a highly selective fashion. The selection process was rooted in a component which became the centrepiece of the colonial system from the latter half of the nineteenth century: the groundnut economy. The crop played a strategic role in the colonial economy. Its cultivation reshaped the environment and forced a revival of socialization patterns linking communal and State environments. Seen as a cumulative process, the colonial system, by producing an indigenous society[10], profoundly influenced the configuration of Senegalese society in its constant re-creation of socio-political behaviour patterns.

In countries under direct rule, the establishment of colonial administration was a two-phase process. The first phase stretched from the end of World War I and the first half of the 1920s. Very early, the colonial authorities became convinced that their subjects could only be ruled through the intermediary of chiefs (Crowder, 1964, 1968, 1978).

The auxiliary status of chiefs affected relations between the State and the population, as well as attitudes towards colonial power and its symbolic paraphernalia. In the Wolof areas where groundnut cultivation developed, for example, chiefs selected by the colonial administration enjoyed varying degrees of political or social legitimacy. But often, areas placed under their jurisdiction were larger than the scope of their former legitimate authority. In an administrative circular issued in 1917, Governor Van Vollenhoven defined the office of chieftaincy quite clearly: 'chiefs had no independent power whatsoever. There was only one chief: only the District Commissioner could issue orders. Indigenous chiefs were only instruments, auxiliaries appointed to transmit orders'.

Given the authoritarian character of the colonial system and the centralizing tendency of its administration, local chiefs had little leeway to legitimize their authority as independent agents and to gain the trust of the population under them. They were not even empowered to use forced labour to accumulate resources and consolidate their power in case the colonial authorities abandoned them. On the other hand, the religious leaders (marabouts) emerged to dominate the Groundnut Basin as large-scale producers. The colonial tradition, characterized by the extreme dominance of State and leadership authority (Ranger, 1986:220-224), was able to establish deep roots in this region by using the chieftaincy system.

The erosion of public administrative institutions in rural society, coupled with the tendency of chiefs to turn public power into hereditary personal privilege, reduced the credibility of chiefs among the population as well as among the colonial administrators.

To reform the system, the colonial authorities replaced traditional chiefs with religious marabouts. This was the beginning of the second phase. It would be hard to date its beginning precisely, but its lasting influence is easy to identify. The end of the chieftaincy system and the transition to the use of marabouts as overseers had decisive consequences on the organization of the colonial administrative system. The change resulted in the creation of a mixed colonial environment comprising communal areas under the control of religious brotherhoods; the four municipalities; the economic matrix of the Groundnut Basin, and a socio-political configuration that became a model and a standard for assessing other societies.

The power of the areas under marabout control thus helped to counter-balance attempts by the *évolués* and those born in the four municipalities to dominate political affairs in the colony. A study of ways and means involved in the creation of religious brotherhoods reveals an incontrovertible fact: the colonial authorities played an active role in the formal shaping of their structures. Such interference was clearly visible as part of the structuring process during ceremonies marking the deaths of El Hadj Malick Sy, founder of the Tijannya movement (1922) and that of Cheikh Amadou Bamba, founder of the Mouride movement (1927). In both cases, the colonial authorities were faced with a choice. They could have deepened the fragmentation of the brotherhoods occasioned by succession crises. Alternatively, they had opportunities to meddle in internal brotherhood affairs in order to safeguard the leadership's cohesion and power. In the event they chose the latter course, because the colonial economic system was eager to benefit from the dynamic situation stimulated by the tendency of marabout power to enforce territorial imperatives. The religious brotherhoods thus set to work helping to order the colonial system by speeding up the integration of Senegalese producers into the capitalist world market (Copans, 1980; Coulon, 1981).

Political reports written by District Commissioners indicate that the colonialists were well informed about the decisive influence of the colonial administration on the shaping of the Muslim religious brotherhoods (Harrison 1988). This attitude contrasted with total official ignorance of 'fetishist' societies. Official records complained about 'our total ignorance of their rites, customs, chiefs' (Harrison, 1988:66). One intriguing aspect of this assessment (the contrast between Muslim and 'fetishist' societies) is that it conditioned the politics of colonial accommodation and variations in mechanisms ensuring connections with local forms of power.

When, in 1946, the Lamine Guèye Act extending citizenship rights to the entire Senegalese population was passed, it gave the religious brotherhoods a much greater political role. But it also made their shaky leadership even less stable. Their participation in networks involving the exchange of favours and services, as well as their juggling of administrative ties to the colonial government and political relationships with the *évolués* and the urban elites, gave them a more substantial status as intermediaries[11]. In this way the religious brotherhoods gained exclusive control of access to the population in the rural areas, as well as to the main political groups and personalities in urban politics. To understand and evaluate their role in the urban arena, we need to understand both the configuration and the political mechanisms at work there.

The four municipalities had a special status in the operative framework of assimilationist policy. Analytical assessments of that policy, in our view, have so far been excessively one-sided. They have been partial to Senghor's characterization of the policy during his power struggle with Lamine Guèye. The four municipalities were run according to metropolitan administrative and political norms. Even before formal conquest, these urban centres, where raw materials were collected for export and manufactured commodities imported for sale, had emerged as venues for the exercise of power, the residential choice of top-ranking colonial officialdom. They also functioned as a school for the acquisition of modern political skills.

The fact that the Senegalese elite struggled to obtain a special status (citizenship without submission to the French civil code) is clear proof of their rejection of assimilation. The bias towards acculturation at the heart of assimilationist policy produced as a reaction, especially in Saint-Louis and Dakar, the reshaping of a colonial memory geared to the assertion of an identity distinct from both extremes of French colonial culture and rural African culture. The highly intellectual version of Islam, less involved with brotherhood links, that developed in the municipalities, was one instance of the process. Indeed, as Wesley Johnson points out, 'Islam, which many Senegalese had considered a foreign intrusion, became a focus of resistance to French authority' (Johnson,1971:125). The tried and tested 'protective power of Islam' worked for the so-called *originaires,* members of the four municipalities. In other words, it would be inaccurate to analyze the ideology of the trading centres in terms of assimilation and acculturation to the French civilizing mission. It was, instead, a reshaping process based, for the inhabitants of Saint-Louis, on commercial realities and, for the Lebu of Dakar and Rufisque, on real estate. This formative approach was reinforced by operational links between *évolués* and the leadership of the religious brotherhoods.

The styles of self-expression thus developed, simultaneously old and new, served as vectors of political identity. They also served as factors for the ordering and installation of mobilization mechanisms for economic and social purposes. These processes tended to destabilize metropolitan norms. Their workings led, as in the Wolof territories, to the emergence of indispensable political entrepreneurs, who ended up pushing the *évolués* off centre stage. Of this development the best illustration was the development of the urban centres of Dakar and Saint-Louis, which occasioned a series of conflicts between the colonial administration, elected local officials and political leaders. As pointed out by Diop and Diouf, for reasons connected to the maintenance of patron-client networks, the municipalities became a bone of contention between different political clans. Real estate allocations and public markets under their management became venues of patronage (Diop and Diouf, 1990:7).

Broadly speaking, a number of emergent characteristics may be identified during the first phase of the colonial period, which ended with the onset of World War II. The colonial system administered society instead of governing it (Mellah, 1984). Its aim was to put the Senegalese to work and to develop trade, at the least possible cost.

With the help of coalitions of subject peoples, the colonial administration succeeded in establishing a tradition of authority, subordination and loyalty. The only options left for those social individuals and groups excluded from the system were to seek protection or to challenge authority, to embark on civil disobedience or to adopt lifestyles of social anarchy. Given the fragmentation of the socio-economic environment, the unequal degree of integration of various social groups into the administrative order created a multi-speed society in which religion and ethnic feeling thrived as unconnected expressions of political development.

Senegalese politicians, like the post-war trade unionists, mobilized their forces for a final accounting with 'the promises of assimilation'. From this perspective, the *évolués*, as products of the colonial educational system in those territories under direct administrative rule, working together with formally educated *originaires* from the four municipalities, attempted to get the French administration to accord them equal status and to lift discriminatory barriers against them. In this last period, political and labour struggles had a definite impact. Strangely enough, the reformation of the French colonial empire accentuated those factors we have identified as contributing to structure the country's political development by the amplifying effect of the adoption of a universal franchise. This new situation followed the passage of legislation by the Second Constituent Assembly in October 1946. In the colony of Senegal, the schism between *originaires* and *évolués* was resolved. Better still, territories under French domination were no longer called colonies; they became 'overseas territories' (Article 60) within a single, indivisible republic (Article 1).

The question is: can these reforms be considered as leading to transformations in administrative procedure? Article 72 of the new Constitution established a legislative body known as the Union Assembly. This was the brainchild of African members convinced that the regular French Assembly never devoted sufficient time to African issues. The result was that the Ministerial Council retained vast prerogatives relating to criminal law, public liberties and political and administrative organization. It was empowered to manage the overseas territories by decree, provided only that it acted within constitutional bounds and consulted the Union Assembly. In concrete terms, this meant that the French government continued to control African affairs.

In trade union and labour matters, the post-war situation and the two strikes of 1946 and 1947 had profound repercussions on Senegalese political and social life (Cooper, 1987, 1989; Guèye, 1990). The principal focus of protest was the right to equal pay for equal work, and the right to family allowances. Senegalese workers thus emerged violently on the political scene, making obsolete the colonial classification scheme which acknowledged only two groups in colonial society: peasants and the *évolués*. They were handled according to classification systems familiar to European industrial and labour sociology (Cooper, 1989: 757). The second Lamine Guèye Act of 30 June 1950 gave civil servants equal pay and working conditions. In 1952, a Labour Code fixing a minimum wage along with a standard working day, family allowances, paid holidays, collective bargaining rights and the legal status of negotiated agreements duly signed, was adopted. As Cooper notes, this was a case in which 'a colonial problem did not lead to a colonial solution. The most direct and plausible solution called for a conception of African workers more as workers than as Africans' (1989:758).

The post-colonial State subsequently found concessions granted in the light of this conception hard to honour. For that reason it added to the pressure on a peasantry entirely under official tutelage. During the social and urban crisis, political leaders like Guèye and Senghor had adopted a wait-and-see attitude. The social fallout from post-war economic and social development programmes was proving hard to manage. These factors combined to create political maneuvering room for labour union leaders. Several of them, including Abbas Guèye and Ibrahima Sarr, stood for election as *Bloc Democratique Sénégalais* (BDS) candidates. During this period, then, in addition to the *originaires* and the marabouts, trade union leaders emerged as partners in the making of political coalitions.

The extension of citizenship status and the influence of the educational system added another group of *évolués*, spearheaded by schoolteachers who, on account of their standardized training, and of the fact that they were recruited from all parts of the colonial territory, formed a stratum of colonial society in tune with democratic ideals. Products of the educational system, they were an elite equipped to confront the trading and bureaucratic elite, stigmatized as advocates of assimilation.

In the light of these developments, it is possible to assess the political crises of the 1950s and the reorganization of coalitions bent on hegemonic power. The 1946 Constitution revived old political cleavages. But it also had a decisive influence on the careers of political parties. With an eye to the imminent extension of citizenship rights to the rural zones, Lamine Guèye had coopted Senghor into the *Setion française de l' internationale ouvrière* (SFIO). The move was intended as a vote-getter. But in 1948, Senghor broke ranks with the representative of the old citizenry and formed the *Bloc des Masses sénégalaises* (BMS) with *évolués* like Mamadou Dia and trade unionists like Abbas Guèye and Ibrahima Sarr. Senghor's ideological apparatus, with its accent on Negritude, succeeded in winning over the marabouts and gaining control of the heart of the colonial landscape, the Groundnut Basin. With help from marabouts, dignitaries enjoying legitimacy in peripheral areas of the colony, and schoolteachers, the BDS was able to align its structures with local power networks. Alliances forged all along the fault lines of the marabout leadership structures gave a characteristically clannish tinge to political maneuvering in the 1950s. For intra-brotherhood rivalries took on more momentous meaning once citizenship rights were extended, as indeed did networks of ethnic solidarity. These factors became the only markers on the political scene as political inclinations were confused with assertions of religious and ethnic identity that served to ensure allegiance to authority.

The political and administrative centre was organized according to imperatives dictated by the periphery. In the 1951 general elections, for instance, the BDS won a resounding victory, leaving the SFIO with only Saint-Louis and Dakar. The BDS actually won Rufisque to boot. The party's victory illustrated the domination of the political scene by local forms of power. It also underlined the power of ethnic identities as mobilizational tools in modern political struggles. Maurice Guèye, the incumbent SFIO mayor, reacting to the selection of his young rival Ousmane Socé Diop as the party candidate for the impending legislative elections, decided two days before voting day to quit his party and stand against its activists as a BDS candidate. He figured, in effect, that the election of Ousmane Socé Diop to the legislative assembly would threaten his hold on the mayor's office (Thiam, 1983:30-40). This victory was a perfect illustration of the way the political game was played at the local level, and of the fact that it would be impossible to democratize it (Creevy, 1977).

Efforts to set up dominant political coalitions were given a boost by the passage of the *Loi Cadre* in 1956, followed by its implementation through a set of decrees. The newly acquired autonomy, along with the granting of fresh powers by the Territorial Assembly, especially with the election of a Governing Council in charge of public services, opened up new opportunities for patron-client manoeuvres. The fledgling administrative bureaucracy adjusted to the ways of patronage. Activist participation in the ruling party determined the pattern of advancement. From 1950 to 1958, the BDS, thanks to its support network of marabouts and its co-optation of *évolués* from the outlying reaches of the colonial system, achieved a level of dominance that shifted the country towards single-party rule.

With the approval of trade union leaders, radical elements were co-opted through the creation of the Senegalese Progressive Union (UPS), which coincided with the organization of the top echelon of the Senegalese bureaucracy. From then on, as the country drew closer to independence, because of the nature of the ruling structure, the main features of the Senegalese political process were to be the following: a bloated, unproductive political centre; the selection of dignitaries with ready-made claims to legitimacy to ensure the allegiance of inaccessible homelands; and the contradiction between the rhetoric of nation-building and the practice of pacification and co-optation of outlying areas of the colony. The same contradiction lay at the heart of the rhetoric deployed by the nationalist movement, which used radically different means in its dealings with Europeans and the indigenous population. The existence of this double standard, and the reasons underlying it, are fundamental elements in any effort to understand the tortuous history of the construction of a sovereign Senegalese State.

The Transfer of Power and the Genesis of the Post-Colonial State

The political movement which articulated the claim of national sovereignty included a variety of ideological currents. In other respects, however, it was remarkably homogeneous. Its seats were invariably in the urban centres; its operational style uniformly involved the use of political and administrative institutions of colonial origin. All its strands used French as the language of communication, and its leadership came just as invariably from intellectual, civil service, business or trade union backgrounds. In the pre-independence period, political leaders, whatever their professional status, never challenged the institutional model of the metropolitan State. Their movement borrowed the concept and structure of the State as envisaged in nineteenth century European ideology. All they objected to, therefore, was the dichotomy between the theory and governmental practice of the French metropolitan State and those of its colonial offshoot, which were based on an autocratic tradition of administration, not government. The nationalists' democratic posturing, of course, contrasted with their own political mobilization techniques, rooted in the use of ethnic and religious networks, while they proclaimed their desire to build an integrated State with full popular participation.

The unstable combination, subject to constant renegotiation, between old forms of power, by nature extremely heterogeneous, and 'modern' political processes, helped to push substantial segments of the society to the margins of political involvement. Political mobilization unleashed an explosive social energy. This really was a new development that saw the emergence of new identities and bonds. The innovation was somewhat dampened by the coolness of the marabouts and chiefs. After all, they had bargained for certain benefits under the colonial system, and were anxious to safeguard them. Old holders of legitimate authority had become skillful at constantly adapting to changes in the authoritarian colonial system, learning in the process to bargain for privileges through direct or indirect pressure. In their connections with elected Senegalese politicians eager to establish strong bonds with them and to obtain financial and political support from them, they had much greater clout. This power was rooted in their central role, if they were Wolof marabouts, within the groundnut economy, and, if they were based in other areas, in the tutelage of the local population. They thus ensured continuity in the political process. In the face of the fragile innovation that was decolonization, their behaviour would necessarily contribute to the definition of political stakes in the time ahead.

National Integration and the Construction of the Patron-Client State

The nationalist movement which took charge of the construction of the nation-State adopted a slate of priorities as from 1960. These included political representation for all communities on Senegalese territory, and the creation of a powerful State designed to whittle down ethnic, cultural and religious differences, thus making the society more amenable to government. In this period both the concept and the structure of the State were borrowed from nineteenth century European ideology, reinforced with two new planks: modernization and nation-building. The result was expected to be a united nation, achieved through the creation of the apparatus and institutions of a sovereign State. Backing up these borrowed concepts was a set of constitutional conditions regulating the transfer of power (Lavroff, 1976; Hesseling, 1985).

The key feature of the established procedures was that they fitted into a historical continuum whose promoters had mobilized their forces very early to defend the colonial status-quo that guaranteed their interests and their power. Such was their power that they prevailed on the country's political leaders, in the 1958 referendum, to campaign for a yes vote (meaning independence modified by association with France). During the constitutional talks, they tried without success to get their ideological and political preferences incorporated in the basic law of the future State. The marabouts saw the triumph of the secular option as a defeat. Nevertheless, in practice they had positioned themselves as indispensable agents on the political scene. In so doing, they had defined the limits of State construction. By the same token, they had signalled their readiness to set up game rules which the nationalist leaders were bound to observe, occasionally even unwittingly reinforcing them.

In order to follow, describe and analyze the post-colonial enterprise in its first phase (covering the 1960-70 period), we have first to decipher the operative codes used and to assess their effect on a political, economic and social landscape that is the product of the cumulative history of various intersecting paths since the colonial period. The territory over which the new political rhetoric was deployed, and over which the political actors of the time strutted, remained a colonial environment. Its Atlantic bias was reinforced by the central importance of the groundnut trade, coupled with the loss of the hinterland after the break-up of the French West African Federation. The nation provided a legitimizing framework for the articulation of a rhetoric of identity. It also facilitated the installation of institutions and mechanisms for the achievement of that identity.

Diaw has accurately described the make-shift ideologizing on which the unifying thrust of this rhetoric of identity depended. One main flaw was that the ideology presupposed an uninterrupted historical process underlying the desired identity, but that historical process had been ruptured by outside forces. The contradiction was introduced by a foreign factor - colonialism. In other terms, the unity implied by the concept of the nation was less an aspect of living reality than a simple antithesis of the colonial presence. Second, even if the concept of the nation as a vehicle for unity was a datum, it could only continue playing that role within the framework of a forward-looking, constructive programme (Diaw, 1990). And it was this constructivist vocation that was manifested in the State, the party and its grassroots organizations for the mobilization of Senegal's communities.

A look at the institutional environment created by the new State makes it clear that the new order maintained its continuity with the old colonial order. Old, wielders of colonial forms of power and leadership consolidated their hold. They did this either by moving directly or through intermediary agents into the new circles of influence and authority. These were now streamlined, with the emerging ruling class dominating the centre of the system, and from there maintaining links with peripheral areas partially reinstated into the political decision-making and management process. The coalition of *évolués* and *originaires* turned itself into a socio-professional group strategically important in the construction of a highly centralized State animated by a colonial mentality. As their power grew, so did the reinforcement and extension of State structures. Indeed, the development process itself came to be identified with the development of the State, period.

The corollary was the demobilization of ordinary people. Growing popular apathy went hand in hand with the recognition of ethnic and religious reference points, whose power had been strengthened both by the development of pre-colonial societies and by colonial policy. In post-colonial society, the leading structural postulates were horse-trading and influence peddling. An analysis of the personnel rosters of party and co-operative agencies, the implementational instruments of 'African Socialism', the official ideology of the Senegalese leadership at the time of independence, illustrates this drift into confusion.

The main feature of the administration was its high degree of centralization, the outstanding legacy of the Jacobin background of metropolitan France and colonial totalitarianism. The Senegalese equivalents of metropolitan circles, subdivisions and cantons were regions, prefectures, sub-prefectures and districts. These territorial structures were supposed to bring rulers closer to their subjects, and to facilitate the participation of the people in development activities. According to Article 19 of the 1960 Constitution, local communities were to enjoy autonomy in their 'administrative procedures, terms of reference and resources'. But in 1972, the Minister of the Interior, explaining the background to the drafting of new legislation governing the rural communities, admitted the failure of past policy in the following terms:

Over the past several years it has become clear that the rural population has not really been involved in our administrative structures - a fact incidentally confirmed by studies conducted by the Bureau of Organization and Methods (BOM). That means that only a tiny minority of the population participates. It is just as clear that if administrative activities are to carried out with genuine efficiency, they have to be based on the active, responsible involvement of the population. After all, they are in the best position to assess their own needs. They will therefore be more inclined to accept certain sacrifices if participatory structures facilitate their understanding of the necessity of such constraints (Collin, 1972a).

Before the National Council of the UPS the Minister was even more emphatic:

The objective of the reform of our territorial administration is to establish new structures and promote new methods so as to create conditions conducive to the responsible participation of the population in government affairs (Collin, 1972b).

How, one might ask, did the country get into the situation deplored by Collin? One cause of the problem was rooted in circumstances at the time of the transfer of power. It had to do with the way in which the top-level administrative structure had been fabricated. Because there was a catastrophic shortage of trained staff, and because the French administration was addicted to colonial ruling habits of an essentially magisterial kind, schoolteachers, civil servants and trade unionists were promoted into top positions. There were four main qualifying standards in the selection process: party membership, connections with traditional authorities, technical expertise or professional experience, and the possession of university degrees. Lower-echelon officials could be seconded for higher training prior to recruitment at higher levels of the administration, provided they belonged to the ruling party or affiliated bodies. The recruitment of army officers followed the same criteria. For that reason, the country's ruling political and administrative agencies became almost completely merged.

The ruling party thus became identified with the State and the administrative system. Party organization was cloned on State structures. The capacity of the ruling party to reach the population came to be determined by its ability to link up with local power bases, negotiating the participatory support of major local power brokers. The fusion of party and administration had a tremendous influence on efforts to institutionalize political and social procedures.

Now even though the BDS and its later incarnation, the UPS, achieved political dominance by using the support of ancient, local power bases, from 1950 onwards their leadership had the imagination to work out methods ensuring direct access to the population. The key dynamo powering the construction of the integral Senegalese State was the co-operative movement. Guidelines for that movement were established in Circular 32 dated 31 May 1962, a brainchild of Mamadou Dia, Chairperson of the Executive Council. The co-operative movement was a state-sponsored movement designed to mobilize the rural population for the achievement of national economic development and African socialism, the doctrinal basis of the regime.

The construction of a co-operative network was a national priority, for the following reasons: It would provide the State with opportunities for nationalizing the groundnut trade, thus securing control over a key economic sector. It would use well-tested State circuits for modernizing and diversifying a rural economy that had grown excessively dependent on the groundnut sector. It would ensure the political loyalty of the rural masses through the distribution of patronage and benefits from the groundnut economy. In the long term the co-operative system was expected to develop into a multi-functional system operating in several sectors. It would thus enhance the country's economic and social integration through the creation of cooperative unions at local, regional and national levels.

The first phase saw the establishment by the State of various ancillary organs of the co-operative movement: a Rural Development Service, Rural

Extension Centres (CER), and Rural Development Assistance Centres (CRAD). Their terms of reference were: to facilitate the achievement of co-operative objectives. To that end they were expected to provide technical aid, popularize new technologies, and help in the training, organization and supervision of operators. A measure of planned obsolescence was incorporated into the design of these structures, because according to the advocates of African socialism, the motive force of rural development would come neither from the State nor from the private sector, but from cooperatives.

A comparative analysis of the objectives and actual accomplishments of the co-operative movement makes it clear that right from the start the movement was confronted with two obstacles. The first was the resistance of the society's political bosses. The second was the skill with which these bosses could entrap and exploit institutions posing a potential threat to their power. The drift in this direction was only underscored by conflicts in economic orientation between the President of the Republic, Senghor, and the Chairperson of the Executive Council, Mamadou Dia. When Dia fell in 1962[12], the conflict ended in the total capture of the cooperative movement by traditional potentates and various tentacles of the State bureaucracy.

The first objective, the nationalization of the groundnut trade, resulted in the elimination of loan sharks, Lebanese middlemen and colonial companies. Much has been made of this, but there was another result: the elimination of accumulation opportunities for traders and contractors from the four municipalities. In the past these agents had enjoyed this source of enrichment that had no political strings attached. Now the bureaucracy stepped into their shoes. State control over such a vital sector of the national economy, together with attempts to modernize practices and to give the rural masses increased responsibilities, had a decisive influence on the power coalitions which clashed in party and State structures in the conflict between Dia and Senghor.

The co-operative movement developed rapidly between 1960 and 1962 because, as compared with the former system, it offered clear advantages to peasants. For instance, they took home the full official price for the produce they sold. They also got rebates and loans that made it unnecessary for them to turn to loan sharks. But efforts to establish modern institutions run on egalitarian principles ran into resistance. From 1963 onwards, organizers of such resistance gained a definitive victory. The co-operative movement, shorn of its multi-functional, multi-sectorial capacities, retreated into the groundnut trade alone. In the process it boosted the political role of the leadership of the Muslim brotherhoods.

As for the State, it restricted itself to promoting agricultural modernization programmes designed to extract increasingly large profits from the rural economy. Local politicians hijacked co-operative facilities to build up their personal support networks, giving their supporters free and easy access to credit and other resources (Cruise O'Brien, 1975; Schumacher, 1975; Barker, 1987). Rural dignitaries boosted their prestige and reinforced their power by getting personally involved in co-operative organization (as did the Mbacke family in Diourbel region, the Niass family in Kaolack, and the Diouf family in the Sine area) or by using placement (as the Sy family did in Thiès region) (Cruise O'Brien, 1977; Copans, 1980; Sy, 1969).

As for the peasants, faced with the incoherence of agricultural policy, they fell back on opportunistic tactics. They supported co-operatives when such support was profitable to themselves. When the going got tough they pulled back. They thus functioned as a force manipulable for mercenary ends. Such attitudes were reinforced as rural development officials from the CRAD rapidly gained a reputation for corruption and subservience to political magnates, rural dignitaries and religious leaders eager to embezzle co-operative profits, loans and sundry resources. While their practice clashed with the ideals of the cooperative movement, the highly politicized Rural Development Centres (CRAD) enabled the ruling party to establish a formidable patron-client network in the rural areas (Gellar, 1987:129). In principle, the CRAD bureaucracy had been expected to wither away. But it had linked up with political and religious power networks in order to perpetuate itself. Subsequently, it trained officials for the administrative control system, bringing the co-operatives to heel as from 1964.

From that date on, even though the co-operatives increased their participation in the groundnut marketing system, their production-centred approach, the abolition of their consumer branches, their domination by the masculine gerontocracy and the traditional elite, entailing the exclusion of women and youth, reduced them to venues of patron-client horse trading, corruption, embezzlement and bribe-sharing. The former dependence on middlemen and colonial banks was now shifted to the State and its bureaucracy. Meanwhile, ethnic homelands and religious bases became factors of greater significance, having broadened their scope by getting integrated into modern structures.

In 1966, the development of state intervention and production-centred priorities at the expense of integrated rural development were pushed to extreme limits by the assignment of the National Development Bank of Senegal (BNDS) to finance agricultural activities, and by the creation of the National Co-operation and Development Assistance Board (ONCAD). ONCAD was supposed to rationalize and coordinate the operations of a range of government agencies active in the groundnut trade. The two organizations, whose style was that of pacifying conquerors in rural society, quickly grew into patronage agencies. Politically they were wonderfully effective; economically they were useless (Caswell, 1984).

In the late 1960s it became clear that the management of the groundnut economy was a shambles. ONCAD and the co-operative movement had grown increasingly unpopular. Furthermore, agricultural policy underwent frequent changes; seeds and other farm inputs were supplied late. Corruption was widespread. Debt collection techniques had grown increasingly brutal. Loans for lean season survival were cut. In reaction, the government decided on a new set of policies. It was high time. The tide of peasant discontent was already in. The vicissitudes of the co-operative movement had left the issues of peasant participation, mobilization and assumption of responsibility up in the air. Even less had been done to resolve the issue of State control over a rural society still under the thumb of traditional authorities. The movement had grown more powerful on account of its involvement in modern sector activities and its articulation of 'peasant discontent'. The solution proposed was a reform of local and territorial administrative structures that complemented the National Domains Act of 1964. It went into force in 1972.

The reform of the local and territorial administration was intended to bring the peasantry into a permanent participatory partnership with State administrative structures, according to the thinking of its initiator, the Minister of the Interior, Jean Collin. The reform was an acknowledgment of the failure of previous efforts to integrate the rural masses in development enterprises. These enterprises were the venues where the fate of the entire society would be decided, along with the role of the top-heavy bureaucracy in the field of agricultural policy. In addition, the reform effort revealed the extent to which local authorities could manipulate the central powers. Directives from the central system were disobeyed, distorted or forgotten. This was not a matter of outright refusal to modernize or innovate. Instead, it indicated a dichotomy between an externally initiated, imposed rationality and the needs and capabilities of the peasantry.

The reform had two objectives. The first was the devolution of power. This objective fell by the wayside after Senghor resigned in 1980. In any case, even during the final decade of his term of office, all that was actually done about it was to set up institutions and mechanisms that remained unworkable because so much power was concentrated in the President's hands. Both the Executive and the Assembly remained under the control of the President, even if the latter regained some of its lost prerogatives. More than ever, the President remained master of the patron-client game, allocator of resources and prestige.

The second objective was decentralization, already envisaged in the National Domains Act (64-46 of 17 June 1864). This land reform measure established the State's proprietary rights over all national lands for which no legal deed existed. By withdrawing recognition from all 'customary' landed property, the reform aimed at the physical liquidation of ethnic homelands. It was a calculated, bureaucratic response of the central system to obstacles mounted at the local level. But local power brokers in the hierarchical societies could suborn or simply frustrate the new law, while the egalitarian societies reacted by stiffening their ethnic and regionalistic reflexes. Indeed, decentralization was intended to spread the central administrative model of State intervention, bringing even the tiniest local unit, the village, under administrative control.

The land reform and the new administrative dispositions were supplemented by a new social code, the Family Code. Passed in 1972 by the National Assembly, the Code was designed to boost State influence at the expense of local dignitaries. The purpose of all these changes was not to enhance popular participation. It was to clamp down administrative controls on society, the better to improve the efficiency of the State's development policy. Of that policy the dynamic heart was the extension of the State's domain. The basic unit of the new administrative structure was the rural community. It was integrated into Senegal's overall administrative system. The way its initiators saw it, the change should signal a clean break with the colonial system of organization, which divided the territory into cantons.

Once the ethnic homelands had been physically liquidated, the next move would be to wipe the ideological landscape clean of past encrustations of values and symbols. For Articles 4 and 12 of Act Number 72-25 dated 19 April 1972, concerning the organization of rural communities, stipulated that in the choice of officials, democratic procedures must be followed. The Act also defined the prerogatives of such officials. They were responsible for defining modalities for the enjoyment of usufruct rights on land under their supervision; they had oversight rights concerning decisions taken by administrative officials regarding budgetary allocations and expenditure; and they were entitled to advise on development projects and the exploitation of natural resources.

The structure of the main administrative organ in the rural communities,[13] the Rural Council, reflected the ambiguous nature of the reform. It was headed by a chairperson caught between two functions. On the one hand he was the representative of his community; on the other hand he served the executive authority. The second function overrode the first because the Government-appointed Sub-Prefect was in charge of the rural community budget, and without his approval, no decision taken by the Rural Council had any force. The central status of this administrative official was a perfect illustration of the real function of the Rural Council: it was to act as a transmission belt for the administrative and technical bureaucracies.

The reform which established the post of Sub-Prefect defined his function: 'to stimulate and guide the responsible participation of the population in the various activities of the administration'. In the interests of democratic equity, sincere or simulated, the law made entrepreneurs, State officials and franchise holders ineligible to sit on Rural Councils. The law also forbade the participation of members of the same family, in order to avoid clannish domination and nepotism. The new system did not spread over all of Senegalese territory until 1982. Any evaluation of its scope and impact done at this point will therefore necessarily be partial. It had a much greater impact on societies in the Groundnut Basin, whose economy was strongly oriented towards the capital and the world economy. In the outlying zones, especially in the Senegal River Valley and the Casamance, the new system came up against resistance because of its integrationist thrust.

An analysis of results achieved against the background of set objectives reveals a number of problems. Decentralization was so organized as to benefit only the State, by facilitating its intervention in the tiniest unit of social organization. There may have been a devolution of powers on the institutional level, but its practical effectiveness was blocked by the context of patron-client relationships in which government officials inexorably moved, sometimes because the State demanded that type of loyalty from them, sometimes because they themselves were keen to preserve their 'sinecures'. In any case, one remarkable feature of the new rural councils was that they were not really operative except in the Groundnut Basin, and there they paid scant heed to official rules. The type of social actors identified as key role players in the new agencies showed clearly that 'responsible participation' worked to the exclusive benefit of local middlemen. Step by step, using the new structures, they were able to operate like an autonomous social group with its own ideology and strategy enabling it to prevail in situations of conflict to maintain its dominance along with the maintenance of certain bargaining norms. The central ruling class depended on this group. So did ordinary peasants. In this way, local leaders were able, whenever the threat of State expansion loomed, to outflank or neutralize the State by disguising their own interests under the grand boubou of communal ideology.

Meanwhile, whatever the particular path[14] taken by individual communities, the general preoccupation was the maintenance of communal autonomy. Senegalese societies thus demonstrated their capacity to absorb the modernizing values the State tried to inject into them, and their ability to adapt to changing situations in the socio-political environment. Their leadership succeeded in turning itself into a special social category of 'political brokers' embracing traditional leaders, traders, major producers and members of leading lineages. Positioned to act as intermediaries for all communications between the apex of the social pyramid and its base, they devised ways of filtering all information, editing out all data that might threaten the status quo, and doing everything to safeguard and promote their own interests.

While Wolof societies and other communities involved in the groundnut economy were able to assess the scope of every attempt at State intervention and to frustrate it, populations in remoter areas, knowing little about cooperatives and being uninvolved in their development, resisted and evaded the National Domains Act, the local and territorial administrative reforms, and the Family Code. Taken as a whole, these three modernizing reforms went contrary to models by which these populations lived. They were contrary, for instance, to the inherently hierarchical, anti-egalitarian model of the Peulhs and the Soninke. They were also contrary to the pluralistic model of Diola political and legal culture. Such differences could only result in irredentist pressures in the long run. The emergent regionalism of the peripheral societies, the assertion of cultural, political and religious claims outside the framework of the State and its traditional connections, all underlined the failure of political integration in rural society. For one thing, these claims and aims were expressed in ways meaningful only in rural society. The gap was all the deeper since the group in strategic control of the State had modeled the reforms in accordance with its own norms and its own logic.

As far as other societies were concerned, the only upshot was the assertion of identity as an aspect of dissidence and protest (Darbon, 1988). These societies had no access to Islamic protection. They were also excluded from the process of fusion and assimilation of the dominant groups composing the mixture of old and new elites. They therefore fell back on ethnic identities as a counterweight to the imperatives of the State, fleshing out their apprehensions by giving Senegalese from the northern regions the image of as invaders. The reshuffling of the unitary mentality was accomplished not only on a basis (and under the stimulus) of regionalism, the spatial and economic expression of cultural particularism, but also on a basis of economic marginalization and ideological unification initiated by the post-colonial State.

On the whole, even though the ethos of ethnicity came under pressure from urbanization and the various processes of assimilation, cultural intermingling and acculturation, it persisted as a significant factor. Several considerations actually contributed to revive it. These included economic development policies based on unequal regional development; discriminatory recruitment according to social and/or ethnic criteria; discriminatory decisions governing the implantation of projects and agencies; the use of diverse political strategies as a means of pressure; and the persistence of patron-client connections and clannish habits in the allocation of power and resources, the development of ethnocentric associations set up to safeguard or develop ethnic heritages. Also, the hegemony of Wolofs and Muslims and its corollary, the reaction from peripheral groups; and the philosophy of national integration, invariably backed up by force or co-optation as a way of dealing with the cultural, ethnic and religious fragmentation of the Senegalese national environment, added to its revival.

The situation in the urban areas was generally similar. But there, State intervention was much more visible, and social pacification correspondingly difficult. The State of Senegal continued to use urban population management techniques developed in the colonial period, especially when it came to handling the urban sub-proletariat and other marginalized groups. Yet the memory of trade union activism among workers, and the fact that their leadership played a significant role in the forging of the post-colonial compromise, imprinted upon the actions of the State authorities in the urban areas a particular dynamic. Because workers were represented within central ruling circles, it was much more difficult to block their political participation, given their social heterogeneity and the difficulty of identifying their spokespersons and representatives. Even in Dakar, where the Lebu ethnic group was able to assert itself as a special partner of the State, their fragmented leadership prevented them from gaining total control over the political environment.

The tortuous trajectory of State intervention in the urban areas was thus based, on the one hand, on attempts to institutionalize professional bodies, age groups and trade unions, and on the other hand on a policy of violent repression and co-optation directed against dissident segments of the social elite. The environment that facilitated this type of management was one of centralization under a single party. But the style was also softened by an economic policy of consumer subsidies. As far as centralization was concerned, the aim was to control municipal institutions and to turn them into venues of patronage. This made it possible to keep elected officials out of the running of urban affairs, to shield the municipalities from political competition, and thus to leave the central ruling class in control of the allocation of funds and power. In 1964, as part of the reinforcement of the presidential regime, most municipalities were shorn of their prerogatives when they were brought under the Ministry of the Interior: 'The municipalities helped consolidate the State system by using their resources to reproduce a mercenary political system. Just as the central civil service establishment adjusted to the neo-patrimonial rule at the structural core of the Senegalese State, all the peripheral authorities (enterprises, party units, etc.) adjusted to the system' (Diop and Diouf, 1990:32).

Because State oversight meant subservience, and because institutions in charge of women's and youth movements were so utterly politicized, they either became discredited or slumped into lethargy. Urban dynamics therefore found outlets in informal, religious and ethnic networks within residential neighbourhoods or factories. Since they were so wide open to patron-client influences, the only way they could express themselves politically was through violence. Violence was all the more unavoidable since political parties were either banned or swallowed up in the ruling party. The only organized groups able to shake the hegemonic power structure[15] were student groups, teachers' unions and workers' trade unions.

In the period from 1963 to 1968, a series of serious social crises broke out. Senghor's regime responded by stiffening its repressive policies and bringing trade unions into the regime, the better to control them. The 1968-69 upheaval, which made it clear that the regime had failed in its attempts to integrate the most dissident sections of the elite, led to a crisis. In the 1970s, this was further aggravated by the phenomenon of 'peasant discontent' and the withdrawn, quasi-dissident attitude of the new head of the Mouride religious brotherhood, Abdou Lahat Mbacké. The changed political circumstances, the ravages of the economic crisis, and the effects of the drought all combined to persuade the regime to change its dominational system. This was all the more necessary since a new generation of university graduates, coming out in the late 1960s, was clamouring for control of the State apparatus on the basis of its technical expertise. The new breed intellectuals created a club called *Nation et Développement* (March 1969) along with a Centre for Socialist Studies, Research and Education (August 1970). They also formulated a 'technocratic' nationalist ideology opposed to 'politics as usual', by which they meant the old patron-client politics that had given the regime its more or less stable base during the first decade of independence (Fatton, 1985). Members of these organizations were of the opinion that the Senegalese people were incapable of designing and sustaining a programme of modernization. They thus disqualified the bosses of patron-client networks (*Club Nation et Développement*, 1972:23).

Thanks to the ensuing brainstorming, the Senghor regime reacted with a series of institutional, political and economic responses to the crisis. The institutional response was the creation of the Senegalese National Confederation of Workers (CNTS), a trade union body affiliated to the ruling party and committed to the ideology of responsible participation. The government was reshuffled and a new post of Prime Minister established in 1970. With the appointment of Abdou Diouf as Prime Minister, the government selection process underwent a profound change. There was now an increasing emphasis on technical expertise, a fact which facilitated the gradual lopping off of dead wood from the political elite and the broadening of the government's base. The new elite group in turn moved to take over local political positions, using its clout within the State apparatus to create a support network for itself.

The new political approach coincided with a supposedly nationalistic policy of support for Senegalese business-managers (Senghor, 1972:71-72) and the appointment of Senegalese executives in foreign companies to posts formerly held by expatriates. Rocheteau has aptly described the new approach as 'the merger of the government superstructure and the industrial techno-structure. In addition to its normal operations, the State was now assigned the role of entrepreneur' (Rocheteau, 1982:375). In this new role, the State lurched heavily into the economic and banking systems. Numerous public and mixed corporations were established. Several financial institutions were brought under State control in order to facilitate access to credit for the future 'national bourgeoisie' (Rocheteau, 1982:368; Gautron, 1979:54-55).

According to Gellar, the Senegalese State set up 70 parastatal corporations between 1970 and 1975. By 1975, these corporations made up 40% of the modern sector, produced 40% of value added in that sector, and employed one-third of its work force (Gellar, 1982:24). Increased State participation in the economy was facilitated by high international market prices for the country's two main export products, groundnuts and phosphates. Under prevailing conditions of social crisis, the proliferation of sinecure posts and embezzlement opportunities helped the ruling party to strengthen its organizational hold on society through the broadening of patron-client networks. Encouraged by the economic upturn, President Senghor launched a policy of receptivity to democratic norms beginning in 1974. There really is no way to understand this policy outside the context of the new economic situation and its effect on the consolidation and expansion of patron-client networks.

The simulated devolution of power, the speeches on the Senegalization of executive personnel, the co-optation of new 'technocratic' segments into the ruling class, the distribution of juicy sinecures and embezzlement opportunities to various 'businessmen', all culminated in the institutional taming of part the intellectual middle class and trade union leadership. First there was the recognition of the Senegalese Democratic Party (PDS), which described its policy as one of 'constructive opposition'. Then came the 1976 constitutional reform which instituted a three-party democracy. The UPS turned into the Socialist Party, while a fragment of the African Independence Party

(PAI) was legally recognized under a Marxist-Leninist label.[16] In 1979, a fourth conservative party, the Senegalese Republican Movement (MRS), was accorded recognition.

The limited multi-party regime did not end the disaffection of all middle class groups. Some rejected the constitutional reform. Political stability was not restored. Students' and teachers' unions kept up the pressure. With the onset of the drought, peasant discontent brought about a drop in groundnut production, and the repayment of farm loans became increasingly problematic. International petrol crises worsened the shock of domestic depression as groundnut and phosphate prices took a dive on the international market. Inflation soared while per capita income dropped, clear signals that the economy was in serious trouble (Gellar, 1982:45-66; Hesseling, 1985:74). The Senghor regime tried to make ends meet by diversifying its sources of international funding. In the process, it increased both the domestic and foreign debt (Rocheteau, 1982:369-377). By the late 1970s, Senegal's debt totalled over a billion dollars, and debt service charges took up 20% of export earnings.

To cope with the dire economic situation, the Senghor regime was obliged in 1979 to seek economic help from the International Monetary Fund (IMF) for re-financing the debt. That international funding agency recommended an Economic and Financial Recovery Programme that required drastic austerity policies. The old post-colonial compromise had been based on the expansion of the State's base, patronage and 'support for sale'. Now it was confronted with technocratic procedures whose advocates had risen to posts within the State structures from 1970 to 1974. These technocrats were in a position to use the leverage of international funding to push aside the old masters of 'politics as usual'. That, at any rate, was what their programme called for. Under those circumstances, Senghor, past master at the game of 'politics as usual', the leader credited with Senegal's political success story (Cruise O'Brien, 1978), had to step down. On 31 December 1980, Senghor resigned (Diop and Diouf, 1990:69). As stipulated in Article 35 of the Constitution, Abdou Diouf, Prime Minister since 1970, was appointed President of the Republic. The 'technocracy' had reached the apex of the Senegalese pyramid. The accession of Abdou Diouf coincided with the establishment of IMF and World Bank economic control over Senegal.

The 'Technocratic' State: Senegal Under Structural Adjustment

The build-up of the 'technocratic' State was very closely linked with the implementation of a new economic policy which required the ascent to power of a new set within the ruling elite, committed to the new logic pushed by the IMF and the World Bank. It was the latter imperative that provided a basis for the power system constructed by the new president. Officially, he had been Deputy Secretary-General of the Socialist Party all along. Nevertheless, he had never been able to assert his unchallenged leadership status in the party. The circumstances under which he came to power were exceedingly difficult. He therefore had to seek a new approach involving much greater institutionalization of political procedures in order safely to implement the austerity measures that were a prerequisite for access to funds.

To get a measure of the impact of the new economic climate on political strategies calculated to restore the hegemony of the ruling class, let us take brief stock of two factors. Our analysis here is not centred on economic policies[17]. What we are interested in is an assessment of the impact of economic policies on the routines as well as the tacit and explicit norms of power, and on the prevalent forms of bureaucratic formality whose function was to provide a structure for Senegalese society.

Technocratic stratagems were worked out as a deliberate method of evading the political game. That meant that in the construction, or at any rate in the recruitment, of the new ruling class, technical expertise was a pre-requisite. Promoters of the new style enforced their claim to national leadership by discrediting the State as an institution and pushing privatization as the gateway to limitless opportunity. Their approach did a great deal to widen divisions between old-style party bosses (nicknamed barons) and lower-level activists. It separated 'conservatives' from 'innovators', thus setting parameters for the reshuffling of the ruling elite.

It should be made perfectly clear that structural adjustment programmes involve something more than a set of technical options for restoring the free play of market forces on a basis of comparative advantages. They also reorder society along different lines dictated by the construction of the new hegemony, in the same way that they infuse new meaning into social struggles. It is this underlying meaning that we intend to analyze in our study of the two main stages of the process. The resulting insights should help us explain why the new regime went to work reforming all sectors but left patron-client networks in the rural areas intact.

The Succession: Change Within Continuity (1981-83)

Abdou Diouf rose to power as the hand-picked successor to the previous head of State. According to Article 35 of the Constitution, by virtue of which he became President of the Republic of Senegal, it was his duty to complete the term of his predecessor. That gave him two years to assert his influence and leave his imprint on the State apparatus. As far as the party was concerned, the great challenge confronting him was to achieve control over it - a feat he had been unable to accomplish in ten years. Since he was after all a hand-picked successor, his freedom of action was circumscribed by the need to maintain a measure of continuity with previous policy. He was thus obliged to keep swinging between two extremes of change and continuity, to the background rumblings of a relentlessly deteriorating social, political and economic situation.

From the word go, the new president came up against the opposition of those who disagreed with his appointment. Some of his opponents were members of his own party. Legal and underground opposition parties furnished the remainder. It was against this background that the Unified and Democratic Teachers Trade Union of Senegal (SUDES) launched a strike in May 1980[18], sparking a crisis. The strike called for a boycott of examinations, with lasting consequences for the Senegalese school system. There were, in addition, political demonstrations by underground political movements and a so-called Islamic reform movement. But the most significant factor was the avalanche of economic and social hardships brought on by the Stabilization Programme (1978-79) and the Economic and Financial Recovery Plan (1980-1985). The two policies affected hiring in the civil service, public corporations and parastatals, as well as price policies. In times past all these sectors and items had provided opportunities for patron-client transactions.

From the moment he was appointed Prime Minister in 1970, Abdou Diouf worked steadily to diminish the importance of political connections and to increase the weight of technocratic expertise in the choice of ministers and top civil servants. As we have pointed out, this shift had an impact on the make-up of the party leadership at both local and national levels. Party connections became increasingly valueless as a passport to high government office. On the other hand, the government took to parachuting its proteges, in classic top-down manoeuvres, into leadership positions at local party levels. The result was either apathy or a sharpening of factional clashes that often provoked members to desert to the opposition. Most went to the PDS. Abdou Diouf was blamed for this turn of events, hence the violent diatribes mounted against him by PS leaders and activists.

Before Senghor's resignation, Abdou Diouf had had a hard time getting accepted within the ruling party. One reason was the long-drawn-out intra-party confrontation with Babacar Bâ, from 1971 to 1978. Diouf won that clash, interpreted as a battle between the 'political' and 'technological' factions within the Senghor regime, with Abdou Diouf representing the technocrats and Bâ the politicians (Diop and Diouf, 1990:88-93). Babacar Bâ's exit from the government confirmed Abdou Diouf's growing strength at the head of the government and the civil service. Using his mastery of these two main pillars of the State apparatus, Diouf moved to consolidate his control, all the while remaining careful to work within constraints imposed by the succession process.

Appointing Habib Thiam and Jean Collin to manage the continuity factor, Diouf used his image as an 'honest, well-bred' fellow and his reputation as a 'peerless, hard-working technocrat' to initiate a series of reforms designed to frustrate every blocking move from within his own party. At the 14 January 1981 meeting, he left intact the strategy of political continuity by keeping all the Socialist Party's founding fathers in the Political Bureau. But he decided to scrap the so-called 'four factions rule', according to which Senghor had limited official recognition to four political persuasions. Instead, he established complete multi-party democracy and freedom of the press. Within the same perspective of pacifying and absorbing middle class opposition within institutional channels, he convened a General Conference on Education and Training Systems.

The intention behind the conference was to use it to take the critical sting out of the country's teachers, who supplied the main leaders of the most determined Marxist and trade union organizations. In organizing the General Conference on a basis of democratic consensus, Diouf took on a sector which had spearheaded all political and social problems in the final decade of Senghor's regime. In February 1981, the new government added a finishing touch: with a view to neutralizing another group of leading dissidents in the educational sector, it set up mechanisms for providing jobs for unemployed university graduates (Diop and Diouf, 1990:187-196).

The consensus ideology at the base of the new President's first moves was articulated in terms of an energizing 'national pride' in his inaugural speech on 1 January 1981 (Diouf, undated:12). The appeal called on national pride as a consensual stimulus to development (Diop and Diouf, 1990:251-281). The novelty of the speech was that it broke with the practice of excluding non-PS members, using the fundamental idea of nation-building, while leaving the door open for the opportunist wing of the petty bourgeoisie to come and form a new segment of the political elite, distinct from the Socialist Party. The manoeuvre enabled Abdou Diouf to broaden his basis of legitimacy to include areas outside the Senghor regime's heritage, but without jeopardizing that core heritage itself. His moves to broaden the basis of his regime, however, were centred exclusively on his person. He therefore nurtured the fable of himself as a person untarnished by his party's history of patron-client relationships and discriminatory practices.

Into the breach opened up by his speech, groups proclaiming their commitment to Abdou Diouf's programme rushed, subjecting the party to criticism, thus sapping its strength at both apex and base. The resulting weakening of the party obliged it to fall in step behind Abdou Diouf during the transitional period. Meanwhile, a series of 'Dioufist' factions fragmented the party, softening it up for subsequent regimentation. These moves culminated in the Illicit Gains Act, a counter-embezzlement sword of Damocles suspended over the heads of PS leaders, accompanied by speeches on the need to inject moral fibre into the nation's political life, served up to rev up crowd support.

By thus pulling out several stops, the new president and his supporters negotiated a safe passage to the February 1983 elections. The president, with help from his support groups, was able to run a campaign distinct from that of his party. He tapped support from patron-client networks run by religious brotherhoods, part of his legacy from Senghor, for support in the rural areas. In this he succeeded all the more easily by exploiting his Muslim identity and his work within the Islamic Conference Organization (OCI).

Diouf's decision to write off peasant debts entrenched him even more solidly within the patron-client environment of Senghor's legacy, this time with his own symbolic paraphernalia and his own package of moves. Simultaneously, support groups, led by the President Abdou Diouf Programme Support Committee (COSAPAD) and the more intellectual New Senegal Seminar and Exchange Group (GRESEN), a think tank, both of which sprouted during the February 1983 election campaign, helped spread the ideology of the State apparatus and the Senghor legacy. These support groups worked to control a section of the intelligentsia while presenting themselves as new-style elements in an emergent set of patron-client networks.

The build-up of Diouf's domination in the transitional phase, as we have attempted to show, involved the use of strategies calculated to shatter all concentrations of power or dissent capable of threatening the survival of the political system set up by Senghor's party. The system underwent some fine-tuning, but nothing was done to upset Senegal's post-colonial configuration, and its Islamic-Wolof base remained intact. Thus, manipulative techniques and the use of repressive mechanisms, together with corruption, all contributed to make the 1983 election entirely fraudulent. After that, bolstered by a presidential mandate acquired through universal suffrage, Abdou Diouf was in a position to consolidate his supremacy and leave a much more personal stamp on his programme.

The Establishment of the Diouf System: The Centralization of Power

The methods used to consolidate the Diouf power system consisted of 'technocratic' economic management procedures, constant reshuffles within the Socialist Party, and firm manhandling of the opposition. The process did not always go smoothly. There were clashes within the ruling party, with the opposition, and among the population at large. It established a new political, economic, social and cultural environment that put a premium on extra-institutional forms of behaviour in the political configuration of post-colonial Senegal. The strategic nerve centre of this configuration was the General Secretariat of the Presidency, which was turned into the country's administrative and political headquarters. The way to this centralization was paved by the elimination of Senghor's political colleagues and their replacement with 'technocrats'. Concurrently, the Senegalese National Trade Union Confederation was brought under control with the promotion of a new leadership drawn from the staff of *Renouveau Syndical*, together with the revival of work-place committees (Diop and Diouf, 1990:115-131). The centralization exercise was also facilitated by the new economic policies dictated by the IMF and the World Bank, with the Minister of Finance and Economic Affairs, Mamoudou Touré as director of operations.

The new liberal policy cut sinecures and expenditure serving to grease the wheels of legitimation. By concentrating resources at the presidency, it facilitated the emergence of a new political configuration. But it also provoked the most violent crises experienced by the State. State withdrawal to the advantage of the private sector was not the only issue at stake in the new policy options. Several factors pointed to the definitive abolition of the post-colonial compromise that had given Senegal's patron-client political system its foundation. Once the compromise ran out, the problem of the distribution of income and power between competing social groups reared its ugly head. Today it stands in all its grizzly nakedness in the form of cutbacks among civil service personnel, who in the past had been the key to social stability in the nation. Furthermore, the State, facing its growing debt mountain, was trapped in endless rounds of negotiations to reschedule payments. Its elbow room and initiative were thus drastically curtailed, for the simple reason that no one can conduct any serious savings policy under such circumstances. Meanwhile, quite apart from their purely economic aspects, the new policies dictated by the IMF and the World Bank had a political and social impact on patron-client transactions and networks.

Several authors have pointed out, with regard to Africa in general, that the new structural adjustment policies are based on a concept that goes somewhat as follows: long term analyses reveal that low levels of savings and productivity in Africa's economies are not the consequence of any deterioration in terms of trade or the subordinate status of the continental economy in the world economic order. They are, instead, simply the result of the failure of Africa's rulers to subject their populations to salutary doses of over-exploitation (Cooper, 1981; Bayart, 1986:320-321). Following this line of argument, IMF and World bank experts, along with their local dependents, have set themselves a single goal: to soak up domestic demand (L'Hériteau, 1986 and Duruflé, 1988). To a certain extent, they are trying to control domestic financial circuits that formerly made up the guts of what Bayart has described as an 'economy of the belly'[19].

Driven by the need to generate domestic savings for paying back debts, yet committed to liberalizing the economy in order to offer optimal conditions to local and foreign investors, the government was forced to tighten its tax structure. The step was inevitable once projected government income fell chronically short of amounts needed to cover recurrent expenditure and debt service payments. A range of measures sent workers' living standards and incomes into a steady downward slide: customs duties, consumer taxes, higher stamp duties, numerous charges and deductions from funds owed to individuals or companies by the Treasury, increased deductions from peasant earnings in the form of constantly falling producer prices after the 1988 riots; the expansion of the tax base, etc. Hence the talk, these last few years, about social costs of adjustment and the need to ease the pressure on the poorest strata.[20]

Adjustment entails a regressive distribution of incomes and wages. The weakest members of society, and those least integrated into patron-client networks, bear the heaviest sacrifices. It would be hard for the Senegalese State to confront directly those components of its own structures that helped to ruin the economy. The entrenchment of the new president's power may be measured in the way in which various types of economic reorganization and their impact on rules governing integration within the political system have led to changes, or to the maintenance of the status quo.

Certain sectors, apparently, escaped untouched from this vast reorganization of the country's political, economic and social landscape: namely, the religious and ethnic leadership groups which played a crucial part in the new alliance. As far as the religious leaders are concerned, it is hard to understand the new regime's policy unless we perceive, for example, that the maintenance of marabouts within the alliance in no way meant any desire to give them a permanent place in the coalition by incorporating them into modern economic circuits. In 1983, contradicting its own economic policy, the government decided to give groundnut producer prices a hefty boost. In terms of constant value, the new price proposed was as good as peak prices paid out in the mid-1960s. The price hike was so patently linked to the 1983 elections that in 1984, just after their victory, the Socialist Party leadership lowered the producer price, justifying the move by pointing to the world market situation (Barker, 1987:10).

The point here is not simply that this manoeuvre could be denounced as opportunistic. It is that it shows clearly how similar the different fractions of the ruling class are. Even if, for the moment, it is still difficult to give a methodical assessment of changes in rural society since the time of peasant discontent and the cycles of drought in the 1970s, it is perfectly clear that while modernizing their agricultural holdings, the marabouts have tended increasingly to shift the prime focus of their economic business into the urban areas, away from the countryside.

The turn towards modern business, together with the modernization of structures and forms which exemplify the power of the religious leadership (bank accounts set up for mosques under construction; the receipt of cash gifts from the Arab States, the establishment of printing presses, libraries, schools, etc.), constituted a new development. The changed circumstances made it necessary to place the old patterns of patron-client interaction on a new basis. For with the groundnut economy in a recession and the civil service lifestyle under stress, the modern elite now for the first time had the upper hand over the religious elite. The new accent on technocratic competence, the cutbacks in legitimacy-bolstering expenditure, and the skill with which the State exploited shifting divisions within the leading Muslim families, pushed religious leaders into abandoning their former role as supportive allies and getting directly involved in politics with increasing frequency. From 1983 to 1988, there were numerous examples of this change. Marabouts gave their official approval (known as *ndiggël*) to groups campaigning for the re-election of the incumbent President. Certain marabouts fought to control local sections of the ruling Socialist Party, especially in the urban areas. Serigne Mamoune Niass in Kaolack was a good example.

These instances were the result of reciprocal attempts by the two elite 'blocs' within the ruling coalition to assimilate each other. They also signalled the gradual acquiescence of marabouts in their role, no longer as political power brokers and intermediaries, but as canvassers and factotums. The capture of the marabout families, and in particular that of their younger branches, was facilitated by their integration into the modern sector, where the State was still boss. One might wonder what form such relationships might take in future. Will the religious leadership be totally assimilated into the modern elite, as a prelude to a complete break between the peasants and existing leadership groups, religious and secular - the kind of rupture that might result from the historical careers of groups whose inspiring models have run out of steam under the changing circumstances created by economic and political liberalization? In any case, the marabouts have had their autonomy whittled down. Their legitimacy is increasingly perceived as arguable.

These are signs that the old networks that worked for Senghor have undergone a shake-up. In the Casamance and the Senegal River Valley, the new political canvassers have had a hard time getting integrated into the environment, and those areas are trouble spots. They are illustrations of the new dynamic, a result of the new 'Dioufist' approach: the reorganization of factions into subordinate units under a single centre that was initially the General Secretariat of the Presidency, and subsequently became the President's Office itself. As illustrations of the dynamics of this approach, let us consider its effects on the ruling party and the government from 1983 to 1988.

After Abdou Diouf won the presidential election and his party the legislative elections, he set about seriously establishing his own mechanisms for controlling the State and party apparatus. First, he decided to abolish the post of prime minister, transferring its main duties to the General Secretary of the Presidency. Concurrently, the old party 'barons' were pushed aside, while non-Party members were given cabinet posts. From 1984, Diouf began to define the issue of the development of the Socialist Party in terms of renovation and openness. In so doing, Diouf gave himself the means to reassure the new breed of activists, while pressuring his support groups to acknowledge the supremacy of the Socialist Party in Senegalese society. In January 1984, while delivering his general policy statement, he attempted to persuade his party colleagues that:

> It is impossible... it is inconceivable for any political body, even one enjoying majority support, to shift towards an exclusive conception of the future of Senegal, by supposing that it is within its ranks, and only within its ranks, that everything ought to be accomplished. As Senegalese socialists, we have always acknowledged that we are not the only patriots, not the only nationalists in this country. Being thus convinced, and remaining true to ourselves in that conviction, in other words, profoundly Senegalese, we have to demonstrate our open-mindedness in our ideas, our generosity in our acts, and thus accept the proffered hand of the Other, whenever that hand is apt to contribute to the strengthening of national unity and solidarity (Diouf, 1984:20).

The philosophy of an energizing national pride changed meaning in the post-election context of 1983. It no longer embraced political groups. It referred solely to qualified personnel willing to join the Socialist Party. Those who wanted to support Diouf should consider it worthwhile to get Socialist Party cards (*Le Soleil*, 19 April 1985:4). The appropriate slogan now was 'Receptivity, But Under Firm Control'. It produced results when key leaders of the COSAPAD and GRESEN support groups joined the Socialist Party.

Their membership and the appointment of ministers from outside the ruling Socialist Party led to the emergence of a new patron-client channel within the State structure. That in turn brought about conflicts with the established channels responsible for recruiting clients for the regime. Several analysts writing about Senegalese political developments from 1983 to 1988 interpreted the resulting political conflicts in terms of contradictions between advocates of 'politics as usual' and supporters of Abdou Diouf within the regime. Some argued that these clashes reflected the problems the new president was having trying to bring the party under control, and the fact that his new plan for a consensus-based politics was arousing resistance.

The fact of the matter is that Diouf and Collin remained on top of the structural reorganization of the Socialist Party throughout this period. By getting themselves acknowledged as umpires of all conflicts, they quietly succeeded in erasing Senghor's stamp from the party and positioning their own personnel, taking care to keep them under tight rein. Jean Collin supplemented the system by encouraging the creation of associations in support of his programme. These Collin support groups were similar to the Abdou Diouf support organizations, except that this time they were intra-party affairs. Collin also took care to give them a key role within the administrative structure.

The same break-and-make strategy was used to take over the CNTS trade union movement and to turn it into a safety valve. At the time of Diouf's accession to power, the CNTS was under stress on account of a power struggle between a 'conservative' faction led by Babacar Diagne and the *Renouveau Syndical* faction led by Madia Diop. Even though Babacar Diagne had once served Diouf as a Minister, the President supported Diop against him. By so doing, and by demanding that work-place committees be set up to keep the *Renouveau Syndical* organizers under check, Diouf was able to use Diop's pseudo-revolutionary verbiage as a safety valve for venting frustration over the sacrifices entailed by structural adjustment policies. The wobbly balance of the trade union policies followed by the *Renouveau Syndical* leader was the 'working class' aspect of the technocracy's rise to power.

Now the stakes moved beyond the simple exchange of services and payments, to include the ability to keep the 'labouring masses' within the CNTS so that it could remain a principal team player toning down the centrifugal tendencies of factions within the trade union movement, or of new, independent workers' organizations. By shuttling constantly between government imperatives and union claims, Diop was able to survive politically in the extremely turbulent years after 1983, especially in 1988. But the non-Socialist-Party wing of the government, which for four years tried to present an alternative channel of patron-client power, was eliminated after the violent disturbances of February-March 1988.

The General Secretariat of the presidency gave permanent and active support to administrative expertise and the technocratic approach. The secretariat became the key reference venue of Senegal's administrative and economic systems. It remained relatively immune to the financial penury that reduced other patronage outlets to ineffective shells. It thus became the single functional deep pocket left in the bribe and kickback economy. Meanwhile, the extreme concentration of power considerably lessened the functions and responsibilities of ministries through the empowerment of entirely independent technical units. That left the administrative and political centre of State power as the final arbiter in all cases of conflict or uncertainty. Thanks to the President's control over all sources of information, Diouf and Collin began to nibble away at the homogeneity of the top echelon of the administrative system. An increasingly large slice of it became somewhat independent of political power plays. This fraction was supported by foreign funding agencies. Here too, developments enforced dependence on the President's office.

Diouf's political style, on the surface, lacked smoothness. Some commentators called it choppy. Oddly enough, however, it helped to achieve the single-party dream that had been the vogue just after independence. By relying exclusively on administrative and juridical management methods, coupled with massive use of repression and coercion, the system succeeded in concentrating authority and placing it at the service of the Presidency. The confusion of prerogatives was worsened by the low level of institutionalization of multi-party democracy, the subservience of elected bodies including the National Assembly to a dictatorial 'technocratic' decision-making process, the instability of top-level administrative and economic teams, as well as the improvisational manner in which personnel were habitually recruited. Within the structures of the ruling party, infighting for the control of the few juicy patronage-dispensing areas left (the President's Office, the National Assembly and the Mayoral offices) became fierce, creating a murderous climate of intra-party violence at both local and regional levels. Judging by the way the various sectors were politically managed, the fundamental vocation of the constitution (to be more accurate, the different constitutions) became clear: to restrict the locus of power and to strengthen the executive branch.

Obviously, the process outlined above was not all smooth sailing. The build-up of presidential supremacy in a regime of political brokers, within the original tradition of support networks, was shaken up by violent crises to which the State opposed an equally muscular style of management. The crises seemed to break out immediately after the 1983 elections. Babacar Sine, in any case, described the change in the following terms:

> Today the honeymoon is over. It lasted two years, from January 1981 to August 1983. From now on relationships between the President and the people will be based on plain truth. Such a relationship deserves deepening, since it is the basis on which the Senegalese people will be committed to the behaviour and deeds of the Head of State and his government.... Furthermore, it is necessary for all work done to be communicated to national public opinion... There, in our opinion, lies the crux: the need to ensure that the President's activities are correctly perceived, apprehended, understood and assimilated by a people who have already expressed a massive preference for him at the ballot box, but who still await convincing proof of the relevance of his policies as Head of State (Sine, 1984).

After 1988, the same voices raised the same problems, proposed solutions or condemned the behaviour of 'a section of the Press' or a 'certain section of the opposition'. Their complaints were a good illustration of the failure to institutionalize democratic practices, and of the persistence of a single-party culture with fresh patron-client imperatives.

Lastly, there is cause to wonder whether the new ruling class did not simply use their claims of technocratic competence to anesthetize members of the old political power structure slowly built up by Senghor and his main colleagues while they hacked away at them with their criticism and pushed them out of the running. The ensuing political reorganization was based on a new rhetoric and a new style of political action focused essentially on the ideology of technocratic expertise. All this was part of the intellectual climate of the time. No doubt the weapons used were the most effective for the critique of the Senghor era.

Today it is clear that the vaunted technocratic nostrums have failed. The political crises symbolized by the opposition slogan *Sopi* (Change) have dragged on too long. Attempts to re-establish macro-economic balances have also proved fruitless. In the absence of a democratic alternative, the outcome of all these failures is a series of increasingly violent confrontations within the Socialist Party and between government and opposition forces. The government flexes its muscle; the opposition responds by taking over the streets. In the beginning, the political change summed up in the opposition's call for *Sopi* and the sociological change invoked by the words *Set Setal*, making common cause, had forced the political authorities to yield a series of concessions after the 1988 upheavals. In the present confusion, though, the two streams seeking change have begun to flow wider and wider apart.

Conclusion

The build-up of the hegemony of the new ruling class came with its share of crises. Some were violent indeed. As we have indicated, the reshaping of patron-client networks did not make giant waves in the rural areas, except in such zones as the Casamance and the Senegal River Valley.

Two conclusions might be drawn from the restriction of crises to selected areas. The first is that during the 1980s, the referential matrices at the base of the post-colonial compromise, that is to say, the areas under the influence of the Muslim leaders with their vote-procuring power, as well as the Muslim-Wolof power model, were running out of steam. The main causes of their exhaustion were the depression hitting the groundnut economy; the hard times faced by the patronage-dispensing agencies, the abolition of some agencies, like ONCAD and the co-operatives; and the entry of marabouts into the modern sector urban economy. The shift from old power bases to new, and the effective use of the rhetoric of the grassroots at the seat of central power, alerted the ruling class to reformulate organizational guidelines behind patron-client networks.

Second, the technocratic style introduced by the new political class, by using its exaggerated emphasis on technical solutions to knock out old network bosses, cleared up space for individual initiatives and new ideologies. Into that space moved youth groups, women's movements, but also marabouts stung in the scandal of their unpaid bank loans. Even if the political coalition built on patron-client networks is extremely stable, its component parts are not particularly well knit. The holes in it are all the wider because the new 'democracy of the literati' emerging in the atmosphere of complete multi-party politics has introduced currents of dissent, especially with the rise of the so-called independent press, likely to print information capable of shaking regimes that formerly enjoyed a monopoly of truth, the kind of regime the State invariably slapped on the nation after consecrating itself the only source of news. Serious distortions between payoffs from power plays and the assimilationist approach of the authorities in the historical career of Senegalese societies provide a means of placing the two biggest upheavals of the decade in perspective.

One meaning of the fact that the urban areas became the really active trouble-spots is that the kind of political violence that came to be associated with the *Sopi* slogan signalled the failure to institutionalize political expression. It also indicated the sudden incursion into the political arena of groups excluded in the pre-colonial and colonial periods: young people and the unemployed. In my opinion, it is perfectly clear that the interstitial spaces that proved such fertile nurseries for autonomous organizations (women's and young people's producer associations in the rural areas, cultural groups and sports clubs in the urban areas) exemplify the difficulties confronting old patron-client networks in their attempt to adjust to the new situation brought on by structural adjustment and intensified in-fighting within the ruling Senegalese Socialist Party.

Patently, then, the technocratic ethos, which ought to have helped in the reconfiguration of the Senegalese political system, merely ended up worsening the crisis of the post-colonial model. By chopping up the country's various power centres in the interests of all-out centralization, and by weakening the component organs of the coalition it headed, the technocratic power structure opened the way for dissident forces. The civil service, that social stratum that had always served the regime as a stabilizing buffer in the social system, now shattered by dismissals and high taxation, gradually withdrew from the mechanisms of political support.

Now the days of the old game of political stabilization through the use of support networks are gone. These days the regime stays afloat thanks to its repressive firepower supplemented with catch-as-catch-can concessions. The disturbances of February-March 1988 were a good illustration of widening cracks in Senegal's institutional edifice. Perhaps that was the necessary price of the post-Senghor hegemonic build-up. In any case, there has been a change. Formerly, members of the ruling coalition staked their claims and negotiated shares from the national bowl. Now ad-hoc brokerage is the rule, the search is for instant pay-offs, and only narrow circles get to participate in the redistribution system.

The new ruling class, after its definitive capture by the central regime, closed ranks. At the same time, efforts to set up countervailing networks rivalling the Socialist Party apparatus failed. In the resulting vacuum, violence became the only form of expression. The regime has rejected democratic dialogue. Now certain sections of the Muslim religious leadership have taken up the role of democratic advocates. The *Sopi* crisis was very cleverly managed, and opposition leaders were backed into a confrontational corner that proved advantageous to the State and its institutions. But the end result was a dead end. The population has been pushed farther towards the fringes of society. People in general still have reflexes acquired from patron-client relationships. But given the dearth of resources, such reflexes no longer bring them any benefits. The range of options has been drastically cut: a desperate forward leap into the void; indulgence in escapist pseudo-solutions, or a search for autonomous environments inaccessible to the State.

Attempts to bring down the ruling regime, spearheaded by the *Sopi* movement, got nowhere. Since then the country has seen a string of confrontations between the opposition and the Socialist Party, itself stressed by internal wrangling. The long political stall has encouraged the emergence of new trends led by the urban youth, lawyers, journalists of the so-called independent press, schoolchildren and university students. It is no easy task interpreting the arcane drift of these new movements. It might be reasonable to suppose that the new approaches they bring to the political and social scene, in line with the strategy of fragmentation initiated by Diouf, will help to redefine the future of democracy in Senegal along corporate lines.

The broker-based patron-client system of the technocrats provided a fertile matrix for the *Set Setal* movement. *Set Setal*, based on a revisionist view of Senegalese history, is designed to redefine urban space and to take it over. Community self-help projects, occasionally diversified with the collective execution of mural paintings, constitute characteristic methods of self-expression used by youth groups intent on telling the political class to rethink its activities and its operational style. By firmly rejecting old top-down organizational styles, young people are defining new norms of social organization opposed to the old habits of the post-colonial compromise. Through a syncretistic output comprising symbols borrowed from distant and varied sources, the youth are in the process of violently rejecting official rhetoric. The urban culture they are shaping has no connection with the memory of the colonial past, or with any remembrance of the nationalist period. In its swing from violence to the drop-out style of the *Set Setal* movement, what the youth are expressing is their refusal to march to the old regimental drumbeat in this new situation of structural adjustment.

Behind the retreating State, new autonomous zones have opened up for the first time. These are spaces facilitating the expression of democratic claims that no longer demand the transformation of all society, but the creation of improved environments for the financial success of social protagonists henceforth committed to the idea that the powers of the ruling regime need to be curtailed. Since resources for bribes and kickbacks, the currency of co-optation, have dried up, co-optation has yielded to the mobilization of the social elite in corporate organizations. Because the broker-based patron-client networks of the technocratic regime failed to deliver the components of a stable, reformed social system, pluralist approaches surged forward in Senegalese society. This pluralism existed all along, but in the past, given the unitarian and centralizing tendencies of the State's political agencies, it had been stifled and disguised through the installation of patron-client relationships as the prime method of socialization and hierarchization.

The crisis of the technocratic system of domination, from that point on, could be seen in the sharp distinction now established between the regime and the society. The crisis makes it simultaneously necessary to differentiate between the self image and that of the society projected by the regime, on the one hand, and the reality of the erosion of society at large by different parts of it in their search for stability. The old patron-client networks facilitated the definition of a common pool from which rulers and ruled all drew a common set of symbols and images. The technocratic regime, on the other hand, wiped out the complicity of rulers and ruled, thus abolishing the old nationalist fable of one indivisible community. Now the only story left is that of an adjustment programme driving everyone endlessly back to square one, a process that does not bother to look for justification. The problem is that increasingly, that process is coming up against resistance from social groups whose approaches do not fit into pre-colonial, colonial or colonial moulds. The behaviour of such groups has so far proved totally impervious to the usual techniques of violent repression and social pacification. It looks as if these social groups have been demanding an alternative democratic structure opposed to the current model, but impossible to interpret, at least for the time being.

The question now is this: what political *legerdemain* can the Senegalese ruling class conjure up to cope with a situation in which their financial backers say the adjustment programme is still unfulfilled, and their elbow room has become excessively tight? The technocratic class rode in on a high tide of hope, but its performance has been woefully limited: the substitution of a broker-based patron-client system for the old orthodox patron-client networks. The technocratic ethos, essentially a symbolic trope, worked initially to open up the political game to a new set of players. That political game meanwhile grew increasingly violent, and the new technocratic players, confronted with the resistance of Socialist Party old-liners, looked rather winded. The regime tried a new experiment, bringing the Senegalese Democratic Party and the Independent Labour Party into the cabinet and parliament, under the Prime Minister, Habib Thiam. The opposition leadership that had led the *Sopi* movement abandoned the streets for the corridors of power, leaving the mob widowed and the general population disillusioned. Some wondered if Diouf had not managed, once again, to outsmart the opposition, thus consolidating his power and putting off the reforms demanded by the funding agencies. Others supposed perhaps that he had simply postponed the social crunch bound to result from structural adjustment by broadening the support base. In whose interests would the new political configuration work?

These are hard questions, difficult to answer. For today, Senegal is involved in a new adventure that will determine the future of democracy in the country. The deadline for the experiment is set for 1993, when new presidential and legislative elections are to be organized under a fresh Electoral Code. Will the new coalition survive the impending test? Or will it explode, as various conflicts between the Socialist Party and the Senegalese Democratic Party indicate, and as the wrangling between the Prime Minister Habib Thiam and the PDS leader Abdoulaye Wade about the expenditure of a F CFA 39 billion loan from the African Development Bank suggests? It may be true that the ruling coalition has worked out a system of 'political pacification'. It is equally true, however, that its economic and educational plans are still somewhat occult, its achievements correspondingly hazy. In the coming period, then, whatever the Senegalese Democratic Party decides, the one inexorable question is going to be this: did the crowd-pulling potency of the *Sopi* movement get weakened in the power-sharing phase?

Notes

1. The very concept of civil society is peculiar to capitalism, in the precise sense that the existence of such a society implies that economic relationships are to a certain degree independent of the political sphere.... In peripheral capitalist societies, however, precisely because of the half-baked nature of capitalism there, civil society is either too weak to stand on its own, or simply non-existent" (Amin, 1988:IV-V).
2. Here I adopt the adjective from Mbembe's title (1988).
3. The homeland concept, referring to a geographical and spiritual entity, a closed, cohesive world, is antithetical to the more open, more heterogeneous concept of a territory. In the environment under study here, Islam and colonial rule were the creators of the latter form. The consequences of the clash between the two conceptual forms are here described as *de-territorialization* when they involve the transformation or destruction of homelands. When homelands adapt, get redefined, or invent new modalities for coping with territorial realities, we call the process *re-territorialization*. Mbembe uses the terms 'indiscipline' and 'rowdiness' to describe this twin process and to measure the capacity for initiative and innovation (1988:29).
4. According to Wilenz (1985:4), all political power is regulated by various *master fictions*, a set of fables providing a basis for imaginary constructs, which then get established as indisputable truths.
5. On the issue of the dislocation of the "original (read pre-colonial) environment," Mudimbe (1987:3) writes with reference to Elisabethville: "There is, on the one hand, the colonial order, established as an absolute recrudescence of history. On the other hand, there is the order of the Extra-Customary Agency, invented as the compulsory transmission channel between traditional memory and the authority of a radically innovative system."
6. The hierarchical societies include the Wolof, Peulh, a section of the Sereer (Sine and Saloum), the Manding and the Soninke.
7. The egalitarian societies include the north-western Sereer, sections of the Malinke, the Diola, Mankan, Balante, Bainut, Basari and Konaji of southern and south-eastern Senegal.

8. This analysis involves the extrapolation of insights from studies on more recent periods conducted by Cooper (1981: 51-52) and Bayart (1988:320-321), and their application to an earlier period.
9. See also Curtin (1975) and Bathily (1988).
10. Moniot (1988:4) emphasizes the challenge faced by analysts dealing with this kind of situation when he writes: 'The colonial system, along with its current sequel, did not wipe out the cultural paradigms of subject peoples. Instead, it proposed and imposed new, functional models for internalization. In the study of contemporary power equations and issues, then, the scholar faces a universe of complex, specific cultural practices...'
11. In the final section of this chapter, focused on colonial territorialization, we shall be returning to this issue.
12. For detailed discussions of the fall of Dia, see Diop and Diouf (1990: 33-35); Lo (1985); Dia (1985) and Senghor (1980).
13. In my analysis of the reform, I have made substantial use of the extremely well-informed study by Magassouba (1984).
14. See the studies on three villages (Fuuta Tooro, Nominka and Mbayar Sereer), published in monograph form by Balans, Coulon and Gastellu (1976).
15. See the chapters by M C Diop and B Diop in this volume.
16. On the system of limited multi-party democracy, see Fall (1977), D. Cruise O'Brien (1978) and Nzouankeu (1984).
17. The economic aspect is given detailed treatment in the chapter by Boye in this volume.
18. See the work of Sylla (1982, 1988), and his chapter in this volume.
19. Bayart describes the 'economy of the belly' as featuring 'predatory practices, underdeveloped productive forces, widespread bribery and the waste of savings in lush, showy spending sprees' Bayart, 1989:320-330).
20. Under present circumstances, the crucial nature of fund-raising can be judged from the following details: in October 1990, a personal income tax was established, featuring a 5% surtax. Concurrently, ministerial and public service budgets were slashed by a presidential directive after the national Assembly had voted the budget. The 5% personal income surtax was rescinded in November 1990 (*Le Soleil*, 26 November 1990:2).

Bibliography

Amin, Samir, 1988, Preface to P Anyang' Nyong'o (ed.), *Afrique: la longue marche vers la Démocratie: Etat autoritaire et Résistances populaires*, Paris, Publisud, FTM/UNU.

Balans, J L, C Coulon and J M Gastellu, 1976, *Autonomie locale et Intégration nationale*, Paris, Pédone.

Barker, Jonathan, 1987, 'Political Space and the Quality of Participation in Rural Africa: A Case from Senegal', *Canadian Journal of African Studies*, 21, 1, pp. 1-16.

Barry, Boubacar, 1988, *La Sénégambie du XVe au XIXe siècle: Traite négrière, Islam et Conquête coloniale*, Paris, L'Harmattan.

Bathily, Abdoulaye, 1989, *Les Portes de l'Or: Le Royaume de Galam (Sénégal) de l'Ere musulmane au temps des Négrier, (VIII-XVIIIe siècles)*, Paris, L'Harmattan.

Bayart, J F, 1985, 'L'Enonciation du Politique', *Revue Française de Science Politique*, 35, pp. 343-373.

Bayart, J F, 1988, *L'Etat en Afrique. La politique du ventre*, Paris, Fayard.

Brunschwig, Henri, 1983, *Noirs et Blancs dans l'Afrique noire française*, Paris, Flammarion.
Caswell, Nim, 1984, 'Autopsie de l'ONCAD: La Politique arachidière au Sénégal 1960-1980', *Politique Africaine*, 14, pp .39-73.
Club Nation et Développement, 1972, *Le Club Nation et Développement*, Dakar.
Collin, Jean, 1972a, 'Projet de Loi sur la Réforme de l'Administration locale et territoriale', Mimeo, Dakar.
Collin, Jean, 1972b, 'La Réforme de l'Administration locale et territoriale', Dakar, Conseil National de l'Union Progressiste Sénégalaise (UPS), Mimeo, Dakar.
Cooper, Frederick, 1981, 'Africa and the World Economy', *African Studies Review*, XXIV, 2/3, pp. 51-52.
Cooper, Frederick, 1987, 'La Question du Travail et les Luttes sociales en Afrique britannique et française 1935-1955', in J. Copans, (ed.), *Classes ouvrières d'Afrique noire*, Paris, Karthala, pp. 77-113.
Cooper, Frederick, 1989, 'From Free Labor to Family Allowances: Labour and African Society in Colonial Discourse', *American Ethnologist*, 16, 4, pp. 745-765.
Cooper, Frederick, 1990, 'The Senegalese Strike of 1946 and the Labor Question in Post-War French West Africa', *Canadian Journal of African Studies*, 24, 2, pp.165-215.
Copans, Jean, 1980, *Les Marabouts de l'Arachide*, Paris, Sycomore.
Coulon, Christian, 1981, *Le Marabout et le Prince*, Paris, Pédone.
Creevy, Berham L, 1977, 'Muslim Politics and Development in Senegal', *Journal of Modern African Studies*, 15, 2, pp.271-277.
Crowder, Michael, 1964, 'Indirect Rule, French and British Style, ' *Africa*, 34, pp. 197-206.
Crowder, Michael, 1964, *West African Chiefs*. New York, Africana Publishing Corporation.
Crowder, Michael, 1968, *West Africa under Colonial Rule*, London, Hutchinson.
Crowder, Michael, 1977, 'A Versatile Charisma: The Mourid Brotherhood 1975-1976,' *Archives Européennes de Sociologie*, 18, 1, pp. 84-106.
Crowder, Michael, 1978, 'Senegal', in J Dunn (ed.), *West African States. Promise and failure*, Cambridge, Cambridge University Press, pp.173-188.
Cruise O'Brien, Donal, 1975, *Saints and Politicians: Essays in the Organization of an Islamic Brotherhood*, Cambridge, Cambridge University Press.
Curtin, P D, 1975, *Economic Change in Precolonial Africa. Senegambia in the Era of the Slave Trade*, Madison, Wisconsin University Press.
Darbon, Dominique, 1988, *L'Administration et le Paysan en Casamance. Essai d'Anthropologie administrative*, Paris, Pédone.
Dia, Mamadou, 1985, *Mémoires d'un Militant du Tiers-Monde*, Paris, Publisud.
Diaw, Aminata, 1990, 'Etat et Nation: La Problématique de la Référence dans une Perspective constructiviste'. Paper delivered at the Colloquium of the African Political Science Association. Mimeo, Cairo, January.
Dieng, A A, 1990, 'La Réunion FMI/Banque Mondiale', *Sud-Hebdo*, 128, October, p.4.
Diop, A B, 1981, *La Société wolof: Tradition et Changement. Les Systèmes d'inégalités et de domination*, Paris, Karthala.
Diop, M Coumba and Mamadou Diouf, 1990, *Le Sénégal sous Abdou Diouf. Etat et Société*, Paris, Karthala.
Diop, M Coumba and Mamadou Diouf, 1990, *Sénégal: Enjeux et Contraintes de la Gestion municipale*. Travaux et Documents du CEAN, No. 28, Université de Bordeaux.
Diouf, Abdou, undated, *Le Sursaut National*, Publications du PS, Dakar.
Diouf, Mamadou, 1990, *Le Kajoor au XIXe siècle. Pouvoir Ceddo et Conquête coloniale*, Paris, Karthala.
Duruflé, Gilles, 1987, *L'Ajustement structurel en Afrique: (Sénégal, Côte d'Ivoire, Madagascar)*, Paris, Karthala.

Fall, Ibrahima, 1977, *Sous-développement et Démocratie multi-partisane: l'expérience sénégalaise*. NEA, Dakar.

Fatton, Robert, 1985, 'Organic Crisis, Organic Intellectuals and the Senegalese Passive Revolution', 28th Annual Meeting of the African Studies Association, New Orleans, November.

Fatton, Robert, 1987, *The Making of a Liberal Democracy: Senegal's Passive Revolution, 1975-1985*. Boulder, Lynne Rienner.

Foucault, M, 1989, 'La Gouvernementalité', *Magazine Littéraire* 269, Paris.

Gautron, J C, 1979 'Les Entreprises publiques, acteur et indicateur du changement social', *Revue Française des Etudes Politiques Africaines*, 158, pp. 43-62.

Gellar, Sheldon, 1982, *Senegal: An African Nation Between Islam and the West*, Boulder, Westview Press.

Gellar, Sheldon, 1986, 'Circular 32 Revisited,' in J Waterbury and M Gersovitz (eds.), *Political Economy of Risk and Choice in Senegal*, London, F Cass.

Guèye, Omar, 1990, 'La Grève de 1946 au Sénégal.' FLSH Master's thesis, History Department, Cheikh Anta Diop University, Dakar.

Harrison, C, 1988, *France and Islam in West Africa, 1860-1960*. Cambridge, Cambridge University Press.

Hesseling, Gerti, 1985, *Histoire Politique du Sénégal*. Paris, Karthala.

Johnson, Wesley, 1971, *The Emergence of Black Politics in Senegal. The Struggle for Power in the Four Communes 1900-1920*. Stanford, Stanford University Press.

Lavroff, Dimitri-Georges, 1976, *Les systèmes constitutionnels en Afrique noire. Les Etats francophones*. Paris, Pédone.

L'Hériteau, Marie-France, 1986, Le FMI et les Pays du Tiers-Monde, Paris, IEDES/PUF.

Lo, Magatte, 1985, *Sénégal. L'heure du Choix*. Paris, L'Harmattan.

Magassouba, Moriba, 1984, 'La Participation en milieu rural dans un Pays en voie de Développement: les Communautés rurales au Sénégal,' *Annuaire du Tiers-Monde*, VIII, (1982-1983), pp. 225-234.

Mbembe, J A, 1990, 'Afrique sub-saharienne: Enjeux de fin de siècle.' Colloquium on 'Youth in the Sahel', Laval University 26-29 September, Quebec

Mbembe, J A, 1988, *Afriques indociles. Christianisme, Pouvoir et Etat en Société post-coloniale*, Paris, Krathala.

Mellah, Fawzi, 1984, 'Le Développement politique: Rôle et limites de l'Administration publique. Eléments pour une analyse de l'Etat moderne au Tiers-Monde,' *Annuaire du Tiers-Monde*, VIII, (1982-83), 1984, pp.77-85.

Moniot, Henri, 1988, 'Une mise en perspective,' in B Jewsiewick and H Moniot (eds.), *Dialoguer avec le Léopard? Pratiques, Savoirs et Actes du Peuple face à la Politique en Afrique contemporaine*, L'Harmattan/Safi, Paris/Quebec.

Mudimbe, V Y, 1987, 'Espace africain et Mémoire,' Paper delivered at the International Colloquium on 'Memory, Identity and Experience in Francophone Societies,' Laval University, 9-12 October, Quebec.

Nzouankeu, J M, 1984, *Les Partis politiques sénégalais*, Dakar, Clairafrique.

Ranger, Terence O, 1986, 'The Invention of Tradition in Colonial Africa,' in E Hobsbawm and T O Ranger (eds.), *The Invention of Tradition*, Cambridge University Press, Cambridge.

Rocheteau, Guy, 1982, *Pouvoir financier et Independance économique en Afrique: Le Cas du Sénégal*. Paris, Karthala.

Schumacher, E J, 1975, *Politics, Bureaucracy and Rural Development in Senegal*, University of California Press, Berkeley.

Senghor, L S, 1972, *Rapport de Politique générale: le Plan de Décollage économique ou la Participation responsable comme Moteur du Développement*. Dakar, GIA.

Senghor, L S, 1980, *La Poésie de l'Action. Conversation avec Mohamed Aziza*. Paris, Stock.
Sine, Babacar, 1984, 'Abdou Diouf entre deux Fronts,' *Le Soleil*, 20 July, pp. 1-5.
Sy, Cheikh Tidiane, 1969, *La Confrérie sénégalaise des Mourides*. Paris, Présence Africaine.
Sylla, Abdou, 1982, 'De la Grève à la Réforme: Luttes enseignantes et Crises sociales au Sénégal', *Politique Africaine*, 8, pp. 61-73.
Sylla, Abdou, 1988, *L'Ecole future pour qui? Crise scolaire et Réforme au Sénégal* (Etudes et Recherches No.108), Dakar, ENDA.
Thiam, Ibrahima, 1983, 'La Vie politique à Rufisque de 1945 à 1958,' FLSH Master's thesis, History Department. Dakar, University of Dakar.
Wilenz, S, 1985, *Rites of Power: Symbolism, Rituals and Politics Since the Middle Ages*, Philadelphia, University of Pennsylvania Press.

8. The Future of Tradition

Souleymane Bachir Diagne

Outlines of a Critique on the Discourse on Culture

At frequent intervals, society is invited to view with alarm the deterioration of so-called traditional values. Sometimes the problem is stated in terms of a failure to hand down said values correctly from generation to generation. In Senegal this issue recently stimulated a number of tentative policy proposals. Proponents of one such proposal, especially anxious to improve the upbringing of the younger generation, at one point suggested the drafting of a 'list of values' which all Senegalese would be expected to live up to. They proposed a corollary list - of negative values that good citizens should avoid.

There is another approach that in many aspects runs parallel to this twin proposal. Its most visible manifestation is the fact that a National Cultural Charter for Senegal is now in the drafting stage. A preliminary draft of its General Report has already, in fact, been submitted to the Government. It's self-appointed mission: 'to integrate the cultural dimension into a comprehensive social plan'. Again, there is a corollary: 'to combat the forces of cultural alienation'.

Now fancy, if you will, the wide range of problems likely to arise from the establishment of a 'list of values'. There is, in particular, one core difficulty from which all the others, ultimately, ramify: it is, to put it mildly, doubtful whether the fundamental social ethic underlying a community of values runs into a crisis simply because the values in question become obsolete. In such situations, which factor constitutes the chicken, which the egg? We might be wiser not to take too seriously the architectural metaphor according to which values might crumble, but can be restored through such determined initiatives as the drafting of a list, if we wish to understand the causal mechanisms of ongoing change.

In its current form, the draft Cultural Charter is based on the hackneyed assumption of Senegal as a society making do with a tattered set of cultural values. The Charter expresses this condition in a formula that on examination seems quite astonishing. It also, in its hazy formulation, aptly encapsulates the bundle of thorny theoretical questions lurking under what is presented as if it were an axiom. In the words of the draft Charter, the crisis in Senegalese cultural life is due to the 'relative success' of the concept of *l'ouverture*, while the twin concept of *l'enracinement* remains 'poorly understood', at any rate so far.

These twin concepts President Senghor used as a formulaic slogan summarizing his prescriptive vision for the development of Senegalese culture. L'*enracinement*, meant a connection to indigenous roots, the basic values of the land. L'*ouverture*, indicated an open receptivity to external influences. Here there is no call to argue either with the slogan or against the vision. What we intend is to take the formula for what it obviously is: just another metaphor, drawn from botany this time, and by the nature of things incapable, like any figure of speech, of working as a substitute for the precise conceptualization of real mechanisms at the core of socio-cultural life in Senegal.

To say that the policy of receptivity to external influences has been successful on the whole, while that of connection to basic roots has been poorly understood, is to make no sense. The implication is that the nation, nourished by avowedly imperceptible internal roots, has nevertheless flowered and opened out quite well to the outside world. The chain of reasoning is patently absurd. Still, these terms have become common currency. For that reason there is no clear awareness of their utter haziness. The reality they mist over is a struggle which itself has become an unavoidable topic, an expression, dramatic in its sheer simplicity, of an immanent tension between identity on the one hand, and 'the forces of cultural alienation' on the other. Let us note, in passing, the exceedingly vague nature of the formula: 'forces of cultural alienation'. In its imprecision it is a perfect example of the kind of meaningless doublespeak which frees its users from deeper analysis.

One consequence of such vagueness can be seen in a proposal put forward in the draft General Report on the Cultural Charter, calling for the organization at regular intervals of initiation festivals. The kindest thing one can say about the idea is that it is contradictory. Doubly contradictory, in fact. The basis of the proposal, after all, is an observed fact: that even in societies practicing initiation, the custom is dying out. From there the illogical leap is made to a call for the institutionalization of the custom. There seems to be no awareness that in the framework of an initiatory culture, the festival as organizational form would be a negation of what the culture is about, or at any rate its reduction to the trivial level of folklore. Second, there is the ignorant, or maybe merely disingenuous, supposition that some time in the past, initiation rites were a traditional part of all ethnic or religious cultures making up the Senegalese community.

The point, however, is that if today, in those cultures still practicing initiation, the custom is gradually dying out, the reason is surely that new modes of social organization (especially urbanization), spiritual organization (mainly Islam and Christianity), and socialization have combined to move the population towards fresh assessments of their values. There is a tendency to forget that values draw their worth only from a specific process of evaluation, and that such an assessment is necessarily a function of ongoing socio-cultural dynamics.

Diouf has pointed out, with sharp cogency, that ethnology played an inflated role in 'the cultural re-creation of Africa' (Diouf, 1989). Indeed the point raised above is a perfect illustration of the promiscuous abandon with which certain Senegalese intellectuals embrace ethnological visions whenever they are challenged to discuss their socio-cultural realities. They behave with a knee-jerk predictability in the trend of what might be called an ethno-logic. That approach leads them to adopt, with undue haste and a 'tradition' which they then turn around to contrast with realities that can only, by definition, be foreign. Thus, for instance, the anthropological notions of the 'essence' and 'soul' of traditional societies have given birth to the idea of 'traditional roots', supposedly the exclusive basis of authentic Senegambian cultures.

This chapter proposes a different point of view. Our argument is that what has taken place in the Senegambian environment is not a unilinear chronicle of foreign values getting precipitated, layer after layer, onto a single cultural matrix belonging to all populations here. Instead, we see nothing less than a history of several processes of evaluation and re-evaluation involving various population groups working constantly to re-establish cultural balances evolving in the face of repeated challenges.

Such a viewpoint presupposes a critique of the kind of ready-made terminology[1] that gets trotted out the moment the issue of culture comes up for discussion. The introduction to this chapter was intended to serve as just such a critique.

Clearly, then, this chapter makes a clean break with the impressionistic anthropologizing that some scholars slip into when called upon to discuss the qualities expected of *Homo senegalensis*[2], a species supposedly threatened by foreign ideas and lifestyles. What we intend here, instead, is to understand the mechanisms at work in all their historical depth. At the end of our appraisal, we hope to present a forward-looking analysis which gives proper consideration to such objective constraints as demography and communications technology, to mention only the main elements.

In place of such hoary conceptual dichotomies as *l'enracinement* and *l'ouverture*, tradition and modernity, authenticity and alienation, which we consider too static and conventional to facilitate a genuine understanding of cultural and symbolic realities, we shall use here the concept of *evaluation*.

This concept comes together with twin corollaries of its own: territorial homelands, on the one hand, and 'de-territorialization', on the other. More metaphors? Certainly. But these metaphors are intended to explain a dynamic process, instead of stalling our thought processes against the dichotomy opposing tradition to foreign values, a dichotomy which, in the final analysis, simply blocks all thought.

The Senegalese Population: A Descriptive Overview

The following data are drawn from the census document entitled *Principaux résultats provisoires du recensement général de la population et de l'habitat du Sénégal* (April-May 1988), published in September 1989 by the National Census Bureau:

Total Population: approximately seven million (7 000 000).

- Population Distribution According to Ethnic Groups (Sénégal/BNR 1989: Table 10):

Wolof:	43.7%
Pulaar (Peulh + Toucouleur):	23.2%
Sérère:	14.8%
Diola:	05.5%
Manding:	04.6%

There are other ethnic groups, but their percentage shares of the country's total population are relatively insignificant. It is instructive to correlate the above list with that of languages spoken (Sénégal/BNR 1989: Table 10):

- Percentages of the Population Speaking Selected Languages:

Wolof:	70.9%
Pulaar:	24.1%
Sérère:	13.7%
Diola:	05.7%
Manding:	06.2%
Sarakholé-Soninké:	01.4%.

Equally relevant to our argument are data from Table 8 of the document, which presents the religious distribution of the population.

- Percentage of the Population Belonging to Various Religions:

Muslims:	94.0%
Christians:	04.9%
Others:	01.1%

Finally, we should recapitulate the following key data: the age structure of the population; and urbanization rates in Senegalese society. From the table on age group distribution, we shall highlight the following data:
- Percentage Distribution According to Principal Age Groups:

    Below 20 years: 57.7%

    20 to 59 years: 37.3%

    60 years and over: 05.0%.

Relevant data on urbanization is as follows: In 1988, the percentage of the country's total population living in the urban areas was 39%; From 1976 to 1988, the urban population grew at an annual rate of 3.8%; Dakar stands out as the urban mammoth, with 80% of the urban population, and 22% of the country's total population.

The age structure of the population, which is predominantly young, calls for the following comments: in strictly generational terms, major basic reference indices tend to be very short-lived. Let us take the fundamental founding act, the Independence of Senegal, with its accompanying ideology of decolonization. It took just a single generation to arrive at a situation where 75% of the population had no experience whatsoever of life before independence. Admittedly, significant events and processes are not meaningful only for generations actually living through them. Still, demographic factors are central to the transmission[3] of such meaning.

Second, a close examination of the urbanization process, which has now attained massive proportions, should lead to the abandonment of the rustic vision which identifies tradition with village life. This is all the more true of urban areas like the four municipalities of Saint-Louis, Rufisque, Gorée and Dakar, where there is a genuine tradition of urban life involving populations which for generations have known nothing other than urban civilization. These people have their 'roots' in the urban areas.

From a different perspective, it should be noted that Senegalese society has been undergoing what might be called a process of 'Wolofization', The reason is not so much that Wolofs are the largest ethnic group. The real reason, no doubt related to this, is that Wolof has grown to mean less and less a distinct ethnic group, and more and more just a language spoken by 80% of the population.

Last but not least, 94% of the Senegalese population are Muslims. This statistic calls for two remarks. The first supplements our critique of the sort of conventional rhetoric on culture whose main themes and reference points are roots, tradition, Black African authenticity, etc. Now this rhetoric seldom addresses the enormous fact that within the socio-cultural environment of Senegal, the dominant prism through which all cultural, axiomatic and even economic meaning must first transit into consciousness is the prism of Islam. The second remark on the 94% statistic applies equally to the various figures cited in the above table. They provide a snapshot of old, ongoing mechanisms and processes. We need to highlight these processes by examining the flow of history.

Mechanisms in history

Islam has been present in Senegal from at least[4] as long ago as the start of the eleventh century. Senegal has also been for a long time integrated into the world network created by the West. Nevertheless, before formal colonial occupation, the entities we know as socio-political and cultural homelands still retained a great deal of potential for initiative, at least in cultural affairs.

This was also true of many aspects of material life, especially those we might term socio-technological. For homelands in this area began long ago, of their own accord, to open up to forms of technological and scientific acculturation. This receptivity was visible in 'changes in agriculture, industrial handicrafts, urbanization and trading techniques, brought about by European-African relations antedating colonialism' (Diagne, 1984). Of that process, the principal lingua franca of West Africa, including Wolof, still bear traces (Diagne, 1984). There was a gradual diffusion of a degree of modernity, along with its accompanying conceptual paraphernalia, between the ethnic homelands and the open environments constituted by the trading towns. In Senegal the main poles of such urban development were Saint-Louis and Gorée, and there a truly mixed cultural mentality began to flourish.

In the light of what we have just pointed out, which incidentally points to the need for more detailed studies on the period in question, it is necessary to revise received notions related to the over-hasty assumption that Africa's traditional homelands were inherently hostile to change. There is nothing peculiar to the Black African mentality that constitutes an obstacle to the idea of progress. Before the colonial era, there were the beginnings of a socio-cultural and technological *aggiornamento*. The process, admittedly tentative, was nonetheless real, and it started because the homelands then still, for the most part, maintained the initiative in handling it. Formal colonialism halted this tentative attempt at modernization. The phenomenon subsequently summed up in colonial writings as resistance to change was not a rejection of progress, but the capacity of traditional mentalities to mount self-preserving reflexes.

A second point is this: the political situation was already critical. It was bound to have direct repercussions on social values. The presence of Europeans having proved sufficient to sharpen conflicts between various local sovereigns as well as between them and their subjects, social instability became the order of the day. The point is that the trans-Atlantic slave trade decimated the population and transformed the nature of political power in its relations with peoples. Henceforth, political power was under pressure to justify itself, as the political philosophy of Kocc Barma well shows, following the realization that political power had been suborned, that family values had been thoroughly taken apart and households destabilized 'from the day merchandise superseded morality' (Fall, 1984)[5]. What justification is there, then, for supposing that the value crisis is something recent, or that the vocabulary used to discuss it is a late invention? In the tension between 'merchandise', (the open space on openess of the marketplace), and 'morality', (the integrity of the spiritual homeland), the contradiction was already clear. And it had begun to unfold in practice.

The Accelerated Phase of Islamization

The accelerated phase was coterminous with the period known to historians, by common consent, as the 'Peulh phase' of Islamization. In the particular case of Senegal, the pivotal event was the 1776 revolution in the Fouta Toro in which the *Torodo* Abdel Kader overthrew the last representative of the Denianké dynasty. The change was significant for the retrospective study of values and mentalities, because the *almaamiya* thus established on part of the territory that later became Senegal installed the concept of a State constituted on the basis of Islam. There, in principle, was an absolute negation of the concept of homelands, since the Muslim *Umma* expresses a totally different philosophy of space, a philosophy we shall call 'de-territorialization'. But only in principle. For it would be erroneous to call a State within which, in the final analysis, power was invariably wielded 'in the name of a purely local tradition', and in connection with which the claim of a genuinely universal Muslim caliphate was never raised (Diagne, 1984:42), a 'theocracy'.

Elsewhere, in the Wolof homelands, this phase saw the rise of Islamic educational institutions, known as *daara,* of which Pire and Coki were the most famous. In the prevailing atmosphere of war, pillage and slavery, and in the face of an increasingly centralized authority, these *daara* gradually took on the character of centres for the dissemination of new Islamic values. In addition, they functioned as socialization venues for populations witnessing the disintegration of an old universe[6]. The idea, then, of Islam as a sure refuge for societies beset by crisis was a long-standing trend. But it took that other factor of de-territorialization - formal colonialism - to give that meaning of Islam its full weight.

The Colonial Phase

The objectives and aims of colonialism are well known: 'the unification of the country; the administration of the territory and its population; economic management; the creation of a capitalist environment; and the suppression of previous forms of production' (Fall, 1984). In short, the physical eradication of homelands. And, by implication, the eradication of intellectual and spiritual homelands as well. Such was the purpose of the colonial educational system, given clear theoretical articulation by Faidherbe, the administrator assigned to establish it. 'We must ensure', he wrote in 1857 to his superior minister, 'that after one generation there shall not be a single chief in Senegambia who has not passed through this school system'.

The establishment of an open physical and intellectual space, standardized according to mercantile norms while destroying the balance of the old homelands, went hand in hand with the construction of a railroad, the installation of telegraph lines, a postal service, the development of a groundnut economy, urbanization, etc. But while thus de-territorializing the space for its own ends, colonialism, without quite desiring to, created a physical and social space for the Islamic *Umma*.

The peasantry, shielded by their isolation and their social system, had for eight centuries resisted Islam. But 'we made this resistance impossible', wrote Froelich (1962). The colonialists opened up paths for pedlars and hawkers. The roads and railways they constructed helped Muslim traders to travel everywhere, preaching by example to populations which had witnessed the collapse of traditional micro-cultures which, outside the homelands they were rooted in, no longer made any sense. And the process was facilitated by the sentiment that in some way, to embrace Islam was to avenge the fact of colonial domination. The same J C Froelich describes Muslims in the area as being 'proud to be members of a community whose real dimensions they were nevertheless far from imagining.... They have no feeling of inferiority whatsoever towards Christians and the West' (Froelich, 1962).

It should be noted that part of the colonial agenda was a drive to convert Africans to Christianity. The Christian religion had, in fact, been long established in the seaboard trading centres and towns such as Saint-Louis and Gorée, which for generations had offered an example of societies harmoniously blending various religions: Christianity, the majority faith of Islam, 'animistic' cults based on belief in local water deities like Mame Coumba Bang and Coumba Castel, etc. During the colonial period, Christian missions moved away from the urban areas and the already Islamized zones to settle 'in the bush', that is to say, in Thiès region, along the coast south of Dakar, and in the Casamance. They went, in other words, mainly into the homelands of egalitarian societies with regimes of centralized power, where right up until the end of the nineteenth century the population had put up the stiffest resistance to colonialism: in particular, in the Saafi area, in Ndut, and in lower Casamance.

The Dialectical Tension

This, then, was the way in which, during the colonial era, the various factors and protagonists active in Senegalese society today, and no doubt set to help shape the unfolding future, evolved into their respective roles in the social drama we here describe as the 'dialectical interaction between the open and the closed'. On one side stood the crisis-ridden homelands with their original values. On the other, there were the ideologies of de-territorialization, born of the combined influences of the West and of Islam.

This much needs to be made quite clear:

- the ethnic homelands were under critical pressure to varying degrees. That did not mean that they were simply withering away. As far as their old values were concerned, these societies were changing, adjusting and regrouping their forces according to new norms, by making inroads into those very Islamic and Christian evaluations working to break down their structures. Developments on the socio-political scene were different, however. On that level,

there was hardly any endogenous dynamism left except in the ethnic group as a form of social organization and as a cultural space, with village communities serving as grassroots units. It was within these two types of venue that the populations involved continued to keep up their identity structures and reference frameworks (Fall, 1984:73).

Here we see a fully operational dialectic between openness and hermetic exclusivity, between de-territorializing and re-territorializing tendencies. On the one hand, the integration of Senegal into the world market through the groundnut trade, urbanization, the development of transport infrastructures, etc. all signalled, at least to a degree, the triumph of the Wolof-Muslim model. But there was also an opposite reaction, the staking of ethnic claims[7]. Such claims ranged from the kind of territorial demands put forward by a section of Diola society to the emergence of associations for the 'defence and exemplification' of one language or the other. Examples of the latter were the associations of *Haal pulaaren*, or Pulaar-speaking groups[8].

The forces most active in the promotion of Western influence were to be found in the school system, the civil service and the various 'development' agencies at work in the country. Western influence, however, was hampered by the circumstance that it could not promote its economic, managerial logic in a vacant socio-ideological matrix. Had that been possible, Western values might simply have proceeded to 'take over' Senegalese civil society. But the ideological and sociological environment was occupied by Islam. That occupation gave Islam 'a clear political edge, plus a growing measure of economic importance' (Fall, 1984:77). Both the colonial administration and the post-colonial State, in many respects heir to the former, have had to and will in future continue to cope with that reality.

Taken purely as a principle, Islam stands for de-territorialization. In practical life, the actual degree of de-territorialization varies from culture to ethnic culture. For instance, among the Haal Pulaaren or the Mandingo, the break with ancient homeland religions dates from long ago, and is profound. By contrast, the Sérères, the Lebu and the Diola, even while accepting Islam, continue to practice such syncretistic rites as visits to the sacred forest, and the memory of their *Tuur* and *Pangool* remains active in the social imagination.

Before proceeding to list constraining factors and attempting to present a forward-looking assessment of the Senegalese socio-cultural scene, it is worth taking a look at the dialectical tension between the open and the closed as far as the Islamic process of evaluation is concerned.

Islam: Aspects of Deterritorialization and Re-territorialization

The phenomenon we have characterized as the dialectical tension between the open and the closed constantly occurs in the process of Islamic evaluation, giving its development an original pattern. Let us repeat: embodied in the very principles of Islam, there is an imperative of de-territorialization. For in place of the 'world' as defined as a spiritual homeland, Islam sets up the ideal of a universal Muslim community supplemented with the reinforcing rationality of a writing system. Furthermore, again on the level of principle, the conversion of Senegambian populations involved no less than an egalitarian revolution directed against caste (or hierarchical) societies. In the colonial period, incidentally, this aspect of social revolution was to become a key feature of the *Hamal* movement within Islam. Lastly, still on the level of principle, Islam introduced and disseminated on a wide scale a set of written rules and a system of law set down in the Koran and the Sunna. In so doing, it gave precision to and popularized a custom which replaced old mind-sets with new, an old evaluation system with a new one. However slow the process, it undoubtedly caused a profound rift with the people's sense of belonging to a homeland, that sense whose perpetuation was the goal of ancestral cults. Islamic society, in short, was forever freed from 'the tremendous pressure of the dead upon the living' (Gouilly, 1952).

Laws regulating family life, marriage, descent and succession changed completely. Among peoples who had previously lived under matrilineal laws, Islam gave a new prominence to patrilineal descent.

There were equally widespread changes introduced by Islamic laws on civil duties, contract law and real estate regulations. People switched to swearing on the Koran to seal reciprocal commitments. Rules of commercial lending that recognized neither interest nor usury became a normal part of economic life. In sum, Islam also brought 'a new legal, social and political culture which made profound inroads into the dynamics of social life' (Diagne, 1984).

We have already mentioned the slow pace of this process. The reason for that lack of speed was the fact that Islam, the de-territorializing process, had to deal with certain re-territorializing trends. It still does, as a matter of fact. And it is the tension between its de-territorializing thrust and the re-territorializing trends of opposing world-views that makes up the dialectic of the open and the closed. Thus, within the context of Islamized African customs, many aspects of law such as the status of women, 'the kinship system, property rights and succession rules constitute a *compromise*'. That compromise was the basis of 'a strain of African law inspired by Islam... which subsequently had to be taken into account under the colonial and post-colonial regimes' (Diagne, 1984). One only has to consider the resistance provoked by the 1972 Family Code, and the criticism levelled at it to this day, to understand that the trend has deep roots.

One of the most important forms taken by re-territorializing tendencies under Islam is the way religious brotherhoods are organized in Senegal. Consider the fact, for instance, that Islamic brotherhoods have sometimes set up veritable homelands around their religious capitals. In these spaces, laws that normally apply throughout the Republic of Senegal are sometimes 'suspended'. Instances range from the regulation forbidding smoking to the statement by the caliph of the Mouride brotherhood, that the national Family Code[9] did not apply to Touba, the Mouride religious centre.

The Muslim religious brotherhoods, in other words, enjoy a degree of autonomy, to give the word its strict meaning, within their own spaces. It has been a characteristic of their existence since the colonial era when in their resistance to domination, they used these spaces as bases for an alternative society, i.e., venues of countervailing power. We see, then, that the public authorities, colonial as well as post-colonial, have consistently had a hard time bringing the space of a new political society under uniform control. One proof of this fact came in the realization, by hindsight, of the quixotic nature of the attempt by former Council Chairman Mamadou Dia to wipe out the reality known to modernizers and Marxists as 'feudal relics'.

As used in this context to describe the personal commitment of disciples to their guiding marabout, the term feudal is wrong on at least one count: feudal relations, in historical terms, became obsolete as a result of the evolution of an economic and production system that replaced the discrete territorial entities of the old system with a standardized and united mercantile environment. In the case of the Senegalese brotherhoods, the outstanding fact is their capacity to ride the tides of socio-economic change. As we all know, by getting involved in groundnut production, the Mouride brotherhood played a role in the integration of the Senegalese environment into the international capitalist network, and by the same token 'acquired an important status in the national economy' (Cruise O'Brien, 1971).[10] Incidentally, the Muslim brotherhoods have a proven capacity to adapt to urban realities, in a situation where one might have supposed that uncontrolled rural migration into the urban areas would contribute to de-territorialization. The function of re-territorialization falls to associations known as *daahira*. Most often these are neighbourhood associations, but they also have a vocational or professional basis, bringing together employees from one enterprise, administrative department, or market (Diop, 1983). Even currents of migration to foreign lands, initially also anarchic, now tend to be organized in *daahira* based abroad. Indeed, these communities have even begun doing some modest missionary work among fringe elements of the African-American population in America, as well as among West Indians in France[11].

These developments have all contributed to the expansion of a phenomenon that might be called 'the brotherhood mentality' beyond the rural centres where it originated. It has provided a basis for economic support networks, some outside the *daahira* groups, most of them in the urban informal sector. These networks operate through support groups and informal contractual arrangements that in the long run are much more reliable precisely because they are informal. And it is not just the Mouride brotherhood that operates this way, though its high degree of centralization makes the phenomenon more obvious within it. The Tijaniyya movement has come up with a sort of imitation of Mouride networks. This has led to a proliferation of urban *daahira* associations, active in missionary work among young people, as part of a mounting movement of positive inter-brotherhood rivalry[12].

The tendency towards re-territorialization in the religious brotherhoods has a second, spiritual aspect, related to the capacity of the mystical Sufi strain in Islam to strike a compromise with homeland-based ideological structures, mental attitudes and cultural norms. For the organizational style of brotherhoods, as a rule, tends to refocus the spiritual energies of the faithful on a series of veritable religious homeland bases and local capitals. This happens to varying degrees from brotherhood to brotherhood, but brotherhood life in general emphasizes religious songfest rituals and regular pilgrimages, opportunities for members to rededicate themselves as conscious members of a committed community.

The trend towards re-territorialization in Islam, as may well be expected, impacts on an 'alternative' dialectic, that of a movement opposed to brotherhoods, dedicated to a self-consciously literate variety of Islam that claims to be more receptive to the *Umma* as the universal community of the Muslim faithful. This movement has a long history, though it was pushed off centre stage by colonial policy regarding Islam, which was rather inclined to manipulate the brotherhood movement as a trump card. The main concern of the colonial powers in this respect was partly to cope realistically with practical developments on the spot, and partly to 'reduce contacts between Black African Islam and North African Islam, reputedly fired up with ill-defined Pan-Arab aspirations' (Froelich, 1962). In short, even if the colonial powers could not prevent the population from being Muslims, they could work to encourage the fixation on a homeland base, a re-territorialization that would insulate Senegalese Islam from the apparent possibility of a 'Muslim peril', the *Umma*.

There was thus a full-blown fundamentalist trend that operated openly sometimes, at other times underground. Its instrument was also its purpose: religious education. What it aimed at was to impart to the large-scale brotherhood movement an aspect of deep cultural awareness, a renaissance of Islamic civilization. As a matter of fact, this fundamentalist trend exists within the ranks of the brotherhoods themselves. In its teething period it was attracted to unrealistic, militantly anti-brotherhood approaches. Subsequently, it seems to have turned to a more judicious programme of educational activism. Its adherents have thus promoted 'Arab schools' and drawn the brotherhoods into the process. That marks a change from the colonial era, when the brotherhoods often opposed the establishment of 'reformist' *medersa*.

One last point: it has been said out before that French colonial policy regarding Islam, by force of circumstance, involved attempts to integrate brotherhood-based Islam into the framework of French colonial strategy. The policy of the secular post-colonial State, in this respect, would seem to be a continuation of colonial policy. One result is the carrying over of what we have called the 'brotherhood mentality' into political and religious patron-client behaviour patterns, and into pressure groups.

What conclusions might justifiably be drawn from this historical overview? Our main finding is that the rhetoric of State construction in general, and the official rhetoric on culture in particular, has long operated as a verbal smokescreen obscuring mechanisms actually at work within Senegalese civil society. The cultural rhetoric of *l'Enracinement* and *l'Ouverture*, from our analytical perspective, stands revealed as a ghost-like fabrication, a conventional fiction without organic substance, when compared to the terms used by the country's population groups themselves to express their significant reference points, the bonds of solidarity linking them, the features by which they choose to identify themselves.

That is why, in this age of the newly emergent civil society, this rhetoric has become definitively inadequate. In place of the old theme of 'identity versus foreign alienation', it is time to turn to cultural meanings and demands expressed by the populations themselves, predominantly young, and increasingly urban[13].

Lastly, and in a general sense, the emergence of civil society, with its train of new patterns of evaluation, poses a challenge to the concept and the objective situation in which the rhetoric of State construction was rooted. The concept of State construction is basically Hegelian. It is the notion according to which the State is not simply one outgrowth[14] of civil society (among others), but the very constituent principle thereof. It is the warder-prisoner view of the State and civil society which is now under pressure with the emergence of a new type of civil society.

This is one aspect of the current social crisis: it is also a crisis brought on by the transition from the kind of thinking according to which the State creates society and officials initiate popular participation, to a new situation in which civil society organizes initiatives on its own, and implements them independently. It is this shift that towards the end of the 1970s propelled Islam to the foreground in social, cultural and political affairs, not some shaky attempt to imitate any foreign model such as the Iranian revolution[15], even if the latter did serve as a catalyst.

It is this that gives Islam the role of what Coulon calls a 'public tribune' responsible for 'articulating in public, in language more accessible than that of politics as usual, the moral and social grievances of a population that no longer really identifies with the heirs of colonialism and their values'[16] Coulon, (1990) believes that the emergent form of politicized Islam could 'raise the stakes'. By that he probably means that in the new situation, the State will be forced to *redefine* its rhetoric on its own nature and purpose. Thus, the constitutional principle that makes the Senegalese State a secular entity will be questioned, if not challenged outright. There is the instructive case of an intellectual, Professor Iba Der Thiam, a former Minister of National Education, emphasizing that it is necessary to harmonize that constitutional principle with the development of civil society. For, as the professor often points out in his public speeches, the secular idea is given a different meaning in America, France, England, etc.

At the end of our historical overview, we would like to add that there is a corollary to the emergence of a civil society: the trend towards autonomous self-organization within it. The trend is visible in the proliferation of associations, 'discovery groups', *daahira* and other religious bodies, etc. But the trend could cut both ways. It could result in the development of a self-reliant, innovative culture within a cohesive national framework. On the other hand, it could degenerate into increasingly pronounced withdrawal into unconnected micro-cultures that would seriously threaten social cohesion. This perspective, then, leads to an open-ended future. We can peep into its possibilities by examining a number of future scenarios factoring in constraints on the cultural system.

Constraints on the Cultural System

As already pointed out, the main focus of our argument is on population as a constraining factor, as well as on problems related to the world-wide development of communications technologies. To take up the population problem first, let us simply outline a number of projections.

Annual urban population growth rates in Senegal have consistently averaged around 5% over almost 30 years. Should that trend hold, it would lead by the turn of the century to a situation where the country's population is evenly divided between the rural and urban areas. Of the urban total 60% would inhabit the Dakar metropolitan area, where problems of hygiene and cleanliness would be enormous in comparison with all other urban centres in the country (Sénégal, 1989a).[17]

Needless to say, this will have important consequences on the country's cultural system, already increasingly urban. Urban culture, as a matter of fact, dominates Senegalese life out of all proportion to the relative size of the urban population alone. People might choose to deplore the fact, but such hand-wringing is useless. It would be much more to the point if we focused on the possible socially negative consequences of such a situation, with the aim of working out a future urban programme designed to remedy them.

With regard to constraints related to the development of communications technologies, it is worth pointing out that this phenomenon is the favourite target of the rhetoric focused on the supposedly tragic combat between identity and 'alienating foreign influences'. Let us offer two observations here. First, it is utterly vain to deplore the culturally and symbolically invasive nature of values transmitted by foreign *media*, since in any case, figuratively as well as literally, such symbols and values are going increasingly to 'rain down on our heads.' It is a situation which should stimulate us to grow beyond slogans and incantations, to design a programme which regards constraints as objective parameters, and deals with them accordingly.

The second observation is really a question: what is the use of the kind of facile rhetoric which automatically treats foreign media as tools of some diabolical force, the better to relax on the notion that there is some set of authentic values now threatened by images from abroad? The flood of foreign images certainly exists; there is no denying that. But we need to go further and point out, first, that the foreign image blitz is no reason why we ourselves should fail to wonder what is wrong with a society that adopts new, borrowed identities as easily as is supposed. Second, we need to admit, to take just one example, that it is partly because of the same development of communications technologies that the demand for democracy has become a world-wide claim. We shall now proceed, on the basis of these constraining factors, to present two scenarios related to 'the future of tradition'.

Urban Culture and the Development of Social Communication

Urbanization has proceeded hand in hand with the process of the de-territorialization going on within the socio-cultural environment. It will continue to do so. This has led to the emergence of a new system of evaluation bringing forth new socio-cultural institutional forms. Of these the most important, no doubt, was the family. In the time taken for the new evaluation system to mature and for the socio-cultural institutions associated with it to find a stable basis, the population is caught between two stools, that is to say, in a transitional crisis best described as a state of bewilderment. Diagne gives a perfect description of a society hanging between two havens:

> *The family as an institution is under stress much more because of social individuation and confusion within exploding communities than because of any individualistic philosophy. In their minds, people have not yet sunk that low. They do not reject blood ties, family bonds or village solidarity. The overwhelming reality is that they find it impossible to live out that solidarity.*[18]

This 'impossibility' is linked to the overall crisis, i.e., the economic and social crisis itself. One wonders whether those who talk of a crisis of values, or of a 'degradation' of values, give sufficient thought to what might be called 'the economic humiliation of fathers?' The transmission of values from one generation to the next, the process through which the social fabric gets woven, goes poorly indeed when parents, whose authority is identified with the force of the values in question, are victims of 'economic humiliation'.

Under these conditions, the urban environment, as well as the cultural identities emerging from it, are bound to be strongly influenced by the following features, listed by Cheikh Bâ:

> *the younger generations, as individuals, casual groups, sports clubs, gangs and groups of all sizes, teams, etc. spontaneously create environments for their own fulfilment, sometimes achieving integration within the urban corpus. In the process they can be seen making use of their*

participatory functions, constantly stimulated and provoked as the official vision of urban areas as a series of intersecting routes (a vision based not on integrated spaces but on the street) develops, and as resources for active participation in urban affairs shrink.

Also visible is the imbalance between the participatory potential of young persons and the lumbering slowness of those traditionally responsible for their support, organization and socialization, such as the family and urban society. This potent youth front, with its many forms and aspects, has been growing ceaselessly. Its growth raises the question of an integrated redefinition of the purposes of urban areas in countries like Senegal. Everyone knows now that perverse forms of youthful group participation are among the main indices of organizational and managerial shortcomings in urbanized environments welcoming massive influxes of the young (Bâ, 1989)[19].

We shall end with a word on what we call here the 'participatory function'. Discussing it, Bâ says, first, that it is 'the main function through which the youth get integrated into society at large'. Second, he says 'it is harder to stimulate under our present living conditions' (Bâ, 1989). Within the framework of a coherent, well-thought-out project aimed at 'an integrated redefinition of the purposes of urban areas', such a function, 'unchained' by an urban development policy, would result in initiatives taken by civil society to establish a genuine 'culture of urban life'. In other words, it would promote a real feeling among urban residents of belonging to harmoniously integrated social and physical environments designed to enhance communication among people. This youthful utopia[20] is already discernible in the self-organizing culture vectored by the *navétane* movement involving neighbourhood sports and cultural clubs.

For it to develop, however, the urban areas, the main cultural context in the times ahead, will have to stop being the dumping ground of motley excrescences proliferating in a process that has more to do with flight from rural misery than with any genuine urbanization. Further, official rhetoric on culture ought to pay greater attention to real socio-cultural mechanisms, and give fresh thought to urban life and the opportunities it offers for a more intense cultural life, along with fresh evaluations thereof.

It is significant that these days communications have become an increasingly crucial issue in Senegal, on the cultural, social and political levels. The fact that the solemn ceremony marking the beginning of the judicial year, and chaired in 1991, as usual, by the President, was focused on the topic of the press, marks this heightened awareness of the importance of communications. Behind the debate on civil liberties and democracy occasioned by the discussion of communications, there is a related issue: relationships between the State and civil society in this new situation marking the end of the old warder-prisoner pattern.

It is already possible to see the outlines of a culture of social *communication* requiring deliberation and free development, as opposed to the traditional policy of centralized, top-down *information*. This claim is a further expression of the current emergence of civil society, which needs the multiplication of communications channels. For it is through such new channels that the various components of civil society will dialogue with and become visible to each other as together they take over new spaces for self-expression.[21]

The genuine development and effective expansion of the communication space would seem to constitute the only valid response to the cultural challenge posed by the world-wide boom in information technology. To see this point clearly, one merely has to look at the emergence of 'a selective preference for local cultural products, an incontrovertible fact even if it is still embryonic, in such fields as music... fashion, culture, hairdressing, etc.' Further, 'it is significant that it is these sectors that are most firmly rooted in the national languages and creativity' (Sénégal, 1989a:104).

To return, then, to our initial proposition, it is clear, from this innovative viewpoint, that the draft of the General Report on the National Cultural Charter lags behind the actual and current evolution of Senegalese culture which in such areas as music, has been able to assert itself on the international level. Those involved in this evolution know that it makes no sense to cling to excessively defensive visions of culture and cultural identity. By the same token, they realize that the irresistible development of communications technology also offers opportunities to those ready to seize them. They understand that in this new world, what we need to do is to achieve a bolder, more active vision of our culture, to take advantage of inevitable advances, and thus project our identity onto the media-dominated environment. They know, in sum, that the best way to defend one's culture is to work for its radiant diffusion.

Conclusion

We come, full circle, to the basic issue: what future lies ahead for tradition? The entire thrust of our argument indicates that to reach a proper answer to the question, we must first recast it: What kind of evaluation system, discernible in embryo today, will prevail tomorrow? The chorus of a hit song by the Senegalese pop music star, Youssou Ndour, says: 'Between the present and the past, there's so little resemblance'. His meaning is clear: in the 30 years that have gone by since the establishment of a sovereign State, the Senegalese social system has changed in its very fabric. For that reason, those who pay close heed to the evolution of civil society will have to understand that traditional identity cannot be a matter of mere repetition. After all, in its root meaning,

> *tradition indicates whatever is suitable for handing down as part of a set of behavioural principles capable of meeting the challenge of new times and new conditions. In terms of inspiration, identity is the capacity to 'reach the very fountainhead of springs, thence drawing whatever resources we need, as active participants in this our age, conscious of our current problems, to work out innovative solutions to them* (Garaudy, 1990:103-104).

Notes

1. The 'ready-made' nature of conventional cultural rhetoric is exemplified by the treatment of one of the greatest novels from Senegal, Cheikh Hamidou Kane's *Aventure Ambigüe*. It has been said that this magnificent book is the novelistic equivalent of the poetry of Negritude. Now it is true that Kane's hero asserts his 'Negritude' in the face of the technological rationality of the West. But from where does anyone fetch the notion that the Islamic metaphysics expressed in the recitation of divine revelation, so superbly described in the book, is identical with 'Negritude'?
2. This sort of humourless discussion, incidentally, could gain a great deal from the self-kidding talents with which Senegalese society so abounds.
3. Old-fashioned anthropology, as we know, used to distinguish between 'warm' societies and 'cold' ones. By its standards, a study of demographic factors and age-group pyramids today would lead to the conclusion that certain 'cold' societies have now become the most 'torrid' on earth.
4. In the words of Gouilly (1952), the people of northern Senegal entered a new era of history 'the day they ran into the mysterious veiled warriors of Abu Bakr Ibn Oumar the Almoravid'.
5. Fall, 1984, here quotes the Abbé Boilat (1853).
6. *The development of these daara was to have considerable consequences. It led to the emergence and consolidation of a religious aristocracy of marabouts which, from the XVIIIth century, got involved in turn in domestic political and social problems, asserted itself as a centre of countervailing power, maintained its hold through a series of fertile dynasties, and gradually evolved a complete strategy for the occupation of the environment* (Fall, 1984: 71).
7. As Bayart has pointed out, 'ethnicity... is a process of cultural and identity structuring, more than any particular fixed structure'. (Bayart, 1989:83). Data from the recent census has stimulated a series of articles from Sérère intellectuals worried about the fact that the number of Senegalese who actually speak Sérère has been declining in comparison to the number claiming to be ethnic Sérères. A good proportion of the voluntary associations and movements now proliferating in Senegalese society consists of groups with a recognizable interest in the discovery of their roots.
8. Coulon (1982). This author points out that the Mouride brotherhood were officially accorded a place of honour within Senghor's rhetoric on 'African Socialism'.

9. Cf. Victoria Ebin, 'A Brotherhood Immigration: Merchants and Missionaries in New York and Paris', Personal communication from the author, Publication pending.
10. Regarding the issue of inter-brotherhood rivalry, Diop and Diouf go much farther. 'Sources close to the regime', they assert,
    have revealed to us that tensions between the Tijaniyya and Mouride communities resulted from attempts by L.S. Senghor to keep the Senegalese Muslim community as a whole off balance, in order to keep it from confronting the State as a united bloc. The monthly paper Ande Sopi made the same argument. Its editors saw the pervasive religious tension in Senegal as a way of weakening the social impact of Islam, whose potential, should it get properly organized, gave the regime cause for concern. "In the opinion of Ande Sopi, the regime's responsibility was indisputable," on account of its policy of keeping Islam divided. The policy has resulted in deliberately fomented inter-brotherhood tensions, leaving aside internal conflicts within each brotherhood. By these tactics the regime sharpened the susceptibilities of the sects, turning healthy competition between them into aggressive rivalries which weakened and unbalanced the community. (Diop and Diouf, 1990:77).
    To this the authors append a note: 'Such interpretations are hard to verify or to analyze in depth'. One would add that intellectual integrity requires such a caveat. What is certain is that as heir to the colonial administration, the secular State learned to deal with the reality of brotherhoods, especially against the background of the world-wide 'Islamic revival' featuring, among various movements, the Iranian revolution.
11. Current developments in Senegalese literature already indicate such a thematic shift.
12. For Hegel, the immediate perceptions whereby populations recognize their identities are merely 'instant feeling', 'contingent imagination', and 'a heartfelt mix of friendship and enthusiasm'. None of them can attain their essential principle except through 'that rich articulation of the moral universe, the State'. Hegel also calls the State 'the active reality of the concept of objective morality'. In many respects, our various African 'founding fathers of the Nation' are unwitting Hegelians. Perhaps the reason is that forced into having to build their nations on the basis of administrations inherited from colonialism, they have become hostages to a mind-set in which civil society is a captive of the State, which in its colonial origins was conditioned to play a supervisory role.
13. Diop and Diouf point out that in the light of this movement, the Marxist-Leninist wing of the Senegalese opposition took note that Islam was a deep-seated and massive reality in Senegal, and that it was 'only natural for it to take its rightful place in the struggle for national and social liberation' (Diop and Diouf 1990: 73). According to the same authors, 'the urban youth, which the State has never been able to mobilize to meet its own political and/or economic objectives, developed a militant commitment to Islam that flourished in the late 1970s at the expense of revolutionary and secular ideologies, as testified by research done in the Faculty of Arts, Dakar', by students focusing on what they considered burning issues of the time for their dissertation topics.
14. The same author adds, in the same article, that African religious culture, forgotten in the design of development policies and nation-building programmes, is making a spectacular come-back in both civil and political societies. Current and future leaders now have to cope with this reality by 'Islamizing' their rhetoric and policies. But, he adds, 'this Islamic revival, however powerful, is above all a counter-culture confronting the Western State that emerged at Independence. Islam, in its rise, took advantage of the failure of that State, and indeed helped to accelerate it' (Coulon, 1990).
15. Sénégal (1989a). Several passages in this chapter are based on data the author gathered for the prospective study listed.
16. Pathé Diagne, *Des Systèmes sahéliens de valeurs*, Paper prepared for CILSS as part of a prospective study in 1985. (Made available by the author - Italics mine). Let us add that the

family as an institution is in a state of transition 'as traditional matrimonial strategies shift in a society whose underlying hierarchical ideologies have been disappearing with urbanization and other developments' (Sénégal, 1989a:88).
17. Cheikh Bâ, public lecture under the auspices of the 'Solidary Association for the Development of Louga', 24 September 1989 (Made available by the author). Right after this observation, Cheikh Bâ adds a number of remarks concerning the 'other' dialectic involved in this urban process of de-territorialization: the fresh concentration of 'the youth factor', as he calls it, around the mosque, in particular, the one at Touba, the Mouride headquarters.
18. In the single concept of a 'participatory function', we encapsulate what Cheikh Bâ separates as a 'participatory function' and an 'innovative function'.
19. It would thus be sheer reductionism to boil the debate down to a simple question of the amount of time to be allotted to the different political parties, all set down in a codified schedule. The real issue is cultural. On this head, Ahmadou Lamine Ly observes that 'it is imperative to change current legislation on the audio-visual media, precisely because the law lags far behind the real evolution of the political system and civil culture' (Ly, 1990).

Bibliography

Bayart, Jean François, 1989, *L'Etat en Afrique. La politique du ventre*, Paris, Fayard.
Boilat, Abbé David, 1853, *Esquisses sénégalaises*, Paris, P Bertrand, (New edition with an introduction by Abdoulaye Bara Diop, 1984, Paris, Karthala).
Coulon, Christian, 1982, 'Contribution étatique et action islamique au Sénégal', in Olivier Carré (ed.), *L'Islam et l'Etat dans le monde aujourd'hui*, Paris, PUF.
Coulon, Christian, 1990 'Mobilisation islamique en Afrique noire', *Jeune Afrique plus*, May-June.
Cruise O'Brien, Donal B, 1971, *The Mourides of Senegal: The Political and Economic Organization of an Islamic Brotherhood*, Oxofrd, Clarendon Press, pp. XXI- 321.
Diagne Pathé, 1984, L'Ouest africain culturel, Etude de l'UNESCO.
Diop, Momar Coumba, 1983, 'Fonction et activité des dahiras mourides urbains (Sénégal)', *Cahiers d'études africaines*, 81-83, XXI, 1-3.
Diop, Momar Coumba and Diouf, Mamadou, 1990, *Le Sénégal sous Abdou Diouf: Etat et société*, Paris, Karthala (Les Afriques), 439 p.
Diouf, Mamadou, 1989, 'Représentations historiques et légitimité politique au Sénégal: (1960-1987)', *Revue de la Bibliothèque nationale*, Paris, 34.
Fall, Yoro K, 1984, 'Crises socio-politiques et alternatives religieuses au Sénégal vers la fin du XIXe siècle', *Revue sénégalaise de Philosophie*, 5-6, pp.69-78.
Froelich, J C, 1962, *Les musulmans d'Afrique noire*, Paris, Orante.
Garaudy, Roger, 1990, *Intégrismes*, Paris, Belfond.
Gouilly, Alphonse, 1952, *L'Islam dans l'Afrique occidentale française*, Paris, Larose.
Kane, Cheikh Hamidou, 1971, *L'aventure ambigüe*. Paris, Union Générale d'Edition 10/18.
Ly, Ahmadou Lamine, 1990, 'Le régime juridique des organes de presse audio-visuelle: radio diffusion et télévision sénégalaises', Master's Thesis, Law Faculty, Cheikh Anta Diop University, Dakar.

Senegal, Republic of, 1979, *Code de la Famille: Loi 72-61 du 12 juin 1972 modifiée par la loi No. 74-37 du 18 juillet 1974 et la loi 79-31 du 24 janvier 1979*, Imprimerie du Gouvernement, Rufisque.

Senegal, Republic of, Ministry of Planning and Cooperation, 1989a, *Etude prospective Sénégal 2015*, Dakar.

Senegal, Republic of, Ministry of Finance and Economic Affairs, 1989b, 'Principaux résultats provisoires du recensement général de la population et de l'habitat du Sénégal (avril-mai 1988)', Bureau National du Recensement, Dakar.

9. The Democracy of the Literati

Aminata Diaw

Relations between ruling authorities and intellectuals, it has been said, are invariably marked by degrees of complicity. For that reason, analyses of the bond are inherently problematic. Still, a history of the concept of the intellectual provides some useful analytical pointers. The French artists, writers and professors who, about a century ago, called for a review of the Dreyfus trial, did so in their capacity as intellectuals. The historic responsibility assumed in that affair definitively linked cultured individuals with protest against the high-handed abuses often related to political power. The concept of the intelligentsia appeared later in Russia, at the beginning of the twentieth century, where it served to identify intellectuals as a class. Beyond these conceptual details, let us add the key characteristics of this social group as analyzed by Marx and Gramsci: the existence of considerable variations within the group, its high level of sensitivity to the imperatives of class warfare, and its capacity to play legitimizing roles. The cogency of these insights becomes clear when we apply them to an analysis of relationships between political power and intellectual thought.

The resulting clarification, though, does not obviate the difficulty. For though conceptual tools may facilitate our grasp of data, they are incapable of elucidating the dynamics of phenomena and processes involving interactions, negation and affirmation, conflict and resolution. It is an essential trait of political power that it seeks to make itself absolute[1]. Political power is absolute to the extent to which it prevails over and transcends all other forms of power. Political power confers a legitimate basis by constituting the founding power *par excellence*. From that role springs a unitary logic operating in the authoritarian mode. All power other than political power must seek authorization therefrom. In other words, all other power must operate on behalf of and in the name of political power. The relationship here is necessarily hierarchical, because it ceaselessly refers back to the political source of legitimacy. It is a relationship calculated to guarantee the domination of political power, since it removes that power from any possibility of challenge and conflict.

One consequence is the endowment of political power with a monopoly of institutionalized physical violence. In the opinion of Max Weber:

It is best to conceive of the contemporary State as a human community which, within the limits of a given territory (for the concept of territory is one of its features), successfully claims on its own account the monopoly of legitimate physical violence (Weber, 1959:101-102).

If political power claims a specific right to be 'the sole source of violence', it also executes this claim in practice. The rhetoric of political power is therefore programmatic. The political environment is an arena where ideas have meaning only to the extent that they embody projections, manifested as future *praxis*, a mode for the appropriation of nature. The interval between project and *praxis* constitutes, for political power, a zone of indeterminate reality. For the fact that *praxis* is of necessity the perversion of the Idea by the Tangible creates room for the evaluation of the equation linking theory with practice. The question then becomes: is the relationship an adequate match, or does *praxis* fall short of theory?

The zone of indeterminate reality is a natural - indeed inevitable - offspring of political power. It gives birth in its turn, to a different kind of power: intellectual power. Of this power the principal functions are evaluation, critical assessment and, in special situations, legitimation.

In Senegal, discussions of the role of intellectuals are made particularly difficult because the concept itself of the intellectual has been thoroughly debased in common usage. Any Westernized fellow with a degree, able to speak and write French, having landed a job in the bureaucracy, feels qualified to pose as an intellectual. This identity, based on a quantum of knowledge plus a set of symbols, confers a right: the right of political self-expression.

We have, of course, presented a rather exaggerated caricature of the Senegalese intellectual here. But the resulting cartoon highlights a fundamental factor: the intellectual's role in the relationship between the *polis* and the political system, which defines the locus of power and domination. In Senegal, the social group made up of intellectuals was fathered by the colonial system. In the post-colonial era, it took over the political environment, along with the assignment of nation-building and the construction of the State. The position was paradoxical, and it gave an oxymoronic twist to the country's political configuration. For here political power and intellectual power were set to function as bedfellows, sharing the same environment. And in the process they defined and circumscribed that environment, determining who should be included, who excluded, using selective standards stressing competence in the handling of technical concepts and instruments in their monopoly. In the first two decades following independence, this arrangement took the form of a three-cornered paradigm at whose summit sat the Senghorian model. The base was occupied by two peripheral models, the Marxist model and the 'Pharaonic' model, to borrow a phrase from Pathé Diagne.

The argument presented here is not intended, we hasten to point out, as a comprehensive treatment of the problem[2]. Our analysis remains primarily focused on political power. Starting from the environment defined by that power, we shall attempt to examine the mechanisms of domestication, integration or neutralization used in bringing intellectual acumen to heel. The principal reason for our option is that we are interested in reaching a clearer understanding of political power, of the State and of its capacity to *instrumentalize* countervailing reality. For we assume, along with Michel Foucault, that real power is the capacity of a programme to impact other programmes, giving them an instrumental bias. The intellectual factor is no exception to the rule of *instrumentalization*. We shall, in short, be looking at ways in which, wittingly or unwittingly, Senegal's intellectuals were turned into allies of the ruling regime in a programme aimed at nation-building and State construction, that is to say, in a drive towards modernity. And we shall see how, in the process, they helped to frustrate democracy and to exclude 'civil society' from the political game.

Image and Paradigm

There is a corner of African fantasy life in which Senegal has always been imagined to be an intellectual breeding ground. Great figures like Léopold Sédar Senghor, Lamine Guèye and Cheikh Anta Diop have marked the stages of the country's political history. True or false, the country's intellectual reputation draws its force from multiple sources in real life. The individual elements contributing to it are so varied yet so intertwined in their interactions as to defy isolation and classification. Their mutual involvements make even simple description difficult, as they interweave with each other to produce a new political and social dynamic.

The implantation of the Western school system in a different cultural environment, by spawning an indigenous intellectual elite, shook up the existing political configuration and possibly changed the factors in the political power equation altogether. The colonial administration consistently based its effectiveness on the build-up of selected poles of evaluation and adaptation set off from the social context. The colonial administration demonstrated the reality of its own dynamics in various ways ranging from the whittling down of the influence of mixed-blood families educated in Catholic mission schools to the official 'indigenization of organic intellectuals belonging to the pre-colonial tradition'[3]. These dynamics enabled colonialism to accommodate intellectuals as a permanent part of its environment, and as a useful cog in its machinery of power.

It was the same calculated approach that led to the education of the first batch of Westernized indigenous intellectuals at the so-called School for Hostages founded in 1857 at Saint-Louis. Behind that move was a discernible desire to speed up colonial conquest. It also revealed the assimilationist assumptions undergirding the colonial thrust. However, the education of this new social stratum went hand in hand with a reassessment of values. The Western school, in effect, became a factory for the production of a colonial society, a colonial culture. The process laid bare the linkage between the integration of a segment of society to the power structure, and its ideological impact, working through the fabrication of a mixed memory feeding on a heritage that was part European, part African. Still, this initial elite did not hesitate to undermine colonial assumptions, since it was aware of the discrepancy between its traditional role[4] and the role henceforth assigned to it. Bathily, discussing the educational arrangements involved, points out that:

the education dispensed went no farther than 'the reading and writing of French, a smattering of arithmetic, and above all a series of daily disquisitions on French power, the French civilizing mission in Africa, etc. (Bathily, 1987:7).

Such was the curriculum dished out throughout the pre-independence period to teachers, nurses, African doctors, civil servants and others. But the social impact of the newly educated stratum is to be measured less in terms of their status within the French colonial dispensation (even if their role there was of decisive importance) than in terms of the part they played in the growing agitation of the Senegalese masses for independence[5].

The successful development of the William Ponty School, and the upgrading of the Institute of Advanced Studies in Dakar to a university, certainly spurred the emergence of this nationalist elite, some of whose members had been trained in metropolitan French universities. As Bathily points out:

colonial intellectuals played a considerable part in the awakening of the toiling masses of Africa to the iniquities of the colonial system. They provided trade union organizers in all the French African colonies. They founded political parties and started various social movements which combatted the colonial system, or worked to modify its basic forms (Bathily, 1987: 8-9).

Being the first to acquire the theoretical tools needed to clarify the workings of colonial domination, these pioneers were confronted with the choice of demanding independence or negotiating it. They did that work in such periodicals as *Présence africaine, La Condition humaine,* and in such youth and student organizations as the Federation of Black African Students in France (FEANF), the General Union of West African Students (UGEAO), the Senegalese Democratic Youth Rally (RJDS), the African Youth Council (CJA), as well as in various political parties. No doubt, too, the image of Senegal as a breeding ground for intellectuals owes something to the part played by the Association of Senegalese Students in France (AESF) within the FEANF. According to Diané (1990:59): 'the FEANF owed its birth and survival in those rough first years mainly to the initiative of the AESF leadership at the time'.

Diané (1990: 16) adds that 'this formative institution, where one learned to live, think and act in concert', provided opportunities for the exchange of experiences, theoretical assessments, and above all the design of activist strategies aimed at the achievement of independence.

These various reasons justify and legitimize the image, whose primary basis is the role of the school system. Cheikh Hamidou Kane describes the situation with profound relevance. The author presents a character in his novel *L'Aventure ambiguë* making up his mind 'to go among them to learn the art of winning even when wrong'. In this way the novelist shows the incursion into Djallobé country of a new social dynamic, a new value system in which the colonial system is the fundamental point of reference, the school the principal vehicle.[6]

It is inaccurate to see the intellectual stratum as the cornerstone of the colonial edifice. It would be much better to see it as a force subversive of the colonial system. It made the political environment coterminous with the intellectual environment. In this way it set up an exclusivist dynamic. Since the prime interface between the intellectual and political environments turned out to be the urban areas, this appropriation of politics by the intellectuals effectively excluded rural society. Thus abandoned, rural society was left under the supervision of organic intellectuals from the pre-colonial era, integrated in a process of indigenization. The organic elite comprising religious leaders, the marabouts, regarded as unqualified according to the standards of the Western educational system and the imperatives of administrative demarcation, was restricted to the protectorate zones inhabited not by citizens but by subjects. In subsequent years there was no real overturn of the distinction established by colonial administrative demarcations. Paradoxically, this dichotomy ended up conditioning participation in the political process, the interaction between those confronting the colonial authority and those collaborating with it, through the mediation of the intellectual stratum.

In any case, the identity of Senegalese intellectuals, as discerned through their history, was shaped in the interface between the hammer of academic and scientific expertise and the anvil of public political engagement. Intellectuals used their expert status, conferred by the power of degrees and the seductive allure of knowledge[7], to establish ties with the masses on the one hand, the colonial authorities on the other, thus giving themselves the aura of political legitimacy. In this game, however, the key factor, since it was the factor conferring the power of exclusion, was the fact that the Senegalese intellectual operated in a linguistic medium determined by colonialism. The prerequisite condition for the achievement of intellectual status remained the ability to speak and write the colonizer's language. French, as the language of knowledge and power, by definition placed the Senegalese intellectual in the corridors of power. That situation was a source of distortions between the social and political planes.

Though its importance was decisive, the criterion of language did not, on its own, suffice to confer intellectual status. That status resulted from the convergence of conditions and situations interacting to produce both a new identity and a new function. To take just three examples, Senghor, Lamine Guèye and Cheikh Anta Diop ceaselessly stressed their intellectual, academic skills, the first as grammarian, the second as jurist, the third as historian. In his preface to his book *Nations nègres et culture*, Cheikh Anta Diop emphasizes this point:

> All these "scientific" theories on the African past are superbly consistent. They are utilitarian, pragmatic. Truth is whatever is useful, and in this case truth is whatever colonialism finds useful. The goal is to manage, under the cloak of scientific objectivity, to get black people to believe that they have never produced anything of value, not even what exists on their own home grounds.... It is imperative, therefore, for Africans to focus on their own history and civilization, to study them in a search for greater self-knowledge, and in this way to succeed, through genuine knowledge of their past, in rendering the cultural weapons deployed against them henceforth obsolete, grotesque and inoffensive, (Diop, 1979:14-15).

Claims of technical competence were meaningful only to the extent that they supported political involvement, in the sense of facilitating the refutation of colonial ideology, in intellectual terms to begin with, then in political terms. Independence was therefore primarily the achievement of intellectuals who made it the organizational focus of rhetoric aimed at demystifying reality and laying the ideational and symbolic foundations for a clean break. The process Senghor called a 'descent into the abysses of the black soul' of course required a necessary linkage of intellectual and political realities. But it also required the integration of intellectually productive work as a value standard. It was Senghor who asserted in 1957 that:

> intellectuals have a mission to restore black values in all their truth and excellence, to awaken in their people a taste for physical and intellectual nourishment, all of which serves to make us men (Senghor, 1964:19).

By that standard, the only theoretical relevance of the thesis of Negritude or Cheikh Anta Diop's theses on a black Egypt lay in their self-imposed political purpose, the basis of their legitimacy. Such an assertion might appear rash were it not for the confirmation given it by what Thomas Hodgkin calls the nationalist answer to the myth of African barbarism, which he explains as follows:

> But perhaps the most important, and deeply felt, aspect of the nationalist answer to the myth of African barbarism is the new stress placed on the qualities of pre-European African societies (Hodgkin, 1957:174).

Strengthened by a messianic vision unencumbered by doubt, Senegalese intellectuals entered the independence era armed with certitudes which history was destined to corroborate or to shatter. Having adopted the role from that point on, they became irreversibly integrated into a logic already imposed by the colonial system. That logic called for their subordination to power as a central, dominant reality. The power structure could not abandon this linkage without dropping the commitment to a kind of modernizing vision which underlay its emergence, but which it has certainly been unable to implement. It is within this perspective that we shall approach the analysis of relationships between the power structure and intellectuals in Senegal from independence to the present. In this process we remain aware, nevertheless, of the difficulty pointed out by Amin Khan in his treatment of the Algerian situation characterized by a dearth of comprehensive visions and a prevalence of piecemeal approaches:

> at the present stage in the formation of the intellectual environment and its analytical tools, any attempt to shape such partial approaches into a well-rounded essay involves a risk of obscuring the fact that it is really impossible to present (the country's) intellectual life as a coherent whole. For the ever-shifting conceptual landmarks borrowed from here and there and strewn over the (national) mindscape seem fixed and steady only from the fictitious perspective of the essay (Khan, 1990:266).

We shall therefore take off from a methodological hypothesis, that of the Socratic paradigm[8], calculated to enable us to define the theme of the relationship between political and intellectual activity. The paradigmatic figure of Socrates is an apt illustration of the conflictual dynamic of alternating expansion and annihilation subtending the relationship between intellectual and political power. Still, the Socratic paradigm calls for two observations. The first is that intellectuals are vectors of real power, the power of thought. Here we think the statement made by Raymond Aron utterly apt: 'The tendency to criticize the established order is, in a sense, the professional ailment of intellectuals' (Aron, 1962:210). Only this intellectual power is capable of providing political power with moral authority. Intellectual inquiry on the present and the future is invariably conducted in the name of Truth and associated values, since 'it is the intellectual who transforms the concept of a world into a meaningful issue'.[9]

The absolute nature of intellectual power flows from the norm of freedom of thought. That is why intellectual power undermines the moral self-complacency of political power. Intellectual power sets itself up as a sanctioning power constantly invoking the judgmental status of ideas and even of expert competence. Furthermore, both political and intellectual power tend towards absolute assertion. There is therefore an eternal temptation for political power to try domesticating intellectual power, using ways and means whose special nature history alone enables us to understand and evaluate.

We have, then, highlighted the conflictual nature of the power bond linking politics and ideation. But here a point of clarification is in order. The universal and universalizing reference of the paradigm tends to void it of all historical relevance the moment its validity transcends all particular, determining situations. Furthermore, its functional usefulness is subordinate to its capacity to impart meaning and intelligibility to a specific set of determining circumstances, to a given historical situation. Our concern here, therefore, will be to see how this paradigm took root and became naturalized in the Senegalese environment, and to assess how it was re-invented in accordance with a given historical situation and a particular set of socio-economic parameters.

The Age of Ideologies: The Establishment of the Triangular Paradigm

The achievement of national sovereignty put all Senegal, especially the ruling class, under a double obligation. The first imperative was to construct the Senegalese State and nation, using the ratified constitution as a foundation. The second was to embark on a programme of economic and social development, with the State providing locomotive power.

The twin project was thoroughly constructivist, and it had to provide an effective impetus on two fronts, one institutional and political, the other economic and social. In that travail it would draw support from what Diop and Diouf have termed 'the ideological triangle" of Negritude, Francophonie and African Socialism' (Diop and Diouf, 1990:251). The re-invention or re-appropriation of political resources was a theoretical construct, an intellectual operation that provided a foundation for the regime's activities. From that perspective, one can immediately assess the impact of Senghor who, to a degree, circumscribed the central issue of political power in Senegal. The man was an intellectual, party leader and head of State all rolled in one. As such he functioned as a theoretical pace-setter, and left his imprint on the institutional framework he occupied as a forum for the practical implementation of Negritude. Hence Diouf's conclusion that:

the intellectual vision of the ruling class was clear. It was of a piece with Senghor's rhetoric of Negritude, whose influence transcended the frontiers of Senegal. It defined an environment for the exercise of power, a modern power with no need whatsoever for ancient historical traditions. The approach was one of the creation of a novel social system of national integration (Diouf, 1989:16).

If Negritude provided inspirational content for power, it did so in the sense that it enabled the regime to fashion a rhetoric of identity as an effective instrument for the construction and consolidation of national unity. Achieved, that national unity was expected to reinstate a Senegalese identity of universal validity. But since this identity did not have a history of its own, it was to be born of some makeshift theorizing coupled with the manufacture of a future memory. To accomplish this feat it would be necessary to wipe out the actual history of the territory, dominated by the urban Wolof aristocracy, and to substitute for it a bundle of values abstracted from their particular territorial roots. Such was the loom for the weaving of Negritude.

This approach became a reference resource for a rhetoric of identity, in the sense that it subverted oral tradition, deconstructed the local history of discrete micro-environments, and in so doing created a collective memory for Senegal. In this way, the do-it-yourself philosophy of Negritude set out, within the framework of a discourse on identity, to process historical data bearing the strong imprint of territorial particularities, turning them into universal values destined to play an integral role in the production of the Idea of the Nation, followed by its practical achievement. One telling instance of this fabrication is the Senegalese national Hymn to Youth, which invokes the hero Lat Dior. In actual history, Lat Dior was defeated. The lyrics of the Hymn, however, 'transmute defeat into victory' (Diouf, 1989).

The resulting 'poaching' described by Diouf is thence legitimized in the rhetoric of identity, with the turf of Negritude mapped out between the twin parameters, *l'enracinement* and *l'ouverture*. After all, the only way to turn the eradication of history into a source of 'Black values valid in both their truth and their excellence' was to license the griot (the intellectual by an older name) to go poaching along the frontier. The booty from that expedition included a gift to Negritude and the rhetoric of identity, the notion of *l'enracinement*, meaning rootedness. But this rootedness turned out to be fake, a straw notion set up to play legitimizing foil to the necessary concept designed to ensure a modernizing linkage: *l'ouverture*. Receptivity, in other words, and openness to foreign influences.

Here we come, perhaps, to an appropriate point where we have to underline what we have described elsewhere as 'the ploy of unitary logic' (Diaw, 1990:5). The parameter of *l'enracinement* thrust forward in the theory of

Negritude is not by any stretch of the imagination a historical construct dug up from the past. Much less is it the fruit of the restorative recollection of basic, genuine African values. In its constant waffling between meanings and reference points, Negritude manages out of one corner of its mouth to deny the existence of African values, and out of the other corner to posit those very values as *a priori*[10] postulates. In any case, the very idea of value is the most glaring proof of the enterprise of fabrication. Value, like tradition, is the fruit of a permanent process of self-creation, a self adjusting mechanism whereby rhetoric refers back to its sources of legitimacy.

If Senghor gave himself the myth-making power of Aristotelian *poesies*, he did so the better to facilitate the acceptance of the notion of Negritude, which is above all a philosophy of fabrication, of creation. Its purpose was to project 'a new vision of the world in which man is integrated, incarnate' (Senghor, 1983:28). It was to provide an environment for the radiant development of 'a new philosophy, a new literature, a new art, a new economy, a new society, in short, a new *Homo Senegalensis*' (Senghor, 1980:236).

With, one might be tempted to add, new values of his own. For Negritude, organized as it was around a scaffolding of newness and modernity, was essentially an attitude of openness to universal history:

> *What needed to be expressed, according to its advocates, were not the ideas of traditional African rulers, the Damels and the Teignes, nor yet the thinking of eighteenth century African peasants. Black Africans, after all, were already integrated into the modern world of nuclear physics and anti-colonial struggles, a world of simultaneous autonomy and interdependence* (Senghor, 1957).

Negritude provided a content for the regime's rhetoric of identity only because the history of *Homo Senegalensis* was not written in the past tense but to be written in the future. The alchemy required to bring the Senegalese nation to birth mined its raw materials from territories beyond ethnic, religious, regional or caste specificities. It also needed to transcend the artificial nature of its imposed boundaries, to become the organizational axis of the regime's programme. It mattered little if this cultural ideology were valid or fake. The important point was that it provided a basis for the regime's political programme, in combination with African Socialism.

At first sight, this ideological option, a response to the need to find short cuts, might be supposed to have offered an acceptable basis for a consensus binding the ruling class, the Marxists, and the left-leaning intelligentsia. But it did not. Senghor, after excoriating believers in 'capsule Marxism', suggested that what was needed was *to construct a type of Scientific Socialism based certainly on Marx and Engels, but enriched with other concepts and other socialist experiences throughout the world, and above all rooted in Black African, Senegalese realities* (Senghor, 1976:38).

The ideological option was a full-scale expression of the philosophy of *poesies*. As a matter of fact, it was an exemplary fulfillment thereof. And yet there was no contradiction between the reference to history, the stipulation of rootedness, and the hostility to Marxist theory that went so far as to endorse a preference for the epithet 'Marxian'. In revising the works of Marx and Engels and launching a Senegalese approach to African Socialism, the official rhetoric was actually performing a damage-control operation on itself. It is not hard to understand the political stakes involved in this ideological choice. In the first place, it offered the regime a solid basis of legitimacy buttressed by culture and tradition. This enabled it to camouflage its economic policy, which made no fundamental attempt to even out inequalities. Second, it denied Marxist and leftist intellectuals any access to cultural reference points, thus cutting off all real contacts between them and the people.[11]

With the ground thus marked out, the Senegalese system was ready to borrow from Marxism three organizational accents, those on man, planning and social justice, while taking care to disconnect them from a key concept, that of the class struggle, so as to rearrange them around that quintessentially political *topos*, the State. Of this approach the content of the first Four Year Plan offered enlightening proof. With hindsight, it becomes clearer in just what way Senghor, using his concept of Negritude, defined the Senegalese scene in such a way as to arrogate to himself the role of 'final' theoretical boundary. The tandem of Negritude and African or Senegalese Socialism became the reference framework for the production of meaning and knowledge, for assessment and criticism. So pervasive was this influence that even some exact disciplines, mathematics for instance, were affected by the unilateral imposition of Negritude. Meanwhile, the regime's attitude to intellectuals followed three interactive scenarios.

The first scenario was purely theoretical, the approach we described in our discussion of the Socratic paradigm, feeding on a degree of conflict. If we emphasize the conflictual aspect of this type of relationship, however, we lose sight of a key aspect, the factor of illusion. The common language used by political power and intellectual power constitutes a frontier within which the two forms of power coexist, and beyond which the uninitiated remain excluded. Now with modernity serving as the legitimizing rationale of the State, while the school system functioned as the vector of modernity, one might wonder wherein lay the potential for conflict. One fact is clear in any case: the rhetoric of Senegalese intellectuals, invariably framed in institutional terms, was never addressed to any institutional entity other than the regime. As far as Laurin-Frenette, (1983:125) is concerned, rhetoric collaborates with the dominant system the moment it gets presented and is supported in venues belonging to that system, and to the related political system, broadly speaking. Some of these venues are occupied by intellectuals, and they include various types in different sectors: the educational system, the university research establishment, journalism and associated media, parties, etc.

The second scenario was economic. The process of nation-building in Senegal, and the reality of the country's development, made it imperative for the regime to accept the collaboration of intellectuals. By that token, the latter came to be defined as development agents. In his closing address at the colloquium on 'Development Policies and the Various Approaches to Socialism', Mamadou Dia long ago highlighted this issue by pointing out that 'the various educational systems were designed more to turn out elites than to ensure the welfare of the population at large'. (Dia, 1962). To Dia, the risk of the happy few turning themselves into a privileged class on the sole basis of their intellectual status was quite clear. However, by happenstance or deliberate amnesia, he did not mention the fact that the regime itself was set to manufacture just such a privileged class through the system of co-optation and the distribution of grants, scholarships and handouts. In the resulting shake-out, all those unequipped to cash in on intellectual credentials were purely and simply marginalized.

The third scenario was political. This, essentially, was the level at which the re-invention of political realities was to take place. The constructivist perspective in Senegal here ran into a problem so thoroughly basic that it proved practically insoluble. The riddle was how to deliver, in practical terms, on the implied promises of democratic socialism. The regime's rhetoric, based on Negritude, had no room for political dissent, or for plural options in ideology or doctrine. It mattered little that the Constitution recognized the right of political parties to organize freely, provided they stayed within the confines of the law and observed democratic norms. The 1962 crisis complicated the situation by resulting in the replacement of a bicephalous executive with a frankly presidential regime. Henceforth, the President alone was responsible for the conduct of national policy. He was both head of the civil service and commander-in-chief of the armed forces. The President's supremacy was underscored by the fact that Parliament had no practical means whatsoever of reining in presidential or ministerial power. All this concentration of power was rationalized by the 'need' to consolidate national unity.

The regime found a way to transcend the contradiction between the constitutional stipulation of political freedom and its own political imperative to curtail that freedom, not by frankly instituting a single-party system, but by claiming it was practicing consensual government[12]. In thus avoiding that unconstitutional step, the regime acted in conformity with its unitary attitude. For, from that viewpoint, 'the important thing is *unanimity* among a people, not the primacy of any particular doctrine, however superb it might be'.[13] To achieve that aim, as Bayart says, a "process of the reciprocal assimilation of elites" was set in motion. The venue for this process turned out to be the State. Now the integration of intellectuals into the political venue was a way of harnessing their critical potential and getting them to fit into an already programmed implementational frame. The usefulness and relevance of unitary thinking depended on its capacity to turn intellectuals into ideologues. In plain words, that meant assigning them 'the task of rationalizing and camouflaging the oppression of the lower classes by the ruling class' (Bon and Bournier, 1971:3).

The construction of Senegal into a materially and culturally developed nation thus became the rationale for a political imperative of collaboration or consensus that reduced intellectuals and the State to a purely instrumental function. The strategy of a national rally aimed at assimilating the country's elites within a single unified party was followed beyond the country's accession to independence, until 1966, when dissidents who had formed the PRA rejoined the UPS. The regime pursued two parallel policies, assimilating cooperative intellectuals, marginalizing others, in order to consolidate and fine-tune its project. Contacts between the PRA and the regime, from 1962 to 1963, ended in a joint admission that there was no deep difference in their doctrines or programmes. The one real point of disagreement concerned the allocation of government and political posts.

Under the circumstances, the creation of the *PRA-Rénovation* and its merger with the UPS in 1964 did not bring about a definitive solution. Certain intellectuals, some quite distinguished, remained outside the party. A second attempt, coupled with the commutation of the sentence on Abdoulaye Ly, was needed before a definitive solution was reached in 1966, a key feature of which was a rigorous allocation of ministerial portfolios. The June 1966 reshuffle which made Amadou Mactar Mbow Minister of National Education, Abdoulaye Ly Minister of Health, and Assane Seck Minister of Culture, was solid proof, if indeed proof were needed, that the regime was bent on a unifying policy, and that intellectuals played a key role in that policy.

It would be wrong to suppose that this integrationist strategy was just an *ad hoc* tactic adopted by Senghor. It was an inherent element of his regime.

It was applied to the *Bloc des Masses Sénégalaises* (BMS), whose Secretary-General was Cheikh Anta Diop. Talks suggested by the General Caliph of the Mouride brotherhood resulted in October 1963 in the absorption of some BMS activists into the UPS, and in a decree abolishing the BMS. In November of that same year Cheikh Anta Diop created the Senegalese National Front, but that was also outlawed by decree. The reason was that it attracted a large number of followers of Mamadou Dia.

The political motivation for this approach was not a genuine search for unity and consensus, even though consensus was the sole goal. The idea was that constructive organizational initiatives and criticism should happen through the co-optation of intellectuals and their integration within the regime, so as to avoid any possibility of plural political expression. It was this approach, more than the strength of the regime, that expressed the regime's determination to deny all possible alternatives to its own policy regarding the emergence of a ruling class. At any rate, the regime's strategy towards intellectuals worked only within a codified environment in which political or ideological preferences were relevant identity tags. The regime's aim was to put down other parties, whether they were called the PRA or the BMS. Still, the main (if not exclusive) motivation behind that aim was to bring intellectuals in those other parties to heel. In its capacity as a mass or rallying party, the only way the UPS could rationalize its dominance was by ensuring the co-optation of significant numbers of 'brains'. Internally, they would help increase the ruling party's dynamism. On the foreign level, they would help to win approval.

The single-party system was based on a process of inclusion or incorporation nourished by a long tradition of compromise, coalition and reconciliation, in a State system harbouring and creating inequalities. With independence it gained direct access to wealth. Economic hardships had a decisive impact on the construction of the post-colonial State, in the sense that they sapped the meaning of nationalist independence slogans. 'Out-of-power' intellectuals came under pressure from the bureaucratic bourgeoisie and their own families. Family pressure was all the more important because it emanated from a social context that did not recognize individuals as autonomous persons with independent powers of decision and action, but instead saw individuals as deeply integrated into the family unit.

These factors were instrumental in the defection of an appreciable number of intellectuals from various democratic organizations into the ruling UPS. Such shifts in allegiance made all the more sense in a society where 'social status, economic role and material wealth still depended on one's relationship to the State apparatus'.[14] Since social prestige was still related to economic status, it was hardly surprising to find that a lot of leftist intellectuals crossed over to the government.

In practice, the post-colonial State managed to make itself substantially independent of society. Instead of promoting its development, the State simply pushed the society off centre stage. Through mercenary allegiances and patron-client networks, with the help of marabouts and trade unionists, Senghor's State distanced itself from the periphery, a society steeped in anachronisms and pop culture, illiteracy and tradition.

Negritude, Francophonie and African Socialism: Senghor's ideological triangle made itself at home in the urban environment, as the President handpicked Western-educated intellectuals to be its spokespersons and negotiators. It mattered little what ideology any particular intellectual claimed to follow. For their part, the intellectual elite willingly went along with Senghor's game plan. Senghor had circumscribed the political arena by making it coterminous with the intellectual environment. He had imposed reference points occult to any but the literate, and thus reinforced the domination of the State apparatus[15] by the petty bourgeoisie. This, perhaps, was why the political system was so stable, and why the regime did not have to use truly authoritarian measures as instruments of government, as in so many other parts of Africa. For the only real crisis the State faced was the 1962 crisis.

The university, a focus of protest and academic freedom, was not spared the visitations of Senghor's strategic arsenal. The regime was unable to defuse university tensions despite increasingly violent and arbitrary reprisals. May 1968 was the climactic crisis. The harshness of the ensuing repression indicated that the stakes went beyond academic issues. The regime came under opposition articulated in Marxist and nationalist terms.[16] The special status of the university and its autonomous style of operation helped more or less to protect faculty members from academic repression. Still, there were occasional cases of ostracism, the most notorious being that of Cheikh Anta Diop. These instances of interference were of special significance. For one thing, they demonstrated, at least circumstantially, that the university as an institution was an accomplice of the regime. Second, they showed how difficult the ideal of consensual politics was in practice. Admittedly, increasingly harsh living conditions, especially for junior lecturers, and the emergence of increasingly radical postures on campus, turned the university into a forum the regime could hardly afford to overlook. The paradoxical coexistence of complicity and exclusion, which showed the way in which the political system doled out the scope of permissible protest, was in a sense a cogent expression of the triangular paradigm.

Senghor's model took over the managerial tools of power in the post-colonial era and arrogated to itself the position of a source of reference. In the process it created a unitary system whose main consequence was the design of a triangular paradigm. The understanding of this paradigm is the conceptual prism that enables us to reach a comprehensive assessment of the Senegalese political process prior to the establishment of multi-party politics. The 'Pharaonic' and the Marxist models, subordinate bases of the triangular paradigm, help to explain the transmutation of the regime's unitary attitude into a closed system. The shift was facilitated by a shared history (with colonialism as the point of reference), and above all by an identical situation within the new political process, inextricably linked with the central role of the State.

As with Senghor's model, the Pharaonic model drew its operative usefulness from a linkage of the theoretical and political environments, with the theoretical environment providing a meaningful grid for the interpretation of political realities. National, political independence, the organizing matrix for the Pharaonic model, was considered meaningless unless it led to the establishment of a federal African State. That progression required a series of legitimating intellectual and scientific postulates.[17] The home turf of the model was the field of historiography and historical revision. In other words, it was an exercise in the revelation of historical truth and meaning long travestied by the universalist pretensions of European civilization and culture. The re-writing of history therefore became a labour of mythological debunking and demystification. The first step in that travail was the analysis of the historical and archaeological background. In this, Cheikh Anta Diop used the exhumed record of Ancient Egypt, backed up with information from such ancient sources as Herodotus, Aristotle and Strabo as an authoritative foundation. On that basis he proceeded to demonstrate the historical precedence and blackness of Egyptian civilization, and then to postulate the historical continuity linking the Nile cradle with Black African societies.

Within that framework, the logical correlation between history and linguistics facilitated the support and legitimation of the idea of shared historical and cultural references, thus making arguments against African federalism moot. Now since, in the first place, the Pharaonic model rode on the idea of the Nation as a political project rooted in an understanding of history as revised and re-written information, the model made sense only to intellectuals, despite the enthusiastic support, status and importance its advocates accorded the national languages. So in this instance too, just as happened with the model deployed by the ruling regime, it was the shared jargon and expertise of academic life that qualified advocates for the expression of political viewpoints.

The trump card of Senghor's model was its skill in pushing every other model into separating the political aspect of reality from the social.[18] Neither did the Marxist model prove an exception: it too got trapped within the confining parameters of the triangular paradigm. It shared with the two other models a common history and a commitment to the undermining of colonialism in the drive towards national independence. But the Marxist model was singular in one respect that perhaps proved its weakness. This was the glaring 'contradiction' between the proclaimed vocation of Marxist groups as working class parties and their real social identity. In Senegal they were often chided as intellectual parties. This identity bind paralyzed their capacity to think through their involvement in mass struggles, or to think as workers' parties. Workers were generally suspicious of intellectuals. The latter, for their part, suffered from internalized guilt feelings. The suspicion and guilt were both related to their petty-bourgeois status and their relationship to culture. Senegal's Marxist parties therefore had a hard time fixating their intellectual potential, even if it was an indispensable part of Marxist ideology (Bathily, 1987:18-19).

It was not until intellectuals rose to leadership positions in their parties that the issue of the status of intellectuals was frankly discussed. The situation of Marxist intellectuals within their parties provided a good illustration of the subordination of intellectual needs to political imperatives. Activists could have their university careers, research foci and time tables all arranged to harmonize with party strategies. This involvement of the party in matters of intellectual expertise was the correlative of a search for some degree of legitimacy in the drive towards the exercise of political power.

The Marxist model faced a second problem. In most cases, it seemed as if activists had embraced Marxism more because of the functionalist myth of its assumed capacity to bring about radical modernization than anything else. For that reason, Marxist intellectuals remained blind to other aspects of the socialization process and other images of socio-political struggle (Diouf, 1990:12).

The Marxist model was also unable to escape the consequences of severed connections between politics and society. That severance focused the political process entirely on the central role of the State. The organization of Senegalese Islam into brotherhoods, and the chummy relations between the regime and the religious leadership, definitely limited the popular appeal of the Marxist model. Marxism did manage to liven up ideological debate, but the model was seriously damaged by being forced underground, and also by the economic hardship that motivated many of its adherents to turn coat and join the ruling party.

So despite constant resistance from the intelligentsia, in the first decade after independence, Senghor's model was able to impose its own system, the triangular paradigm. Because it occupied the centres of power, ran the administrative structure and controlled the economy, the Senghor regime was able to push the Pharaonic and Marxist models off to the fringes. However, this political configuration in Senegal reached its limits in the 1970s, when the internal workings of the regime's adaptive strategies were laid bare amid mounting protests. In 1968 and 1969, social protest reached unprecedented intensities. Underground opposition forces grew more radical from 1970 to 1975. Strike after strike shattered the school and university system. As far as the regime was concerned, Marxist and leftist intellectuals had a hand in the wave of troubles[19].

The salient development of this period was the irruption onto the political scene of a new generation of university graduates, sure of their knowledge and skills, eager to challenge the first generation of leaders. These two factors obliged the regime to set up a two-phase damage-control mechanism. In the first phase, it tried to recover the ideological initiative in political debates by setting up think tanks. In 1966 it set up the *Club Nation et Développement*, unusual in that it was open to all comers. In 1970 it set up the Socialist Studies and Research Centre. As part of the same process, teaching staff in the UPS were reorganized.

The second phase saw the creation of the *Parti Démocratique Sénégalais*, defined as a contributory party. Significantly, the draft manifesto signed by 200 Senegalese executives that led to this development was originally not principally aimed at the creation of that party (Wade, 1975:6). The question was whether this response to the challenge really enabled the regime to regain the initiative and adjust to the new situation. Apart from the regime's success in marginalizing the Marxist left, wracked by internal disputes of increasing bitterness after the legal recognition of Majmout Diop's PAI, the answer has to be no. For the co-optation of moderate intellectuals through the PDS did not defuse the bomb of political agitation, as proved by the arrest in 1975 of the organizers of *Xarebi*. Within the *Club Nation et Développement*, the new party intelligentsia designed a theoretical scheme basing its legitimacy wholly on technocratic expertise. It was asserted that the strengthening of the role of intellectuals within the ruling party would lead to the demise of 'politics as usual'. Arguments highlighting the absence of effective democracy subjected the existing modernization scenario to scathing criticism, and the old pioneering activists were ridiculed as 'pre-fabricated elites'. It would have been naïve to take all this with undue solemnity. The intention of the new critics was not really to bring the State together with 'civil society' or whatever passed for such. The new generation of intellectuals did fit intellectual acumen within a framework of nationalist ideology. But their nationalism was thoroughly elitist.

The limited political pluralism established in 1976 did not mean a fundamental break with the old-style political approach revolving around the State as central institution. Instead, it involved a shuffling of the cards to give the new technocrats a better deal. As a matter of fact, the *Club Nation et Développement* served to launch a number of intellectuals into government posts. Now all this new jockeying left a bitter taste in the mouths of Senghor's old guard. But it harmonized snugly with World Bank and International Monetary Fund options, which tended to short-circuit both the political parties and the people in their enthusiasm for technocratic solutions. Meanwhile, the leftist parties did not let up in their fierce struggle for official recognition for political parties, the basis of their attempts to break the hegemonic hold of the regime. Through forums ranging from the ASD to the COSU, the intellectual left brought all debate to bear on one central point: the need to give practical shape to the aspiration to freedom, by installing a democratic regime.

The era of ideology ended with one generation handing over with visible ill grace to a generation of heirs calling themselves technocrats. Various parameters combined to put the finishing touches on the process. First, the world economy entered a recession, with unpalatable effects on the national scene. Second, the regime, in its hustle to consolidate its power through influence-peddling and political patron-client games, committed a series of management blunders. Third, it was realized that the development policy followed was flawed in its undemocratic approach, and that the necessary linkage between the State and 'civil society' just was not there. Fourth, despite its manipulation of the triangular paradigm, the regime never totally succeeded in neutralizing the intellectual factor.

The construction of the post-colonial State on the model put forward by Senghor showed his shrewdness in the way he was able to circumscribe the political environment by fixing the game rules. Senghor did a lot to support intellectual, cultural and artistic effervescence. Part of the reason was surely that he himself was a humanist, a cultivated man of letters. But there was just as certainly the additional consideration that the left has never separated intellectual production form political activism. The film-maker and novelist Ousmane Sembene provides a good example of this attitude. Furthermore, as far as many opposition intellectuals were concerned, political dissent in this period was limited to disagreement with the man Senghor.

From the Dusk of the Idols to the Technocratic Dawn

Senghor's resignation and the death of Cheikh Anta Diop marked, in a sense, a 'break' in Senegal's political and intellectual history. The disappearance of the two great figures from the Senegalese scene ushered in the 'dusk of the idols'. The two men had played the role of intellectual idols by serving as poles of reference. In so doing they had marked the fault lines in the landscape of Senegalese political and intellectual life. They presented two different intellectual constructs, represented two ideological schools of thought. But they also projected two political visions, one based on Negritude, the other on Egyptology. The two visions ran parallel to each other, always avoiding convergence, taking precautions against undue contact, as if the two could only continue to exist if they remained separate and apart, inevitably antithetical.[20]

Behind the surface hostility, nevertheless, there lurked perhaps a family likeness, an identity neither side dared acknowledge. For in asserting the unity of African culture, Cheikh Anta Diop was moved, like Senghor, to downplay both oral traditions and monographic studies which did not fit into the Egypto-Pharaonic framework (Diouf, 1989:17). The theoretical output of both Senghor and Cheikh Anta was characterized and legitimized by the rejection of a Wolof model crammed with traditions and values totally out of sync with the concept of modernity, the putative form to be taken by Africa's reinstatement in history as a universal process. From that perspective, the ways in which Cheikh Anta Diop, author of *Nations nègres et culture*, used history and linguistics, and in which Senghor, bard of Negritude, used anthropological lore and linguistic concepts, differed only in degree. Both, in the end, worked within the same modernizing paradigm.

Let us be clear on this. We have no intention whatsoever of presenting the theories of Senghor and Cheikh Anta Diop as if they were mere mirror images of each other. Our intention is simply to elucidate the functional nature of the intellectual constructs deployed by the two men, both operating within a modernizing paradigm. For the discourse of both men sprang from 'a social order, that of bearers of philosophical, literary and scientific knowledge' (Diop and Diouf, 1990:274). In both cases, the arguments invoked transcended the local environments known to these scholars, replete with oral traditions and traditional norms, to produce a universal construct based on rational, scientific values. In this connection, there are two arguments that need emphasizing, since they shed light on the relationship between these two men, these two intellectual giants.

The first is this: Cheikh Anta Diop, against the advice of a section of the intelligentsia, supported Abdou Diouf in the 1983 elections, even though that candidate's platform was different from his. Senghor had said that Cheikh Anta Diop only opposed him for 'crypto-personal' reasons. Did the latter's behaviour in the 1983 elections bear out that assessment? Admittedly, on the intellectual level, Abdou Diouf had no reason to treat Cheikh

Anta Diop the way Senghor did. The fact that Senghor shut him up in his IFAN laboratory, thanks to the tacit acquiescence of the intelligentsia, meant that his intellectual expertise could be acknowledged without giving him a chance for full political self-expression.

Possibly, the abortive posthumous attempts to evaluate and seriously criticize Diop's work are part of an attempt to make up for the ostracism to which the man was subjected while alive, coupled with the compromising behaviour of the university as an institution. The debate between Amady Aly Dieng and Mariétou Diop Diongue in the Senegalese press, quite apart from the valid criticism and the 'adulation' involved, exemplifies a certain uneasiness with which, in one way or another, people approach the work and status of Cheikh Anta Diop. After his death, Dakar University was renamed Cheikh Anta Diop University. That also, in another way, was an expression of a clear desire to honour him as a great intellectual. Whether it was a final gesture of a guilty conscience or a historical irony, the consecration put the final touch to Senghor's systematic treatment of Cheikh Anta Diop. For even after the man's death, the move confined him to a single environment, the university campus.

Once the twilight of the idols came round, Senegal negotiated a new turn in its history on a note of deep economic gloom and unprecedented social upheaval, symptoms of the failure of the me-too ideology to stimulate development and national integration. The impact of the 1973 petrol crisis, the long-lasting drought of the 1970s, the erosion of public finances and the litany of mismanagement, all spelled a depressed economy. In spite of huge infusions of foreign aid, the downward trend continued steadily. Of the resulting social tension, there were two illustrative indices.

The Mouride brotherhood, a faithful objective ally of the regime, began to take up the tale of peasant discontent. The new Caliph, Abdou Lahad Mbacké, gave government policy short shrift when he made it understood that the peasants were 'worn out'. Indeed, from 1960 to 1967, the purchasing power of peasants had dropped by 20% despite a rise in groundnut production. When France cut off groundnut export subsidies, the government passed the burden on to the peasantry. To this must probably be added the list of embezzlements and sleazy deals at the ONCAD from 1966 to 1980, involving tens of billions of Francs CFA. ONCAD was a State corporation supposedly set up to manage 'cooperation and development aid'. What it actually did was to provide a slush fund for the ruling party at the expense of the peasantry. The system of patron-client networks that grew up around the ONCAD bonanza was in truth a looter's paradise for rural traders, transport owners, loan sharks, plantation owners and big-shot marabouts belonging to the ruling Socialist Party's power base.

Administrative reforms were sidetracked from their stated objectives. One way this happened was through implementational tricks that turned the administration into a mechanism for political control of a rural environment in which marabouts played key roles as representatives of the authorities and grand electors. A second manner was to use administrative resources to finance political patron-client networks. Meanwhile, the cooperative movement crashed. From its ruins rose the bitterness of peasant discontent.

The second parameter, the school system, was certainly the more important factor. It crystallized all the dreams and nightmares of a society to which it offered the premise of equal opportunity and the promise of social mobility. Beyond this psychological impact, the Senegalese school system was a political prize of unparalleled importance, from both the government and opposition points of view. In his *La poésie de l'action*, Senghor identified two main resources for the attainment of the objectives of the Social and Economic Development Plan: the rural sector and the educational system. And education was allocated 30% of the State's recurrent budget.

The student movement, traditionally inclined to the political left, tended to adopt recalcitrant attitudes to the Senghor regime. That stance hardened in the late 1970s. Student protest had no shortage of issues to coalesce around: unemployment, problems with scholarship allocations and food allowances, inadequacies of syllabus content, overcrowding on the campus, etc. The government was able to defuse tensions caused by the January 1980 student demonstration in Ziguinchor and the SUDES[21] teachers' union call for a strike. But the underlying causes of the crisis in the school and university system were not dealt with in a clear-headed, definitive manner. The crisis was all the more complex because it rode on a political undertow which influenced its topical focus. The student movement was prey to the same in-fighting fissuring the Senegalese left. Paradoxically, because it consistently used such authoritarian and repressive measures as whippings, arrests, the closure of university dormitories and the drafting of dissident students into the army, the government helped to bridge over some political differences between student factions.

The teachers' movement suffered likewise from internal political divisions. The sidelining of the PAI-Senegal activist Magatte Thiam during the 1979 teachers' union congress, and his replacement by the Democratic League activist Mamadou Ndoye; the sacking of the same Mamadou Ndoye at the Third Congress (late 1981) and the accession of the MNR activist Madior Diouf to leadership of the SUDES (the Unified Democratic Teachers' Union of Senegal), testified to the extreme politicization of the Senegalese educational system in general and to the commitment of leftist intellectuals to the opposition in particular. The fact that there was a measure of 'consensus among leftist intellectuals concerning the analysis of the university crisis' was proof that the university worked as a haven for a section of the intellectual elite opposed to Senghor's model. It also showed that the university functioned as a context for the expression of an alternative solution.

On that point, the SUDES contribution to a colloquium organized as early as May 1977 was emphatic[22]. The crisis could only be resolved through a radical break from 'a Senegalese school system serving to perpetuate Western capitalist cultural and socio-economic models...an elitist French-speaking educational system... an elitist school system designed to ruin the social structure'. These three characterizations signalled a determination to break away from the Senghor model, a vehicle of neo-colonialism, in a search for an alternative to the development goals put forward at the time of independence. Focusing on the educational system as an instrumental institution, a section of the intellectual elite proposed a development model designed to shift Senegal from Senghor's external orientation *(l' ouverture)* to a much more serious focus on national culture. For the shift to be effective, it would have to fit into the framework of a determined search for justice and social equality. The new approach would therefore discredit an educational approach that catered to the exclusive interests of the privileged, and which accentuated social imbalances.

The SUDES proposal included a section on 'Educational Expenditure and Working Conditions for Teaching Staff'. The section was particularly important because it implicated the country's economic structure and impinged on the overall implementation of educational policy.

With this 'break' we come to the intellectual factor identified by Jean Copans (1990) as a component of the paradigm of modernity. The trend is to challenge the colonial pact in the sphere of research, a pact condemned by Paulin Hountondji (1990), along with extroversion and scientific dependence. It may sound paradoxical, but to a certain extent, ongoing socio-economic changes had a lot to do with the crisis of the educational system, the solution adumbrated by a section of the intelligentsia, and the extreme politicization of the intellectual stratum as a whole. Unemployment among graduates, for instance, and the deterioration in middle class living standards, including teachers' living conditions, certainly played a part.

Abdou Diouf's accession to power under these conditions, thanks to a constitutional technicality, was proof of the regime's ability to adapt to shifting political circumstances in its determination to hang on to absolute power. The regime moved in several different but ultimately far from divergent directions. There was the organization of a General Congress of Educational and Training Staff in a bid to defuse the crisis in the school and university system. Then there was the installation of an open multi-party system. The two moves constituted a perfect illustration the shrewdness of the unitary approach.

The new consensual approach in politics and the drive to achieve full democracy should in no way obscure the regime's vital objective. That was to confirm its grip on intellectual power without jeopardizing the established separation of intelligentsia and society, the very basis of the status quo. In combination with the leftward tilt of the intelligentsia, these various factors ended up snapping the alliance of forces that had previously been more or less united in opposition to the Senghor regime. Of this breach the principal consequence was, to some extent, a dissipation of intellectual power caused by a proliferation of platforms.

Meanwhile, the new economic policy brought in by Abdou Diouf, basically focused on State disengagement, was proving incompatible with the me-too ideology and the instrumental role of the State within the Senghor model. The overhaul of the ruling political class and the reshuffling of cards within the government power structure seemed unavoidable if the old Senghorian hegemony was to be broken. For that reason, there was a concerted effort to accent technical competence as a way to winnow out Senghor's old guard, nicknamed 'barons', with the simultaneous induction of new blood into the politico-administrative system.

The new President achieved control over the government apparatus by overturning the rules of access to the party. Hitherto, party membership was the gate to government positions; henceforth, the itinerary would be reversed. The position of the new breed of so-called technocrats, in reality executors of pre-set programmes, was strengthened by the increasingly open interference of funding agencies in the definition of the country's economic objectives. The political consequence of this change was an increasing tendency to 'parachute' political leaders from the governmental apex onto the disenfranchised base. The phenomenon called for the application of grey matter. The urgent need for a new ideology became clear in a context of thorough-going multi-party politics, with the General Conference on Education in full swing.

The following factors facilitate an understanding of power relationships between the political and intellectual spheres in the formative period of Abdou Diouf's hegemony. First came the energizing appeal to 'national pride'. Next came the declaration of 'an urgent need to produce' a set of genuinely Black African principles in the creative and interpretive arts, 'through the use of the national languages' (Diop and Diouf, 1990:275).

The new President may have been in no position to claim untarnished historical and political legitimacy. Nevertheless, he did take pains to distance himself from the ideology of Negritude. Once the founding father Senghor had 'resigned', it was time for some quick-fix ideologizing. A germane question here: should the ideology of an 'energizing national pride' be viewed as part of an attempt to summarize and transcend Senghor's political philosophy? From the regime there was no precise theoretical answer to this query. For the initial use of the slogan was remarkable mainly for the absence of definitional clarity and semantic precision.

The build-up of a technocratic identity and hegemony went hand in hand with the consecration of a new myth of 'development'[23], the key term in the effort to create a consensual base for the new political programme. The idea was to get all social actors and economic operators, with no exception, to cooperate in the weaving of the nation's past as a springboard to a distinctive national future.

Thus, as with L.S. Senghor and Cheikh Anta Diop, history, revised and re-written, was assigned a role in a radical process of distancing and legitimation achieved by rotating the old triangular ideological paradigm so that another of its conceptual corners, formerly a base, became the apex. There was a further touch. At the bottom, tradition supplemented the new political dream, thus making *l'enracinement* the foundation. In place of the poet's prosody and the scientific disquisitions of theoreticians, the new fashion highlighted the griot's chronicle with its vivid images and striking metaphors, its mesmeric rhythms and catchy melodic lines. Thus was the griot re-introduced into the structural scaffoldings of modern politics thanks to the media. In this incarnation his assignment was to fabricate a fresh political legitimacy to compensate for the lack of any serious ideology.

The confusing merger of roles between praise-singing griots and journalists was no doubt the reason why a number of communications professionals fled the State media. The emergence of the private or independent press, and the dynamism of the new papers, had a great deal to do with a determination to create an environment in which intellectual power could come into its own, and take initiatives in the arena of political debate. The fact that academics expressed their views in the columns of the independent press on such issues of public import as the institutional crisis or the Casamance problem indicated that the intelligentsia were now determined to bridge the gap between themselves and society maintained since independence. The ubiquitous use of the concept of a 'civil society' in discussions was eloquent proof of this change. Now the mere mention of 'civil society' seemed sufficient to give the concept the weight of authority. For the time being, however, the concept itself was not very precisely understood, beyond a sense that it had an instrumental function: the harnessing of social forces for political purposes.

The make-shift tinkering characteristic of the griot's work was not restricted to emotional content. That was true even if the National Cultural Charter envisaged a take-over of responsibility for pop culture. Oral traditions and emotional intensity were to be combined with a third factor, this time scientific. The combination, using the General Congress on Education as a springboard, led to the idea of promoting a New Educational System. This second pole gave a clear view of the way in which a section of the Senegalese intelligentsia played a legitimizing role in the build-up of Abdou Diouf's hegemony. It also showed how Abdou Diouf used that part of the intelligentsia in his effort to dominate his own party.

The consolidation of Abdou Diouf's hegemony involved a number of initiatives and the creation of various structures such as the GRESEN, the Committee of 1500, the Studies and Research Group, and *Abdoo ñu dooy*. All these initiatives and organizations were manifestations, in varying styles, of strategies of domestication and control deployed by the regime. They also expressed the notion of a personal legitimacy inherent in Abdou Diouf, in the form of direct fealty. Whether calling themselves 'the cream of the intelligentsia' or more simply, a collection of 'competent, patriotic intellectuals', these intellectuals entered the political arena on the basis of a single criterion: their technical expertise.

It did seem rather illogical, though, given a context of complete multi-party politics, to claim for any single political party the status of prime instrument if the aim was to accent an all-embracing, consensual approach. It became fashionable to accept, even to claim, a lack of political affiliation, as long as it was the only way to create the consensus that would make the myth of development an operational reality. The new movements recruited members from the upper echelons of the civil service and the university. Never before had the university been tapped for so many posts in government. The roster of appointees included Iba Der Thiam, Ibrahima Fall, Balla Moussa Daffé, Ndioro Ndiaye and Sakhir Thiam.

Beyond these developments, we must remember also that democracy, like development, had been reduced to a purely technical aspect. In the new vision, popular, political support mattered little. The government wangled itself a new recruitment environment in which technical expertise was the sole criterion. Abdou Diouf did not discourage the emergence of this new type of patron-client power play, since for one thing it enabled him to control a section of the intelligentsia assigned to create a custom-made legitimacy for him. Furthermore, it enabled him to manipulate the political weight of a fringe group within the Socialist Party. The rivalry between the GRESEN and the *Club Nation et Développement* fit nicely into this control strategy.

Now, while intellectuals used support groups and think tanks to create or improvise some legitimacy for Abdou Diouf, they were not free to act in parallel networks outside institutional channels. That explains why a good number of them ended up joining the ruling party. Some, by aspiring to play the role of an opposition within the ruling party, weakened it by bringing certain conflicts into it. Babacar Sine (1990:4-5), the Socialist Party ideological guru, touched on this problem in his contribution to the debate in the *Soleil* under the title 'Renovation and Openness'. Presenting a critical analysis of his party, he pointed out that 'after the 1983 elections, and after the formation of a government including new members with no party affiliation, in the process of opening out to embrace selected executives and intellectuals such as the GRESEN group, the Party suffered its first internal crisis'. The blame was put on certain obstructive tactics and defensive reactions.

The recommendation was to make renovation and openness central planks in the Socialist Party approach after the 1983 elections. In the event, despite the help of intellectuals sought and given, Abdou Diouf's regime botched the run-up to the February 1988 elections. The ruling party was accustomed to a 'single-party culture'. The intellectual patron-client networks established did not operate within a conscious framework of a radical break with past practices involving a fundamental rethinking of the issue of modernization. For these and other reasons, the system drifted towards violent confrontations in February-March 1988.

The Senghor and Abdou Diouf regimes had different styes of adjustment and re-adjustment to the socio-political context. But no one could parlay such nuances into a fundamental break between Senghor's hegemonic system and Diouf's. In both cases, the use of patron-client networks and the effort to woo intellectuals showed that the political approach in question revolved around the State as central institution. The one difference that marks each regime's originality was the treatment of the intellectual environment. But in both cases, that intellectual environment remained cut off from 'civil society'.

On now to the intellectual left. What can be said of it apart from that it stumbled into a double trap? It was trapped in the first place because it failed to work out an innovative conceptual approach capable of challenging the existing political approach and designing an improved model. Despite the failure of modernization under both Senghor and Abdou Diouf, the left continued to define itself in relation to the central role of the State, that heirloom from the colonial past. The intellectual left failed to create and manage the instruments of a genuine autonomy that might have ensured a participatory involvement in society commensurate with its stature. The absence of independent publishing or distribution networks endowed with financial resources from non-governmental sources, and the almost total lack of research outfits with independent financial backing, also contributed to the atomization of the intelligentsia. Rare exceptions like the Sankore Publishing House, now out of business, underscored the lack and proved there was a real need for such facilities.

The intellectual left was trapped in a second sense by the introduction of multi-party politics. The shift led to a proliferation of platforms, diluting the force of ideas in an environment where speakers and audiences were often interchangeable. Meanwhile, so-called civil society, ghost-like in its lack of substance, or perhaps merely voiceless, existed only in the speeches made about it. In the period after February 1988, the intellectual left presented the sad spectacle of a movement whose key reference points - democracy, human rights, freedom of association and self-expression - had all been hijacked. Once again, the unitary approach had done its work, practically in a flash, with the help of a speech marking a Muslim religious feast, the *Korité*.

According to the paper *Sud Hebdo,* Senegal's intellectuals have entered a catatonic state of breakdown. Is that assessment right? It is a fact that whether as duly invited luminaries or rowdy gate-crashers, the country's intellectuals have been known to invade the political scene as idols or ideologues, technocrats or experts, critics or censors. They have always needed opposition to or collaboration with the regime as reference points and yardsticks for their own performance. Unfortunately for them, the constructivist prospect opening out on the morrow of independence, along with the modernizing dream riding on it, lost steam in the dead end of State construction and nation-building. In place of the old unitary approach, the new trend favoured a variety of antagonistic stances ranging from ethnic to religious, regional to homeland claims. At the moment, the irredentist movement in the Casamance and the Muslim fundamentalist trend have the highest profiles. The Mauritanian crisis showed in what violent directions such claims could lead. The opposition's repeated attempts to design a policy alternative to the regime's programme within a unitary framework show how incapable the political system is of handling such antagonistic approaches. The General Congress on Education was expected to give birth to a New Educational System. But that brainchild proved still-born. The bankruptcy of the educational system has turned chronic.

That is the depressing report card the country's intellectuals share with the regime. Real or imagined, their silence has contributed to the impasse Senegal has been in, especially after the February 1988 elections. Instead of working out a new approach to modernity, they allowed themselves to get locked into the modernization approach inherited from colonialism, an approach that assumed an organic linkage between knowledge and intellectual expertise, the right to self-expression, and participation in political life. It seems clear enough that the two types power, one intellectual, the other political, have mated to produce a democracy. The catch is in the qualifier: Only for the Literate.

Still, if Mamadou Diouf is to be believed, new vistas lie ahead. He sees hope in the shape of what he calls professionalization. He raised the issue of professionalization publicly during a televised post-1988 election debate when, in answer to a query from Sokhna Dieng, Director of Television, he retorted: 'I am an intellectual. It is my business to think. That's what I'm paid for'. It was a response that expressed a return of the country's intellectuals to their natural habitat. Breakdown and catatonia, the refusal to play the thorny role of messiah, can be interpreted as a decision to desert the political arena, at least as currently demarcated. Those words have been echoing in other venues: the university, the bench, the independent media. By stressing the sole identifying criterion that matters to them ('to think, and to think productively'), the country's intellectuals are trying to get out of the bind of patron-client relationships and cooptation arrangements.

The new trend is significant when juxtaposed to the movement for *Sopi* (change). We surmise that both trends were born of attitudes favouring a radical break, dated February 1988. *Sopi* should not be seen as a protest limited to the political arena. It is more like a social implosion, or better still, the eruption of the social sphere into the political. The fact that *Sopi* became the rallying cry of youths taking over the streets was a taste of things to come. This nation is pregnant with a 'civil society' conceived outside the channels of institutional wedlock. Possibly, once born, it will prove to be the only entity capable of imposing a democratic system not hijacked by the formally educated, a complete democracy.

The contempt of this 'civil society' for the institutional environment, and its boycott thereof, took clearer shape in the movement known as *Set-Settal*[24]. Instead of the spontaneous and violent seizure of the streets, there was a different kind of occupation, a composite blend of art and ecology. The murals painted by participants in this movement work like a challenge to piece together a puzzle. Only those who take the time to rearrange the pieces get to understand them. It must be said that at first sight it is hard to make out linkages between Mandela, Ahmadou Bamba, Senghor, Galandou Diouf, Blaise Diagne, Abdoul Aziz Sy and Lat-Dior. The one clear impression the observer carries away is the absence of opposition leaders on the murals, and the solitary, understated presence of the President of the Republic. The young painters, through these works, are challenging the remainder of

Senegalese society to come up with new ideas on politics, to rethink the issue of modernity. Possibly, the trend towards professionalism and academic commitment is part of the response[25], in the sense that it is an attempt to re-examine the 'democracy of the literati'.

Notes

1. 'It is therefore entirely plain to me, by virtue both of reason and of Scripture, that Sovereign Power, whether it reside in an isolate individual as in a Monarchy, or in an Assembly as in popular or aristocratic Republics, is such that one might not imagine men establishing a greater power'. Hobbes, (1971:219). We might deduce from this that the absolute nature of political power is not a matter of its form but of its essence.
2. We shall not be discussing the role of traditional intellectuals and their interactions with religious brotherhoods or the ruling regime. What we intend here is to describe and analyze the establishment of a democracy of the literate by the Western-educated political and intellectual elites of Senegal.
3. Mamadou Diouf (1990: 8) uses the term 'indigenization' to refer to 'the measures whereby the colonial State succeeded in integrating organic intellectuals belonging to the pre-colonial tradition into its system by neutralizing them and putting them at its own service after redefining their roles and functions in the colony'.
4. The so-called hostages were in fact children of rulers.
5. Lo (1985) shows how important a part teachers played in stimulating awareness among their people, thanks partly to the nature of their work itself, and partly to their special bonds with the population.
6. In this connection, Bayart (1989:157-158) shows how the tooroodo oligarchy successfully appropriated such innovations as the school system, the political process, etc.
7. The seduction of power reminds us of what Gramsci called 'eloquence, the external, momentary agent of feelings and passions'.
8. The condemnation of Socrates was symptomatic of the inherently conflictual nature of the relationship between political power and intellectual power. Socrates was condemned to drink hemlock. Nevertheless, his dialogues on the immortality of the soul argue that the best way "to get rid of critics" is not to silence them. See Plato, *Apology: The Defence of Socrates* (1989).
9. See Weber (1963:124-125). In the light of this definition it becomes easier to understand the definition put forward by Souleymane Bachir Diagne when he describes the intellectual as someone 'carrying greater moral weight than an ordinary citizen. This is not merely the interested opinion of a university graduate. It goes somewhat beyond that, because people are entitled to expect the behaviour of intellectuals to have a certain moral dimension', *Sud Hebdo*, 88, January 1990.
10. This denial is less a negation of Negritude itself as a particularistic cultural trait than a negation of various micro-particularisms within Black culture. This is the basic assumption that facilitates both the mythic fabrication and the presence of Negritude at the Banquet of the Universal.

11. 'The major problem facing Socialism is not so much the need to abolish class-based inequalities between people of the same nation as the need to even out imbalances between wealthy peoples and proletarian peoples, between developed and developing countries' (Senghor, 1976:24). The gimmick was to deny the domestic aspect of the problem of inequality (class struggle) and to focus solely on its international aspect.
12. Following the 1962 crisis, Senghor came right out and said the country needed single-party rule. see Lo (1985:95).
13. See Senghor (1971:261). Apart from the institutional fallout from the 1962 crisis, the most serious of which was the installation of a monocephalous Executive, there was also an attitudinal shift away from exclusion towards inclusion. The new attitude favoured the cooptation of opponents, not their elimination. See Bayart (1989:210).
14. Balandier, quoted in Bayart (1990:99).
15. See the chapter by Mamadou Diouf in this volume.
16. See the chapter by Momar Coumba Diop in this volume.
17. See Cheikh Anta Diop (1974:5-6). 'There are those who think that by such behaviour they can make up for their lack of revolutionary ideas, stamina and foresight by resorting to insulting, wild and woolly language. They forget that the essential tone of genuinely revolutionary language comes from the cogency of facts and ideas interlinked in dialectical arguments of such persuasive clarity that they inexorably convince the lucid reader'.
18. The Senghor regime never forgot the pivotal factor of the Pharaonic model as expressed in the following statement: 'The African revolution must be achieved through the restoration of historical consciousness'. It is possible that it was because of the momentous intellectual implications of such a revolution that Cheikh Anta Diop was carefully side-tracked in his university career, a manoeuvre which cut him off from permanent, fruitful contact with young students. There is no doubt that the regime was motivated by the receptivity of the student body, real or imagined, to the challenge against the Western intellectual tradition, and against a kind of Africanist outpouring seen as a 'theoretical manifestation of imperialism'. On the other hand, a purely conceptual approach to decolonization, or the reform of perceptions in such a way as to make Africa a subject of discourse, became an academic and political programme presenting no real danger to the regime. The government, in fact, imposed the institutional venue for that discourse: the Institut Français de l'Afrique Noire, rebaptized the *Institut Fondamental de l'Afrique Noire* (IFAN). By definition, as a research institute, it provided no room for dialogue and persuasion. On this topic, see Ela (1989).
19. See the analysis by Momar Coumba Diop in this volume.
20. An illustrative point, of anecdotal interest, was the dispute between Senghor and Cheikh Anta Diop on the proper spelling of the word *siggi*, a Wolof word meaning to stand tall. *Siggi*, incidentally, was the title of the journal published by the *Rassemblement National Démocratique*.
21. See the analysis by Abdou Sylla in this volume.
22. *La voix de l'éducateur*, No. 2, July 1977.
23. The new myth, in reality, was reheated from old leavings. The old approach to development was now stripped of its political accoutrement. Thus undressed, it was re-appointed in the finery of technical expertise, calculated to attract consensual support. The university, incidentally, provided another instance of such recycling. With no fundamental change whatsoever, it was re-baptized a 'Development University'.
24. The literal meaning of *Set-Settal* is: Clean and Cleansing. It refers to neighbourhood self-help projects and urban beautification campaigns. One characteristic feature is the painting of murals depicting distinguished political figures in Senegal's history. Sometimes the fame of those thus honoured is limited to a single neighbourhood.

25. The regime understands the revolutionary aspect of this phenomenon, likely to escape its control. All the regime's latest public utterances have included enticements to intellectuals and to civil society.

Bibliography

Aron, Raymond, 1962, *The Opium of the Intellectuals*, New York, Norton.

Bathily, Abdoulaye, 1987, 'Contribution à l'histoire des rapports entre les intellectuels et l'Etat en Afrique de l'Ouest, de l'époque précoloniale à nos jours', Paper presented at the International Seminar on 'Intellectuals, the State and Imperialism: Towards Intellectual Decolonization', University of Zimbabwe, Harare, 19-23 October.

Bathily, Abdoulaye,1990, 'Rapport de politique générale du Comité Central au $3^è$ congrés ordinaire de la LD/MPT', Mimeographed document, Dakar.

Bayart, J F, 1989, *L'Etat en Afrique: la politique du ventre*, Paris, Fayard.

Bon, F and M A Burnier, 1971, *Les nouveaux intellectuels*, Paris, Seuil et Cujas.

Copans, Jean, 1990, *La longue marche de la modernité africaine. Savoirs, Intellectuels, Démocratie*, Paris, Karthala.

Dia, Mamadou, 1962, 'Discours de clôture du colloque sur les politiques de développement et les diverses voies vers le socialisme', Mimeographed document, Dakar.

Diané, Charles, 1990, *La FEANF et les grandes heures du mouvement syndical étudiant noir*, Paris, Chaka.

Diaw, Aminata, 1990, 'Etat et Nation: la problématique de la référence dans une perspective Constructiviste', Paper delivered at the AAPS Seminar, Cairo, 20-22 January.

Diop, Cheikh Anta, 1974, *Les Fondements économiques et culturels d'un Etat Fédéral d'Afrique noire*, Paris, Présence Africaine.

Diop, Cheikh Anta, 1979, *Nations nègres et culture*, Paris, Présence Africaine.

Diop, Momar Coumba and Mamadou Diouf, 1990, *Le Sénégal sous Abdou Diouf: Etat et société*, Paris, Karthala.

Diouf, Mamadou, 1989, 'Représentations historiques et légitimités politiques au Sénégal (1960-1987)', *Revue de la Bibliothèque Nationale*, 34, Paris, pp.14-23.

Diouf, Mamadou, 1990, 'Les intellectuels, l'Etat et la société civile au Sénégal: la quête perpétuelle d'un paradigme', Paper presented at the Colloquium on 'Academic Freedom', Kampala, Uganda, 26-29 November.

Ela, Jean-Marc, 1989, *Cheikh Anta Diop ou l'honneur de penser*, Paris, L'Harmattan.

Hobbes, Thomas, 1971, *Léviathan*, Paris, Sirey.

Hodgkin, Thomas, 1957, *Nationalism in Colonial Africa*, New York, New York University Press.

Hountondji, Paulin, 1990, 'La dépendance scientifique hier et aujourd'hui', *Revue Sénégalaise de Philosophie*, 13-14, pp. 17-28.

Kane, C A, 1982, *L'aventure ambigüe* [Prèface de Vincent Monteil], Paris, Union Générale d'éditions. [lère édition 1961].

Khan, Amin, 1990, 'Les intellectuels entre identité et Modernité', in El-Kenz, Ali (ed.), *L'Algérie et la modernité*, Dakar, CODESRIA.

Laurin-Frenette, Nicole, 'Les intellectuels et l'Etat', *Sociologie et Sociétés*, XV, 1, pp. 121-129.

Lo, Magatte, 1985, *L'heure du choix*, Paris, L'Harmattan.

Platon, 1984, *Apologie de Socrate*, in Platon, oeuvres complètes, tome I, Paris, Gallimard.

Senghor, LS, 1957, 'Le problème de la culture ou pourquoi la page culturelle', *Unité Africaine*,11.
Senghor, L S, 1964, *Liberté I Négritude et humanisme*,Paris, Seuil.
Senghor, L S, 1971, *Liberté II Nation et voie africaine de socialisme*, Paris, Seuil.
Senghor, L S, 1976, *Pour une relecture africaine de Marx et Engels*, Dakar, NEA.
Senghor, L S, 1980, *La poésie de l'Action: conversations avec Mohamed Aziza*, Paris, Stock.
Senghor, L S, 1983, Preface to Ndaw, Alassane, *La poésie africaine*, Dakar, NEA.
Sine, Babacar, 1989, 'Révolution et ouverture: contribution au débat,' *Le Soleil*, 6 February.
Wade, Abdoulaye, 1975, 'Discours d'ouverture à la première conférence nationale', Special issue of the publication *Démocrate*, Dakar.
Weber, Max, 1959, *Le savant et le politique*, Paris, Plon.
Weber Max, 1959, *The Sociology of Religion*, Boston, Beacon Pres

10. The Regime and the Press

Moussa Paye

Over the past 30 years, relations between the Senegalese regime and the press have weathered numerous transformations. Throughout these changes, however, one aspect has remained constant: daily news, printed in the press or broadcast on the air, has stayed a monopoly of the ruling regime. The country's major newspaper started life in 1933 as the *Paris-Dakar*, a weekly. It subsequently became a daily, and at independence changed its name to *Dakar Matin*. In September 1960, following the break-up of the Mali Federation, Senegal's Ministry of Information and the Press took over the federal infrastructure. The new state of Senegal used it as the basis for an information policy emphasizing mass education. The necessary resources were marshalled. The new broadcasting service started with six low and high frequency studios, a 100-kilowatt short wave transmitter, a 25-kilowatt medium wave transmitter, two 4-kilowatt tropical wave transmitters, and an 8-kilowatt medium wave transmitter in Rufisque.

At the end of 1960, two transmitters were beamed towards the Casamance, and the regional broadcasting station at Ziguinchor went into operation on 4 April 1961. The Saint-Louis station had formerly served Mauritania, but when the Mauritanian transmitter went into operation in June 1961, it was transferred to Dakar. Changes made at the time included the creation of the Senegalese Press Agency. Working with ten teleprinters set up in various agencies and administrative offices, it transmitted a daily total of 18 000 words in addition to local news items. From this point on it enjoyed a monopoly over information throughout the territory. It also served the radio broadcasting system and the Ministries through the distribution of a daily news bulletin, *Info-Sénégal*, with a print run of 256 copies.

The Information, Radio and Press Board was assigned a pivotal role. Its information service vetted all news disseminated in Senegal, censoring out items when the powers that be thought such action necessary. Its press service put out several publications: *Sénégal Magazine*, later renamed *Sénégal Aujourd'hui*, which had a print run of 5,000 copies; *Sénégal documents*, a monthly wall newspaper with a print run of 2,000 copies; *L'ère nouvelle*, an Arabic-language publication also with a print run of 2,000 copies; and a daily press digest printed in 120 copies for distribution to the ministries and other public services. Within the Communications Board, there was a cinema section responsible for producing newsreels, publicity films, prestige documentaries and educational footage. The popular 'Senegalese Newsreel' series, shown twice a week on cinema screens throughout the country, was among the products of this board.

The Press and the Nation-Building Process

Given that the population was mostly illiterate, the principal vehicle for the nation's information policy became a series of regional information centres radiating from a headquarters unit in Dakar. A total of 130 audio centres were set up in the main district towns. They were run by groups of 'independence volunteers' trained and equipped by a Regional Information Commissioner presiding over a Regional Information Committee. The programme had a set of instructional materials designed to put across the official message, made up of nationalist and socialistic themes echoed by middle-level party organizers. Across the literacy divide, the print media were devoted exclusively to the government point of view. For the official press, this was natural enough. It was, after all, what they had been set up to do. But there were other publications such as *Afrique nouvelle*, a missionary paper designed for an all-African readership, *Africa*, and *L'Observateur africain*, which, though in principle non-official, saw eye to eye with the regime.

The Senegalese Government's determination to establish a powerful state-controlled media system was clear from 1961, during the First Four-Year Development Plan period. Out of a total national budget of FCFA 92,067 million, the Ministry of Information got an allocation of FCFA 450 million. Of this, the bulk went to the radio broadcasting system, which got FCFA 335 million to help it purchase a powerful 200-kilowatt transmitter costing FCFA 150 million, FCFA 100 million worth of reporting and broadcasting equipment, and FCFA 40 million for improving premises and facilities. A total of FCFA 35 million were provided for the installation of long range short-wave antennae, and FCFA 10 million were set aside for building a regional station in Saint-Louis. A subsidy of FCFA 15 million was allocated for establishing a Cinema Board. A similar sum was provided for the purchase of printing and photographic equipment, and FCFA 10 million went into the installation of a teletype unit connected to the Reuter network. A further FCFA 75 million was set aside for the installation and equipment of 28 regional information centres, designed to operate as the backbone of a mass education system. The equipment included mobile film projection vans. Over the four-year programme period, annual budgetary allocations followed a rising curve: 1961: 52 million; 1962: 128 million; 1963: 132 million; 1964: 138 million.

The Senegalese government had a second preoccupation in its dealings with the media: the Africanization of media staff. As of the first year after independence, the situation was rather negative. Top level personnel, those with university-level qualifications, classified in category A, included only four Senegalese. Category B, comprising higher school certificate holders with some specialized training, included 27 Senegalese. In category D there were 139 Senegalese. Africanization schedules and recruitment projections stood as follows: 1961: 14; 1962: 90; 1963: 81; 1964: 71. A look at the government gazette, *Le Journal Officiel*, of 29 September 1962, shows how French journalists dominated the Senegalese media. Alain de Mazières, Georges Giraud and Jacques Janvier, all technical advisors, were made members of the National Order of Merit, along with the Editor-in-Chief of *Dakar Matin*, Danie-l de Bergevin. On 22 October that same year, *Dakar Matin* published an advertisement inviting job applications from young Senegalese school certificate holders.

Around this time, El Hadj Ousseynou Seck became a star radio announcer. His 6:50 a.m. news in Wolof and his florid tributes to the big shots of the day, Léopold Senghor and Mamadou Dia, were extremely popular. In the unsettled early years after independence, there was no doubt that the two leaders owned the radio waves. It was perfectly normal, then, for this hot medium to figure at the eye of the storm when, in the morning of 17 December 1962, the constitutional crisis in which the two men opposed each other came to a head. A radio announcement said 'Alioune Tall would give a press conference, and that Mamadou Dia would address the nation at 20 hours to explain the measures he had taken'. Supporters of Mamadou Dia, Chairman of the Council of State, knowing how strategically important control of the media was, occupied the radio station in Dakar, protected by members of the gendarmerie faithful to Dia.

But President Senghor outmanoeuvred them. From the Yeumbeul studio came Senghor's appeal. Dia's supporters at the Radio Senegal headquarters in Dakar cut off the end of that speech, their idea being to broadcast a speech by Mamadou Dia, recorded two hours earlier. But then the Dia address was in turn interrupted from Rufisque after a few seconds[1]. Magatte Lo (1986) recounts how, with a parachutist as bodyguard and Théophile James at his side, he gained entry into the station attached to the Rufisque transmission centre at about 15 minutes past midnight:

> *Giving listeners the impression I was speaking from the Dakar studio, I read the message twice. And to make sure that the entire population would clearly understand it, I translated it into Wolof. It was late, but all Senegal was listening. The moment I finished reading the President's message on the radio, crowds poured into the streets of the capital and in the smallest villages, to acclaim Senghor* (Lo, 1986:79).

These political circumstances lent legitimacy to the control of the media by the faction of the state apparatus that won out in the confrontation. It tended to favour Radio Senegal. Around 6 a.m. on 18 December, radio announcer Ousseynou Seck began recording his commentaries on Senghor's victory over Mamadou Dia, using a few items supplied by Magatte Lo. For some time thereafter, El Hadj Ousseynou Seck, propaganda shock trooper that he was, worked hard to exorcise the demons of 'Diaism' from Senegalese minds. He condemned the fallen Dia with the same conviction that had characterized his praise songs to that same dignitary when he was still in power.

As may easily be surmised, the resulting state control over the main information and news media affected the prospects of multi-party democracy. In February 1963, there was a campaign for a constitutional referendum in which the ruling *Union Progressiste Sénégalaise* was opposed to the *Bloc des Masses Sénégalaises* (BMS) led by Cheikh Anta Diop. Cheikh Anta Diop, with the BMS, conducted a fierce campaign against the planned constitutional changes designed to establish a personalized regime in which the President would be the sole source of power. His speech, delivered in Wolof on the radio, had such an effect on the population that he was never again allowed to use the radio[2].

Returning from Paris to Dakar on 11 September 1963, on the eve of the UPS congress scheduled for 10 October, and prior to the December elections, President Senghor announced that thenceforth he would make a radio address to the Senegalese people every week. 'In Senegal', he added, 'since God gave us a gift for telling tales, the gossip mills work full time. But that is no reason for taking them seriously'. It was his way of denying rumours of a possible ministerial reshuffle[3].

Meanwhile, the legislative and presidential elections of 1 December were drawing near. Eight days before the opening of the campaign, President Léopold Sédar Senghor, speaking on the radio, promised that all legally registered parties would be free to contest the elections. 'Better still', he added, 'each party will be entitled to one half hour of air time'. However, a Ministry of Interior circular added some fine print, and it was less generous. First, opposition parties would have to make their presentations before the ruling party. The idea was that since the ruling party had spoken first during the 3 March 1963 referendum campaign, it was its turn now to have the last word. Second, all speeches would have to be delivered in French; they would also have to be recorded at least half a day in advance.

Even before the start of the electoral campaign, the *Parti du Regroupement Africain (PRA)*, the only opposition party still in the running against the ruling party, rejected the conditions laid down by the Ministry of the Interior.

The PRA, in a communique published on 23 October, explained 'Why the PRA-Senegal Refuses to Use the Radio in the Election Campaign': The PRA-Senegal refuses to use the facilities of the national broadcasting system under the above conditions, laid down solely for the only opposition party recognized by the UPS, PRA-Senegal, which has handed in a list for a national union known as *Démocratie et Unité Sénégalaise*.

There is no need to expatiate on this refusal. Everyone knows, after all, how the 'ruling party' continuously uses and abuses the radio in French, the 'vernacular languages' and other national languages. PRA-Senegal activists will continue to speak to their compatriots in the languages they understand. In any case, the Senegalese people have little left to learn concerning Senghor's 'strong-arm democracy' and his 'dominant party'.

The electoral campaign, needless to add, turned out one-sided. The radio broadcasting system and the daily newspaper *Dakar Matin* both gave exclusive coverage to the government point of view, broadcasting and publishing appeals to vote for the ruling party, seasoned with threats against the opposition. Apart from the Wolof speeches of El Hadj Ousseynou Seck, the radio also broadcast the fire-breathing editorials of an astonishing journalist on whose performance the opposition Manifesto poured scorn, dubbing them 'the ridiculous and tiresome ratiocinations of Lamine Diakhaté'[4].

In somewhat understated tones, the 28 November issue of *Dakar Matin* announced that 'unknown assailants attacked the house of a UPS dignitary'. The dignitary was no other than the ruling party's resident Wolof radio announcer. The 29 November issue of *Dakar Matin* carried a 'Warning from the Minister of the Interior to the Opposition'. The next day, there was an article on opposition violence under the headline 'UNTS Condemned'. As far as the paper was concerned, the only source of violence was the opposition.

The elections turned out to be bloody, with opposition demonstrations being put down by force. Reporting on them the next day, before official results were out, *Dakar Matin* put out a headline saying the UPS had won 96% of the vote, and printed a front page editorial by the Minister Lamine Diakhaté: 'A Victory for Courage'. Quite carried away, *Dakar Matin* published a special issue that same day highlighting a front page communiqué from the Ministry of the Interior entitled 'Total Victory for the UPS'. The next day, 3 December, it was the turn of the newly elected President to appear on the front page with a transcript of his speech broadcast the day before. The 4 December issue was devoted to expressions of 'UPS Gratitude to the Senegalese People'.

Mass Diokhané, Director of the Radio Broadcasting System, had stood as a UPS candidate for a parliamentary seat and won. He would be leaving his job on 7 December. It was an appropriate opportunity for the award of Knight of the National Order medals to Nicolas Sané, Jacques Gerling and Paul Benoît. Paul Pyaubert and Léonce Glèze were made Officers of the National Order of Merit. As usual, with just one exception, those honoured were expatriate officials on technical aid missions. To judge by the ruling party's attitude, Senegalese citizens would have to wait some time before being deemed worthy.

During these early years of independence, the Senegalese State could well have adopted the witticism attributed to Sidy Lamine Niass: 'I own the paper, not the journalists'. For while the State had total control over the information media, its control over journalists was rather shaky. After the break-up of the Mali Federation, a number of the country's first generation of journalists went over to Modibo Keita: Doudou Guèye, Racine Kane, Mamadou Talla. And Moctar Kébé worked in Mali as a teacher. The remainder, about 30 journalists, founded the National Press Union of Senegal, unaffiliated to the government. One of them, Cheikh Bara Lô, was described by a French paper as a Trojan horse working for Communist penetration in Black Africa, because he had been Vice-President of the World Federation of Democratic Youth from 1957. Four months after its creation, the Senegalese National Press Union attended the eleventh Congress of the Pan-African Union of Journalists in Accra. For reasons related to its internal structure, its Secretary-General declined the offer of a PAUJ Bureau post. Cheikh Bara Lô, who formerly worked in the office of Alioune Tall, was a survivor from the old days when the first Senegalese government followed a determined anti-imperialist policy. Back from the Accra Congress, the Secretary-General of the Senegalese Press Union, in a *Soleil* interview, described the trip:

> The Congress lasted 4 days, from 12 to 16 November. It opened with a superb keynote address from Kwame Nkrumah, President of the Republic of Ghana, in which he defined the role assigned us.... Then Doudou Guèye, a member of the Malian delegation, presented a historical backgrounder starting with the May 1961 Congress in Bamako.

The Congress had the charged atmosphere typical of great anti-imperialist, anti-colonial and anti-neocolonial get-togethers, a far cry from the political stance of the Senegalese government.

In May 1964, the Senegalese National Press Union, at a general assembly meeting held in Dakar's Chamber of Commerce, expressed its disappointment that ever since Senegal attained independence, despite repeated attempts, no precise legislation setting out the rights and duties of journalists had been passed. The general assembly urged that representatives from the journalists' union be included in the drafting team working on such legislation, and that the laws in question be passed within the year. Furthermore, the general assembly deplored the fact that 'the collective bargaining contract currently regulating the journalistic profession, apart from being discriminatory in practice, dated from 1948, and had never been updated to bring it in line with current living conditions'.

The union further[5] deplored the fact that it had always been disconcertingly easy for anyone to acquire a press card. It requested that the National Press Card Commission be immediately reorganized, that henceforth its chairman be an African journalist, that cards already issued be cancelled, that a new set of cards be issued immediately under conditions of strict adherence to rules regulating the commission. The crunch, as far as relations between the Union and the authorities were concerned, was yet to come:

> *In the present situation of our nation, and bearing in mind the imperatives of the country's development, the General Assembly considers that the Press should by definition be assigned a vanguard role, with Senegalese journalists playing a signal part. It is profoundly distressed that the authorities have so far chosen to be aloof, thus relegating Senegalese journalists to a subaltern position that frustrates their development. It is the intention of Senegalese journalists henceforth to assume their responsibilities fully. To that end, they urge the authorities to help them by cooperating closely with them in the higher interests of the country*[6].

At this crucial juncture the Minister of Information, Lamine Diakhaté, closet poetaster and writer of monumental editorials, fell from grace. A terse statement issued from the President's Office on 29 May 1964 ended his 18-month term of militant office: 'Mr. Lamine Diakhaté, Minister of Information and Communications, handed in his resignation to the President, who accepted it'. Whatever other underlying reasons there might have been, it was clear that by the final implementational year of the First Four-Year Plan, the ministry had failed to achieve both quantitative and qualitative personnel recruitment goals. Yet as of 28 December 1964, official periodicals published in Senegal numbered no less than 43 titles of widely varying quality, covering diverse fields of interest (Senegal,1965).

Leaving nothing to chance, the authorities opened the Centre for the Study of Information Sciences and Technology at Dakar University. Its purpose was to train journalism students from the sub-region, beginning in the 1965-66 academic year. The Senegalese Press Agency (APS), reorganized by presidential decree, was placed under the Minister in Charge of Information. Article 3 of the Statutes regulating the agency went so far as to stipulate the following terms: 'Under no circumstances shall the APS tolerate influences or considerations likely to compromise the accuracy and objectivity of information. It should not under any circumstances fall under the *de facto* or *de jure* control of any ideological, political or economic group'.

The Consolidation of Control
From 1965 to 1970, Senegal had no television apart from a single educational television channel, a UNESCO pilot project experimenting with the use of mass media for educational purposes. The reason given by Jacques Janvier, Technical Adviser to the Senegalese Ministry of Information, Radio Broadcasting and the Press, was this: 'On account of the high costs involved, plans for the installation of a television station in Dakar have had to be shelved for the moment in the expectation that private investors might take the initiative'. A number of journalists had been selected for training pending the establishment of a television service. Now they had to champ on the bit for a few years.

In the wake of a process of national reconciliation achieved through carrot-and-whip tactics, the Political Bureau of the *Union Progressiste Sénégalaise*, now a single party, initiated studies on modalities for the creation of a national daily. Meanwhile, the State moved to control the organization of the nation's journalists. In April 1966, a constituent meeting was held on the premises of the magazine *Awa*, to set up a 'National Union of Professional Journalists in Senegal'. The journalist elected chairman turned out to be none other than Doudou Guèye, Editor-in-Chief of *L'Unité Africaine*, central organ of the ruling UPS. The former pro-Malian dissident had rejoined the dominant party fold and was now ready to serve the good cause, flanked by a solid phalanx of ruling party stalwarts: Alioune Fall, Deputy Director of Radio Senegal, Henri Mendy, Administrative Officer of the Senegalese Press Agency (APS), and Moctar Kébé, a journalist serving in the Press Office of the Ministry of Foreign Affairs, a rising star at the time.

The new union was named with transparent ambiguity. The first part of its appellation, the 'National Union of Professional Journalists', gave the impression that only Senegalese belonged. But the coda said 'in Senegal'. That left a loophole through which the Frenchman Pierre Biarnès, Managing Editor of the *Moniteur Africain*, wriggled in. He was elected General Treasurer. Jean Chalet, the *Agence France Presse* bureau chief, and Jean Roux, Personal Advisor to the President of the Republic, also became members. Cheikh Bara Lô, former Secretary-General of the Senegalese National Press Union, fell in behind his boss in the official pecking order, Mamadou Seyni Mbengue, Director of Information Services. In 1966, then, the new power equation signalled a change in government policy design as far as the press was concerned.

In 1967, a confidential memo from the Minister of Information, Abdoulaye Fofana, to the Interministerial Council convened to examine plans for the

creation of a national daily, indicated that it could be built on 'a press corporation comprising the UPS, the SNEP and *Dakar Matin*'. Alternatively, it might include 'the UPS, the SNEP and possibly 2 local printing presses'. At the Interministerial Council meeting on 30 November, Léopold Sédar Senghor decided that the national daily would have to meet three conditions:
1. It would have to be worthy of the name;
2. It would have to reflect government if not ruling party policy;
3. It would be endowed with startup funding, but after that it would have to be sufficiently well managed to cost the State nothing.

Meanwhile, the National Union of Professional Journalists in Senegal put out a here-today-gone-tomorrow paper called *Le journaliste sénégalais*. A year later, a preliminary protocol was signed between the Government of Senegal, the *France Edition et Publication* Company (belonging to the Pranpar group, publishers of *France Soir, Paris Presse, Elle, France-Dimanche* etc.,) and the publishers of *Dakar Matin* (SEPA). Shortly thereafter, the *Société Sénégalaise de Presse et de Publication* was set up, bringing together the *Société Sénégalaise d'Edition, France Edition et Publication*, SEPA, and the *Société Nationale des Entreprises de Presse*[7].

The May 1968 crisis, however, upset all plans made by the Senegalese government and its ruling party. Following clashes on the university campus, the Centre for the Study of Information Sciences and Techniques was closed and its students sent to Strasbourg to continue their studies. Whether as a result of the situation, or by happenstance, in August 1968, eight months after the Tenth Congress of the ruling UPS, *L'Unité Africaine* ceased publication. One intriguing point: in a section devoted to the party press, the Congress recommended that the editing and management of party papers be made the responsibility of a team of qualified executives assisted by professional journalists. In the confusion, the regime once more found itself in a crisis where its allies had to stand up and be counted. The National Broadcasting Service, under Moustapha Niasse, trusted man of the regime, Director of Information and the Press, rose to the occasion. Radio Senegal was perhaps the only whole-heartedly pro-regime institution. So unconditional was its loyalty that the underground strike committee set up after the arrest of practically all trade union leaders reserved some particularly harsh words for it:

> Radio Senegal broadcasts nothing but lies. No enterprise, no government service, no establishment, no worker has gone back to work. The strike call has drawn a 100% response throughout the territory[8].

At the onset of disturbances at the University of Dakar in 1968, the first groups of striking students took to the streets, making for the home of the inevitable Wolof-language radio announcer El Hadj Ousseynou Seck. Unflappable as usual, the propaganda storm trooper gave his answer on the radio waves at dawn and dusk: 'If the regime gave your father as much as it gives me, he too would praise it as highly as I do'. Giving its readers a taste of what was to become the standard journalistic style of the *Soleil*, the newspaper *Dakar Matin*, formerly content to lie discreetly by omission, now pulled out all stops. When, after the liberation of its leaders, the various bureaux of the National Union of Senegalese Workers finally met, the National Bureau devoted its first declaration to a castigation of the daily *Dakar Matin*:

> Since the start of strike action on 30 May 1968, the daily newspaper Dakar Matin has conducted a systematic campaign of scurrilous accusations and insults against the trade union leadership in an attempt to distort their activities and to poison the social climate.
>
> After claiming, with a frivolity bordering on irresponsibility, that the movement was inspired by a foreign power, Dakar Matin piled up accusation upon false accusation, day after day. The least one can say about these accusations is that they did nothing to bring about the calm recommended by the trade unions and the government. The National Bureau deplores the fact that despite initiatives taken to resolve the social crisis, which recommended the abandonment of unwarranted accusations and declarations, in its 10 June 1968 issue, Dakar Matin published an article entitled 'My Ticket', hurling new calumnies at trade union leaders. In the atmosphere of mass arousal created by the persistence of this scurrilous campaign, the UNTS demands an immediate end to these provocations, and held the daily Dakar Matin responsible for any eventual worsening of the social climate^9.

At the end of 1969, the Gordian knot of a national daily newspaper remained uncut. Thierno Diop, secretary to the Press Commission of the seventh UPS Congress, discussed the issue after a survey of publications appearing in the country at the time:

> The creation of a national daily worth its salt requires careful work. This is not the first time the issue has been raised in our sessions. Certain activists, indeed, have cracked that our national daily is as rare a creature as the sea serpent. No matter. The decision to create it was taken at the Vth Congress. At the VIth Congress, we had hoped to announce that the daily would start publication before the end of 1968. Nothing came of that. We therefore need to tread carefully before making fresh promises. That said, and with all necessary precautions taken, we are in a position to announce here and now that Senegal will have its daily newspaper before

July. If all goes according to plan, we may have it on the 10th anniversary of our independence.

What Thierno Diop said next made it quite clear what degree of autonomy the projected national daily would have in its relations with the regime:

> The paper shall maintain permanent liaisons with the Party, to facilitate the coordination of educational and organizational activities. As a matter of fact, if proposed draft amendments are approved by the Congress, the Editor-in-Chief of the national daily will automatically be a member of the Political Bureau.

On 16 May 1970, the managing editor of *Dakar Matin* announced that his paper was ceasing publication. On 20 May, *Le Soleil* burst on the Senegalese scene. Prior to taking over from *Dakar Matin,* the paper had been incorporated since 4 May. Initially, its offices were drab. They were located in a building at the end of the former Rue Thiers, now renamed Amadou Assane Ndoye. There, in a single room, the manager, the editor-in-chief and seven journalists, three of them seconded from the French technical aid agency, worked around a long metal table.

The Media War

Early in 1970, a third organization of professional journalists saw the light of day with the election of Moctar Kébé as head of the National Association of Senegalese Journalists. On 21 June, *Le Soleil,* no doubt confused about the association's real name, printed a notice about the general assembly meeting of an 'Association of Journalists in Senegal'. It also printed a three-point agenda: approval of statutes and bye-laws; programme report; and questions arising. The meeting was to be held at the African Cultural Centre. That same year the Centre for the Study of Information Sciences and Technology (CESTI) was revived. Its priority objective was to train staff for press, radio, television and news agencies as well as for ministries of information. The centre was expected to provide multi-disciplinary training for journalists capable of plotting out the path of media development in their countries, in order to make such media increasingly responsive to the requirements of public opinion.

Outside *Le Soleil* editorial boardroom and the CESTI lecture halls, however, there was an atmosphere of social agitation that took on the proportions of a media war. On one side stood the government; on the opposing side stood various trade union and student organizations. It was a lopsided fight. The regime, using *Le Soleil* and the radio, saturated public opinion with the government point of view. On the other side, trade union and political opponents scarcely had anything beyond fly-by-night publications and occasional tracts. Still, President Senghor himself took note of the intense agitation at the time, describing it in these terms:

> We note that from the beginning of 1970, and especially from the end of the farming season, tracts proliferated, heroic in their anonymous attacks on the Head of State, the Government, the Party. You know as well as I do whence these sheets originate. Some come from ambitious individuals afraid that power has definitively escaped their grasp. Some come from the underground PAI, still unaware that the independence they seek was won some time ago. Some come from unrepentant conspirators dreaming to be carried to power in foreign vehicles. The only new twist is that some tracts are merely copies of articles, originally by-lined, and letters, some of them private, written by French politicians unable to mind their own business instead of interfering in the internal affairs of Senegal[10].

The fact was that repercussions from the May 1968 disturbances were still felt in 1970. The break-up of opposition trade union organizations was accompanied by a violent media campaign. In July 1970, Le Soleil thought a turning point had been reached when the central organ of the National Union of Senegalese Workers (UNTS) published a resolution passed at an extraordinary session of its national executive committee expelling a number of its leaders including Alioune Cissé and Bassirou Guèye for collaborating with the regime. Peering into the entrails of the future, the editor-in-chief pronounced a prophecy:

> In the weeks ahead, Senegalese trade unionism will present a less ambiguous profile. In all likelihood, there will be on the one hand a group of die-hard Marxists dreaming of world-wide revolution. On the other hand there will be an autonomous central trade union organization. It will be up to the latter to assume its responsibilities[11].

Poles apart from the trade union concerns agitating other sections of the intellectual petty bourgeoisie, the National Association of Senegalese Journalists (ANJS) held its national executive session in November 1970, under the auspices of the Prime Minister Abdou Diouf. At the general assembly meeting held a month later at the African Cultural Centre on the Avenue El Hadj Malick Sy, the faction most interested in autonomy, which had set itself the goal of making the journalists' organization genuinely democratic, was overwhelmed by 'a phalanx of screaming, gesticulating militants determined to impose their will through loud assertions of political commitment'[12]. In short, the faction led by Moctar Kébé defeated the followers of the two Vice-Presidents Abdou Rahmane Cissé and Mame Less Dia, who both resigned subsequently.

On 26 February 1971, Gabriel Jacques Gomis held an evening press conference at the Church of the Ugandan Martyrs. The profession, he said, was swarming with mediocre journalists who were giving it a bad name with both the public and the government. 'Journalism is a noble profession deserving respect and consideration. It should not be a stepping stone to the achievement of selfish goals'[13].

In the ensuing discussion, a student asked the speaker from what sources the national daily got its information on the university. Abdoulaye Bâ's report published in *Le Soleil* on 1 March did not mention an answer from the speaker. But the same issue of the newspaper gave an answer of sorts: the banning of the two main student organizations, the UED and the UDES. Bara Diouf, as a matter of fact, had prepared public opinion for the move the day before, in an editorial aptly titled: 'Showdown':

> *Agitation at the university, veiled until recently, has openly erupted now. Step by escalating step the group of die-hard students whose avowed aim is to destroy the current regime and the Senegalese State, have raised the stakes to the point of all-out conflict*[14].

From that point on the State handled the crisis through a series of vindictive communiqués, including a 16 March announcement expelling 49 students from the university. Before the national assembly, the Prime Minister Abdou Diouf referred vaguely to all these events and to the campaign of denigration directed against the public authorities, the head of state and his collaborators. The aim, he said, was 'not to remove us physically from power in this country, but to attack our moral integrity, weakening us through discouragement'[15].

On Monday 26 April 1971, the Minister of Information, Ousmane Camara, was interviewed in a revived radio series entitled 'Live With ...'. He took the opportunity to make sure the audience got the point of the policy he was appointed to implement:

> *Whatever the situation may be elsewhere, in Senegal the public authorities are aware that a free and objective press can be of considerable service. That is why they go to great lengths to ensure that where government activities are concerned, the press is not maltreated, jostled or misinformed.*

But the monument of liberal tolerance had a craggy down side:

> *The press can also prove harmful when it turns nasty, fabricates rumours and misinformation, disseminates doctrines and ideologies likely to endanger the State or to unbalance Senegalese society. That is why we have taken care to provide legal safeguards against the emergence and proliferation of that type of press here in Senegal.*

The Minister of Information announced that television transmission would begin before December 1971. Initially there were only three or four hours of programming a week, but as facilities were set up, coverage increased until by 1975 the service was available throughout the country. Three months later, speaking from the eminence of the International Information Summit held in Helsinki on 10 June 1971, Abdou Diouf presented a much more liberal and enlightened vision:

> We have opted to convince, not to coerce; to argue convincingly when we are right, but also to leave ourselves open to persuasion when we happen to be wrong. Here we come to one more decisive role information can play: its capacity to reveal reality as it actually is, especially in presenting a balance sheet of State activities. I should add right away that our information resources are still very under-developed. That, of course, is perfectly understandable. After all, it is easier to propagate information about the activities and statements of State officials, to simply echo them, than to anticipate news as it breaks out there in the remote regions. Sometimes, because they are so few journalists, and because their training is inadequate, they have a hard time stepping off the beaten track. Still, I have not the least intention of denigrating them. The fact is that our press is in a process of full scale development[16].

That same day, Boubacar Latmingué Faye, a former leader of the Student Federation of the *Union Progressiste Sénégalaise* (UPS), was appointed Director of Information and the Press. In August 1971, Bara Diouf was given the double responsibility of editor-in-chief and political director. That made him the chief decision-maker at *Le Soleil* over and above the manager who had run the national daily from its April 1970 gestation to that date. For some time, various ministerial departments had been abuzz with rumours of plans for reshaping the structural facilities and operational modalities of the Senegalese press.

The individual promotions turned out to be a prelude to the reforms. Among its proposals, the draft called for the abolition of regional information centres through their transformation into branch offices of the Senegalese Press Agency (APS). In a memo (Niang, 1971) addressed to the Minister of Information in charge of liaisons with the Assemblies, officials working for the regional information services, who incidentally were very close to the ruling party, deplored the fact that they had not been consulted at the drafting and planning stages:

> Despite the principle of responsible participation proposed by the Head of State and ratified by the last UPS Congress. Worse still, the plan in question provides us with no guarantees whatsoever in our capacity as officials of the information service. Instead, against all considerations of

social equity, and regardless of the inevitable consequences such an eventuality would entail, it threatens us with dismissal or dissolution (Niang, 1971).

The memo continued:

The regional information service is a branch of the civil service. We wonder, therefore, to what extent it is feasible, in legal terms, simply and purely to transfer the movable and fixed assets of such an administrative service to a commercial, industrial agency such as the APS. Such a move is all the more questionable since the APS, despite State subsidies, has operated chronically in the red, a fact the BOM report, incidentally, points out (Niang, 1971:2).

The reform went ahead nevertheless, and the regional information service was assigned a new role within the framework of the APS. 'Originally a bureaucratic organization conceived with no regard for the most basic professional standards, it ended up making our national news agency a key tool in the social communications strategy in force'[17].

On 15 June, the first genuinely independent professional paper of the post-colonial period hit the streets. It was called *Lettre fermée*, and its publisher was one of the pioneering crop of Senegalese journalists, Abdou Rahmane Cissé. His inaugural editorial was bursting at the seams with optimism:

We trust the Head of State will allow us to extend to him our gratitude for having thought it worthwhile to take the trouble to write to the Soleil following its publication of a brief notice by our journalistic colleagues concerning the impending birth of our Lettre fermée. *We hope the poet, knowing how bohemian and inclined to artistic spontaneity we of the Fourth Estate tend to be, will have the grace to forgive us journalists this outburst of spontaneous exuberance that is merely our professional stock in trade.*

Disillusionment, however, was lurking in the wings. It pounced as soon as issue number 2 appeared. A short advertisement for which the paper paid FCFA 5,000 was censored in spite of its innocuous air. It said: 'Shut-down at the CAPA Factory. Abdou Cissé Reveals Why in *Lettre fermée*. On Sale at All Kiosks'. By the sixth issue the cup of the new journal's grievances was overflowing:

They talk of democratic liberalization, holding up Lettre fermée *and its publisher as proof. What a hollow honour. As if a single swallow sufficed to start the spring, or a single slogan to spark a revolution. As if those hailing the lone swallow were not in fact busily weighing down the same bird's wings with the grossest lead.*

From the eighth issue, dated 8-21 September, the publisher announced the establishment of his own sales outlets, because 'the local press and foreign advertising agencies refuse categorically to advertise our journal, even when we pay top rates'. In its tenth issue, *Lettre fermée* crossed the red line of government tolerance. It carried an editorial and an open letter on the condition of the journalists' organization. But the key article was one condemning 'the most pernicious neocolonial attitude' that took the form of the systematic liquidation of the linguistics scholar Pathé Diagne, doomed to swell the ranks of academic outcasts of whom the most famous were Cheikh Anta Diop, Abdoulaye Ly and Amady Aly Dieng, all of them African lecturers.

To top it all, the issue carried an investigative think piece on the possible existence of a Pretoria-Abidjan-Dakar axis. This added up to more than sufficient reason for the prohibition of the sale and distribution of the journal throughout Senegal by a joint decree from the Ministries of Information and the Interior dated 23 October 1972.

By the time the public authorities 'sank' *Lettre fermée,* the television service had been transmitting for a month. Considering the almost total control the Senegalese government exercised over the media, one might have supposed it would not have needed to go so far as to destroy a little magazine appearing once every two months with a tiny print run. True, the magazine did carry some spirited articles, but that need not have worried the government unduly, since it managed to prevent the little journal from placing advertisements in the daily newspaper and on the radio as well. The most reasonable conclusion may be that interactive dynamics between the independent journal and the official press were conditioned not so much by print as by the factor of relative credibility.

Meanwhile, an open letter written in October by Amadou Moctar Wane, a journalist at the Senegalese Press Agency, revived the struggle for control of the ANJS headed by Moctar Kébé. Confronted with the crisis within the ANJS, the regime tried some damage control by setting up a so-called Committee of Sages under the chairmanship of Alioune Fall, Director of the Radio Service. The Committee actually got to discuss the situation of the press with the President of the Republic and his Minister of Information. But because it failed to understand conflicts between the two opposed factions within the ANJS bureau, it crashed. Mame Less Dia, the second dissident Vice-President (the first being Abdou Rahmane Cissé), followed Amadou M. Wane's open letter with a second, scorching in its criticism of the Committee of 'Sages':

> No doubt the so-called Sages themselves became aware of the pointlessness of their mission. That was most probably why they dared not reveal

their findings to the rank and file. In any case, it was not the rank and file that invited the good offices of this august committee. Significantly, the main parties in the case, the two Vice-Presidents who handed in their resignation, were never invited before the Committee of "Sages".

The journalists' organization thus relapsed into its habitual lethargy. By a weird coincidence the issue of *Lettre fermée* carrying the views of the dissidents was the last to be published. The dissident wing of the ANJS also found itself deprived of a mouthpiece. The only independent journal in the country had been summarily wiped out. The most disturbing aspect of its execution was that it laid bare the duplicity of the official rhetoric claiming liberal information policies. Speaking of the almost total absence of private papers in Senegal, Ousmane Camara, Minister of Information, in a 'Live' interview broadcast on 26 August 1971, advanced no better rationalization than the high cost of newspaper publication:

No publication can survive on fine prose alone. It takes money. In this country money is short, and the State cannot subsidize everyone. It may still be reasonable to write off peasant debts. After all, peasants are the majority, and they are poor. But for the State to fund private newspapers - that would require a huge leap.

Yet Abdou Rahmane Cissé had asked no one for money. He did not even ask his readership for financial support. In his touchy honesty, he had written in the maiden issue of 28 February 1972 bearing the number 00 and distributed free of charge: 'For reasons of moral probity and professional ethics, we shall take no subscriptions until we are sure that this newsletter can survive its teething period'. Five months later, in February 1973, the State bought the *Moniteur Africain*. In March 1973, the President of the Republic accorded members of the executive committee of the ANJS an audience. By the evidence of a haphazard report in the national daily, the meeting seems to have drifted from a request for a press club to a discussion of the role of journalists.

Referring to the press club, which would serve as a meeting place for all Senegalese and foreign journalists, the President pointed out that the intention of the association was to enable Senegalese journalists to play their correct role as transmission belts between the regime and the people[18].

In line with this hope, the Senegalese State took a series of significant measures in 1973. In September *Le Soleil* established a printing company, the *Nouvelles Imprimeries Sénégalaises* (NIS). In December, a month after the creation of the National Audio-visual Council, Act 73-51 transformed the National Radio Broadcasting Service into the Radio and Television Broadcasting Board of Senegal (ORTS). That same December, *Afrique Nouvelle* reappeared after a one-year hiatus. Intriguingly, the new manager, a Guinean Muslim by the name of Tayère Diallo, was a protege of Bara Diouf. In February 1974, the Supreme Court, responding to an appeal lodged by Abdou Rahmane Cissé, cancelled the 1972 Ministerial decree prohibiting the sale and distribution of *Lettre fermée*. But the 16-month publication ban had killed that newsletter outright. The State had destroyed the first attempt to set up a really independent press enterprise. The paper was dead, but its initiator was very much alive. When the Manifesto of 200 intellectuals advocating multi-party politics and the democratization of the country's political life appeared, Abdourahmane Cissé was among the signatories.

On 5 June 1974, the French daily *Le Monde* published an interview with President Senghor. In the same issue, the Office of the President added a clarificatory note, to which *Le Monde* appended a terse response: 'The President raises no query as to the accuracy of the substance of the interview as printed'. The incident was only one more example of the authoritarian attitudes of African heads of state towards the press. More astounding was the intrusion of Bara Diouf into the discussion, and the terms he used. According to him, 'a journalist from the French daily, who had been welcomed more like a relative or a friend than like a man of the media, saw fit to dish out for public consumption a series of deliberately distorted statements attributed to President Senghor'[19].

People in power find it so much nicer if journalists only publish flattering portraits provided by themselves along with positive assessments of their actions, supplied in the form of official press releases. Journalists rash enough to ask a single embarrassing question can find themselves targets of official anger. Senegalese journalists learned to cope with this reality by asking the most harmless - and the silliest - questions. A student called Pape Malick Fall, writing to the Editor of *Le Soleil*, complained:

One would suppose, to judge from their questions, that these journalists never studied their discipline. Consider this example. During the last press conference, broadcast on 4 June 1974, one journalist asked the government's ministerial spokesman to describe the cabinet's reaction to the election of Miss Senegal. As if the cabinet did not have more important problems to deal with[20].

When a constitutional amendment introduced a multi-party system limited to four political tendencies, the country's media environment underwent a change. Abdoulaye Wade's Senegalese Democratic Party (PDS) put out an organ called *Le Démocrate*, with a print run of 5,000. Summarizing the reaction in ruling circles, *Le Soleil* wrote:

It could be that the revival of L'Unité africaine was catalyzed by the appearance of a new paper, Le Démocrate, house organ of the Senegalese

Democratic Party. This maiden entry into the Senegalese press environment has clearly drawn a positive response from a curious public[21].

On a different level, the regime continued to strengthen its alliances with other African countries. At that time, one stratagem was to prevent liberal politicians in the Ivory Coast from joining forces with their Senegalese counterparts, led by the lawyer Abdoulaye Wade. So despite a tradition of rivalry between Senegal and the Ivory Coast, the two States set up a joint press enterprise, *La Société Ouest Africaine de Presse*. In an exclusive release to the Senegalese Press Agency, the Chairman of the new corporation's administrative board, Laurent Dona Fologo, referring to the *Moniteur Africain*, said:

> We consider the joint operation of this press organ a practical proof and a symbol of cooperation between our States, and even among the States of West Africa. We are determined to ensure that this organ functions at a level of quality and importance commensurate with its stature[22].

In the initial years, the national daily left such peripheral production tasks as printing, distribution and advertising to outside specialists. But now it began to move into those areas. The first step was the establishment of the *Nouvelles Imprimeries Sénégalaises* (NIS). *La Société Sénégalaise de Presse et de Publication* (SSPP), publisher of *Le Soleil*, owned 75% of NIS capital, in partnership with a French parastatal, *La Société Nationale des Entreprises de Presse* (SNEP). Printing equipment was purchased with loans from the State of Senegal and the French Aid and Co-operation Fund. The enterprise thus set up was pretty solid, whatever changes the future held in store for it. And it practically gave the Senegalese State a monopoly of high quality printing capacity in the country. For that reason, it became difficult for the independent or opposition press to operate outside the NIS trap. To leave no stone unturned in its effort to wrap up economic control over press production circuits, the State created a Senegalese Press and Advertising Company (SPT), in which the national daily, *Le Soleil*, and the Senegalese Radio and Television Corporation (ORTS) jointly owned majority shares. That meant that the major State media were now in a position to supervise in close detail the implementation of their publication and advertising policies.

The SPT went into operation in the second half of February 1975, under the chairmanship of the Director of Information Services, Saliou Fall. Its General Manager was Claude Cherot, with Tidiane Daly Ndiaye as his deputy. The ruling party chalked up another success: Moctar Kébé was re-elected chairman of the National Association of Journalists on 1 February 1975.

The resulting configuration of the Senegalese press gave the opposition little elbow room, but hostilities began as early as issue three of *Le Démocrate*. It carried an article focused on *L'Union Sénégalaise des Banques* (USB), entitled 'Tough Times for the USB'. After pointing out that several billion FCFA had 'disappeared from the Bank, the article concluded: 'It is time for those Senegalese guilty of serious misdemeanours to be sanctioned and replaced with more competent, more serious personnel. God knows there is no shortage of qualified citizens'. The facts might have seemed clear enough in the case, yet *Le Soleil* took it upon itself to answer the article by sending a staff journalist, Papa Hamet Diop, to interview the Director of the USB, Amadou Sow. Sow took the opportunity offered by the friendly national daily to expatiate on the 'immaturity' of the opposition lawyer Abdoulaye Wade, presenting detailed personal gossip to prove his point. After some remarks on the Senegalization of his bank, Sow concluded with a rather surprising admission of the point raised by the PDS paper, the *Démocrate*: 'At the moment it is not feasible to evaluate the size of the loss to which the *Démocrate* refers'[23].

The State was well aware that it stood to lose credibility if it left rebuttals of what it termed opposition 'attacks' to the national daily alone. The UPS Central Committee was therefore all ears when, on 12 March 1975, Habib Thiam, its Secretary for Information and Press Affairs, presented a report on the state of the party press. He highlighted *L'Unité Africaine*, saying its revival had been well received by party activists. 'Confusionists', he said, were busy trying to mislead Senegalese public opinion. The mission of *L'Unité Africaine* would therefore be 'to explain and popularize the ideology of the UPS, to inform and to train activists'[24].

Multiparty Politics and the Strategy of Control

L'Unité Africaine was not the only organ working towards this set goal. In 1975, when the ruling party was already beginning a three-year campaign in preparation for the first multi-party elections for a decade, planned for 26 February 1978, that organ was overshadowed by the State media. Government officials proclaimed that the State media would be neutral, but the atmosphere in the media told a different story. On 1 August 1975, *Le Soleil* set a precedent by covering a press conference given by the rising opposition leader Abdoulaye Wade. On 20 October, the new Director-General of the ORTS, Assane Ndiaye, having replaced Alioune Fall when the latter died in March, went on a tour of regional stations. In Saint-Louis he was received by the regional administrative authorities along with the Director of Radio Channel III, Massamba Niang. Significantly enough, the welcoming committee also included Insa Coulibaly, Deputy Secretary-General of the Saint-Louis municipal branch of the UPS, accompanied by male and female party activists. Coulibaly rendered a vibrant tribute to the Director of the Regional Radio Service, 'Mr. Massamba Niang, known for his indisputable commitment to the ruling party, the UPS, and for his devotion to the public welfare'.

The author of the report emphasized what he called the double role played by Massamba Niang: 'As head of the regional Channel III, he plays an administrative role; as UPS Municipal Advisor for Saint-Louis and Political Commissioner for Saint-Louis region, he plays a political role'.

Journalists meeting this profile of the model ruling party operative were understandably few. Properly defined, professional standards and ethics did not go well with the portrait of the journalist as transmission belt so dear to Léopold Sédar Senghor, who incidentally forgot to modify his views to match changing political realities. As chance would have it, with the retirement of the last French managing editor, Bara Diouf took over supreme control of the national daily at the end of August.

In 1975, a decree from the Governor's office banned private buses, known as *cars rapides*, from the streets of Dakar. 'If we leave Dakar', the drivers told *Le Soleil* journalist Magassouba Moriba, 'we die'. The reporter covered the drivers' strike extensively, reporting some tense events: 'Fights broke out in several places, and the police intervened. At one point they used tear gas to disperse trouble-makers'. Magassouba Moriba noted that after this clash 'six drivers were arrested and taken to the central police station. They were freed the following morning after pleas from the Road Transport Workers' Union'. Journalists often develop a degree of sympathy for the people they cover. Moriba put in a few lines on behalf of the transport owners:

> To want to abolish at one stroke the means of transport needed so urgently by the working population, without providing any substitute for the vehicles thus withdrawn, is to mount a particularly risky operation, with inevitably serious consequences[25].

Magassouba Moriba's reportage on the '*car rapide* affair' infuriated the authorities, who considered it subversive. The very next morning, the Governor of Cape Verde (Dakar) region, El Hadj Malick Bâ, appeared on the front page of *Le Soleil*. He gave an official speech, reported as follows by Ibrahima Gaye:

> The Governor pointed out that tear gas was never used, and that its use had never been considered. Likewise, there were no fights; they just never happened. The only way the police intervened at Colobane and on the Avenue Blaise Diagne was to show up. Their mere presence brought the situation under control[26].

The Governor admitted, nevertheless, that the police seized 53 *cars rapides*. The difference between the journalist's and the Governor's accounts was the price of State security. So Moriba Magassouba's head had to roll. Someone at the top, whose every wish was law to Bara Diouf, wanted it. A month later, *Le Soleil* appeared with a front page photo and an evocative caption: 'The Rush Hour Jam'. In tone the article sounded like an echo to Magassouba's, a discreet tribute to a loser, another man defeated despite being right:

> *Since the regulation of urban transport within the capital, a large number of cars rapides have been banned from the city. The consequence is that now, after a long wait, passengers have to elbow their way and deploy athletic skills to get onto already overloaded vehicles. At several points the rush produces an enormous jam. One feels most sorry for women in the melee. In these circumstances how they wish men were more gallant*[27].

Moriba Magassouba was dismissed in accordance with a fixed, implacable attitude of the regime: political commitment, even in the theoretically neutral national media, was more important than professional standards. 'Subversives' and others indifferent to the charms of the ruling party, condemned by this measure, were sent off to seek sustenance elsewhere. The official stance, a Manichaean one, gave Senegalese journalists only one choice: pro or con the regime. In its drive to obtain strategic control over the future development of newspapers and periodicals in Senegal, the regime went so far as to define a model for independent journalism. The paragon selected was *L'Ouest Africain*, a paper close to the ruling Socialist Party, run by the former Minister of Information, Boubacar Obèye Diop. The man was a sophisticated politician and a formidable advocate. He could have been a great theoretician. Instead, he chose the easy road of political fealty and the defence of the regime's authoritarian methods.

Seizing the opportunity presented by his position in the overall system of the regime's control over the media, Obèye Diop brought out his paper in a new format on Friday 21 November, in the presence of a distinguished guest invited for the occasion, Mr. Daouda Sow, Minister of Information. After welcoming this last-born member of the Senegalese media community, Sow announced plans to organize periodic conferences with the press to discuss professional issues, and invited journalists to observe the nation's new information policy.

The journal *L'Ouest Africain* was presented as a new-born, but it was only a new version of an old paper, a regression, in fact, since the old version had been a weekly, the new only a monthly. But the game was worth the candle. The bottom line was that it gave Obèye Diop a platform. Surrounded by his board, he proceeded to publish a few home truths:

> *Considering the number of worthwhile publications which might have been created or saved if the large sums paid out to certain foreign publications had been invested in them, we cannot help regretting that such a lot could have been accomplished in Senegal and in Africa, but was not, because the resources and the political will were lacking*[28].

Obèye Diop's monthly paper had a team of experienced journalists with a history of political struggle. It could certainly have matched the challenge posed by the *Démocrate*, had it been accorded the resources needed to maintain a degree of autonomy, no matter how superficial. In any case, the combat would have been more loyal, even if not necessarily balanced. The regime, however, was not particularly interested in ethical arguments. The government chose to give priority treatment neither to Obèye Diop's monthly nor to the central organ of the UPS, *L'Unité Africaine*, in its confrontation with opposition papers, but to *Le Soleil*.

For the time being, the *Démocrate* remained the major source of worry. When the PDS paper raised the issue of the bribing of its activists in Sine-Saloum region, citing the example of Matène Fall, the *Soleil* sent Mame Less Dia to interview that protagonist. In the columns of the national daily, the latter denied the accusations laid against him:

> *The first time I heard about such an amount being paid to me to join the UPS was when I read it in the Démocrate'. Matène Fall admitted he had resigned from the PDS on 22 November, but not to join the UPS. His intention was 'to help a home boy pump fresh life into the region*[29].

The home boy referred to was none other than the Secretary-General of the Regional Union of Sine-Saloum, Babacar Bâ, also, incidentally, the Minister of Finance and Economic Affairs.

A week later, Matène Fall, Ahmed Khalifa Niass and a few hundred PDS activists joined the UPS in the presence of Babacar Bâ and the regional political secretariat. This provided an opportunity for Matène Fall, in an interview with the same accommodating journalist, Mame Less Dia, to deny his earlier denial: 'I've come to join the UPS, but the reason is far from the one advanced by backbiters claiming I was bribed'. This from the man who had initially argued against the accusation of bribery on the grounds that he was not about to join the ruling party. It was not until its 23 December issue that the *Soleil* revealed the goal of the press campaign for which its columns and its journalist Mame Less Dia, appointed Special Correspondent in Sine-Saloum for the nonce, had been used:

> *Right now in the Senegalese Democratic Party ranks, it's each for himself and the devil take the hindmost. Just after his return from Abidjan, Babacar Bâ, continuing his efforts to undermine and dismantle the opposi-*

tion, begun since he was elected head of the regional union of the UPS, dealt the opposition party a fatal blow seriously jeopardizing its capacity to hold its planned congress in Kaolack on 29 January 1976.

It looked as if the regime had decided to finish off the Senegalese Democratic Party in 1975, and had appointed Mame Less Dia to deliver a series of obituary notices entitled 'Sine-Saloum: The PDS Losing Steam: Birth, Growth and Decay of the PDS'. Throwing self-control to the winds, Mame Less Dia went all out to express the hope that the PDS would go ahead and hold its congress in the 'pacified' region under the difficult conditions he himself had described. In undisguised glee he looked forward to a political fiasco: 'We would be disappointed if, as rumour has it, the PDS decided to postpone its congress'[30].

Given the credibility associated with its pioneering history and its refusal to participate in the usual rituals of political rhetoric, the *Démocrate* was a formidable political adversary of the regime. But it was not the only opposition organ. In December 1976, the National Democratic Rally (RND) forced underground by the law permitting only four political currents, published *Siggi*, a legal journal that continued the long struggle of Professor Cheikh Anta Diop: 'Our intention is to stand tall, to make this paper a medium of opinion serving a vast community of dissidents'. *Siggi* was a cyclostyled paper, with a circulation limited to campus circles. Possibly for that reason, President Senghor decided to assault it with grammatical artillery. The word *Siggi*, he decreed, ought to be written with a single 'g'. The tactic, after a series of epic linguistic battles featuring Pathé Diagne and Cheikh Anta Diop, forced a name change on the paper, which became *Taxaw* (stand up).

In July 1977, the alliance between Mamadou Dia and the underground PAI in its turn brought out a publication called *Ande Sopi* (unite for change). In addition to these papers, a few other sheets appeared, but their readership was small. One was *Mom-sarew*, a PAI organ since 1958. There were two versions of this paper, one published by Majmouth Diop's legal wing, the other by the underground section of the party. *Le Militant* was the central organ of the Democratic League; the Unified Democratic Teachers' Union (SUDES) published *L'Educateur Sénégalais*, while the Free Workers' Union published *Liberté*. And then there was *Le Politicien*, which brought out its maiden issue in January 1977 with the motto: 'Democracy begins with freedom of the press'. It sold like hot cakes, rising from an initial print run of 7,000 to 30,000 with the sixth issue. Ordinary people found it amusing as it dished out the rumoured peccadilloes of targeted members of the ruling class. The first victims of the satirical journal were opposition leaders, pilloried for the entertainment of the masses.

In its August issue, *Le Politicien* published a number of legal documents purloined from the Court at Thiès, exposing deals involving a leading businessman, Ousmane Diagne, who had written an attack on *Le Politicien* in defence of the Minister of Finance in *Le Soleil*. The Editor of *Le Politicien*, Mame Less Dia, was arrested on 23 September. Issue nine of the paper, headlining his arrest, sold 70,000 copies. The court was about to release him on bail when it received a complaint from the President of the Republic concerning an article in that same issue about some property owned by the President in Normandy. Mame Less Dia was kept in jail.

While the controversy raged, stern warnings were issued with the incumbent Chairman of the National Association of Senegalese Journalists, Moctar Kébé, at the centre of the storm:

There is no doubt that we have learned a lot from the copious explanations recently showered on us. In my opinion, however, the debates would have been more worthwhile had they been pitched at a higher level of seriousness, instead of degenerating into personal attacks[31].

That did not keep the ANJS from adopting an extremely tough resolution at its 30 September General Assembly:

demanding the liberation of Mame Less Dia from detention.... While continuing to trust in the capacity of the Senegalese judiciary to ensure the triumph of justice, the General Assembly condemns the methods of intimidation used against the Managing Editor of the Politicien at the time of his arrest, as well as the refusal to allow him to contact his lawyer.

On Tuesday 11 October the Steering Committee of the ANJS met the Minister of Information, Daouda Sow, who handed them a letter from the President of the Republic along with an explanatory note indicating the threshold of tolerance: 'Respect the independence of the judiciary'[32]. On 2 November, President Senghor withdrew his complaint against *Le Politicien* after receiving apologies from the managing editor and the political affairs editor of the satirical journal. To make sure everyone understood the dissidents had cracked, the *Soleil* that same day printed the abject apology:

I have come respectfully to repeat my apologies along with those of the entire Board of Le Politicien *for the unfortunate technical error which, today, has brought us to accepting responsibility for the spread of "information" we know to be false. Owing to considerations beyond our control, the article was printed without our accompanying remarks, to our profound regret. The mistake has distressed us all the more deeply because of the serious damage to the honour of a man who to us is both father and protector.*

Soothing words indeed, for an old poet just past his 70th birthday, especially since Samba Dioulde Thiam, writing in the October issue of *Ande Sopi*, had so lampooned the President's birthday celebrations as to draw a shocked response from Moustapha Niasse:

> The journal *Ande Sopi* has once again brought itself to public attention through an article entitled "Gifts of Old Age". ... The article, focused on a 71-year-old man, alleges that his 70th birthday was organized at State expense, that for his trips he purchased an aeroplane worth several billions, and that all that was left for him to do was to wait for the mists of senility. The article ends with an invocation to the angel of death. It is simply obscene[33].

The horror felt by senior government and party officials was real. It was a point of pride with them that they were right, their opponents wrong. After all, they were in power. There never had been any other way of running things but theirs. Delivering a lecture on the promising topic of 'The Press and Democracy' on Saturday 17 December, Obèye Diop gave short shrift to a questioner, Serigne Diop, criticizing the regime's monopoly over the media and the refusal to broadcast PDS announcements. His answer was dizzying:

> There is no question whatsoever of treating the PDS differently from the PS. All listeners can hear statements from the two political parties on the radio. But the PS issues short, precise statements. Why should the other party be enabled to turn the radio into its mouthpiece, by allowing it to broadcast statements that read more like feature articles in the press? We are for equal opportunity, but with moderation[34].

After a year of political pluralism, then, it was clear that the power of the press would continue to be curtailed. The British journal *New Africa Development*, in its December 1977 issue, presented a sobering assessment of the Senegalese experience: 'Lately, we have received disturbing news from Senegal which bodes ill for that country's ongoing experiment with freedom of the press'.

Following the bringing of *Le Politicien* to heel, President Senghor told the French daily *Le Monde* (4 November 1977) that in Senegal there was no prospect of the media constituting a fourth estate. This judgment was a taste of things to come, as the regime tried to rein in a press hoping to enjoy full freedom after the democratic opening. Meanwhile, the February 1978 elections were drawing close. During the campaign the National Association of Journalists crashed. In their jockeying for political positions, a number of the association's members set up an Organization of Socialist Journalists. It proved to be a kick in the rear for Moctar Kébé, administered by Obèye Diop, who was elected Chairman. Moctar Kébé, who happened to be abroad at the time, only got the post of Deputy Secretary-General, under Obèye Diop as Chairman, Bara Diouf as Vice-Chairman, Gabriel Jacques Gomis as second Vice-Chairman, and Tidiane Daly Ndiaye as Secretary-General.

Within the ANJS, Moctar Kébé's credibility diminished. Various factions used *Le Politicien* to push their views. Most active were those highlighting the conflict of interest between the chairmanship of a non-political corporate body and membership of the executive committee of an association based on sectarian criteria, self-defined as 'established within the Socialist Party framework, and, of course, committed to democratic socialism'[35]. Moctar Kébé was obliged to resign his chairmanship of the ANJS. From that point on, the old ANJS was definitively gone. The new executive committee was a finicky team led by a journalist from the national radio service, Mbaye Sidy Mbaye.

As 1978 dawned, the election campaign heated up. For the first time since independence, the campaign turned the State media into a genuine forum for the interchange of information. But the experiment lasted only a few days. The population did not get the hoped-for debate between the two leading candidates, President Senghor and his rival Abdoulaye Wade. Face-to-face debates were scarce, and after the campaign they died out altogether, even though Moctar Kébé, a journalist with close ties to the regime, wrote a think piece a few months before the election advocating their adoption as a permanent feature:

> *I have been wondering if the time is not ripe now to start a series of real face-to-face encounters in the press, with members of the ruling party and government on the one side, and opposition leaders on the other, debating the entire range of national issues*'[36].

The old policy was maintained, however, and thus the media war remained a lopsided struggle between the opposition press and the official media. In its April 1978 issue, *Taxaw* took rueful note of the state of affairs:

> *It is rather odd that while Mr. Senghor talks endlessly about democracy, he deploys a wide array of threats and tricks against organs of the democratic press and all those trying to exercise their right to freedom of thought and expression.*

The National Democratic Rally had called for a boycott of the elections. In the post-election period, the fact that large numbers had stayed away from the polling booths improved that party's stature. Its paper, *Taxaw*, took up the cause of freedom of speech, including freedom for the foreign press. The government, offended that it carried an interview with Professor Cheikh Anta Diop, had just banned sales of the February issue (155) of the magazine

Afrique-Asie in Senegal. Content was not the sore point. The probable reason was the fact that a foreign magazine had given coverage to Cheikh Anta Diop. The government seemed convinced that it should have a monopoly of foreign approval. All the more so since, on the eve of the election, it had helped out the weekly *Jeune Afrique* with a FCFA 100 million loan carrying a 7% interest rate, some 11% or 16% below the standard bank rate in Senegal, meaning a shortfall for the national treasury.

Given the stature of the two combatants, Cheikh Anta Diop and Léopold Sédar Senghor, the controversy initiated by *Taxaw* made international waves, with sharply defined black-and-white positions. July was an especially busy time. President Senghor had presented a motion on foreign intervention in Africa at the OAU summit in Khartoum. Cheikh Anta Diop had analyzed the resolution in an article entitled 'Words and Reality'. On his return from Khartoum, Bara Diouf seized the opportunity to print a peremptory rebuttal: *'Taxaw* is Wrong'. No doubt he intended to emulate the Permanent Secretary in President Senghor's office, Djibo Kâ, who had written a vituperative article against issue 11 of *Taxaw*, which contained a report on a demonstration against President Senghor at a poetry reading session at the Poetry Center in New York. The article made much of 'the poverty of a certain section of the press', and ran alongside a reprinted article from the *New York Times* that did not mention the demonstration. In sum, Djibo Kâ figured that if the *Times* did not print it, it did not happen. There is little doubt that ten years later, when President Abdou Diouf was casting around for his first Minister of Information, he remembered the agility with which Djibo Kâ had conjured up that denial.

The war on *Taxaw* had repercussions in the State media. A journalist from the Ministry of Information was reprimanded by his superiors for attending a press conference called by the leader of the National Democratic rally. A number of journalists working for *Le Soleil* and the Ministry of Information signed a petition calling for the recognition of the RND; they were placed under covert surveillance. These were psychotic times, and it was that paranoid atmosphere that led to the dismissal of Alain Agboton from *Le Soleil*. His name beginning with an A, he found himself listed at the top of the recognition petition. He was among the first trainees to graduate from the CESTI, condemned by a categorical verdict delivered from a press boss: 'CESTI trains Communists'.

Alain Agboton was ordered to move to Sine-Saloum to head the regional office. He explained his refusal to the General Manager of *Le Soleil* during a 5 May interview, confirmed by a letter dated 16 May. The board replied the same day. The correspondence ended with a letter from the Personnel Chief, dated 24 May 1978:

Your behaviour is tantamount to a case of absence without leave. We therefore request that you kindly present yourself at the Accounts section to receive emoluments due you subsequent to your breach of contract, i.e., your severance pay plus annual leave allowance calculated according to legal rates for the appropriate period.

Two days later, employees at the *Soleil* held an extraordinary general assembly meeting at which they issued a resolution condemning Alain Agboton's dismissal. They decided on strike action lasting until 17:00 the next Sunday unless he was reinstated. Then came a message from Colonel Waly Faye, commanding officer of the Gendarmerie and the military tribunal, that showed the high degree of State involvement in the affair: 'The State is invariably justified. It never retreats'. So three years after Moriba Magassouba, Alain Agboton was in his turn shoved out into the cold. The general manager of the *Soleil* refused to rescind the dismissal order. As for the employees, they were in no position to match their brave words with deeds. A different message, labelled No. 1851 T and dated 1 June 1978, narrates the sequel to the showdown.

In line with its customary practice, the State used litigation as its principal weapon against the so-called independent press. The previous year, the *Politicien* had been taken to court and had its feathers clipped. Next into the plucking machine went *Promotion*. The scenario was the same as for the *Politicien*. First, on 25 September 1978, the Prime Minister served a writ against the paper for defamatory information published in issues 47 and 48 alleging that Abdou Diouf had purchased State buildings for peanuts, and that he or a relative of his had been given a loan. When the publisher of *Promotion*, Boubacar Diop, arrived at the printer's to take delivery of 20,000 copies of his paper, he was asked to pay all arrears plus the cost of the current issue on the spot. This was contrary to past practice, but Boubacar Diop paid up and got ready to pick up his papers. Bara Diouf then presented him with a decree confiscating the whole issue.

The publisher of *Promotion* hardly knew what kind of trap he had fallen into. He had scraped to make ends meet throughout 1978, and his paper had suffered along with him. Working alone on *Promotion*, Boubacar Diop had based his articles on rumour without ever checking his sources. He was reported to be a spokesperson for the former Minister of Finance and Economic Affairs, Boubacar Bâ, who had been elbowed out of the line of succession behind Senghor. Whatever the truth of that claim, Boubacar Diop had made sensational rumours his stock in trade, coming out with an avalanche of alarmist and titillating headlines: 'Senegal Bankrupt', 'Senghor Near Death', 'The Head of State No Longer Trusts Prime Minister Abdou Diouf', 'Night of Long Knives in the State Establishment', etc.

With such an impressive backlog of yellow journalism, Boubacar Diop was a ripe target for a Bara Diouf editorial. On 18 September 1978 it came under the headline: 'Is Nazism Really Dead?' This was followed by a flood of letters to the editor of *Le Soleil* castigating the publisher of *Promotion* for his lack of seriousness. The flood lasted well into October. On 23 October, in an interview with Bara Diouf, President Senghor transfixed the offending journalist with a contemptuous reply:

> *Pardon me, but I have no desire to discuss such a blackmailing rag, or its director, a man not famous for his integrity in the past, who now presumes to preach morality and honour, when he is not busy, in his typically uncouth fashion, dispensing lessons in grammar.*

Still, Boubacar Diop kept raising the ante until July 1980, when he was jailed for publishing allegations under such headlines as 'Prime Minister Acquires 169 Million Francs of Real Estate in Caen', 'Unpunished General Gets One Billion Francs', and 'Marabout Given 300 Million Francs'. The persons alluded to were well known, but the allegations were totally unverifiable. In his determination to poison the atmosphere in such a way as to block Abdou Diouf's chances of acceding to power, Boubacar Diop fought tooth and nail, but in the end he could not escape a sentence of 18 months in prison plus a FCFA 500,000 fine.

This was a time of unfettered freedom of the press; it was also a time the government used to sharpen its regulatory tools. As early as 1975, a task force had been set up under Jean Pierre Biondi, Technical Advisor in the President's Office. It comprised nine members: the Minister of Information, the General Manager of *Le Soleil*, the Director of the Radio and Television Service, the Director of the Senegalese Press Agency, the President's Press Officer, two Members of Parliament from the ruling party, and the Editor-in-Chief of the *Moniteur Africain*. Their terms of reference required them to produce a report capable of serving as a basis for a projected press code.

One circumstance rendered the press code suspect right from the start: all members of the preparatory task force belonged to the same school of thought. In January 1979, the *Politicien* organized a dinner-debate chaired by the Minister of Information, Daouda Sow. Participants included agency directors, representatives of various political parties, and high State officials. The topic was the assessment of the new press code. The ensuing discussion was stormy. Only government supporters found nothing wrong with the Code. Everyone else found its stipulations disturbing. It provided harsh penalties for offences committed by the press. Upon request, editors were obliged to name authors of unsigned articles. Where fines had sufficed in the past, offenders would now be jailed.

According to Article 28 of Act Number 73-44 on the Press Code dated April 1979, the Commission overseeing press organs was empowered to audit the accounts of every organ, to vet recurrent expenditure, to monitor print runs on a permanent basis and to publish its findings. It stipulated prison terms for the publication of defamatory articles, information likely to weaken the morale of the armed forces, and items disrespectful of the President of the Republic. Further penalties included confiscation of assets, the suspension of organs for no more than three months, and seizure of all copies of offensive journals. The National Assembly passed the bill in March 1979. Throughout the controversy surrounding its passage, the ANJS remained mute because its leadership was weak and its vision misty.

The Search for Hegemony and the Dissident Response

Once, on a visit to Port-au-Prince, Senghor was welcomed with a witticism by his friend Césaire, who said he had 'a lion's mouth, a sage's smile'. The phrase was a perfect expression for the ambivalent relationship between Senghor and the press during his last years in office. In October 1980, the French daily *Le Monde* announced that the President of Senegal planned to retire on 3 December that year. In his weekly press review, the Senegalese journalist Gabriel Jacques Gomis mentioned the fact. He was forthwith forbidden ever to speak on the radio again. In due time Senghor explained why:

> It is true that in the 21 October 1980 issue of Le Monde, that newspaper's Dakar correspondent wrote about my impending resignation. I had not seen the correspondent in question for some six months. But I had, early in 1980, informed the Prime Minister, Abdou Diouf, of my intentions, and, on the eve of the holiday season, I told those Ministers most entitled to know. These are the facts[37].

Two weeks later, Senghor pardoned the publisher of *Promotion*, the man he had turned into an enemy with a sarcastic answer at his 7 April 1978 press conference. It was from that day that the humiliated journalist became a member of the critical opposition. On 11 December 1980, President Senghor decorated four journalists: Bara Diouf, Aly Kheury Ndaw, Abdou Salam Kane and Serigne Aly Cissé. He thanked Bara Diouf 'for having, along with his three colleagues, made *Le Soleil* a paper of international stature'. This was Senghor's last significant interaction with the press.

After Abdou Diouf took over power, one of the first significant moves of the Senegalese press was the convening of a series of meetings aimed at reviving the National Association of Senegalese Journalists. The meetings took place on 7 and 8 March. Cherif El Walid Séye, editor of the national affairs page of *Le Soleil*, devoted his editorial to the event:

Senegal's journalists, whose work is to serve others all year long, are today meeting to take stock of their achievements in the effort to improve their professional performance and status, as well as of the problems facing them. These are important issues.

In his opening address, the Minister of Information repeated the beloved official definition of journalists as development agents, urging them 'to help consolidate the nation'[38]. The most influential contribution to the discussions, however, came from the association of CESTI graduates. They presented a report which led to the creation of three commissions which decided to meet on 28 March to present the General Assembly with a working paper focused on the burning issues of the day:
1) The situation of journalists in the work place;
2) Professional standards and ethical rules;
3) Orientation and structure.

The last was the most important item. It involved a decision as to whether to reinforce the status of the journalists' group as a voluntary association or to transform it into a trade union, as recommended by the CESTI graduates.

The substantive assembly was held on 9 May. After a lively debate lasting from 10 hours to 23 hours, the issue was put to a vote. A total of 58 were for revitalizing the association or turning it into a union; 33 wanted it to join the democratic trade union movement, and two were for the status quo. When the time came to elect the Executive Committee, the trade unionist faction abstained. Some speakers thought the slate of candidates for the executive committee unrepresentative. To avoid the risk of a split, Moctar Kébé and Tony Stephen withdrew. At that point, numerous speakers called for an infusion of new blood as well as for the incorporation of the trade unionist wing into the executive. But because the trade unionist wing refused to work with the Steering Committee, this initiative failed[39]. For almost two hours the discussions stalled. The general assembly then rejected the slate of candidates and fixed another date for a meeting.

The journalists' organization, unable to choose an executive committed to reform, postponed the time of decision. Meanwhile, however, new graduates fresh from the CESTI were coming into the profession, and the principle of autonomy was making headway, however hesitantly. On 6 May, Abdou Diouf signed an amnesty pardoning all press offences committed before 1 January 1981. His Minister responsible for Information disseminated Circular 523 of 10 September 1981, asserting the equality of citizens and political parties before the State media. In practice, however, the media remained partial to the regime, and the opposition reacted by holding a joint press conference on the partisan use of the State media by the ruling party. To this dull recitation of the obvious, Djibo Kâ, Minister of Information, responded in the National Assembly by saying that the necessarily frequent appearances of figures in the regime in their capacity as members of the government should not be confused with their appearance as party members. The argument, typical of the reasoning of politicians, nevertheless succeeded in diverting attention from the real issue.

Early in 1983, with a month to go before the elections, the association of CESTI graduates organized a round table discussion on 'The Media and Pluralism'. The format called for equal representation for all political parties, with freedom of speech assured all round. The ruling party naturally boycotted the discussion. It did not want to go and get told that:

> *in a pluralist society, the role of the media should be to facilitate the expression of every point of view, even if considerable disquiet results. For that is the only effective way to give democracy sturdy foundations in our society* (CESTI, 1983).

At the start of the campaign, Decree No. 83.138 dated 31 January stipulated the following broadcasting time schedule for the parties contending the legislative round: 21 minutes daily for the majority party; 21 minutes for all opposition parties. Since there were seven, this gave each a total of 3 minutes per day to put its message across. The Supreme Court ruled the allocation unconstitutional, on the grounds that the Constitution guaranteed equal access to the means of propaganda for all candidates. The regime then covered its tracks by passing another law in which the phrase "majority party" was amended to "majority parties." The change from singular to plural only made the fraud more glaring.

For the presidential campaign, the Minister of Information issued a ruling, No. 850 dated 2 February 1983, allotting 5 minutes of air time per day to each candidate. The period following, from 6 to 25 February, was a high time of free speech, even if there were a few hitches. When it was over, it left a bitter taste in the public mouth. For it seemed as if the deposits paid by the various parties had merely served to purchase air time for a few short advertisements and announcements. *Xarebi* (No. 2, 1983), the central organ of *Ande Jëff*, spoke for the entire opposition when it stated:

> *The regime refuses stubbornly to enable us to broadcast bulletins and other announcements concerning our movement. For example, our policy statement on Abdou Diouf's call[40] for an energizing spurt of "national pride" was brazenly cut from the communiqué issued by our Permanent Bureau issued on 9 August 1983.*

Ten days before the elections, the Senegalese Democratic Party decided to publish an evening paper, *Takusaan*, as a means of breaking *Le Soleil's* monopoly. The new paper came out three times a week and never became a daily. After a year it folded. With a print run of 12,000, it built up a considerable readership between January 1983 and February 1984. But a covert campaign organized by the all-powerful Permanent Secretary to the President of the Republic, Jean Collin, undermined the editorial board, finally splitting it off from the Senegalese Democratic Party. That done, Jean Collin planned to replace *Takusaan* with a new paper called *Carrefour*, edited by Mamadou Tamimou Wane. The maiden issue of *Carrefour*, which Pathé Mbodj, Abdourahmane Camara and Tidiane Kassé, all formerly on the board of *Takusaan*, helped to produce, came out in April 1984. On the front page it carried a surprise: a photo of Abdoulaye Bathily, leader of the left wing LD/MPT. Offended, Jean Collin ordered Wane to sack certain members of the editorial board suspected of hobnobbing with left-wing extremists.

The year 1983 was the tenth anniversary of the collective bargaining contract for journalists and technicians. The implementation of its provisions was lax, at least as far as communications professionals were concerned. Breaches of Article 2 were especially rampant. State media were in the habit of hiring staff not on the basis of professional competence but in line with political considerations. The profession had thus been thrown open to would-be journalists slithering out from the underbelly of the ruling Socialist Party. Among them the best educated came from the teaching profession, but they took up posts which in principle should have gone to qualified CESTI graduates, some of whom now went unemployed upon graduation. Employers also disregarded Article 7, designed to prevent discrimination in hiring, work load distribution, promotion and retrenchment. Priority treatment was regularly reserved for so-called journalists with ruling party patronage.

To take an outstanding example, at the Ministry of Information, one schoolteacher turned journalist after a two-year course in Lille was appointed Senior Reporter immediately after his course, even though management had long refused to promote serving journalists, claiming there was no room on the organizational ladder. Alioune T Dia (1985: 151) summed up the situation as follows:

> The Ministry of Information does not observe the collective agreement with journalists. Neither does the national daily, Le Soleil. At the Senegalese Radio and Television Service (ORTS), the situation is the same. Graduate journalists from CESTI have been working there full time, presenting individual feature programmes and peak hour newscasts for two years and more, all without pay.

Such were the circumstances under which employees at the *Soleil*, at their general assembly meeting on Friday 22 July, decided on a 24-hour strike that kept the paper off the stands the following Saturday. The outcome, as evaluated by personnel representatives at the *Soleil*, proved bitter:

> *The management of the Soleil wants to personalize the dispute by satisfying selected individuals, thus dividing the movement and sabotaging its objective: the comprehensive observation of the provisions of the Journalists' Collective Agreement* (Dia, 1985:151).

The strike, which failed to gain the active support of other sectors, happened when the National Union of Communications Professionals was stagnant, its executive organs non-existent.

On 5 October 1984, the authoritarian policies governing State media made no allowances even for allies of the regime: the Director of the Radio Broadcasting System, Pape Racine Sy, was sacked for refusing to broadcast a communiqué from the General Caliph of the Mouride religious brotherhood announcing that the Muslim feast, *korité,* would be celebrated on Friday 7 September, even though part of the Muslim community would celebrate it on the 6th. Interestingly enough, the stand he took was exactly that recommended in a Ministry of Information circular dated 19 September 1984.

On 26 and 27 September, the Communications Minister invited press attachés and advisors to a seminar on the functions and operational resources of press attachés and advisors. The participants adopted a series of resolutions, never subsequently implemented, except that it gave them the illusion of being in a position to discuss problems confidentially with the minister. In times to come that perception was to make them a fifth column within the journalists' trade union. The union got started in mid-December, when the UNPICS disintegrated after congress participants, asked to make a clear choice between recognition as a voluntary association and as a regular trade union, opted by acclamation for an Information and Communications Professionals' Trade Union (SYNPICS). Mamadou Diop, a journalist at the ORTS, was elected Secretary-General in place of Abdou Rahmane Cissé, appointed Director of Information Services shortly before.

The general resolution adopted by the congress held on 15 and 16 December was the statutory indication of the victory of the radical wing of the journalists' organization. It urged the national executive board to see to the renegotiation of the collective agreement of journalists and affiliated technicians in Senegal in order to end abuses by employers and to guarantee the regular and systematic promotion of professionals in the work place. It urged the administrative committee and the national executive to look unsentimentally and critically at legislation concerning the journalistic profession and the publication of newspapers and magazines, with special reference to the Press Code, notorious for its infringements on freedom of speech and press freedom. It further recommended the drafting of a professional code of ethics. In addition, it urged initiatives to democratize criteria governing the allocation of press cards and to ensure the adoption of equitable guidelines in the allocation of professional credentials for all media. The novelty of this general resolution was that it openly recognized the normal conflict of interest between employers and employees, and stipulated that media owners and management were not qualified for membership of the professional journalists' union, SYNPICS.

The SYNPICS Manifesto of 1 May highlighted problems facing Senegalese journalists. It also dealt with the record of State practices in the area of free speech. The regime reacted swiftly. On 30 April 1985, 22 journalists with Socialist Party affiliations signed an appeal published in *Le Soleil* calling the manifesto bizarre and bewildering on the grounds that by using intemperate language and taking crudely sectarian positions, it revealed a leftward drift likely to damage the credibility of the SYNPICS and the genuine interests of its members. The appeal went on to pronounce the incumbent executive of the union unfit to act as self-appointed spokesmen in any dealings with the regime.

All signatories to this appeal were more or less avowed members of the ruling party. But some members of the SYNPICS, though also Socialist Party militants, did not go along with the 22 after the national executive issued a firm clarificatory statement and the rank and file followed suit with a consistent rebuttal of the appeal. The SYNPICS executive pointed out that those signatories of the appeal who happened to be card-carrying members of the union were entitled to express their viewpoints at union meetings. They had chosen to forget this in their 'unfortunate outburst', thus contravening SYNPICS bye-laws. They would therefore have to answer to the appropriate bodies. But there were other signatories about whose involvement the SYNPICS executive raised a query: Amadou Dieng (Director, APS), Tidiane Daly Ndiaye (General Manager, SPT), Ibrahima Dem (Presidential Advisor), Birassy Sow (Principal Secretary to the Minister of Information), Amadou Matho Ndiaye (Editor-in-Chief of *L'Unité*, central organ of the Socialist Party), El Hadj Laba Sow (Chief Radio Programme and Channels Officer, Member of the government-affiliated CNTS union executive at the ORTS), and Aly Kheury Ndaw had also signed the appeal. The question was: in what capacity did they feel so involved in the matter of a manifesto issued by a trade union to which they did not belong?[41]

The 22 signatories of the anti-SYNPICS appeal had come out swinging with a spectacular show of bravery. But in 24 hours they turned tail. They had promised to publish a longer list of signatories in the next issue of *Le Soleil*, but they did not, and 22 remained the final number. When the National

Assembly sat on 23 May, the Minister of Information, Djibo Kâ, called the SYNPICS Manifesto a 'courageous, patriotic document'. The fact that his declaration amounted to a scathing rebuke of the 22 signatories faithful to the regime seemed not to have bothered him.

While journalists were moving into the social and entrepreneurial arena, the *Soleil* put the finishing touches to its own transformation into a full scale corporation with an unchanged capital investment of FCFA 27,400,000. The State auditors had recommended the change, which began back in 1983 with the absorption of new shareholders and the establishment of the *Nouvelles Imprimeries Sénégalaises* (NIS) as a separate company. Bara Diouf became Managing Director and Chief Executive Officer of *Le Soleil*. Another journalist, Tidiane Daly Ndiaye, became head of the NIS. There were structural changes: a post of Deputy Editor responsible for the national affairs page was created and 1984 was a good year for *Le Soleil* in business terms. The staff took up a percentage of shares, and the balance sheet showed a modest surplus, 12%. Bara Diouf was expected to retire; individuals and factions got busy jockeying for the succession.

The Rise of a 'Peculiar Type of Press'

Over the past five years the manners and methods of the Senegalese press have changed remarkably. One reason is that a new generation of journalists, coming of age, brought a different spirit to its work. Even the State media underwent some change. Early in the afternoon of 22 August 1985, at a time when a coalition of opposition parties had scheduled an anti-apartheid march ending at the presidential palace, the telephone rang in the radio newsroom. The caller said the Minister of Communication, Djibo Kâ, would be issuing a communiqué soon. The communiqué turned out to be a Senegalese Press Agency dispatch fulminating against "the handful of 50 demonstrators. The journalists on duty were Lamine Touré for the 8 pm shift and Demba Ndiaye for the news bulletin after that. The Director of the Radio service, Pathé Dièye Fall, and the Editor-in-Chief, Ibrahima Sané, tried to force the journalists to read the dispatch without mentioning the fact that it came from the APS. The two journalists refused. They were subsequently transferred to Saint-Louis and Ziguinchor, after some weak-kneed resistance from the radio section of the SYNPICS, in the ineffectual form of a signed petition protesting the transfers.

Still, there was no doubt that a new spirit was emerging among younger members on the periphery of the Senegalese journalistic establishment. That spirit led in time to the creation of the pioneering papers that grew to constitute the country's independent press. Different projects were incubating:

It happened one Sunday morning in December 1985. Holiday time all round. Five unrepentant, overweening buddies met in a suburban living room, arguing heatedly, as usual, in order not to have to change. This time the issue was how to create the kind of journalism we dreamed about. The solution came eventually. Over the next six months, each of us would save FCFA 100,000. The total would constitute the startup capital for our project[42].

That was how *Sud Magazine* was born, its first number appearing in March 1986. A year later, in February 1986, *Le Cafard Libéré* began publication.

On 11 and 12 April 1987, at the SYNPICS congress, Abdoulaye Ndiaga Sylla, formerly a journalist at the *Soleil*, founding member of the Sud Com group and publisher of *Sud Magazine*, was elected Chairman of the National Executive Bureau. The union's 1 May manifesto was an opportunity to warn the authorities not to go ahead with their decision to cut the annual subsidy given to the Senegalese Press Agency. That agency was entering its twentieth year under depressing circumstances. Even though it had 50 subscribers, including civil service departments, information agencies, diplomatic missions and private companies, its finances were in poor shape.

The SYNPICS Manifesto also revealed that the State planned to maintain a monopoly over the audio-visual media, and condemned that attitude. In a further significant move, the SYNPICS condemned the collective agreement that had regulated the profession since 1973:

The draft collective agreement presented by our Union corrects important anomalies in the old agreement. Under the old agreement, professional promotion depends on the employer's good will, and the only other determining criterion is an appointment to a specific position. These provisions are restrictive because they disregard competence, seniority and educational credentials, thus encouraging bootlicking and mediocrity[43].

Noting the vigorous growth of the independent press, the SYNPICS urged the government to implement effectively and without discrimination the principle of subsidies for independent press organs, and to guarantee access to credit for legally established press enterprises. In July 1987, a delegation of the national executive bureau led by the national Secretary-General had an audience with the President of the Republic, who promised to instruct the ministers and officials involved to give due attention to a memorandum presented a fortnight earlier as well as to the Union's draft agreement.

In September, three members of the SYNPICS national executive bureau left their posts at the national daily, *Le Soleil*, under the circumstances reported below:

> *The Le Soleil moved into high gear with the intensification of the witch hunt invariably reserved for those of its journalists who, being 'wrongheaded,' find flunkeyish behaviour unattractive. Such people are an endangered species at the Le Soleil. After much harassment, the management of the Le Soleil found no better tactic than to inflict a de facto demotion on Sidy Gaye and myself, in September 1987. Sidy Gaye had been head of the foreign desk, while I was a senior reporter. That meant we were in Category 4. We were suddenly transferred to head the Saint-Louis and Thiès offices. Those posts were Category 3 positions (Sud Hebdo, 38, 2 February 1988, p.8).*

Most of those sacked went to work for *Sud Magazine*, and constituted the work force for *Sud Hebdo*, launched three months later. This was a time when the independent press scene in Senegal was getting configured, with the former editors of *Takusaan* and *Carrefour* going to *Wal Fadjri* in November 1987. Abdourahmane Camara had been working as a correspondent for *Wal Fadjri*, but he now took a permanent post running it, and also hired a team of editors whose professional competence helped raise their paper to the top, beside *Sud Hebdo* and *Le Cafard libéré*.

The second generation of the independent press played a preponderant role in so eclipsing the State press that for the first time the opposition began to think it feasible to bypass it. But as opposition papers became an increasingly active part of the independent press, the first generation of opposition journalists and editors tended to relapse into support for the government, forgetting their former trials and tribulations. Boubacar Diop, for instance, went so far as to perjure himself in this fulsome eulogy to the new President:

> *Even those who burrow into the record of the final ten years Abdou Diouf spent in the shadow of Senghor will not find a shred of evidence indicating that he was ever guilty of any conflict of interest, any dereliction of duty, or indeed any immoral act in his private or public life*[44].

The regime had more to be pleased about. The promoters of *Ande Sopi* having switched alliances, their paper stopped publication at the end of February. On January 1988, a Senegalese television crew was barred from entering the El Mansour cinema hall to report on the closing session of the Senegalese Democratic Party congress. At the same time, reporters from the independent paper *Sud Hebdo* got harassed in the course of their work. SYNPICS took the opportunity to reassert its position:

> *While not denying the need for wider coverage of national events, SYNPICS would like all political parties to understand that journalists working for the State media in general, and for the audio-visual media in*

particular, have no influence whatsoever upon the policy decisions and options of their official superiors[45].

To mark the start of the election campaign, the PDS published the first issue of *Sopi*. The paper, run by a team of media professionals, succeeded beyond the dreams of the PDS politicians who had organized it for electioneering purposes. In the hectic post-election period of April, the paper *Combat pour le Socialisme*, the central organ of Socialist Party work-place committees, attacked *Sud Hebdo*, most recent of the Sud Com group, which had started publication in March 1988:

> We were among the first to congratulate promoters of Sud Hebdo right after its creation for their exemplary initiative. We thought the paper would have no political ties, and that it would publish objective information. Things have worked out otherwise: Sud Hebdo has in practice been extremely cosy with our opponents. And it has made a daily habit of publishing systematic attacks against the regime, unbacked by any evidence. This state of affairs is no longer tolerable to Combat pour le Socialisme.

The reason for the anger of *Combat pour le Socialisme* was apparent in the following passage:

> There is no rule, no professional code of ethics justifying the continuation of certain attitudes such as those of Moussa Paye, a press attaché working for the Chairman of the Economic and Social Council, 3rd in the order of State precedence. In issue No. 7 of Wednesday 2 March 1988, he gave vent to his dishonest, vile and cowardly animosity towards Senegalese democracy. It would be understandable if Sud Hebdo belonged to a political party[46].

The offending article was entitled: 'Did Dakar Switch Sides?' It was an analytical piece about voting patterns in selected polling centres in Dakar. Based on statistics, it pointed out an emerging trend: in some constituencies that had traditionally been ruling Socialist Party strongholds, Abdoulaye Wade of the opposition PDS had outpulled President Abdou Diouf. The same journalist wrote an article raising questions about the arrest of opposition leaders and the use of the army to maintain order during the state of emergency. One immediate outcome was that on 21 April 1988, the Chairman of the Economic and Social Council signed a decree 'relieving a certain journalist of his responsibilities as press attaché'.

Sud Hebdo had refused to lower the standard of free speech during a state of emergency when other papers had found it prudent to tread more cautiously. Its stance had brought it into a confrontation with an energetic sector of the ruling party. *Combat pour le Socialisme* turned out to be an enthusiastic and influential point organ for the repressive machinery of the State. First, it warned the radio journalist Demba Ndiaye about his articles in the *Devoir*. Mame Less Dia wrote a scorching defence of Demba Ndiaye in the columns of the same *Devoir*. But *Combat pour le Socialisme* did not wait long to hit back at Demba Ndiaye. Pouncing on an article of his in the *Devoir* of October 1988, the ORTS management sacked him.

In another instance, two weeks after *Sud Hebdo* No. 24 came out with an article by Kader Boye asserting that the country's institutions were in a state of crisis, the *Soleil* on 14 January 1988 published a rebuttal by Jacques Mariel Nzouankeu stating the official viewpoint: 'No, our colleague, Professor Kader Boye, is quite wrong to argue that our institutions are in a state of crisis'. Serigne Diop also provided a supporting refutation. In the 17 November 1988 issue of *Sud Hebdo*, Kader Boye answered both men, thus signalling a break in the debate which apparently raised certain scruples in the highest circles of the State. The government was fast losing credibility because of the exaggerated toadying typical of the State media. Frustrated readers were therefore turning towards the so-called independent press, better able to deliver information they could trust. It was in this atmosphere that the CESTI and the Friedrich Ebert Foundation organized a seminar on 'The Media in Senegal', on 29 and 30 August.

The seminar was planned to give the regime's communications policy a fresh and solid base. With much media hype it was organized by Babacar Siné, then Director of the CESTI and the regime's backroom media czar. Participants came from all media, including central organs of political parties. As they took turns spelling out criticisms and claims, Babacar Siné listened with a Buddha's impassivity. The seminar ended with a set of generous resolutions calling for the full, unfettered development of the Senegalese press. A digest of SYNPICS claims, suggestions from press publishers, and even proposals from political organizations, the report was submitted to the President of the Republic, who on Wednesday 11 January accorded an audience to seminar delegates at which various media bosses were also present.

On the eve of this audience, the Ministerial Council devoted a considerable part of its deliberations to press matters. In particular, according to a report in *Le Soleil* of 12 January 1989, it strongly deplored 'the tendency of part of the press to dabble in defamation, disinformation, moral subversion of the nation and the casting of discredit on republican institutions'. It also asked the Ministers involved 'to ensure the strict application of laws and regulations governing the press, especially those related to punishments for excesses and infractions'.

In support of these directives, *Le Soleil's* CEO, Alioune Dramé, wrote an op-ed piece in the national daily that same day entitled 'Ringing the Alarm'. To the *Sud Hebdo* editorial board it sounded more like bloodhounds baying at the kill. Their paper was the target. After all, no less a person than the President of the Republic had, during an audience that same hectic day, taken time to condemn 'certain pseudo-scholarly articles', a transparent reference to the series by Kader Boye. So the editorial board took up the challenge in issue No. 36 of 19 January 1989, in an editorial against 'government threats against the press'. There followed a lively exchange in *Le Soleil* of 25 January and *Sud Hebdo* of 2 February 1989. As public insults mounted in intensity, the State saw the escalation as potentially damaging, especially since the opposition journal *Sopi* was becoming a source of serious anxiety. Various initiatives were therefore taken to bring about a cease-fire.

Abdoulaye Wade, Secretary-General of the PDS, had been out of the country. On his return, *Sopi,* which subtitled itself 'the paper for change', published a front page article under the headline: 'Presidential Elections: The Real Results'. The gist: Abdoulaye Wade had won. For publishing that issue, Number 52 of *Sopi,* the Publishing Director, Cheikh Khoureissy Bâ, was jailed for six months. From that point on, the State had its sights trained on *Sopi*. Injunctions and trials followed in thick succession as top opposition and government leaders fought it out. At stake was one key demand: the dismissal from the government of the almighty Secretary-General in the President's Office, Jean Collin. As the man celebrated his 60th birthday in September 1989, *Sopi's* attacks turned more sarcastic while the government tightened the screws on the opposition organ. In October, a member of the *Sopi* editorial board, Madior Sokhna Ndiaye, was jailed in a murky affair in which he was accused of publishing a letter from a reader who had used someone else's name. In the ensuing crisis, the attitude of the NIS printers had little to do with commercial norms, as survivors from *Sopi* who created the journal *Le Témoin* well remember:

> *It was with genuine pleasure that Tidiane Daly Ndiaye admitted that during his term as Director of the Nouvelles Imprimeries du Sénégal, he went out of his way to give* Sopi *and* Le Cafard Libéré *a tough time, adding that indeed,* Sopi *had still to recover from its problems*'[47].

As 1989 ended, the atmosphere was dominated by the legal tussle between the State and *Sopi*. The eventful months of February, March and April gone, the independent press dropped back into the groove of ordinary work, the routine of accounting and management details. In the atmosphere of detente, the SYNPICS hosted the Steering Committee seminar of the West African Journalists' Union on 18 December. Its contacts with the authorities had grown more cordial, so all seminar proceedings were chaired by the Minister of Communications. Still, the so-called independent press did not long remain bogged down in weekly routines. On 1 April 1990, the NIS raised printing costs by 34%. At their press conference the following day, various publishers were bitter and disappointed. Sidy Lamine Niasse spoke for them when he said: 'We are now up against the real obstacles in the way of journalism. As far as our ability to do our work goes, we've been pushed against the ropes. Any day now, we could fold'. (Press conference of publishers of the so-called independent press, Monday 2 April).

In spite of these difficulties, one week after the hike in printing costs another journal joined the Senegalese press. *Le Témoin*, which began publication on 10 April, apparently got some behind-the-scenes support from individuals close to the regime, delighted to see that Ousmane Ngom, second in command in the Senegalese Democratic Party and publisher of *Sopi*, was embroiled in quarrels with his staff. One thing is clear: after the team that had started it left, *Sopi* never again attained its peak print run of 35,000. Its influence dwindled accordingly.

On 19 April, the new Minister of Communication, Moustapha Kâ, toured the offices of the NIS, *Le Soleil*, the Senegalese Press Agency, the *Politicien*, the *Cafard Libéré*, *Wal Fadjri* and *Sud Hebdo*. Such courteous solicitude did not mean that future prospects for the independent press were any clearer. In August the NIS was taken over by the French Hersant group. Its former Senegalese Director, Tidiane Daly Ndiaye, appointed Director of the ORTS, was replaced by one Madame Simonet, as French as they come. Thus one of the few rotary presses in West Africa came under foreign control. The publisher of *Sud Hebdo* had cause to muse out loud: 'We should not be surprised if tomorrow the new owners, as part of some adjustment programme, impose even more draconian conditions on the national press, forcing it to fold for lack of resources'. (*Sud Hebdo* 116, 3 August 1990)[48].

In the resulting fluid situation, plans by the Hersant group to bring out an evening paper were postponed. The Minister of Communication explained that care should be taken to ensure that the new paper did not threaten the circulation of *Le Soleil*. The government, never one to let such inconsistencies bother it, was dithering about approving a move that, for the first time since independence, would have broken the State monopoly over the daily press. It would be pure illusion to suppose that the regime's hesitations had anything to do with a desire to preserve the country's independence and national sovereignty. For at the time professionals in the communications sector were discussing the Hersant project, foreign interests had already moved into the audio-visual media. On FM radio, Radio France International was already broadcasting 18 hours daily in the 92 metre band; the ORTS broadcasts for only six hours daily on FM.

FM 92 launched its programmes with an interview in which the President of the Republic expressed a determination:

> to democratize and strengthen the information system by pluralizing and diversifying it...In any case, we live in an open world environment. Ours is the age of satellite communication. Clearly, no country can protect itself from that environment, and such protection would in any case not be a good idea. I think we can benefit from this diversification of our media environment. The quality of our output will improve not only because of your presence, but also because the Senegalese media will have to adapt to it[49].

This rosy vision of future prospects looks less hopeful in the light of certain constraints. Among them are a number of legal and administrative moves and regulations forming a policy framework for the communications sector: the drafting of a press code, the establishment of a High Commission on Audio-visual Media, and the creation of a Press Support Fund. Good intentions notwithstanding, uncertainties have arisen. Journalists have been tossed between the hope of seeing the new collective agreement implemented and that of being rid of the most repressive clauses in the Press Code. As for the High Commission on Audio-visual Media, all political parties are dead set against it. And the Support Fund has created more problems than it has solved. Some so-called independent journalists have gone so far as to accuse the Ministry of Communication of favouring *Sud Hebdo*, *Wal Fadjri*, *Le Cafard Libéré* and *Le Témoin*, on the grounds that those papers are to receive larger allocations than others.

The Support Fund is a State subsidy. There are those in the press, as well as some readers, who see it as an instrument the government will use to compromise the independence of the private press. The threat is real. Already, the most unlikely hustlers, drooling at the prospect of millions in State subsidies, are crawling into the press sector. New papers are emerging at mind-boggling speed. And the ministry in charge of the sector is all the less sure of its control because certain groups, including the SYNPICS and some parts of the independent press suggest that the Ministry of Communication be abolished, as in the United States. The suggestion ignores the fact that for the first time in the history of Senegal, the Minister is a fellow journalist, Moctar Kébé.

In the 30 years since independence, the Senegalese press has developed at a pace matching the country's. In this environment, more than anywhere else, the trend towards political and economic liberalization seems to have changed basic realities. If progress in media development over the past several years proves irreversible, the forward drive will mark an intense phase in our progress towards modernity. Along the route, stiff challenges may provoke occasional doubts and hesitations, but of one fact there is no doubt: all minds are bent on reaching the goal.

Notes

1. *Dakar Matin*, 19 December 1962.
2. *Nomade*, Special issue on Cheikh Anta Diop, p. 195.
3. *Dakar Matin*, 12 September 1963.
4. Abdoulaye Ly, 'Pour les candidats, le 15 nov. 1963', in 'Manifeste des candidats de la liste Démocratie et unité sénégalaise patronnée par le PRA-Sénégal'.
5. *Sénégal d'Aujourd'hui*, 8 May 1964. p. 10.
6. *Ibid.*
7. *Le Soleil*, Special issue, 4 April 1975.
8. Central Strike Committee, 'Instruction No. 2', Dakar, 3 June 1968.
9. Quoted by Paye (1978: 11).
10. *Le Soleil*, 7 December 1971.
11. *Ibid.*, 11 September 1970.
12. *Lettre Fermée*, No. 10, October 1972.
13. *Le Soleil*, 1 March 1971.
14. *Ibid.*, 27-28 February 1971.
15. *Ibid.*, 23 April 1971.
16. *Ibid.*, 11 June 1971.
17. *Ibid.*, 1 August 1986.
18. *Ibid.*, 7 March 1973.
19. *Ibid.*, 8 June 1974.
20. *Ibid.*, 10 June 1974.
21. *Ibid.*, Special issue, 4 April 1975.
22. Quoted in *Le Soleil*, 3 January 1975.
23. *Le Soleil*, 29 January 1975.
24. *Ibid.*, 15 March 1975.
25. *Ibid.*, 5 November 1975.
26. *Ibid.*, 6 November 1975.
27. *Ibid.*, 5 December 1975.
28. *Ibid.*, 25 November 1975.
29. *Ibid.*, 10 December 1975.
30. *Ibid.*, 24-25 December 1975.
31. *Ibid.*, 13 October 1977
32. *Ibid.*
33. *Ibid.*, 3 November 1977.
34. *Ibid.*, 22 December 1977.
35. *Le Soleil*, 12 and 14 November 1977.
36. *Ibid.*, 3 August 1977.
37. President Senghor's farewell address, 31 December 1980.
38. *Le Soleil*, 9 March 1981.
39. *Ibid.*, 11 May 1981.
40. *Xarebi*, No 2. August 1983.
41. SYNPICS, *Bulletin de liaison*, May 1985. p.21.

42. Babacar Touré, 'L'aventure', in *Sud Hebdo an 1*,*Sud Hebdo*, p.1.
43. SYNPICS, *Manifeste du 1er mai 1987*.
44. *Promotion II*, No. 2, February 1983.
45. SYNPICS declaration entitled 'Liberté d'informer', 5 January 1988.
46. '*Sud Hebdo* ou la désinformation', *Combat pour le socialisme*, No. 8, p.6.
47. *Le Témoin*, No. 13, 26 September 1990.
48. *Sud Hebdo*, No. 116, 3 August 1990.
49. *Le Soleil* du 12-9-1991.

Bibliography

CESTI, (Amicale des Anciens du), 1983, 'Rapport de la commission de réflexion et de documentation', Mimeographed.

Dia, Alioune Touré, 1985, 'Le pluralisme de la presse au Sénégal', Dakar, UNESCO.

Janvier, Jacques, 1965, 'Une expérience africaine: le ministère de l'Information, la radio et la presse'.

Lo, Magatte, 1986, *L'heure du choix*. Paris, L'Harmattan.

Niang, Massamba *et al.*, 1971, 'Avis et suggestions des agents de l'Information régionale sur le projet de réforme des structures et du fonctionnement de l'information et de la presse au Sénégal', Mimeographed, Dakar.

Paye, Moussa, 1968, 'Evolution du syndicalisme au Sénégal depuis 1968', Final Year Thesis, CESTI, Mimeographed.

Sénégal (République of), 1965, Ministry of Information, Tourism and Telecommunication, 'Liste des journaux et revues paraissant au Sénégal', Mimeographed, Dakar.

11. Reform Options for the Educational System

Abdou Sylla

The 1981 General Conference on Education and Training was a first step towards the reformation of the Senegalese educational system. Yet as late as 1990, that system was still regulated by statutory guidelines laid down in Act No. 71-036 of 3 June 1971. The National Commission on Educational and Training Reform (CNREF) drafted a new set of statutory guidelines as a replacement for the 1971 Act. But so far, the 1971 Act, itself slow in the passage (it took over a decade after independence), remains the only law spelling out principles, guidelines, objectives and curricula for the educational system. As it stands, the law is riddled with problems and shortcomings. The Head of State acknowledged as much in his address to the nation on 1 January 1981. It is the perception of those shortcomings that led to a reform process that began in 1985.

Several educational experiments and instructional innovations have been tried out as part of this reform process. But all this activity has gone on in the absence of an organized legal framework and guidelines designed according to clearly defined priorities. For that reason, current educational policy in Senegal is rather incoherent. Given the large number of ongoing programmes and projects in the pipeline, it seems clear that the central need in this time of financial and economic crisis is to find ways of making the resources, structures and personnel that are still available to the educational system more cost-effective.

Meanwhile, the World Bank has taken over the bulk of funding for educational projects. Confronted with a staggering array of urgent problems while Word Bank intervention increases steadily, the State stands open to the suspicion that as far as the educational system is concerned, it has abdicated its sovereign responsibilities, and given up the planned management of educational investments and programmes. Some teachers, accusing the state of dereliction of duty, have taken to quipping that henceforth the system should be called the World Bank School System.

Such a situation throws up two queries: what lies ahead for the Senegalese educational system? What kind of school will the country develop? A look at the educational system as of 1990, with due attention to the plethora of problems and hardships it has had to face over the past decade, and the numerous protest movements and strikes that shook it in that period, resulting in the loss of an entire academic year in 1987-88, is likely to lead to the conclusion that education in Senegal has a dim future, unless basic factors causing imbalances, stresses, fault lines and malfunctioning within the system are rooted out.

Moreover, it does seem as if, faced with a truly endless array of problems, the public authorities decided back in 1988 to give up the idea of forward planning. To all intents and purposes they adopted a new credo: to let problems come as they may, and to cope with or adjust to them as far as momentarily possible, one day at a time. In such a situation any attempt to circumscribe the many problems at issue within the limits of a brief study would be unrealistic, downright impossible, in fact. What is feasible, we think, is to start with a selective analysis of basic data and key parameters, to use that analysis to delineate an accurate profile of the educational system, and then to argue that the aimless drift in which the system is caught now is a consequence of the improvisational style of policy design, and that in the long run that myopic drift[1] might plunge the Senegalese people as a whole into disaster.

The Choice of Educational Policy

In 1960, when the French-speaking African countries attained independence, most of the crowd-pulling slogans of the time were focused on the urgent need for economic and social development, the preservation and consolidation of national unity, the imperatives of nation-building, and the construction of a State strong enough to take charge of all these urgent processes. In the heat and hurry, certain sectors such as industry, agriculture, fisheries and infrastructural facilities were defined as productive. Priority attention was therefore focused on them, and they duly got the lion's share of investment resources. In the Senegalese case, one can get a clear idea of the starting priorities and initial policy preferences of the State from Chapter 2, Title I of the Eighth Economic and Social Development Plan (October 1989). That section of the Plan document presents an assessment of economic policies initiated since 1960 (see Senegal, 1989b). It shows that for at least two decades, the two main priorities of Senegalese economic policy were rural development and industrial development. From 1960 to 1975, the State was the initiator and organizer responsible for the design and implementation of all rural development activities, ranging from production through marketing to consumption.

At the time of independence, Senegal had a more substantial industrial infrastructural base than other French colonies in West Africa. But most industrial units then belonged to foreign businessmen. Quite a few were subsidiaries of multinational corporations. The State decided to enter the industrial sector and to leverage the entry of Senegalese nationals into it by setting up State corporations, acquiring shares in other corporations, and nationalizing colonial companies operating in sectors like the electricity and water supply systems considered to be vitally important to the national economy. Sizeable industrial units, industrial areas and an industrial free zone were established between 1960 and 1975.

At the end of the second development decade, such was the diversity of State operations in the economy that its portfolio covered 150 enterprises and corporations. Overall, in both the rural and industrial sectors, "the State was determined to do a lot, trusted in its capacity to achieve a lot, and did invest a lot.." (Senegal, 1989b:24). In the rural sector, the State set up a large number of extension and supervisory agencies. Its activities were remarkably coherent, multi-faceted and diverse, and their technical and economic coverage was comprehensive. In the industrial sector, the State invested directly or indirectly in a large number of projects, promulgated various Investment Codes offering a variety of advantages and exemptions, and protected local industries through a range of tariffs and quantitative measures.

From the Colonial to the National Educational System

No doubt because of this emphasis on economic priorities, but also because the so-called social sectors (education, housing and health) were not perceived as presenting urgent needs, they were accorded no particular attention in the first post-independence decade. As far as the educational system was concerned, this 'neglect' had other causes. At the time of independence in 1960, Senegal inherited a modern educational system that had been in operation for a long time, and covered the entire national territory. The various levels of that educational system were relatively well developed. By 1960, for instance, school attendance rates had reached 36%, according to a World Bank study (1988a). Senegal, after independence, tended to rest on past laurels, quite forgetting that the colonial educational system was designed for a specific purpose: to serve the interests of the colonial power[2]. At the onset of independence, then, the following crucial elements were lacking:

- An educational policy[3] presenting a clear definition of principles, aims, objectives and syllabuses, time-tables and structures, organizational charts, examination schedules, competitive examinations, certificates and degrees within the Senegalese educational system;
- An educational development plan precisely defining short, medium and long term developmental phases, necessary investments, requisite school maps, classrooms and school buildings to be constructed, and teacher training programmes.

Everything was done as if the school system was not expected to develop at all. Hence the habit, at that time, of seeing the Senegalese school system as an appendage of the French school system. Every year the educational system dished out copies of French curricula and time-tables, cloned French administrative and instructional styles, imitated French examinations, and presented competitive examinations identical to those in France. From 1963 to 1965, the system saw only two significant moves. Both emanated from the 1961 Unesco Conference of Ministers of Education from independent African countries, held in Addis Ababa, which adopted a resolution calling for universal primary education in Africa.

The first move was the drafting and implementation of a large-scale school construction programme that produced general secondary schools in all regional and district capitals. The second involved the recruitment of young candidates with only one to three years of secondary education supplemented by short training courses lasting two to three months, organized in the long vacation periods. These became the generation of pupil teachers. The two moves combined to boost intake capacity in the middle reaches of the educational system, which meant a rise in the school population at that level. Simultaneously, there was a remarkable rise in overall school attendance levels from 1960 to 1970.

The 1971 Reform

In the midst of all this activity, some key aspects of the educational system were overlooked or neglected outright: aims and objectives, structures and methods, teacher training, refresher courses, etc. Not surprisingly, the first demand of the May and June protest movements in 1968 and 1969 was that the school system and its curricula should be reformed to reflect national and African realities[4]. But the moment they were faced with the imperative of implementing the necessary reforms, the Senegalese authorities discovered, as if by magic, a series of obstacles blocking the development of our educational system[5]:

- The record and achievements of the educational system did not match the effort made to support it. One quarter of the national budget went into education, training and culture. Yet at the start of the implementation period of the Third Social and Economic Development Plan, fewer than one-third of children of school-going age were in primary school.
- There were deep disparities from region to region. In the Cap Vert region, for instance, school attendance rates were almost 60%; but in Tambacounda and Diourbel regions it was lower than 15%.

- The number of repeaters was becoming alarming; the overall rate stood at 17%, and in the last two years of the primary cycle it was as high as 40%.

Primary school enrolment had grown steadily since 1958, practically doubling overall. Yet the percentage of pupils passing the secondary school entrance examination had fallen constantly, from 39.2% in 1961 to 17% in 1967. If the two trends continued, thousands of young persons would be jettisoned onto the streets. Furthermore, the rise in enrollments was not matched by increases in educational facilities. Classrooms had therefore become overcrowded, working conditions had deteriorated, and textbooks and instructional equipment were in short supply.

Progress in the educational system had not kept pace with profound social and political changes since independence. The system's aims were therefore no longer attuned to such new requirements of the development process as suitability, efficiency, profitability, social welfare and individual advancement. To the list of official reasons for the deteriorating situation, schoolteachers added the following: the reduction of the teaching vocation to a low-status occupation, with the attendant loss of prestige; the degradation of material, social, psychological and other working conditions; inadequate professional training, and the shake-up in administrative and academic hierarchies.

The educational system, in short, had stalled, blocking the smooth development of society. Such were the circumstances under which the May-June upheavals broke out. The crisis led to the design of a major reform process by technicians of the Research and Planning Board (DRP) working behind closed doors[6], yielding in turn the National Educational Orientation Act, No. 71-036 of 3 June 1971.

According to the principles of this Act (Title 1, Article 1), the reformed educational system was to help raise the cultural standards of the majority of the national population, boost national income, abolish inequalities left over from past times, and promote richer inputs of African culture into the pool of universal civilization. In effect, the new educational system was expected to do more to ensure the country's economic growth and improve returns on investment within the limits of budgetary constraints, through the more rational organization of educational and training expenditure. In future, it would have to train youths useful to the nation, ready to fit smoothly into various sectors of national life, conscious of African cultural values, and capable of contributing to scientific and technological advancement. Firmly rooted in local realities, they would nevertheless be receptive to foreign influences and the contributions of other peoples, in keeping with the twin inspirational guidelines of our entire educational process: *l'enracinement* and *l'ouverture*.

In pursuit of these goals, Title 2, Article 6 stipulated that curriculum content would have to give priority to the Senegalese natural and social environment, the immediate surroundings of the population. The content of disciplines such as history, geography, the natural sciences and French would therefore have to be Africanized and Senegalized. In other words, in their teaching, the emphasis would shift to Senegalese historical realities, the African environment, African literature and, most centrally, Senegalese literature. For the aim was to enable young Senegalese to reconnect with and to understand the cultural values of the black world, an indissociable part of their cultural heritage.

L'enracinement was to be achieved through a second process: the introduction of national languages into the school system. In the long run, the supposition was that this would lead to the use of these national languages[7] as instructional media. *L'ouverture*, the second prong of the educational philosophy, would come about through the teaching of science and technology, coupled with non-African languages and cultures, all of which would be on the curriculum.

The teaching system would allocate subject matter to various levels and cycles depending on the learners' ages and the desirable level of instruction (Title 3, Articles 8-13). The entire system would comprise the following levels: nursery, elementary, middle, secondary and university. One major innovation was the creation of a practical middle school cycle. In theory, 80% to 85% of all elementary school pupils would pass through that cycle. It would be compulsory for all children not going on to study in general or technical secondary schools. The five-year cycle was designed to meet the following objectives:

a) To train progressive peasants using efficient techniques for the growing of food and industrial cash crops common in their regions; running market gardening and dairying enterprises, and maintaining orchards, thus ensuring a rich and balanced diet as well as adequate incomes for themselves;

b) To train fishermen, herders, traders, craftspersons and workers capable of using modern techniques and making their output competitive;

c) To produce well-informed mothers and fathers leading productive economic lives and capable of managing their household budgets (Article 11).

The Practical Middle School experiment was tried out in various centres throughout the national territory for over ten years. But it drew tremendous flak from teachers and parents alike. No attempt was made to extend it, and in the end it was abandoned.

The new educational system was supposed to use active teaching methods designed to train children to become resourceful learners instead of making them receptacles apt to parrot encyclopaedic quantities of rote data, as in the old school system.

We can sum up the main features of the reformed school system as follows (Title 1, Articles 2-5): it would tend to raise the cultural standards of the population; to train free men and women able to create conditions ensuring their own fulfillment in all respects; to advance scientific and technical knowledge, and to devise effective solutions to national development problems. It would be democratic in the sense that it would recognize the right of everyone to education and training, and also because, being free of charge, it would provide equal educational opportunities for all children. By that token it would also be a mass educational system. It would be secular, but would also encourage and support all private individual or collective initiatives contributing to the achievement of its objectives. Its prime vocation being to ensure an awareness of firm roots *(l'enracinement)*, it would be an African educational system. But since *l'enracinement* had a twin aspect, *l'ouverture*, the system would simultaneously incorporate universal values and civilization. Lastly, it would be a permanent educational system.

The General Conference on Education and Training (EGEF) and the National Commission on Educational and Training Reform (CNREF)

Various sources agree that the Orientation Act was, generally speaking, positive. Strictly and correctly enforced, so goes the judgment, it would have made the Senegalese school system a worthy national educational establishment. Unfortunately, it had some shortcomings and problems, a fact in the end admitted by the highest authorities in the land. It was after a tumultuous academic year, 1979-80, in which the teachers' union, SUDES[8], launched a strike, the culmination of several years of struggle waged by various teachers' trade unions[9], that the authorities reached the critical conclusion that our educational system was ill suited to the needs of the country. One upshot was the convening of a General Conference on Education and Training.

Over 70% of the country's teachers were involved in the strike. It marked the beginning of a full-scale rift between the SUDES and the government, and played a decisive part in the unfolding crisis of the educational system. For the government responded with a range of punitive measures, transferring targeted teachers from their bases, withholding salaries from others, sacking yet others[10]. The crisis aroused national opinion, leading to calls from religious leaders, dignitaries, political parties and ordinary citizens for dialogue and moderation. Meanwhile, the Senegalese nation entered a time of severe economic problems that resulted in the design and implementation, starting from 1979, of an economic and financial recovery plan. Other austerity programmes and measures followed: a New Agricultural Policy (1984), a New Industrial Policy (1985), then a Structural Adjustment Programme (1988).

The year 1980 was particularly tumultuous. The school system was in a state of crisis, as was the social system, the economy, and the State. In the face of so many threatening situations on all fronts, the only viable option seemed to be a change of leadership at the top of the State structure. In the end that change was accomplished in a dialectical process based on a multiplicity of varied contradictions. The result was the replacement, on 31 December 1980, of Léopold S. Senghor by Abdou Diouf. The first decision taken by the new President, announced in his televised address to the nation, was to convene a General Conference on Education and Training (EGEF). The scheduled date was 28 January 1981. (Sylla, 1983, 1987).

The four-day conference was intended to conceive and define a new educational system, national and Senegalese in character, democratic and popular in orientation, secular in its inspiration but still sensitive to local socio-cultural realities, especially the religious factor. The conference did produce consensual findings and recommendations[11], and the Minister of National Education, in his closing speech, summed up the satisfaction of all participants:

The Senegalese educational system, in the form now emerging, is truly a product of the national will, not the result of a speculatory exercise involving a small circle of specialists, though, of course, specialists helped design it.... I would like to say how impressed we were with the detailed nature of the discussions, the warmth of commitment to the ideas expressed, the sincere, frank and loyal attitudes of all involved.... That is what I call the spirit of the General Conference, typified by a concerted, loyal and open-minded determination to succeed in a common search for feasible solutions. For this we have cause to be grateful. Thanks to your efforts, this spirit of sincere cooperation, a spirit generous enough to acknowledge differences, prevailed from start to finish of our deliberations. The Government has taken note of all proposals here advanced. It confirms the recognition that teaching is a special function, and re-emphasizes the imperative need to reassert its value. I hereby make a solemn pledge to you. Nothing humanly possible will be left undone in our endeavour to ensure that the teaching profession regains its dignity and its prestige.

In February 1981, the government followed up these promises made by the Minister of National Education by announcing its determination to implement 'with loyal intelligence'[12] the recommendations of the General Conference. Next, the government created the National Commission on Educational and Training Reform (CNREF), with a mandate 'to explore the findings, proposals and recommendations of the General Conference on Education as approved by the Government, with a view to their practical implementation'[13].

For four years the CNREF commissioners pored over the findings of the General Conference, touching up details where necessary, considering practical conditions and modalities for the implementation of a new educational system designed to be radically different from the old system both in its basic features and in its innovative aspects. There were specific implications: the old educational system was elitist, selective, exclusive; the new system would have to be democratic, inclusive and mass-oriented. The old system was outer-directed and derivative, an appendage to the French system; the new system was expected to be inner-directed, national and African[14] in its originality.

As a *national* institution, the educational system would have to be rooted in the national and cultural realities of Senegal and Africa; it would be based on a resolute policy for the training and advancement of national personnel; it would contribute to endogenous national development, and raise the level of awareness of national unity (Title 1, Articles 4 and 5, Orientation Bill). As a *democratic* institution, the educational system would have to provide equal educational opportunities for all. It would therefore be universal, compulsory and free of charge, catering to all school-age children with no discrimination whatsoever. All children from 3 to 16 years old would be entitled to compulsory and free education. The system would encourage and provide facilities for continuing education (Articles 1,3 and 5). As a *popular* institution, the educational system would make a clean break with past practices characterized by exclusive selection. It would express and reflect the people's cultural needs, offer appropriate solutions and promote the people's cultural, scientific, technological, moral and spiritual advancement, while remaining open to life in the surrounding environment (Articles 3 and 5).

As a *secular* institution, the new educational system would enshrine respect for the citizens' freedom of thought. But it would also incorporate specific aspects of our socio-cultural realities, especially the religious dimension (Title 1, Article 2). Its various structures, levels and cycles would dovetail harmoniously into each other (cf. the new organizational chart; Title 2, Articles 6-10). The new educational system would be a comprehensive one. It would provide education in the orthodox mode, as well as in a continuing process. And it would provide literacy training in informal facilities linked with its formal structures (Title 3, Articles 11-17).

A Code of Professional Ethics would be drawn up, along with a set of Statutory Guidelines defining and guaranteeing teachers' rights and duties and ensuring the obligatory and permanent maintenance of the proper status of the teaching profession (Titles 4 and 5, Articles 18-25). A policy for the retrenchment of expatriate personnel and adequate training for Senegalese nationals would guarantee the Africanization of staff positions and the effective assumption of responsibilities by African personnel. A permanent determination to maintain its independence would be a feature of the new educational system. At the same time, it would endeavour to remain in tune with our realities and, in its polytechnical orientation, ensure permanent links between education and production.

If the new educational system was going to be independent, it would necessarily have to be underwritten by a National Educational and Training Fund, and both education and training would cease to be considered the exclusive preserve of the State. The new system would provide special education for the physically and mentally handicapped, ending their isolation from the educational mainstream. Elitist examination barriers would be abolished. In their place, an original, flexible system of academic and vocational guidance would be instituted.

Once implemented, in short, this new educational system would signal a radical, qualitative break with past practices, a revolution, no less, in Senegal's educational system as well as in society as a whole. It looked good on paper but the question remained: was it feasible? What was the government's real attitude? At a press conference on Friday 18 January 1985, the Minister of National Education answered the last question by separating those recommendations the government considered acceptable from those it could not accept.

Acceptable Recommendations[15]

The government considered acceptable the following recommendations:

a) The principle of a national, democratic and popular educational system;

b) The incorporation of informal structures into the formal educational system, as democratic enhancements and instruments of cultural, economic and social development;

c) The introduction of special educational facilities for the handicapped, as an integral part of the overall system;

d) The idea of making cost-effective use of existing facilities by creating multi-grade classes and running double-shift classes;

e) The reorganization of administrative structures, university institutions, scientific and technical research facilities, in such a way as to draw maximum advantage from available resources;

f) The Code of Professional Ethics and all personnel-related proposals intended to reassert in significant ways the value of the teaching profession and to ensure a high-quality educational and training system;

g) The overall structural organization of the system based on a three-cycle organizational chart comprising a basic, a general and vocational secondary, and a higher educational cycle;

h) The integration of the school system into the environment, in line with a multi-faceted educational and training approach;

i) The introduction of religious education, provided the secular character of the system as a whole was respected, and the representation of multiple religions within the State acknowledged.

j) The introduction and promotion of national languages;

k) Recognition of the importance of the Arabic language, and its encouragement;

l) The creation of a special Education Fund.

The Minister took care to point out, however, that these proposals were acceptable only within a rationally programmed process. No one should therefore be surprised if, in certain particulars, the educational reform process seemed in the initial stages to proceed with excessive caution, from certain points of view.

Unacceptable Recommendations

The government rejected the following recommendations:

a) The statutory separation of teaching staff from the civil service establishment;

b) Cumulative increases in housing, teaching and in-service allowances;

c) The abolition of private educational establishments;

d) The reopening of boarding facilities at educational institutions;

e) The dichotomy, on the organizational chart, between the general and technical branches of the secondary school cycle;

f) The immediate abolition of competitive and other examinations.

The press conference stimulated considerable comment. Most questions concerned the kind of New Educational System the government wanted to establish, the reassertion of the status of the teaching profession, the resources available to the new system, etc. Some wondered whether the package of recommendations deemed acceptable by the government would really suffice to institute the reform process as projected by the General Conference on Education and Training and by the CNREF. How could the new educational system be national, democratic and popular as long as private institutions flourished, and elitist selection processes, competitions, examinations, etc. were maintained? How would it be possible to reconcile the goal of a national, democratic and popular educational system based on socialist principles with a capitalistic economy and a social structure characterized by constantly unfolding classes and class struggles?

How, moreover, would it be possible to reassert the status of the teaching profession if, among the measures adopted by the government, none was calculated to produce any significant financial improvement in the living conditions of teaching staff? What did the special status of teachers mean if in statutory terms they were denied terms separate from the civil service as a whole, and if their claims for cumulative increases in housing, teaching and in-service allowances were turned down?[16] According to the Minister, it would cost hundreds of billions of francs CFA to establish and run the new educational system. Where would such resources, particularly heavy in the area of funding, come from if the population were to be exempt from any contribution or participation, if recurrent expenditure incurred by the National Education Fund was to be met principally through State subsidies, and if, given the ongoing economic crisis, it was no longer possible to increase State budget allocations for educational and training facilities?

Whatever criticisms might be levelled at the government, it must be admitted that despite the crisis and its attendant shortages, budgetary allocations for national education remained the highest. In the 1990/91 financial year, the allocation reached FCFA 60,446,802,000. That was double the armed forces allocation, next in size with FCFA 30,452,960,000[17]. Large as the national education budget may be, the fundamental problem facing the educational system is a problem of resources. That problem can only be solved, as Barber Conable pointed out, by 'an increase in resource flows' (World Bank, 1988a: VI). With population growth at high and rapidly rising levels (3.2% according to the World Bank), the country's school-age population and actual school enrolment keep going up. Educational needs rise just as steadily, while in all cycles enrolment levels are far higher than can be reasonably accommodated with the existing infrastructural, equipment and personnel base.

That is why all solutions imagined and all projects initiated since 1985 seem to have focused on one problem: the gap between educational needs and available resources. We shall be looking at various proposed solutions and projects, but before that we need first to examine the existing situation, to survey the material condition of the Senegalese school system, and to assess its needs.

When Senegal attained independence, the State did not define a comprehensive and coherent educational policy covering all aspects of the educational process. The General Conference on Education and Training, through its proceedings, as well as the CNREF, which designed a basic framework for the organization of educational aims, an organizational chart and implementational structures, resources and personnel, provided further opportunities for the design of an overarching educational policy. The State let that opportunity also slip. The Orientation Bill, designed to serve as the key statutory text in the school system, was drawn up by the CNREF, but did not get promulgated as a legally binding Act. Iba Der Thiam, who served as Minister of National Education from 1983 to 1988, explains why:

> *Jean Collin, the former Principal Secretary in the President's Office, considered the New School System a pipe dream. He therefore shelved the motion for the Orientation Bill. He was against the promotion of national languages, and for that reason he systematically sabotaged my programme (Le Témoin,* 31 July 1990. p.2).

The Orientation Bill referred to was approved by the Ministerial Council on Tuesday 23 October 1990 and voted into law by the National Assembly on 30 January 1991. The decree establishing the CNREF was definitely promulgated. Once that body had submitted its findings, the Head of State decided to retain its Executive Committee and Secretariat as official national structures. Since then, however, the structure has been given nothing to do. As for the General Conference on Education and Training, as instituted by decree, it was supposed to meet every four years. Had that rule been followed, there would have been a second General Conference in 1985, a third in 1989. In fact, though, there has so far been only the one session held in 1981. And there is, indeed, a National Commission for the Study, Coordination and Monitoring of General Conference programmes. From time to time it actually meets. But what can it do in a situation where the CNREF and the General Conference are both inoperative, and where there is no statutory programme to be studied, coordinated or monitored? In the void left by these serious shortcomings, the Senegalese educational system can only drift.

The Current Condition of the Educational System

We shall use the Orientation Act of 1971 as a starting point for an assessment of the current condition of the Senegalese educational system. Our evaluation, needless to say, will take into consideration the development of all factors and parameters at work in this educational system from 1970 to 1990.

Preschool Education

Preschool education was introduced into Senegal by Christian nuns running various religious establishments (Notre-Dame, Saint Joseph's, Saint Theresa's, Saint Peter's, etc.). It remained a private sector activity until some time after independence. In 1975, even though the Orientation Act was theoretically in force, and the school reform programme supposedly in the implementational phase, practically all preschool institutions were still Christian missionary establishments under religious and private management. Furthermore, most such institutions were located in the national capital, Dakar, where they were concentrated in middle class residential areas.

According to Title 3, Articles 8 and 9 of the Orientation Act, preschool education was officially the first level of the educational system as from 1971. In the words of Article 9, preschool education, using appropriate teaching methods, prepared children below elementary school age for entry into the primary school system. Yet it was only in 1977 that the State created its own kindergartens in the regional capitals. They comprised a three-year cycle divided into three sections to cater for children aged three and above. Kindergartens were run by preschool teachers of both genders trained at a National Preschool Teacher Training College (ENEP). The College, established in the town of Louga in 1977, took in candidates from two qualifying categories: those with O-Level equivalent + 4 years, and those with A-Level equivalent qualifications + 1 year. Preschool educational inspectors and secondary school teachers trained at the Advanced Teacher Training College in Dakar were in charge of supervising and monitoring the work of kindergarten teachers.

As stipulated in Article 9, cited earlier, the sole purpose of the preschool system is to prepare children for the school system, using such interactive methods as drawing, graphics and painting. There is no provision for examinations or tests. After three years, kindergarten children may enter the regular school system, provided there are vacancies.

In comparison with other cycles and levels of the educational system, preschool education is still embryonic. Preschool establishments exist only in the urban centres, and even there it is only children from middle class and bourgeois families who get enrolled. A DERP/MEN document gives a good idea of changing enrolment patterns at this level of the educational system over the past decade (see Table 1).

Table 1 shows that while the public sector has made visible progress, preschool education is still dominated by the private sector, with 63.7% of enrolment. Part of the reason is that so far, the State is not obliged to provide formal education for children until they are 6-7 years old. At that age, children enter the primary school cycle, the focus of attention for both the colonial regime and its successor, the State of Senegal. At the moment, the public preschool system faces a range of problems likely in the long term to compromise its development. These include:

a) A split between public preschool institutions which use the national languages as instructional media, and their private counterparts, which use French;

Table 1: Preschool Enrolment Figures: 1978-1979 - 1987-1988

	1978/79	79/80	80/81	81/82	82/83	83/84	84/85	85/86	86/87	87/88
Public	437	1103	1656	2389	2897	3631	4546	5543	6088	6688
Private	5179	5016	6789	6696	6227	6009	6169	7221	7072	7814
Total	5616	6119	8445	9085	9124	9640	10715	12764	13160	14502

Source: Senegal, 1989b.

b) Inadequate and insufficient practical and theoretical training for preschool teachers, coupled with insufficient in-service monitoring;

c) The widespread practice of inflicting on children teachers who do not speak their language;

d) The lack, in the case of some teachers, of training in linguistics;

e) An absence of linkages between the linguistic content of ENEP courses and the practical demands of classroom work;

f) The absence of kindergartens in rural zones. This raises questions about the principle of the democratization of the educational system, supposed to ensure equal educational opportunities for all children. For if, as Article 9 of the Orientation Act stipulates, the role of the preschool system is to prepare children for the educational system through the use of appropriate interactive techniques such as graphics, painting, singing, writing, reading and arithmetic, then children from the urban areas, given greater access to preschool education, are privileged as compared with rural children.

Elementary School

The elementary school system is the second step up the educational pyramid. It is the oldest cycle and the most developed. It covers the entire national territory, with classes in the remotest villages. Title 3, Article 10 of the Orientation Act defines the purpose of elementary education as follows:

a) To stimulate the minds of children through classroom exercises in order to enhance the discovery, development and fulfillment of their aptitudes and potential;

b) To ensure the physical, intellectual and moral training of children in such a way as to arouse their sense of initiative and critical thinking;

c) To enable children to learn basic skills and aptitudes indispensable for their subsequent education;

d) To rehabilitate manual work as a key to the development of intelligence and as a basis for the future integration of children within the economic and socio-cultural environment, thanks to close linkages between school life and social life in general.

Education at this level emphasizes adaptation to the environment. Its curricula therefore give priority to mathematics, language and the environment. School establishments might be of the traditional type, or consist of new structures. The cycle lasts six years, one per class. The schools, variously called elementary or primary, are run by teachers and assistant teachers. Each school is under a headteacher, normally a senior teacher. Elementary school teachers are trained at regional teacher training colleges and vocational training centres, by elementary school inspectors and secondary school teachers, with inspectors in charge of instructional supervision and administrative management.

The elementary school cycle developed by leaps and bounds during the first decade after independence. Mental attitudes in general were changing. Among the population the demand for education was intense, universal education had become an official imperative, and the authorities were putting in a great deal of work in the sector. School enrolment tripled between 1960 and 1975. Still, in the development of this cycle, there were imbalances between geographical areas in the number of classrooms and schools as well as in enrolment figures:

a) The Cap-Vert region alone possesses nearly one-third of all classrooms in the entire country (2039/6893). Enrolment there is more than a third the national total (36.4%);

b) Three regions, (Cap-Vert, Casamance and Sine-Saloum) have over 4635 classes, more than double the total in the remaining four regions, even though the latter have a larger total population and are geographically bigger.

There are therefore discrepancies in school attendance rates and educational coverage.

At the end of the sixth year of elementary schooling, there are two examinations, a school-leaving examination resulting in the award of a Primary School Leaving Certificate (CEPE), and a competitive common entrance examination leading to the secondary school cycle. Table 2 shows changing patterns of results in these examinations from 1968 to 1975.

Table 2: General and Competitive Examination Results: 1968 to 1975

Year	1968	69	70	71	72	73	74	75
CEPE*								
Candidates	36713	39315	39455	35961	-	38800	39700	41631
Passes	15323	17622	21898	21031	-	15442	15800	16276
Percentage	42	45	55	58	-	39.8	39.8	39.1
2nd School Entrance								
Candidates	44749	41575	42984	44315	43062	43724	44200	45610
Passes	8574	7492	7463	7778	7677	7878	8884	8994
Percentage	19	18	17	17	18	18	20.1	19.7

Source: Sylla, 1987:52.   * Elementary/Primary School Leaving Certificate

As the Table 2 shows, for the secondary school entrance examination, the pass percentage remained low and constant over the years, ranging between 17% and 20%. These figures are an accurate reflection of the elitist nature of the school system. The fact is that access to secondary schools depends on the number of places available, and it is the government that determines this number every year. Since 1975 there has been no significant change in these percentage figures. If anything, the success rate has fallen. For instance, in the 1988-1989 school year, out of 111,415 candidates, only 16,945 passed, meaning a success rate of 15.2% (Senegal, 1989b). Out of the 16,945 successful candidates, between 4,000 and 5,000 would go to private secondary schools; the remaining 10,000 to 11,000 or so would enter the public secondary school system. They would be entitled to fee-free education and free materials and books, but only theoretically. In practice, what they actually got would depend on what the State could afford.

Out of the 95,000 failures, about 35% would repeat the final year of the elementary cycle, 35% being the recorded national repeater rate for that class. A total of 10% would enroll in private secondary schools. The remaining 55% would simply drop out of the educational process, their parents being unable to pay the cost of further schooling. At the end of the second tier in the educational pyramid, then, existing social inequalities are maintained and reinforced.

From 1968 to 1975, the percentage of passes registered at the school leaving examination (CEPE) increased remarkably. The reason was that examination standards were lowered, and questions became much easier than before. Reacting to the devalued standard, many pupils from well-to-do families no longer bother to take this examination.

Anyone looking at elementary school enrolment levels over the period from 1977-1978 to 1987-1988 without correlating them to corresponding population statistics for the age group from 7 to 12 years old might suppose there has been a steady rise in percentage intake figures over the years. But as Table 3 shows, that is not the case. Instead, the rapid growth of the school-age population has intensified the demand for schooling.

As far as infrastructural facilities and enrollment levels are concerned, this Table shows the situation of the elementary educational cycle as of 1986-87.

In correlation with preceding tables, Table 4 indicates a series of significant changes between 1974-75 and 1986-87. Over this period, enrolment doubled from 308,526 to 610,946. The number of classes, however, did not increase accordingly. In 1974-75 there were 6,893; by 1986-87, the number had increased, but only to 10,836. The overall school attendance rate rose from 30.6% to 54.6%. The number of pupils per class rose from an average of 46 in 1974-75 to 56 in 1986-87. Meanwhile, enormous discrepancies remain between the urban and rural zones. Overall school attendance rates are twice as high in urban zones (86.8%) as in the rural areas (34.7%) The number of pupils per class is much higher (66) in the urban areas than in the rural zones (46). In sum, the demand for education is much higher in the urban areas.

Table 3: School-Age Population, School Enrolment Figures and Attendance rates 1977-1978 to 1987-1988

	1977/78	1981/82	1983/84	1984/85	1985/86	1986/87	1987/88
Population	847800	958500	1019050	1052050	1085400	1119800	1154200
Enrolment	346373	452679	533394	567059	583890	610946	642063
Attendance rate (%)	40,9	47,2	52,3	53,9	53,8	54,6	55,6

Source: Senegal, 1989b

Table 4: Situation of the Elementary Educational Cycle as of 1986-87

	Total	Urban zones	Rural zones
Number of schools	2.373	637	1.736
Number of classes	10.836	5.653	5.183
Number of pupils	610.946	371.787	239.159
Pupils per class	56	66	46
Overall school attendance rate (7-12 year-olds)	54.6%	86.8%	34.7%
Average annual rate of increase, 1981-82 to 1986-87	+ 6.2%	+ 4.2%	+9.8%

Note: Generally, schools in the rural areas tend to be small, just two or three classes on the average. Many do not cover the complete elementary cycle.
Source: Senegal, 1989b.

To sum up, the elementary school system currently shows the following typical features:

a) Too many pupils, leading to overcrowded classrooms, especially in the urban areas, where classes sometimes have to accommodate as many as 80 to 100 pupils, often crammed three or four to a desk;

b) Extremely intense demand for education in the urban areas, with facilities in short supply and the State rendered impecunious by the economic crisis;

There is a terrible shortage of desks[18], sundry equipment and textbooks (the national average is 0.61 book per pupil), and schools are far too few. As part of the reform package initiated immediately after the General Conference on Education and Training, alternative solutions were tried out. A noteworthy example was the system of double-shift and multi-grade classes. We shall be discussing them in the third part of this chapter. On the whole, however, given the factors delineated above, especially the population explosion producing an average annual growth rate of 3.2%, according to World Bank figures already cited, meaning intensified demand for education without a commensurate expansion of the infrastructural base (schools, classes, equipment, etc.), conditions in the elementary and secondary school systems have become alarming. Problems, mainly material and financial, have continued to bedevil the system as a whole. As primary causes of protests, disturbances, upheavals, wildcat and unlimited strikes, they have helped to plunge the educational system into a chronic crisis.

It is certainly on account of the many problems confronting it, and the constant disturbances that have become part of its routine, that parents no longer believe the public school system capable of delivering on the promise

Table 5: Junior Secondary School Enrolment, School-Age Population and School Attendance Rate

	1977/78	1981/82	1983/84	1984/85	1985/86	1986/87	87/88
Enrolment	62.987	79.408	89.890	94.633	99.522	102.771	106.509
Population	451.550	532.300	533.750	567.050	599.300	623.450	674.700
Gross attend. rate (%)	13,9	14,9	16,1	16,4	16,6	16,5	15,8

Source: Senegal 1989b

of education. As a consequence, private kindergarten, elementary, middle and secondary school establishments have developed spectacularly. As of 1987/88, private elementary school enrolment made up 10% of the public school total, private middle enrolment was 44% of the public total, and private secondary enrollment amounted to 18% of the public secondary school total (MEN/DRP).

Junior Secondary (Middle) School

Considering its national coverage and the number of pupils and staff involved, the junior secondary or middle educational cycle is the second largest cycle after the elementary cycle. It is an urban-based system, catering to children aged 12-13 to 16-17, in establishments known as middle-level colleges (CEM), i.e., junior secondary schools. To gain access, pupils have first to pass the competitive entrance examination. They are then directed to various schools by national and regional orientation committees. Parents of unsuccessful candidates may opt to send them to private schools, provided, of course, they can afford the fees. The junior secondary system is a four-year cycle. Classes are numbered, following the French style, in reverse order: Year 1 is called the sixth form, Year 2 the fifth, Year 3 the fourth, while the final year in the cycle, Year 4, is called the third form.

Article 11 of the Orientation Act, dealing with the junior secondary cycle, defines the cycle as comprising a general stream, a technical stream and a vocational stream. It comes after the elementary cycle. It prepares students either to enter the general, technical or vocational high school cycle. Or they can enter the job market. As we noted earlier, however, the vocational stream was abandoned at the pilot stage, so the junior secondary cycle essentially is a preparation for the high school cycle (general, technical or vocational). Admission to the higher cycle depends on 4th-year junior secondary students passing the O-Level equivalent certificate examination called the *Brevet de Fin d'Etudes Moyennes* (BFEM), and getting streamed by national and regional selection committees.

Available statistics indicate that in the decade from 1977-78 to 1987-88, there were substantial advances in this cycle. Enrolment nearly doubled, from 62,987 to 107,024. However, when correlated with the school-age population at this level, the rise in enrolments looks less impressive (see Table 5).

The low school attendance rate is primarily a consequence of the low admission rate into secondary school (fewer than 20% passes). That low admission rate is in turn caused by the small number of available places in the junior secondary cycle. The cycle had the following capacities as of 1986-87: a total of 231 establishments, 123 of them public; a total of 2,146 classes, 1,424 of them public; a total of 102,771 students, 71,303 of them in public schools. Plant and facilities are so tight that even regular students have to squeeze in. Classrooms have become crowded, teaching standards have fallen. The staff has a hard time fitting large numbers of students into small schools originally planned to contain four to six classes only, but now accommodating eight to ten. Some classes have to be scheduled late in the evening, sometimes as late as 7pm.

A further serious consequence of the state of the junior secondary cycle is that pressure on the next higher cycle, the A-level equivalent cycle that in the French system comprises the second, first and *Terminale* classes, is intense. Year in, year out, under normal circumstances, large numbers of students who pass the BFEM examinations are directed upwards into this pre-university cycle. Thus, at the start of the 1989-90 school year, seeing that the number of high school establishments in the regional capitals was too small to meet the high demand from students who had finished the preceding cycle, Ministry of National Education officials tried out two solutions. First, without constructing any new classrooms, they opened new first year high school classes in the existing establishments. Secondly, some existing junior secondary schools were promoted to the status of high schools through the addition of first-year high school classes. But no simultaneous arrangements were made for second and final year high school classes.

To understand this situation, and to get a good idea of the pressure on the secondary school system as a whole coming from mounting junior secondary enrolment (which, incidentally, parallels the pressure on the junior secondary cycle from the elementary cycle), we think it necessary to reassess the development of the Junior Secondary School Leaving Diploma Examination since 1977. That was the year in which that Certificate replaced the original Certificate that under the French colonial system had signalled completion of the first cycle of the school system (BEPC).

From 1960 to 1976, changes in the system produced a situation in which pupils' educational standards and abilities dropped substantially. At the same time, they passed the increasingly easy examination in droves, then moved up into the second cycle, jampacking all classes. The solution lay in a reduction of enrollment in the second cycle. This was achieved through the design and implementation of a reform scheme instituting the Primary School Leaving Diploma in 1976-77. Unfortunately, the solution incubated a problem. For, as Table 6 shows, the evidence of the results suggested that the new examination was more like a competitive examination that a school-leaving examination.

Table 6: Junior Secondary School Leaving Diploma (DFEM) Examination Results: 1977 to 1984

Year	Registered	Sitting	Passes	Passes (%)
1977	13,936	13,521	2,343	17.32
1978	17,625	16,351	3,727	22.76
1979	18,981	18,221	3,607	19.78
1980	20,176	19,312	5,793	20.99
1981	22,093	21,245	5,477	25.78
1982	26,339	25,335	7,174	28.31
1983	27,929	26,919	7,696	28.14
1984	30,474	29,183	10,011	34.30

Source: Sylla 1987

The results in Table 6 shocked parents. Teachers thought they were terrible, and their unions attacked the examination. It was therefore replaced, as from the 1984-85 school year, by a Junior Secondary School Leaving Certificate Examination (BFEM), considered less hostile to final year junior secondary students. As compared with the previous examination, the BFEM introduced three major innovations: the correction process provided for a second opinion from a second assessor; the entire examination was taken in a single session; and priority was given to oral evaluations, especially in check-up routines. In 1986, out of 26,730 candidates, 12,601 were declared successful. In 1987, out of 27,774 students, 14,344 passed (*Le Soleil*, 28 July 1987).

These results were clearly better than the old BEPC results. Their main consequence was a massive influx of students from the junior secondary cycle into the high school cycle. Since the only condition governing passage into the high school cycle was success in the BFEM examination, high school enrolment soared, saturating the system. The experience of the junior secondary and high school cycles, their general and competitive examinations, and the enrolment levels resulting therefrom, all suggest the following conclusions:

- There is no justification for turning all examinations into competitive trials, or for making ordinary evaluative examinations and competitive examinations identical in practice;
- There is no justification for making the number of places available in the educational system the factor determining success or failure in examinations, competitive or otherwise. Examinations are supposed to test students' knowledge and aptitudes. It is therefore untenable to subordinate them to the material capacities of the school system.

The time has come, quite clearly, to rethink the design and functions of ordinary and competitive examinations within the educational system. So far, examinations have been modified, reformed or cancelled simply because public opinion did not like them, the authorities were against them, or the results were discouraging. The educational system is a functional gestalt. That means that high enrolment rates necessarily imply shortages of textbooks and teaching equipment, problems with classroom discipline, a deterioration in instructional standards, etc. The root solution to the problem of high enrollment levels and the attendant problem of ordinary and competitive examinations, then, would be to build new schools and classrooms and to increase the volume of resources allocated to the educational system.

Unfortunately, African governments cannot afford to increase the resources already allocated to education. To do so, they would have to make drastic cuts in allocations to other, equally strapped ministries and departments with their own heavy demands. The fact is that on account of the current economic crisis, African governments no longer have any extra cash to invest in education. The only possible way out, under these circumstances, is to come up with alternative solutions of the type pioneered by the General Conference and CNREF experiments. In the design and implementation of such innovative approaches, it would be essential to mobilize and involve competent individuals and groups, organized or not, throughout the nation.

High School

The high school cycle takes in students who complete the junior secondary cycle, pass the BFEM examination, and are then directed into high school establishments known here as *lycées*. These are sited in the regional capitals. As indicated by Title 3, Article 12 of the Orientation Act, the purpose of high school education is partly to train middle-level personnel for jobs in the public and private administrative and economic sectors, and partly to prepare students for higher education. There are three high school streams: general, technical and vocational.

The cycle is a three-year one, the first to final years being known respectively as the *deuxième, première* and *terminale*. Each class is in turn subdivided into several streams (A, B, C, D, E, F, G) covering such specialized disciplinary areas as the humanities and literature, the social sciences and economics, the natural sciences, medicine and pharmacy, technical and commercial courses. Students are free to make their own options.

At the end of the third and final year of the high school cycle, students take an examination organized by the High School Certificate Board *(Office du Baccalauréat)*, responsible to the Vice-Chancellor's Office at the University. Successful candidates are awarded the A-Level equivalent high school certificate. Slightly less than 50% of junior secondary school students get through to the high school cycle. Correlated to the total school-age population in the relevant age group, the numbers actually educated at this level are paltry indeed. Over the period from 1977-78 to 1987-88, increases in enrollment at this level of the educational system have been slow, as indicated by Table 7. This slow progress is well reflected in the low school attendance rate at this educational level.

As Table 7 shows, the higher up one goes in the educational pyramid, the lower the rate of actual school attendance. In other words, the national educational system suffers from very serious incidences of failure, drop-out rates, dismissals, etc. One noteworthy fact: the general high school stream has always been and remains by far the most developed stream at this level. Total enrolment at the country's various technical, vocational and teacher training establishments at this high school level make up hardly a third of the total opting for the general stream. The low number of students in the technical, teacher training and vocational streams raises a query concerning the cost-effectiveness of structural investment in these streams for training facilities, staff emoluments, recurrent expenditure, capital expenditure, scholarships and various allowances. There are 36 such schools in the country, serving a total of only 6,590 students. That means a mere 183 students per school on the average. Worse still, such a system trains very few technically qualified persons to serve a developing economy, and equally few teachers for a school system with steadily increasing yearly enrollments.

In its technical and vocational streams, then, the educational system faces a crucial problem: existing teaching and training establishments are unnecessarily numerous and scattered. Some are tiny, and several seem to offer similar or identical courses. A long-term solution would require their structural reorganization, as already suggested by the General Conference on Education and Training as well as the CNREF.

The situation in the general stream is quite the opposite. The *lycées* or high schools are too few for the already huge enrollment, and new students enter the system yearly after passing the junior secondary school leaving diploma examination. To handle surplus enrolment, in 1989-1990 certain junior secondary schools were turned into high schools, and others simply had first year high school classes tacked on to them. On the whole, results registered for the A-level equivalent *baccalauréat* examinations from 1979 to 1989 seem middling, the pass rate ranging from 46.37% to 57.72%. There was one exceptional year, 1987-88, when public high schools remained closed and only private high school students took the examination. The pass rate then was 38.87%. Judged against the total school-age population at the high

Table 7: School-Age Population, Enrolment Levels and School Attendance Rates 1977-78 to 1987-88

Year	1977/78	1981/82	1983/84	1984/85	1985/86	1986/87	87/88
Population	294.000	346.300	371.550	386.450	401.950	418.050	434.850
Enrolment	15.481	20.297	24.127	26.431	30.342	34.102	38.308
Attendance rate (%)	5,3	5,9	6,5	6,8	7,5	8,2	8,8

Source: Senegal 1989b

school level, however, these results are indisputably low. Table 8 presents the evolving pattern of results.

The *baccalauréat* examination was recently reformed one more time. The changes, established in the 1989-90 school year, involved the cancellation of Part One examinations, which in past years second-year high school students were expected to take. An early French test was also established for second year students, and oral evaluations were given predominant weight in Group 2. The new schedule called for a single session in June-July, with a make-up session in October for students who for valid reasons were unable to take the ordinary session. Right from the start, the new *baccalauréat* examination was perceived by teachers as easier than the old. It led to a substantial increase in the university intake, because the selective barriers formerly constituted by the two-part examination were now abolished. Still, no doubt because candidates were unfamiliar with the new format, the pass rate at the June-July ordinary session was only average, 42% (5,421 passes out of 12,831 candidates (*Le Soleil*, 13 August 1990, p.2).

So far, the Senegalese educational system has not found a solution to the problem of ordinary and competitive examinations. At the transition point between each cycle and the next, therefore, the issue crops up, creating static. For that and other reasons, the high school cycle is beset with the same problems as the preceding cycles: shortages and inadequacies regarding premises, enrolment levels, resources and equipment, etc. Such problems naturally have a psychological impact, and the habitual tension of the classroom atmosphere, unsatisfactory student-teacher relationships, the high incidence of strikes, etc., are only symptoms of the underlying malaise. On the purely instructional level, also, there are serious consequences: educational standards have fallen, tests are rarely administered, and sometimes it is downright impossible for teachers to assess how much their students have actually learned.

Higher Education and Research

The first step towards the establishment of a system of higher education in Senegal was taken in 1918 with the establishment of a Medical School in Dakar. The school took in African students from the former French West African colonies for training as 'African doctors'. In 1938 the French Institute of Black African Studies (IFAN) was established, followed in 1950 by the Institute of Advanced Studies. The University of Dakar was officially opened on 24 February 1957. At that time it had four autonomous faculties: medicine and pharmacy; law and economics; humanities and literature; and science.

Table 8: A-Level Equivalent *Baccalauréat* Examination Results 1979-1980 et 1988-1989

Years	1979/80	80/81	81/82	82/83	83/84	1984/85	85/86	86/87	87/88	88/89
Presented	5.156	4.666	4.167	5.126	5.235	6.288	6.976	6.802	1.232	08.186
Admis	2.877	2.360	2.084	2.773	2.976	2.921	3.887	3.840	0.479	04.586
Percentage	55.79	50.57	50.01	54.09	56.84	46.37	57.72	56.45	38.87	56.02

Source: University Statistics Bureau, Dakar.

From the moment of its accession to independence, Senegal endeavoured to complete the system by creating new university and higher educational structures. Up until 1971, France gave the University of Dakar substantial subsidies for its recurrent, capital and development budgets, for salaries and emoluments (faculty, administrative staff, technical staff and service personnel), and for various scholarships and fellowships awarded students and faculty. France also provided teaching and research staff under periodically renewed cooperation agreements. In the decade from 1970 to 1980, this programme of French financial and staff aid was gradually scaled down, ending in 1981-82. In principle, the State was supposed to use the intervening period for getting a grip on the development of the university. In other words, it was expected that the university would find a solid basis in the national realities of Senegal and in the African environment in general.

So far, so good. After all, right from its inception, the purpose of the university of Dakar had bee to serve the sub-region and region, and it did this by taking in students from the former French colonies of West Africa. In consequence, the first laws and statutes regulating the university were French texts. That was the situation until independence. From that point on, co-operation accords covering higher education replaced the old texts, until managerial sovereignty and autonomy over the university shifted wholly to Senegal.

At present, the university and higher education system in Senegal is regulated by Senegalese laws and statutes. Right now the entire higher educational system in Senegal is funded, managed, administered and controlled by the State. So far the country has no private institutions of higher education. Existing legal provisions allow private educational establishments only at the four lower cycles. While such a system offers certain advantages, it also presents a number of drawbacks. The current consequences of such drawbacks are severe. Halls and lecture rooms are overcrowded, institutional premises are small and in disrepair, instructional materials and equipment are insufficient. All this brings up a query of central importance these days: is the State, all by itself, capable of funding the system of higher education in particular, and the entire educational system beyond that?

The issue is crucial, for behind this question of educational financing lies a question of principle: will education and training be provided free of charge, thus ensuring the right of all citizens to education and training as guaranteed in the constitution? Whether or not the educational system is democratic, in the sense of giving all children equal access to and equal chances of success in the school system, depends furthermore on the enforcement of this right as stipulated in the Orientation Act.

In the Senegalese system of higher education and research, there are lecturers and researchers of diverse national origins. For some time now, however, Senegalese teaching staff have predominated in number, with staff from other countries in the sub-region (Mali, Guinea, Burkina Faso, Togo, Benin, Cameroon, etc.) decreasing in number over the past decade. The same pattern is discernible within the student body, with students from other countries in the sub-region becoming rarer. Senegalization within the higher educational system has proceeded more rapidly than in other areas, mostly on account of external factors[19]. These factors included the drop in French student enrolments after the onset of African independence and the withdrawal of French staff from Africa. The number of students from other African countries also dropped as a result of the post-independence creation of universities and higher educational institutions in many African countries. Since the lost academic year of 1987-88, with the increasing frequency of campus disturbances and strikes, foreign student enrollment has decreased more rapidly.

To cope with the rapid increase in the student population, three approaches were adopted and tried out. The first was to expand old buildings and construct new ones on the same old campus. The second was to create new higher educational structures such as the CESTI, EISMV, ENSUT, ENSEPT and EBAD. The third was to open a new university at Saint-Louis. This was done at the start of the 1990-91 academic year.

The higher educational system faces other problems apart from the high enrollment level. Its educational and training facilities are too many, too small and too scattered. Often, they duplicate each other's functions. For example, the ENEA, ENCRB and INDR are all involved, simultaneously, in training rural development staff. Similarly, engineering courses are dispensed redundantly by the ENSUT, EPT and IST; as for teacher training, it is handled not only by regional teacher training colleges, but by the CFPS and the CFPP, the ENEP, ENS and ENSEPT. Needless to say, such a situation raises questions about the cost-effectiveness of the facilities involved. As currently structured, they employ relatively large numbers of staff yet cater for few students per unit, the average number of graduating students being from 20 to 50 per year. In any case, the graduates cannot all find work in the production system. And it is not feasible to envisage attracting foreign students to fill such establishments.

The fact is that the higher educational system is in a state of crisis, as can be seen from the regular cadence of strikes making its institutions non-functional for months on end. The crisis itself is rooted in numerous causes. From the students' point of view, there are various material and infrastructural problems such as the shortage of lecture rooms and accommodation, and chronic overcrowding in those that exist. Scholarship and other aid funds are also inadequate. Educational and scientific resources such as textbooks and documents are in short supply, and the number of teaching and supervisory staff is low. Enrolment levels keep rising, but job prospects after graduation are grim, and student attitudes towards the university are accordingly lukewarm. Because several months each year are devoted to strikes, curriculum and syllabus content is never fully dealt with, students' achievement levels have slid downwards, and examination results are chronically horrendous.

The teaching faculty have their share of problems. The teaching profession has been steadily down-graded, job tenure and security have become ever more chancy, and working conditions have deteriorated. In reaction to all this, and for the first time in the history of Dakar university, the Autonomous Faculty Union (SAES) was pushed into organizing a general strike involving all university teaching staff. The strike brought an improvement in teaching, research, training and housing allowances, as well as increases in allocations for study tours. In addition, there was a promise to improve working conditions and equipment.

As for the administration, caught between faculty and students, it is constantly embroiled in system management problems. Available resources are so inadequate that it is common for various supplies to run out in the middle of the financial year. Obviously, in the face of high needs and crippling shortages, the higher educational system cannot continue limping along on the same old bases, along the same old lines, trying to attain the same old goals. We return, then, to the question raised earlier: can the State, on its own, continue to fund the higher educational system and, even more ambitiously, the entire national educational system?

Up to this point, issues related to plant, premises and equipment, administrative supplies such as paper and stencils, instructional materials such as textbooks, chalk, dusters, exercise books and rulers, personnel for basic and continuing education courses, staff promotion and management, instructional content and methods, tests and examinations, supervisory procedures, legislative and statutory texts, have not been treated analytically. One main reason is that there are no statistical data on these heads. That does not make these issues any the less crucial. For when the State is no longer in a position to provide the educational system with the most basic equipment and supplies in adequate quantities; and when it is no longer able to train the teachers the system needs (since 1984, the State has been unable to train more than a yearly total of 250 teachers, even though 600 are needed per year)[20], then the system can no longer function smoothly.

A breakdown, in other words, is imminent, given the current economic crisis. Now there are hopes of saving the educational and health systems. The fact, though, is that the educational system is not an island unto itself. Its existence is conditioned by other sectors, and dominated by the economic and social health of the nation. In a situation, for instance, where large numbers of parents are unemployed, children can no longer go to school; much less will they be able to afford textbooks and educational materials. The 10 August 1990 issue of *Sopi* reported that the Head of State, in his Circular No. 008/PR dated 25 July 1990 and addressed to all Ministers, ordered 'an across-the-board 40% cut in all budgetary allocations intended for materials, maintenance and miscellaneous expenditure' less than two months after the National Assembly had voted its annual budgetary allocations. It was logical, under such circumstances, to expect shortages in the educational system to continue during the 1990-91 school year.

There is, in short, an urgent need to understand that the educational system cannot be insulated from the country's overall socio-economic situation. Neither can it remain indifferent to the future social; and economic prospects of its graduates. For nearly a decade now, people in this country have been growing increasingly disenchanted with the educational system. That disillusionment, without a doubt, is a consequence of the failure to take linkages between the educational system and society as a whole into account.

Policies and Projects

A number of programmes designed since 1981, along with certain implementational achievements, could give the impression, on the surface, that the Senegalese educational system is undergoing effective, irreversible reform. Notable among these programmes and achievements are the following:

a) The convening and effective organization of the General Conference on Education and Training, and then the work done by the CNREF, together with the conclusions flowing therefrom. Today, these events and processes feature as definite milestones in the itinerary of the Senegalese educational system, key phases in the qualitative transformation of the system. Thanks to them, the authorities now have an excellent set of innovative legislative and statutory texts to work from.

b) The public authorities have gone on record as being determined to reform the educational system by making 'intelligent and loyal use' of findings from the above reform processes.

c) Since then, numerous innovative educational programmes and activities have been initiated, and some are in the implementational phase.

d) One Minister of National Education, Iba Der Thiam, displayed a fierce, dogged determination to implement the reform programme.

e) The national media have shown an unfailing interest in the educational system and its prospects.

f) Various active groups within society, especially teachers' unions and parent-teacher associations, have been regularly involved in the search for solutions to educational problems. This raises the hope that some day the nation as a whole will rise to the challenge of taking control of the educational system, opening the way to a new age.

On the other hand, a look at actual practices and realities on the ground leads to the conclusion that instead of a coherent reform process conducted with systematic determination under accurate control, what our educational system has really been going through is a long slide backwards. First, educational standards and general achievement levels among pupils and students have been deteriorating from year to year. This is a consequence of overcrowding in the classrooms, and the shortage and inadequacy, at all levels in the school system, of infrastructural facilities, textbooks and instructional materials. Another reason is the chronic recurrence of strikes and upheavals. These factors are of course linked to material and financial shortfalls, but shortages and inadequacies of personnel also play a part. Teacher training programmes are no longer up to scratch; the number of teachers turned out is low, and doubts have been expressed about their competence, since some take up teaching simply to make a living, and the status of the profession is low in any case.

The high population growth rate stresses the educational system by increasing educational and training requirements at exponential rates. In some rural areas, numerous classes have been closed for lack of teachers or pupils. Meanwhile, in the urban areas where school population densities are high, the system of double-shift classes throws large numbers of pupils and students into the streets because no extra-mural programme exists to keep them occupied while their shift is out. The children have grown tired and cynical. So have some teachers. But increasingly, in the urban zones, significant fringe groups among students and pupils are fed up with the chaos and are determined to get on with their studies, even in the teeth of strikes.

The situation of the Senegalese school system is, to say the least, confused. It teems with such a host of problems and conflicts that it is hard to say which way it is drifting. It is a curious fact that as far back as 20 April 1983, less than three weeks after his appointment as Minister of National Education, Iba Der Thiam presented a programme indicating lines along which the educational system could develop in future, along with his own Action Plan as head of the ministry. In the history of the Senegalese educational system, this was the first time a Minister had, on his appointment, presented a programme and policies he intended to implement in the post given him by the Head of State. Right up until his dismissal in April 1988, Iba Der Thiam continued to give the impression that he knew perfectly well what he was about as Minister of National Education, the reasons for his programme, and the direction he intended it to take.

The Term of Office of Iba Der Thiam (1983-1988)

Iba Der Thiam's Action Plan (1983-88) for National Education was organized around four priority objectives (*Le Soleil*, 21 April 1983, pp. 1,4,5 and 6). First, the minister promised to observe faithfully all findings of the General Conference on Education and Training approved by the Government. Second, he would co-operate in all good faith with all teachers' unions. Third, he would work continuously to improve the status of the teaching profession. In the fourth place, he would demonstrate a burning and constant desire to improve living and working conditions for students and teachers. Simultaneously, he would explore, in cooperation with all interested parents, all possible career openings, a major concern of both students and parents.

These four priority policy guidelines, the standard for all educational projects and programmes from 1983 to 1988, made up a package referred to as the democratization reform project. Through it and his Action Plan, Iba Der Thiam expressed his policy design for the school system and the educational system in general.

The Democratization Process

Democratization is a long-standing claim put forward by the Senegalese teachers' union movement. It was pioneered by the African Teachers' Union of Senegal (SPAS, 1960-68); reaffirmed by the Senegalese Teachers' Union (SES, 1969-73), and handed down to both the Unified and Democratic Teachers' Union of Senegal (SUDES, 1976-90) and the Democratic Teachers' Union of Senegal (UDEN, 1984-90). Clearly, the reason why the SUDES took up the old democratization claim right from its inception in 1976 was that the politicization of the educational system was leading to widespread and serious consequences. Later, in 1981, the General Conference on Education and Training acknowledged the claim as necessary to the achievement of a national and democratic educational system[21]. Iba Der Thiam's appointment as Minister of National Education, then, came at a time (1981-83) and in an atmosphere of change characterized by the dynamics of the General Conference on Education and Training, when the Senegalese educational system was in the throes of qualitative change, and the political system was shifting gears from the Senghor era to the Abdou Diouf era.

Iba Der Thiam defined democratization in his Action Plan, as involving not only students and pupils, teachers and parents and their associations, but also the administration and management of the entire educational system.

As far as educational administration and management were concerned, democratization meant the involvement of all partners of the school system in consultation, decision-making, programme design and implementational processes. In specific terms, such matters as appointments of headteachers, transfers of teaching and other staff, and the whole range of issues related to the school system would be examined and deliberated upon within sovereign commissions on which all partners (Ministerial representatives, trade union delegates and representatives from parents' associations) would sit. In matters of school management, personnel management and staff recruitment, old habits of favouritism and exemptions would be out, equal opportunities for all in. Access to all scarce resources would be determined by competitive selection, the only ruling criteria being competence and merit.

As far as teachers were concerned, democratization would mean improved prospects of professional and social advancement as the status of the teaching profession got boosted, the moral authority and social prestige of teachers were enhanced, educational monitoring, testing and refresher courses were systematized, regular examinations and competitive evaluations were organized, scholarships and fellowships were awarded for training and advanced courses, and schools and teachers were given adequate educational equipment and materials of all types, etc. Finally, teachers, students and pupils would be accorded all their rights (salaries, allowances, etc.) with no delays.

Students and pupils, for their part, would be given responsibilities through their parents, who would be given seats on the management councils of their schools and on committees set up to manage contributions from them or from their parents. In five years' time all students and pupils would be supplied free of charge with equipment and materials for their studies and games. Their parents would be represented on scholarship allocation committees, along with trade union delegates and officials from the Ministry of National Education. No Senegalese pupils or students would henceforth be allowed to duplicate registration, a practice common at the first year primary level. Failures would not be readmitted, and no exemptions would be allowed for repeaters. Everyone would be subject to examinations.

A tall order indeed, by the looks of it. For Iba Der Thiam's Action Plan challenged a long-standing situation. It aimed to change mental attitudes, to turn habits and prejudices inside out. Still, despite problems and fears, Iba Der Thiam, in his speech marking the opening of the 1983-84 school year (*Le Soleil*, 10 October 1983, pp.4-7) claimed to have implemented his Action Plan and to have kept his promises. Time has passed and the dust has settled some. From our vantage point today, and with hindsight to help us, how do we assess the democratization effort as conceived and tried by Iba Der Thiam?

Taken as an educational technique for inculcating habits of freedom and responsibility, the democratization process was a noble ambition. It was precisely because of that, and on account of the sincerity, integrity and determination with which Iba Der Thiam promoted that goal, that he attracted veiled or frank hostility leading sometimes to outright obstructionism and enmity from the most determined adversaries, while gaining the admiration of those in favour of the scheme. The democratization process upset all those who stood to gain from the status quo, just as it pleased believers in social justice and a progressive educational system.

But the process also risked getting off the rails. For there were those, especially among the younger students and pupils, who were only too eager to mistake democracy for anarchy, to confuse the assumption of responsibilities in consultative and decision-making bodies with simple permissiveness, and to let freedom degenerate into licence. But there was a profounder question left unanswered: how could the educational system be isolated for democratization when all around it, in the political and social systems of national life, old habits and practices that made power plays, favouritism, exemptions and nepotism the order of every blessed day at every level? Lastly, there was some worry as to whether the democratization process was not a screen for new discriminatory practices in educational management.

At any rate, it was while the process of educational democratization was getting under way that the post-electoral disturbances of 1988 took place. Student strikes, protests and attendant upheavals added up to a whole academic year lost. From February to May 1988, a tidal wave of discontent swept through the Senegalese educational system and society as a whole. It swamped Iba Der Thiam, accused by his enemies of having conjured up the storm in the first place by bringing too much democracy into the educational system, by others of having failed to soothe the waters once they rose. He was accordingly sacked from the post of Minister of National Education. Two years after his dismissal, it seemed as if the idea of democratization had already become a buried past of the heritage of the Senegalese educational system (see below). There were no systemic arrangements for its implementation. Whether the principles of democratization were applied or not depended primarily on the conviction, sincerity, determination and perseverance of its promoter. Once Iba Der Thiam was gone, the future of the democratic ideal within the Senegalese educational system, now looking more like a bed of nails than a bandwagon, found no new promoters willing to jump on it.

The Issue of Free Educational Supplies
Iba Der Thiam's Action Plan included a set of well publicized decisions scheduled to enter the implementational phase at the start of the 1983-84 school year. Of these the most popular was the plan to provide free educational materials for all pupils within five years. It was also the most impractical. Giving reasons for the decision in the 7 October 1987 issue of the *Soleil*, Iba Der Thiam pointed out that it was not he who made the decision to provide educational materials free of charge but the ruling Socialist Party, whose doctrine was based on democratic socialism. He argued that as far as he was concerned, the application of this principle in the educational system necessarily meant the following guarantees:

a) Equal opportunities for all. Unless educational supplies were provided free of charge, social imbalances were bound to be reflected within the educational system. Commitment to democratization necessarily implied the abolition of the non-egalitarian factor constituted by the failure to supply educational materials free of charge.

b) Access to education for all: this meant that educational resources should not remain the exclusive privilege of a minority or class.

The measure, in short, was based on the principle of social justice, the motive idea behind the Action Plan. The plan was given a five-year deadline. Was it completed on time? Are we in a position to assess its performance now?

Tambacounda region was selected for the trial run in 1983-1984. One reason was the region's remoteness, but another was the fact that in the 1982-83 examinations, ordinary as well as competitive, students and pupils from there had performed brilliantly. The scheme subsequently spread out to other regions in stages, until it reached the final stage, Dakar, at the start of the 1988-89 school year. Given that the decision went into force when the country was undergoing economic and financial difficulties, it looked a bit like a demagogic ploy. For instance, all it meant, in specific terms, when it got to Dakar region at the start of the 1988-89 school year, was that each pupil returned home at the end of the day with two or three textbooks and the same number of exercise books. Furthermore, according to a 1988 survey conducted by the Studies, Human Resource and Planning Board of the Ministry of National Education, over the 1987-88 school year the national average of textbooks issued per capita was 0.61. In plain words, the average Senegalese pupil got less than a single textbook (Sénégal, 1989b).

As a measure intended to institute social justice, the scheme failed. The prime reason, of course, was that the country was under economic and financial stress. But a contributory factor was the failure to observe implementational corollaries envisaged by Iba Der Thiam. One such provision was that all schools should follow a strictly planned policy of textbook purchases, upkeep and lending. Had that been done, it was envisaged that after a few years each school would have acquired a complete stock of textbooks needed by its pupils. Future purchases would only be needed for replacing worn-out copies.

Most probably, this failure will have a negative impact on the qualitative development of the Senegalese educational system. The point is that most educational innovations being tried out at the moment (double-shift classes, multi-grade classes, experimental classes) suffer from the shortage, and sometimes the total absence, of textbooks. The situation is especially serious in the rural zones where parents might not quite see what useful purpose such books can serve. Even those who care to have them might be unable to buy them in villages without bookshops or documentation centres. Rural schools depend entirely on State allocations for educational materials.

Double-Shift and Multi-Grade Classes

Double-shift and multi-grade classes were recommended in the first place by the General Conference on Education and Training. Technical Commission Number 1 (CT 1) of the National Commission for Educational and Training Reform (CNREF), assigned to survey educational resources, explored their feasibility, potential, conditions and modalities. The diagnosis was based on an exhaustive diagnosis of the school system focused on its personnel, material and financial resources as of 1981-82. The findings indicated various disparities and inequalities, an inefficient system, overaged and neglected buildings and furniture, irrational use of available resources, a tight State budget, and a steadily increasing school-age population, meaning a correspondingly steady rise in the demand for education.

The General Conference on Education, as well as the Technical Commission of the CNREF, concluded that there was a need to explore alternative solutions and directions. The Technical Commission forthwith drew up a series of scenarios for double-shift classes, as follows:

Scenario I: Maintenance of Current Trends;

Scenario II: Flex Time Option with one teacher, two sets of pupils in one classroom;

Scenario III: Flex Time Option with two teachers, three sets of pupils, two classrooms.

Scenario I, in which current arrangements would be maintained, would obviously entail enormous expenditure, and the State could not possibly afford it. Quick to recognize that fact, the First Technical Commission rejected this option and turned its attention to Scenarios II and III, involving double-shift classes. The decision was that double-shift classes would be tried out in the urban areas, where enrolments were so high as to constantly outstrip all efforts to construct new classrooms and schools. In Dakar and Thies the situation was particularly critical. In the rural zones, educational demand was not as intense, so multi-grade classes could be tried out. The idea was to have a singe teacher handle two or three different classes of pupils within a single classroom.

Anxious to satisfy the demand for education, to raise school attendance rates and to make more rational use of personnel (teaching staff in particular) and material resources (with the accent on local materials), the Ministry of Education, without waiting for the CNREF to finish its feasibility studies, and without meeting preconditions set by the First Technical Commission, began experimenting with two-shift classes as early as the opening of the 1982-1983 school year, that is to say, just a few months before Iba Der Thiam was appointed Minister of National Education[22]. Multi-grade classes were also started. The double-shift format actually used had two teachers using a single classroom for two sets of pupils. The system was in operation until October 1986[23].

An evaluation of the double-shift system conducted by a survey unit within the ministry itself came up with positive findings, according to which primary entry-level pupils in double-shift classes matched or outperformed pupils in the old-style classes, at least in the basic subjects (reading, writing, arithmetic). The results were positive even though teachers and parents raised strong objections to some of its aspects. They pointed out, for instance, that the system meant half the pupils were unoccupied for a great part of the working day when their shift was out, and were thus exposed to the risk of delinquency. Teachers were given an incentive allowance to go along with the system, but that did not seem to motivate them sufficiently. There was no significant change in teacher-pupil ratios, and classroom time also remained practically the same. There was likely to be a 50% drop in school attendance rates in 1986, and by the year 2000 the figure could be down to 40%, given the combination of high educational demand and increasing pressure to cut educational expenditure.

Despite these problems, and in the face of intense demand for education and pressure from anxious parents, the Ministry of National Education tried to milk the double-shift system for all it was worth by starting a new type of double-shift classroom system in October 1986. The new system had one teacher teaching two different sets of pupils in a single classroom. It was in line with Scenario II as designed by the First Technical Commission of the CNREF. The system was tried out in the first three classes of the primary school system. A total of 780 classes throughout the national territory were involved, covering a total of 88 165 pupils. Real teaching time was cut from the 26 hours normal in old-style classes to a total of 18 hours per week. Each set of pupils was unoccupied part of the day, some in the afternoon, some in the morning, but there were no planned extra-mural activities. The experiment went on for three school years, from 1986-87 to 1988-89. At the end of that period the system was evaluated, in the 1988-89 school year, by the Evaluation Unit of the National Institute for Educational Development Studies and Programmes (INEADE), in cooperation with the French group SODETG-CIEC (Senegal, 1989d). An analysis of data from the evaluation survey leads to four main conclusions:

a) Despite a widespread misapprehension due to the fact that double-shift classes take less classroom time and leave pupils unoccupied for half the day, the new system does not result in lowered academic achievement levels. Quite the contrary: in the first three primary classes, achievement levels are actually higher in the instrumental subjects (reading, writing, arithmetic).

b) Parents and teachers both have a negative image of the double-shift system. The reasons, apart from the misperception listed above, include the absence of extra-mural activities, insufficient information about the system, and the feeling that it somehow expresses social inequalities.

c) Assistant teachers generally get better results than senior teachers.

d) Pupils in the double-shift system who possess their own copies of arithmetic or reading textbooks do significantly better than those without.

Conditions under which the new scheme was tried out were so poor that 75% of the teachers surveyed said they did not want to take that kind of class, or to repeat the experience. Many teachers and parents thought the system should be abolished, on the grounds that pupils did not get sufficient classroom time under the new schedule, and that their achievement levels were low.

In our opinion, double-shift classes may be a realistic alternative for the Senegalese school system. However, there are instructional and material conditions to be met if the innovation is to succeed. In the first place, there should be a clear and precise experimental plan. Secondly, once designed, such a plan should be strictly adhered to. Teachers should be well informed about the system, and motivated to make it work. Their performance should be monitored and supervised by competent educators. Parents and the population at large should be sensitized and accurately informed. And in the schools themselves, appropriate educational and material conditions should be created to make the process viable. For instance, textbooks and instructional materials should be supplied, school-yards and time tables should be reorganized, extra-mural activities planned, etc.

In the mean time, however, in the 1989-90 school year, the Ministry of Education, without issuing any precise directives, went ahead and imposed yet another newfangled experiment on the fledgling double-shift system.

Since then, both innovations have been extended in practice, but as far as guidelines are concerned, the system is flying blind. So there is reason to fear that the makeshift nature of the system will get accentuated, and that it will be pushed recklessly forward until it crashes. There is no good reason why the urgency of material and political demands should be allowed to compromise educational innovations. After all, the issue at stake is the future of the youth.

No evaluation has been done on multi-grade classes, those in which a single teacher working in a single classroom handles two or more classes of different levels. The system has been tried out in the rural regions (Fatick, Kaolack, Kolda, Louga, Saint-Louis, Tambacounda, Thies and Ziguinchor). According to the Division of Educational and Training Reform in the Ministry of National Education, in the 1988-89 school year the experiment involved 163 classes with a total of 7 037 pupils. Like the double-shift system, it offers the following main advantages:

a) It helps to maintain existing school attendance rates, even if it cannot help raise them;

b) It facilitates optimum use of teaching staff and classrooms;

c) It helps to meet the demand for education in the rural areas.

On the other hand, it has disadvantages that could prove deleterious in the long run:

a) The actual amount of teaching time per class is less than in the regular system. For the single teacher handling two or more classes at different levels deals by turns with one class at a time.

b) The level and quality of instruction goes down.

c) Teachers, overworked, get exhausted.

At the moment, with these two experimental systems going on, the Senegalese educational system is a three-speed system. There are single-shift classes, double-shift classes and multi-grade classes, each running according to its own specific time-tables, enrollment levels, teaching methods, etc. This means that within the public school system inequalities persist. The private school system has its peculiarities too. It could be argued that double-shift and multi-grade classes are no more than experiments. But the fact is that as far as the authorities are concerned, they have become a permanent feature of the national educational system. Throughout the colonial period, incidentally, there were multi-grade classes. In any case, pupils who have gone through double-shift and multi-grade classes are in no position to experience the orthodox system.

Experimental Classes

The experimental classes scheme, begun in the 1987-88 school year, involved the introduction of new curricula into the preschool and elementary school cycles. The new syllabuses were drafted by seven commissions[24] made up of teachers from all levels, headteachers and inspectors. They covered the following subjects: french, mathematics, history and geography, civics, natural sciences, art education, practical work, physical education and sports. In these new curricula, objectives set in each educational cycle are defined with a view to enabling each pupil to achieve a precise set of skills at the end of each cycle. Second, in place of the old-style content-oriented instructional methods, the new methods are objective-oriented. According to the Division of Educational and Training Reform in the Ministry of National Education (as of 31 March 1989), in the 1988-89 school year, there were 150 experimental classes in the elementary cycle and 50 in the preschool cycle. In other words, the project had maintained its experimental status up to that date.

Originally, there had been plans to extend the experiment in the 1989-90 school year in a bid to achieve a qualitative jump from leading edge experimental classes to entire experimental schools. The plan fell through, however, on account of the pupil-student strike and the change of minister. A new Minister of National Education was appointed in March 1990, and, following the structural overhaul of the State system, the Educational and Training Reform Board was demoted to the status of a division. For that reason, it is no longer in charge of anything. As a matter of fact, it no longer has any idea what happened to the experimental[25] classes. Neither has it received any directives concerning that innovation.

The new curricula and teaching methods were also tried out in selected double-shift classes. In such cases, in other words, the two experiments ran concurrently.

An evaluation of the pilot classes scheme was conducted in the 1988-89 school year by the INEADE (Sénégal, 1989d). The principal findings were that: the result was positive overall; and the majority of participants wanted to follow through with it, provided certain modifications could be made. Of these the most important had to do with arrangements for training teachers, headteachers and inspectors to take charge of instructional methods, evaluation, classroom approaches, training syllabus design, educational research, etc. There were also suggestions for improving logistical, instructional and financial resources.

A second assessment, however, conducted by INEADE (Sénégal, 1989d), and covering both double-shift and pilot classes, came up with somewhat less flattering findings. In any case, all prior surveys[26] had pointed out that while success was within the reach of the various educational experiments in the school system, they all suffered from a series of drawbacks: shortages affecting the school system as a whole and the experimental schemes in particular; overlapping experiments; a tendency to push recklessly ahead with new methods, sometimes resulting in their widespread application without prior evaluation; inadequate teacher training programmes; increased work loads with no real compensation; and the failure to involve all participants, etc. These shortcomings were all too likely to hamper the experiments. As far as the educational bureaucracy was concerned, however, the various experiments were complementary components of a single, indispensable reform package.

There is little doubt that the inspiration for these various educational experiments came from the spirit and findings of the General Conference on Education and Training, as well as from the recommendations of the CNREF. In practice, though, preconditions and prerequisites posited by the General Conference and the CNREF were shoved aside. Yet it is part of the current management style to claim that whatever is initiated, implemented and carried out in the educational system is done in accordance with General Conference and CNREF stipulations. Everything, in short, is blamed on the two bodies, for no good reason.

The Status quo - Ibrahima Niang

Strictly speaking, during his two-year term from 1988 to 1990 as Minister of National Education, Ibrahima Niang initiated no educational innovations. He merely continued whatever he found in progress on his accession, including double-shift, multi-grade and experimental classes. He certainly took office in an awful period, when the educational system was riven by a serious crisis. His first assignment was therefore to tackle the crisis, and to try and resolve it.

The 1987-88 School Crisis

Ibrahima Niang was appointed Minister of National Education in April 1988. The country's schools and university had been closed since 28 February. He did his best to get classes and courses going again throughout the system. First, he tried to tame the tempest through press releases, announcements of measures designed to appease the aggrieved parties, and decisions to reorganize the academic year and teaching schedules, including internal examinations and continuous assessments, time schedules, etc. All these attempts failed. He then decided to negotiate with the striking pupils. These, drawing upon their experience of struggles and strikes as well as from the taste of practical in-school democracy under Iba Der Thiam, had organized a Senegalese Pupils' Group (CES) and drawn up a list of demands. They acted in concert with secondary and high school students who had also organized their Senegalese Students' Group (CED) with its own demands.

In the ensuing negotiations, attended by various witnesses from the spectrum of Senegalese society, the authorities agreed to 90% of these demands.

To enable the educational establishment (which had meanwhile been reorganized into two ministries, the first of National Education, the second of Higher Education) to keep its promises to students and pupils, the Head of State, at a Ministerial Council meeting on Thursday 15 September 1988 convened to lay the groundwork for the opening of the academic year, adopted a series of unprecedented measures (*Le Soleil*, 16 September 1983). Taken together, the package of measures would cost over FCFA 1.5 billion, with expenditure for the higher educational system alone totalling nearly FCFA 1 billion. Modifying the tradition according to which, at the start of every academic year, the Ministry of National Education addressed the nation, the Head of State himself, in an address delivered on the night of Sunday 2 October 1988, restated the Government's determination 'to find lasting solutions to the problems facing our educational system'[27].

School Premises Rehabilitation

In the effort to follow through on agreements hammered out between the Ministry of National Education and students and pupils' representatives, Ibrahima Niang conducted two major operations aimed at rehabilitating school establishments. Dubbed respectively ORES I and II, the first took place in 1988, the second in 1989.

Rehabilitation work had been a key demand put forward by negotiating pupils and students. In 1988 it certainly was a crying need, for school buildings were everywhere dilapidated, and both plant and furniture in the country's educational establishments were in a state of disrepair. Since independence, there had been no maintenance and repair service in educational establishments. Every passing year saw the educational infrastructure deteriorate steadily, especially since some buildings had been constructed back in colonial times. With the State chronically impecunious after independence, many schools had been making do with makeshift shelters, especially in the rural areas. In some places, parents anxious to get their children into school had banded together to construct school buildings, with scant regard for technical or educational norms. So there were schools unprotected by walls or watchmen, classrooms with no doors. Thieves frequently helped themselves to windows and doors, vandals broke windows. Urinals, toilets and washrooms were unknown in some schools, and where they existed, they were often out of order. Walls of dubious construction frequently collapsed, good roofing was stolen, and often, what was left leaked. Under such conditions, questions of hygiene, cleanliness and calm, the kind of conditions indispensable for the learning process, became an acute problem.

ORES I, the first school-building and equipment rehabilitation project, was conducted in August, September and October 1988. With help from the Military Engineering Corps, and a budget of FCFA 619 million, the Ministry of National Education was able to rehabilitate 50 educational establishments, some partially, some completely[28]. The rehabilitation project involved a range of activities: strip-cleaning of masonry, paving, painting, installation of electrical fixtures, the making or repair of doors and windows, walls, fences and sanitary blocks, etc. ORES II took place in August, September and October 1989. It involved the same activities, funded to the tune of FCFA 600 million. This time also, the project got help from the Military Engineering Corps. It resulted in the partial or complete rehabilitation of 100 elementary, middle and secondary schools. ORES I and II covered the entire national territory.

Alongside ORES I and II, a number of significant projects were also conducted, which endowed several schools with equipment and supplies. For example, in 1988-89, 11,075 desks were supplied; in 1989-90 a further 15,000 were provided to schools. A total of 450 ordinary, multi-use and specialized classrooms were constructed and equipped, along with high schools, secondary schools, workshops and scientific laboratories. Taken together with all similar activities and programmes aimed at safeguarding and maintaining the educational heritage, it is clear that ORES I and II helped in significant ways to improve working and studying conditions for teachers, students and pupils. From that perspective, they may be assessed as having contributed to the improvement of our educational system.

Savings and Economics - Djibo Kâ

Djibo Kâ, a pure scion of the ruling Socialist Party, having risen from being a Socialist Youth Wing activist to the Executive Bureau and other commanding bodies within the Party, was appointed Minister in late March 1990. Under him the Ministries of National Education and Higher Education were yoked. At his accession the situation in the educational system was peaceful, for the pupils' and students' strike had ended. During his official tenure, he did not initiate any educational programme of national scope. Rumour had it that he intended to hand over management of the elementary school system to the municipalities. If so, the move could be significant, in that it would lead to substantial savings for the State. However, a number of queries would have to be addressed before its implementation. To begin with, existing legal provisions and statutes would have to be reorganized and amended; new terms of reference would have to be drawn up empowering different officials and agencies; and the municipalities would have to be reorganized to enable them to handle their new responsibilities. Second, new financial arrangements would have to be made, for the fact is that right now, every municipality in the country is financially strapped.

These are real problems. Nevertheless, the project deserves serious consideration and experimentation, especially since some developed countries like France have made it work, and their experience could prove useful.

The Education IV Project

The full title of this project is The Elementary Education Development Project. It is a pilot project run by the Education and Technical-Vocational Training Bureau (BPE). It was initiated by three partners: the Government of Senegal, the African Development Bank, and the World Bank (working through its subsidiary, the International Development Association). Scheduled to run from 1987-94[29], it is planned to dovetail into a subsequent project. It was designed to fit into the framework of the reform of the Senegalese educational system. According to project officials, the first objective of the reform process as defined by the General Conference on Education and Training and the CNREF, is to make elementary schooling universal in Senegal by the year 2000. The project comprises two basic phases, the experimental and the sectorial adjustment phase

The first phase was the experimental phase. It covered Diourbel, Fatick and Louga, three regions with the lowest school attendance rates, but where the population was apparently eager to catch up fast. The challenge there was to construct 400 classes. There was no rigid deadline: implementational speed would depend on the degree of awareness and involvement of the population. In the event, even though the original experimental project was not fully implemented, it was followed by a sectorial adjustment programme, which in turn comprised two aspects, a physical operational aspect and an institutional reinforcement aspect.

In the physical operations part of the sectorial adjustment programme, the idea was to continue and expand the classroom construction programme initially begun in the regions of Diourbel, Fatick and Louga, while at the same time constructing offices for the INEADE project along with buildings for selected inspectorates. Other buildings would be repaired, instructional materials would be obtained for classes, and textbooks would be produced.

In the institutional Reinforcement aspect, project activities and programmes were designed to strengthen the institutional framework. They therefore had to be based on prior studies and assessments of educational policy. After all, the fundamental mandate of Educational Project IV was to help establish structures technically organized and equipped to manage the educational system efficiently. Within that perspective, all Ministry of National Education structures responsible for elementary school administration were to be reinforced. They included the Directorate of Elementary

Education (DEE), the Planning, Human Resources and Studies Board, the School Buildings and Equipment Board (DCC), and the INEADE.

The basic, overall objective of Educational Project IV was to reinforce the operational and management capabilities of the Ministry of National Education. It covered all sectors of the elementary school system, and involved all structures responsible for its administration and development. Designed, negotiated and implemented by Senegalese executives in collaboration with Ministry of National Education officials, the project, when all is said and done, was *rather unimaginative*. It could have been initiated and implemented entirely by Senegalese nationals. The only real external input was funding. In its current implementational phase, it involves the services of only three expatriate experts.

Conclusion

From the first days of independence, the Senegalese State failed to define a coherent educational policy incorporating precise guidelines for the creation of an educational system designed to contribute to an endogenous, national development process. The 1971 Orientation Act was botched in its implementation. The result was a serious crisis afflicting the educational system. To this date there is no Orientation Act based on findings and proposals presented by the CNREF. No one has any idea, in practical terms, what kind of reform programme the government happens to be implementing. Certain key aspects of the CNREF reform design have been ignored or hazed over. For instance, the introduction of national languages is still bogged down in the experimental phase; the CNREF suggested the abolition of private educational institutions, but the government refused; the issue of religious instruction is no longer even discussed in the educational system. This is probably because of opposition from secularists who would interpret its introduction as a triumph for Islamic fundamentalists. The issue of the re-opening of boarding schools, shut down by the government in 1981-82, remains unresolved. The issue of the phasing out and winding down of French technical assistance hangs in the balance. The CNREF had suggested the abolition of such competitive and other examinations as the Junior Secondary Entrance and Certificate examinations, but the government turned the proposal down.

Meanwhile, the State has concentrated on its own set of priorities: double-shift classes, multi-grade classes, pilot classes, the emphasis on elementary schools and Educational Project IV, etc. All these priority options are essentially aimed at making optimum use of structures, resources and personnel. In the design and implementation of the attendant programmes, teachers' unions and their activist members have felt uninvolved and unconsulted. Their opinion is that the government has been obeying World Bank and International Monetary Fund dictates. Meanwhile the programmes and reforms remain stymied at the experimental stage, no doubt because prerequisite conditions for take-off and generalization are not yet ripe. The question, then is: has the Senegalese educational system been advancing or backtracking?

Over the years the Senegalese educational system has muddled through a series of increasingly severe problems and strikes. Such a constantly recurring scenario has nothing accidental about it. On the contrary, it is a perfectly explainable result of the way the system runs, which sometimes has little to do with the subjective quarrels and polemical attitudes of those embroiled. The fact is that the educational system has to function, and it does lurch on from year to year, whatever the circumstances. If those in charge of it make no reasonable arrangements to provide maintenance services for buildings and infrastructure, furniture, textbooks and instructional materials, etc., and if they make no serious master plans directing the development of the educational system as a whole, then shortages of equipment and educational materials are bound to arise when the State no longer has the means to cope with the educational crisis. Makeshift solutions then proliferate, but the respite they provide is temporary and piecemeal. The educational system has been drifting aimlessly, and the national press, reporting on the July 1990 examinations, hit the nail on the head when it encapsulated the mess under such headlines as 'Madness in the School System' and 'Butchery at the University'.

Hustling to cope with crisis conditions, the State has often made promises it could not keep. Various decrees, including those on the General Conference, the CNREF and the National Conference on Education, have been issued but not implemented. The General Conference on Education and Training was supposed to meet every fourth year, but in 1985 and again in 1989 it was not held. Nothing has been done to set up the National Education Fund. Negotiations between the government and pupils (CES) and students (CED) have dragged on. According to the students and pupils, the reason is that the State is in the habit of breaking agreed pledges, or only partially fulfilling its contractual obligations.

Still, the gravest troubles confronting the educational system do not all emanate from the system. Apart from the specific difficulties of the educational system, the State itself is in crisis, and the fallout is enormous: structural reorganization, enterprises going bankrupt, workers getting laid off, rising unemployment, etc. No matter how determined people may be to safeguard the educational system, no matter how much energy and resources get invested in the system, shortages persist, and the system will crack under imposed constraints once parents in droves are unemployed, when neither the society nor the economy can produce sufficient resources for investment in the educational system. At this juncture when the country already counts hundreds of unemployed graduates, such a scenario is no longer remote. The State is busy sacking employees and encouraging thousands of others in whose education the Nation has invested heavily to leave the civil service under their own steam. One might wonder, at such a time, if it makes sense to continue investing so intensely in the educational system. Quite obviously, there is no way the development of the educational system can be envisaged independently of the development of the economy and society as a whole.

The current drift of the educational system can be remedied through the resolutely responsible use of national resources and skills. However, the educational system cannot be salvaged in isolation.

Notes

1. The most obvious symptom of this drift is the inability to bring the development of the educational system under control. The normal operation of the system is under permanent threat of disruption occasioned by student protests and activism.
2. The following words from Maurice Delafosse, quoted by Abdou Moumouni (1964) put the issue of principles, guidelines and objectives of the colonial educational system in a nutshell: *"Just as we require interpreters to enable natives to understand us, we also need intermediaries belonging to native society by their origins but to European society by virtue of their education, to make people in this country understand and adopt this new and foreign civilization towards whose introduction they show, quite understandably, a die-hard hostility.* (*Bulletin de l'Education en A.O.F.*, No. 3, June 1917. Italics ours). The colonial school system may have undergone modifications, but by and large, neither its spirit nor its objectives have changed, and it still serves the same interests as in the past.
3. A collection of administrative regulations commissioned by the Ministry of national Education's Bureau of Technical and Vocational Training Projects (BPE, September 1989, 3 volumes), and compiled by an expert consultant, Souleymane Ndiaye, makes no mention of official regulations governing the organization of the school system prior to 1967 (Act No. 67-51 on the Status of the Private Educational Sector, Volume 2, p.451).
4. The student strikes that shook so many societies in 1968 and 1969 had an unprecedented impact in Senegal. The need to understand their deep-seated causes as well as their political consequences and implications opened the way to a perception of the extent to which an ill-adapted educational system could pose a threat to society.
5. Opening statement on the reform process by the Minister of National Education at the top-level intra-Ministerial meeting of 11 February 1969. See also our forthcoming book, *L'Ecole Sénégalaise en Gestation: De la Crise à la Réforme. 1ère partie: la crise (1960-1980)*. The Minister ended his opening statement as follows: "The combined effect of the factors I have outlined constitute part of the reason why our urban areas, especially in the Cap Vert region, contain such large populations of unemployed youths aged between

14 and 18. The unpredictable reactions of these youths have sometimes disturbed the balance and smooth progress of society."
6. A national commission charged with the drafting of reforms for the primary, middle and secondary school cycles was created by Decree No. 69-332 of 27 March 1969.
7. It is now two decades or so since officials began talking about the scheme to introduce national languages into the educational system. The plan is still on paper.
8. SUDES: *Democratic Teachers Union of Senegal*. Following a severe crisis lasting from 1981 to 1984, this trade union broke up, and was succeeded by another union, the Democratic Union of Senegalese Teachers (UDEN).
9. For our account of these struggles and the political implications thereof, see Sylla (1982, 1987).
10. In a declaration issued in December 1980, the SUDES spelled out the vast range of sanctions imposed on union activists from June to December 1980: the suspension of 38 teachers in June 1980; the withholding of 110 teachers' entire salaries in July and August; the dismissal of 23 teachers in September; the suspension of 38 more in September; the arbitrary transfer of 500 teachers in October; the dismissal of 51 teachers in October; and the arbitrary transfer of 200 secondary school teachers in November and December.
11. Credit for the consensus was generally given to the SUDES. It did a fine job of mobilization, and the determination of its activists went a long way to ensure the success of the historic General Conference. On this and attendant issues, see our works, cited above, as well as the special issue of the SUDES organ, *La voix de l' Educateur*, published in February 1981.
12. This was the expression used by the government spokesperson after the first Ministerial Council meeting of the first week in February 1981, that is to say, following hard upon the General Conference.
13. Article 2, Decree No. 81-644 of 6 Huly 1981 on the establishment of the CNREF. Two other decrees were issued around the same period: Decree No. 81-624 of 24 June 1981 on the establishment of the general Conference, and No. 81-625, also of 24 June 1981, setting up the National Commission for the Study, Coordination and Monitoring of the General Conference.
14. Our presentation here is a summary of the draft National Education Act produced by Technical Commission No. 2 of the CNREF, responsible for studying general educational policy.
15. Presentation copy on the Minister, in *Le Soleil*, No. 4417, Saturday 19 January 1985, p.4. We here summarize ideas and propositions, accepted as well as rejected, as presented in the text.
16. The cumulative increases in question, refused in 1985, were finally accepted in April 1989 following a strike by the Autonomous Union of University Teaching Staff (SAES) and an agreement with the government.
17. *Le Soleil*, No. 6011, Wednesday 6 June 1990, p.2. For the 1990/1991 financial year, the total State budget for all Ministries was FCFA 516,436,000,000.
18. The Chairman of the Action Committee for the Defence of the Senegalese Educational System (CIDES), speaking during the 8:30pm. television news broadcast on Sunday 27 November 1988, said there was a shortage of 150,000 desks. Assuming a ratio of two pupils per desk, the number of pupils needing desks would be 300,000. At the normal ratio (in the urban areas) of three pupils per desk, the number would rise to 450,000. Hence the 'Operation Classroom Desks' appeal launched by CIDES. Even by conservative estimates, 300,000 to 450,000 pupils would make up half the actual enrollment at this level.
19. The increase in Senegalese student enrollments was a normal result of developments in the educational system and enrollment levels lower down in the pyramid. According the World Bank study previously cited (1988a), this increase, when correlated with the total school-

age population of the relevant age group, was not particularly, rapid. In 1960, the overall school attendance rate was 0.5%; in 1970 it was 1.3%; in 1980 it was 2.8%, and in 1983 it was 2.2%. As for the percentage of examination passes, it was still below 50%. An article in *Le Témoin* Number 9 of Tuesday 31 July 1990, under the title "Hecatomb" gives the following details: "Pass rates in first and second year undergraduate examinations at the Cheikh Anta Diop University (Dakar) ranged between 3.88% in Philosophy and a high of 40% in Portuguese. For final year students, the worst results were in English where the pass rate was 20%. The best were in Classical Literature, where the pass rate was 33%. Other Senegalese papers including *Sud Hebdo, Sopi and Fagaru* also commented on these catastrophic results.

20. This issue is so vitally important that the Head of State, taking cognizance thereof, ordered the Ministry of National Education, in his directive reported on page 2 of the Saturday 14 and Sunday 15 July issue of the *Soleil*, to send more than 700 teachers into the schools each year and to open 320 extra schools. The fact of the situation since 1984 is that the only reason school attendance rates have not fallen below the current level (54.6%) is that double-shift and multi-grade systems have gone into application. The yearly intake of 250 teachers barely makes up for losses of teachers due to resignations, dismissals and retirements.

21. The claim was reflected in Point 8 of the platform of SUDES demands drawn up in 1978. It was taken up by all three component commissions of the General Conference on Education and Training, and approved by the Government through the promulgation of Decrees 81-624, 81-625 and 81-644. The first decree established the general Conference, the second established the National Commission for the Study, Coordination and Monitoring of the General Conference, and the third established the National Commission for the Reform of the Educational and Training System (CNREF).

22. Strictly speaking, then, Iba Der Thiam did not initiate the double shift classroom system. Nevertheless, he defended it with such energetic enthusiasm that people came to think of him as the originator.

23. In the end, then, the format adopted did not follow either of the double-shift scenarios laid out by the First Technical Commission. Since it used two different teachers for two classes, the only resource economized was the single classroom. The teachers were in fact under-utilized. While one of them taught, the other did nothing.

24. The Commissions produced the following documents: Curricula for Preschool Pilot Classes; Curricula for Elementary School Pilot Classes; Teachers' Handbook for Preschool Pilot Classes; Teachers' Handbook Elementary School Pilot Classes.

25. We interviewed the official in charge of this Division on 13 June 1990.

26. The INEADE surveys, it must be said, suffered from some methodological inadequacies. The sample interviewed was small, and coverage of the national territory was incomplete, with certain zones left out altogether.

27. It was in line with this determination that the appropriate measures cited above were taken, in addition to the disbursement of 2 billion F CFA for their implementation. See *Le Soleil*, No. 5514, Monday 3 October 1988, p.3.

28. For more detailed information on ORES I and II, see *Le Soleil*, No. 5518, Friday 7 October 1988, pp. 1 and 2; as well as No. 5512 of 1 October.

29. We know nothing about the funding aspect of this project. For one thing, documents relating to the project cannot be published without prior permission from the World Bank.

Bibliography

Dakar University, 1976, Office of the Vice-Chancellor, 'Textes relatifs à l'Université', Dakar, June.

Moumouni, Abdou, 1964, *L'Education en Afrique*, Paris, Maspero.

Senegal, (Republic of), 1984, Commission nationale de Réforme de l'Education et de la Formation (CNREF), 'Rapport général et Annexes', (Volumes 1 to 6), Dakar.

Senegal, (Republic of), 1988, 'Tableau de Bord, Année scolaire et universitaire 1986-87', Dakar, Fliers.

Senegal, (Republic of) Research Division, 1989a, 'Recherche relative aux programmes et à la pédagogie dans les classes double flux classes pilotes', Dakar, July.

Senegal, (Republic of), Ministry of National Education/DERP, 1989b, 'Demande et offre d'éducation en zones rurales', Dakar.

Senegal, (Republic of), 1989c, Bureau of Educational, Technical and Vocational Training Projects.

- 'Dossier I: L'innovation pédagogique', Dakar, May.
- 'Dossier II: Administration et Gestion des Inspections', Dakar, May.
- 'Dossier III: La Décentralisation', Dakar, May.
- 'Dossier V: Guides Méthodologiques', Dakar, May.
- 'Dossier VI: L'Evaluation', Dakar, May.
- 'Dossier VII: Comment préparer un document de projet', Dakar, May.
- 'Recueils des Textes administratifs',(Volumes I, II and III), Dakar, September.

Senegal, (Republic of), 1989d, INEADE, Evaluation Division, 'Rapport d'évaluation des classes à double flux', Paris, June.

Senegal, (Republic of),1989e, 'Evaluation des nouveaux programmes dans les classes pilotes', Dakar.

Sylla, Abdou, 1982, 'De la grève à la réforme: luttes enseignantes et crise sociale au Sénégal', *Politique africaine*, II (8), pp.61-73.

Sylla Abdou, 1987, 'L'Ecole future pour qui?', (*Etudes et recherches*, No. 108), Dakar, Enda.

Sylla Abdou, 1985, *L'Ecole sénégalaise en gestation. De la crise à la réforme*, Dakar.

World Bank, 1988a, *L'Education en Afrique subsaharienne. Pour une stratégie d'ajustement, de revitalisation et d'expansion*. Washington, D.C.

World Bank, 1988b, *Rapport sur le développement dans le monde*, Washington, D.C.

World Bank, 1989a, *Rapport sur le développement dans le monde*, Washington, D.C.

World Bank, 1989b, *L'Afrique subsaharienne. De la crise à la croissance*, Washington, D.C.

12. Student Unionism: Pluralism and Pressure Politics

Momar Coumba Diop*

Reasons Behind a Long Silence

The crisis now ravaging the African continent has generated impressive quantities of print. So far, however, few works of excellence have dealt with its impact on the continent's political and trade union bureaucracies, the mechanisms of domination at play, and the social movements which, during the 1980s, drew particular attention on account of their peculiarly violent activities. Yet, as Mamdani (1990:3) has aptly pointed out, the current African crisis is also the crisis of the mass movements and organizations of the continent. For even though in the post-independence period various commentators and spokespersons strained mightily to present the working class or various peasant groups as key players in the process of historical transformation (Dieng, 1985:112-117), these supposedly strategic groups have failed to deliver as 'the real protagonists of African history'[1].

The African crisis is above all the crisis of those radical intellectuals, who in the 1960s, opposed the continent's new States in their integrationist drive. Today they fulminate against the ravages of regimes they openly call 'mystificatory'. The obvious difficulties confronting various 'socialist' regimes, together with changes in international relations, have combined to push such radical thinkers, now cut adrift from the lost umbilical cord of the eastern countries and no longer able to fall back on the comforting paradigms of the 1860s, farther onto the fringes of social discourse. At the same time, changes have shaken the European social-democratic left which formerly ran the cultural factories from which African intellectuals normally imported their intellectual staples. These days the majority of Africa's thinkers subscribe to neo-liberal ideas. Along with these shifts, there has also been a change in relations between the continent's intellectuals and Western aid agencies, the North American outfits in particular. For the aid agencies now feed the intelligentsia with resources denied them by their States. In the resulting velvety dynamic of cooptation and corruption, the Western aid donors manage to defuse potential anti-Western attitudes, deflecting criticism onto local political elites.

---

*I would like to thank the following for their valuable criticisms and suggestions: Ibrahima Thioub, Ousseynou Faye, Djibril Samb, René Collignon and Babacar Fall Baker.

The donor agencies provide selected African intellectuals with financial cushions that enable them to resist the blandishments and pressures of the State. They thus remain immune to the temptations of local-level corruption. This enables the sponsors, in return, to deepen the pro-Western tendencies of beneficiaries among the African intelligentsia, including leftist recipients. In his masterly analysis of the 'metamorphosis' of Latin American intellectuals, Petras (1990) offers a brilliant explanation of the process. One outcome is now a major aspect of African political life: the conversion of selected radical intellectuals. Normally, the transformation follows labyrinthine paths sophisticated enough to camouflage underlying realities. But Issa Shivji, for one, has seen through the maze: 'In Africa, the radical, logical or not, has invariably adopted more of a comprador attitude than a liberal or revolutionary one in his choice of theories and points of view' (Shivji, 1989:12).

At the same time, there has been a change in the status and relationships of radicals both within political networks and in the nexus of their interactions with foreign forces directing the development process. That change has had an impact on paradigms of social modernization. It has also had a particularly strong impact on the working class vocation and the bias towards 'peasant points of view'.

The paradigms in question set apart some chosen group among the ordinary people, conferring on it some historic role denied other groups. For that reason they have long put a clear spin on the study of social movements. It is mainly on account of this powerful pull that so few studies have so far focused on certain social groups which have worked energetically to bring about the shift away from totalitarian modes and norms in most African countries since 'independence'. Students have been particularly under-studied on account of this bias.

While the old paradigms were collapsing, something else was happening: notwithstanding their determination to frustrate every independent organizational initiative from the people themselves, the States were confronted with mass movements that spilled over beyond the established channels of political activity sanctioned by the ruling class. Thanks to these changes, new research prospects opened up in which students were given increasingly serious attention. The theoretical rehabilitation of students[2] as a social group took place in the late 1980s.

In many African countries students helped to break down old, established systems of social and political control. For that reason they became the focus of sustained attention. Student radicalism provided an outlet for general social discontent and for protest against the educational system, caught up in a widespread crisis that became patent from the 1970s onwards. In

Senegal, however, the study of student radical movements was a difficult matter. One reason was that the country's university system was so young. A second was that information on the issue was rather limited. Furthermore, the documentary output of student unions, especially from the 1960s, has not been properly preserved. One reason was that for a time, the possession or distribution of 'subversive' documents could get students into hot water. The situation was similar in many African countries, and it affected other unions and groups as well. The police carried out systematic search-and-destroy operations targeted at the production presses and distribution depots of such documents. Student unions were not immune to these attempts to snuff out dissent. Since leftist organizations were obliged to operate entirely or partially underground, research on them was difficult. For under the circumstances, certain scholarly questionnaires could look uncannily like police dossiers.

In Senegal the emergence of students as a social group was historically linked to colonialism[3]. Students played a considerable part in the nationalist movement and in the creation of the elite now running the various States of Africa. Student unions served as training grounds for large numbers of professional spokespersons working for leftist organizations. Yet because Africanists long looked askance at students, preferring to focus on groups they considered nobler or more relevant, their scholarly output did not reflect the importance of students. In Senegal, the main reason why scholarly works paid relatively little attention to students was that for a long time, a complex imperative of silence worked to protect selected aspects of the operational lifestyles of opposition groups from systematic scrutiny.

Our aim in this chapter is to describe the role of students in Senegalese politics, with special reference to their input into the political plans of left-wing organizations. We do not intend here to produce a detailed history of the radical student movement. What we intend is to identify its interests and stakes *vis-à-vis* the network of local political structures. In addition, we shall attempt to delineate government reactions to student struggles.

Readers looking for traces of neo-evolutionist paradigms in which the existential development of the student union movement is schematically divided into discrete 'stages' and 'phases' will be disappointed. So will those hoping to glean titillating (but ultimately pointless) anecdotes. We are quite aware that certain first-person reports on the student union movement affect a breezy, impressionistic style. That is a trend we have deliberately avoided. Instead, we have aimed to highlight key characteristics of the student union movement by analyzing it within the framework of domestic power relationships, placing a special emphasis on its connections with university faculty unions, another section of the petty bourgeoisie projecting a leftist agenda

(Diallo, 1986). The closeness of student and faculty stances is the result of linkages making it possible for university faculty to take up in their later development business earlier left unfinished in the struggle to meet student aspirations. Bianchini explains the process well:

There is an ironclad sociological necessity that forces students to end their careers as campus revolutionaries if they aspire to take the plunge into professional careers. The academic profession offers an escape hatch from that conundrum (Bianchini, 1988:239).

Our leading hypothesis is that the construction of the neo-colonial State goes hand in hand with a wide-ranging process designed to prevent the emergence of any power centres with a potential for an independent existence, and therefore capable of functioning outside the control of the State. The State took such strenuous care to bring opposition parties and labour unions to heel that students' and teachers' unions were left as the main channels for the expression of left-wing points of view. For that reason, beyond the maze of specific details, the struggles of these movements were focused mainly on the recovery of democratic rights. The student union leadership was in the forefront of the political movement that made it its permanent vocation to frustrate Senghor's attempts to achieve complete hegemony. That is why it came in for more than its fair share of repression. In its struggles it defended values derived from the anti-imperialist tendencies of the late 1960s.

The Rise of a Political Force

The development of the educational system produced an elite that aspired to self-expression and also had a taste for power. Students, with their virulent anti-colonialist critique, acted as a pressure group pushing the ruling class to restore the country's dignity. They played a leading role in the struggle to establish a democratic system. And in stimulating other social forces, they contributed to political change.

Within the State structure, students occupy a transient position, that of the budding intelligentsia. Nevertheless, as Peter and Segundo (1986) point out, even though students are in training for a defined status, they themselves have no well-defined role in the production process. So far, that fact has not kept them from playing a relatively important part in political struggles. In the nationalist struggle, student activists fought alongside nationalist militants. For that reason, the radical student movement enjoyed constant support from the left-wing intelligentsia. To a certain degree, the movement represented the aspiration of large sectors of the middle classes. In time it came to identify itself as the conscious factor within a movement impelling the entire country in the direction of greater liberty. In Senegalese political life, the university has always been a centre for active dissent. The roots of this activist tradition go back to the struggle for independence and the transformation of the country's development options.

Intellectuals created the best organized, most coherent and most articulate forms of political protest. To contain them, President Senghor used a combination of repressive tactics and cooptative tolerance, within both his ruling party and the State, for a populist movement based on a tendency represented in the UPS by Samba Guèye. And he was able to present leftist claims, especially those coming from students, as demands from "privileged" groups (Diop and Diouf 1990). A further ploy Senghor used to counter radical left-wing protest was ridicule. For instance, he quipped that whenever the Senegalese opposition painted his party, the UPS, as a reactionary, anti-nationalist force, 'all baobab trees in Senegal laughed so hard they tore out their roots' (*Le Soleil,* 9 November 1974).

Still, students and teachers challenged the legitimacy of the power structure, pouring criticism on Senghor and his international backers. They put forward demands based on meritocratic and sometimes straightforward ethical values. They tirelessly attacked the foundations of the regime, repeatedly castigating its leaders as 'incompetent'. But even though they belonged to a handful of groups that put up the stiffest resistance to the totalitarian designs of the State, their propaganda was unable to mobilize the population at large against the regime.

The State's success in coopting the Muslim religious elite (marabouts) did a great deal to blunt the impact of Marxist-inspired revolutionary schemes. Groups of intellectuals camouflaged their concerns and claims by presenting them as attempts to secure the common interest. Their aim was to cloak their individual ambitions under the spurious claim of being tribunes of the masses. Often, they themselves did not understand the jargon they spouted. Still, it remains an open question whether the appeal to "the masses" in the agitational rhetoric of the urban petty bourgeoisie was not aimed at securing greater legitimacy for the activities of that group.

During the early 1960s, the intellectuals made up the frustrated portion of the anti-colonial front. In their attempt to develop an organized opposition, they relied on Marxism laced with various brands of nationalism. In the process they forged themselves an identity, but also clashed with the ideology of Negritude in the person of the intellectual lord of the ruling class, Léopold Sédar Senghor. Since there was no local tradition of adequate analysis bearing on the nature of the State or on social stratification, the left fell back on theories which were often irrelevant in the local situation. The power base of the leftist intellectual leadership was derived in part from the manipulation of book learning as developed by Western cultural production bureaucracies or by their counterparts in Eastern Europe. For that reason,

African leftist intellectuals, with a handful of exceptions, played second fiddle to the managers of these foreign intellectual bureaucracies. In many cases the latter, to all intents, assumed the prerogatives of established opinion makers.

Prey to the repressive power of the State, and torn between their militant commitments and their professional duties, intellectuals in Africa's leftist organizations had little time to devote to theoretical profundities, to judge from the evidence of their published output. For this lack of productivity there is a plethora of excuses. But we might justifiably wonder whether one key cause of the intellectual barrenness of Africa's leftist thinkers was not the influence of the paradigms mentioned above. The problems raised by the assimilationist model had become obvious by the late 1960s. On top of that, the clear situation of economic crisis and the discontent of the urban petty bourgeoisie led to the construction of a cultural model typified by attempts to play down the influence of the colonial cultural legacy. Hence the aptness of Bianchini's observation that the 1968 crisis was really an attempt at cultural decolonization, a process postponed until then.

At the same time there was a vast reform movement within the anti-colonial front that had emerged in the late 1950s. The front was originally made up of broad alliances between nationalist or Marxist groups active at the time. They took part in the struggle for independence, but ideologically their sense of direction tended to be hazy. Especially in the 1940s and 1950s, there were significant differences both within and among the various political organizations. There was, for instance, the clash between the SFIO and the Senegalese Democratic Union (Bathily, 1986).

The first test this kind of alliance faced was the issue of neo-colonialism. Some political forces refused to turn into imperialist clients. The opposition, attempting to get organized, erupted into violence during the election campaigns of 1961 and 1963. Because the working class was small, and because it proved impossible to set up a peasant organization strong enough to wield decisive influence on the country's political direction, the power base of forces capable of challenging the regime was narrow. One faction within the alliance broke off to become managers of the system of economic exploitation. The others, in a response typical of African nationalist organizations, as pointed out by Mandaza (1986), undertook to purge the nationalist movement. The Marxists, along with selected nationalist factions, gradually distanced themselves from the broad alliances of former years, the better to concentrate on the defence of workers' rights in various political and trade union organizations. Apart from those in the student movement, such organizations generally had a hard time surviving the repressive onslaughts of the State apparatus and the left-wing organizations' own suicidal taste for schisms. Whatever their shortcomings, though, they did succeed in mobilizing the urban intelligentsia permanently in the anti-imperialist, nationalist cause.

The ruling class failed to wipe out of the popular consciousness the lessons of the struggle against the colonial administration. That experience had tended to show that State power was vincible. On account of its authoritarian style, the ruling class got steadily isolated from radical intellectuals. Yet the radicals could not find a way to formulate political claims with mass appeal. They did try to move beyond the level of elitist factions of Westernized activists, but in vain. One reason was the factor Bianchini calls 'the total domination of the popular strata by Islam' (1988:174). A second was 'the addiction of Leninist organizations to sectarian splits' (1988:166). It was the kind of situation that led to the decline of those intellectuals formerly known as radicals, as Shivji (1989) makes clear.

Beginning in 1960, the expansion of State power, coupled with power struggles within the regime itself, made the State intolerant towards any competing power centre (Bianchini, 1988:239; Diop and Diouf, 1990). Between 1960 and 1963, the country's institutions were severely shaken by opposition challenges and by power struggles within the ruling class. From 1963 onwards, the State began to restructure itself to deal with a situation of permanent conflict between factions of the elite that had led the independence struggle. The period saw the emergence of authoritarian techniques designed in the first place to repress left-wing intellectual protest. In time the authoritarian trend came to penetrate and dominate the institutional apparatus of the State, preventing them from facilitating the development of any independent power base. By roping selected groups into mergers and banning others, the government pushed opposition groups into a corner where it became practically impossible for them to oppose it and still remain within the law (Hesseling, 1985:257).

The Senegalese authorities forbade all political demonstrations where radical intellectuals could make public statements. That ban turned the university campus into the prime venue for the expression of organized opposition viewpoints. By the same token, the university became the battleground for conflicting leftist groups. Various factions within the student movement reflected viewpoints of different left-wing parties. The student movement remained true to a local opposition tradition of habitual challenges to institutional values. It was characterized by extremely intense ideological debates raging over the underlying assumption that the outbreak of a revolutionary movement was imminent. Discussions in the 1960s' were dominated by one issue: the need to oppose the neo-colonial State and its subservience to imperialist interests.

When the student movement adopted objectives hostile to the interests of the ruling class, the State deployed a repressive machinery that combined manipulative techniques with ideological police tactics designed to head off any direct challenge to its domination. A study of the way the Senegalese State managed student union movements reveals that it was steered by a guideline similar to that identified by Abdalla in his work on the student movement in Egypt: there was a constant effort to marginalize the movement by cutting it off from dissident groups within the emergent social order. Abdalla (1985: 214) quotes the Cairo University Vice-Chancellor's advice to his students:

> Here in the university, you can discuss everything and express any opinion. But if you go into the streets you will lose your immunity, since you are no longer in the university precincts, and will not be able to ensure that events will turn out as you want them to.

The crisis of the educational system in general and the university system in particular, and the break in the normal transitional flow from student life to professional careers, were both intensified after 1960. They thus became an issue of national political debate. To understand the political and cultural stakes involved in the situation, we have to look into the historical background. The rise of the French school system in Senegal, especially the coming of the university, shook up the local power structure along with its cultural bases. Before the emergence and expansion of the Western educational system, Senegalese societies had created a sub-system of intellectual production and accumulation with its stock of technical, magical and religious data on various aspects of life. This sub-system was a key component in the machinery of social reproduction. A number of social groups owed their emergence and status to their mastery over and control of the available knowledge and technical know-how. The regime that rose to manage the social and political system depended on the ability to keep the majority of the population from gaining access to the fundaments of the kind of knowledge and expertise involved. That was the way in which the authorities ensured their strict control over the social and cultural bases of the distribution of power. An uncontrolled spread of knowledge and technical know-how was likely to undermine the expert status of established groups. It would also surely sap the very foundations of the cultural system.

In the wake of independence, the political establishment was faced with the challenge of limiting the impact on the social structure of the accumulation of various kinds of knowledge. It therefore worked out a way to place taboos on selected forms of intellectual criticism, on the grounds that such ideas threatened the fundaments of what they defined as "tradition". The attempt to manipulate "tradition" in this way was no easy task. Social and political changes in the period after 1960 forced component groups within the Westernized elite to define fresh objectives. Economic structures had changed, and the Senegalese economy had become increasingly integrated into the world market. This led, quite early, to a demand for specialized labour. Traditional educational systems were not equipped to meet that need. The same changing social context gradually transformed the functional role of the educational process. Where in the past education had mainly served to ensure the strict defence of tradition, now it began to focus on training people to cope with social change. Simultaneously, the changed situation brought about a differentiation between various sections - political, intellectual, administrative, technical - of the elite. In these circumstances, higher education rapidly emerged as the dominant mechanism for a system of social distribution based on individual merit.

The university's role in the creation of the elite was accentuated by the characteristic traits of the country's economy at the time of independence. The economy then was dominated by foreign companies established back in colonial times[4]. Culturally speaking, given the fact that it had only been in existence a short time, there was no way the university could claim to be an institutional venue for the affirmation of the national cultural heritage. As the public sector expanded, the university became the main corridor leading to higher-echelon jobs in the civil service. It also became an important wheel in the promotional machinery of the nation-State. It was in part on account of the development of the university that a middle class bourgeoisie grew up and began to reproduce itself. Because no one in Senegal was in a position to mount a direct challenge to foreign capital, and also because the country did not have a national bourgeoisie worthy of that description, the new ruling class found itself with no field of self-expression beyond the political, ideological and cultural spheres of life. It therefore moved to take over those spheres, while continuing to bargain for more economic elbow room.

In the process, the importance of the university in the self-perpetuation of different factions within the middle class became patent. The fact that the university functioned as the leading instrument for the training of elite groups from day one was no longer disputed. The institution was therefore a major prize with ramifications beyond the purely economic area. For its operations impacted directly on the cultural, political and social configuration of the country.

The moment it became clear that the university was a key to social control, the country's colonial and neo-colonial rulers spared no effort to dominate it. Their efforts became all the more strenuous as students kept tirelessly challenging the status of the ruling class by trying to strip Senghor of his legitimizing charisma. And the clash was all the sharper since Senghor played a key role in determining the direction of the educational system. Senghor was, in all practical terms, his own Minister of National Education, and in that sense he was fundamentally different from his successor, Abdou Diouf.

To begin with, campus protests focused on political claims coupled with attacks on the instructional curriculum and demands for conformity with the French model. As Bailleul (1984) has observed, in the history of the university institution, key protagonists had always been sensitive to personnel-related issues. Certain student and faculty claims were based on the metropolitan French educational model. Indeed, discrepancies in hiring methods for French and overseas faculty were extreme (Bailleul, 1984:34). In the early days the colonial authorities seem to have been rather lax as far as recruitment standards were concerned. Students and politicians alike therefore condemned the mediocrity of faculty hired to teach in the colonies. And students demanding faculty capable of giving them indisputably top-class instruction used the metropolitan educational standard. Their ideal, in sum, was elitist. The demand was made as far back as the establishment of the Dakar Institute of Advanced Studies in 1949-50. One more reason behind the claim was that the majority of students attending that institution at the time were Europeans. Because top-notch French academics were uninterested in jobs overseas, the faculty had a large number of secondary school teachers moonlighting as part timers. When the University of Dakar was created in 1957, the institution was brought more closely into line with the metropolitan system, and there was an improvement in the quality of the teaching faculty (Bailleul, 1984:36, 38).

The University of Dakar, then, became comparable in status to a metropolitan university. Student demands did not stop for all that. The political and ideological context was dominated by the anti-imperialist independence struggle, and there were courageous men pushing the idea of a University at the service of Africa, not a sterilized factory for the production of culturally alienated individuals. But the ruling class, never having opted for a national identity at variance with the colonial cultural scheme, was in no position to underwrite any such vision of the University. All in all, after twenty years of independence the policy followed by the ruling class was a continuation of the old colonial policy (Fatton, 1985).

Both the educational and top civil service systems were under direct, open French control. Students and faculty members protesting French cultural domination made this an issue. So between the State and those Senegalese who advocated struggle against acculturation, a conflict developed. The ruling elite was all the less inclined to meet such demands since the university depended heavily on France for both funding and aid personnel. The struggle for the country's economic and political independence, a cause dear to leftists, spilled over into the cultural sphere, with the university becoming one of the main battlefields. Linkages between various aspects of this struggle and other social movements were not unduly difficult, because in any case students already played an active role in political struggles. Thus, in the challenge it posed to the university, the student protest movement pointed to stakes beyond campus issues. One reason was that it indicated paths for other forms of political expression, attacked the power structure, and whittled away at the foundations of the regime's domination.

Campus opposition provoked a repressive reaction that led to a head-on collision between Senghor and the academic community. That opposition became a constant fixture in Senegalese political life. The State exerted unrelenting pressure in an effort to snuff out student organizations potentially capable of serving as vehicles for leftist challenges to the regime's hegemony. Partly on account of this repression, and also because opposition organizations had such a habit of splitting into warring factions, campus organizations tended to be notoriously short-lived.

The General Union of West African Students (UGEAO) was not the first student association (Bailleul, 1984:124). But it left a decisive imprint on the independence era both because of the huge area from which it drew its membership and because its propaganda was consistently internationalist, anti-colonial and anti-imperialist. Diané offers an accurate description of the part played by the UGEAO in the political and trade union experience of African students:

The UGEAO as a political and labour organization was to play an important part in the development of Dakar university. Its history was peppered with numerous clashes with the central government authorities in Dakar. It went through a series of poignant confrontations with political leaders thought to be collaborators or stooges of the regime. The UGEAO worked closely with the Federation of Black African Students in France (FEANF). Their cooperation was greatly facilitated by the fact that all students at the budding University of Dakar were at that time expected to continue their studies in France. Apart from cooperation at the leadership level, the UGEAO also provided the black African student movement in France with seasoned, militant and committed leaders (Diané, 1990:38-9).

The UGEAO had a pan-African membership. Its leadership also had a pan-African cast. The organization was therefore subjected to strict security surveillance, leading in 1961 and 1962 to a repressive assault that deprived it of its leadership structure:

> *Quite clearly, it would have been unrealistic to expect the Senegalese political authorities to tolerate the existence of a countervailing power centre just a few kilometers from the presidential palace, especially since that power centre seemed alien to them, partly because its policy focus was so radically different from the Senegalese government's own policy objectives, and partly because there were so few Senegalese on the UGEAO's executive committees. It seemed as if the UGEAO were under the control of foreign students, most of them from Dahomey (Bailleul, 1984:126).*

Despite official repression, the student leadership was able to set up strong organizations. Thus, after the UGEAO was dissolved in 1964, the Dakar Students' Union (UED) and its Senegalese branch, the Democratic Union of Senegalese Students (UDES) were created in 1966. Both played key roles in providing students with valuable political and trade union experience and training (Bailleul, 1984:132). The organization had an explicit rationale for such training:

> *We consider training in trade union matters inseparable from political education. That is why the ultimate aim of training for work in student unions ought to be the efficient preparation of African students for active integration in the life of their society.... It is therefore absolutely necessary for us to make use of the context of student union organization as a venue for effective decolonization. That means we have to be careful to block the infiltration of reactionary ideologies into the University (UED, 1966:10).*

On 28 February 1966, the UED organized a march on the American and British embassies to protest the overthrow of Kwame Nkrumah. The march came to be remembered as the 28 February movement[5]. The following is a student account of the event.

> *At 1 p.m. on Monday 28 February 1966, the student body attended a meeting on campus to protest the recent string of putsches in Africa. The meeting turned into a peaceful march towards the British and American embassies. But the forces of repression (police and gendarmerie) halted the students with tear gas grenades and batons. Some marchers got arrested. On Tuesday 1 March, students decided to strike until their 47 arrested comrades were released. They were released, and on 2 March lectures resumed as usual. That same day, however, the authorities summoned eight students to the Ministry of National Education. There, five were arrested by the police. Five students, three of them from Dahomey, the remaining two from Upper Volta, were banned from the campus and their scholarships withdrawn (UED, 1966:2).*

The 1960s saw the rise of anti-imperialist student organizations, with the African Independence Party (PAI) getting a solid footing among students and lecturers. That led to the suspicion that the PAI had infiltrated the UDES and the Senegalese Teachers' Union (SES). In his work on socio-political conflicts in the 1960s, Abdoulaye Ly analyzes the student movement and its role in that context:

Following the dissolution of the General Union of West African Students (UGEAO), the struggle of the Dakar student body came to a halt. In 1966, it picked up again with the emergence of two new organizations after the decision to go on a 45-day strike on 28 February that year, the day after the suppression of a planned march on the British and American embassies in protest against the fall of Nkrumah. The Dakar Students' Union (UED) was a supra-national organization, but it seems to have been under the influence of the PAI student movement MEEPAI. And the Senegalese national student organization, the Democratic Union of Senegalese Students (UDES) was under its direct control. That, at any rate, seemed to be the case, to judge from the fast-breaking events of 1968 involving the Senegalese movement (Ly, 1979:12)[6].

In the course of the 1968 strike, the UDES played a clearly catalytic role. Its leadership included students who belonged to the MEEPAI (Thioub, 1990:10). In various student organizations, the most highly politicized members rose to leadership positions. Their activities were structured by the political context in which they worked. So the presence of Marxist students in the UDES leadership was not the consequence of a devilish plot but a result of the highly conflictual relationships between the government and the intellectual left organized within the PAI. Among the activities of the banned UGEAO taken over by the UED, the People's African University did some significant work. The authorities accused that organization of being a centre for communist propaganda:

The People's African University (UPA), an organization entirely run by students connected in the past with the UGEAO and now with the UED, was without doubt the most brilliant contribution of militant students to classroom education in Africa. It was no secret that schoolchildren attending courses run by the UPA achieved fine results in both the primary school leaving examinations and the A-Level equivalent certificate examination. Unfortunately, the Senegalese authorities decided nevertheless to ban the UPA school in December 1965. By that stroke they denied over 600 schoolchildren an opportunity to get a free education. This year we have to do all we can to get the UPA courses restarted (UED, 1966:12).

The UGEAO served as a dominant role model for protest organizations in the 1960s. Campus organizations followed its lead, and the General Union of Senegalese Students (UGES) was among the most faithful in this respect. One of the pressure tactics the State used against these organizations was to deport extremist leaders if they came from other countries, and to stop them from registering for courses if they were Senegalese. Such repressive tactics escalated the political stakes involved in campus struggles and gave a more violent twist to protests, making them spill over beyond the campus context proper. The consequence was the emergence of groups with anti-assimilationist ideas expressing them in struggles for the advancement of national languages, the reassertion of Senegalese cultural values, and the development of a more African or more Senegalese University. Throughout the 1960s, this struggle led to the maintenance of lasting antagonisms and claims. Combined with the growing frustration of the urban petty bourgeoisie, it led to the May 1968 crisis. As Fatton (1985) observes with admirable cogency, May 1968 proved that independence had disappointed the people as a whole. For that reason, the argument that the May 1968 movement in Dakar was simply a copy-cat reflex based on the French student upheaval of that year is hard to sustain. There is plenty of evidence against that claim. As early as October 1967, the UDES had issued a 'UDES Memorandum on Events at the University of Dakar'. That memorandum shows clearly that the Dakar campus was already a hotbed of protest. The reason was that the government had defined a new set of guidelines for scholarship awards, now scheduled to cover ten months, not the entire year:

> Students with relatively well-off parents living in Dakar will only be entitled to half scholarships. Two-thirds of all scholarships will be awarded to students with relatively well-off parents living outside Dakar, and to students with parents living in Dakar but belonging to low-income groups. Students whose parents live outside Dakar and also earn low incomes may be awarded full scholarships (Dakar Matin, 13 October 1967).

Negotiations between students and the authorities from February to April 1968 broke down, leading to a warning strike on 18 May 1968. On 26 May, the UDES Executive Committee decided to bring all work on campus to a halt, beginning on 27 May 1968. The strike would be unlimited, examinations would be boycotted, and pickets would be organized outside the various faculties (UDES, 1968). The student union also appealed to all democratic organizations and all patriotic forces to come together in a broad united front for the struggle to rid the country of neocolonialism and its lackeys (UDES, 1968:8).

From 28 May, the social situation at the University worsened fast. The police moved in with force and arrested several student leaders. Labour unions called for a general strike from 31 May (Lo, 1987:46). The government reacted by arresting several leaders of the National Union of Senegalese Workers (UNTS). According to Lo, who was then in the government, the idea was 'to disrupt the trade union movement by attacking its leadership' (Lo, 1987:46-47). This situation, lasting until 4 June, was from the ruling class viewpoint extremely serious, as Lo aptly points out:

A colleague came, personally and very confidentially, to inform me that the President had just agreed with the French Ambassador that should the situation degenerate to the point where extraordinary measures were needed to rescue him, he would be "picked up" by helicopter from the presidential palace and put on a plane bound for France (Lo, 1987:54-55).

Official explanations for the 1968 strike include the assertion that foreign agents and the PAI manipulated the Senegalese involved (Lo, 1987:39). Bathily counters this supposition with a precise statement:

Naturally, among the leaders of the 1968 student movement, there were people like us. But we were a mere handful. Those of us who were MEEPAI members at the University of Dakar were scarcely ten, out of a student body numbering 3000 at the time. The 1968 movement was primarily a spontaneous protest movement pushing student demands. But it also put forward claims on behalf of the entire working class (Ndiaye et al., 1990:114).

In the late 1960s, the Senegalese political scene went through a particularly instructive process. Certain leaders mainly products of the post-independence student union movement, attempted to reorganize the opposition by formulating claims increasingly antagonistic to government policy objectives. The consequence was a clash that continued well into the 1970s. On account of it, the government made all opposition political organizations and activities illegal, leaving underground work as the only possible mode for dissidence. The situation moved the most radical leftist groups to distribute tracts and newspapers attacking the government. Some also engaged in violent acts.

Within trade union organizations, teachers stated their claims in the Senegalese Teachers' Union (SES) and later in the Senegalese Unified Democratic Teachers' Union (SUDES), which left a lasting imprint on teachers' minds. These claims were put forward at a time when the teachers' unions were getting reformed. Where in the past the activist membership of such organizations had come mainly from primary school teachers, now young high school teachers and university lecturers took the lead. A new style developed in which attempts were made to harness selected political organizations to local traditions of anti-colonial struggle[7] and to a symbolic imagery derived from those traditions. In this attempt to break with the State-centred collective memory and to regain lost historical terrain, the dominant names that kept cropping up included Lamine Senghor, Mamadu Laamin Daraame, C. Sidia Léon Joop, Aliin Sitoë Jaata, and Ndatte Yalla.

Opposition members in the Maoist organization *Andë Jeff* dropped the thematic and symbolic approaches favoured by the remaining opposition groups in their confrontation with the State. In the process, they abandoned the working class focus central to the paradigms of Marxist intellectuals. In the 1970s, several programmes were designed to implement the new strategies of radical rift: a "Cultural Front" organization was set up as a research, production and propaganda structure. Sports clubs and cultural associations were established to ensure links with the 'masses'. The town of Thiès was a particularly active centre in the ensuing cultural ferment.

There had been a tendency for radicals in the country to be marginalized because their theories were so far removed from local realities. *Andë Jeff* slowed down that trend. Through a process of calculated historical revision, its leaders attempted to bring heroes forgotten or neglected by the State into the limelight. Using accounts of outstanding feats of resistance in local history, they tried to assert dissident cultural values. This helped reduce the impact of the historical narrative projected by 'the State as historiographer'.[8] By the same token, such work stopped the marginalization of radical intellectuals by significantly reducing the gap between living realities and their theoretical reflections thereon.

At this point there was a crystallization of dissident political and cultural issues. A new crop of political and labour leaders emerged whose ideological make-up was dominated by clashes between positions derived from East bloc alliances, and a series of particularly lively confrontations between left-wing communist factions. In this way they also helped to accentuate the segmentation of the left. Maoists facilitated the resurgence of left-wing opposition rhetoric. Their main ideological parameter was a cultural protest against the values projected by President Senghor, the 'bard of Negritude'. This leftist faction, led by such former students as Marie Angelique Savané, was able to gain a foothold in the working class, especially at the CSS sugar factory in the north of the country. It also made inroads into the student body through the Patriotic National Union of Senegalese Students (UNAPES), which succeeded in dominating competing factions.

It was the UNAPES[9] which projected the anti-assimilationist message of cultural resistance on campus. It persuaded students to adopt its opposition viewpoints thanks to a set of leaders drawing their charisma from the handling of learned jargon and popularized versions of the "scientific knowledge" on which the power of certain intellectual gurus was founded. The UNAPES was successful in part because of a resurgence of trade union agitation, in part because of significant changes in student enrollment and intellectual intake, and partly because it knew how to manipulate the burning political issues of the day. Its operations coincided with the crisis in the hegemonic power of the regime during the late 1970s, which led to rising dissatisfaction and protests, especially among students and teachers, leading role players on the Senegalese left.

The Campus Crisis
The crisis shaking Senegalese society as a whole did not leave the University untouched. It was thus in a period of the institution's decline that the UNAPES emerged on campus. Among the hallmarks of the crisis, there was the deterioration of teaching and research establishments while they faced acute operational problems, saw their academic standards fall as their enrollment levels soared and cash became even scarcer, and a new crop of unemployed graduates emerged (Senegal, 1989:89). The shortage of textbooks and teaching equipment made lecture room note-taking the dominant form of intellectual transmission, placing a heavy accent on the oral mode in academic discourse. One remark made by Copans concerning the situation of African universities is particularly relevant here:

Schools and universities were plunged into an unprecedented crisis. The demagogic fashion for populist democratic posturing had glorified formal education as a supreme value to the point of making content irrelevant. Above all, with the passage of time the educational establishments were also shorn of all efficiency. Real doubts were raised by the proliferating institutions, skyrocketing enrollments with no proper preparation, and the cheapening of the learning process. Rote learning and shoddy work became the order of the day. Instead of reading books, students copied lecture notes. And in place of accurate monitoring of degree standards, favouritism and trickery became highways to academic credentials (Copans, 1990:312).

It is probably inaccurate to blame lecturers for the fall in standards. But it must be said that their attitudes did nothing to stop the rot. Hirji's observations on the University of Tanzania (Hirji, 1990) seem applicable to the Senegalese situation. The campus crisis provoked reactions aimed at ensuring financial survival. Hirji points out that in trying to cope with the crisis, lecturers made a show of keeping up instructional standards in grading their students more rigorously, but that this strictness contrasted with lackadaisical attitudes towards their research, publication and teaching duties.

An analysis of the distribution of the meager resources available to the university over the past several years between staff, the administration and academic requirements (World Bank, 1992) shows that the proportion of the Ministry of National Education's budget allocated to higher education rose from 16% in 1983-84 to 25% in 1990-91. Concurrently, social expenditure was seen to have increased rapidly as compared to allocations for instructional equipment. According to World Bank estimates, in one decade university expenditure apart from emoluments dropped from 53% of the budget to 27%. One wonders what kind of coalition of forces took the decisions thus leading step by step to the transformation of lecturers into scapegoats of the crisis.

Students in the 1960s had a consciousness shaped by the combined experience of labour union and revolutionary party activism. Students in the 1970s, however, did not have a consciousness geared to the expectations of any revolutionary movement. They had the consciousness of student unions waging short-term struggles. The shift coincided with a decrease in the influence of the African Independence Party (PAI) (Hesseling, 1985), weakened by infighting among its leadership. The localization of consciousness took place at a time when the student movement was busily involved in the practical business of rebuilding and reorganizing itself. As always, however, student politics were marked by intense ideological debate. And the movement spread rapidly among the youth, because the public school system had a mass enrollment base.

In the absence of reliable data on the social backgrounds of students, we can only surmise that some came from poor, rural families. For young people, especially those from the lower classes, the university was a key rung on the social ladder, a path to the fulfillment of dreams. Children from the politico-bureaucratic bourgeoisie and the wealthier strata sought to cash in on their economic legacy by converting it into intellectual capital. They did this by opting out of the local elite training system and going instead to universities in France and, more recently, North America. With increasing costs and enrollment levels, competition for available financial assistance grew fierce. Students challenged the quality of the financial aid system and the subsidized arrangements for providing such services as board, lodging and health care. And yet budgetary allocations in the higher educational system had on the whole favoured student aid expenditure to the detriment of expenditure for faculty and instructional equipment (World Bank, 1992). According to World Bank estimates, nearly half the higher educational budget goes routinely into such social expenditure as scholarships and allocations for board and lodging. Under these circumstances, the demand for instruction rises, leading, when frustrated, to strikes.

The University has no private endowments. Students contribute little to recurrent costs. The State is therefore increasingly hard pressed to maintain operational standards. The situation is likely to get worse. The educational policy component of the structural adjustment programme has already come up with the verdict that it is too "costly" to keep African universities running. Furthermore, graduates' credentials are considered inadequate, mainly on the grounds that 'studies are not properly oriented towards development'. Orivel (1988) presents a telling caricature of the deprecatory rhetoric on the dysfunctional impact of the mass-scale university[10]. It was partly because funding agencies made such a fuss about the inefficiency of the University and the fact that its linkages with the economy were weak that the educational reform plan inspired by the General Conference on Education got stalled. Meanwhile, discrepancies between objectives set by the technical services in charge of the State budget and those working in the National Commission on Educational and Training Reform (CNREF) have grown more serious.

In the face of radical positions taken by teachers' and students' unions, the State offered certain concessions regarding salaries. But this meant cuts in allocations for educational materials and equipment, supplies of which have become increasingly dependent on the availability of foreign aid. It also meant worsening student-lecturer ratios, particularly at the undergraduate level. In the past, university lectureships had provided a path towards upward mobility for some social strata; now the prospect looks grim. Intense demand among students from wealthier families for places in foreign universities indicates increasing insecurity about the likelihood of their being able to "cash in on their intellectual capital" in the near future.

The financial crunch within the university (Coordination des étudiants de Dakar, 1991:3-8) came at a time of tremendous growth in school enrollment levels. It also coincided with large-scale unemployment among university graduates. The main consequence of the latter development was the devaluation of academic credentials and the posts they formerly led to[11]. Among the most unsettling consequences was the change in the status of students. In the past, university students in Senegal represented a modern elite. They were living images of the shape of things to come. In the current crisis context, however, there is no longer any definite prospect that students will graduate to fill those positions that their status formerly entitled them to. With the disappearance of posts, attendant opportunities also dwindled. Caught with no clear view of their future prospects, students have tended to get mired in the present. Their union aspirations have become accordingly short-term. That is one reason for the protests against the legitimacy of the university institution and the selection process on which it is based. In effect, students are using radical methods of struggle to combat the imminent likelihood of their own social exclusion.

Bourdieu puts the situation nicely when he describes the new forms of struggle, a far cry from the elitist methods that became an invariable hallmark of the old left, as a form of 'secessionist movement' involving students threatened with exclusion: 'Formerly, their status implied a guaranteed place as starters in the race towards the future. Now they have been reduced to non-starters. In reaction, they intend to challenge the validity of the race itself'. (Bourdieu, 1984:225). Such struggles were all the more effective because during the 1970s, when jobs were Africanized, large numbers of young lecturers were hired. In the beginning, on account of the draconian selection and advancement process in force, which kept them from getting promoted, the young lecturers did not develop any great feeling of attachment to the university as an institution. Indeed, promotion hassles tended to embitter them. For though they had joined a profession considered prestigious at the time, their personal advancement remained a chancy business. So they had little sense of an *esprit de corps* with their senior colleagues on the faculty. In Bourdieu's phrase, they did not 'bond in anticipated identification' (Bourdieu, 1984:225). In sum, the younger lecturers felt closer to students than to professors.

The problems involved in the search for tenure at the University were exemplified by power struggles in the faculties (*Wal Fadjri*, 186-189), especially in the Humanities Faculty, as well as by the attempt, in the late 1970s, made by teachers' unions to loosen the tight monitoring system under which junior lecturers laboured. In the 1980s the tenure battle was won, but then the new lecturers found themselves facing further problems: their living conditions kept deteriorating. Such problems were all the harder to understand since in some faculties, lecturers were handling courses that normally should have been handled by full professors[12].

Disillusionment among the teaching staff merged with the discontent of students increasingly anxious about the devaluation of academic credentials. The result was the generalized crisis that shook the university in the late 1980s. One upshot was the wasted academic year of 1988. As far as 1960s-style opposition groups were concerned, the lost year was a disaster, a levelling action from the ground up. This assessment, by itself, pointed to the rise of a new type of student consciousness relatively independent of the elitist hold of the traditional leftist leadership. It also made mincemeat of the supposition that student groups were manipulated by outside forces. The crisis caused a significant shortening of the academic year, thus emphasizing the devaluation of university credentials.

These developments gave vent to a degree of student animosity towards society. Their demands, decidedly radical, showed a thorough distrust of official statements and a readiness to challenge the competence of lecturers and professors. Demands for the establishment of a university educational service[13] to monitor teachers' qualifications, for instance, were to a certain extent motivated by such vindictive attitudes. In putting forward such demands, student leaders pushed claims similar to those made by the first generation of Dakar University students, in the sense that they wanted to draw closer to the French educational model.

One issue of particular importance is the degree of Africanization of Dakar University teaching staff. In 1970, out of a total faculty of 192 lecturers and professors, 91 were Africans (Senegal, 1984:96). In 1989, according to available data on the faculty (Statistics Bureau, Vice-Chancellor's Office, UCAD), 493 out of a total staff complement of 573 were Africans. Over the decade, variations within faculties were significant. In the Arts Faculty, the level of Africanization rose from 41.1% in 1978 to 91.59% in 1989. In the Faculty of Medicine, the increase was from 57% to 87.20%. In that faculty a large number of lecturers qualified for upgrading in the competitive bar examinations held in the 1980s. For that reason, out of a total of 184 Africans on the teaching staff in 1988-89, 62 were full and associate professors.

Some young lecturers in the Faculty of Medicine rose to prominence in their fields of specialization with remarkable speed. But the same thing happens, as a rule, in French medical faculties. Still, one wonders if the notoriously intense rat race in various faculties has not compromised the quality of research and teaching. Meanwhile, it has become clear that students' studies and their general intellectual development is narrowly focused on present needs. At the level of student unions, this focus is reflected in activist strategies which have contributed to the impasse of the university as an institution. Because students vote in elections for faculty deans[14], they have considerable clout during these campaigns marked by internecine rivalries between groups of lecturers and professors. They therefore know that their power comes from the electioneering connected with these contests. The alliances formed in the process are not calculated to reinforce the institutional authority of the university.

In combination with the relative effectiveness of student union activism, this is among the reasons why students who fail their courses (they are known as *cartouchards*) can renew their course registrations with such ease. Faculty deans are victims of a system that affords them no protection from pressure mounted by students wanting exemptions from regular re-inscription standards. In the past, left-wing student unions fought hard to obtain the Africanization of university jobs. Today their success has created a situation in which students are increasingly hostile to African lecturers and professors. Politicians like Abdoulaye Wade, incidentally, are quick to point an accusing finger at the university:

> *Standards at our university keep falling year by year. To raise them, we have to raise the standards of teaching staff. Unfortunately, what we find more frequently these days is that side by side with eminent professors, some of them learned indeed, we have lecturers and professors of doubtful quality. Some, to call a spade a spade, are downright mediocre. That's what the students themselves say (Sopi, 1 March 1991:5).*

Beyond the rhetorical violence of student leaders, the increasingly radical strikes and the chronic atmosphere of protest and confrontation on campus all indicate that they are battling against a fate that seems more and more ineluctable: their slide into an ever-lower social status. Official sources indicate that out of every 1000 students registered in each of the main faculties, the number making it into the fourth year, and the number of students who graduate with a master's degree, are as follows (Senegal, 1981:91):

Law:	275 and 265;
Economics:	397 and 389;
Arts and Humanities:	308 and 195;
Natural Sciences:	244 and 156.

In effect, by opting out of the race for degrees and defining claims of an increasingly political nature, student leaders raise the stakes in their confrontations with authority, making settlements all the harder. One consequence is that some students, faced with failure year after year, have lost faith in the university. Their parents go along with this disillusionment. For that reason, attacks against the university have become a form of protest.

Factional Struggles in the 1970s

With the exception of students in the youth wing of the ruling Socialist Party[15], the student body, taken as a whole, has been much closer to the intellectual left than to the regime. And the Socialist Party group on campus, though benefiting from hefty injections of financial incentive, has remained relatively small. There is every indication that the terrible deterioration in the status of students facilitates the outbreak of increasingly drawn-out conflicts. In any case, the fact that the student body is so close to the intellectual left has occasioned serious leadership problems over the past several years. The recent history of the student movement bears this out.

In January 1971, political tension soared following the publication of tracts attacking government policy. On 18 January 1971, a tract entitled *A Call to the People* published by an extremist left-wing group condemned the "hypocritical show" being prepared for the scheduled visit of G Pompidou the following month. In February 1971, a sensational sortie by a group of schoolchildren and students called "The Arsonists" ended in the torching of the French Cultural Centre. The official press reported the event in these terms:

> *February 1971. President Georges Pompidou was scheduled shortly to visit a number of States, including Senegal. There was the smell of cordite in the air, however. It exploded a few days later. Fifteen youths raided the French Cultural Centre and set it on fire. In short order they were arrested (Le Soleil, 27 March 1974).*

A number of militant students who had fled to neighbouring countries, especially to Mali, were extradited on 4 February 1972 and tried on 22 March by a special court. One of them, Omar Blondin Diop, a charismatic student leader, died in jail under murky circumstances in May 1973, aggravating social tension. The UPS Centre for Socialist Studies, Research and Education strained to offer explanations, but Blondin Diop's death discredited the government. It was forced to cope with fierce criticism from such academics as P. Fougeyrollas, who declared:

> *None of Senghor's humanistic or pseudo-humanistic statements will ever make people forget the heroic resistance of Omar Blondin Diop, and the martyr's fate he suffered. He was a militant African with clear and generous ideas which, together with his radical activities, presage the coming of mass struggles that will soon end the corrupt reign of French capitalists in Senegal* (Fougeyrollas: Senegal, 1973: 13).

Meanwhile, the Special Court meted out increasingly harsh sentences against students accused of torching school buildings (*Le Soleil*, 6 October 1973) as well as distributors of tracts considered subversive. Some of the trials were nothing short of sensational. At the session held on 2 November 1973, for instance, the defendants were accused of circulating tracts reporting that the head of State, during a visit to the Vatican, had assured Pope Paul VI that 'even if he failed to make Senegal a Catholic country, he would do his best to make the Senegalese bad Muslims' (*Le Soleil*, 7 November 1973). The defendants responded by saying: 'We found this tract so stupid as to be insignificant. We reproduced it only to satisfy our intellectual curiosity' (*Le Soleil*, 7 November 1973). There were other trials of student leaders accused of having tried "to run an illegal association," the AGES (*Le Soleil*, 6 and 9 October 1973). These trials were held at a time when the government was doing its best to dismantle revolutionary unions. To a considerable extent, they also involved teachers' unions. (Cf. *Le Soleil*, 21 July 1971; 9 October 1973; and Paye, 1978).

After the UDES and the UED[16] were dissolved on 28 February 1971 (JORS, 17 April 1971: 379), the government drafted legislation designed to block protest movements on campus. Penalties ranged from two-year enrollment bans to complete dismissal. Implementation began on 17 March 1971, when a group of fifty students were forbidden to re-enrol. It was reinforced in 1973 and 1977, when dozens of students in academic and specialized institutions were banned. On 6 September 1971, the government drafted legislation for the creation of a university police corps with the following terms of reference (Decree 71-993, 6 September 1971):

a) To monitor the observance of general rules pertaining to law and order formulated by the Vice-Chancellor, as well as bye-laws issued by faculties and institutes;

b) To monitor regular attendance by students at lectures, under conditions laid down by the Vice-Chancellor;

c) To safeguard university property;

d) To ensure a calm atmosphere conducive to the normal work of the University;

e) To monitor infringements of University rules, and in general to provide the University authorities with all information likely to help prevent the outbreak of such infringements (JORS, 1971:961).

Along with these measures, there was a notable proliferation, from 1968 to 1973, of training colleges established under the supervision of the armed forces and subject to military discipline[17]. The attempt to dismantle revolutionary student movements also involved the enforcement of stricter discipline in national training colleges as well as the manipulation of financial incentives and penalties. It gradually achieved a separation between the student movement on the university campus and that at the national training colleges.

The disbandment of the UDES and the UED pushed student union activists underground. The General Association of Senegalese Students (AGES), founded in May 1972, called itself 'an anti-imperialist union defending the material and spiritual interests of students and advocating the creation of a genuinely democratic University at the service of the African peoples' (AGES, 1972). The first public meeting of the AGES, scheduled for 26 January 1973, was brutally broken up by police forces following fights between militants of the new organization and UPS activists. The official press described the meeting in the following terms:

To mark the death of Amilcar Cabral, Secretary-General of the PAIGC, students requested permission to hold a protest meeting. The government, considering this normal, agreed. It turned out, however, that at the meeting little was said about the deceased PAIGC leader. The students spent most of their time talking politics, with each national union heaping insults on its government. Worse still, the protesters prevented a dissenting student from speaking, and threatened him. Furthermore, before adjourning the meeting, they decided, without requesting permission, to hold a meeting at 21 hours on 26 January for the purpose of forming an association.. On 26 January, then, the protesting students, bent on holding their meeting, began with a public gathering. Students belonging to the UPS decided to participate actively in this meeting, with the intention of frustrating this attempt at provocation. That was when the fighting began. The police intervened and broke up the student gathering... Subsequently, the protesters formed commando squads of ten, sometimes twenty each, and went through dormitories and lecture rooms assaulting those who disagreed with them, sometimes right before their professors (Le Soleil, 3 February 1973:3).

From 1971 to 1974, a number of radical students took to torching school buildings and writing and distributing tracts considered subversive by the State. The authorities reacted by arresting students and teachers in droves. "Support Groups for Victims of Repression in Senegal" condemned the resulting human rights abuses (*Le Monde*, 22 October 1975). To defuse the situation, the government proclaimed a political amnesty in 1974. After that, President Senghor authorized the creation of the Senegalese Democratic Party (PDS). At its inception, that party defined itself as a 'contributory party'. The new measures, however, did not entirely stop the activities of underground groups, whose membership included current and former students. In 1975, the police was able to identify and arrest several underground political leaders. The press then began issuing reports on a so-called *Xarebi* affair. Meanwhile, the urban petty bourgeoisie was growing increasingly frustrated. Various student and teachers' organizations sprang up to push its demands, with the SUDES and the UNAPES playing leading roles. Hence the severity of government repression.

The expulsion of student leaders from schools and the University destabilized their organizations. The authorities no longer allowed any student associations to operate unless they were patently apolitical friendly associations (cf. Diop, 1975; Joop, 1975). In 1975, during the segmentation of the student movement, this type of organization flourished in the Arts Faculty, especially in the Department of Classical Literature. The Law Faculty was also active. These friendly associations played a considerable part in reorganizing the student movement as well as in defending student interests. Their development went hand in hand with the restructuring of student unions organized by underground political organizations. Incidentally, there was a similar process going on in the teachers' unions following the dissolution of the SES by Decree 73-279 of 28 March 1973 (Paye, 1978).

To begin with, these associations limited their activities to simple cultural events such as lectures, film shows and plays. But soon, pressure built up for turning them away from their official purpose and into propaganda organs. As some student leaders explained, 'our experience with these organizations showed that once deviated from their cultural orientation, they could become nothing less than structures for combatting the very people who set them up' (UDED, undated: 5). On the whole, government repression in the early 1970s did not stop the creation of a student organization dedicated to the defence of the interests of students, like the ones typical of the first decade after independence. The official management approach emphasized the need to contain and depoliticize the student movement. These objectives were very clearly expressed in legislation on student organizations drafted after May 1968.

Within a collective volume of this kind, considerations of scope and space make it impossible to present an exhaustive analysis of the full range of tactics deployed towards that objective. We can, however, indicate that as from 1968, the State reinforced its measures of political control over student affairs by amending legislation and rules governing the University. The disciplinary code for students was toughened. Student representation at Faculty and university meetings was abolished. In 1971, an Interim Council was appointed to handle work normally done by the university Assembly and the Disciplinary Committee set up in October 1970. Modalities for the application of disciplinary authority in cases involving students were spelled out.

The intention behind these regulations[18] was to push students out of decision-making organs and to contain their demands[19]. That was why the State took care to redefine university freedoms in such a way as to give the concept of administrative police autonomy within the university environment a much more restrictive meaning. By manipulating the concept of university freedoms through the multiplication of loopholes in legislative and regulatory texts, the public authorities facilitated incursions of police forces into the university environment, giving the Vice-Chancellor substantial prerogatives denied other components of the University Assembly.

Factional fights within and among left-wing organizations hampered the reorganization of the student movement. Initiatives taken after 1975 concerning the orientation of the Student Association were not unanimously approved, and divergent attitudes remained unreconciled. Some students advocated the creation of 'a patriotic, anti-imperialist association'. Others wanted an 'independent democratic association'. The agenda called for the creation of a supra-national organization, and on this issue two viewpoints emerged. The first position, advanced by the UES, advocated the organization of such a body on the basis of the existing structure of friendly associations. The AGES, however, argued that it would be better to reorganize the movement on the basis of existing national students' unions on campus. Underlying the difference, naturally, was the problem of leadership. For behind each position lay the ill-concealed issue of the type of following that would dominate the resulting group. This was the dominant issue in debates within the Steering Committee for the Reorganization of the Senegalese Student Movement (CIRMES).

Between leaders advancing straightforward political demands and claims, and those whose main concern was the improvement of working and living conditions for students, the cleavage was sharp. Priorities diverged. Students took to characterizing the difference as a dichotomy between a *patriotic line* and a *bread-and-butter line*. In short, the cleavage was ideological. It pitted activists from various PAI factions against Maoist militants busy building up a power base in the student organizations. There was also a tactical dimension to the disagreement. Two opposing points of view were involved: one envisaged the reorganization of the student movement through a merger of friendly associations. The other called for the reorganization of a democratic student movement on the basis of national unions. Proponents of the latter viewpoint thought it a matter of urgent priority, a prerequisite in fact, that the Senegalese Students' Union itself be reorganized beforehand into a Senegalese National Union (UNAPES, 1986a).

The patriotic line was defined as follows:

The orientation of the UNAPES is anti-imperialist and patriotic. That is the ruling philosophy of the union. Through this combative stance, the UNAPES functions as the organization leading the struggle of Senegalese students for the defence of their material and spiritual interests. Under present circumstances, this means the struggle against their current living and working conditions; the struggle against the multi-faceted ideological misinformation directed at them, and the struggle to retrieve the democratic freedoms and prerogatives of the university (UNAPES, 1980:3).

The UNAPES leadership further stressed that:

As far as the UNAPES is concerned, the Senegalese educational system is basically anti-national, anti-democratic, and against the people. An analysis of these three characteristics clarifies our concept of a new Senegalese educational system, which would have to be national, democratic, and for the people. The same analysis gives us a set of

> *ineluctable guidelines for our union. Those guidelines are anti-imperialist, patriotic... Our option in favour of patriotism is eminently legitimate. For it is the nurturing sap of all our aspirations, the navel connecting us to our people, as we demand its fulfillment in an independent, prosperous Senegal in full control of her destiny* (UNAPES, 1980:5).

A second group of students advocated an antithetical position:

> *We have to work hard to develop guild-type friendly associations in the various faculties and institutes. Then we have to consolidate, re-orient and merge them. That will endow students with a vast, unifying organization capable of highlighting their practical problems and then solving them.... Those who think friendly associations are ineffective, and those who suppose that struggle within the framework of friendly associations is nothing better than legalistic corporatism, are making a mistake fraught with serious consequences. Similarly, those who say that before we can set up the Democratic Students' Association we first have to create a strong Senegalese National Union are wrong* (UES, 1978:4).

According to this group 'there was only one condition for bringing together all forces concerned with the struggle: we must start with their material and spiritual interests. On that basis, judging from results, support for their struggle is anti-imperialist work. The factor that determines the justice of this union line, as compared with the so-called anti-imperialist or patriotic line, is that it facilitates the creation of the one condition for an anti-imperialist struggle:

> *the bringing together of the largest possible number of students. After that, they can participate more widely in the struggle. By contrast, when students are brought together in ideologically defined groups, a large number of those forces likely to contribute to the struggle are excluded from the start. That hampers the fulfillment of the one condition in whose absence anti-imperialism is but an empty slogan. Anti-imperialism is not the starting point; it is the goal* (UDED, undated:9).

On 7 March 1977, a strike began from the Faculty of Science in protest against the government requirement that students sign an undertaking to work for the government for a 15-year period before they could receive scholarships. Differences crystallized from that point on. The moment the strike order was lifted, the UES mounted a harsh critique of its handling (UES, 1977). Yet throughout the strike, slogans on unity and the re-organization of the student movement had been key themes because there was no strong union on campus. Following the disbandment of the UDES and the UED, the AGES leadership had gone underground, and the UES, founded in 1976, was still structurally weak.

A document called the *Manifesto for a Patriotic Association of Senegalese Students* contained the following observation regarding the period:

> *Our objective analysis shows that the principal flaw of this movement, the cause of its failure, was the prevalence of divisions within its ranks. These divisions, the result of profound differences between the AGES and the UES, as both organizations indeed acknowledged, had a disastrous impact on all our initiatives. For a variety of reasons, the two campus groups were incapable of offering the vast majority of students a dynamic, clear-sighted organizational framework that could have guaranteed the success of their struggles* (CIRMES, 1979:5).

In their declaration on 9 January 1979, students belonging to the PAI accused the AGES of following 'a sectarian, dogmatic strategy and tactics out of sync with the broad democratic struggle'[20]. As for the UES, it was condemned for its role in the 1977 strike:

> *In 1977, students turned their backs on established channels of struggle and mounted a spontaneous uprising based on a set of 12 clear demands. Such spontaneity was a symptom of organizational immaturity on the part of the students, but the culprit was the UES. After all, it was the one organization with a serious mandate to organize Senegalese students*[21].

Such accusations were symptomatic of differences within the student leadership. Data covering the period from 1978 to the present shed useful light on these differences. As is well known, the Steering Committee on the Reorganization of the Student Movement (CIRMES) was elected on 5 November with the following terms of reference:

a) To conduct a broad publicity campaign on the creation of an association of Senegalese students reaching all venues where students might be found;
b) To monitor debates and thinking on the Senegalese student movement, the student movement at the University of Dakar, and the direction of the association;
c) To publish a Manifesto, followed by the convocation of a General Assembly;
d) To keep the student body well informed;
e) To facilitate discussions concerning the organization.

Structures were set up with a view to making the CIRMES more functional. These structures, known as Action Groups for the Reorganization of the Student Movement, did not meet with the approval of all student groups (UES, 1978:5).

Out of the debate between the CIRMES and the GARMES coordinating group emerged the *Manifesto for a Patriotic Association of Senegalese Students* in March 1979. The 18 March 1979 meeting between the CIRMES and the GARMES coordinating group resulted in a 23 March 1979 declaration proclaiming the founding of the Patriotic Union of Senegalese Students. The new body defined itself as 'anti-imperialist and patriotic'. One noteworthy point: in a document entitled *Declaration of the General Assembly of GARMES Coordinators in Favour of a Constituent Assembly to Form the UNAPES*, students who wanted the latter organization established decided, before the first UNAPES congress, to set up an Interim Executive Committee made up of CIRMES members.

A study of this document and the CIRMES programme report prepared for the constituent assembly meeting on 23 March reveals a great deal of disagreement within the CIRMES concerning the creation of the UNAPES, especially with regard to the policy direction of the planned organization. These differences were brought into the open in published tracts as well as during general assembly sessions like the one held on 21 December 1979[22]. One such broadside, dated 6 March 1980 and bearing the imprint of a body calling itself the 'El Mansour Nucleus'[23], condemned 'the anti-democratic tactics of sabotage and obstruction used by the Interim Executive Committee and the UNAPES faction falsely described as patriotic'. The group went on to pass a motion "defying the UNAPES, and breaking with it." The move was the culmination of political conflicts for the leadership of the student body.

The declaration of the 'El Mansour Nucleus' led to the foundation of the National Democratic Union of Senegalese Students (UNDES). This showed the extent to which the student movement was riven with political conflicts between the various schools of the leftist intelligentsia to which it belonged. This type of segmentation emerged first within the AGES in 1976 when members of the underground PAI, together with students belonging to the so-called *Patte d'Oie* Group, organized a schism resulting in the creation of the UES. On 16 March 1980, students close to the underground PAI created the UNDES. On 4 June 1980, students belonging to the Democratic League created the UDED. Prior to the first UNAPES congress, the El Mansour Nucleus, together with a similar body of underclass Philosophy majors, organized a breakaway movement. In the same year, after the UNAPES was consolidated, leaders of the AGES group, who had worked extremely hard to facilitate the reorganization that produced that union, founded the Revolutionary Detachment of Senegalese Students.

The build up to the creation of the UNAPES was marked by numerous conflicts and schisms. From the first UNAPES congress on 22 and 24 March 1980, divergences between various student groups widened. The upshot was the creation of rival organizations that made the campus scene a microcosm of the wider Senegalese political environment. This was when the group called le Collectif was set up. As early as May 1980, differences[24] surfaced between UNAPES militants and students belonging to PAI-Senegal. The issue was that of appropriate support for teachers in the SUDES union. The clash, in a way, reflected differences within the SUDES between pro-Soviet and Maoist members.

SUDES activists had scheduled a warning strike for 13 May 1980, and the UNAPES had called on its militants to conduct a half-day sympathy strike. Other student groups rejected the strike call, arguing that it might give the government a pretext for dissolving the SUDES. But UNAPES leaders, now accused of being "trade unionist anarchists and extreme leftists," gave the following reasons for the strike in a declaration dated 13 May 1980:

> *The UNAPES, in its capacity as a patriotic, anti-imperialist organization, works and will forever work towards the unity of the students' and teachers' movement, on the basis of just principles. To that end it asserts its independent and autonomous right to state its position on all international and national issues, especially those involving the Senegalese educational system. For that reason, it is our duty as students, in our support for the SUDES in its struggle, to assume all our responsibilities, leaving no loopholes for provocation, in order to help the teachers achieve their objectives.*

Following the debate on appropriate support for the teachers' struggle, students belonging to the *Rassemblement National Démocratique* left the UNAPES.

In the late 1970s, Maoist leaders gained increasing influence over students. Between 1979 and 1980, they tried unsuccessfully to turn SUDES activists against the union leadership in a bid to weaken the influence of the PAI and the Democratic League[25]. Many of their militants were reprimanded at the time. But in 1982-1983, the UNAPES entered a time of open crisis brought on by factional fights among its leaders. In 1983 a group of dissidents called a general assembly meeting to set up a Steering Committee for the Reorganization of the Senegalese Student Movement (CIRMES).

The UNAPES crisis actually signalled a transitional shift between two types of student organization. The first type, strongly anti-imperialist, represented the left wing point of view, which had a majority following on campus. The dominant issues it rallied around were clearly political. At the onset of the UNAPES crisis, the university institution was facing ever-worsening problems in its operations. Issues mobilizing students were becoming less and less political. Yet the public expression of this indifference to politics was met with brutal police violence and threats of unemployment. Students reacted by adopting combative, anti-government attitudes.

Reorganization and Confrontation

The differences described above did not stop student leaders from getting together in front organizations to conduct strikes of considerably long duration. In 1984, such structures consisted of national unions, friendly associations and the Social Commission. The 1984 strike, for instance, was led by a coordinating body representing different factions, known as the 'Combat Committee'. In 1983, a 'Committee for Struggle and Reorganization' was formed and placed under UNAPES control. As expressed in various tracts and organizational mouthpieces, the debate between student leaders indicated that despite divisions in this segment of the left, government strategies designed to tame the left had failed. Students remained refractory, protesting against the Senghor regime, and even more against that of his successor. It is hard to understand this situation unless we place events within the context of a profound economic crisis affecting the country and aggravating the already precarious status of students.

A second reason for the failure of government policy was that its approach to the student movement was characterized by an insensitive reliance on brute force. Published eye-witness accounts of the brutal manner in which the police and security forces treated students between 1984 and 1988 show how extensive government repression was. In this connection, it would be hard for students to forget the muscular police intervention on campus on 22 January 1987 following the outbreak of a strike that same day (*Wal Fadjri*, 5 February 1987:1-11). During that period, this repression was worsened on account of infighting within the government, in which the main antagonists were Jean Collin, Secretary-General to the Cabinet, and Iba Der Thiam, Minister of National Education.

Iba Der Thiam's political and union values were diametrically opposed to those of the majority of people in the ruling regime. He did his best to create within the government a faction owing no fealty to Jean Collin or the Socialist Party but basing its claim to legitimacy on the direct confidence reposed in it by the President. Numerous observers have speculated that the disturbances were calculated to weaken the position of Iba der Thiam during his tenure as Minister of National Education. In that case they would seem to have been designed to foment a particularly unmanageable conflict that would have triggered the resignation of a Minister determined not to yield to the hoary authority of Jean Collin, the apparent foreman of the neo-patrimonial regime. In the event, Iba Der Thiam survived the particular crisis in question, but only for a while. For events on campus merely served as a backdrop for various serious and complex upheavals in the country's political life. These included a police strike and the dismissal of leading political figures from office. In the end Iba Der Thiam had to leave office in April 1988.

The disturbances also showed that a number of social conflicts had been seized on by warring factions within the government, without the original protagonists involved being aware that they were being used. At any rate, the disturbances of January 1987 further alienated students from the ruling class and its programme of social pacification. At the same time, they helped to paper over certain political divisions, thus paving the way for the organization of increasingly radical struggles.

We would like to point out that harsh as government repression was, it had little resemblance to the bloody brutality typical of the Zairian government's approach as described by Bapuwa Muamba (1990). In the reorganizational period of the late 1970s, the most dynamic student groups were divided into several political schools of thought. The differentiation dated back a long time, and it affected the entire process of reorganization from 1978 to 1980. Relationships among leftist groups were intensely conflictual. This state of affairs spilled over into campus politics through the rise of highly politicized sub-groups identifying with various trends in the wider spectrum of national politics. In the 1970s, the student union movement, just like the Senegalese opposition, was riven by a series of schisms related to ideological and personality conflicts touched off by the collapse of the PAI and a series of power struggles within the left. In documents produced by the student leadership, this fragmentation was acknowledged and its deleterious impact admitted. The campus literally crawled with large numbers of organizations and fronts, friendly associations, national unions, the Social Commission, etc. None of them, on its own, had any real hold on the student body as a whole. Hence the crucial necessity of an umbrella organization[26].

The period saw the emergence of deep ideological confrontations. Theoreticians in the UNAPES called them struggles about political lines (UNAPES, 1986:6-8). Student leaders presented the situation in the following light:

> Over the two decades of the 1970s and the 1980s, the Senegalese student movement was victimized by certain political tendencies. It was bombarded with factional propaganda of unprecedented intensity, with the result that the involvement with factional politics came to override any focus on the students' own problems. This disorientation of the student union movement ended with the dissolution of national unions (CED, 1991:23).

Attempts at reorganization made in the 1980s resulted in greater centralization at the end of the Delegates' General Council meeting in Soweto Hall on campus on 26 May 1987. In an effort to halt the fragmentation brought on by the 1978 reorganization, the General Council called upon the various national unions (UNAPES, UDED, UNDES) 'to declare their own dissolution, and to implement that declaration'. In the course of the January 1987 strike, students founded the Dakar Students' Section (CED, 1988). This union (CED, 1988) emerged after the fragmentation of student unions and the collapse of the UNAPES under the impact of frequent infighting and multiple schisms. To ensure the efficient functioning of the new structure, branches known as Struggle Committees and Neighbourhood Committees were organized in faculties and neighbourhoods (CED, 1988). The history of the student movement is peppered with attempts to organize leadership structures off campus to cope with problems arising from the closure of the campus. Results, however, were never satisfactory. Effective co-ordination always remained a problem.

Structurally, the CED was based on a series of faculty general assemblies. On the surface, its most important decisions were taken during these general assembly meetings, which served the CED as a propaganda forum. On occasion they also turned into battlefields where opposing student leaders clashed. This duplex function gave them considerable importance. For that reason, when faced with a strike, the government adopted the tactic of isolating the union leadership from its base (CED, undated) by prohibiting all general assembly meetings within faculty precincts. Alternatively, the government, taking advantage of the fact that there was no intermediate structure linking the union leadership with the general assemblies, used other means to pressure and weaken the strike movement: it shut down the university dormitories.

The absence of intermediary structures affects the way crises get managed. Given the hegemony of political militants over the general assemblies, decision-making procedures during these sessions tend to be undemocratic. Factional clashes between political activists often make crises intractable. In 1984, for instance, political divergences concerning modalities for the organization of the student movement caused clashes which tempted certain factions to manipulate possibilities of dragging out the strike as a way of proving the movement's leadership incompetent, or of proving that it had "capitulated." There were cases in which, for some factions, important stakes rode on the cancellation of the strike call. On occasion, groups opposed to the movement's leadership might consider it in their interests to interfere with the handling of strikes. When, on 15 May 1984, the strike was called off, there were disagreements within the leadership, as shown by the subsequent flood of accusations traded by various leaders. Frequently used insults included words like 'opportunists, bitter-enders, union anarchists and leftists', as well as 'collaborators' and 'agents of the Trilateral Commission'.

The debate heated up again over the issue of student representation on the Dakar University Administrative Council.

All this in-fighting within the student movement's leadership left a strong imprint on the literature produced by the Struggle Committee in 1984[27]. The incessant clashes slowed down and further complicated the process of agreement among factions of the student movement. With the coming of hard economic times, however the most politicized groups were motivated to explore common grievances and to review divergences with other groups.

A further noteworthy fact concerns changing structural patterns in university enrolment. Available sources indicate that in 1959-60, 33% of the 1,012 registered students were Senegalese. Ten years later the percentage of Senegalese students had risen above 50%. In 1975-76, out of a total of 7,312 enrolled students, Senegalese nationals made up 71.2%. In 1988-89, 12 871 out of 14,833 registered students were Senegalese. The Senegalese percentage had reached 86.77%. The percentage of non-Senegalese students has been going down steadily. One reason behind the trend, no doubt, is the creation of university institutions in other African countries. But it also has something to do with the high incidence of strikes at the university of Dakar.

Under these circumstances, Senegalese students have come to dominate the student movement as a whole. Increasingly now, priority is given to local political issues. Students tend to be mobilized around specifically Senegalese preoccupations, of which the job crunch is among the most serious. Local political rivalries thus tend to spill over into student politics. The issues of unemployment and deteriorating living conditions figure prominently in all strike situations. The ravages caused by government economic policies have made it easier to mobilize forces outside the campus in protests against unemployment. Trade unions as well as political parties consider the university itself a burning issue for political debate. In this debate, leftist groups on the whole see eye to eye in their critique of the university crisis. Meanwhile, the stakes involved have escalated. Their crucial importance is one clear reason why the routine operations of the University were so frequently paralyzed, and for such long periods, between 1984 and 1992.

Problems have frequently surfaced regarding the handling of strikes. The government has a habit of waiting until a showdown, and then making miserly concessions. This tends to prolong crises. Judging from the student approach to the 1988 strike, which resulted in a lost academic year, it would seem that transformations in the student movement have been facilitated by the emergence of national conflicts. Frustrated students have tended to stick intransigently to their demands, pushing the public authorities into a corner. It is a way of hitting back at the State. And the State, by not addressing structural shortcomings at the bottom of chronic clashes with students but opting instead for repressive responses, has brought upon itself the most serious political crisis since 1980. The sudden outbreak of youth uprisings during the 1988 election campaign was a poignant warning. Young people played a key role in protests against the political system. In the process, they also demonstrated a capacity to resist government moves intended to discredit or divide them.

Student unions were unable to maintain lasting contacts with the working class, effectively controlled by the ruling regime. They also failed to create bonds with the peasant population, especially after May 1968. On the other hand, they did succeed in developing special ties with high school students. The latter gave the student movement an aura of power by bringing it a wider geographical base. With the centralization of the student movement, affiliated high school students also got better organized. The creation of the Senegalese Students' Coordinating Group dates back to the January-February 1987 strike organized by the CED. Before then, social and educational groups and struggle committees had taken charge of strikes. High schools functioned as centres of political dissidence. Each high school had a structure called the Executive Committee, made up of students elected by an assembly of delegates from each class. It was this committee that was responsible for leading the protest movement. Representatives of various executive committees from regional high schools formed combat organizations called regional and national coordinating groups.

It was probably the desire to halt the rise of this type of force that led ruling party officials to organize strike-breaking groups within the country's schools. The intention became especially clear after the creation of the Committee for the Defence of Educational Interests. One result was the installation of serious violence in the school system. As early as December 1990, the ruling party organ called *Combat pour le socialisme* published an article under the headline: 'Plot Against the School System'. The article accused leaders of the Dakar Region Students' Coordinating Group (CRED) of having sold out to opposition party leaders, presented as fomenters of strikes (*Combat pour le socialisme*, December 1990: 1). Around the same time, the *Soleil*, the semi-official government mouthpiece, publicized the opinions of Babacar Sine, then member of the ruling Socialist Party's Executive Committee, according to which strikes within the school system were all "a small part of a carefully laid plan" hatched by "obscure forces" (*Le Soleil*, 24-25 February 1990: 1). In 1991, a series of clashes occurred in various schools as a result of this attempt by the government to regain control there (*Wal Fadjri*, 11 January and 15 February; *Le Soleil*, 22 January 1991).

Most of the leaders of the high school student movement came from the "student aristocracy" of sixth formers. Some went on in later years to become student leaders on the university campus. Because they were so close to university students, they developed bonds of solidarity focused largely on anxiety about the impending doom of unemployment. The rise of young high school teachers, some with student union activist backgrounds, played a significant role in the spread of influential leftist ideas among high school students. In the imagination of most such students, the prestigious status of university student necessarily involved a high degree of dissent. Protest was presented as the ultimate behavioural lifestyle for a whole age group. The State's unpopularity among youth merely reinforced the trend. A constant feature of the neocolonial State has been the repeated failure of its attempts to co-opt youth organizations into the regime's power structure. From the government point of view, control over student unions was of secondary importance compared to the need to bring the rural population and the working class under administrative control through networks of religious organizations, rural extension agencies and regime-affiliated trade unions.

The State tried to isolate students from other social groups. Along with this effort, it also restricted freedom at the university, especially after May 1968. Attempts to exert control over the student movement were based on a policy of coercion tempered with dollops of social welfare assistance. The State was thus able to coopt selected leaders, but those who went along with the regime also lost the moral authority indispensable to their credibility. The failure[28] of attempts to corrupt[29] targeted leaders of the Senegalese High School Student Coordinating group in 1988 was mainly due to the students' own ability to generate and circulate information, to ensure a broad collegial leadership, and to refer constantly to the grassroots for support[30].

Against the backdrop of the trouble-fraught February 1988 elections, students were able to mobilize their activists around slogans centred mainly on their material and intellectual working conditions. The list of demands presented during the protests of 19 April 1988, signed by the Student Coordinating Group (Senegal, 1968), placed a special emphasis on a grievance at the root of the structural instability of the University: jobs[31]. Graduate unemployment had become an important issue in political discussions. Through their list of demands, leaders of the Student Co-ordinating Group were able to draw in groups like medical students, who in the past had been lukewarm towards protracted protest movements. They thus succeeded in reinforcing the strike.

A lot of energetic action has been taken in the drive to deal with graduate unemployment. Both the private and public sectors have been involved (Senegal, 1985). Yet the problem has remained acute. In its superb study on the educational system, the Economic Council (1980) drew the government's attention to the issue, stressing its seriousness. The Council wondered, in practical terms, what would become of the cohorts of recently trained graduates in Law and Economics, especially the latest groups, given the fact that credentials from competing courses at the National Civil Service Training Centre and the doctoral-level section at the University's Technological Institute were considered superior, and public sector job opportunities were so rare. The public sector was already as saturated as the private, where openings created by the Senegalization of executive posts were getting rapidly filled up. In any case, the large number of degrees awarded in some disciplines meant a risk of degrees losing their value, with the consequent loss of social standing on the part of affected graduates (Senegal, 1980:39).

Frustration with this situation, coupled with the Islamic revivalism of the late 1970s and the weakening of secular ideologies, constituted part of the explanation for the emergence of a Muslim movement at the university. Attempts to organize Muslim student movements at the University of Dakar date back a long time (Timéra, 1986:32). However, such efforts have in recent times been consolidated. A Mouride Students' Association was established on campus in 1975-76 (Sy, 1984). Several other groups were subsequently organized on the basis of affiliation to Muslim religious brotherhoods. Simultaneously, a Muslim organization seemingly independent of the brotherhoods began to gain ground. It was called the Dakar University Association of Muslim Students. It conducted varied activities, including the publication of a paper, the provision of meals for students fasting during the Ramadan season, the provision of transport for students attending Friday prayers, the building of a mosque on campus, and Koranic recitation sessions. On the last point, Samba Sy points out:

> *In June 1984 regular Koranic recitation sessions followed by translations and commentaries were organized during the month of Ramadan. It is only just to point out that the sessions attracted large and enthusiastic audiences* (Sy, 1984:75-76).

Thrive though they did, these Muslim movements did not succeed in becoming dominant organizations on campus as far as student mobilization was concerned. Among university students their impact was comparable to the influence of so-called "fundamentalist" sects within Senegalese society at large. In the first place, they have been unable to shatter the old system of marabout-led and brotherhood-based control which is substantially tied to the dominant State system. Second, they have been unable to mount an effective challenge to dissident movements based on secular ideologies.

Conclusion

To a degree, our inquiry confirms Fatton's (1988) analysis of the nature of African states. The ruling class was able to implement its hegemonic aspirations only through reliance on neo-patrimonial methods. The State, meanwhile, failed to grow into an all-embracing corpus, even if it succeeded in coopting selected leftist challengers of ruling class legitimacy. The increasing marginalization of the State could be seen in the kind of social movements described by Bayart (1983) as 'the revenge of African societies'. For our part, we shall stop short of the extreme formulation according to which, to quote Mbembe (1988: 22), the behaviour patterns observed express 'the revenge of pagan values' over formal norms established in African countries since independence.

An examination of relations between the ruling class and the opposition shows that the former proved incapable of asserting its moral and intellectual leadership over the rest of society. The lack of legitimate status under which the ruling class laboured meant that it never got certain segments of the intelligentsia to acquiesce in its rule without coercive force. Relations between students and the ruling class exemplify the difficulties the ruling class faced in its attempts to achieve its political aims.

Meanwhile, events had pushed the student union movement to a historical crossroads. The university as an institution had deteriorated so sharply that its adjustment had become a priority agendum. The government had come under increasing pressure from funding agencies and their "technocratic constituency" of local placemen. Such pressure risked shattering the old system of budgetary allocations under which the lion's share of resources had gone to the higher educational system. The pressure developed in the wake of the identification of structural bottlenecks hampering the efficient running of the university, especially financial constraints. In the hope of initiating thorough-going changes in the situation, a series of low-profile but quite strict austerity measures were proposed, including the tightening of university entrance requirements and the curtailment of student scholarships, subsides and allowances.

The basic principle behind these proposed changes was the need to abandon the commitment which, the structural adjustment programme notwithstanding, provided relative immunity for higher educational expenditure as compared, say, with expenditure on health care, or even with expenditure on the other cycles of the national educational system. Under pressure from international funding agencies, the government suggested that a national conference be convened to discuss the needs of the university (*Le Soleil*, 13 April 1992). It appointed a moderator for the exercise. The reform was targeted in part, as a careful reading of the World Bank report on the

University of Dakar indicates, on a decision to curb the relative effectiveness of student unions. As a matter of fact, a study of implementational conditions accompanying structural adjustment packages in other sectors of national life shows that the division of trade union movements into discrete bodies, a way of atomizing politically recalcitrant forces, is a standard prerequisite for the implementation of structural adjustment programmes. The crux of the matter, then, is to determine whether the government has sufficient political clout to stop any group or groups from blocking the implementation of the measures proposed, especially those measures related to demands that had figured consistently at the top of student claims throughout the 1980s.

Students were an important instrumental force in the development of a left-wing challenge to the hegemony of the ruling regime. They mounted a permanent opposition to the leadership of the ruling class, and frustrated the attempts of the State to co-opt the intelligentsia as a whole. Within the labour union movement, by contrast, the ruling class succeeded in setting up a union affiliated to the regime and controlling the majority of workers through rather complex mechanisms we have described elsewhere (Diop and Diouf, 1990).

Students belonged to radical groups aspiring to speak for society as a whole. It is merely just to point out, however, that they were effectively cut off from other social groups, notably from peasants and the working class, especially after May 1968. On the whole, instead of working together with such social groups, students have tended much more to operate along their fringes.

The urban intelligentsia benefited from the initiatives and activities of students. They profited most from student demands for a more democratic political system. Bonds between students and teachers were especially close. The struggles of teachers' unions in the late 1970s, covering the entire range of problems confronting the educational system, were in the main led by veterans of the May 1968 student movement, in a context marked by changes in the sociological make-up of teachers' unions. These struggles peaked in the convocation of the General Conference on Education and Training (EGEF), which challenged both the design and functioning of the educational system in the post-independence period. The radicalism of the teachers' union movement, however, was insufficient to paper over the exceptionally deep ideological cleavages that divided the left at the time. The student movement reflected such divisions with particular sharpness, turning the reorganization of student unions in the late 1970s into a peculiarly difficult process. In the end the process produced a union which had a powerful impact on the consciousness of students at the time, the UNAPES.

Neither the ruling class nor the leftist opposition had any tradition of democratic debate. The political climate therefore put a premium on energetic propaganda, with different factions notoriously reluctant to cooperate with each other. Heightened repression after 1968 encouraged the rise of determined leaders who gradually dropped their openly anti-imperialist rhetoric and the usual revolutionary myths to concentrate instead on the gritty realities of daily life, such as the improvement of living and working conditions for students. But a constant feature of student union politics since independence was the desire among students, born of their consciousness of their own power as a group, to get involved in activities designed to influence national affairs.

The construction of the post-colonial State was punctuated with a series of strikes in schools and the University, the peak period being May 1968. For that reason, from then on the State beefed up its repression and surveillance of the unions. First it banned the National Union of Senegalese Workers (UNTS), the Dakar Students' Union (UED), and the Senegalese Teachers' Union (SES). Then it set up a regime-affiliated trade union, the National Confederation of Senegalese Workers (CNTS).

While this was going on, the country was experiencing structural economic difficulties typified by a fall in agricultural output so steep as to disturb the government and the vegetable oil industry (Senegal, 1976:44-48). Students too were the target of vigorous government attacks designed to stop them from developing any potential for countervailing power against the regime. They nevertheless survived the repressive onslaughts of the State. But their radical protests did not have much impact upon the rest of the society. For one thing they were handicapped by their essentially transient status. For another, as Mamdani (quoted in Asowa Okwe, undated: 6) points out, they laboured under 'the illusion that they could, all by themselves, transform society'. Ousmane B. Diop (1982:87-89) presents a telling description of student relations with other sections of the country's youth. In these encounters 'it is invariably the student who speaks on behalf of all youth,..., Students do not exclude non-students. They simply keep them from speaking up, or at any rate from interrupting them'. Hence the absence of a common political environment[32] in which students and non-students could work together against the established political order.

Young people in the urban sub-proletariat suffer nowadays from unprecedented poverty. Galled by the showy opulence of wealthier groups, they have tended to react with extreme violence (Diop and Diouf, 1990). The peak period of such violent behaviour came during the April 1989 Senegalo-Mauritanian massacres. Because such violence occurs outside any political framework, it is uncontrolled. It is thus a sign that the social fabric is in

Mauritanian massacres. Because such violence occurs outside any political framework, it is uncontrolled. It is thus a sign that the social fabric is in tatters. Periodic acts of violence give people otherwise barred from the enjoyment of wealth, the social pariahs long confined to the fringes of national life, opportunities for stealing or simply smashing goods forbidden them.

Despite the wild flavour of student activism, it is doubtful whether student militants have really succeeded in firing the imagination of the youth as a whole. The clear lack of involvement of young people in regular party politics (save during election campaigns) shows the extent to which left-wing parties have failed to develop strategies and a rhetoric capable of appealing to something larger than a 'bookish avant-garde minority'. If the Senegalese Democratic Party has had a measure of success, it is because it has consistently refused to confine its programmes within the unique framework through which the Westernized elite has always maintained its 'highfalutin' status symbols. The problems confronting political organizations and trade unions attempting to organize unemployed urban and rural youth constitute a massive parameter in Senegalese politics. These problems are indications of the refusal of such youth groups to blindly trust the judgment of avant-garde leaders.

Using a complex array of stratagems, the State succeeded in the past in coopting selected opposition leaders. Some of the latter were former students or 'revolutionary' teachers. The record so far casts discredit on political leaders. In its current state of political and ideological demobilization, the population at large therefore tends to see all the factional infighting between different sections of the elite as a lot of sound and fury ultimately signifying nothing higher than a competition to grab shares in 'the economy of the belly'.

Notes

1. M Mamdani, T Mkandawire and W Dia-Wamba (1988).
2. More and more studies are now centred on this issue. Bianchini's work contains relevant information on Senegal. Historians and sociologists have published less comprehensive studies. Reports on the Black African Students' Federation or the Association of Senegalese Students in France published by leaders from the pioneering generation of the student movement indicate that African students maintained close links with forces campaigning for the decolonization of their respective countries. Despite the general penury of studies, there are some good general studies on Egypt and a number of anglophone countries: Abdalla (1985); Peter and Mvungi (1986); Asowa-Okwe (undated).
3. See Bathily, Diouf and Mbodj (1990), as well as Diagne (1990).
4. Cf. Conseil économique et social (1981).
5. See UED (1966).

6. As far as the supposition that the students were manipulated by the PAI goes, Ibrahima Thioub shows that in 1968 the PAI was in a state of crisis, and that its leadership was neither sufficiently cohesive nor strong enough to try to seize power. "The PAI was in no position to take power, and the possibility was never for a moment considered. The PAI's weakness, however, did not prevent certain political activists trained within it, some of whom left its ranks, but some of whom remained members, from playing signal roles in student organizations. This was one of the main reasons why the UDES stance became so highly political." See also the explanations given by Dansokho in Ndiaye *et al.* (1990:90-91).
7. One organization that turned this cultural struggle into a key plank in its platform of political struggle was the *Andë Jeff*. See Bianchini (1988).
8. On this issue, see the precise and erudite analysis of Achille Mbembe (1988).
9. See CIRMES (1979).
10. For a critique of this approach, see the analysis of the French case put forward by Luc Boltanski (1988: 76).
11. Two studies provide valuable information on operational problems facing the University of Dakar. The first was conducted following the 1968 campus crisis. The second was conducted shortly before the 1980 strikes, and was used by the government to prepare the ground for the 1981 General Conference on Education and Training (Conseil Economique et Social 1968; 1980). The 1980 study gives a clear explanation for the current impasse in educational policy. It seems clear that as far as educational budgeting is concerned, the State has no more resources left. Moreover, several funding agencies are unwilling to finance the University as currently configured. It has therefore become impossible to cope with the mounting intake of new undergraduates. At the moment, there is no telling how young Senegalese students can continue enjoying free access to the University unless there is a substantial influx of fresh funds.
12. There was a parallel protest against recruitment criteria for lecturers, as well as against conditions governing their admission to or exclusion from the CAMES aptitude rolls, and calling for greater regularity in the election of deans. Such protests were sharpest at the Faculty of Humanities in December 1988 and at the Faculty of Sciences in January 1989.
13. See the Faculty of Arts publication entitled "Jalons autour d'une plate-forme" (1986: 11 pages), and the Faculty of Arts executive document: "Les enseignants évaluent et s'auto-évaluent" (19 July 1990, 2 pages).
14. To take the Faculty of Arts as an example, in 1988-89, full, associate and assistant professors had 24 seats on the Faculty Board. Lecturers had 6, instructors had 7, students 9, and technical and administrative staff 2.
15. The UPS Students' Federation (FEUPS) was created on 8 August 1961. Notable among its founding members were Moustapha Niasse, Daouda Sow and Pascal A. Sané. Djibo Kâ, a second-generation leader, played a key organizational role in the federation. According to information published by Matar Dia, then Political Affairs Director in the Socialist Party's Permanent Secretariat, the movement grew from 8 members in 1961 to over 500 in 1976, including 176 scholarship holders (Dia: 1985).
16. Before the two associations were disbanded, Decree No. 68-860 of 24 July 1968 (JORS 10 August 1968: 979) on student associations in university-level institutions was promulgated. The decree was very clearly aimed at depoliticizing student organizations. The government's moves can only be understood when related to parallel attempts to control labour unions under the guideline of "responsible participation." Simultaneously, arrangements to control "equipment used for foreign political propaganda" were set up (Act 69-31 of 29 April 1969; Decree 69-579 of 13 May 1968. See *JORS*, 10 May 1969: 576 and 31 May 1969: 651).
17. See UNAPES, "Bref aperçu de la situation de notre pays," undated. 15 pp.

18. Owing to lack of space, we are able here neither to cite these regulations in full nor to present a list thereof. Interested readers are advised to consult two sources: Université de Dakar (1973) and Senegal, 1977.
19. Similar reactions were observed in other African countries. See, for instance, Bazaara (1990: 1).
20. Declaration of Students affiliated to the African Independence Party (PAI Senegal), 9 January 1979: 2-3.
21. Hard as it tries, this declaration fails to paper over programmatic cracks in the UES platform. See the "Declaration of the UES Interim Executive Committee: Clarification Concerning the Document Published by the So-called Interim Executive Committee of the UES," 25 January 1979.
22. Examples included *Le Cartouchard, La Voix de l'UDED* and *Echos des Lettres*.
23. The "El Mansour Nucleus" was formed by a group of students living in the university dormitory near the El Mansour cinema in the lower-class Grand Dakar neighbourhood. It was considered a minority faction within the Interim Executive Committee.
24. See UNAPES (1980); Executive Committee of the Friendly Association of the Law Faculty, "Declaration on the 13 May 1980 Strike Call;" *Jappō ji*, 5: 3; GOR (1980).
25. One tract in particular, entitled "Towards a National Day of Vigorous Action For the Radicalization of the SUDES Struggle," issued in December 1979, was especially virulent in its attacks on the PAI and the Democratic League.
26. See in addition, UDED (undated) and *Renaissance*, journal of the PAI student movement, No. 1: 5-7).
27. On this issue, see the document produced by the Friendly Association of the Arts faculty, entitled "Unity and Struggle for the Satisfaction of our Demands," undated, 2 pages; "Un anniversaire dans la lutte," 5 June 1984, 2 pages; Struggle Committee of the Arts Faculty, "Appeal to All Students of the University of Dakar," 9 May 1984; UNDES, "Complete Strike Report," *Cartouchard*, No. 5, August 1984: 3-7; Students in the Struggle, "The University: Current Situation and Future Prospects."
28. *Le Cafard Libéré*, 37 and 38, June 1988.
29. *Ibid.*, 39, July 1988.
30. *Ibid.*, p.4.
31. CED (April 1988); CED (September 1988).
32. During the post-election riots of February 1988, students played a catalytic role in getting many unorganized groups involved. They thus created a large-scale social movement that proved difficult for the State to bring under control. It must be pointed out, however, that instances of such joint action are rare.

Bibliography

Abdalla, Ahmed, 1985, *The Student Movement and National Politics in Egypt*, London, Al Saqi.
AGES, 1972, 'Le bilan de l'expérience, la situation actuelle, notre tâche d'organisation', Conseil général du 25 mai.
Amicale de la Faculté des Lettres, 1986, 'Jalons autour d'une plate-forme', Dakar.
Asowa Okwe, C, (undated), 'Le mouvement étudiant et les luttes pour la démocratie dans le Kenya néo-colonial', Research proposal submitted to CODESRIA.
Bailleul, André, 1984, 'L'Université de Dakar: institutions et fonctionnement (1950-1984).' Post-doctoral degree thesis in Law, University of Dakar, July.

Bathily, Abdoulaye, 1986, 'L'Union Démocratique Sénégalaise (UDS), section sénégalaise du RDA, contexte politique et base sociale de ses activités (1946-1955)', Paper presented at the Colloquium marking the 40th anniversary of the RDA, Yamoussoukro, Ivory Coast, 16-25 October.

Bathily, Abdoulaye, M Diouf and M Mbodj, 1990, 'Le mouvement étudiant sénégalais, des origines à 1989', Paper contributed to the CODESRIA project on 'Social Movements, Social Transformation and the Democratization of Development in Africa', Dakar, February.

Bayart, J F, 1983, 'La revanche des sociétés africaines', *Politique africaine*, 1, pp.95-128.

Bazaara, Nyangbyaki, 1990, 'The Struggle for Democracy at Makerere University 1986-1989: An Assessment', Paper presented at the CODESRIA Colloquium on Academic Freedom, Research and the Social Responsibility of the Intellectual in Africa, Kampala, 26-29 November.

Bianchini, Pascal, 1988, 'Crises et réformes du système d'enseignement sénégalais (1968-1986): contribution à une sociologie politique de l'éducation en Afrique noire', 2 volumes, Doctoral dissertation, IEP, Bordeaux.

Boltanski, Luc, 1980, 'Croissance universitaire et montée des cadres en France 1960-1975', *Sociologie et Sociétés*, XII, 1, pp. 67-100.

Bourdieu, Pierre, 1984, *Homo Academicus*, Paris, Minuit.

CE de l'Amicale de la Faculté de droit, 1980, 'Déclaration à propos du mot d'ordre de grève du 13 mai 1980'.

CIRMES, 1979, 'Rapport d'activités du CIRMES pour l'assemblée générale constitutive du 23 mars', Dakar.

CIRMES, 1979, 'Manifeste pour une Association Patriotique des Etudiants Sénégalais', Dakar, March.

Conseil général des délégués étudiants de l'Université Cheikh Anta Diop, 1987, 'Résolution générale', May, 2p.

Copans, Jean, 1989, 'La crise de l'Afrique noire au miroir des études africanistes', Paper presented at the colloquium marking the 50th anniversary of the IFAN, Dakar, 27 February-3 March, Extracts from this paper were reprinted in *La crise de l'africanisme africain*, in Jean Copans, 1990, pp. 317-326.

Copans, Jean, 1990, 'La formation et la déformation des classes ouvrières africaines: sur l'orientation de quelques recherches récentes', *Le Mouvement Social*, 151, pp.39-52.

Copans, Jean, 1990, *La longue marche de la modernité africaine*, Paris, Karthala, 406 p.

Coordination des Etudiants de Dakar (CED), 1988, 'Extraits du bilan de la grève de janvier 1987', Dakar, 5 February.

Coordination des Etudiants de Dakar (CED), 1988, 'Procès-verbal des négociations entre le ministre de l'enseignement supérieur et la CED', Dakar, 1 September.

Coordination des Etudiants de Dakar (CED), 1991, 'Mémorandum', Dakar.

Dia, Matar, 1985, *De Senghor à Abdou Diouf ou l'évolution du Parti socialiste du BDS au renouveau actuel*, Tivaouane (Senegal), 19 January.

Diallo, Kalidou, 1986, 'Syndicat unique de l'enseignement laïc du Sénégal (SUEL). Contribution à l'étude du mouvement syndical à la veille et au début des indépendances', Master's degree thesis in History, Faculty of Humanities, University of Dakar. 65 p.

Diané, Charles, 1990, *La FEANF et les grandes heures du mouvement syndical étudiant noir*, Paris, Chaka.

Dieng, Amady Aly, 1985, *Le Marxisme et l'Afrique noire: bilan d'un débat sur l'universalité du marxisme*, Paris, Nubia.

Diop Ousmane Blondin, 1982, *Les Héritiers d'une Indépendance*, Dakar, NEA.

Diop, Momar Coumba and Mamadou Diouf, 1990, *Le Sénégal sous Abdou Diouf: Etat et Société*, Paris, Karthala.

Diop, Taïfour, 1975, 'Pour un climat sain à l'Univesité de Dakar', *Agora*, I.

Faculty of Law and Economics, *Jappōo ji*, (Faculty Newsletter), No. 5, pp. 3.

Fatton, Robert, 1985, 'Organic Crisis, Organic Intellectuals and the Senegalese Passive Revolution', Paper prepared for presentation at the 28th annual meeting of the African Studies Association, New Orleans, Louisiana, 23-26 November.

Fatton, Robert, 1988, 'Bringing the Ruling Class Back In: Class, State and Hegemony in Africa', *Comparative Politics*, April, pp. 253-264.

Groupe Ouvrier Révolutionnaire (GOR), 1980, 'La récente mobilisation des élèves et étudiants: un prélude aux grands affrontements sociaux', 24 January.

Hesseling, Gerti, 1985, *Histoire politique du Sénégal*, Paris, Karthala.

Hirji, Karim, 1990, 'Les études universitaires et les relations', *Bulletin du CODESRIA*, 1, pp.9-15.

Joop, Buba, 1975, 'La prolifération des amicales: psychodrame ou fruit d'une réflexion mûre', *Agora* I & II.

Le Brun, Olivier, 1979, 'Education and Class Conflict', in Rita Cruise O'Brien (ed.), *The Political Economy of Underdevelopment: Dependence in Senegal*, Beverly Hills, Sage.

Lo, Magatte, 1987, *Syndicalisme et participation responsable*, Paris, L'Harmattan.

Ly, Abdoulaye, 1978, 'Pour l'unité du mouvement patriotique. Quelques aspects méconnus de l'évolution politique et syndicale au Sénégal de 1966 à 1970', *Andë Sopi*, 28, September, pp. 4-5 and 8.

Mamdani, Mahmood, 1990, 'Les mouvements sociaux, les mutations sociales et la lutte pour la démocratie en Afrique', *CODESRIA Bulletin*, 3, pp.3-6.

Mamdani, Mahmood, T Mkandawire and W Dia-Wamba, 1988, 'Mouvements sociaux, mutations sociales et lutte pour la démocratie en Afrique', CODESRIA *Working Paper*, 1, 26 p.

Mandaza, Ibbo, 1986, 'Introduction: The Political Economy of Transition', in Ibbo Mandaza (ed.), *Zimbabwe: The Political Economy of Transition 1980-1986*, Dakar, CODESRIA.

Mbembe, Achille, 1988, *Afriques indociles: Christianisme, pouvoir et Etat en société postcoloniale*, Paris, Karthala.

Muamba, Bapuwa, 1990, 'Zaire : Pourquoi ce bain de sang dans les campus?' Paper presented at the CODESRIA Colloquium on 'Academic Freedom, Research and the Social Responsibility of the Intellectual in Africa', Kampala, 26-29 November.

Ndiaye F, M Prinz and A Tine, 1990, *Visages publics du Sénégal*, Paris, L'Harmattan.

Orivel, François, 1988, 'Coûts, financements et efficacité des Université de l'Afrique subsaharienne francophone',Washington, Institute of Economic Development Working Paper.

PAI-Senegal Student Group, 1980, 'Halte à la surenchère spectaculaire et aux manoeuvres de liquidation', in *Renaissance* [Organe des élèves et étudiants du PAI], 1.

Paye, Moussa, 1978, 'Evolution du syndicalisme au Sénégal depuis 1968', Graduate thesis, Dakar, CESTI.

Peter, Chris and Sengondo Mvungi, 1986, 'The State and the Student Struggles', in Issa Shivji (ed.), *The State and Working People in Tanzania*, Dakar, CODESRIA.

Petras, James, 1990, 'La métamorphose des intellectuels latino-américains', *CODESRIA Bulletin*, N°1, pp. 6-9.

Senegal, (Republic of: Economic and Social Council), 1968, 'Les problèmes de l'emploi des diplômés de l'Université', November, pp. XIV-75.

Senegal, (Republic of: Ministry of Information and Legislative Affairs), 1973, *Livre blanc* [sur le suicide d'Oumar Bondin Diop], Dakar, [GIA], 31p.

Senegal, (Republic of: Economic and Social Council), 1976, 'Etude sur les mécanismes de réajustement des prix et des salaires: périodicité et niveau des réajustements', Mimeographed document, Dakar.

Senegal, (Republic of: Economic and Social Council), 1980, 'Etude sur l'enseignement en général, l'enseignement technique et professionnel en particulier', Dakar, 172 p.

Senegal, (Republic of: Economic and Social Council), 1981, 'Etude sur la promotion des Petites et moyennes Entreprises', 2nd Annual Ordinary Session Report, Mimeographed document, 72 p.

Senegal, (Republic of: Ministry of Planning and Cooperation), 1989, 'Plan d'orientation pour le développement économique et social 1989-1995', Dakar, October.

Senegal, (Republic of: National Commission on Educational and Training Reform), 1984, 'Rapport général', Annexe, Volume I. Mimeographed document, 140 p.

Senegal, (Republic of: National Labour Board), 1985, 'L'insertion des diplômés d'études supérieures dans la vie active (1980-1984). Bilan descriptif', Dakar, 38 p.

Senegal, (Republic of: Office of the President of the Republic), 1977, *Répertoire des textes législatifs et réglementaires*, Dakar, NEA.

Shivji, Issa, 1989, 'Les embûches de la réflexion sur la démocratie', *CODESRIA Bulletin*, 2-3, pp.12-13.

Sy, Samba, 1984, 'Les étudiants mourides à l'Université. Essai sur l'association des étudiants mourides', Master's degree thesis, Faculty of Humanities, University of Dakar.

Thioub, I, 1990, 'Le mouvement étudiant de Dakar et la vie politique sénégalaise: la marche vers la crise de mai-juin 1968', Mimeographed document, Dakar.

Timéra, Mahamat, 1986, 'Jeunesse urbaine et renouveau religieux au Sénégal', Graduate research report in Anthropology.

UDED (undated), 'Document sur la réorganisation actuelle du mouvement étudiant de Dakar dans le contexte de crise du système néo-colonial'.

UED, 1966, 'Le mouvement du 28 février, signification et perspectives', Dakar, 13 p.

UED, 1966, 'Mémorandum sur les événements de l'Université de Dakar', Dakar, 11 march.

UES, 1977, 'A la mémoire de tous ceux qui ont payé de leur vie dans le combat pour une école démocratique dans un Sénégal meilleur', 26 May.

UES, 1978, 'Sur la situation à l'Université de Dakar', Dakar, December.

UNAPES, 1980, 'Communiqué final du premier congrès de l'UNAPES', Dakar, 24 March.

UNAPES, 1980, 'Soutenons la juste lutte des enseignants', 12 May.

UNAPES, 1986a, 'Document préparatoire du troisième congrès', Dakar, January.

UNAPES, 1986b, 'Note introductive au 3^è congrès', Dakar, January, p. 6-8.

UNAPES, undated, 'Bref aperçu sur la situation de notre pays', Mimeographed document.

University of Dakar, 1973, 'Textes relatifs à l'organisation et au statut de l'Université de Dakar', Dakar, GIA.

World Bank, 1992, 'Revitalisation de l'enseignement supérieur au Sénégal: les enjeux de la réforme', Washington, March.

13. Trade Unions, Political Parties and the State

Babacar Diop Buuba

It is the role of workers, acting as individuals or in organized groups, to produce the wealth that ensures the self-perpetuation and development of societies. Similarly, but within given limits, it is the role of established authorities (economic, political, spiritual) to order and direct the functioning of States. In the fulfilment of these roles, relations between workers and the authorities may be official or informal, conflicts between them open or disguised. Conflicts are often mediated through *ad hoc* or permanent consultation and bargaining, depending on the socio-economic context of a given country, its political traditions, and the power equation linking the different social forces involved.

In the history of workers' organizations, there is a pattern, shifting normally from spontaneous forms of organization and struggle to better structured, more stable forms. That shift is paralleled by a movement from rudimentary, basically economic protest to a focus on more precise, more political objectives. Thus, from 1847, when the *Communist Manifesto* was drafted, and especially as from 1864, when the International Association of Workers was created, the relationship of workers to the political process took on a more explicit aspect. The authors of the *Manifesto*, arguing from the premise that 'all class struggles are political', urged the proletariat to get organized not simply 'as a class but also as a political party'. Nearly a century and a half later, Lech Valesa, leader of the 'Solidarity' union movement, a man famous for his criticism of his country's Communist regime, became President of the Polish Republic. His ascent to power was proof that one did not have to be an avowed Marxist or to belong to any Communist Party to understand the impact of trade unions on the direction of the political process.

The history of relationships between trade unions and politics in Senegal is part of the history of humanity, contributing its share of constant and variable data and insights. Several interesting studies have been conducted on the dynamics of inter linkages between trade union movements and the political process in Senegal's colonial and post-colonial history (Thiam, 1983; Martens, 1983; Ndiaye, 1990). Their existence is an indication of the lively interest surrounding the issue. In this chapter, we shall be examining major questions raised in these studies, with special attention to the context of relations between the State and trade unions. Additionally, our focus will embrace not only relations between trade unions and political parties in general, but also interrelations between various trade unions themselves. Our motivating hope is that such an approach will help to clarify the potential role of trade union forces in the social, political and economic development of Senegal as the country enters the final decade of the twentieth century.

Pointers from the Colonial Past
Like most of their counterparts throughout the world, Senegalese workers did not wait until the rise of unions to commence their struggles against the economic and political establishment. Back in 1885, the Carpenters' and Shipwrights' Guild in Upper Senegal forced employers to recognize its right to represent members of the trade[1]. Workers' protest movements got off to an early start in Senegal, as the record of railroad strikes in 1919, 1925, 1938 and 1947-48 shows (Ndour, 1990). However, for a long time these movements were limited in their impact. The main reason was the absence of trade union legislation. To be more precise, workers had no recognized legal status. True, in theory, the relevant labour law in France, the Act of 21 March 1884, was supposed to apply to the colonies, as stipulated in its Article 20. In practice, however, it was not enforced. As for the principle of trade union freedom promulgated by the International Labour Organization as early as 1919, it was utterly ignored by French colonialists in their overseas territories. Only after the Popular Front acceded to power in France was the 11 March 1937 Decree promulgated, fixing conditions for the enforcement of Titles I and II of Book III of the metropolitan Labour Code. The authorities then took a tentative step, empowering literate workers to form or join unions. Better still, the 20 March 1937 decree explicitly recognized the right of workers not qualified under this provision to join vocational associations (Brun, 1964). The groundwork for this acceleration of trade union development in Senegal had been laid through the early dissemination of Marxist ideas in the country.

> *The first Senegalese to learn the principles of trade union organization were two sailors who went to work in Marseille, Magatte Codou Sarr and Moïse Bâ. Having worked with French colleagues belonging to the CGT, these activists spent the years after World War I propagating trade unionist ideas in West Africa. On his return to Senegal in 1919, Sarr set to work organizing recently demobilized soldiers and sailors who had returned to join the ranks of the wage-earning work force at the time*[2].

French trade unionism was traditionally pluralist. That tradition was extended into Senegal. In 1937 there were already some 40 unions. Naturally, there were attempts to unify African unions. But existing barriers separating black workers from white, and legislation separating enfranchised inhabitants of the Four Municipalities from ordinary colonial subjects in the rest of the country, prevented the trade union movement from playing a decisive role in the emancipation of workers. Worse still, once the Vichy regime took power in France, there was a general backlash against political liberties in general and trade union rights in particular. Not until the 7 August 1944 decree were the rights of trade union movements re-established in the colonies.

African and European workers, moving towards a merger to promote their interests, set up a coordinating unit for French West Africa known as the French West African-CGT Confederated Trade Unions. The body was headed by two Secretary-Generals, one each from the African- and French components.

From December 1945 to February 1946, a series of strikes moved African workers in the public and private sectors to overcome their differences. The strikes also provided opportunities for the African and French communities, now working together, to inflict heavy blows on the colonial administration. A large-scale movement covering several French West African territories, the strikes gained support from traders, the unemployed, and all those eager for change. In time, however, serious disagreements[3] arose within the confederated body. The conflict was mainly about attitudes to relations between the union and the French Communist Party. By implication, it also involved connections between the union and the African Democratic Rally (RDA), an African ally of the French Communist Party. The short-lived nature of this alliance, coupled with the development of other political groupings, signalled the beginning of challenges to Communist domination of the trade union movement. By raising the principle of equal treatment for Africans and Europeans, the major railroad strike of 1947 underscored a more pronounced 'nationalistic' tendency. Furthermore, since the movement was led by political activists from the BDS, a party created by Léopold Sédar Senghor after he quit the SFIO, it was equally indicative of that party's rise.

From that time on, there developed a clear tendency for trade unions to adhere to political party positions, or vice versa. For instance, to counter BDS activities, the SFIO urged its activists in large numbers to join the CGT-FO, which served as a cooptation station for activists of the original CGT at odds with the French Communist Party. Now even though the 1949 and 1950 strikes were sparked by economic claims for salary increases and democratic demands for equal pay for equal work for Africans and Europeans, the administration interpreted them as politically motivated movements. A number of leaders, including the Communist Suret-Canale, then teaching in Senegal, were expelled from the colony. Links between BDS politicians and CGT unionists became closer. In the 1951[4] territorial assembly elections, Senghor chose as his running mate the trade union leader Abbas Guèye, and his party won both seats. Meanwhile, radical members of the CGT, including Ablaye Guèye and Gabriel d'Arboussier, were active in the UDS-RDA. Persistent attempts to achieve working class unity culminated in the general strike of 3 November 1952, a resounding success. The Overseas Labour Code was adopted through Act 52-1322 of 15 December 1952.

Various political leaders, including Senghor, still held on to the idea of splitting the trade union movement from the French Communist Party. In November 1955, the CGTA was created. The UDS leaders Abdoulaye Ly, Assane Seck and Gabriel d'Arboussier reinforced the trend towards autonomy from French influence by putting their intellectual skills at the service of the workers. When, in 1956, the BDS was transformed into the much larger BPS, the change signalled the new alliance between political leaders from the former BDS and UDS, as well as between trade unionists with ties to the two bodies. Links between the trade union movement and the drive towards political emancipation were more clearly articulated. The BPS was seen as:

the first organized detachment of the West African masses, the Senegalese section of the unified movement of workers and peasants, the only grouping capable of destroying all forms of domination and achieving the modernization of Africa (Martens, 1983:29).

Efforts to bring various African movements together led to the creation of the UGTAN on 16-20 January 1957. When, in 1957, the BPS won 47 of the 60 Assembly seats, the elected deputies included Ibrahima Sarr, Abdoulaye Ba, Ousmane Ngom and other UGTAN leaders. The UGTAN continued the struggle for democratic and economic rights by organizing an action programme from 6 to 13 August 1957, in December that same year, and in January-February 1958. The Ministerial Council included political leaders led by Mamadou Dia as well as trade unionists such as Latyr Camara of the UGTAN, Minister of the Civil Service establishment. From that point on, relations between trade unions and political parties took on a new aspect. When the UGTAN, growing more radical, began to agitate for total and immediate independence, the gap between that union's leadership and the BPS political leaders grew wider. The latter merged with Lamine Guèye's PSAS to form the Senegalese Progressive Union on 4 April 1958. Characteristic differences between the UPS, which opted for a Yes vote in the 1958 referendum, and the UGTAN leadership, which campaigned for a No vote, confirmed the break. Radical trade unionists such as Latyr Camara went into a new party, the PRA-Senegal, while Ibrahima Sarr, a former railway union organizer, was appointed Minister of the Civil Service establishment.

The general strike organized by the UGTAN from 4 to 6 January 1959 further soured relations between trade unionists and politicians. The UPS tried to weaken the UGTAN from within. Splits ensued. From 23 to 25 October 1959, dissident former members of the UGTAN and representatives of the CASL-FO, along with certain railroad workers, created the Senegalese Workers' Union. The movement expanded, leading to the birth of the General Union of Senegalese Workers from 21 to 23 January 1961. The finishing touches to trade union unity came with the creation of the UNTS on 28 and 29 April 1962. The unitary, expansionist trend, however, never meant an end to opposing tendencies. While remaining within the umbrella movement, industrial workers like Madia Diop maintained a parallel membership within an autonomous national trade union. Similarly, teachers outside the ruling party had their own union, the SUEL[5]. The Senegalese General Confederation of Workers (CGTS), led by Abdoulaye Thiaw, for its part, tried to rekindle the torch of struggle.

Facing the Test of National Construction

The ongoing process of the territorialization of trade unions gained momentum following the passage of the *Loi cadre* of 1956. The proclamation of independence speeded it up further. Leaders taking up political power saw a need to reshape the trade unions, and Senghor made no bones about it:

> Following a record of past services rendered, indeed on account of said services, the time has come for the trade union movement to change. It needs to get a clearer idea of its proper role, its appropriate duties. For today there are well-organized political parties. In the general realm of politics, these parties represent the Nation in its entirety. The trade union movement, therefore, should revert to its natural role. That role, before all else, is the defence of the purchasing power of its members (Senghor, 1961:125-126).

The question was whether all sections and factions within the UNTS would toe the new line. There were, of course, certain trade union leaders at headquarters who found it quite acceptable. But at regional and local levels, it had little chance of acceptance, because the structures of the old trade union movement were still active there. Internal struggles within the UPS, which peaked in the December 1962 crisis, were set to rekindle conflicts within the trade union movement. The split in the UNTS ranks became an open reality during the 26 May 1963 Congress.

It was in this atmosphere of general confusion, against a background of mounting risks, that the 4th Congress of the UPS, held in October 1963, came out with a more systematic statement of the ruling party's theoretical approach to trade union affairs:

> Gone are the days when the point was to defend workers' interests against a foreign State. Now the task is to increase the national income, while ensuring a more equitable distribution of that income through protection for all in accordance with the maxim: "To each according to his work." The overriding need, in other words, is to raise production levels (Dakar Matin, 12 October 1963:11).

In October 1963, a faction of Cheikh Anta Diop's BMS defected to the UPS. The move enabled the UNTS once again to coopt former members of the UGTS. But a confrontation with the PRA-Senegal produced casualties among workers. Madia Diop, a member of the PRA-Senegal as well as a UTS leader, fled the police. Workers who had taken part in a march on the presidential palace were attacked. Ten people died and some sixty were wounded. The UTS called for a general strike, but the strike failed. In 1964, some of its members joined the UNTS. Having learned from the crisis, the ruling party consolidated its links with the trade union under its control. In January 1964, a Coordinating Committee of the UPS and the UNTS was established, with a schedule of regular meetings.

From this point on, the opposition began to make a definite political showing. To counter the activities of the FNS, a new organization led by Cheikh Anta Diop, as well as those of the PRA-Senegal led by Abdoulaye Ly, the State beefed up its security and legislative arrangements. A 21 May 1965 law outlawed seditious organizations. When in June 1966, the PRA got integrated with the UPS, the UNTS was also expanded and strengthened. The CST, CGTS, SUEL, SPAS and the Confederated Labour Cartel now all functioned with the same aims in view: 'the urgent need to create a single trade union organization independent of all political parties and international sponsors, able to defend workers' interests by integrating them into the national interest' (Martens, 1983:50).

Merger negotiations continued until 1967 and were concluded in April that year. The resulting influx of workers from outside the ruling party inevitably affected the direction of the UNTS. Now the organization lost no time condemning the loss of workers' purchasing power.

Revelations of the May 1968 Crisis
The radical shift within the trade union movement was encouraged by the schoolchildren's and students' protest movement that began in March 1968. A general assembly meeting of the Cap-Vert region UNTS leadership condemned rising prices and unemployment. The national conference, at its meeting, concluded that the movement's co-operation with the ruling regime

had produced disappointing results. A 3 May declaration urged activists to prepare for action. The critical turn taken by protest movements among schoolchildren and university students heightened tension throughout the country. One student was killed and more than sixty wounded. In support of the schoolchildren and students, the UNTS declared an unlimited general strike. Clashes between police and demonstrators grew increasingly frequent. Trade union leaders, including Alioune Cissé, Bassirou Guèye and Madia Diop, were arrested. After a series of negotiations the strike ended and on 4 June 1968 the detainees were freed.

The strike brought striking workers considerable gains. The national minimum wage went up by 15%, while allowances for Ministers' and Members of the Assembly were cut. The resumption of trade union activities in 1969, beginning in the banking sector, deepened the gulf. Much more than the 1963 crisis, the 1968 crisis led to deepening reflection on linkages between the State and the trade unions. The government, having concluded that the UNTS was strongly influenced by Communist members of the illegal PAI, encouraged the creation of the UNTS in 1969. Doudou Ngom became the boss of the new body, assigned a clearly spelled-out revisionist task:

The formula supposing that trade unions can be a-political often serves to camouflage an ideology whose proponents lack the courage for forthright political expression. That is why, in every country, each trade union organization is an offshoot of a specific political party (Martens, 1983: 58).

In December 1969, the Seventh Congress of the UPS modified the party statutes. Thenceforth, the CNTS was integrated into the political organization with the same status as the regional unions. The trade union was allotted two cabinet posts, along with 10% of National Assembly seats. Meanwhile, there were continuing protests in the educational sector, with strikes in high schools and at the University of Dakar. Rampaging youths set fire to the French Cultural Centre, and dissatisfaction among workers peaked with a strike at the Mbao refinery. In reaction, the government clamped down on selected branches of the remnant UNTS and CNTCS. In June 1971, the UNTS was dissolved; its leaders Abdoulaye Thiaw, Iba Der Thiam, Mbaba Guissé, Ousmane Diallo and Bakhao Seck were arrested. The government amended Article 249 of the Labour Code to provide for a compulsory period of arbitration and settlement before any strike could be declared. The year 1972 saw the consolidation of links between the CNTS and the UPS. President Senghor opened the first ordinary congress of the trade union organization on 22 September 1972. In 1973, the trend towards closer collaboration between the ruling party and the trade union organization was accentuated. After winning the legislative elections, the party once again sent a batch of trade union representatives to the National Assembly.

The year 1973, however, also saw the resurgence of protest movements. There were student strikes in February and march that year, and the SES was dissolved. The teachers' union leaders Séga Seck Fall, Mbaba Guissé and Babacar Sané were arrested. Senghor accused the union of frustrating his educational policy. An epic legal battle ensued. The SES took the case all the way up to the Supreme Court, with the result that to this day "the Warrant for Séga Seck Fall" remains a landmark case in the nation's law books. The flames of discontent were fanned meanwhile by rising prices and increasing poverty in the rural areas, a consequence of the drought. To defuse the crisis, the regime adopted a parallel set of economic and political measures. Wages were increased by 15% in 1973, and the next year there was a further 15% rise. The former Chairman of the Ministerial Council, Mamadou Dia, arrested after the 1962 'coup d'état', was released.

The Democratic Opening and the Return to Pluralist Trade Unionism
There has been considerable speculation as to the real reasons for the democratic opening. Was it the regime's way of proving to its international partners that it could keep the situation in hand? Certain commentators were quick to link Senghor's decision to recognize Abdoulaye Wade's Senegalese Democratic Party with his wish to join the Socialist International. Others saw it as an attempt to deflect popular anger caused by the rising cost of living. Incidentally, following negotiations with the CNTS, the government was obliged to raise wages and salaries by 30% in October 1974. Underground opposition groups turned to new forms of struggle. A Maoist organization called *Andë Jeff* appeared on the political scene, advocating protracted struggle against the Senghor regime. Its leaders were arrested in 1975.

In other respects, the regime continued to broaden the scope of the official opposition: the PAI faction led by Majmout Diop was recognized in 1976. With the recognition of the MRS in June 1979, Senghor decided to close the charmed circle of officially acceptable political viewpoints. The UPS would represent socialism, the PDS would represent liberalism, Boubacar Guèye's MRS would represent conservative thinking, and the PAI would stand for orthodox Marxism. Other political tendencies refused to go along with this scheme. Nationalists banded together in Cheikh Anta Diop's RND. The former Chairman Dia and the militant rump of the PAI that had stayed underground started a paper called *Andë Sopi*. Since the authorities refused them legal recognition, various political groupings decided to make their presence felt through propaganda broadsides and in the trade union movement. Thus the UTLS, closely associated with the PDS, was created in 1975. In the next presidential and legislative elections, some of its activists worked with the opposition lawyer Abdoulaye Wade, while the CNTS campaigned for the ruling party.

Still, the UTLS did not manage to incorporate underground opposition viewpoints. Other trade unions emerged. One was the new teachers' union SUDES, whose organizers included former SUEL, SPAS and SES activists. The technicians' union SDTS was a later addition which, along with the CGTDS, asserted an independent orientation. All these organizations applied for official recognition. The rural areas also jumped on the trade union bandwagon. In 1977 the RND-affiliated Union of Farmers, Herders and Fishers was created. The UPS responded by setting up a similar union the next year. The new configuration naturally affected the development of the UPS and the CNTS. At the extraordinary party congress of 27 December 1976, the UPS took on a new name: the Socialist Party. Meanwhile, discontent had been gaining ground within the CNTS. To cope with it, and to find a way out of serious disagreements within the leadership, the ruling party decided to review its links with the trade union. The stipulation calling for the merger of the two was dropped, and the organizers agreed to accept simple affiliation.

The regime had planned to gain greater control over legal procedures governing the recognition of trade union organizations by amending Article 6 of the Labour Code. Events proved it wrong, with unions unaffiliated with the ruling PS gaining ground instead. In 1978, elections of workshop delegates ended in substantial victories for the UTLS. At the same time, tensions between leading CNTS figures intensified. The UTLS itself was not immune to bitter internecine conflicts[6]. Its first congress, held on 4 January 1979, was marked by the clash between the faction led by Puritain Fall, who had in the meantime become a Member of the Assembly on the PDS ticket, and other factions led by Mamour Diallo and Oumar Ndiaye. The last-named enjoyed the support of certain former railroad unionists from the CNTS. The PDS had tried to gain control over the UTLS, but now it began to lose whatever influence it had. Indeed, it even lost its hold on Puritain Fall, who, though elected to the Assembly on the PDS ticket, nevertheless quit the party.

The disintegration of the UTLS was speeded up by the assaults of the regime and the rivalry between various factions of the legal and underground opposition. But the weakening of the UTLS did not mean the end of social struggles. On 13 May 1980, the SUDES called a 24-hour warning strike that drew a substantial response. From other sectors the regime came under sustained attack: there was a terrible strike at the Richard Toll sugar complex, and a series of student strikes occasioned instances of police brutality, particularly in the Casamance. Strikes by Senegalese students abroad amplified the scope of these protests.

Workers, having watched their purchasing power fall to 73% of 1960 levels, were on the whole sympathetic to these protest movements. After all they had their own worries, worsened by continuing job losses: 3,000 workers had already lost their jobs at the BUD-Senegal agricultural complex, and the giant ONCAD parastatal had been shut down. This was the background against which, in late November 1980, Senghor announced his decision to retire from the political scene, after taking care to amend Article 35 of the Constitution so as to facilitate the rise of his Prime Minister, Abdou Diouf, to the presidency.

Life Under the IMF and the World Bank
When Abdou Diouf rose to the presidency, he was fully aware of the array of challenges facing the nation, crying out for urgent solutions. In the economic sphere he would have to conclude the financial stabilization plan started in 1979, then begin a medium term economic and financial recovery plan lasting from 1980 to 1984. That would be followed by a medium and long term adjustment plan from 1985 to 1992. All this would mean decreasing State[7] intervention, a policy of privatization, and the encouragement of voluntary retirements in a bid to cut down the national wage packet.

On the social level the challenge was to defuse the bomb of trade union agitation ticking away loudly in such traditional sectors as education. At the same time it was necessary to forestall protest movements provoked by the adjustment process. In January 1981, President Diouf convened the General Conference on Education and Training. Participants included political authorities, all teachers' unions, and traditional and religious dignitaries.

On the political level, the authorities decided in favour of open democracy. This meant that the former limitation imposed on the number of officially permissible political tendencies was scrapped. In short order the number of political parties rose above ten. In addition to the three already recognized, that is to say, the PDS, the PAI and the MRS, others got their registration papers. They ranged over a pretty wide spectrum, from the nationalist RND through various Marxist tendencies such as the pro-Soviet PIT and LD-MPT, the Maoist *Andë-Jeff*-MRDN and the Trotskyite OST and LCT to the socialist worker-management advocates of the MSU. All this while, as usual, the opposition continued to flow and ebb between the urge to merge and the temptation to split into further factions[8]. The trend towards multiple organizations also affected the trade union movement. The SUTSAS thus emerged in 1982, along with the SUTELEC. Next came the SATJUS in 1983 and the SYNPICS in 1984. Nor was this sector immune to the temptation to split into factional groups: the parent body SUDES produced the SAES in 1985 and the UDEN in 1987.

Without a doubt, the dominant trend within the Senegalese trade union movement during the 1980s was the creation and consolidation of autonomous unions. Some, such as the SUTELEC, SUTSAS and SUDES, were created as a result of the more openly democratic atmosphere. Some split off from older autonomous unions following internal conflicts or disappointments. Some were splinter formations from the CNTS, as was the case with the posts and telegraphs union, the urban transport corporation (SOTRAC) union, and the SONEES water utility workers' union. Yet others were started by workers simply anxious about their future. In 1990, for instance, computer programmers in the civil service established the SINFAD. That same year, the Committee on Initiatives for the Defence of Civil Servants' Interests (CODIF) was formed. In some cases the motivation was a combination of survival reflexes and political commitment. Some observers have pointed out that the regime had a hand in the state of chronic fission within the trade union movement, because it weakened workers' organizations and thus made it easier for the government to implement World Bank and IMF measures.

It is true that the government did take a number of measures calculated to unbalance such autonomous unions as the SUDES. For example, when in 1984 it appointed the SUDES activist Professor Iba Der Thiam, as Minister of National Education, it pulled off a grand coup. Uncertainty about the right attitude to take towards the new minister was a contributing factor to an internal crisis within the SUDES. That crisis was aggravated by power struggles between various opposition factions within the union. Once the political arena was opened up to all parties and formerly underground organizations, especially the Marxist groups, were legalized, the stakes became much clearer as far as trade union organizations[9] were concerned. In an attempt to forestall union domination by political parties, the SAES inserted a clause in its statutes declaring that at top national levels, the holding of union positions was incompatible with acceptance of similar responsibilities in political organizations. Taking advantage of this confused state of affairs, the government pushed forward its plans. And in the face of these new challenges, the CNTS and various autonomous unions embarked on some soul searching.

New Assignments in the Period of Responsible Participation

There were various attempts to rouse the umbrella trade union organization out of its habitual lethargy. The period from 1981 to 1984 saw the structuring of the *Renouveau* revivalist movement within the union. The primary issue in the struggle was democracy. The Third Confederal Congress held on 17 and 18 April 1982 accepted the principle of the coexistence of plural tendencies within the union. Simultaneously, a further move was made to loosen links with the ruling party: the Congress ended up affirming that the union post of Secretary-General was incompatible with any government ministerial appointment.

These changes, however, did not mean an end to union turmoil. In the end a number of members left the umbrella organization. For example, the FRODULES organizers Babacar Diagne and Alioune Sow, along with others, resigned from the CNTS and set up the UDTS in 1987. Others chose to remain in the umbrella organization and work for reform. For example, organizers of the Committee for a Militant Democratic Trade Union Movement (CISDL), including some opposition activists, established their group. In other words, differences between the CNTS and the autonomous trade unions did not exactly reflect the dichotomy between the ruling Socialist Party and the opposition. Certain opposition groups considered it necessary to work within the CNTS, since its 70 000 registered members made it the organizational focus for the majority of workers. Others thought it more important to concentrate their energies on the organization of an umbrella union that would serve as an alternative to the CNTS.

At the sixth CNTS congress[10], the last to date, held on 10 and 11 March 1990, the CNTS did not hesitate to emphasize its achievements over the period: it had negotiated and signed a national inter-professional collective bargaining agreement in 1982; got Act 80-01 rescinded; obtained amendments to stipulations in Articles 47 and 188 of the Labour Code; organized a demonstration of Members of the Assembly in front of the National Assembly to protest against Article 35 of the revised Labour Code; and led all trade union organizations in opposition to Articles 22 and 23, of Act Number 29-89 amending the Investment Code. It would be possible to argue that the CNTS did try to adapt to the changing situation by getting involved in new activities and restructuring itself. Decisions taken at the Congress included the generalization of the federal model and the creation of an Economics and Statistics Department. The CNTS asked the State to ratify the agreement on the National Unemployment Solidarity Fund, to revise the schedule of payments for State loans to enterprises, to identify new job-creation opportunity areas, to bring together small and medium industrial enterprises, to organize joint management programmes, etc. (*Le Soleil*, 12 March 1990). In this connection, it tried to stimulate various initiatives in production plant management. But the experiment[11] was marred by clashes with workers.

Still, the CNTS retained its reputation as the most representative workers' organization. That gave it strategic clout as the key defender of workers' viewpoints in negotiations with the authorities and in international organizations. In that capacity it also got substantial grants and subsidies. This could ensure a measure of longevity for the CNTS, but the question remained: could it survive if it failed to meet workers' needs in these hard times? It is the necessity of working within these two parameters that also makes the challenge facing the autonomous unions so difficult and interesting.

The Issue of Autonomy

Independent trade unions in Senegal had been trying since the early 1980s to set up a central inter-union body. But it was only in August 1987 that the structure got set up. Now known as the Co-ordinating Group, it had a draft joint platform, a somewhat stabler structural form, and a joint action programme.

Most of the organization's meetings were hosted by the SUTELEC, with the UDEN and the UTLS taking turns to provide the secretariat. Among the coordinating body's achievements was the organization of a seminar on economic and social issues on 13 and 14 August 1988. This seminar enabled the independent trade unions involved to pay closer attention to the government's new policy package: a New Agricultural Policy, New Industrial Policy, New Health Policy, New Educational Policy, etc. It also provided an opportunity for a comprehensive evaluation of the coordinating body itself. The conclusions were as follows:

> *The general opinion of seminar participants was that the inter-union body's record was negative on balance. The coordinating group itself, however, earned a high approval rating for having adopted a set of key operational regulations. It was also given credit for selected activities. Still, it was pointed that the work done so far was less than might have been expected, given the seriousness of the circumstances. To remedy the situation, it was suggested that a task force be set up to prepare the ground for the organization of an independent umbrella union. At the same time, care was taken to point out that the organization of the planned inter-union umbrella body would not preclude the survival of the coordinating body, which would continue to serve members unprepared to join the new grouping. It was also pointed out that we had not exhausted all opportunities for joint action within the coordinating body, and that we needed to make further efforts in that framework*[12].

Following this meeting, the co-ordinating body slumped into deep lethargy, waking up sporadically to participate in major struggles led by the SUTELEC in 1988, the SAES and UDEN in the higher educational system in 1989, and the SUTSAS, also in 1989. The autonomous unionists did their best in the closing weeks of 1989 to respond positively to the CNTS call to try and block the passage of laws detrimental to trade union interests. On the whole, though, the main conclusions were as follows:

a) Active solidarity between unions mainly took the form of bilateral interaction. It was essentially up to each individual union to judge how much support it actually got from any other particular union in its past struggles.

b) The co-ordinating body wasted precious opportunities for showing its clout and credibility when factories were shut down, prices went up and new taxes were slapped on wages and salaries[13].

c) It was also handicapped in its routine operations by deep cleavages that surfaced through the publication of contradictory conference minutes, the issuing of unilateral public statements in the name of independent trade unions, etc.

In the face of all these shortcomings, the various participants in the independent trade union movement decided the time had come for a hard-nosed assessment. It came on 8 and 16 April 1990. In the course of the two meetings, two things became clear. First, of the ten groups originally in the co-ordinating body (CGTDS, SAES, SATJUS, SUTELEC, SUTSAS, SUDES, SYNPICS, UDEN and UTLS), some, like the SATJUS, no longer played an active role. On the other hand, some new groups, like the SNTPT and SUTS, had come in. The second observation was that the cause of the rift was the decision-making procedure followed. Since its formation, the coordinating body had taken decisions by consensus. Unions like the UDEN and the SAES were convinced that this was just a ploy used by persons determined to prevent the organization from achieving its objectives. They therefore suggested that where there was no consensus, decisions be taken by a simple majority vote or some acceptable voting formula. Other unions such as the SUDES and the faction of the UTLS led by Djibril Diop, disagreeing with this viewpoint, asserted that published guidelines for the projected umbrella organization should be given priority.

In the event, one trade union group embracing the SAES, SNTPT, SUTSAS, SUTELEC and UDEN formed the Trade Union Conference for the Creation of an Autonomous Central Organization. In a declaration dated 12 August 1990, the Conference expressed satisfaction at progress made towards the establishment of a National Union of Independent Senegalese Trade Unions. Once the work done in various committees (Guidelines, Statutes, Bye-Laws, Organization, Claims, Press and Information, Trade Union Education and Finances) had been assessed, it was considered feasible to schedule a constituent general assembly meeting within the year. A faction of the UTLS-Mayoro joined the group, which also received support from such new trade unions as the SINFAD. In May 1990, teachers belonging to the group (from the SAES and UDEN) were able to organize an Education and Research Federation.

A second trade union grouping made up of the SDTS, SUDES, SUTS and UTLS (Djibril Diop), though determined to hold on to their independence, resolved 'to continue working together in pressing for the satisfaction of workers' demands'[14]. The grouping continued calling itself a Coordinating Body, and currently publishes a newsletter called *Echos de la Coordination*. Other organizations such as the CGTDS and the UDTS, which already saw themselves as umbrella bodies, thought it more advisable for other unions to join them. In any case, attempts at liaison were made, and a number of group activities conducted. For example, in July 1990, there was a joint session for communications workers that brought together unionists from the autonomous SNTPT, which at the time belonged to the conference that became the UNSAS; the SUTS which belonged to the CNTS, and the UTLS-Djibril Diop, which belonged to the Co-ordinating Body.

Observers often suppose that conflicting viewpoints within the trade union movement reflect differences between political parties. One such observer is the journalist A. Camara. According to him, "in reality, what we find within the union movement is the same configuration of alliances as on the political scene. This leads, quite naturally, to a rekindling of the hoary debate about the right attitude towards the CNTS. Points of view projected by the SUTSAS and the UDEN, in particular, as well as the SUDES viewpoint, brought up deep-seated differences between the LD/MPT and the PIT. The latter organization was likely to find entirely congenial the development of bilateral relations by SUDES with unions involved in the process of 'responsible participation.' The LD/MPT was in a similar mirror-image situation regarding the position adopted by the UDEN and SUTSAS. Was all this due to simple coincidence? Possibly, just possibly' (Camara, 1990:3).

The journalist, however, once he had interviewed the Secretary-Generals of various unions, most of them political party activists, was moved to modify his premise. Such a modification became all the more pertinent after he examined their attitudes towards the order for a general strike contemplated by opposition parties in 1990. The SUTSAS and the SAES were lukewarm. This could only have displeased members of the eight-party opposition grouping. On the other hand, the PIT must have found the SUDES position quite congenial. In its most extreme form, the UDEN viewpoint was closer to that of those leaders interested in organizing a political strike (Camara, 1990:3).

It is no secret that the political parties deployed their most powerful arsenals in the 1988 and 1989 campaigns, during and after the presidential and legislative elections. They supported student struggles and those of the university teaching faculty in 1989. In their conduct and results, these campaigns showed that initiatives from political parties had not been decisive in starting the struggles, nor in waging them. The parties, for their part, having seen how tepid a response the call for a general strike had drawn (*Sopi*, 4 May 1990: 1) maintained that the time had come for mobilizing their followers for a 'final assault'. They took pains to add, however, that this time the assault was 'no longer simply the task of political parties and activists' (*Sopi*, 10 August 1990:1). This obvious come-on intended to entice unionists was actually interpreted as a reproach during the 14 August 1990 press conference of the National Conference of Heads of Opposition Parties (CONACPO)[15]. Other interpretations, however, were crystal clear:

> The CONACPO appealed urgently to trade union organizations and their members to take an active part in this struggle whose outcome would shape the destiny of everyone among them (*Sopi*, 17 August 1990:5).

Conclusion

As the year 1990 drew to a close, the political and labour scene in Senegal presented a variety of possible scenarios. The ruling party could try and re-establish a dialogue with the opposition as a whole and with the various social forces active in the country, including the trade unions. Such a scenario might indicate a determination to seek comprehensive and lasting solutions to the crisis devastating Senegal. On the other hand, there was the temptation to regress into old power plays in which the ruling Socialist Party constituted, to all intents, a single-party State. This boded ill for the future[16]. The opposition, by contrast, had analyzed its problems in more sophisticated fashion. It was therefore better placed to take advantage of popular discontent and push the government into making more substantial concessions than in the past. Indeed, opposition branches abroad had made good progress towards a merger of political and trade union forces[17]. The situation back home was somewhat more complex, so the State could continue to take advantage of contradictions within the opposition in order to maintain its hegemony. Lastly, there was the possibility that other social protagonists, the trade union in particular, would get fed up with the endless guerrilla warfare between the government and the opposition. In that case they could decide to take their disaffection to its logical conclusion and wage decisive struggles while counting on their own strength. That would mean the opening of new channels towards a fresh division of labour and power.

In the trade union movement, each of the various poles was perfectly aware of its strengths and weaknesses. The CNTS still counted on posts in the private sector, while the independent unions had gained strategic positions in the public and parastatal sectors. There was some uncertainty as to whether they could make inroads into the traditional strongholds of the CNTS, overcome their differences, and mobilize workers to present a serious alternative. Beyond that, it would also be necessary to find out if the CNTS and the independent unions could agree on the main issues, that is to say, the defence of the material and spiritual interests of workers, along with leadership in meeting the people's aspirations. Only on those terms could the trade union movement hope to exert any decisive influence on the social, economic and political development of Senegal in the 1990s.

From late October 1990 onwards, events broke fast. In a decree published in the 25 October 1990 issue of *Le Soleil*, the government announced the imposition of an income surtax. Two days later, on 27 October 1990, the UNSAS secretariat decided to issue a strike warning to back up its demand for lower income tax rates, the total abolition of the surtax, and lower prices for food staples and essential commodities. When the Secretariat met on 13 December 1990, it fixed two periods for strike action. The first would run from 14 to 15 December, the second from 18 to 22 December 1990. The opening salvo from the UNSAS came in the form of a set of reasoned claims. The union attacked the government on grounds of mismanagement, condemned it for wasting money on prestige projects, and put forward proposals for meeting workers' needs. Meanwhile the SUDES, which belonged to the second pole within the independent trade union movement, decided to make its move on 3 December. Many workers hoped the unions would take joint action on key issues, but they were disappointed. The struggles, nevertheless, provided useful insights as to the real power of the unions and the options available to them.

UNSAS got support in its struggles from the faction of the UTLS led by Mayoro, now renamed SDTS, as well as from selected sections of the CNTS including the SONACOS-EID local of the National Union of Oil Industry Workers, the School and University Staff Union (STESU), the Taiba workers, and railroad workers from Thiès. Some workers from these support groups actually organized specific skirmishes during this campaign. An example was the strike organized by the STESU at the Inter-State School of Veterinary Science and Medicine on 8 and 9 January. The objective was to obtain a cost of living allowance pegged to current prices, subsidized annual medical check-ups, and the cancellation of three arbitrary sanctions.

A number of local union branches took the Confederal Bureau to task. But the UDTS refused to take part in the struggle on the grounds that it was an adventuristic initiative. In its declaration of 11 December 1990, it appealed to workers to ignore the UNSAS strike call. As for the government, reacting with unusual speed, it cancelled the surtax. The decision was presented as a result of discussions between the President of the Republic and the CNTS Secretary-General. By the looks of it, the State had hit upon a new method of crisis management. In the past it had had a habit of waiting for the situation to degenerate before taking any action. Now it was quick to invite trade unions to negotiate.

In separate negotiation sessions, the President operated as umpire. The UNSAS was asked to attend a series of meetings focused on its three-point agenda. Another series was devoted to the CNTS and the CSA and their 14-point agenda. At the end of the UNSAS negotiations, an agreement was signed on 16 January 1991. The government agreed to set up working commissions to discuss a new tax schedule, but refused to bring down commodity prices. Thanks to the agreement, the negotiating parties were able to avoid the showdown of an indefinite strike. So the third phase of the UNSAS struggle, scheduled to start on 17 January, did not proceed. As for the agreement between the government and the joint CNTS-CSA team, it was signed on 11 March 1991. There was agreement on numerous points. Admittedly, some union claims were precisely what the government itself wanted. Examples included the demand for a single-shift day and arrangements to put the IPRES[18] back on a sound financial footing. Taking advantage of the last demand, the State raised the deduction rate without consulting the CNTS and the CSA.

These developments constituted proof that the trade union movement was stirring, reshaping its internal dynamics along two poles, with the UNSAS forming one pole, the CNTS and the CSA the other. At one point it seemed possible that strikes by workers and traders[19] might merge with a planned march by the joint opposition grouping CONACPO on 19 January 1991, during the outbreak of the Gulf War (in which Senegal participated). Such an eventuality could have sent Senegal into a tailspin of uncertainties. There are those who think it was on account of the outbreak of the Gulf War that the CONACPO called off its march. Others, however, think the reason was the cancellation of the strike order by the UNSAS.

The different component parties within the CONACPO took dissimilar views of the country's political situation and the prospects ahead for themselves. Given these differences, a rift was inevitable. Now that it has happened, we are living through a different configuration of the Senegalese political scene. In the changing situation, what lies ahead for the trade unions? Will the CNTS be able to maintain its commitment to 'responsible participation?' Of the CSA and UNSAS, which union is likely to come up with an autonomously developed policy strategy geared to struggle and capable of influencing the majority of workers? And when confronted with coming developments, how will the State and the various political parties react?

For two reasons these are hard questions to answer. First, there are times when workers' reactions take even the major trade union organizations by surprise. One such occasion was the crippling wildcat strike called by private urban minibus drivers on 23 and 24 April 1991. Secondly, it seems clear enough that trade union activities do not always follow the same direction as political party activities. In this connection, the May Day celebrations in 1991 provided several intriguing insights. For example, the CNTS and the CSA marched jointly in the parade, as if to illustrate their joint programme. The new-found unity went down particularly well with leaders of the Socialist Party and the PIT. On the other hand, the PDS, even though it was now a member of the ruling majority, did not seem unduly displeased at the liaison between its allies in the SDTS and the UNSAS, considered close to the opposition. Lastly, the protest struggle launched in December 1991 by the FEDER grouping (comprising the SAES, the UDEN and some independent unionists) along with the SUDES showed that workers could transcend their structural and circumstantial differences.

Several questions remain. Do all these signs indicate the unfolding of a carefully designed strategy and a set of appropriate tactics? Or are they simply the outcome of pragmatic, *ad hoc* stances? A pertinent Wolof proverb likens the process of struggle to a tuber likely to fracture suddenly at some unexpected point. After that there remains the task of healing whatever can be salvaged. Given the endless range of current challenges, the mythic figures of Prometheus and Sisyphus would make apt heroes of the working class movement now.

Notes

1. *Le Soleil*, 2-3 May 1987, p.5. See also Thiam 1983, Volumes VI and VII.
2. Martens (1983: 7). These pioneering migrants played a constant part in anti-colonial struggles between the two world wars. Outstanding among them were Lamine Senghor of Senegal, Tovalou Quenum of Dahomey (Benin), and Garang Kouyaté of Mali. Cf. Sagna (1986).
3. Thanks to his analysis of imperialism, Lenin was able to highlight the divisive culture established and developed within the working class: "Imperialism also tends to create privileged groups among the working class and to cut them off from the main mass of the proletariat..." (Lenin, *oeuvres*, Editions Sociales, Paris. Editions du Progrès, Moscow, 1976. Volume 22. p. 305). Maintenance of a labour aristocracy is facilitated by profits from capitalist exploitation. But there is a further contributing factor: "imperialist ideology also penetrates the working class, which is not sealed off from other classes behind a 4. Great Wall of China." (Lenin, *Ibid.*, p.308).

4. Subsequently, when Senghor dropped Abbas Guèye, he created the Democratic Rally before going on to join Lamine Guèye's Senegalese Social Action Party.
5. On the history of the teachers' trade union movement, see Diallo (1985).
6. At one point no less than four factions claimed to be sole legitimate representatives of the UTLS. The faction formerly led by Cheikh T Fall, thought to be closely affiliated with *Andë Jeff*, after having announced that it was disbanding in order not to have to participate in "this sad show prepared for the working class," resurfaced as the "UTLS-Front" during the constituent general assembly meeting of the UNSAS on 7 April 1991. At its congress on 12 and 13 January 1991, the UTLS under Djibril Diop, close to the PIT, changed its name to the Senegalese Workers' Union (UTS). The reason given was that this would end "the confusion a certain megalomaniac who has usurped our acronym has been trying to foment." The reference was to Puritain Fall. The faction led by Mayoro, close to the PDS, renamed itself the Senegalese Workers' Democratic Trade Union (SDTS). That left only the faction led by Puritain Fall, incidentally also the UDS/R Secretary-General, carrying the original acronym UTLS.
7. See the chapter by François Boye in this volume.
8. The PDS, for example, spawned the PDS-R and the UDSR. The RND gave birth to a splinter group, the PLP. The LCT first joined the worker-management advocates of the MSU, then abandoned them. AJ-MRDN, the UDP and the OST, along with a group known only as "readers of *Suxuba* tracts," set up a "Steering Committee to Unify the Revolutionary Left," from which sprang the AJ/PADS. In the heat of the 1988 elections a *Sopi* alliance emerged from the collaboration of the PDS, the LD/MPT and the PIT, but before the PDS joined the government in April 1991, the movement embraced only the two first-named parties. The National Conference of Opposition Party Leaders (CONACPO), comprising the leadership of the AJ-MRDN, the LD/MPT, MSU, OST, PAI, PDS, PLP, PPS and the UDP, shrank when the PDS switched over to the government coalition in 1991. Other forces (RND, PDS-R) joined the opposition front, giving rise to a new acronym, CONACPO PLUS.
9. After the purge of Maoists from the union, the internal power struggle shifted to a straight rivalry between the LD/MPT and the PIT. The upshot was the breakup of the SUDES.
10. Cf. the address delivered by Omar Sané, Deputy Secretary-General in Charge of the Cap Vert Regional Union at the last congress. Its gist: the government had not let up in its efforts to come up with a thoroughly revised Labour Code (See *Le Soleil*, 11 May 1991, p.2; *Le Témoin*, Nos. 34 & 35, March 1991, and No. 38, April 1991).
11. One example comes to mind: the clash between the CNTS leadership and the *Bok Jom* cooperative bakery in the Dakar suburb of Guediawaye. The project was begun in 1984 by a group of professional bakers who asked the CNTS to provide supervisory services. The CNTS in turn contacted the International Confederation of Free Trade Unions. The Institute for Trade Union Cooperation (ISCOS) was assigned to handle project implementation. Achievements were considered excellent until a dispute broke out on the issue of managerial autonomy. Cooperative members were against a manager the CNTS leadership wanted to impose on them. The CNTS partners (ISCOS) were called in to arbitrate, along with the ILO. When the dust cleared, the former cooperative members had been pushed out and the CNTS had the upper hand (*Sopi*, No. 129, 20 April 1990; No. 133, 18 May 1990; and No. 140, 13 July 1990).
12. See the publication entitled "Objectif: unité des travailleurs," Coordination des Syndicats Autonomes, June 1987 - August 1988. p.22.
13. The innovation was the Personal Income Tax, which superseded the General Income Tax and the Tax on Wages and Emoluments.
14. *Echos de la Coordination*, No. 01, August 1990, p. 10. Cf. Interview with Amara Seck, Deputy Secretary-General, SUDES.

15. In the 16 August 1990 issue of *Sud hebdo*, Demba Ndiaye, in his report on the CONACPO press conference held on 13 August 1990, defended the trade unionists: "Incidentally, it is tactically clumsy to blame the unsatisfactory situation on the lack of trade union involvement in the struggle against the government's highly unpopular policy."
16. The satirical weekly, *Le Cafard Libéré* (5 September 1990, p.1) put this regressive tendency in a nutshell: "Looking at the last appointments to central government and parastatal posts, one gets a strong impression that the Socialist Party is again at its old game of reaching out in all directions with its tentacles in a bid to colonize the administration. In France, in the peak period of de Gaulle's power, the party-State of the UDR laid such a stranglehold on the civil service that certain wags quipped that France had become the Republic of Cronies and Clowns. Here in Senegal, we wonder whether we are heading in the same direction in this period when multi-party democracy is getting rooted, and the hegemony of any single party over the workings of the State system ought therefore to be disappearing."
17. In cooperation with workers' and students' organizations in France (RETSEF, OTESF, UTSF Action Revendicative and other French and African trade union and political organizations), representatives of the 9 opposition parties (CONACPO) organized a demonstration on 19 June 1990, to coincide with the French-African summit held in La Baule. The organizational framework was the Pan-African Democratic Forum, and the topic was "SOS for Democracy in Africa."
18. When elections to the new executive bureau were held on 14 March 1991, Madia Diop, Secretary-General of the CNTS, was elected Chairman of the Administrative Council, while Youssouph Diop of the National Council of Employers was elected Vice-Chairman.
19. The Senegalese National Union of Traders and Industrialists rejected a set of new measures related to the Value Added Tax schedule. J.P. Dias, at that time a member of the opposition, gave the following analysis of their position: "Yesterday it was the wage earners organized within independent trade unions who got the 5% surtax on net wages and salaries cancelled, and went on to mount a struggle against the new personal income tax schedule. Today it is the traders who are resisting the attempt to strangle them. In this struggle, it is significant that the live wires come from the informal sector. This means the people are waking up. (Cf. *Sopi*, No. 167, 18 January 1991).

Bibliography

Brun, Charles Francis, 1964, 'Vers l'unité syndicale au Sénégal', *Afrique Documents*, pp. 125 et seq.

Camara, A, 1990, 'Autonomie et politique', *Wal Fadjri*, No. 212, May, p.3.

Diallo, Kalidou, 1986, 'Syndicat unique de l'Enseignement laïc du Sénégal (SUEL). Contribution à l'étude du mouvement syndical à la veille et au début des indépendances', Faculty of Humanities, University of Dakar, 65 p.

Martens, Georges R, 1983, 'Les relations professionnelles et l'évolution des rapports Etat-syndicats sous l'effet des mutations économico-politiques au Sénégal', Graduate thesis in Anthropology, Faculty of Humanities, Cheikh Anta Diop University, Dakar.

Ndiaye, A I, 1990, 'Syndicalisme et ajustement structurel: évolution des rapports Etat-syndicats sous l'effet des mutations économico-politiques au Sénégal', UCAD, FLSH, mémoire de DEA d'anthropologie, 72 p.

Ndour, Birame, 1990, 'De l'histoire des cheminots du Sénégal (1890 - 1948)', *Pratiques Sociales et Travail en milieu urbain*, No. 12, pp. 9-18.

Sagna, O, 1986, 'Les pionniers méconnus de l'indépendance: africains, antillais et luttes anti-colonialistes dans la France de l'entre deux guerres (1919 - 1939)', Doctoral dissertation, Paris VII, 2 volumes, 937 p.

Senghor, Lépold Sédar, 1961, *Nation et voie africaine du socialisme*, Paris, Présence Africaine.

Thiam, Iba Der, 1983, 'L'évolution politique et syndicale du Sénégal colonial de 1840 à 1936', Advanced doctoral thesis in History, Paris I Sorbonne, 9 volumes.